Athenian Religion

Athenian Religion

A HISTORY

Robert Parker

CLARENDON PRESS · OXFORD

OXFORD

UNIVERSITY PRESS

Great Clarendon Street, Oxford OX2 6DP

Oxford University Press is a department of the University of Oxford.
It furthers the University's objective of excellence in research, scholarship,
and education by publishing worldwide in

Oxford New York

Athens Auckland Bangkok Bogotá Buenos Aires Calcutta
Cape Town Chennai Dar es Salaam Delhi Florence Hong Kong Istanbul
Karachi Kuala Lumpur Madrid Melbourne Mexico City Mumbai
Nairobi Paris São Paulo Singapore Taipei Tokyo Toronto Warsaw

with associated companies in Berlin Ibadan

Oxford is a registered trade mark of Oxford University Press
in the UK and in certain other countries

Published in the United States
by Oxford University Press Inc., New York

British Library Cataloguing in Publication Data
Data available

Library of Congress Cataloging in Publication Data
Athenian religion : a history / Robert Parker.
Includes bibliographical references.
1. Athens (Greece)—Religion.   2. Greece—Religion.   I. Title.
BL793.A76P37   1995   292.08—dc20   95-20279
ISBN 0-19-815240-X

3 5 7 9 10 8 6 4

Printed in Great Britain on acid-free paper by
Biddles Ltd., Guildford and King's Lynn

For Jo

Preface

For financial assistance I am grateful to Oriel College, Oxford, and the Craven Committee. Another institution to which I feel deeply indebted is the library of the Ashmolean Museum in Oxford. My text has benefited greatly from the attention of the staff of Oxford University Press, in particular Margaret Clarke and Rita Winter. Several debts to individual scholars are acknowledged in their place; many other people who have contributed to the book (organizers of seminars in particular) can only be thanked collectively. But I must certainly mention Professor Jan Bremmer, Professor Anna Davies, Sir Hugh Lloyd-Jones, Robin Osborne, Simon Price, and Richard Rutherford with warm gratitude for their advice or friendly interest. It is a great grief that I can no longer so thank David Lewis, a master both of scholarship and of the art of helping other scholars. My greatest debts, for the learning that comes through friendship, are to Simon Hornblower and Christiane Sourvinou Inwood.

R.C.T.P.

Oriel College
1 August 1995

Contents

Conventions and Abbreviations

The dates offered in this work for archaeological and epigraphic evidence are, failing contrary indication, those given in the publication cited, with two exceptions: those for inscriptions of the period 229 to 86 BC have been adjusted in accord with the results of S. V. Tracy's study of letter-cutters (see 'Tracy' in the list of abbreviations); and for inscriptions dated by archonships, in the periods in the third and second centuries where the sequence of archons is still controversial, the proposals of the authorities cited in *A Lexicon of Greek Personal Names* (*LGPN*), II, p. x, n. 21 have been accepted.

Abbreviations of periodicals and works of reference are those recommended in the *American Journal of Archaeology* (*AJA*), 95 (1991), 1–16. For ancient authors the abbreviations in *The Oxford Classical Dictionary*² (1970), supplemented by those in Liddell/Scott/Jones, *A Greek English Lexicon*⁹ (Oxford 1940) (LSJ), have been followed, with a few trivial divergences. Abbreviations of papyrological and epigraphical publications are from LSJ (with some supplements listed below).

On much-debated topics, I sometimes cite only a recent contribution, adding the symbol [+] to stress that this work refers to earlier studies which remain important.

Where works are cited by a short title that does not appear in the list below, the full form has been given earlier in the notes to the same chapter.

Agora   *The Athenian Agora: Results of Excavations Conducted by the American School of Classical Studies in Athens* (Princeton 1951–). Note esp. *Agora* XI (1965): *Archaic and Archaistic Sculpture*, ed. E. B. Harrison; *Agora* XV (1974): *Inscriptions: The Athenian Councillors*, eds. B. D. Meritt and J. S. Traill; *Agora* XIX (1991): *Inscriptions: Horoi, Poletai Records, Leases of Public Lands*, eds. G. V. Lalonde, M. K. Langdon, and M. B. Walbank.

Agora Guide	*The Athenian Agora: A Guide to the Excavation and Museum*³ (American School of Classical Studies at Athens 1976).
Aleshire, *Asklepieion*	S. B. Aleshire, *The Athenian Asklepieion: The People, their Dedications, and the Inventories* (Amsterdam 1989).
Aleshire, *Asklepios*	S. B. Aleshire, *Asklepios at Athens: Epigraphic and Prosopographic Essays on the Athenian Healing Cults* (Amsterdam 1991).
Austin (after a fragment number)	C. Austin, *Nova Fragmenta Euripidea in Papyris Reperta* (Berlin 1968).
Badian, 'Deification'	E. Badian, 'The Deification of Alexander', in *Ancient Macedonian Studies in Honor of C. F. Edson* (Thessalonike 1981), 27–71.
Boardman, *Black Figure*	J. Boardman, *Athenian Black Figure Vases* (London 1974).
Boardman, *Greek Sculpture: Archaic*	J. Boardman, *Greek Sculpture: The Archaic Period* (London 1978).
Boardman, *Red Figure: Archaic*	J. Boardman, *Athenian Red Figure Vases: The Archaic Period* (London 1975).
Boersma, *Building Policy*	J. S. Boersma, *Athenian Building Policy from 561/0 to 405/4 B.C.* (Groningen 1970).
Borgeaud, *Pan*	P. Borgeaud, *Recherches sur le dieu Pan* (Bibliotheca Helvetica Romana 17, 1979).
Bourriot, *Génos*	F. Bourriot, *Recherches sur la nature du génos: Étude d'histoire sociale athénienne—périodes archaïque et classique* (Lille 1976).
Brickhouse/Smith, *Socrates on Trial*	T. C. Brickhouse and N. D. Smith, *Socrates on Trial* (Oxford 1989).
Bruneau, *Recherches*	P. Bruneau, *Recherches sur les cultes de Délos à l'époque hellénistique et à l'époque impériale* (*BEFAR* 217, Paris 1970).
Bruneau/Ducat, *Guide de Délos*	P. Bruneau and J. Ducat, *Guide de Délos*³ (Paris 1983).
Bull. Ép.	*Bulletin Épigraphique*, in *Revue des études grecques*.

Burkert, *Greek Religion* W. Burkert, *Greek Religion: Archaic and Classical*, tr. J. Raffan (Oxford 1985; German orig. 1977).

Burkert, *Homo Necans* W. Burkert, *Homo Necans: The Anthropology of Ancient Greek Sacrificial Ritual and Myth*, tr. P. Bing (Berkeley 1983; German orig. 1972).

Burkert, *Mystery Cults* W. Burkert, *Ancient Mystery Cults* (Cambridge Mass. 1987).

Calame, *Thésée* C. Calame, *Thésée et l'imaginaire athénien* (Lausanne 1990).

Carlier, *La royauté* P. Carlier, *La royauté en Grèce avant Alexandre* (Strasburg 1984).

Castriota, *Myth, Ethos, Actuality* D. Castriota, *Myth, Ethos and Actuality: Official Art in Fifth-Century B.C. Athens* (Madison 1992).

CEG P. A. Hansen, *Carmina Epigraphica Graeca Saec. VIII–V a. Chr. n.* (Berlin 1983) and *Carmina Epigraphica Graeca Saec. IV a. Chr. n.* (Berlin 1989). (The numeration is continuous in the two vols., the second beginning at no. 466.)

Clinton, *Sacred Officials* K. Clinton, *The Sacred Officials of the Eleusinian Mysteries* (*TAPS* NS 64, Philadelphia 1972).

Coldstream, *Geometric Greece* J. N. Coldstream, *Geometric Greece* (London 1977).

Coldstream, *Geometric Pottery* J. N. Coldstream, *Greek Geometric Pottery* (London 1968).

Coldstream, 'Hero-cults' J. N. Coldstream, 'Hero-cults in the Age of Homer', *JHS* 96 (1976), 1–12.

Conomis *Lycurgi Oratio in Leocratem cum Ceterarum Lycurgi Orationum Fragmentis*, ed. N. C. Conomis (Leipzig 1970).

Cook, *Zeus* A. B. Cook, *Zeus: A Study in Ancient Religion* (3 vols., Cambridge 1914–40).

Crux P. Cartledge and F. D. Harvey eds., *Crux: Essays Presented to G. E. M. de Ste. Croix on his 75th Birthday* (= *History of Political Thought* 6/1–2, 1985).

Culley, *Sacred Monuments* G. R. Culley, *The Restoration of Sacred Monuments in Augustan Athens* (Diss. Chapel Hill, NC 1973).

Davies, *Propertied Families* J. K. Davies, *Athenian Propertied Families* (Oxford 1971).

Dentzer, *Banquet couché* J.-M. Dentzer, *Le motif du banquet couché dans le proche-orient et le monde grec du vii*e *au iv*e *siècle avant J.-C.* (*BEFAR* 246, Rome 1982).

Derenne, *Procès d'impiété* E. Derenne, *Les procès d'impiété intentés aux philosophes à Athènes au V*me *et au IV*me *siècle a. J.-Chr.* (Liège 1930).

Desborough, *Greek Dark Ages* V. R. d'A. Desborough, *The Greek Dark Ages* (London 1972).

Deubner, *Attische Feste* L. Deubner, *Attische Feste* (Berlin 1932).

D/K H. Diels, rev. W. Kranz, *Die Fragmente der Vorsokratiker*[6] (Zurich 1951–2).

Dodds, *Greeks and the Irrational* E. R. Dodds, *The Greeks and the Irrational* (Berkeley 1951).

Dow, 'Law Codes' S. Dow, 'The Law Codes of Athens', *Proc. Mass. Hist. Soc.* 71 (1953–7).

Early Greek Cult Practice R. Hägg, N. Marinatos, and G. C. Nordquist eds., *Early Greek Cult Practice* (Stockholm 1988).

Edelstein, *Asclepius* E. J. and L. Edelstein, *Asclepius: A Collection and Interpretation of the Testimonies* (2 vols., Baltimore 945).

Faraguna, *Atene nell'età di Alessandro* M. Faraguna, *Atene nell'età di Alessandro: Problemi politici, economici, finanziari* (*Atti dell'Acc. naz. Lincei* 382, 1992, Scienze morali, storiche, filologiche, Memorie ix.ii.2 pp. 165–445, Rome 1992).

Ferguson, 'Attic Orgeones' W. S. Ferguson, 'The Attic Orgeones', *HThR* 37 (1944), 61–140.

Ferguson, *Hellenistic Athens* W. S. Ferguson, *Hellenistic Athens* (London 1911).

Ferguson, 'Orgeonika' W. S. Ferguson, 'Orgeonika', in *Commemorative Studies in Honor of Theodore Leslie Shear* (*Hesperia*

	Suppl. 8, Princeton 1949), 130–63.
Ferguson, 'Salaminioi'	W. S. Ferguson, 'The Salaminioi of Heptaphylai and Sounion', *Hesperia* 7 (1938), 1–74.
Ferguson, *Treasurers*	W. S. Ferguson, *The Treasurers of Athena* (Cambridge, Mass. 1932).
FGE	D. L. Page ed., *Further Greek Epigrams* (Cambridge 1981).
Floren, *Griechische Plastik I*	J. Floren, *Die geometrische und archaische Plastik* (Munich 1987) = vol. I of W. Fuchs and J. Floren, *Die griechische Plastik.*
Foucart, *Mystères d'Éleusis*	P. Foucart, *Les mystères d'Éleusis* (Paris 1914).
Garland, *New Gods*	R. Garland, *Introducing New Gods: The Politics of Athenian Religion* (London 1992).
Gauthier, *Bienfaiteurs*	P. Gauthier, *Les cités grecques et leurs bienfaiteurs (IVᵉ–Iᵉʳ siècle avant J.-C.)* (*BCH* Suppl. 12, Athens 1985).
Gifts to the Gods	T. Linders and G. Nordquist eds., *Gifts to the Gods* (= *Boreas: Acta universitatis Uppsaliensis* 15, Uppsala 1987).
Goody, *Logic of Writing*	J. Goody, *The Logic of Writing and the Organisation of Society* (Cambridge 1986).
Graef/Langlotz, *Vasen von der Akropolis*	B. Graef and E. Langlotz, *Die antiken Vasen von der Akropolis zu Athen* (2 vols. in 4, Berlin 1925–33).
Graf, *Nordionische Kulte*	F. Graf, *Nordionische Kulte* (Biblioteca Helvetica Romana 21, 1985).
Graf, *Orphische Dichtung*	F. Graf, *Eleusis und die orphische Dichtung Athens in vorhellenistischer Zeit* (Berlin 1974).
Habicht, *Gottmenschentum*	C. Habicht, *Gottmenschentum und griechische Städte*² (*Zetemeta* 14, Munich 1970).
Habicht, *Studien*	C. Habicht, *Studien zur Geschichte Athens in hellenistischer Zeit* (*Hypomnemata* 73, Göttingen 1982).
Habicht, *Untersuchungen*	C. Habicht, *Untersuchungen zur politischen Geschichte Athens im 3. Jahrhundert v. Chr.* (*Vestigia* 30, Munich 1979).

Hägg, *Greek Renaissance*

R. Hägg and N. Marinatos eds., *The Greek Renaissance of the Eighth Century B.C.* (Stockholm 1993).

Hansen, 'Trial of Sokrates'

Forthcoming English version of M. H. Hansen, 'Hvorfor Henrettede Athenerne Sokrates', *Museum Tusculanum* 40/3 (1980), 55–82.

Hedrick, *Demotionidai*

C. W. Hedrick Jr., *The Decrees of the Demotionidai* (*American Classical Studies* 22; Atlanta 1990).

Hedrick, 'Phratry Shrines'

C. W. Hedrick, 'Phratry Shrines of Attica and Athens', *Hesperia* 60 (1991), 241–68.

Herter, 'Theseus'

H. Herter, art. 'Theseus' in *RE* Suppl. vol. XIII (1973), 1045–238.

Hornblower, *Commentary*

S. Hornblower, *A Commentary on Thucydides*, I, bks. 1–3 (Oxford 1991).

Hornblower, *Greek World*

S. Hornblower, *The Greek World 479–323 BC* (corrected imp., London 1985).

Hornblower, *Mausolus*

S. Hornblower, *Mausolus* (Oxford 1982).

Humphreys, 'Genos'

Ch. in S. C. Humphreys' forthcoming *Athenians and their Kindred* (provisional title, Oxford).

Humphreys, 'Lycurgus'

S. C. Humphreys, 'Lycurgus of Butadae: An Athenian Aristocrat', in J. W. Eadie and J. Ober eds., *The Craft of the Ancient Historian: Essays in Honour of C. G. Starr* (Lanham, Md., 1985), 199–252.

IG I³

Inscriptiones Graecae I³: *Inscriptiones Atticae Euclidis Anno Anteriores* (Berlin: fasc. 1 ed. D. M. Lewis, 1981; fasc. 2 ed. id. and L. Jeffery, 1994). For details of other vols. of *IG* see LSJ, p. xlii.

Inscr. Dél.

Inscriptions de Délos. To the details in LSJ, p. xii, add *Inscr. Dél.: Période de l'Amphictyonie attico-délienne, actes administratifs* (nos. 89 to 104–33), ed. J. Coupry (Paris 1972).

Jacoby, *Atthis*

F. Jacoby, *Atthis: The Local Chronicles of Ancient Athens* (Oxford 1949).

Jameson et al., *Selinous*

M. H. Jameson, D. R. Jordan, and R. D. Kotansky, *A* Lex Sacra *from*

Selinous (GRBM 11, 1993). 'A 4'
refers to line 4 of face A of the
sacred law itself.

Jeffery, *Local Scripts* — L. H. Jeffery, *The Local Scripts of
Archaic Greece*[2], with suppl. by
A. W. Johnston (Oxford 1990).

Jensen — *Hyperidis Orationes Sex cum
Ceterarum Fragmentis*, ed. C. Jensen
(Stuttgart 1917).

Jones, *Public Organization* — N. F. Jones, *Public Organization in
Ancient Greece* (Philadelphia 1987).

Judeich, *Topographie* — W. Judeich, *Topographie von Athen*[2]
(Munich 1931).

K/A (after a fragment number) — R. Kassel and C. Austin, *Poetae
Comici Graeci* (Berlin 1983–).

Kearns, 'Continuity and Change' — E. Kearns, 'Change and Continuity
in Religious Structures after
Cleisthenes', in *Crux*, 189–207.

Kearns, *Heroes of Attica* — E. Kearns, *The Heroes of Attica*
(*BICS* Suppl. 57, London 1989).

Kolb, *Agora und Theater* — F. Kolb, *Agora und Theater: Volks-
und Festversammlung* (Berlin 1981).

Kolb, 'Baupolitik' — F. Kolb, 'Die Bau-, Religions- und
Kulturpolitik der Peisistratiden',
JdI 92 (1977), 99–138.

Kraay, *Greek Coins* — C. M. Kraay, *Archaic and Classical
Greek Coins* (London 1976).

Kron, *Phylenheroen* — U. Kron, *Die zehn attischen
Phylenheroen* (*AM-BH* 5, Berlin
1976).

Kurtz/Boardman, *Greek Burial
Customs* — D. C. Kurtz and J. Boardman,
Greek Burial Customs (London 1971).

Kutsch, *Heilheroen* — F. Kutsch, *Attische Heilgötter und
Heilheroen* (Giessen 1913).

Kyle, *Athletics in Athens* — D. G. Kyle, *Athletics in Ancient
Athens*[2] (Brill 1993).

Lambert, *Phratries* — S. D. Lambert, *The Phratries of
Attica* (Ann Arbor 1993).

Langdon, *Sanctuary of Zeus* — M. K. Langdon, *A Sanctuary of
Zeus on Mount Hymettos* (*Hesperia*
Suppl. 16, Princeton 1976).

Lauter, *Landgemeinden* — H. Lauter, *Attische Landgemeinden
in klassischer Zeit, MarbWPr* 1991
(1993).

Lauter, *Turkovuni* — H. Lauter, *Der Kultplatz auf dem
Turkovuni* (*AM-BH* 12, Berlin
1985).

Lévêque/Vidal-Naquet, *Clisthène* — P. Lévêque and P. Vidal-Naquet, *Clisthène l'Athénien* (Paris 1964).

LGPN — *A Lexicon of Greek Personal Names*, I: *The Aegean Islands, Cyprus, Cyrenaica*, ed. P. M. Fraser and E. Matthews (Oxford 1987); II: *Attica*, ed. M. J. Osborne and S. G. Byrne (Oxford 1994).

LIMC — *Lexicon Iconographicum Mythologiae Classicae* (7 vols. in 14 pts., Zurich 1974–).

Lloyd-Jones, *Justice of Zeus* — H. J. Lloyd-Jones, *The Justice of Zeus*[2] (Berkeley 1983).

Lohmann, 'Country Life' — H. Lohmann, 'Agriculture and Country Life in Classical Athens', in B. Wells ed., *Agriculture in Ancient Greece* (Stockholm 1992), 29–57.

Loraux, *L'invention* — N. Loraux, *L'invention d'Athènes: Histoire de l'oraison funèbre dans la 'cité classique'* (Paris 1981).

LSA — F. Sokolowski, *Lois sacrées de l'Asie Mineure* (Paris 1955).

LSCG — F. Sokolowski, *Lois sacrées des cités grecques* (Paris 1969).

LSS — F. Sokolowski, *Lois sacrées des cités grecques, suppl.* (Paris 1962).

Maass, *Prohedrie* — M. Maass, *Die Prohedrie des Dionysostheaters in Athen* (Munich 1972).

Manville, *Citizenship* — P. B. Manville, *The Origins of Citizenship in Ancient Athens* (Princeton 1990).

Mark, *Athena Nike* — I. S. Mark, *The Sanctuary of Athena Nike in Athens: Architectural Stages and Chronology* (AIA monograph NS 2 and *Hesperia* Suppl. 26, Princeton 1993).

Meiggs, *Athenian Empire* — R. Meiggs, *The Athenian Empire* (Oxford 1972).

Metzger, *Recherches* — H. Metzger, *Recherches sur l'imagerie athénienne* (Paris 1965).

Meyer, *Urkundenreliefs* — M. Meyer, *Die griechischen Urkundenreliefs* (*AM-BH* 13, Berlin 1989).

Michel — C. Michel, *Recueil d'inscriptions grecques* (Brussels 1900).

Mikalson, *Athenian Popular* — J. D. Mikalson, *Athenian*

Religion	*Popular Religion* (Chapel Hill, NC, 1983).
Mikalson, *Calendar*	J. D. Mikalson, *The Sacred and Civil Calendar of the Athenian Year* (Princeton 1975).
Millett, *Lending and Borrowing*	P. Millett, *Lending and Borrowing in Ancient Athens* (Cambridge 1991).
Mitchel, 'Lykourgan Athens'	F. W. Mitchel, 'Lykourgan Athens: 338–322, in *Lectures in Memory of Louis Taft Semple*, 2nd ser. (University of Cincinnati 1973).
M/L	R. Meiggs and D. M. Lewis, *A Selection of Greek Historical Inscriptions*, rev. edn. (Oxford 1988).
Moretti	L. Moretti ed., *Iscrizioni storiche ellenistiche* (2 vols., Florence 1967, 1976). Reference is to vol. I unless otherwise indicated.
Morris, *Burial*	I. Morris, *Burial and Ancient Society* (Cambridge 1987).
Murray/Price, *Greek City*	O. Murray and S. Price eds., *The Greek City. From Homer to Alexander* (Oxford 1990).
Mylonas, *Mysteries*	G. E. Mylonas, *Eleusis and the Eleusinian Mysteries* (Princeton 1961).
'Myths'	R. Parker, 'Myths of Early Athens', in J. Bremmer ed., *Interpretations of Greek Mythology* (London 1987), 187–214.
Nauck (after a fragment number)	A. Nauck, *Tragicorum Graecorum Fragmenta*[2] (Leipzig 1889).
Naumann, *Die Ikonographie der Kybele*	F. Naumann, *Die Ikonographie der Kybele in der phrygischen und der griechischen Kunst* (*IstMitt-BH* 28, Tübingen 1983).
Nilsson, 'Bendis'	M. P. Nilsson, 'Bendis in Athen', *From the Collections of Ny Carlsberg*, III (1942), 169–88 = Nilsson, *Op. Sel.* III.55–80.
Nilsson, *Geschichte*	M. P. Nilsson, *Geschichte der griechischen Religion*, I[3], II[2] (Munich 1951, 1969) (the reference is to I unless otherwise stated).
Nilsson, *Griechische Feste*	M. P. Nilsson, *Griechische Feste von religiöser Bedeutung mit Ausschluss der attischen* (Leipzig 1906).

Nilsson, *Op. Sel.*	M. P. Nilsson, *Martini P. Nilsson Opuscula Selecta* (3 vols., Lund 1951–60).
Ober, *Mass and Elite*	J. Ober, *Mass and Elite in Democratic Athens* (Princeton 1989).
Osborne, *Demos*	R. Osborne, *Demos: The Discovery of Classical Attika* (Cambridge 1985).
Osborne, *Naturalization*	M. J. Osborne, *Naturalization in Athens* (4 vols. in 3, Brussels 1981–3). Numbers preceded by a D or T refer to items in the catalogues of Decrees (vols. I and II) and of Testimonia (vol. III).
Ostwald, *Popular Sovereignty*	M. Ostwald, *From Popular Sovereignty to the Sovereignty of Law: Law, Society and Politics in Fifth Century Athens* (Berkeley 1986).
Parker, *Miasma*	R. Parker, *Miasma* (Oxford 1983).
Paroem. Graec.	E. L. Leutsch and F. G. Schneidewin, *Corpus Paroemiographorum Graecorum* (2 vols., Göttingen 1839, 1851).
Payne/Young, *Archaic Marble Sculpture*	H. Payne and G. Mackworth-Young, *Archaic Marble Sculpture from the Acropolis*² (London 1950).
Pečírka, *Enktesis*	J. Pečírka, *The Formula for the Grant of Enktesis in Attic Inscriptions* (Prague 1966).
Pélékidis, *Éphébie*	Ch. Pélékidis, *Histoire de l'éphébie attique des origines à 31 avant Jésus-Christ* (Paris 1962).
Petrakos, Ἱερὸν τοῦ Ἀμφιαράου	B. C. Petrakos, Ὁ Ὠρωπὸς καὶ τὸ Ἱερὸν τοῦ Ἀμφιαράου (Athens 1968).
Pickard-Cambridge, *Dithyramb*	A. W. Pickard-Cambridge, *Dithyramb, Tragedy and Comedy* (Oxford 1927).
Pickard-Cambridge, *Dramatic Festivals*²	A. W. Pickard-Cambridge, *The Dramatic Festivals of Athens*, rev. J. Gould and D. M. Lewis (Oxford 1968; reissued with suppl. 1988).
Placing the Gods	S. E. Alcock and R. Osborne eds., *Placing the Gods: Sanctuaries and Sacred Space in Ancient Greece* (Oxford 1994).

PMG	D. L. Page ed., *Poetae Melici Graeci* (Oxford 1962).
Poland, *Vereinswesen*	F. Poland, *Geschichte des griechischen Vereinswesens* (Leipzig 1909).
de Polignac, *Naissance*	F. de Polignac, *La naissance de la cité grecque* (Paris 1984).
Pouilloux, *Rhamnonte*	J. Pouilloux, *La forteresse de Rhamnonte* (*BEFAR* 179, Paris 1954).
Price, *Rituals and Power*	S. R. F. Price, *Rituals and Power: The Roman Imperial Cult in Asia Minor* (Cambridge 1984).
Prinz, *Gründungsmythen*	F. Prinz, *Gründungsmythen und Sagenchronologie* (Munich 1979).
Pritchett, *Greek State at War*	W. K. Pritchett, *The Greek State at War* (Berkeley 1979 [III] and 1985 [IV]).
QS	*Quaderni di Storia.*
Radt (after a fragment number)	See *TrGF*.
Raubitschek, *Dedications*	A. E. Raubitschek, *Dedications from the Athenian Acropolis* (Cambridge, Mass. 1949).
Reinmuth, *Ephebic Inscriptions*	O. W. Reinmuth, *The Ephebic Inscriptions of the Fourth Century B.C.* (*Mnemosyne* Suppl. 14, Leiden 1971).
Rhodes, *Boule*	P. J. Rhodes, *The Athenian Boule* (Oxford 1972).
Rhodes, *Commentary Ath. Pol.*	P. J. Rhodes, *A Commentary on the Aristotelian* Athenaion Politeia (Oxford 1981).
Richardson, *Hymn to Demeter*	N. J. Richardson, *The Homeric Hymn to Demeter* (Oxford 1974).
Ridgway, *Archaic Style*	B. S. Ridgway, *The Archaic Style in Greek Sculpture* (Princeton 1977).
Ritual, Finance, Politics	S. Hornblower and R. Osborne eds., *Ritual, Finance, Politics: Democratic Accounts Rendered to D. M. Lewis* (Oxford 1994).
Robert, *Heldensage*	C. Robert, *Die griechische Heldensage* (Berlin 1920–6).
Robert, *OMS*	L. Robert, *Opera Minora Selecta* (7 vols., Paris 1969–90).
Robertson, *Festivals and Legends*	N. Robertson, *Festivals and Legends: The Formation of Greek Cities in the Light of Public Ritual* (*Phoenix* Suppl. 31, Toronto 1992).
Robertson, *History*	M. Robertson, *A History of Greek*

Art (Cambridge 1975).

Rosivach, *Public Sacrifice* V. J. Rosivach, *The System of Public Sacrifice in Fourth-Century Athens* (American Classical Studies 34, Atlanta 1994).

Roussel, *Tribu et cité* D. Roussel, *Tribu et cité: Études sur les groupes sociaux dans les cités grecques aux époques archaïque et classique* (Annales littéraires de l'université de Besançon 193, Paris 1976).

Ruschenbusch (after a fragment number) E. Ruschenbusch, *Die Fragmente des solonischen Gesetzeswerkes* (*Historia* Einzelschriften 9, Wiesbaden 1966).

Schachter, *Cults* A. Schachter, *The Cults of Boiotia* (*BICS* Suppl. 38, London 1981–   ).

Schmitt Pantel, *Cité au banquet* P. Schmitt Pantel, *La cité au banquet: Histoire des repas publics dans les cités grecques* (*CEFR* 157, Paris 1992).

Schrader, *Marmorbildwerke* H. Schrader (with E. Langlotz and W. Schuchardt), *Die archaischen Marmorbildwerke der Akropolis* (Frankfurt 1939).

Schwarz, *Triptolemos* G. Schwarz, *Triptolemos: Ikonographie einer Agrar- und Mysteriengottheit* (*Grazer Beiträge* Suppl. 2, Horn 1987).

Schwenk, *Age of Alexander* C. J. Schwenk, *Athens in the Age of Alexander* (Chicago 1985). 'Schwenk 22' means inscription no. 22 in Schwenk's collection.

Schwyzer E. Schwyzer, *Dialectorum Graecarum Exempla Epigraphica Potiora* (Leipzig 1923).

Seaford, *Reciprocity and Ritual* R. Seaford, *Reciprocity and Ritual* (Oxford 1994).

Shapiro, *Art and Cult* H. A. Shapiro, *Art and Cult under the Tyrants in Athens* (Mainz 1989).

Shapiro, *Personifications* H. A. Shapiro, *Personifications in Greek Art* (Kilchberg 1993).

Shear, *Kallias* T. L. Shear Jr., *Kallias of Sphettos and the Revolt of Athens in 286 B.C.* (*Hesperia* Suppl. 17, Princeton 1978).

Shipley, *Samos* G. Shipley, *A History of Samos, 800–188 B.C.* (Oxford 1987).

Simon, *Festivals* E. Simon, *Festivals of Attica: An*

	Archaeological Commentary (Madison 1983).
Simon, *Götter*	E. Simon, *Die Götter der Griechen* (Munich 1969).
Smarczyk, *Religionspolitik*	B. Smarczyk, *Untersuchungen zur Religionspolitik und politischen Propaganda Athens im Delisch-Attischen Seebund* (Munich 1990).
Snodgrass, *An Archaeology*	A. M. Snodgrass, *An Archaeology of Greece* (Berkeley 1987).
Sourvinou-Inwood, 'Polis Religion', (1) and (2)	C. Sourvinou-Inwood, 'What is *Polis* Religion?', in Murray/ Price, *Greek City*, 295–322; ead., 'Further Aspects of Polis Religion', in *AnnArchStorAnt* 10 (1988), 259–74.
Stahl, *Aristokraten und Tyrannen*	M. Stahl, *Aristokraten und Tyrannen im archaischen Athen* (Stuttgart 1987).
Stupperich, *Staatsbegräbnis*	R. Stupperich, *Staatsbegräbnis und Privatgrabmal im klassischen Athen* (Diss. Münster 1977, 2 pts. in 1: references are to Pt. 1 unless otherwise indicated).
Tagalidou, *Herakles*	E. Tagalidou, *Weihreliefs an Herakles aus klassischer Zeit* (Jonsered 1993).
Tausend, *Amphiktyonie*	K. Tausen, *Amphiktyonie und Symmachie* (Stuttgart 1992).
Thomas, *Oral Tradition*	R. Thomas, *Oral Tradition and Written Record in Classical Athens* (Cambridge 1989).
Thompson/Wycherley, *Agora*	H. A. Thompson and R. E. Wycherley, *Agora*, XIV: *The Agora of Athens: The History, Shape and Uses of an Ancient City Center* (Princeton 1972).
Tod, *GHI*	M. N. Tod, *A Selection of Greek Historical Inscriptions* (2 vols., Oxford 1933, 1947).
Todd, *Athenian Law*	S. C. Todd, *The Shape of Athenian Law* (Oxford 1993).
Töpffer, *Attische Genealogie*	J. Töpffer, *Attische Genealogie* (Berlin 1889).
Tracy	S. V. Tracy, *Attic Letter-Cutters of 229 to 86 B.C.* (Berkeley 1990).
Traill, *Political Organization*	J. S. Traill, *The Political Organiz-ation of Attica* (*Hesperia* Suppl. 14, Princeton 1974).

Travlos, *Bildlexikon*   J. Travlos, *Bildlexikon zur*
                                    Topographie des antiken Attika
                                    (Tübingen 1988).

Travlos, *Pictorial Dictionary*   J. Travlos, *Pictorial Dictionary of*
                                    Ancient Athens (London 1971).

Tresp, *Kultschriftsteller*   A. Tresp, *Die Fragmente der*
                                    griechischen Kultschriftsteller
                                    (Giessen 1914).

TrGF   *Tragicorum Graecorum Fragmenta*,
                                    I: ed. B. Snell, *Tragici Minores*; III:
                                    ed. S. Radt, *Aeschylus*; IV: ed.
                                    S. Radt, *Sophocles* (Göttingen 1971,
                                    1985, 1977).

Vanderpool Studies   *Studies in Attic Epigraphy, History*
                                    and Topography Presented to Eugene
                                    Vanderpool (*Hesperia* Suppl. 19,
                                    Princeton 1982).

van Straten, 'Gifts'   F. T. van Straten, 'Gifts for the
                                    Gods', in H. S. Versnel ed., *Faith,*
                                    Hope and Worship (Leiden 1981),
                                    65–151.

van Wees, *Status Warriors*   H. van Wees, *Status Warriors: War,*
                                    Violence and Society in Homer and
                                    History (Amsterdam 1992).

Vermaseren, *Corpus Cultus*   M. J. Vermaseren, *Corpus*
Cybelae II   *Cultus Cybelae Attidisque*, II:
                                    Graecia atque Insulae (Leiden 1982).

Versnel, *Ter Unus*   H. S. Versnel, *Ter Unus* (Leiden
                                    1990).

Veyne, *Les Grecs ont-ils cru à*   P. Veyne, *Les Grecs ont-ils cru à*
leurs mythes?   *leurs mythes? Essai sur l'imagination*
                                    constituante (Paris 1983).

Veyne, *Pain et cirque*   P. Veyne, *Le pain et le cirque:*
                                    Sociologie historique d'un pluralisme
                                    politique (Paris 1976).

Veyne, *Writing History*   P. Veyne, *Writing History*, tr. M.
                                    Moore-Rinvolucri (Manchester
                                    1984; French orig. 1971).

Vidal-Naquet, *Black Hunter*   P. Vidal-Naquet, *The Black Hunter:*
                                    Forms of Thought and Forms of
                                    Society in the Greek World, tr. A.
                                    Szegedy-Maszak (Baltimore 1986;
                                    French orig. 1981).

Wallace, *Areopagos Council*   R. W. Wallace, *The Areopagos*
                                    Council, to 307 B.C. (Baltimore 1989).

Walter, *Akropolismuseum*   O. Walter, *Beschreibung der Reliefs*
                                    im kleinen Akropolismuseum in Athen
                                    (Vienna 1923).

Welwei, *Athen*	K. W. Welwei, *Athen: Vom neolithischen Siedlungsplatz zur archaischen Grosspolis* (Darmstadt 1992).
West (after a fragment number)	M. L. West, *Iambi et Elegi Graeci*[2] (2 vols., Oxford 1989–92).
West, *Orphic Poems*	M. L. West, *The Orphic Poems* (Oxford 1983).
Whitehead, *Demes*	D. Whitehead, *The Demes of Attica, 508/7–c.250 B.C.* (Princeton 1986).
Whitley, *Style and Society*	J. Whitley, *Style and Society in Dark Age Greece* (Cambridge 1992).
Wilamowitz, *Antigonos*	U. von Wilamowitz-Moellendorf, *Antigonos von Karystos* (Berlin 1881).
Wilamowitz, *Glaube*	U. von Wilamowitz-Moellendorf, *Der Glaube der Hellenen* (2 vols., Berlin 1931–2) (cited from 1959 Darmstadt reprint, which has slightly different page-numbers).
Wycherley, *Stones of Athens*	R. E. Wycherley, *Stones of Athens* (Princeton 1978).
Wycherley, *Testimonia*	R. E. Wycherley, *Agora* III: *Literary and Epigraphical Testimonia* (Princeton 1957).
Yunis, *A New Creed*	H. Yunis, *A New Creed: Fundamental Religious Beliefs in the Athenian Polis and Euripidean Drama* (*Hypomnemata* 91, Meisenheim 1988).

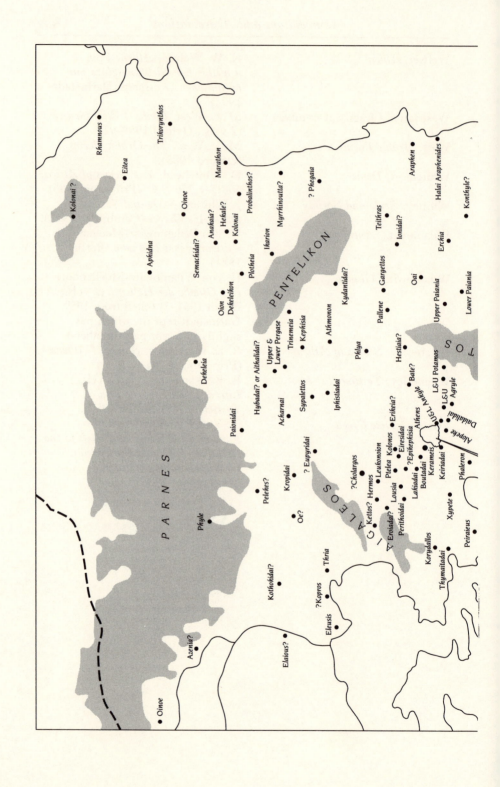

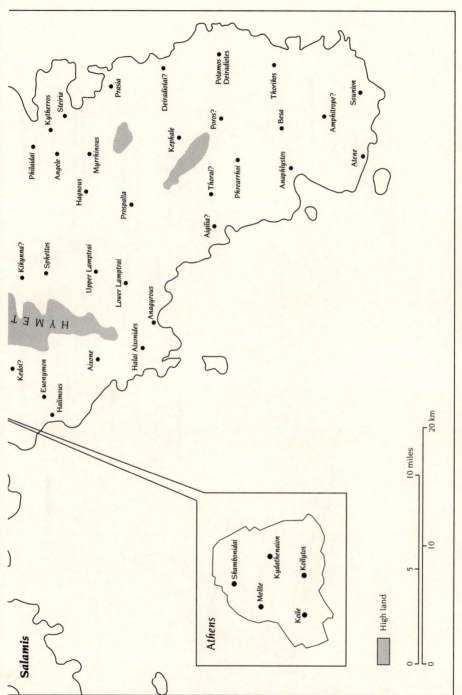

Salamis

Kedoi?

Εμονymon
Halimous

Kikynna?

Sphettos

Upper Lamptrai

Aixone

Lower Lamptrai

HYMET

Halai Aixonides

Anagyrous

Philaidai

Angele

Hagnous

Myrrhinous

Prospalta

Kytherros

Steiria

Prasia

Aigilia?

Thorai?

Phrearrhoi

Deiradiotai?

Kephale

Poros?

Potamos
Deiradiotes

Besa

Thorikos

Anaphlystos

Amphitrope?

Sounion

Atene

Athens

Skambonidai

Melite

Kydathenaion

Koile

Kollytos

High land

0   5   10

0   10

10 miles

20 km

MAP I. The Demes of Attica, after J. S. Traill, *Demos and Trittys* (1986)

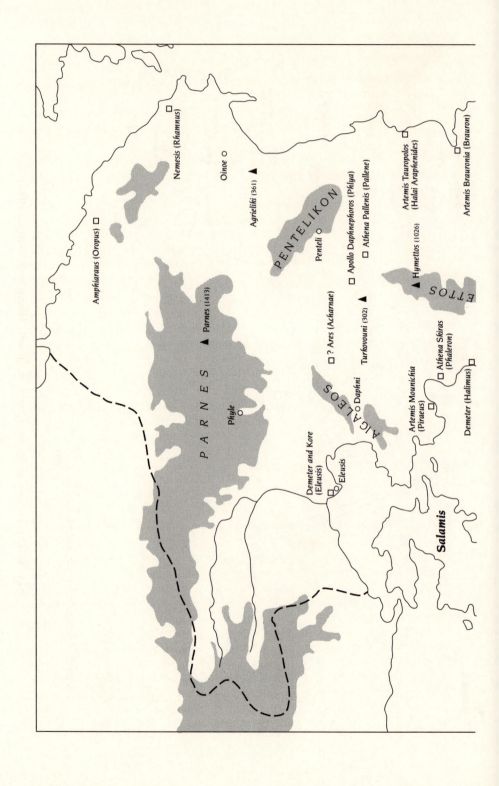

Nemesis (Rhamnus) □

Oinoe ○

▲ Agrieliki (361)

Amphiaraus (Oropus) □

P E N T E L I K O N

Penteli ○

Apollo Daphnephoros (Phlya) □

Athena Pallenis (Pallene) □

Artemis Tauropolos
(Halai Araphenides) □

Artemis Brauronia (Brauron) □

Hymettos (1026)

▲ Parnes (1413)

P A R N E S

? Ares (Acharnae) □

▲ Turkovouni (302)

H Y M E T T O S ▲

Athena Skiras
(Phaleron) □

Demeter (Halimus) □

Phyle ○

A I G A L E O S

Daphni ○

Artemis Mounichia
(Piraeus) □

Demeter and Kore
(Eleusis) □

Eleusis ○

Salamis

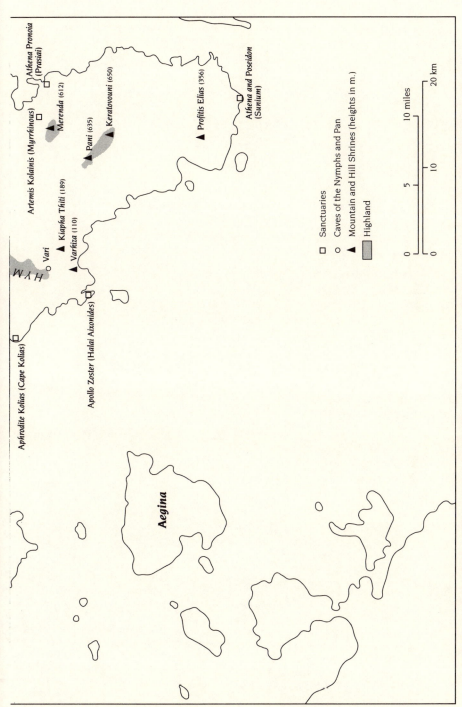

MAP II. Caves of Pan, Mountain and Hill Shrines, and Principal Sanctuaries outside Athens and the Piraeus

1

Introduction

'The general conclusion of the book which the reader has before him is that religion is something eminently social,' writes Durkheim in the introduction to *The Elementary Forms of the Religious Life*. To a Greek, the great sociologist's revolutionary thesis might have seemed a little tame. A society which commonly expressed the idea of 'belonging to the same social group as' in terms of 'sharing lustral water with' or something similar evidently in one sense took the 'eminently social' character of religion very much for granted. Even the philosophers (when not thinking theologically) constantly see religious practice as a medium of association not between man and god but between man and man.[1] Indeed, religion's most important function in their eyes is as a vehicle of κοινωνία, fellowship, at many different levels.

Among students of Greek religion, Durkheim's position is far from being controversial. To insist on the 'eminently social' character of that religion is in fact something of a cliché. How radically Durkheim's insight has affected the way in which the subject is commonly studied is another matter. To speak very crudely, in a religious act a group of worshippers approach a god via a set of traditional procedures, acting on the basis (or at least 'as if' on the basis[2]) of certain beliefs. 'Gods', 'traditional procedures' (rituals, festivals), and 'beliefs' of course form the standard material of studies of Greek religion. 'Groups of worshippers', on the other hand, tend to be simply taken for granted.[3] It is as if, in the proposition 'Greek religion is social', 'social' can be interpreted simply as 'not

---

[1] See e.g. the passages cited (very revealingly for our argument about 'embedded' religion) in a study of *Lending and Borrowing in Ancient Athens* (by P. Millett, Cambridge 1991), 151. For the pressure towards harmony created by shared participation at sacrifices see e.g. Xen. *Hell*. 2.4.20–21; Isaeus fr. 4 Thalheim *ap.* Dion. Hal. *Isaeus* 10; Men. *Dysc.* 560–62; n. 9 below; Schmitt Pantel, *Cité au banquet*, 249.

[2] Cf. Veyne, *Writing History*, 196–97.

[3] See, however, C. Sourvinou-Inwood, *'Reading' Greek Culture* (Oxford 1991), 147–51, and more generally her very important studies 'Polis Religion'.

individual', without any further need arising to analyse the many different forms of grouping that in fact make up society.

This neglect is in part a product of certain long-established demarcations in the study of the subject. Comprehensive accounts of Greek religion, the great 'Histories', are typically Panhellenic. As syntheses of material from hundreds of Greek cities, each with its own social structure, they obviously cannot attempt to relate these practices very closely to particular social groups. Local studies tend to proceed piecemeal, cult by cult. Often they treat not the full range of religious activities of a given city or region, but a special subset, the festivals. This tradition of hiving off 'festivals' as a separate object of study, which goes back to antiquity,[4] isolates them from the broader life of the society in which they are performed. The festivals of the various Greek states, torn from their place of origin, float in a sea outside time and place, occupied only by other festivals.

Numerous exceptions exist, of course.[5] In the French-speaking world in particular, Durkheim's work was taken as an incentive to study particular social forms and institutions of the historical period,[6] not (as in Britain) to scurry back across the millennia in search of the hypothetical social 'origins' of Greek religion. And vagueness about the social context of Greek religious practices is often a product not of choice but of brute necessity. Most obviously, archaeologists are much more likely to be able to identify sacred sites and, with luck, the god they belonged to, than the particular social groups that made use of them; but the bias of the evidence is much broader than this. Again, it is scarcely the fault of modern students of Greek festivals that no equivalent to *Le Carnaval de Romans*[7] exists. The choice is largely between writing accounts of Greek festivals that are somewhat ahistorical and abstract, and writing none at all.

For Attica, however, the situation is much less unfavourable, and the worshipping groups can be studied in some detail. (Distinguished studies of them have in fact been made, but normally by historians rather than by specialists in Greek religion.[8]) Surely one

---

[4] See Tresp, *Kultschriftsteller*, 27–28.

[5] A notable Attic one is Kearns, *Heroes of Attica*, to which the present work seeks to be a kind of complement.

[6] By Louis Gernet above all (cf. S. C. Humphreys, *Anthropology and the Greeks*, London 1978, 76–106), to whom the so-called 'Paris school' owes its sociological cast of mind. Contrast the subtitle of Jane Harrison, *Themis: A Study of the Social Origins of Greek Religion* (Cambridge 1912). Admittedly much in Durkheim's *Elementary Forms* itself encouraged the concern with 'origins'.

[7] E. Le Roy Ladurie's celebrated study (Paris 1979) of an uprising during the Carnival at Romans, south-east of Lyons, in 1580.

[8] In this regard the contribution of W. S. Ferguson is outstanding. The valuable short study by Mikalson, *Athenian Popular Religion*, is primarily about religious attitudes.

ought to seize the opportunity of fitting, for once, an account of rites and gods upon the underlying social framework that is the armature of all Greek religious practices. Again, religion in Athens has much more of a history than it has in Greece as a whole or in any other state. The origins of many cults are known, as are the dates of the most fundamental reorganizations of the whole structure. It is a history which even contains events, such as the trial of Socrates, and personalities, such as Lycurgus, whose religious position can be described. Where histories of Greek religion and histories of Greece commonly pursue parallel paths at some distance from one another, an account of Attic religion constantly intersects with ordinary Athenian history. The normal isolation of the two spheres is a necessity that still impoverishes; the chance of escaping from it in the special case is again surely to be welcomed.

There are further reasons, one may more tentatively suggest, why it might in principle be desirable to take the individual city as the basic unit of analysis in any study of Greek religion. Of course, in certain senses what we conventionally term 'Greek religion' is indeed Greek; but if one specifies those senses one also sees their limitations. First and perhaps least important, certain shrines and festivals were in principle open to all Greeks, participation in such rites being in fact fundamental to such sense as the Greeks had of a shared national identity.[9] Athenians went outside Attica for religious purposes, or might do; and non-Athenians flocked to the Eleusinian Mysteries. Secondly, all Greek cities to our knowledge were heirs to a common religious tradition, consisting most obviously of the names of the principal gods, basic ritual procedures such as sacrifice, and numerous Panhellenic myths. Thirdly, the Greek cities' sense of cultural identity with one another imposed a certain pressure towards homogeneity: innovations were very likely to be imitated, the cults of an individual city were rather unlikely to develop in a way that was wholly alien to the Panhellenic norm. These factors were important constraints upon the development of religious life in the individual cities. But it is precisely as 'constraints' upon the active and organizing principle, the cities, that they should be viewed. The religious experience of the individual was almost entirely shaped by his or her city and the subgroups of which it was made up. As in political life, the lesser units formed a pyramid, of which the pinnacle was not nation but city. As for innovation and change, they came either from the cities or (as with

---

[9] See e.g. Hdt. 8.144.2 (and several appeals by speakers in him to 'shared' [9.90], or 'Hellenic' gods); Ar. *Lys.* 1129–31; Thuc. 3.59.2; Isoc. *Paneg.* 43; Pl. *Resp.* 470e.

Orphism) from forces that lay outside the formal structures altogether: never from 'Greece'.[10]

'History of Greece' is in effect an abbreviated expression for 'history of the interaction of the individual Greek states'. Greek consti-
tutional history likewise is the history of individual Greek
constitutions; and the case is much the same with Greek law. What
then is a 'history of Greek religion'? Simply a history of the religious
practices of individual Greek states? The analogy, it may be
objected, breaks down here: all Greek states have much more in
common with one another in their religious practices (a shared
acknowledgement of Zeus as king of the gods, for instance) than they
do in their laws or constitutions. It may also be objected that the religious practices of individual Greek cities cease to be an adequate
unit of analysis once it is acknowledged that there is interaction
between them; for members of a group of interacting individuals
may be profoundly influenced by belonging to it even if it takes no
collective decisions.[11]

The issue is delicate, and need not be pressed to the point of resolution here. It is clear that, of the phenomena that we study under
the name 'Greek religion', some at least are such as can only be
investigated in relation to individual states; and rather few are so
general and invariable that a local perspective is simply a pointless
restriction of viewpoint. One might assume, for instance, that
sacrifice is the same always and everywhere in the Greek world. But
the Athenians seem normally not to have sacrificed to heroes according to what are commonly conceived as the norms of heroic
sacrifice.[12] The narrowed perspective is never misleading (provided
one recognizes that Athenian practice was not in fact wholly isolated), often advantageous. 'Athenian religion' is there to be studied
with profit, even if the phrase should in fact be understood as an
abbreviation for 'Greek religion as practised in Attica'.

But how is 'Athenian religion' to be defined? A short definition
would be 'the religious outlook and practices of Athenian citizens'—
who were to be found, of course, throughout Attica, not in Athens
alone. Though lacking most political rights, women are citizens for
our purposes (as they were according to one Athenian interpretation
of citizenship, that which specified, for instance, that birth from 'a
citizen woman', ἀστή,[13] was a condition of a child's legitimacy). The

---

[10] Classification of oracles is problematic: but they are certainly not mouthpieces of Greece.

[11] The 'peer polity interaction' model; for our purposes it is not a decisive objection that
Greek cities were not 'peers' in size and influence.

[12] See A. D. Nock, *HThR* 37 (1944), 144–45 = id., *Essays on Religion and the Ancient World*
(Oxford 1972), 578–79.

[13] Even the word πολῖτις occasionally occurs, as in Isae. 8.43, Dem. 57.43.

practices of other residents of Attica could in principle be excluded to the extent that Athenians ignored, or were ignorant of, them. But the opening of Plato's *Republic* shows us Socrates watching the festival of a Thracian goddess in the Piraeus,[14] then withdrawing for social purposes into the house of a Greek metic where sacrifice has just been performed. The various sectors of society were in constant contact, and very little that happened in Attica can be declared certainly irrelevant to the potential religious experience of an Athenian citizen. Doubtless the mining-slaves in Laurion who clubbed together to make dedications to Phrygian Men can be left on the fringes of the subject, just as they were on the fringes of Athenian awareness.[15] But even against them the city might in principle have intervened, if it had judged their doings impious or subversive.

Is the object of study to be 'public' or 'private' religion? Antitheses of this type sometimes appear in Greek texts, and may have clear meanings in specific contexts; but a general distinction between 'public' and 'private' in religion cannot be maintained.[16] The most important Greek word that suggests the idea of 'public' cult is δημοτελής, 'paid for by the people', which can be applied to sacrifices, festivals, sacred precincts, and even gods. A religious place or act so funded is one over which 'the people' has rights and which it can use to make statements about values; women convicted of adultery, and 'draft-dodgers', for instance, were excluded from 'publicly funded' shrines.[17] But private individuals were, of course,

---

[14] The disapproval that doubtless underlies the text's infinitely urbane surface (cf. C. Montepaone, *AnnArchStorAnt* 12, 1990, 105–109, with citation of Proclus and P. Vidal-Naquet) does not concern us here.

[15] See Ch. 9, n. 146.

[16] See the brilliant arguments of Sourvinou-Inwood, 'Polis Religion' (2), 270–73; she points out *inter alia* that the Pythia traditionally advised *individual* enquirers to honour the gods νόμῳ πόλεως (Xen. *Mem.* 1.3.1, 4.3.16). I air some views on another troublesome antithesis, that between 'popular' and 'literary' religion, in *CR* NS 35 (1985), 90–92 and in a contribution to C. Pelling, *Tragedy and the Historian* (Oxford forthcoming); but the issue is not of central importance to the present volume.*

[17] The early Attic uses are Thuc. 2.15.2 (of the festival *Synoikia*); Pl. *Leg.* 935b (of state sacrifices); Dem. 21.53, where an oracle of Dodona is quoted which prescribes offerings to Dionysus Demoteles (Dittenberger long ago noted, *Hermes* 26, 1891, 474–77, that *LSCG* 102.5, *IG* XII.9.20 attest the adjective as an epithet for gods, even if not at Athens; the old conjecture Διονύσῳ δημοτελῆ ἱερά should therefore have been abandoned); [Dem.] 59. 85–86; Aeschin. 1.183, 3.176 (exclusions from δημοτελῆ shrines). *LGPN* II now lists seventeen attestations of 'Demoteles' as a proper name. For the concept see too *LSS* 19.20 and 19.86 (victims provided by 'the city'). Early non-Attic instances are Hdt. 6.57 (sacrifices in Sparta) and probably *LSCG* 56.15 (shrines: Cleonae). J. K. Davies, *CAH*² IV.2 (1988), 379, notes that several early Attic texts distinguish between private and δημόσια offerings: *IG* I³.35.11–12, 255 B 15–21, 136.32; cf. Aesch. *Sept.* 177 (δήμιος), *Eum.* 655; Xen. *Lac. Pol.* 15.2, *Apol.* 11; [Xen.] *Ath. Pol.* 2.9; also the new instances from Selinous (Jameson et al., *Selinous*, A 18, B 10) and e.g. *SIG*³ 1015. There are numerous fourth-cent. and Hellenistic instances of δημοτελής, which becomes in effect synonymous with δημόσιος: see e.g. the

free to make dedications and perform sacrifices in public temples; indeed, in so far as individuals can be said to have cultivated personal relations with gods, it would most commonly have been with those of public shrines.[18]

At the opposite extreme lie the targets of a famous veto of Plato in *Laws*:[19] 'Let nobody possess shrines in private houses. Whenever anyone is disposed to sacrifice, let him go to the public shrines [δημόσια].' Plato goes on to claim that irrational elements in society, women and the sick in particular, cram 'every house and every village' with altars that, ignorantly and impetuously, they have vowed to establish, whether in anxiety or desperation or, by contrast, in high elation. But in what senses are even 'shrines in private houses' private? Plato ignores the many types of such shrine that, far from being products of individual impulse, were recommended, and even prescribed, by tradition: the well-known household cults of Apollo Agyieus and Hermes and Hestia and, above all, Zeus Herkeios. Even though their cult was not 'publicly funded', these were most emphatically among the 'gods whom the city recognizes'; 'do you possess a Zeus Herkeios?' was among the questions put to candidates for a magistracy.[20] Even when, in the manner deplored by Plato, an individual did found an altar to a less familiar power, the expectation was often, and perhaps normally, that it would be open for use by Athenians at large. An altar dedicated to 'Cephisus and the gods who share his altar' by one Xenokrateia in Phaleron around 400, for instance, declares that 'anyone who wishes may sacrifice on it [?] after achieving benefits'.[21]

Thus the antithesis between 'public' and 'private' proves not to be absolute even at its extreme points. And between these extremes lies

entry in LSJ; G. Busolt, *Griechische Staatskunde*[3] (Munich 1920), 521, n. 6; J. and L. Robert, *Fouilles d'Amyzone en Carie* (Paris 1983), 123. Lexicographers often so describe Attic festivals: *Anecd. Bekk.* I.86.20 = *FGrH* 328 F 168 (*Genesia*); Σ Ar. *Ach.* 146 (*Apatouria*); Σ Ar. *Plut.* 627 (*Theseia*). Their usage is not necessarily reliable: Σ Dem. 19.199 describes the rites led by Aeschines' mother as μυστήρια δημοτελῆ καὶ κοινὰ καὶ οὐ πάνυ σέμνα; Σ Ar. *Lys.* 1, by contrast, rightly observes καὶ γὰρ πολλὰς ἑορτὰς αἱ γυναῖκες ἔξω τῶν δημοτελῶν ἦγον ἰδίᾳ συνερχόμεναι (and similarly on the rites of Adonis, *Lys.* 389).

[18] See e.g. Men. *Dysc.* 260–63. On the individual, not the *oikos*, as the minimum unit in Greek cult, see Sourvinou-Inwood, 'Polis Religion' (2), 264–67.

[19] 909d–910e.

[20] Arist. *Ath. Pol.* 55.3. Sourvinou-Inwood, 'Polis Religion' (2), 270–73, argues that the household cults were felt to be dependent on the public cults of the same gods. Commentators point out that even Plato elsewhere countenances 'private' cults of these traditionally sanctioned types (*Leg.* 717b, 885a; n. 23 below). (The main point is not affected by doubts about the actual frequency of household cults: M. Jameson in Murray/Price, *The Greek City*, 192–95.)

[21] *IG* I[3].987 (*CEG* 744). One might compare the activity of Archedemus in the 'cave of the Nymphs' at Vari (*IG* I[3].974–82; W. R. Connor, *ClAnt* 7, 1988, 155–89); but such individual foundations are much harder for us to identify than Plato's attack would lead one to expect.

a large area of ambiguity. Lexicographers distinguish 'publicly funded' (δημοτελῆ) sacrifices and shrines from those of demes (δημοτικά) for which the demesmen pay,[22] and it is true that in usage the word δημοτελής is applied to rites and shrines of the city as a whole. But the cults of the demes, political subdivisions of the city itself, were in no sense private; and it is scarcely credible that a woman of the Piraeus taken in adultery could have gained entry to the Thesmophorion of her deme on the plea that it was not 'publicly funded', i.e. funded by the city of Athens, in the strict sense. There would probably have been more inclination to apply the term 'private' to the shrines of phratries and groups of *orgeones* and religious clubs of other types; indeed it is likely that these are the bodies envisaged by Aristotle when, in a famous passage, he advises the democratic reformer to amalgamate 'private' (ἴδια) into 'few and common' (κοινά) cults.[23] But in different degrees even cults such as these, those of the phratries above all, were products, like the household cults mentioned earlier, of publicly sanctioned convention. To sum up: in terms of finance and ownership and administrative responsibility, there are important distinctions to be drawn between 'public' and 'private' and various intermediate categories; but the traditional practices of the city, the cults of 'the gods whom the city recognizes', flow round and over such divisions. A final argument confirms from a different side that there could exist no authentically private religious domain in Attica. No act, howsoever private, was exempt, it seems, from the possibility of being arraigned as 'impious'.[24] But if the danger of impiety penetrated the innermost recesses of the household, so too did the religion of the city.

The Athenians had little to say about the history of their cults, except in mythological terms. Two ancient observations have, however, been very influential. According to the Aristotelian *Constitution of the Athenians*, the *archon basileus*, most ancient of all

---

[22] So most fully *Anecd. Bekk.* I.240.28–30 (more briefly Harp. and other lexicographers s.v. δημοτελῆ καὶ δημοτικὰ ἱερά); rites funded by groups of *orgeones* and *gene* are noted as further categories. Deme documents tend in fact to refer to their common rites as κοινά: *IG* I³.258.34, *IG* II².1214.11; cf. *Prakt* 1990 (1993), 36, no. 20.5.

[23] *Pol.* 1319ᵇ24–25. In Pl. *Leg.* 885a, by contrast, ἱερὰ ἴδια are those of individual households, in contrast to those of κοινωνίαι of whatsoever type; but diversity of usage in this area is to be expected. The ἱδρύματα ἴδια πατρῴων θεῶν κατὰ νόμον ὀργιαζόμενα of *Leg.* 717b could belong either to households or perhaps to phratries. [Arist.] *Oec.* 1346ᵇ13–15 distinguishes τεμένη δημόσια from θιασωτικά and πατριωτικά (of phratries).

[24] On impiety cf. Ch. 10 below. Sourvinou-Inwood, 'Polis Religion' (2), 270–73, stresses that Leocrates was attacked by Lycurgus in the surviving speech for exporting his own private 'ancestral sacra' from Athens; she also points to the city's legislative control over private burial practices.

the officers of the state, 'administered almost all the ancestral sacrifices'. The eponymous *archon*, by contrast, the youngest, had authority over no ancestral rites but only 'the additions'.[25] It seems in fact to have been a common belief that 'the solemnest and most ancestral of the ancient rites' were in the charge of the *basileus*, who had originally, a true king, 'performed all the sacrifices'.[26] And in most modern accounts this belief has been taken over as an uncontroversial statement of fact. Some, however, have begun to doubt whether a hereditary kingship of the type postulated ever existed in Attica. Even if these doubts are too extreme, the *Thargelia* is an instance of a festival apparently of high antiquity that was in the charge of the eponymous *archon*; to save the Aristotelian principle, we have to suppose that it passed from control of the *basileus* to that of the eponymous *archon* as part of an otherwise unattested reform.[27] And that supposition surely brings out how implausible it is that no adjustments or exchanges or reinterpretations should have occurred in the many centuries of unrecorded history that intervened between the first establishment of magistracies at Athens and the time of the fourth-century sources that for us describe their functions. The hardest fact with which we are left is one about Athenian perceptions: the association between the *basileus* and everything in religion that is archaic, ancestral, authentic.

The other influential ancient text is a passage of Thucydides, where that archaeologically minded historian argues that the city of Athens expanded from a primitive nucleus consisting of the acropolis and the region to the south of it; for here are sited the precincts of Zeus Olympios, Apollo Pythios, Dionysus in the Marshes, Earth, and 'other ancient shrines'.[28] The direction of Thucydides' argument can be reversed, so that the presumed history of the growth of the city becomes a kind of guide to the history of its cults.[29] New possibilities were opened with the publication in 1983 of a text that finally, perhaps, allows the elusive 'old *agora*' and several associated shrines to be pinned down, east of the acropolis and close to the

---

[25] Arist. *Ath. Pol.* 57.1, 3.3 (the latter passage, however, gives the polemarch too a share in τὰ πάτρια). On the πάτριος/ἐπίθετος distinction cf. Ch. 9, n. 3; cf. Arist. *Pol.* 1285ᵇ 14–19.

[26] Pl. *Pol.* 290e6–8; [Dem.] 59.74.

[27] That such a reform occurred is quite plausible on other grounds: see Ch. 6, n. 119. And it must be allowed that all the other rites administered by the eponymous *archon* (*Ath. Pol.* 56.3–5) are, or may be, recent. On the case of the *Epidauria*, a new festival controlled by the *archon* and intercalated within a traditional festival controlled by the *basileus*, cf. S. Dow, *RhM* 113 (1970), 273–76. Kingship at Athens: cf. Ch. 2, n. 19.

[28] 2.15, on which A. W. Gomme has valuable long notes in his commentary (Oxford 1956).

[29] This is one reason why Jane Harrison interrupted her famous studies of Greek religion to write *Primitive Athens as Described by Thucydides* (Cambridge 1906); for a recent application of the approach see Robertson, *Festivals and Legends*, esp. 9–31.

region identified by Thucydides as the primitive core of the city.[30] From whatever theoretical perspective one approaches ancient religion, such questions of topography and spatial relations can prove of inescapable importance. But there are several reasons why the book that follows is not laid out as, so to speak, a commentary on Thucydides' brief text. The chronological indications that Thucydides offers are completely vague; numerous details of topography remain maddeningly obscure; and we must surely doubt Thucydides' over-hasty assumption that where the primitive Athenians worshipped they also necessarily lived. That inference having been removed, what we have is a judgement—an important one, to be sure—about the identity and location of early sacred precincts in Athens.[31] Above all, Thucydides cannot be our guide, because an approach via physical remains is inescapably limited, as we noted earlier, in its ability to trace the history of worshipping-groups.[32] But theirs is the history we wish to write.

This book has grown to its present size from what was intended as a brief historical introduction to a thematic study of Athenian religious practices and attitudes. The thematic study will, it is hoped, eventually follow as Part 2. Of course the division of material between two such parts is somewhat arbitrary. The present work is long and detailed. But the reason for presenting evidence rather fussily and fully is simply a feeling that, where little is attested, it is important to be clear and specific about this little: if more were known, less detail would suffice. It would be foolish, for many reasons, to dream of writing a definitive book on a subject such as this. Of these reasons, the most striking is perhaps that the possibility of a single, transforming discovery of new evidence is far from being a mere fantasy (or nightmare). Undoubtedly the most revealing document that we could possess would be the full sacrificial code of Solon, as republished by Nicomachus at the end of the fifth century. Fragments of Nicomachus' work, some sizable, have in fact been found in the excavations of the *agora*, a great enterprise that still continues.[33] It is much to be hoped that further large sections of this enormous text will one day re-emerge, to render large sections of this study obsolete.

[30] See G. S. Dontas, *Hesperia* 52 (1983), 48–63.*

[31] Cf. Gomme, 61. 'Over-hasty': contrast the diagrams in Morris, *Burial*, 64 and 66, which, rightly or wrongly, find much more evidence for 'settlement' north of the acropolis than south.*

[32] Of course many contemporary archaeologists pose sociological questions, sometimes with considerable success. But it remains to be shown that archaeology can trace anything remotely resembling the detailed picture of Attic social structures that is available from written evidence.　　　　　　　　　　　　　　　　　　　　　[33] Cf. Ch. 4, n. 3 below.

2

Out of the Dark Age

In the fifth century, Athenian religion offers itself vividly to the imagination, through literature and art; and, in the fourth, evidence of various kinds is abundant enough to encourage the hope that here, uniquely, the workings of religion in a classical Greek city can be observed in detail. As one moves back in time from 472, date of the first surviving play of Aeschylus, the sources of information are progressively stripped away; and beyond about 600 there are left only a few slight scraps of non-contemporary literary evidence, and archaeological remains. In large measure we must rely on retrojection, comparison, and conjecture.

As we shall see, even archaeological evidence for religious life almost dies out beyond the eighth century. This century, therefore, must be our effective starting-point. But an event of the utmost importance, probably the most important in Athens' long history, seems to have occurred before then. A book treating the same area as this one might well have borne the title 'Attic Religion' and have described the cults of four or five or even more independent *poleis*, like those of Boeotia. Instead, Attica was unified, early and finally.[1] The unification—what the Athenians called the synoecism of Theseus—determined the whole scope and structure of subsequent religious life. When did it happen, and what did it entail? Those questions cannot be finally answered; but a brief review of earlier life in Attica may at least help to identify the possibilities, and provide a context for the developments of the eighth century.[2]

Mycenaean remains are richly spread throughout the region that was later to be known as Attica. (The date of the cultural unification of Attica, expressed above all in a common dialect, is just as uncer-

---

[1] Eleusis was held by oligarchs from 403 to 401, Piraeus by a Macedonian garrison for much of the third cent. But these divisions were caused by war, not by the disintegration of a federation.

[2] For a recent and much fuller account, with abundant bibliog., see Welwei, *Athen*. For the post-Mycenaean period, there are helpful site-lists in Morris, *Burial*, and Whitley, *Style and Society*.

tain as that of the political unification.[3] Before it, of course, no Attica existed.) By the thirteenth century, Athens was evidently much the most important settlement: graves are abundant in the lower town, while the acropolis was apparently terraced to bear substantial buildings, very probably a palace-complex, and by the end of the century had been protected by 'Cyclopean' walls. But the country-side flourished too. Ten or so settlements (mostly on hilltops or hill-sides) have already been identified, including places familiar from later myth and cult such as Acharnae, Eleusis, Thorikos, Brauron, Spata (Erchia), Marathon, and Aphidna. There is, of course, no direct evidence about the relation of these townships to Athens itself. If, as is sometimes thought, impressive *tholos* tombs must contain the remains of independent kings, Athens had not managed to swallow up her near-neighbour Acharnae even in the thirteenth century, when the famous Menidi *tholos* was probably constructed. (Other *tholoi*, from Thorikos, Marathon, and Spata, are earlier.) But it is not obvious that a splendid tomb is an index of anything but wealth, which can be found even in a dependency. There is no sign —from fortifications, for instance—that any other Attic town was remotely comparable to Athens in power in the late Mycenaean period.[4]

According to myth, Athens was unaffected by the Dorian invasion; and we can scarcely infer from the building of the fine monumental fortifications of the acropolis, an expression of power above all, that immediate danger threatened. None the less, the acknowledged marks of Mycenaean civilization vanish, though gradually, here too.[5] (In eastern Attica, in particular, late Mycenaean sites are quite numerous.) The only settlement which was certainly occupied without a break was, predictably, Athens itself; and even Athens probably suffered a substantial drop in population. What happened in the countryside is less certain. There is at the moment some gap in the archaeological record even at sites, such as Thorikos, Eleusis,

[3] The two processes are distinct, as is clear from culturally unified but politically divided Boeotia. The Athenians themselves assumed that there had always been an Attica, which had perhaps extended further westwards, to take in the Megarid: see Soph. fr. 24 Radt; Philochorus *FGrH* 328 F 107, with Jacoby's note; Pl. *Criti.* 110d–e; Smarczyk, *Religionspolitik*, 376, n. 123.

[4] See M. A. Pantelidou, Ἀι προϊστορικαὶ Ἀθῆναι (Athens 1975); R. Hope Simpson, *Mycenaean Greece* (Park Ridge, NJ 1981), 41–51, 245 (fortifications) [+]; S. E. Iakovidis, *Late Helladic Citadels on Mainland Greece* (Leiden 1983), 73–90; S. Diamant, 'Theseus and the Unification of Attica', in *Vanderpool Studies*, 38–47; Hornblower, *Commentary*, 263; Welwei, *Athen*, 32–39.

[5] See V. R. d'A. Desborough, *The Last Mycenaeans and their Successors* (Oxford 1964), 112 19; O. Broneer, 'Athens in the Late Bronze Age', *Antiquity* 30 (1956), 9–18; Pantelidou, Ἀι προϊστορικαὶ Ἀθῆναι, 258; Welwei, *Athen*, 50–53, 60–65 (who cites the newest evidence).

Brauron, and Marathon, where evidence for post-Mycenaean occupation or use resumes early;[6] and the centre of the post-Mycenaean
site often seems to have moved. Other comparable places, mostly in
east Attica, were apparently inhabited for the early part, at least, of
the missing centuries.[7] An absolute gap remains in the eleventh to
tenth centuries (the 'Early Protogeometric' period). Is this gap
sufficient to demonstrate that Attica outside Athens was at one time
almost totally depopulated? It would scarcely be surprising if one of
the eastern townships were eventually proved to have existed without a break.[8] On the other hand, if arguments from the absence of
archaeological finds ever have value, the years from the twelfth to
the tenth century were certainly a period of displacement and very
considerable depopulation. Though a few settlements re-emerge in
the late tenth century, archaeologists see the remanning of the countryside as a process beginning substantially around 850, and gaining
greatly in momentum in the second half of the eighth century.

When, therefore, did the 'synoecism of Theseus' occur? According to Thucydides, the first and much the most important source, it
was not a physical but a political unification: people continued to live
in their towns throughout Attica (what were later identified as the
'twelve cities of Cecrops') but looked henceforth to Athens as the
sole centre of political life.[9] That is evidently correct, since towns
and demes continued to flourish within the unified state; but if no
transfer of population was involved, it follows that the synoecism
cannot be tracked down archaeologically.

Most scholars today suppose that a united kingdom could not
have survived the turmoil and poverty of the Early Dark Ages. The
synoecism (whether an event or a process) will therefore have
occurred somewhere in the period 950–700, probably, on the most

---

[6] In the late Protogeometric period: see Desborough, *Greek Dark Ages*, 159–60, 363–64.
For other Attic PG sites see Snodgrass, *CAH*[2] III.1 (1982), 668; *AR* 1984–5, 11.

[7] See n.5 above, and the entries for LH III C in Hope Simpson, *Mycenaean Greece*, 41–51.

[8] H. Lauter's extensive investigations in the Vari region have been partly inspired by the
hope of detecting continuous habitation in the region: *Lathuresa* (Mainz 1985), 67; id. (with
D. K. Hagel), *MarbWPr* 1989 (1990), 5. But so far he has not succeeded. On the 'Skourta
plain' on the borders with Boeotia (probable site of classical Panakton) habitation continued
into the PG period, perhaps without a break, but then ceased: M. H. Munn and M. L.
Zimmermann Munn in A. Schachter ed., *Essays in the Topography, History and Culture of
Boiotia* (*Teiresias* Suppl. 3, Montreal 1990), 33–40 [+].

[9] 2.15.1–2; Thucydides' interpretation (for such it is) was perhaps influenced by Thales'
similar proposal to unite the Ionians, Hdt. 1.170. For later sources see M. Moggi, *I sinecismi
interstatali greci* (Pisa 1976), 44–81. Cities of Cecrops: see Philochorus *FGrH* 328 F 94, with
Jacoby; the list is not tradition, but a 'Versuch, die Zustände Attikas vor der Bildung des
Gesamtstaates auf Grund von Sagen und unter Anlehnung an noch bestehende Kultverbände
nach Analogie der ionischen Zwölfstadt zu schematisiren' (Busolt, cited by Jacoby).

recent views, early within it.[10] (It has often been thought, but on insufficient grounds, that Eleusis escaped the main synoecism and was not incorporated until the seventh century.[11]) The archaeological evidence, however, introduces a serious complication. According to the ancients' own conception (which has great intuitive appeal), primitive Attica was divided into small independent communities, which were eventually brought together politically by the act of synoecism. Moderns too often suppose that regional cult-associations still active in the classical period, the Marathonian Tetrapolis above all, inherited religious traditions of the originally independent townships (as the tribes and demes of Rhodes and Cos were to do after those islands' much later synoecisms).[12] But archaeologically, as we have just seen, it is only from about 850 BC that most of the townships of historical Attica become visible at all. We have therefore four choices: to dismiss the archaeological record as seriously defective; to suppose that the synoecism concerned only those 'cities of Cecrops' (some, in fact, of the most famed) that existed by 900 or a little later;[13] to down-date it to, say, 750, to allow other settlements time to grow into thriving independent communities before they are united; or to abandon the notion that a political unification of Attica needed to occur at all (in the post-Mycenaean period at least). On this last view (a kind of 'synoecism by default') the 'new towns' of ninth-century Attica would always have recognized some measure of subordination to Athens itself.[14] All that is certain is that the synoecism is already taken for granted in 'Homer' (but the date at which

[10] For extensive bibliog. and doxography see Moggi, *I sinecismi*, 44–81, and, on the various meanings attached to synoecism, P. Musoliek, *Klio* 63 (1981), 207–13. Add now A. Andrewes, *CAH*² III.3 (1982), 360–63 (by 900); Whitehead, *Demes*, 8–9 (ninth/eighth cent.). For various dissentient views (mostly favouring a Mycenaean or Dark Age synoecism) see E. Meyer, *Geschichte des Altertums*, III² (Stuttgart 1937), 312; J. Sarkady, *Act. Class. Univ. Debreceniensis* 2 (1966), 9–27; R. A. Padgug, *GRBS* 13 (1972), 135–50; M. Sakellariou, *REA* 78/79 (1976–7), 11–21; H. van Effenterre, *La cité grecque* (Paris 1985), 168–74.

[11] See Andrewes and esp. Padgug, as cited in the previous note. To judge from pottery styles, Eleusis was looking culturally to Attica rather than the Megarid by c.900, when relevant evidence is first available: see Coldstream, *Geometric Pottery*, 402, 404.

[12] Whence the title of S. Solders, *Die ausserstädtischen Kulte und die Einigung Attikas* (Lund 1931), still a valuable work of reference on cults outside the city. The central thesis can be neither proved (see Padgug, *GRBS* 13, 1972) nor disproved. Rhodes and Cos: see Jones, *Public Organization*, 236, 243.

[13] Sites that have yielded PG material include Eleusis, Marathon, Thorikos, and Acharnae: see n. 6 above.

[14] So A. M. Snodgrass, *CAH*² III.1 (1982), 668, dates to the late tenth/early ninth cent. a synoecism which he redefines as 'the recognition that the new cultivators of the Attic countryside, even as far afield as the plain of Marathon, could retain their citizenship of Athens'. Cf. W. G. Cavanagh in J. Rich and A. Wallace-Hadrill eds., *City and Country in the Ancient World* (London 1991), 107–108, Welwei, *Athen*, 66; Whitley, *Style and Society*, 58. In a very modified sense this brings us back to the old theory (n. 10) of a Mycenaean synoecism (for which Sarkady, there cited, argues on these archaeological grounds).

the relevant passage entered this 'fluid text' must be in doubt): in the Catalogue of Ships, while the troops from other regions of Greece are drawn from a cluster of cities, the Attic contingent comes from Athens alone.[15]

Though many other Greek states underwent synoecism in one of its various guises, the Athenians were unique, it seems, in celebrating the event, or supposed event, at a public festival, the *Synoikia*. (Some moderns doubt the association, which goes back at least to Thucydides, of *Synoikia* with synoecism.[16] But the festival must certainly relate to a decision of communities in some sense to 'live together', συνοικεῖν.) It was held, naturally, on the acropolis, and in honour of Athena; it almost certainly antedates 508/7, because sacrifices are performed by one of the old Ionian tribes, which lost most of their importance in that year.[17] Does the existence of the festival create a presumption that the event from which it is named actually occurred? Or did the myth of Theseus' synoecism create the ritual, at a time when the myth had some present significance? Synoecism was still a living issue in the Greek world in the classical period. It meant strength, in the judgement of Herodotus, Thucydides, and many another Greek; Sparta was to break up the synoecisms (διοικίζεν) of troublesome allies to keep them weak.[18] The *Synoikia* proclaimed the political vision of Theseus that had laid the foundations of Athenian power.

From the festival (the relation of which to actual history must remain uncertain) we revert to the synoecism itself. To speak of the 'unification' of Attica is much easier than to imagine its actual meaning, in the political and social conditions of the Dark Ages. There

[15] Hom. *Il.* 2.546–56; cf. Andrewes, *CAH*[2] III.3 (1982), 360; and for possible Attic influences on this and other passages, Seaford, *Reciprocity and Ritual*, 144–54, 183, and n. 38 below.

[16] So H. T. Wade-Gery, *CQ* 25 (1931), 9, n. 6; M. P. Nilsson, *RE* s.v. *Synoikia* (*contra*, Deubner, *Attische Feste*, 37, n. 1); N. Robertson, *RhM* 128 (1985), 238–39; K.-W. Welwei in G. Binder and B. Effe eds., *Mythos* (Trier 1990), 162–64. But their attempts to make the meaning something like 'assembly or common festival of the *oikoi*' seem misguided linguistically: one must start from the verb. For the occasional use of συνοικέω and derived words in relation to synoecism see the indices to Moggi, *I sinecismi*, and esp. his no. 43 (*IG* V.2.343; *Schwyzer* 665), a record of the συϜοικία of Euaimon with Orchomenos in the fourth cent.

[17] See Deubner, *Attische Feste*, 36–38, and for the old tribes *LSS* 10 A 31–58, with W. S. Ferguson, in *Classical Studies Presented to E. Capps* (Princeton 1936), 155–56, and Dow, 'Law Codes', 22–23. For reasons that are unknown, only one of the old tribes is involved, and in alternate years only; nor is it clear how to interpret the role of an old tribe at this particular festival: a special association, because of the unifying role of the tribal structure, or just one survival of a broader role of the old tribes in pre-Clisthenic religious life? Or a survival preserved because of the special association? Nothing is known of the ritual except that it involved sacrifice. The city deme Skambonidai made an offering (*IG* I[3].244 C 16), but the festival has left no trace in other deme calendars.

[18] See e.g. Hdt. 1.170, Thuc. 2.15.1–2, with Hornblower, *Mausolus*, 79–81.

are, very broadly, three current views of the political structures of Dark Age Greece. On one, much influenced by anthropological comparison, it is a society of local 'big men' or 'chiefs' (Greek *basileis*), each with his own followers; no effective supra-local structures exist, and even the chiefs are not such by ancestral right but have constantly to struggle to maintain the allegiance of their retainers.[19] The second view still starts with 'chiefs', but superimposes a 'paramount chief', whose primacy is recognized in certain contexts (military above all).[20] 'Paramount chief', however, is not an office that exists independently of the person who at any given time is recognized as such, and like an ordinary chief the paramount has permanently to work to retain allegiance. A system of this type might, of course, readily evolve out of the first. The third view substitutes at the top something much closer to 'kingship': a position with traditional prerogatives and duties that is taken up and passed on by the individual king, and is in fact often transmitted by inheritance.[21]

Historians tend to speak as if in the Dark Ages, almost uniquely in Greek history, political structures were the same throughout Greece. It seems almost inevitable that there were in fact considerable regional variations.[22] It is obviously tempting to align Attica, which contains a substantial and stable town, with whatever paradigm offers the most centralization and stability. But for our purposes the similarities between the three positions just outlined are as important as the differences. All start with an emphasis on local communities, and a plurality of local *basileis*. Positions two and three add explicitly that local communities are grouped together into larger geographical units, those over which the paramount chief or the king exercises some measure of authority. Position one is not in principle committed to such larger units, but in practice will probably do well to assume them (as Homer does[23]): the followers of the various Attic *basileis* would therefore have felt themselves different from their Boeotian equivalents, even before Attica had any political identity. (For Attica, that probability becomes a certainty if, as is normally believed, the region already had a tribal system—a form of unifying political organization—in the Dark Ages. We must return

---

[19] See e.g. B. Quiller, *SymbOslo* 56 (1981), 109–55 (who cites abundant ethnographic literature); R. Drews, *Basileus* (New Haven 1983); Stahl, *Aristokraten und Tyrannen*, 150–55. For some critics see Welwei, *Athen*, 80, n. 9.

[20] See e.g. W. Donlan, *SymbOslo* 64 (1989), 5–29 (and other scholars cited by van Wees, *Status Warriors*, 282).

[21] So e.g. Carlier, *La royauté*, 210–14; van Wees, *Status Warriors*, 281–94 (an important discussion). For further bibliog. on this much-debated question see Welwei, *Athen*, 80, n. 9.

[22] So J. Whitley, *BSA* 86 (1991), 341–65 (on Athens as a 'stable settlement', ibid. 352).

[23] See van Wees, *Status Warriors*, 36–40.

to this point.) On the other hand, even position three will not rate the power of the king or the degree of effective centralization very highly.[24] Jurisdiction, for instance, on this view probably still rests with the local *basileis*.

If there was a king or a paramount chief in Attica before the synoecism (to assume for the moment that one occurred), there was also some measure of centralized authority. But even if there was not, it is entirely possible that men from all Attica engaged in some activities in common, provided, of course, that they had some sense of a shared cultural or ethnic identity. Cult is obviously a main area (along with warfare and, perhaps, marriage exchange) where such a pre-political sense of being Attic might have been fostered and expressed. In principle, therefore, there could have been '*Panathenaea*' even before Attica existed politically, like the *Pamboiotia* at which the ethnically related but politically independent cities of Boeotia assembled, or the *Panionia* of the Ionians.[25] On the other hand, even after synoecism, most of life's important activities for most inhabitants of Attica were probably still played out in the local community. The chief tie created by synoecism between a farmer of Eleusis and one of Marathon was perhaps that they occasionally now fought in the same battleline, and never in opposite ones. Nobles, no doubt, attended a council of some kind in Athens, but even they may have spent much of their life on their lands. Centrally celebrated festivals were probably still few, and may have been largely a preserve of nobles and their followers. Most of the religious activities of most farmers are likely to have been conducted in or near their own villages. And if no synoecism ever needed to occur (because the townships were never independent), we doubtless have still to imagine a society that was strongly decentralized in most of its habits of life.

We should raise here the issue of the Attic tribal system. The old orthodoxy whereby primitive Greek society was dominated by supra-familial kinship-structures—tribe or phratry or clan—lies in ruins. Recent reconstructions start from the individual household and the dependants (not normally real or fictive kin) attached to it.[26] It remains true, however, that the population of archaic Attica was

---

[24] Cf. W. G. Runciman, 'Origins of States: The Case of Archaic Greece', *Comparative Studies in Society and History* 24 (1982), 351–77 (on *inter alia* 'semi-states').

[25] See in general V. Ehrenberg, *The Greek State*[2] (London 1969), 120–31; on Boeotian federal festivals see P. Roesch, *Études béotiennes* (Paris 1982), 218, 224; on the *Panionia*, S. Hornblower, *Historia* 31 (1982), 241–45; and cf. Tausend, *Amphiktyonie*, 26–34, 90–95. Note, however, C. Morgan's warning (*PCPS* 37, 1991, 131–32) against the back-projection of later federal arrangements to the Dark Ages.

[26] See e.g. van Wees, *Status Warriors*, 26–28.

distributed among four 'tribes' (*phylai*), the names of which recur, with considerable variations, in other Ionian communities (Miletus, Ephesus, and Samos, for instance).[27] The *phylai* of historical Greece are invariably not independent entities but subdivisions within a larger structure, like the 'houses' of a boarding-school. Both the military and religious life, for instance, of many classical cities was largely organized 'by tribes'. A Greek 'tribal society' is therefore, paradoxically, one that in theory possesses a centralized political organization. Unless the primitive Attic *phylai* worked on quite different principles,[28] they too must have been the parts out of which 'the Athenians' were constituted. The commonest explanation for the coincidence in names between Attic and Ionian tribes is that the tribal division antedated the 'Ionian migration' (of the eleventh century?). In that event, we have, with difficulty, to weave this unifying, 'political' structure into our mental picture of the Dark Age world of small communities and *basileis*. The alternative is to suppose that the Ionian tribal system, created on one side of the Aegean in, say, the eighth century,[29] was copied on the other by a community that felt close cultural ties with the originator.[30] In that case, the introduction of the tribal system at Athens (whether as an invention or in imitation of, say, Miletus) was a crucial though still undatable event in the political unification of Attica.

We turn now to the evidence for religious life. Scarcely any physical evidence survives from before about 750, except in the special area of the treatment of the dead. From the Mycenaean period there seems to be none at all. If Athena once lodged in the royal palace on the acropolis, she has left no trace of her presence; and the supposed Mycenaean initiation-house at Eleusis has now been reclassified as a secular building.[31] Cults of Demeter Eleusinia were widely diffused in the historical period, in Ionia in particular, and it has been suggested that the goddess must already have been honoured under this

[27] See Jones, *Public Organization*, 11–12, and M. Piérart, *REA* 87 (1985), 169–88.

[28] They certainly do not once their operations become, very slightly, observable: see pp. 193–208 of Roussel, *Tribu et cité*, an epoch-making work which, by establishing the dependence of 'tribe' on 'city', made urgent for the first time the problem we are here considering.

[29] The *terminus ante quem* on this view becomes the near-certainty that Miletus already possessed tribes at the date of the colonization of Cyzicus, around 700 (M. Piérart, *MusHelv* 40, 1983, 2–5).

[30] For older opinions on both sides see Smarczyk, *Religionspolitik*, 380–81. Jones, *Public Organization*, 11–12, still seems to assume a common Ionian inheritance; Roussel, *Tribu et cité*, 209–20 (see the qualifications of Piérart, *REA* 87, 1985, 167–88), followed by Welwei, *Athen*, 119–20, argues for borrowing. And see now W. R. Connor, 'The Ionian Era of Athenian Civic Identity', *ProcPhilSoc* 137 (1993), 194–206, who treats 'Ionian identity' itself as an east-Greek construct which 'only gradually exerted its influence in Attica'.

[31] By P. Darcque, *BCH* 105 (1981), 593–605.

title before the Ionian migration.[32] But the inference is very uncertain. What may be a hearth altar on the Nike bastion of the acropolis has been dated to the sub-Mycenaean period only on the basis of
a clutch of crude figurines found within it: but these have now
slipped to the early seventh century, and take the altar with them.[33]

Only four or five sacred sites have produced pottery of the tenth
to ninth centuries: the sanctuaries of Zeus on Mount Hymettus and
on Mount Parnes, of Artemis at Mounichia and (perhaps) Brauron,
and of an unidentified god or hero in the Academy region of
Athens.[34] But Attica shared in the 'eighth-century renaissance'
(though not, in the main, until near the century's end), and by about
700, religious activity is demonstrably under way at most of the great
sacred centres of the classical city: on the acropolis, and in the sanctuaries of Demeter at Eleusis and of Athena at Sunium, as well as
those of Artemis at Brauron and Mounichia. 'Geometric' sherds are
also reported from what became the precinct of Nemesis at
Rhamnus. Zeus' shrines on Hymettus and Parnes are now joined by
a remarkable abundance of further mountain-sanctuaries; and hero-
cult too is certainly attested.[35] (We will return to these last two forms
of cult in the following chapter.)

At most sites of this date the evidence consists merely of votive
offerings or the remains of sacrificial pyres. The early history in
Attica of true religious architecture, which appears elsewhere in
Greece at about this time, remains tantalizingly obscure. Some
'sacred houses' of the period that have been identified are secular in

[32] See Graf, *Nordionische Kulte*, 274–77: cf. *Early Greek Cult Practice*, 102.

[33] See Coldstream, 'Hero-cults', 16; Travlos, *Pictorial Dictionary*, 151; I. B. Romano,
Early Greek Cult Images (Diss. Pennsylvania 1980), 61; and for the date of such
'Stempelidolen', M. Küpper, *MarbWPr* 1989 (1990), 17–29. Mark, *Athena Nike*, 32, n. 7,
now tolerates an even later date.

[34] Cf. Desborough, *Greek Dark Ages*, 137. Hymettus: abundant late PG pottery (Langdon,
Sanctuary of Zeus, 74–76). Parnes: a few PG vessels (E. Mastrokastas, *ASAtene* NS 45, 1983
[1984], 340). Academy: a cache of over 200 late PG vessels (P. D. Stavropoullos, *Prakt* 1958
[1965], 8–9). But the association between these finds and those at the 'sacred house' 150 yds.
south-east (cf. Ch. 3, n. 19) is very uncertain. Brauron: late PG vases found in the sanctuary
area, very deep, to the north-east of the later stoa (Desborough, *Greek Dark Ages*, 159; P. G.
Themelis, *Brauron*, Athens 1971, 10, 46). Mounichia: L. Palaiokrassa, τὸ Ἱερὸ τῆς
Ἀρτέμιδος Μουνιχίας (Athens 1991), 53, 64, 90 (but the PG finds are sparse).

[35] Acropolis: fragments of LG votive plaques (J. Boardman, *BSA* 49, 1954, 196–97); sherds
from monumental Geometric vases (Graef/Langlotz, *Vasen von der Akropolis*, I.23–34); late
eighth-cent. bronzes (B. Schweitzer, *Greek Geometric Art*, tr. P. and C. Usborne, London
1971, 138–42; E. Touloupa, *AM* 87, 1972, 57–76; Floren, *Griechische Plastik I*, 37–43). Eleusis:
n. 37 below and ('sacred house') Ch. 3, n. 19. Brauron: LG pottery (J. Papadimitriou, *Ergon*
1961 [1962], 28); Geometric gold ornaments (id., *Ergon* 1962 [1963], 30, fig. 37; cf. Coldstream,
Geometric Greece, 128). Sunium: a votive pit in the *temenos* of Athena (H. Abramson, *CSCA*
12, 1979, 9), with material starting *c.*700 (Abramson's ninth-cent. *incipit* seems too high). The
deposit perhaps comes from a hero-cult of Phrontis (Ch. 3, n. 24), in which case the main cults
of Sunium remain unattested. Rhamnus: B. C. Petrakos, *Ergon* 1982 (1983), 35.

design, though they seem to have been put to use (occasionally at least) for sacrificial meals.[36] Of actual temples, two have been tentatively identified. Terracing was built at Eleusis in the eighth century, to bear, it is argued, an apsidal temple of which a small length of curved wall remains. On an older view, the terrace was merely intended as a level area for ritual activity. And on the acropolis, two archaic column-bases are a harbinger of the future: they may come from a first temple of Athena built in the eighth century or not much later.[37]

Two famous literary references perhaps date from this period. (Both passages have, not implausibly, been suspected of having entered the text under Attic influence, presumably in the sixth century, but the case falls short of proof.)[38] In the Catalogue of Ships in the *Iliad*, the Athenians are:

> the people of great-spirited Erechtheus, whom Athena
> the daughter of Zeus reared, and the grain-giving earth bore him
> and Athena set him down in Athens, in her own rich temple,
> where the young men of the Athenians propitiate him [her?[39]]
> with bulls and lambs as the seasons come round.

And in Book 7 of the *Odyssey*, Athena

> came to Marathon and broad-streeted Athens
> and entered the well-built house of Erechtheus.

In both passages, Athena and Erechtheus share a house or temple, as on the most widely accepted view they were still to do in the classical Erechtheum. This cohabitation, it has been suggested, went back to Mycenaean times: Athena had been worshipped in a house-shrine in the Mycenaean palace on the acropolis, an arrangement recalled in the *Odyssey* passage, where she 'enters Erechtheus' well-

---

[36] See Ch. 3, n. 19 below.

[37] Column bases (in the area of the 'Dörpfeld temple' near the Erechtheum): C. Nylander, *OpAth* 4 (1962), 31–77 (? early seventh cent.); S. E. Iakovidis, Ἡ Μυκηναϊκὴ Ἀκρόπολις τῶν Ἀθηνῶν (Athens 1962), 62–65. I. Beyer, *AA* 1977, 56, n. 37, argues for an eighth-cent. date, which better suits Hom. *Il.* 2.549, if genuine. E. Touloupa, *BCH* 93 (1969), 862–84 identifies a bronze shield-shaped Gorgoneion (Nat. Mus. Inv. 13050: ? seventh cent.) as an *akroterion* of the primitive temple. But N. Valmin, *AA* 1964, 143–45, suggests that the two columns may have stood in the open, with an image of Athena Promachos. Eleusis: Mylonas, *Mysteries*, 56–63, cf. *AR* 1982–3, 10.

[38] Hom. *Il.* 2.546–51, *Od.* 7.80–81. Attic influence: see Kron, *Phylenheroen*, 33–37; S. West in A. Heubeck, S. West, and J. B. Hainsworth, *A Commentary on Homer's Odyssey* (Oxford 1988), 38, n. 15; n. 15 above.

[39] For 'him', the accepted rendering (cf. Kron, *Phylenheroen*, 35, n. 113) cf. Eur. *Erechtheus* fr. 65.94 Austin, φοναὶ βούθυτοι in his honour. But 'her' is not impossible: for Athena receiving a bull, not the normal cow, cf. the Boeotian BF lekanis, Nilsson, *Geschichte*, fig. 32.1; and for ἔνθα δέ (strictly 'and there') scarcely differentiated from ἔνθα τε ('where') see e.g. Hom. *Il.* 8.48, and cf. C. J. Ruijgh, *Autour de 'te épique'* (Amsterdam 1971), 476–80, 691.

built house'. In the *Iliad*, by contrast, the relation has been reversed in accordance with the later norm, so that the goddess now owns a temple, and the mortal becomes her lodger. (This would be the temple from which the two-column bases survive.)

The theory is elegant, but uncertain.[40] Was the Mycenaean 'palace-cult' as important as it postulates? Even if it was, is a recollection of it likely to have re-emerged about half a millennium later in the *Odyssey*? Or are we to suppose that a cult of Athena persisted in the perhaps now ruined 'house of Erechtheus' until a true temple was built for her in the eighth century? Unfortunately, the fortunes of the palace and the acropolis in the Dark Ages are completely unknown.

What emerges more clearly from the passages is the predominant position of the ancestor-hero Erechtheus in early Athenian myth and cult. He remained an important figure, and the myth of his birth first told here was still in the fifth century precious proof of his descendants' claim to be autochthonous, earth-born.[41] But later he had to share with other national heroes a glory that here is his alone.

Such, in outline, is the contemporary evidence for Attic religion in the early centuries. In many ways the development is typical of what can be observed throughout the Greek world. No cult can be shown to have persisted unbroken from the Mycenaean period. Evidence of any kind for religious activity is entirely lacking in the early Dark Ages; it appears in the tenth and ninth centuries, and increases sharply in quantity in the eighth. Sanctuaries begin to be marked out, with walls and terraces, and temples built (this is at least a probable development at this date in Attica, as we have seen); hero-cults suddenly proliferate; luxury objects that had hitherto often found their way into graves are now dedicated in shrines,[42] and these new sanctuaries are, it seems, often not built over older, rougher sacred places, but planted in virgin soil. A surprising number of the 'ancestral traditions, coeval with time' of the classical period appear in fact to have been created in the eighth century.

Some scepticism about the limits of archaeological argument is

[40] The theory: M. P. Nilsson, *The Minoan-Mycenaean Religion*[2] (Lund 1950), 488; id., *Geschichte*, 248 (and on the Erechtheum recently E. M. Stern, *Boreas* 9, 1986, 51–64). The view that Mycenaean cult-places were concentrated in the palaces has since been shaken: see Burkert, *Greek Religion*, 31–32. C. Kardara, *ArchEph* 1960 (1965), 165–202, seeks a different home for Erechtheus, in the supposedly sub-Mycenaean shrine on the Nike bastion; nothing supports the identification (cf. n. 33 above).

[41] Cf. 'Myths', 193–95; and on Erechtheus' special status in the Homeric passages, Kearns, *Heroes of Attica*, 133.

[42] Cf. Seaford, *Reciprocity and Ritual*, 195. The tendency is less clear in Attica than at the Panhellenic shrines, but see n. 35.

certainly in order, here as everywhere; but it would be hypercritical to deny the importance of the 'eighth-century renaissance' in religious life. Can it be explained?

According to a theory that has been advanced of late from several sides, the solution lies in 'the rise of the *polis*'. This, it is argued, was inseparably associated with a transformation in the forms of religious life. It was through collective rituals performed at newly established sanctuaries that the nascent city acquired and expressed its identity. These rites welded the whole populace together for the first time: the first form of citizenship was 'cultic citizenship'.[43] (What had gone before? On one variant of the view, a monarchy so dominant that its subjects could develop no separate sense of civic identity; on another, by contrast, conditions so turbulent that no political community encompassed more than a handful of men.)

The 'rise of the *polis*', however, is one of history's more elusive turning-points. The *polis* in the sense in which we refer to it today, an ideal synthesis of various political, cultural, geographical, and economic elements, first arose in 1898, in the pages of Burckhardt's *Griechische Kulturgeschichte*. Such an abstraction has not had a history in the real world like that of meander decoration on geometric vases. Only the individual elements in the synthesis have histories; and these may be various (within individual cities, to say nothing of divergences between *poleis*). Faced with actual societies, historians cannot agree when or whether they became *poleis*.[44] We cannot identify any 'pre-political' state of society in Greece subsequent to the Mycenaean kingdoms. Thus any attempt to treat the 'birth of the *polis*' as a datable occurrence is in danger of compacting a long history into too short a space.[45]

The ancients knew nothing of any such happy event. They saw instead a gradual fading of monarchy into oligarchy; and the historical instances at Sparta and Cyrene of decayed kingships that survived amid forms of oligarchy suggest that they may have been

[43] See esp. A. M. Snodgrass, *Archaic Greece* (London 1980), 33; C. Bérard, 'Récupérer la mort du prince: Héroïsation et formation de la cité', in G. Gnoli and J.-P. Vernant eds., *La mort et les morts dans les sociétés anciennes* (Cambridge 1982), 89–105; id. in *Architecture et Société* (*CEFR* 66, Rome 1983), 43–62; de Polignac, *Naissance, passim*; and for a good (though broader) summary of archaeologists' approaches, Whitley, *Style and Society*, 39–45. There is an interesting slippage from Snodgrass's observation that archaeologists can better study the rise of sanctuaries than the death of kings to de Polignac's claim that the city was in fact constituted in religious rather than political terms.

[44] On the chaos of conflicting definitions in which the debate is conducted see van Effenterre, *La cité grecque*, 39–41; on Burckhardt, W. Gawantka, *Die sogenannte Polis* (Stuttgart 1985). On Homer's relation to the *polis*, opinion is revealingly divided: see the survey in Seaford, *Reciprocity and Ritual*, 1–10.

[45] For more gradual approaches see e.g. Donlan, *SymbOslo* 64 (1989), 5–29; Welwei, *Athen*, 76–132.

right. In this case, there was no single moment when monarchic authority yielded to that of the collectivity; nor, on the other hand, did a state emerge where hitherto there had only been disunited families. As the aristocratic council grew in power, so the *polis* grew—perhaps rather slowly—around the king. And the point is strengthened if we see kingship not as a primeval form but as one of transition, a product itself of a growing need for central authority. The transformation is dramatic only if a wholly fragmented society of competing *basileis* suddenly acquired a centre. But in Attica above all, with one town always much larger than the rest, it is not at all tempting to postulate such a development.

Athens had been a centre of population since the Mycenaean period. In the early Dark Age, admittedly, it may have been little more than an unfortified scatter of villages grouped around a stronghold; but it was apparently not to become a city of ideal classical shape, with walls and a place of public assembly, until well into the archaic period, long after we would acknowledge its claim to be a *polis* in the political sense.[46] It is surely plausible that the men of this primitive Athens came together occasionally to sacrifice a cow to Athena. It is surely also plausible that at such a rite the king (if king there was) presided. A confusion needs to be cleared away here. A god, it is often said, becomes monarch of a Greek community when the mortal king is deposed.[47] Thus monarchy and civic religion are seen as incompatible elements, like oil and water. Athens was, in fact, one of the cities where the main civic temple was probably built on the actual site of a Mycenaean royal palace. To keep that antithesis in sharpest focus, however, one needs to block out an intervening period of some 400 years. Dark Age *basileis* certainly did not exercise the same kind of dominant authority as a Mycenaean *anax*; nor is it likely that they monopolized sacral functions in a way that made it impossible for a public religion to develop. On the contrary, one of the most characteristic functions of a *basileus* seems to have been or become that of conducting communal rites. The Attic 'king' of later times, the annual magistrate, supposedly 'organized almost all the ancestral sacrifices', as did the similar elective 'kings' of other states; at Sparta, true kings still did the same. In Homer too we find kings coexisting with such institutions of civic religion as temples, priests, festivals, and public sacrifices.[48] In Greek perception, the public

[46] See A. M. Snodgrass, *Archaeology and the Rise of the Greek State* (Cambridge 1977), 26–30 (the 'old *agora*', however, has now to be taken more seriously: Ch. 1, n. 30 above); id., *Archaic Greece* (London 1980), 154–56; Whitley, *Style and Society*, 61–64. Welwei, *Athen*, 62, estimates the population of Dark Age Athens at 2,000–3,000, I. Morris (in Rich/Wallace-Hadrill eds., *City and Country*, 33) at 2,500–5,000.

[47] A much-quoted remark of Ehrenberg, *The Greek State*[2], 15.

religion of the classical period had its origin at the hearth of the king. Even if we efface kings in the familiar sense from our own imaginings about Dark Age Attica, we are left with a town—by Dark Age standards a metropolis—and the strong likelihood that its inhabitants were bound together by communal structures of some kind.

It is too absolute, therefore, to see whatever transformation occurred in the eighth century as the creation of a public religious domain. That it was probably a period of rapid political and social change in Attica is not in dispute—though specific and reliable evidence, whether archaeological or literary, is hard to find. A population explosion has been claimed because of the numbers of eighth-century graves, denied because of their character (and on broader demographic grounds).[49] According to schematic later reconstructions (but that is all they are), it was in this century that oligarchic rule was formalized, with the introduction of a primitive form of the central principle of 'rule in succession, by turn' (a ten-year archonship).[50] Formalization above might have been balanced by formalization below, with the recognition of certain elementary powers of a popular assembly. The effect of both changes would have been to give more Athenians a clearer stake in the state. But the rise of the sanctuaries in eighth-century Greece can scarcely be explained in any simple way by the political consolidation of the individual cities; for Delphi and Olympia, among early sanctuaries not the least glorious, were of course Panhellenic,[51] that at Thermon in Aetolia and others served not a city but an ethnic group. The development must be cultural and economic, not narrowly political.

It has not so far been questioned that a form of public religion did exist in the eighth century. Just this, however, is by implication denied by a still-influential tradition of scholarship. We must raise

---

[48] See esp. *Il.* 6.86–311 (note particularly 300); *Od.* 3.4–61, 20.276–78, 21.258–59; cf. van Wees, *Status Warriors*, 323, n. 12. Attic 'king': p. 8 above, and cf. Carlier, *La royauté*, 555, index entry 'Rôle religieux du roi'.

[49] By, respectively, A. M. Snodgrass in several works, and Morris, *Burial*: cf. R. Osborne, *BSA* 84 (1989), 314–15; N. Purcell in Murray/Price, *Greek City*, 44–45; J. K. Papadopoulos in *JMA* 6 (1993), 188.

[50] Reconstructions: see Rhodes, *Commentary Ath. Pol.*, on 3.1.

[51] It is true that Delphi and Olympia can be characterized as retarded architecturally (as οἱ περὶ Snodgrass stress: see e.g. C. Morgan, *Athletes and Oracles*, Cambridge 1990, 16); but they count against de Polignac's argument that the emergence of fixed cult-sites (commoner in fact in the Dark Ages than he allows: see C. Sourvinou-Inwood in N. Marinatos and R. Hägg eds., *Greek Sanctuaries*, London 1993, 1–17, and now the contributions of de Polignac himself and Morgan to *Placing the Gods*) is in itself to be associated with the birth of the *polis*. As for *ethne*, 'there is no clear chronological discrepancy between the beginnings of sanctuary development in *poleis* and *ethne*' (Morgan, *Athletes and Oracles*, 7). The argument sometimes offered that it is precisely the rise of the *polis* that creates a need for supra-*polis* sanctuaries seems to me suspiciously *ad hoc*.

briefly the controversial issue of the *gene*. The *genos* of classical times
was a hereditary association normally entrusted with the priesthood
of a cult or cults; the hierophant of the Eleusinian Mysteries, for
instance, was recruited from the *genos* of the Eumolpids. The relation of the *gene* to their cults has often been seen as much like that of
the English aristocracy to their houses: what had originally been private property was eventually opened to the public, the family living
on, however, as privileged caretakers. On this view the *genos* was primarily a form of social grouping, an aristocratic clan, and the original function of the cult was to give the group its religious centre. The
implication for religious life is that, since early priesthoods were
assigned apparently without exception to *gene*, all the cults of Athens
must have been privately owned in early times. A strange polytheism, in which the gods were shared out one by one for private use,
and no worshipper had free access to them all!

One has in fact only to make the full implications of this view
explicit to see that it can scarcely stand. The priestess of Athena
Polias on the acropolis was recruited from the *genos* of the
Eteoboutads. But it is inconceivable that the cult of this goddess, the
protectress, the symbol of the city's life, had ever been confined to a
single clan—as if, without Eteoboutads, there would have been no
Athena Polias. A newer interpretation should therefore prevail:[52] to
the *genos* were assigned the honours and obligations of priesthood,
but the cult served by the priest was open to all. The Eteoboutads
enjoyed the privilege of selecting from their number a priestess to
pray to Athena Polias on behalf of all the Athenians. It was, indeed,
precisely the public character of the service, the possibility of display that it conferred, that made the office so worth having. Such a
priesthood was a kind of magistracy.[53] And it would be hard to show
that any of the priesthoods held by the *gene* lacked this public character.

The cult centres outside Athens itself raise similar issues. In the
classical period, many great festivals held in the country, those at
Sunium, at Brauron and Eleusis, for instance, formed part of the
public religion of Athens. They were administered by public
officials, and attracted celebrants from throughout Attica; often a
semi-formal procession went from the city to the outlying sanctuary.
Here too it has often been assumed that the city only gradually
absorbed autonomous local sanctuaries and rites (whether of

---

[52] See esp. Roussel, *Tribu et cité*, 65–78, and cf. Ch. 5 below.

[53] A very unusual kind, certainly, being vested in perpetuity in a group. For possible explanations (such as collective responsibility of the *genos* for rites and, perhaps, for upkeep of the
shrine) see Ch. 5.

Athenian villages, or of towns that had been independent before the synoecism).[54] It was, therefore, only as a secondary development that these sites became places of pilgrimage, approached from afar. An example from the full historical period shows that the assumption is not absurd. A few years after reacquiring Oropus, and with it the Amphiareum, from Thebes in the 330s, the Athenians appointed a distinguished commission to perform a great four-yearly festival for the first time, and showered the god with attentions and honours. Thus both territory and god were brought firmly back within the Attic orbit.[55]

It is not at all clear, however, that all the countryside cults of Attica had become Athenian by such a process of incorporation. (And where incorporation did take place, this may have been very early.) In all our documents, those we have mentioned are always under Athenian control. We must at least consider an alternative conception, that the web of religious life in Attica was spun by the spider at the centre. If rites are celebrated away from the city, that is partly because, for religious reasons, they belong in the countryside, partly because a city should exploit the whole of its territory. Why are three separate cults of Artemis located on the coast? Are coast-dwellers so especially fervent in their devotion to the goddess? It is surely rather that Artemis herself loves wild places, especially for the rites in which she prepares young (human) animals for adult life in the city. The cult of Demeter at Eleusis is very generally believed to have once been independent: so the ancients say (though they set the incorporation far back in the mythological period), and until recently few moderns have ever doubted them. But it can scarcely be coincidence that the corn-goddess' sanctuary lay in some of the finest cornland of Attica, the Thriasian plain. And if that is why Demeter was worshipped at Eleusis, it becomes unnecessary to assume that the Eleusinian cult had ever existed outside the framework of Athenian religion. As we have seen, on present archaeological evidence none of the best-known country sanctuaries was frequented before the ninth century, and few before the eighth. It can be argued that the growing city of Athens marked out its claims to the whole of Attica in the ninth and eighth centuries by implanting precincts on virgin sites far from the capital. Doubtless the truth is in fact complex: the shrine of Nemesis at Rhamnus, for instance, is under local administration in the fifth century, even though we can scarcely doubt that it was also of interest to Athenians from the city,

---

[54] See particularly M. P. Nilsson, *Arch. Jahrb.* 31 (1916), 313–14 = id., *Op. Sel.* I.172–73.

[55] See Ch. 11, n. 102 below. The case is not quite parallel with what is postulated for Eleusis, since Oropus was not a part of Attica by origin.

and in the fourth the deme of Halai Araphenides was able to honour its benefactors by proclamation at the *Tauropolia*, a local festival but one that attracted celebrants from all Attica.[56] We cannot investigate all the possibilities here. About the history of any individual shrine one can make no very confident claim. But the general proposition is plausible that Athenians from the city were already going to worship throughout Attica in the eighth century.[57]

We have surveyed the fragments. Let us conclude by attempting a 'conjectural reconstruction', after the manner of archaeologists, of the forms of Attic religious life in—when should it be? If we choose the year of the first Olympiad (776), most traditional of dates, qualifications and reservations will have to be multiplied. The year 700 will be a safer choice. First, however, we must mention a crucially important development that cannot be pinned down in time.

In the archaic period there were three main magistracies,[58] of which that of *basileus* seems to have been invested with far less secular power than the archonship and the post of 'war-leader' (polemarch). Pre-eminent religious authority and immediate political power were therefore divorced (whether by division of the inheritance of a true king or by creation of a set of magistracies with functions so distributed). When such a division of authority occurs, who receives the city's centre? The symbolic centre of the archaic and classical city, as is well known, was the 'common hearth' in the Prytaneum. Public guests, both human and divine, were invited to dine there (along with the very few uniquely honoured citizens who enjoyed the privilege in perpetuity); religious processions started from there; magistrates, according to Aristotle, derived their authority to perform sacred functions 'from the common hearth'; while Herodotus restricts the 'most true-blooded' Ionians to those who had 'set out from the Prytaneum at Athens'.[59] The obvious pre-

---

[56] Rhamnus: *IG* I³.248, cf. 247 bis (addenda, p. 957), and for local devotion to the goddess 522 bis. The case of Rhamnus comes close to fitting the 'incorporation' model; but it does not seem that the city ever assumed administrative responsibility for the shrine. (A reference to *epistatai*, hitherto unattested in demes, in *IG* I³.247 bis 14 is noteworthy; but the δημόται of Rhamnus still lease out a *temenos* of the goddess in *IG* II².2493 [for the provenance see *SEG* XXXIV 123] of 339/8.) Halai: *SEG* XXXIV 103.15.

[57] This way of viewing extra-urban sanctuaries is due to de Polignac's important study, *Naissance*. It has been applied to Attica (which de Polignac excluded as untypical) by C. Sourvinou-Inwood in a lecture in Oxford (10 Mar. 1987), to be developed in her 'Reconstructing Change: Ritual and Ideology at Eleusis', in P. Toohey and M. Golden eds., *Inventing Ancient Culture?* (London forthcoming). See too Osborne, *Demos*, 154–82 and in *Placing the Gods* (where he stresses that early public rites outside Athens itself are attested, not of course with absolute reliability, by Solon fr. 83 Ruschenbusch and Hdt. 6.138).

[58] Cf. Welwei, *Athen*, 101–10.

decessor to the city's common hearth is, of course, the hearth of a king (at one of which Themistocles crouched, in flight from the democratic city). But the building at Athens that contained the common hearth was the seat not of the *basileus* but of the *archon*,[60] and it was associated through its name with *prytaneis*, executive rather than religious officers, whatever their precise functions in archaic Athens may have been. Were it useful to speak of 'the birth of the *polis*', one might identify as the birthday of the *polis* of Athens that day on which a common hearth was consecrated over which no king presided. When that day may have been, however, we cannot say within a hundred years.

We revert to the reconstruction of Attic religious life in the year 700. At the centre of public cult was the 'king'. He was either a king of very attenuated powers, or in fact a magistrate. He presided at public sacrifices in Athens, and led processions to sacred sites in Attica. Such public rites might have resembled the sacrifice that Homer imagines in Book 3 of the *Odyssey* (5 ff.), one shared by almost 5,000 Pylians. How they were organized and paid for we can only guess. It is very probable that participation was by tribe, and that the 'tribe-kings' took a lead.[61] For some rites, perhaps not yet very many, an effort was made to attract celebrants from all Attica. Priests were provided by *gene*, and these associations may have borne some of the expenses of the cult. If a new rite was established, it was no doubt the *basileus* who assigned the priesthood to an appropriate *genos*.

The petrefaction of religious sentiment into stone structures was just beginning; temples, artefacts of culture, were mounting sacred hills and entering sacred groves. The expense—or at least the burden of organization—may have been borne by aristocrats.[62] Aristocrats no doubt also represented Athens in her international religious relations. Athens was a partner in two of the archaic 'amphictyonies'—interstate organizations charged with the administration of a shrine or shrines—and surely participated in the Ionian rites on Delos. She thus had a public interest in Poseidon of Kalaureia,

[59] *IG* I³.131, with Jameson's commentary; Arist. *Pol.* 1322ᵇ26–29; *IG* II².1283; Hdt. 1.146.2. Cf. above all L. Gernet, *Anthropologie de la Grèce antique* (Paris 1968), 382–402; also Rhodes, *Commentary Ath. Pol.* 105 [+]; I. Malkin, *Religion and Colonization in Ancient Greece* (Leiden 1987), 114–34; Schmitt Pantel, *Cité au banquet*, 145–77.

[60] Arist. *Ath. Pol.* 3.5 says this explicitly (though the *basileus*' seat, the *boukoleion*, was 'nearby', and he presided over the 'court at the Prytaneum', ibid. 57.4). Themistocles: Thuc. 1.136.3.

[61] On them see Carlier, *La royauté*, 353–59; Rhodes, *Commentary Ath. Pol.*, 150–51, 649; and pp. 45–46, 112–13 below.

[62] Note how in Homer some 'public' expenses are initially met by *basileis*, then recouped from the people: see van Wees, *Status Warriors*, 35, on e.g. *Od.* 13.14–15.

Demeter of Anthela, and the Apollos of Delphi and Delos.[63] Indeed, such international connections had perhaps once been even more extensive. We learn by chance that in the fifth century two further un-Attic gods, Zeus Kenaios of Euboea and Athena Itonia of Thessaly (or Boeotia), had small public shrines in Athens (as did Poseidon of Kalaureia). Are these last faint traces of vanished archaic amphictyonies to which Athens had once belonged?[64]

A peasant from the Attic uplands will not have been very interested in Kalaurean Poseidon. Nor will public rites performed by the *basileus* in Athens have been the centre of his religious life. Worshipping-groups other than that of the city must have been even more important in the eighth century than in the fifth, important though they still were then. This is not the place to review them; for the moment let it be said curtly that rites were also performed by individuals, by households, by phratries (smallish hereditary groups), and, no doubt, by local associations, the predecessors of the demes. (But some would argue that the 'local associations' of this date were in fact the phratries.) These must have been the levels at which were conducted most of the surprisingly numerous ancient Attic festivals that we can name. (Some ten of those attested later have equivalents in other Greek, usually Ionian, communities, and therefore probably date back to before the Ionian migration.[65] They must already have been hallowed by time in the eighth century.) There may also have been more exclusive worshipping-groups. *Gene* perhaps celebrated rites of their own, distinct from the public cults for which they provided priests; and possibly associations of *orgeones* already existed, hereditary religious clubs honouring particular minor gods or heroes. Such may have been the forms of religious life, in barest outline. How humans established relations with the diverse powers of polytheism through these various groups, thus giving religious shape to their lives, how through the same groups they dominated one another and shaped the hierarchies of society, it remains to enquire.

---

[63] See Tausend, *Amphiktyonie*, 12–19, 34–55. These associations doubtless existed by 700, though the question of how far back they stretched into the Dark Ages (so crucial for an attempt to imagine that world) is controversial.

[64] *IG* I³.383.131, 151–52; 369.74; *Agora* XIX H1. An amphictyony, but of Boeotians only, is in fact attested at the shrine of Athena Itonia in Koroneia (Tausend, *Amphiktyonie*, 26); the same goddess's shrine at Philia was centre of the Hellenistic Thessalian league (D. P. Theochares, *ArchDelt* 19, 1964 [1966]/*Chron.* 248; cf. *SEG* XXVI 688, XXXIV 558.64).

[65] For a list see Sarkady, *Act. Class. Univ. Debreceniensis* 1 (1965), 12.

3

Mountain Peaks and Tombs of Heroes

In the main, as we have seen, the religious practices of the eighth century can only be described in the most general terms. Two forms of early cult that can, unusually, be discussed in some detail have been kept for this separate chapter. Both are already attested in or before the eighth century, but persist into the seventh and even grow in importance; they provide in fact most of the little that can be said about our theme in a notoriously ill-documented period.[1] We will treat them as a bridge, which leads at the end of the chapter to the few developments that are specific to the seventh century itself.

We begin with mountains. Pausanias mentions several of the mountain sanctuaries of Attica,[2] but it is still a surprise to discover quite how abundant they were in the archaic period: if we admit hills as well as true mountains, the tally of plausible instances stands at the moment at eleven.[3] Almost all these shrines were certainly in use in the eighth or seventh century, and two, the precincts of Zeus on Mounts Parnes and Hymettus, have yielded material going back to the ninth or tenth. In the classical period their fortunes become

---

[1] Cf. R. Osborne, *BSA* 84 (1989), 297–322.

[2] 'On their mountains the Athenians also have statues of gods. On Pentelikon is a statue of Athena, on Hymettus one of Zeus of Hymettus, and also altars of Zeus of Rain [Ὄμβριος] and of Look-Out Apollo [Προόψιος]. On Parnes there is Zeus of Parnes in bronze and an altar of Zeus of Signs [Σημάλεος]. There is another altar on Parnes, and when they sacrifice on this they invoke Zeus sometimes as of Rain, sometimes as Unharmful [Ἀπήμιος]. There is also a small mountain, Anchesmos, with a statue of Zeus of Anchesmos': Paus. 1.32.2. See in general Cook, *Zeus* II.2, 868–97, 'The Mountain-Cults of Zeus'; Nilsson, *Geschichte*, 393–401; Langdon, *Sanctuary of Zeus*, 78–112; and Map II above.

[3] For eight sites see Langdon, *Sanctuary of Zeus*, 100–106; one of these has now been fully studied by Lauter, *Turkovuni*. Add H. Lauter (with H. Lauter-Bufe), 'Ein attisches Höhenheiligtum bei Varkiza', in R. Hanauer et al. eds., *Festschrift zum 60. Geburtstag von W. Böser* (*Karlsruher geowissenschaftliche Schriften* A2/B2, Karlsruhe 1986), 285–309; id. (with D. K. Hagel) *MarbWPr* 1989 (1990), 14–15 on one at Kiapha Thiti; M. Küpper, ibid. 20 [+], on the hill bearing a chapel of the Panagia about 1 km. east. A little information about the sanctuary on Mt. Parnes is now available in E. Mastrokostas, *ASAtene* NS 45 (1983) [1984], 339–44 (*SEG* XXXIII 244). Note too the two small '6th c. temples' identified at Profitis Elias, on the east slope of Hymettus above Koropi, by N. Kotzias, *Prakt* 1949, 51–74; id., 1950, 144–72 (cf. Langdon, *Sanctuary of Zeus*, 5–6; Travlos, *Bildlexikon*, 194–95).

more uncertain (evidence from the Hymettus shrine, for instance, is very sparse after the early sixth century), and none seems to have been regularly visited beyond the early Hellenistic period. In Attica, as elsewhere, the mountain shrine appears as a characteristic centre of post-Mycenaean but, in the main, pre-classical religious activity. To judge from volume of finds, the boom period of the shrine on Hymettus, the best known, was the seventh century.[4]

The predominant god of the mountains in Pausanias' account is Zeus. Athena has a statue, and Apollo an altar in association with his father, but no god other than Zeus has a sanctuary of his own. A shrine of Apollo of Parnes is mentioned in a resolution passed by a private body in 324/3, but one may wonder whether a true mountain-shrine would have been used, as this is, as a site of display for a decree.[5] In the admittedly rare dedications actually found in peak sanctuaries, Zeus alone is certainly attested. We cannot assume that all the shrines known anonymously, from archaeology alone, necessarily belonged to him; but, to judge from analogies in the rest of Greece, the majority probably did, particularly those situated on real heights distant from human habitation.[6] If that is so (and even,

---

[4] At Turkovuni, Lauter recognizes two phases of cult activity, late eighth–late seventh cent., mid-fifth–late fourth cent.; at Varkiza material is quite abundant from the seventh cent., appreciable in but not after the fourth, slight for the interim; from Mt. Parnes there is material from PG down to a few scraps of BF (see Mastrokostas, *ASAtene* NS 45); pottery 'mostly geometric, but ranging through the entire first millennium B.C.' is mentioned in connection with the scarcely studied site on the east slope of Agrieliki (Langdon, *Sanctuary of Zeus*, 104–105); Kiapha Thiti provides evidence from the late eighth cent. to the late fourth., Panagia Thiti goes back at least to the early seventh cent. and has yielded a Doric capital from the fifth. The other sites have been studied too little to allow chronological conclusions. For mountain shrines elsewhere in Greece that flourished in the eighth–seventh cent. see Langdon, *Sanctuary of Zeus*, 106. Langdon's explanation for the decline of the Attic mountain-shrines, by reference to a supposed decline in indigenous Attic agriculture, is unconvincing, as imported grain supplemented but did not supplant the native product (cf. Lauter, *Turkovuni*, 156, n. 218, and P. D. A. Garnsey in *Crux*, 62–75). For one hill-sanctuary founded, by contrast, in the third cent., see H. Lauter, *AA* 1980, 242–55.

[5] *IG* II².1258 (cf. p. 336 below). For Παρνήσ(σ)ιος as ethnic from 'Parnes' cf. *SEG* XXXIII 244; *IG* I³.1057 bis; Ar. *Ach.* 348. On θ→σ, see M. Lejeune, *Atti e memorie del primo congresso internazionale di Micenologia* (Rome 1968), 737; on σ and σσ, L. Threatte, *The Grammar of Attic Inscriptions* (Berlin 1980), 525. Note too Hesych. s.v. Ὑμήττης· ἐν Ὑμήττῳ Ἀπόλλων τιμώμενος, and App. 2 A s.v. *Kunnidai* (on Apollo Kynneios).

[6] For Zeus see the works cited in n. 2 above. Note too the sacrifice of the Erchians to 'Zeus Epakrios, on Hymettus' (*LSCG* 18 E 58–64); the cult of this god on Hymettus and Parnes is also mentioned, without details, in lexicographers (e.g. Photius ε 1323), who cite Polyzelos fr. 8 K/A, and he was apparently mentioned in the fragmentary orgeonic decree *IG* II².1294 (Ferguson, 'Attic Orgeones', 93 f.). For 'Highest Zeus' (Ὕπατος) in Attica see Paus. 1.26.5 (the acropolis, the highest spot in Athens), (?) *IG* II².1358 (*LSCG* 20, Marathon calendar) B 13; elsewhere in Greece the epithet is regularly associated with high places and sometimes actual mountain-tops (cf. Graf, *Nordionische Kulte*, 202–203 and esp. *LSCG* 109). But for other gods favouring elevated, conspicuous sites see e.g. *Hymn. Hom. Aphr.* 100 and *Hymn. Hom. Dem.* 272 (with Y. Béquignon, *RA* 1958, ii, 149–77); R. G. A. Buxton, *JHS* 112 (1992), 5, n. 46; even hero-shrines could be so situated (E. Kearns in *EntrHardt* 37, Geneva 1992, 69,

though less emphatically, if it is not), these mountain cults represent only one form of worship among the many that must have been practised in the seventh century. Other gods will have been honoured at vanished sites, more liable to destruction and harder for us to detect, in the plains.[7]

Elsewhere in Greece, a hilltop Zeus sometimes developed into one of the leading gods of a city or larger region. A dominant mountain could obviously serve as a symbolic centre of a territory that was perhaps politically divided. Thus Zeus Atabyrios was probably honoured throughout Rhodes before there existed a Rhodian state; Zeus Lykaios was the greatest god of Arcadia, Zeus Ithomatas of Messenia.[8] The powers of such a Zeus were no doubt accordingly broad.

The Zeus of Hymettus or Parnes was never a national symbol like the Atabyrian or the lord of Mount Lykaion. None of the Attic mountain-shrines was ever equipped with elaborate buildings;[9] and it has been inferred from the most specific of the epithets attested in Pausanias—Zeus *Ombrios*, 'of Rain', and *Semios* 'of Signs'—that these cults were of specialized, agricultural appeal.[10] Zeus of Rain was normally approached in times of drought, as we see, for instance, from a fragment of a calendar from Rhodes which prescribes offerings to 'Zeus of Rain when necessary'. (His feared opposite, 'Withering Zeus', was acknowledged in Attica at Thorikos. 'Harmless Zeus', another Attic mountain-title, was possibly an optimistically named counterpoise to the Witherer.[11]) Zeus of Signs was

and cf. n. 19 below). Asclepius eventually penetrated Pentelikon, but not, to our knowledge, before the Roman period (S. Dow, *Phoenix* 36, 1982, 313–28, on *IG* II².4531).

[7] For one see *MarbWPr* 1989 (1990), 20: early seventh-cent. 'Stempelidolen' at a site where deme decrees were later displayed near Trachones.

[8] For refs. see H. Schwabl in *RE* X A s.v. *Zeus*, 253–376. Other mountain-Zeuses of broad fame include Zeus Panhellenios on Aegina, Zeus Idaios on Crete, Zeus Pelinnaios on Chios, Zeus Kenaios on Euboea.

[9] According to Lauter's reconstruction, there was at Turkovuni a modest Geometric oval cult-building (?), beside a tumulus-shaped structure; at the time of the fourth-cent. revival, a *peribolos* and altar were added. At Kiaphi Thiti and the site above Varkiza there were rough altars on terraces (LG/sub-geometric, according to Lauter); at Panagia Thiti a *temenos* was marked out by *horoi* and received a building in the fifth cent. Even Hymettus offered only 'three humble structures' (Langdon, *Sanctuary of Zeus*, 1), of problematic interpretation (Lauter, *Turkovuni*, 135–36).

[10] See Langdon, *Sanctuary of Zeus, passim.*

[11] Rhodes: *LSS* 103; for further evidence see e.g. Langdon, *Sanctuary of Zeus*, 79–87 (much of this relating to mountain shrines), H. Schwabl, *RE* Suppl. vol. XV. 1046–48. For Attica cf. the prayer cited by Marc. Aur. 5.7; Alciphron, *Epist.* 2.33 (3.35); Paus. 1.24.3; and two Roman altars from the *agora*, *Hesperia* 37 (1968), 291, no. 32. Withering Zeus (Αὐαντήρ): *IG* II².2606. Harmless: above, n. 2. The dedication to Earth from the Hymettus shrine belongs in this context (cf. Paus. 1.24.3) if correctly identified: Langdon, *Sanctuary of Zeus*, 15, no. 10 (where justified doubts are expressed). On the uncertain rainfall of Attica see R. Osborne, *Classical Landscape with Figures* (London 1987), 31–34.

probably, in practice, a closely related figure. Cloud formations around mountain-tops provide 'signs' of weather, particularly of rain: in his work *On Weather-Signs*, Theophrastus regularly refers to the Attic mountains, and actually speaks of the group of 'sign-giving mountains'.[12] As worshippers we should therefore imagine smallholders, going up to the mountain shrines in procession like the Coan 'association of those who walk together to Zeus of Rain'; and doubtless also the occasional shepherd.[13]

Beyond a doubt these are indeed among the worshippers we should envisage. What is much less clear is that all others should be excluded. In early poetry, Zeus is not associated with mountain-tops merely because he controls the weather; these high seats are a symbol of the pre-eminent power of the 'highest of lords', and from them he looks down on all the doings of mankind.[14] Men could thus petition him on the heights about any of their needs. And there are hints that this may have occurred in Attica, at least in the early period. At the sanctuary on Mount Parnes, one, and perhaps two, of the very few specific dedications were apparently made to 'Zeus of Suppliants'. A recently discovered boundary-stone shows that the same 'Zeus of Parnes' had acquired a further precinct, in Athens itself, early in the fifth century. For what it is worth, members of the cult-society associated with Apollo of Parnes in the fourth century were evidently not drawn from the shepherd classes.[15]

Again, the finds from the precinct on Mount Hymettus display one remarkable feature. In this rustic shrine, writing is extraordi-

---

[12] 51, τὰ ὄρη τὰ σημαντικά; for other Attic instances see 20, 24, 43, 47, and cf. the comment of Nilsson, *Geschichte*, 393. Zeus is Σημαλέος on Parnes (Paus. 1.32.2), and Σήμιος too on a graffito dedication from Hymettus, Langdon, *Sanctuary of Zeus*, 13, no. 2. Of course in principle the 'signs' of Zeus were not of importance only to farmers (cf. e.g. Hom. *Il.* 8.170–71; Philochorus *FGrH* 328 F 113).

[13] Cos: *SIG*³ 1107, cf. Nilsson, *Geschichte*, 394, n. 2. For processions to mountain shrines cf. e.g. those to Mt. Pelion (Nilsson, *Geschichte*, 396), and Cithaeron (Paus. 9.3.7); note too οἱ ἀναβαίνοντες to the precinct of Poseidon Helikonios on Samos, *BCH* 59 (1935), 478. On supplication for rain in modern Greece see Cook, *Zeus*, III. 284–96; Langdon, *Sanctuary of Zeus*, 5 (with the citation of Milchhöfer) and 82, n. 13; for the collective nature of such acts cf. Alciphron, *Epist.* 2.33 (3.35). Shepherds: Apollo Proopsios, 'Foreseeing', of Hymettus (Paus. 1.32.2), sounds like the shepherd of epic similes watching the weather from the heights. The Munns (in A. Schachter ed., *Essays in the Topography, History and Culture of Boiotia* [*Teiresias* Suppl. 3, Montreal 1990]) ascribe the abundant Corinthian wares supposedly found in the shrine on Mt. Parnes to transhumant Corinthian shepherds. M. H. Jameson in C. R. Whittaker ed., *Pastoral Economies in Classical Antiquity* (*PCPS* Suppl. 14, 1988), 103, attractively suggests that the Erchians' offering to Zeus Epakrios on Hymettus (*LSCG* 18 E 58–64) in Thargelion marks the opening of the summer pastures.

[14] See e.g. Hom. *Il.* 7.202; 8.47–52, 75–77.

[15] See *SEG* XXXIII 244 (there is also a dedication to Zeus Parnesios); *IG* I³.1057 bis; n. 5 above.

narily conspicuous. Numerous graffiti and specimen alphabets of the seventh century have been found, and several details suggest that dedicators may have been self-consciously offering specimens of their skill in the difficult art to the god: '*X*. . . wrote it himself', one sherd boasts.[16] (The marks on an inscribed sherd could be called a *sema*, sign,[17] and one may wonder whether a relation of serious punning existed between such inscribed signs and Zeus of Signs, the god of the shrine: 'receive this sign that I offer you, and send fair signs in return'. No sherd, however, says that, or even describes itself as a *sema*.) Would farmers in quest of rain have left such traces of their presence? Perhaps the shrine had originally attracted a broader clientele, until they were drawn off in the sixth century by the fine temples of Athens itself.

It is hard to get beyond such tentative conclusions, when we can identify the original worshipping-group of no single one of these mountain shrines. Two extreme positions are possible: that they all belonged to Zeus and were frequented for purposes linked with agriculture alone; or that they met needs of every kind and were in fact a principal context of religious activity in the early centuries. It seems impossible to determine just where between these poles the truth may lie.

For hero-cults, the evidence is of various kinds. It begins in the second half of the eighth century, and becomes more abundant in the seventh. Offerings were laid, regularly it seems, in the *dromoi* of monumental Mycenaean tombs at Menidi and Thorikos;[18] in the Academy region, a cult association appears to have met for sacrificial meals in a building of several rooms, close to a contemporary graveyard and next to the remains of a Helladic house which was, perhaps, identified as the house or tomb of the hero of the locality,

---

[16] See Langdon, *Sanctuary of Zeus*, 46 (and on dating L. H. Jeffery, *JHS* 98, 1978, 202–203). 'Himself': Langdon, *Sanctuary of Zeus*, 20, no. 30. Zeus also on one graffito receives the general honorific title ἄναξ (ibid. 13, no. 1), and there is fragile evidence that Heracles was associated with him (15, no. 9; 41, no. 173).

[17] Hom. *Il.* 6.168, 7.189 (noted by Jeffery, *JHS* 98, 1978, 202–203; cf. R. Thomas, *Literacy and Orality in Ancient Greece*, Cambridge 1992, 60).

[18] See Coldstream, 'Hero-cults', 11–12 [+]. Add, on Menidi, R. Hägg, 'Gifts to the Heroes in Geometric and Archaic Greece', in *Gifts to the Gods*, 93–99; on Thorikos, M. Devillers, *An Archaic and Classical Votive Deposit from a Mycenaean Tomb at Thorikos* (*Miscellanea Graeca* 8, Ghent 1988); and in general J. Whitley, *JHS* 108 (1988), 176. The evidence: at Menidi, numerous offerings (pottery, *pinakes*, etc.) from the late eighth–fifth cent., no trace of sacrificial meals (Hägg in *Gifts to the Gods*, 96); at Thorikos, an offering-table and *bothros* constructed in the *dromos*; pottery from mid-seventh–mid-fourth cent. (most abundant from 550–425). Coldstream also mentions a much less clear instance of the same phenomenon from Aliki.

Hekademos;[19] in or near the *agora*, three deposits of early votive material have been found which look as if they had been offered to heroes, because of the character of the offerings or because a modest shrine of heroic type was later built on the same site.[20] The *agora* had long been a burial ground, and excavators suggest that the heroic cults that sprang up there in the seventh century, just when it was losing that character, honoured those ancient (and not so ancient) dead amid whose graves they were celebrated.

How comparable are these various phenomena? The regular offerings brought to the inhabitants of the Mycenaean *tholoi* at Menidi and Thorikos look like clear instances of homage paid to 'heroes' (though even this has been disputed[21]). The early graves of the *agora* were not impressive monuments like these. But the belief doubtless existed that the area contained tombs;[22] and the offerings

[19] See H. Drerup, *Griechische Baukunst in geometrischer Zeit* (Göttingen 1969), 31 [+]; Lauter, *Turkovuni*, 159–62; and for the Helladic house, and Hekademos, Travlos, *Pictorial Dictionary*, 44, fig. 52; P. D. Stavropoullos, *Prakt* 1958 (1965), 8 (but cf. Ch. 2, n. 34 above). Lauter argues that the LG seven-roomed house in question was secular in form and use, but doubled up as a locale for hero-cult performed by a 'gentilician' group in association with the cemetery; numerous traces of sacrifices were found in, under, and around it (*Ergon* 1962 [1963], 5; *Prakt* 1963 [1966], 7, cf. *BCH* 88, 1964, 682; for nearby pits containing votive deposits see *Prakt* 1956 [1961], 52–53 [40 LG vases]; ibid. 1958 [1965], 8, n. 1 [12 vases]). Evidence for post-Geometric cult (? *c*.600) has proved fragile: *Ergon* 1962 (1963), 7 f. The 'sacred house' at Eleusis just south-west of the sanctuary (K. Kourouniotis and I. Travlos, *Prakt* 1937 [1938], 42–52) was, according to Lauter (*Turkovuni*, 163–69), a similar dual-purpose building, but there are no specific grounds here for supposing the cult to have been heroic. Lauter also argues, because of the presence of a round tumulus-shaped structure (? tomb ? cenotaph), that the late eighth–seventh-cent. cult on Turkovuni was in part heroic (136–39).

[20] See Thompson/Wycherley, *Agora*, 119–21 ; H. A. Thompson, 'Some Hero Shrines in Early Athens', in *Athens Comes of Age* (Princeton 1978), 96–108 [+]. The instances are: (1) a stone-curbed pit just north of the altar of Ares, amid Mycenaean burials, with votive material going back into the seventh cent. (Thompson, *Hesperia* 27, 1958, 148–53); (2) a fifth-cent. tri-angular structure (with a *horos* inscribed τὸ hιερô), amid EG graves, over an earlier rectan-gular structure, with which LG and Proto-Attic material is associated (G. V. Lalonde, *Hesperia* 37, 1968, 123–33: perhaps a *Tritopatreion*, according to Bourriot, *Génos*, 1155, n. 217); (3) 20 yds. south-east of this, amid EG graves, the 'Geometric house on the N. slope of the Areopagus' (probably rather, it is now thought, a religious structure: see Thompson/Wycherley, *Agora*, 17, n. 50) from which a large deposit of seventh-cent. votive material was recovered (D. Burr, *Hesperia* 2, 1933, 542–640; the material would suit a heroic cult; see Hägg in *Gifts to the Gods*). Other presumptive hero-shrines in the *agora*—the 'classi-cal shrine at the Northwest Corner', near Mycenaean and PG graves (T. L. Shear Jr., *Hesperia* 42, 1973, 360–69); the rectangular structure with *horoi* below the middle Stoa, amid Mycenaean graves (G. V. Lalonde, *Hesperia* 49, 1980, 360–69)—cannot be shown to go back to the seventh cent., likely though that is.

[21] By C. Antonaccio, 'The Archaeology of Ancestors', in C. Dougherty and L. Kurke eds., *Cultural Poetics in Ancient Greece* (Cambridge 1993), 46–70 (a book of the same title is forth-coming; cf. too *AJA* 98, 1994, 389–410); cf. J. Whitley, *AJA* 98 (1994), 225–27. Her attempt to dissociate true hero-cult from tombs can scarcely stand in the face of the literary evidence (for which see e.g. Seaford, *Reciprocity and Ritual*, 114–23).*

[22] For a much clearer Corinthian instance of association between heroic cult and a PG cemetery see C. K. Williams II, *Hesperia* 42 (1973), 1–12 and 43 (1974), 1–6; and perhaps cf.

and emplacements are certainly of heroic type. One must, however, allow the possibility that they honoured Tritopatores, for instance, the collective ancestors of particular groups, rather than heroes.[23] About the cult association of the Academy nothing can be said with confidence except that it met, scarcely by chance, close to a grave-yard.

Very seldom in Attica, unfortunately, can hero-cults known from archaeology be linked with the really abundant literary and epi-graphical evidence. None of the sites just mentioned have yielded inscribed dedications that would have permitted certain identifications. Two suggestions have, however, been made in addi-tion to the very speculative one about Hekademos already men-tioned. We learn from the *Odyssey* that Menelaus' steersman Phrontis son of Onetor, 'he who was most skilful among mankind at steering a ship, when the storm-winds blew hard', died and was buried at Sunium. That is perhaps an allusion to a cult of Phrontis that already existed at Sunium; and if not, the passage itself might easily have encouraged such a cult to arise. Near the temple of Athena at Sunium, a rich votive-deposit has been discovered, including a fine Proto-Attic plaque showing a ship with a very prominent helmsman. Is this Phrontis, and do these votives derive from the hypothetical cult? The suggestion is alluring.[24] Secondly, in the west cemetery at Eleusis—in about the year 700, according to the excavator—an enclosure was built around a group of some six Helladic graves. It is suggested that they had been identified as belonging to six of the Seven against Thebes, who, according to an Attic tradition first attested in Aeschylus, were buried at Eleusis, and whose tombs there were later shown to Pausanias. That Eleusinians or Athenians were already seeking reflected glory from this foreign myth would scarcely have been predicted on general grounds. But the enclosure, if correctly dated, is certainly another instance of respect shown in this period to ancient tombs.[25]

L. C. H. Morgan, *AJA* 41 (1937), 545–46. And note the 'apology' offerings left (twice) when a chamber tomb below the *agora* was disturbed in the fifth cent.: Coldstream, 'Hero-cults', 11, with an earlier Eleusinian parallel (cf. too *Hesperia* 22, 1953, 47).

[23] So Antonaccio, 'Archaeology of Ancestors', 58 (cf. n. 20; and on Tritopatores Ch. 7, n. 25).

[24] See H. Abramson, 'A Hero Shrine for Phrontis at Sounion ?', *CSCA* 12 (1979), 1–19, who finds a new site for the cult of Phrontis first postulated by C. Picard, *RA*, 6th ser., 16 (1940), 5–28. The deposit (from a pit south-east of the temple of Athena) may belong to Phrontis even if the small temple that Abramson quite plausibly ascribes to him (8.5 m. north of the temple of Athena) does not. The Homeric passage is *Od.* 3.278–83. Phrontis may have presided over the ἄμιλλα νεῶν (Lys. 21.5) celebrated at Sunium, suggests Picard, 13.

[25] See Mylonas, *Mysteries*, 62–63; id., Τὸ δυτικὸν νεκροταφεῖον τῆς Ἐλευσῖνος, II (Athens 1975), 153–54, 262–64, 326, citing Paus. 1.39.2. The date depends, insecurely, on the

It was not just in Attica that heroes were being discovered in such abundance at this time, but in most of Greece. Many were the Mycenaean tombs to which offerings were now brought, and never does the practice begin before the late eighth century.[26] The 'hero of Lefkandi', it is true, received what might be termed 'heroic burial' in the tenth century;[27] but such funerary honours for a contemporary are not exactly the same phenomenon as regular cult paid to a more ancient inhabitant of the land (though the two things are no doubt related). The archaeological evidence still strongly suggests that the regular cult either began, or at least assumed radically new forms, in the late eighth century. And even if one insists that classical hero-cult had complex origins, of which such consecration of Mycenaean tombs was only one, there is still a development here to be explained.

As an explanation, or part of one, the influence of Homeric epic has often been suggested, and often rejected.[28] The strongest objections appear to be the following. There are probably a few references to hero-cult in Homer;[29] but the poet cannot have caused a phenomenon which he also reflects. Secondly, in all contexts other than this, it is a truism to insist that Homer represents not the origin of a tradition but its culmination; tales of Troy divine are not, therefore, a new causal factor in the eighth century. And finally, the two groups 'Homeric heroes' and 'heroes of cult' do no more in the classical period than overlap, even if one gives 'Homeric hero' a broad generic sense as 'warrior of the Trojan-war period'; in Hesiod's account, it is the men of the gold and silver ages rather than of the age of heroes who after death take on functions that recall those of the heroes of classical cult.[30] Many attested heroes (of Attica above

discovery of LG sherds in the area. On the myth see Jacoby on Philochorus *FGrH* 328 F 112–13 [+], who interestingly had argued before Mylonas's discovery that 'at that time [the late sixth cent.] the Eleusinian tombs may have had their name for a long time' (p. 445, top). The missing seventh hero might have been Amphiaraus (who disappeared underground at Thebes) or Adrastus (who in some versions survived). See further Kearns, *Heroes of Attica*, 130 (and 41–42 on Phrontis). Antonaccio 'Archaeology of Ancestors', 68, n. 49, dismisses the case as one of 're-use', not hero-cult.

[26] See Coldstream, 'Hero-cults'.

[27] See M. Popham, E. Touloupa, and L. H. Sackett, *Antiquity* 56 (1982), 169–74, and the comment of C. Sourvinou-Inwood in Hägg, *Greek Renaissance*, 42, n. 55.

[28] *Pro*: e.g. Coldstream, 'Hero-cults'; Burkert, *Greek Religion*, 204; *Contra*: e.g. de Polignac, *Naissance*, 130, with n. 12; Snodgrass, *An Archaeology*, 160–61 and in *AnnArchStorAnt* (= *AION*) 10 (1988), 19–26 (though his argument from tomb-types is perhaps too rational).

[29] See Th. Hadzisteliou-Price, *Historia* 22 (1973), 129–44.

[30] Hes. *Op.* 122–23, 141, 170–73 (a point stressed by I. Morris, *Antiquity* 62, 1987, 750–61). But a popular argument based on the different usage of the word ἥρως in epic and in cult is not decisive: see van Wees, *Status Warriors*, 8.

all) neither feature in Homer nor could readily be imagined as doing so.[31] Hero-cult cannot, it is true, be understood in isolation from myth, since the same conception of a past time of heightened reality underlies both phenomena. But Homer did not create the one any more than he created the other.

Others connect the change in various ways with political developments, in particular (of course) the 'rise of the *polis*'.[32] According to this theory, a society is emerging that is, for the first time, of a certain scope, ordered, but not monarchic. Within the new political structure, new forms of political self-assertion become possible and necessary. The 'big men' of the emergent *polis* invent a category of special beings, the heroes, who, if duly honoured, will be powerfully active for the collective good. The unspoken implication is that they are themselves beings of the same nature. There is a connection between the cult newly paid to heroes and what were (to judge from grave-goods) the novel splendours of the aristocratic funerals of the eighth century. A recently dead aristocrat could even perhaps be added to the ranks of the heroes by his successors, as may have been the fortune of the Eretrian warrior whose tomb was discovered in 1965. Or the commemorative rites performed by a particular family could grow into a hero-cult—one shared by the community at large—as happened, it has been suggested, at Grotta on Naxos.[33] Thus the heroes arise (as did the Saints, or so it has been argued[34]) not as champions of the poor, but as clients of the great and good.

Another approach starts from the link between the hero and the land in which he lies. Offerings at Mycenaean tombs predominantly occur in regions inhabited by free peasants: they are therefore a device by which free but insecure smallholders stake their claim to

---

[31] So Kearns, *Heroes of Attica*, 131.

[32] See C. Bérard, 'Récupérer la mort du prince: Héroïsation et formation de la cité', in G. Gnoli and J.-P. Vernant eds., *La mort et les morts dans les sociétés anciennes* (Cambridge 1982), 89–105; Bérard, in *Architecture et Société* (*CEFR* 66, Rome 1983), 43–62; and (with different emphasis), de Polignac, *Naissance*, 127–51. Seaford, *Reciprocity and Ritual*, ch. 4 and 180–82 (similarly Burkert, *Greek Religion*, 204), sees these cults as a communal transposition of older, family-based funerary rites and the associated emotions. The chronological relation is, however, complex, as private funerals and funerary monuments were perhaps gaining in importance in the late eighth–seventh cent.

[33] Eretria: C. Bérard, *Eretria*, III; *L'Hérôon à la porte de l'ouest* (Berne 1970), and in *Eretria*, VI (Berne 1978), 89–95 (but the view that the cult was familial only is not strictly refutable). Novel splendours: see Coldstream, *Geometric Greece*, 349–52. Grotta: V. K. Lambrinoudakis in *Early Greek Cult Practice*, 235–46; similar phenomena are discussed in an unpub. paper by R. Hägg, 'Grabzeremonien, Ahnenverehrung und Heroenkult in der frühgeschichtlichen Argolis'.

[34] By P. Brown, *The Cult of the Saints* (London 1981).

the soil by attaching themselves to its ancient inhabitants.[35] (In Attica, it has been suggested, we should think of established communities using this means to assert their traditional title against parvenus.[36]) The theory can be transposed from an individual to a collective level, much to its benefit: the cults are a means by which a community takes symbolic possession of its territory, the territory which is also that of the 'heroes who occupy the land'.[37] A closely related and uncontroversial proposition is that, since heroes, unlike gods, are commonly specific to a particular group, their cult is a fundamental mechanism by which a group's sense of shared identity may be forged.

The heroes of the historical period certainly worked in most of these ways. Every reader of Pindar's epinician poetry knows that the relation of living aristocrats and dead heroes could be one of mutual benefit; and even in democratic Athens, Theseus and Cimon to some extent gained new prominence together. Again, the role of hero-cults in binding members of a group to one another and to their territory is very clear—to take a particularly sharp small-scale example from Attica—in the calendar of the deme Thorikos: the Thorikians worshipped themselves, as it were, in the two heroes Thorikos and Cephalus, and they worshipped their land in the several cults (that of 'the hero over the plain', for instance) that related to actual features of their physical environment.[38] But one may hesitate before allowing that the 'origin of hero-cult' is now explained.[39] The heroes of the classical period, in Attica above all, are of a spectacular diversity. The theories we have looked at tend to give primacy to a single type—that of the founder-hero and national symbol such as Erechtheus, for instance. Even if we combine the various approaches and their characteristic heroes, important types remain excluded, such as those linked with seafaring and healing. It is not clear that functions as prominent as these can be dismissed as sec-

[35] See A. M. Snodgrass in Gnoli and Vernant eds., *La mort et les morts*, 107–19, and in his own *Archaic Greece* (London 1980), 38–40. But in a paper given in Oxford in autumn 1987 he stated a preference for the Francophone approach (n. 32 above). The distribution map of hero-cults on which his argument depends alters drastically if the much more abundant (but of course chronologically unstratified) literary evidence is included, with due regard to the special character of the main source, Pausanias: see K. Tausend, *Gymnasium* 97 (1990), 145–53.

[36] See Whitley, *JHS* 108 (1988), 173–82: he argues that Thorikos, for instance, had long been settled when the cult at the Mycenaean *tholos* begun, but was increasingly surrounded by new settlements.

[37] So I. Malkin in R. M. Rosen and J. Farrell eds., *Nomodeiktes: Greek Studies in Honour of Martin Ostwald* (Ann Arbor 1993), 225–34.

[38] See *SEG* XXXIII 147, with my comments in *Gifts to the Gods*, 144–47.

[39] What follows depends heavily on Kearns, *Heroes of Attica*, 129–37.

ondary, when the supposed primary functions are merely being established by scholarly conjecture. Heroes' powers were probably already diverse in the seventh century, to judge from the quantity of hero-cults even then attested. Who knows what groups or individuals approached the three hero-shrines (if that is what they are) in the *agora* in the seventh century, or what they asked for?

This objection disappears if the problem is redefined[40] as no longer the origin of hero-cult but the crystallization of the category of heroes: the emergence, that is, of the practice of classifying under this rubric a range of figures some of whom might long have been honoured under a different title, as minor gods, for instance. 'Hero' thus becomes from the start a river into which flow many tributary streams. But there remains the problem of explaining how the crystallization occurred when it did. Here, plausible general theories may lose their lustre when applied to specific cases. Let us allow, for instance, that the hero-cult newly established at a Mycenaean tomb in Thorikos around the year 700 may have served as an 'identity cult' for the Thorikians. But the social unit that needed new emphasis at this date was surely that of the Athenians. An answer could, of course, be made, along the lines that the process of state-formation gives new prominence not just to the whole but also to its parts. (Alternatively, the Thorikians might be seen as resisting centralization.) But if anything can be explained, then nothing can. The more one considers the diversity of the political contexts in which hero-cults emerged up and down the Greek world in the eighth century,[41] the harder it becomes to find a socio-political explanation of any simple type. Suitably complex accounts of mental phenomena cannot, however, be given on the basis of archaeological evidence alone.

We cannot leave the eighth and seventh centuries without mentioning the enigma of 'Lathuresa', a complex of rough buildings on a hillside above Vari. An excavation conducted there in the 1930s, the results of which were scarcely published, yielded thousands of figurines and other small dedications, and in the opinion of one investigator the whole complex served purposes of cult. A thorough recent study of the surface-remains concludes that the site was a habitation, for some 80–100 souls, built all at once in the late eighth century; the religious activities centred around a single building, the '*tholos*', which continued in use down to the fifth century, even

---

[40] With Kearns, ibid.
[41] A point stressed by Whitley, *JHS* 108 (1988). But we are then left with diverse causes producing the same result at the same time.

though the settlement itself was abandoned soon after it was built.[42] (A small 'extramural' shrine has also been identified.) The jumble of buildings at Lathuresa resembles no known Greek *temenos*, and the interpretation as a habitation is doubtless (despite the absence of an obvious water-supply) to be preferred. But the postulated miniature village, built as a unit, with its own shrines for a group based, it is suggested, on kinship or pseudo-kinship, is equally unparalleled. The site remains for the moment an anomaly which coheres with no other of our guesses about the modes of life in Attica around 700 BC.

Mountain cults and hero-cult, as we noted at the start, flourished in the eighth and seventh centuries alike. Very little that is absolutely new in the seventh century can be recorded. (But we should not allow arbitrary periodization to create an impression of 'stagnation' or 'regress'. Many of the effects of the 'eighth-century renaissance' manifest themselves so late in Attica that the great period of change can be said to spill well over into the seventh.) No major new religious site emerges,[43] and the architectural transformations that existing sanctuaries may have undergone have left few traces. Nothing can be said with confidence even about the acropolis, except that a first temple was almost certainly now built if one had not been before. A few fragments of roof-tile and other architectural terracottas are the only memorials to the elegant constructions that perhaps arose;[44] even these, on recent views, do not antedate the last quarter of the century.

The one area of major change is iconography.[45] The history of mythological vase-painting effectively begins in the seventh century; and very little can be said about modes of representing the gods before this, whether in painting or in the plastic arts.[46] But even here the sense of transformation may in part be a product of our perspec-

[42] See H. Lauter, *Lathuresa* (Mainz 1985). For various doubts see A. Mazarakis-Ainian in *Early Greek Cult Practice*, 112–13; Osborne, *BSA* 84 (1989), 308. One investigator: C. W. J. Eliot, *Coastal Demes of Attika* (Toronto 1962), 39–41.

[43] One minor one does, the shrine of Nymphe below the acropolis: see Travlos, *Pictorial Dictionary*, 363; and cf. n. 7. No stagnation: I owe this point to an OUP reader, who suggests 720–620 rather than 820–720 as 'the period of rapid change and growth'.

[44] See Ch. 2, n. 37 above; for the tiles see N. A. Winter, *Greek Architectural Terracottas* (Oxford 1993), 64–65 [+]; she places the vast majority of the archaic material later than earlier scholars, after about 560. Note too the marble acroteria, Payne/Young, *Archaic Marble Sculpture*, 68 and pl. 17.4–5. Seventh-cent. pottery finds from the acropolis are rather sparse (S. P. Morris, *The Black and White Style*, Yale 1984, 9), as are terracottas (D. Brooke in S. Casson (ed.), *Catalogue of the Acropolis Museum*, II, Cambridge 1921, 322), but bronzes appear numerous (Floren, *Griechische Plastik I*, 301–304).

[45] Cf. Osborne, *BSA* 84 (1989), 309–13.

[46] This is not, however, to say that no representations existed: see C. Sourvinou-Inwood, *CR* NS 40 (1990), 129–31.

tive. A new style of painting unquestionably emerged, marked by a reduction in repetitive ornament, a greater concentration on the main narrative scene, larger, fleshier figures more individually characterized. And mythological subjects certainly increase enormously in frequency. Whether the painters of the eighth century had been able to present, within their own conventions, a narrative scene, is another question, one that art historians debate with vigour. On one answer, 'Proto-Attic', the style of the seventh century, becomes a working-through of experiments made by the late Geometric painters.[47] However that may be, for us it is in Proto-Attic that a mythological world first comes clearly into view. It proves to be strikingly free of any prejudice in favour of local heroes: Theseus first slays the Minotaur on non-Attic pieces, while the works of his homeland show Heracles busy against Nessos, or Odysseus blinding Polyphemus, or the Gorgons in fierce pursuit of Perseus.[48]

In the plastic arts, a few small figures can be claimed, rather unreliably, as 'goddesses'.[49] Much the most striking is one who holds up her arms in the old Minoan manner on a snake-bordered polychrome plaque (of the seventh century) found in a votive deposit in the *agora*. The same archaic gesture (perhaps of blessing) seems also to be shown on cruder terracotta figurines found on the acropolis and at Eleusis, and it reappears spasmodically on objects of this period and a little later from elsewhere in Greece. We would gladly know what perishable medium (or was it cult practice?) had preserved the iconographic tradition from the Mycenaean period.[50] Such hieratic images tend to conservatism: a famous vase of the seventh century from Eleusis shows a much freer and more modern Athena, the first certain Athena in Greek art, with a lance in her

---

[47] So Snodgrass, *An Archaeology*, ch. 5 [+]; and see now G. Ahlberg-Cornell, *Myth and Epos in Early Greek Art* (Jonsered 1992), 17–40 [+].

[48] On Theseus see Ahlberg-Cornell, *Myth and Epos*, 122–30 (and on his possible presence on Geometric vases, 26–27).

[49] See *LIMC* s.v. *Artemis*, 630–31 nos. 80, 84a–b, 85 (all from Brauron). For eighth-cent. 'goddesses' see R. A. Higgins, *Greek Terracottas* (London 1967), 22, 140, with pl. 7; Coldstream, *Geometric Greece*, 130–32, with Robertson, *History*, 44.

[50] Plaque: Burr, *Hesperia* 2 (1933), 604, no. 277, figs. 72–3; E. T. H. Brann, *Agora* VIII (Princeton 1962), 87, no. 493; E. T. Vermeule, *Götterkult* (*Archaeologia Homerica* 3.V, Göttingen 1974), pl. 10b. As snake-borders occur on other plaques (J. Boardman, *BSA* 49, 1954, 197, n. 149), it is not certain that ours shows 'one of the rare recurrences of the Minoan and Mycenaean snake goddess' (J. N. Coldstream, *Deities in Aegean Art*, London 1977, 14). Figurines: F. Winter, *Die Typen der figürlichen Terrakotten* (Berlin 1903), I. 24, no. 4 (cf. Brooke in Casson, *Catalogue of the Acropolis Museum*, II.345–46, no. 1215). Revival of the archaic gesture: see R. V. Nicholls, 'Greek Votive Statuettes and Religious Continuity, c. 1200–700 B.C.', in B. F. Harris ed., *Auckland Classical Essays Presented to E. M. Blaiklock* (Auckland 1970), 1–37 [ı], Burkert, *Greek Religion*, 365, n. 14.

hand as, always a helper of heroes, she protects Perseus from the Gorgons.[51]

Such is the sparse account of a hundred years of religious history that the archaeological evidence enables us to present. It does not seem possible to correlate these religious phenomena, such as they are, with the great historical process of the period, the 'enslavement of the poor to the rich' through debt-bondage.[52] And yet it is inconceivable that drastic and ever-growing inequities were not in fact reflected in religious life. For this radical partiality of archaeological history there is no cure; but it is well to recognize the disease.

[51] Eleusis Museum 544 = *LIMC* s.v. *Athena*, 958, no. 5; cf. Shapiro, *Art and Cult*, 37.

[52] Arist. *Ath. Pol.* 2. I know that many other views of the social situation are possible. But the point remains that hektemorage, whatever it was, is archaeologically invisible.

4

Solon's Calendar

In contrast to its predecessor, the sixth century seems like the great age of transformation. By the end of it, Athens was equipped, at last, with temples of truly monumental scale; and near the beginning had occurred, perhaps, one of the great landmarks in the history of Greek religion—the drafting by Solon of a written calendar of sacrifices, possibly the first such that existed and the only one from archaic or even classical Greece that is known in any detail.[1] Whether or not it was in fact Solon who drew up a systematic programme for the religion of the state, a corpus of written prescriptions on religious matters evidently built up during the course of the century. A traditional, pre-literary religion therefore made its first, limited contact with the art of writing.

'Solon's' calendar is a prime document for our theme, but the approach to it must of necessity be oblique. Apart from a few fragments quoted in literary sources,[2] we know it from surviving portions of a revised version that was inscribed in or near the year 401, as part of a general revision of the laws.[3] It has long been controver-

[1] Other early calendars are *SEG* XI 53 + *Hesperia* 45 (1976), 230–31, pl. 52e (Corinth: inscribed on the wall of a temple which was destroyed *c*.570, according to H. S. Robinson in *Hesperia* 45); *LSA* 41 (Miletus); *LSCG* 146–47 (Gortyn); (?) *IG* XII.3.450 (Jeffery, *Local Scripts*, 323, no. 14: Thera). Allusions to religious legislation by Draco are hopelessly vague: see R. Stroud, *Drakon's Law on Homicide* (Berkeley 1968), 81.

[2] Solon frs. 81–86 Ruschenbusch. Evidence about religious life occurs incidentally in frs. of other laws, e.g. 72 (the funerary laws), 76a (religious associations: cf. Whitehead, *Demes*, 13–14 [+]), 88 (the right of heralds from the *genos* of Kerykes to παρασιτεῖν ἐν τῷ Δηλίῳ for a year), (?) the testimonium to fr. 79 (= Androtion *FGrH* 324 F 36: payments for *theoroi* to Delphi), (?) fr. 50b (the concept of ἀγχιστεία ἱερῶν).

[3] It appears in fact that the sacred, like the civil, code was revised twice, first in 410–404 and again in 403–399. (On the many related problems see most recently P. J. Rhodes, *JHS* 111, 1991, 87–100 [+].) The two revisions were inscribed respectively on the two sides of (on the majority view) two walls in the Royal Stoa. What seem to be frs. from the earlier revision (but for other views see Rhodes, *JHS* 111, 1991, 94) are now *IG* I³.237 bis–241. Those of the later revision are *LSS* 10, *LSCG* 17 B, C, and the tiny frs. *Hesperia* 10 (1941), 34–36, E, F, C. It is generally accepted that the later revision did not supplement the earlier, but replaced it; for both *IG* I³.241, col. II (earlier revision) and *LSS* 10 A 19–28 (later revision) appear to treat the same subject: annual sacrifices made in Skirophorion (so first W. S. Ferguson in *Classical*

sial whether laws that passed for Solon's were so in fact; more recently it has been argued that early Greek laws were specific responses to specific problems, the great archaic lawgivers, authors of comprehensive codes, being creations of the anachronistic imagination of later ages.[4] On an extreme view, Athens' first true sacrificial code would then be the one assembled at the end of the fifth century.

Some fragments of sacred law survive from earlier in the fifth century and even perhaps late in the sixth; but their character and origin (for date of inscription need not be date of composition) are too ill-established to do more than complicate our uncertainties.[5] The problem has therefore to be approached through the fragments of the revised code; and a slightly pernickety discussion unfortunately cannot be avoided.

One of the revisers, Nicomachus, was prosecuted for abuse of his office; according to the prosecutor, the task of the revisers was to ensure that the city performed 'the sacrifices from the *kurbeis*' (a distinctive archaic form of inscription) and 'from the *stelai*, in accord

Studies Presented to Edward Capps, Princeton 1936, 144–51). About the earlier revision (cf. N. Robertson, *JHS* 110, 1990, 57) we know that it listed sacrifices, almost certainly in calendar order (L. H. Jeffery, *Hesperia* 17, 1948, 108), with prices, some information about the responsible priests or magistrates, and perquisites. It sometimes appealed to the authority of συγγραφαί (*IG* I³.238.4) and so can scarcely have been a mere republication of Solon's laws; there is no evidence whether it anticipated such divisions as that into annual and trieteric sacrifices. Unlike the later revision, it shows no sign of citing its sources for each sacrifice (the reference to συγγραφαί aside): this may in part be why, though politically less sensitive than the secular law-code, it none the less received a second revision (itself, according to Lys. 30, deeply flawed). On the history of the calendars see esp. Jeffery, *Hesperia* 17 (1948), 106–11; Dow, 'Law Codes'; and Robertson, *JHS* 110 (1990), 67–68.

[4] So K. J. Hölkeskamp, *PCPS* 38 (1992), 87–117 (who, however, takes no specific position on Solon). Tempered faith in the authenticity of many Solonian laws is expressed by e.g. A. Andrewes, *CAH*² III.3 (1982), 376; Rhodes, *Commentary Ath. Pol.*, 133. Debate about the physical form of Solon's laws continues: see R. Stroud, *The Axones and Kyrbeis of Drakon and Solon* (Berkeley 1979); H. R. Immerwahr, *Bull. Am. Soc. Papyrologists* 22 (1985), 123–35. For our purpose, the critical issue is whether a new religious regulation (or a revision of an older regulation) of say 525 would have been in some sense added to the *kurbeis*, or would have been clearly distinguished from them as a separate *stele*. The revisers would not necessarily have been misled by the fact that a sacred law of *c*.500 might still, being inscribed *boustrophedon* through religious conservatism, have looked like the *kurbeis* (Jeffery, *Hesperia* 17, 1948, 110); they presumably considered also such factors as place of display.

[5] See *IG* I³.230–35. Inscrs. 231–32 (of *c*.510–480), found in the city Eleusinion, contain regulations, not in standard calendar-form, relating broadly to cults associated with Eleusis; 232 A 43 probably mentions the tribe-kings. Jeffery argued, *Hesperia* 17 (1948), 110, that they were too discursive to be actual extracts from Solon's *axones*, but, being inscribed *boustrophedon*, would doubtless have been mistaken for such by the revisers of 410–399. But cf. n. 4. Inscr. 234 (*LSCG* 1) is a fragment of a calendar, but not necessarily of one issued by the city rather than a subgroup. The other texts are too tiny to discuss.

with the draft proposals'.[6] This probably means that they were required to integrate the code of 'ancestral sacrifices' on *kurbeis*, which will have been ascribed to Solon, with other rites established more recently by popular decree and recorded on marble *stelai*. Such decrees of the assembly creating new sacrifices are familiar: a surviving instance from about 500, for instance, establishes or modifies the ritual programme to be followed at one of the Eleusinian festivals.[7]

Fortunately, each entry or group of entries in the surviving calendar is accompanied by a rubric; and these rubrics must be fundamental in any reconstruction. Those that appear in the surviving portions (of course only a fragment) of the revised code are:[8]

'From the Tribe-Kings' ⟨sacrifices⟩'
(ἐκ τῶν φυλοβασιλικῶν)   (attested 4 times)

'From those ⟨arranged⟩ month by month'
(ἐκ τῶν κατὰ μῆνα)   (attested 3 times)

'From those on no fixed day'
(ἐκ τῶν μὴ ῥητῇ)   (attested once)

'From the *stelai*' or 'From the draft proposals'
(ἐκ τῶν σ[τηλῶν] or ἐκ τῶν σ[υγγραφῶν])   (attested once)

These rubrics are, in all seeming, citations of authority, explanations of the title by which a given sacrifice earns its place in the revised code.[9] As we noted, the new code was seen by contemporaries as a collection of sacrifices ancient and modern, an amalgam of rites from Solon's *kurbeis* and the more recent *stelai*. 'From the *stelai*' (or an equivalent that means much the same) duly appears as one of the rubrics. On an optimistic view, it will follow that the remaining rubrics represent the subdivisions, or some of them, of the

---

[6] τὰς θυσίας ἐκ τῶν κύρβεων καὶ τῶν στηλῶν [so eds: εὔπλων or ὅπλων MSS] κατὰ τὰς συγγραφάς, Lys. 30.17; cf. 18 and 20 for *kurbeis* (these sacrifices are treated in 19 and 20 as 'ancestral'), 21 for *stelai*. (The suggestion of Rosivach, *Public Sacrifice*, 46–48, 54–57, 160–61, that Nicomachus was invited to codify only the 'ancestral' sacrifices appears irreconcilable with these texts.) The συγγραφαί (also mentioned in 21) have been taken in three ways: (1) as a 'compilation from earlier sacrifice lists', perhaps that which underlay the revision of 410–404 (so Jeffery, *Hesperia* 17, 1948, 108: cf. Ostwald, *Popular Sovereignty*, 407, n. 249; 416); (2) the draft regulations according to which new sacrifices (subsequently recorded on *stelai*) were first established (so Robertson, *JHS* 110, 1990, 73–74, with parallels); (3) the 'draft of the decree which specified the sources' that the revisers were to use (Rhodes, *JHS* 111, 1991, 95) . (3) best suits Lys. 30.21, where the συγγραφαί are contrasted with Nicomachus' actual practice.
[7] *IG* I³.5 (*LSCG* 4).
[8] Cf. Robertson, *JHS* 110 (1990), 67–68.
[9] As Dow, 'Law Codes', first demonstrated. Previously the ἐκ rubrics had been interpreted as identifying the funds from which the sacrifices were paid for.

Solonian code inscribed on the *kurbeis*.[10] A plausible further inference might be that the 'month by month' and 'on no fixed day
sacrifices' were subsections of a broader category of 'king's
sacrifices', an equivalent, under the charge of the chief religious
magistrate, of those administered by the much less important tribe-
kings.[11]

On this view, we know not a little of the structure of Solon's code.
But even on a less optimistic assessment the rubrics provide important information. Since they are appeals to authority, it ought to follow that lists of sacrifices under the headings 'month by month', 'on
no fixed day', and (probably) 'of tribe-kings' existed before the revision occurred.[12] We should still therefore reject the extreme view
whereby the revisers were confronted with nothing but a vast array
of particular rules, into which they introduced system for the first
time. The 'month by month' and other lists must have been the
product of an earlier codification or codifications. And it will remain
likely that this codification, which, late in the fifth century, was
understood as Solon's, was of some antiquity.[13]

Very probably then, we can speak of the 'sixth-century code' even
if we hesitate—in a spirit of caution, rather than because any specific
evidence outlaws the traditional attribution—to call it Solon's. And
the rubrics illuminate the organization of the sixth-century code, or
at least the divisions into which sacred law at that period fell. There
was a list of sacrifices associated with the tribe-kings, and two of
public sacrifices that were perhaps the responsibility of the *basileus*.
Of these two, the 'month by month' calendar was surely of central
importance: it defined the public ritual year. It must have inspired
the similar 'month by month' calendars of the demes, the oldest of
which dates apparently from around 430, before the revised code
was available as a model.[14] 'In [the month] Hekatombaion. On the
tenth. For Athena, a sheep' was probably the minimum form of a
typical entry, to which a variety of further items might be added:
rules for age or colour or sex of the victim; its price; secondary offerings such as cakes; the officiant(s); perquisites for the officiants; brief
ritual details; rules for the distribution of meat. How systematic the

---

[10] So Dow, 'Law Codes', 30.

[11] But the βασιλέως νόμος concerning cult at Acharnae cited in Ath. 235b–d from Crates
is irrelevant, being, in its existing form at least, post-Solonian (R. Schlaifer, *HSCP* 54, 1943,
43).

[12] The rubric 'from the *stelai*' of course does not imply a prior codification of material from
the *stelai*. But *stelai*, however uncodified, are an authority to which appeal can be made in a
way that uncodified 'sacrifices arranged month by month' are not.

[13] For 'month by month' lists found in other states *c*.500 see n. 1 above.

[14] That from Thorikos, *SEG* XXXIII 147 (*IG* I³.256 bis, p. 958).

old list was in providing such rules is uncertain[15] (the earliest deme-calendar is haphazard, the city's revised code of 401 much more thorough); and we can only guess how non-annual sacrifices were dealt with.[16]

The second list is known only from a single entry under an unidentifiable month in the revised calendar: 'On the sixth. From the ⟨sacrifices⟩ on no fixed day. To Athena.' But even this curt notice seems sufficient to prove that Solon recognized movable feasts. There are no obvious Greek parallels, but at Rome the main mass of fixed festivals, *feriae statae*, were accompanied by a smaller group of *feriae conceptivae*, of varying date.[17] These were in the main agricultural festivals, and their date was announced annually by the pontiffs or magistrates according (in theory) to the progress of the particular agricultural year. (If the Greek institution worked similarly, did the right of fixing the dates lie with the *basileus*?) It is plausible in itself that the movable festivals of Attica were also mostly agricultural (though the hypothesis finds no support in the one attested case, where the deity honoured is Athena). The celebration of the 'pre-ploughing festival' (*Proerosia*) was 'proclaimed' in the fourth century, even though it in fact took place on a fixed day.[18] This flexibility is obviously appropriate, both practically and symbolically, when working farmers perform the rites. But when such festivals are taken up by the city, the association with immediate agricultural realities is liable to be loosened; and it looks as if in the revised code of 401, in ratification perhaps of what was already conventional, the floating sacrifices of Solon were fixed to particular days.[19]

A complication should now be noted. In certain 'month by month' calendars of demes and other subgroups, including the earliest document of this type, it is the exception rather than the rule for

---

[15] Some prices were mentioned: Plut. *Sol.* 23.3 (Solon fr. 81 Ruschenbusch). One substantial section of the revised code (*LSS* 10 A 31–58, from the tribe-kings' list) comes from a 'Solonian' source; but it must have been retouched in detail (to revise prices, for instance) and so is not a sure guide.

[16] In 401 they were listed separately: *LSS* 10 A 30.

[17] The parallel is drawn by J. Triantaphyllopoulos, *REG* 95 (1982), 291–96; on the *conceptivae* cf. e.g. J. Scheid, *Romulus et ses frères* (Rome 1990), 457. The connection between floating festivals and agriculture is stated explicitly by Ovid, *Fasti* 1.657–62; not all the *feriae conceptivae*, however, were agricultural.

[18] *LSCG* 7.6. The fluctuation in the date of *Proerosia* in different demes (*Gifts to the Gods*, 141, n. 39) may be a related phenomenon. For 'proclamation' of festivals see *LSA* 41.12 (an archaic calendar from Miletus), *LSCG* 151 A 35; Eur. *El.* 172; many Roman festivals were still 'announced' even after fixing in the calendar (J. Scheid, *PCPS* 38, 1992, 119 f.).

[19] In the one attested case, this occurred; and if other sacrifices continued to float, it is strange that we do not hear of it. Flexibility: cf. W. Warde Fowler, *The Religious Experience of the Roman People* (London 1911), 102–103.

sacrifices to be pinned to a fixed day within the month.[20] One such calendar specifies that certain sacrifices are to be performed 'before' others, though whether this marks one rite as a preliminary to another or simply indicates their proper sequence is unclear.[21] Have we really to suppose that within these small communities the majority of sacrifices still floated, though within the confines of a single month, and were fixed year by year through proclamation by a relevant magistrate? And would it once have been thus in Athens itself? On this view the role of the published calendars was to establish a sequence for festivals,[22] and not, except within broad limits, an absolute dating; and the 'on no fixed day' sacrifices differed from the others only in not even being tied to a particular month. Or did the draftsmen of these vague calendars simply assume knowledge of the exact traditional date on the part of some members, at least, of the group concerned?

What of the content of the code? To what extent was the codification merely a record of the practice of the day, and to what extent a refashioning of it? Unfortunately we cannot advance beyond posing this question—especially urgent, of course, if the codifier is identified as Solon. From the few fragments, no pattern emerges. It has, indeed, been argued strongly that in religion as in politics Solon sought to limit aristocratic influence, and to establish cults in which the people could participate as of right, not merely through the condescension of well-born proprietors.[23] Thus it is suggested that the *Genesia*, an annual commemoration of dead parents, had always been celebrated privately in aristocratic households: Solon instituted a public *Genesia*, and so opened the traditional ritual of aristocratic family solidarity to Everyman. Or perhaps he established the cult of 'Aphrodite of the Whole People' ('Pandemos'), who declares her constituency in her name. Or again it was Solon who set up the

---

[20] So in *SEG* XXXIII 147 (Thorikos); *LSCG* 20 (Marathonian Tetrapolis); and *LSS* 19 (the *genos* of *Salaminioi*); cf. S. Dow, *BCH* 92 (1968), 170–86.

[21] *LSCG* 20 B 5, 30, 51: cf. 'before the *Kotytia*' in Jameson et al., *Selinous*, A 7 (with comments on pp. 26, 109).

[22] It is not, however, strictly demonstrable that within the month such calendars list festivals in order.

[23] F. Jacoby, '*Γενέσια*: A Forgotten Festival of the Dead', *CQ* 38 (1944), 65–75; id., *Atthis*, 36–41, where (p. 38) it is said that 'the numerous alterations of existing conditions' in Solon's code were 'to a wide extent aimed at weakening the position of the aristocracy in matters of cult'. Cf. *Atthis*, 23: 'The ἄξονες of Solon gave a list of the State festivals with the sacrifices to be performed; i.e. they founded (to put it exactly) a religion of the state'. Contrast Dow, 'Law Codes', 27: 'Solon, reducing to writing for the first time Tribe-Kings' law which already went back over a millennium, could hardly make many radical changes.' The most recent discussions of Solon seem not to raise the subject.

board of 'exegetes appointed by Apollo' (*pythochrestoi*) in rivalry to the traditional body of Eupatrid exegetes.

Though it underestimates the scope of public religion before Solon,[24] the argument has a certain plausibility. We may concede, for instance, that Aphrodite Pandemos was probably consecrated in the archaic period, in a spirit that was in a broad sense political;[25] or that the same spirit animated the festival of *Synoikia*. The difficulty is that there is no solid independent ground for associating either Aphrodite Pandemos or any other such cult with Solon himself or with any other specific figure, or century.[26] Even where particular cults unquestionably had a place in the sixth-century code (as did the *Genesia* and the *Synoikia*), it cannot be shown that they were his creation.[27] We know far too little of the political history of the seventh and sixth and indeed eighth centuries to be able to identify Solon as the only possible inventor of unifying festivals. And nothing about the code suggests that it disturbed the vested religious interests of established groups such as the *gene*.[28]

We have by contrast good reason to believe that Solon was the first of a series of Attic (and non-Attic) legislators who sought to restrict the ostentation of private funerals. His motives have been

[24] See Ch. 2 above.

[25] Cf. Apollod. *FGrH* 244 F 113, and, on the goddess, Graf, *Nordionische Kulte*, 260, with the new Erythraean decree, *SEG* XXXVI 1039 (XXXIX 1238). The goddess has been speculatively identified on coins of (?) the Clisthenic period: see E. Simon, *SNR* 49 (1970), 5–19, with the comment of J. H. Kroll, *ANSMN* 26 (1981), 31.

[26] Fortunately a passage of Nicander which ascribes the temple of Aphrodite Pandemos to Solon is quoted by Athenaeus (569d) along with its wholly unreliable source in fourth-cent. comedy; it can therefore be ignored. Jacoby's case for associating the ἐξηγηταὶ πυθόχρηστοι with Solon rested, apart from general probabilities, on the suggestion that Plato's law for the selection of exegetes in *Leg.* 759d reproduced one of Solon's: Plato carelessly repeated Solon's allusion to 'the four tribes' in his own law for his own twelve-tribe state, an error which betrays the borrowing. The passage is puzzling, as the explanations offered (see T. J. Saunders, *Notes on the Laws of Plato*, London 1972, 35–40) scarcely account for Plato's reference to 'the four tribes'; but it is hard to accept that artful Plato worked in the way Jacoby suggests. The supposedly prior Eupatrid exegetes are unattested (Jacoby, *Atthis*, 10, 27–28) before the 'Eupatrid renaissance' of the late second cent. BC (see Ch. 12, n. 45), which must create suspicion. On the other hand, the view that the *exegetai pythochrestoi* can be shown not to have existed before the late fifth cent. (see Ch. 11, n. 10) relies too much on an analogy with the history of the Eumolpid exegetes which proves nothing. Jacoby also, without argument, associates Solon with the cult of Apollo πατρηῷος (which has now been connected, no less speculatively, with Pisistratus by C. J. Hedrick, *AJA* 92, 1988, 206 f.).

[27] *Genesia*: see Solon fr. 84 Ruschenbusch (the word δημοτελής there used of it will not be Solon's: cf. Ch. 1, n. 17), and an unpub. study by S. Dow cited by S. Georgoudi in P. Gignoux ed., *La commémoration* (Louvain 1988), 80, n. 40. *Synoikia*: *LSCG* 10 A 31–58 (cf. Ch. 2, n. 17). Jacoby's polarization of the hypothetical private, aristocratic *Genesia* and the later public, democratic festival is anyway tendentious (at Rome, the public *Parentalia* as it were acknowledged the private rites): see Bourriot, *Génos*, 1126–34 and esp. Georgoudi, in Gignoux ed., *La commémoration*, 73–89.

[28] Cf. *LSS* 10 A 73–74 and 19.86.

much discussed[29]—a wish to curb extravagance; to strike at a symbol of aristocratic power; to remove a source and centre of tension between great houses; a response to broader changes in attitudes to death in the archaic period—and none of these factors, except perhaps the sumptuary, can be eliminated. Plutarch, a main source, rather disconcertingly dockets the relevant measures under a different rubric, this too of real concern to ancient lawgivers: 'control of women'. He also speaks in a related context of 'removing what is harsh and barbarian from mourning practices'; and we might claim Solon's bans on, for instance, self-laceration and prepared laments as instances of such cultural censorship.[30] (One can, of course, argue that control of the funeral necessarily entailed control of women and of ways of expressing grief. But this simplifying stratagem is not necessarily correct.) What is clear is that Solon, or the anonymous archaic legislator, here and elsewhere took for granted his right and duty to regulate the 'private' affairs of the citizenry. The totalitarian side of the classical city and its religion is here for the first time on display.

Let us mention here another 'event' of the 590s, since to pass it by entirely would be all too austere: the coming of Epimenides the Cretan to purify the city by novel sacrificial ritual from the 'Cylonian pollution'.[31] One cannot imagine the Athens of the fifth or fourth century entrusting its problems to a holy man come from abroad; such a one would perhaps scarcely even appear in a fiction that was set in the classical period. But there is no more history than this to be extracted from the doings of a figure whose very nature it is to be wrapped in swathes of the fabulous.

We revert to the code, and a final crucial question. Why record a ritual calendar in writing at all?[32] The problem that the question raises is less that of the relation between writing and religion than that of the relation between writing and law: for the most fundamental fact about 'Solon's calendar' is that it formed, in later Athenian perceptions at least, part of a comprehensive civic code,

---

[29] See the excellent full survey by Seaford, *Reciprocity and Ritual*, 74–92 [+], which encourages me to be brief. The sources are Solon frs. 72 (Plut. *Sol.* 21.5 etc.) and (?) 109 (Dem. 43.62) Ruschenbusch.

[30] *Sol.* 12.8–9 (on Epimenides, who is seen as having prepared the ground for Solon). Control of women: ibid. 21.5, which finds some support in Dem. 43.62 and a striking parallel in *LSA* 16.*

[31] Cf. Parker, *Miasma*, 211, n. 23; West, *Orphic Poems*, 45, 51; Hornblower, *Commentary*, 518.

[32] On the 'social history of writing' in Greece see esp. M. Detienne ed., *Les savoirs de l'écriture en Grèce ancienne* (Lille n.d.), and R. Thomas, *Literacy and Orality in Ancient Greece* (Cambridge 1992). Our particular topic has been somewhat neglected, but Detienne (70, n. 151) promises a study.

drafted by a lay politician. The ritual practices of a community were part of its customs/laws (νόμιμα), and whatever pressures led to the codification and publication of 'secular' law inevitably led to the publication of religious rules too.[33] The state festival-programme was part of the publicly defined conditions of life for an Athenian no less than were the laws on inheritance and adultery.

The issue becomes more complicated if we accept the argument that the early Greek law-codes existed as such only in later perception, being in fact no more than accumulations of specific enactments passed in response to particular crises.[34] We would then need to find a more specific motivation for the religious legislation too. That argument, however, is doubtless too extreme: at Athens, for instance, there was perhaps a development by generalization from Draco's enactment on the single topic of homicide to a fuller Solonian code.[35] But even if we stay with the traditional view that the religious calendar was drafted as part of a general codification, there are still questions to be asked about the specific form that it assumed. Ritual laws were recorded, we may allow, because all public laws were: but how exactly was a religious law in this sense defined?

There is a striking contrast between the first Greek texts, calendars such as Solon's, and the elaborate prescriptions found among ancient near-eastern texts. Calendars of Solonian type fix dates and costs, identify the individual recipients of sacrifice with care, and sometimes handle questions of sacral responsibility and privilege; but on the conduct and content of the ceremony they spend few words. The furthest they normally venture into the sphere of ritual symbolism is a requirement that a victim should be of a particular age or colour, or should be 'burnt whole' or 'without wine-offerings'. By contrast, the 'Temple Program for the New Year's Festival at Babylon' covers over 460 lines and is still incomplete.[36]

Clearly the calendars were not designed as 'do it yourself' guides to conducting the rites concerned. One may allow that Greek ritual was often in fact rather simple. There were no long sequences of libations to perform, no elaborate formularies to recite with verbatim precision: in many instances an instruction such as 'For Athena a full-grown victim' did indeed get to the heart of the matter. And

---

[33] So Detienne, *Les savoirs*, 70.   [34] Cf. n. 4 above.

[35] On the restricted scope of Draco's legislation see S. C. Humphreys in M. Gagarin ed., *Symposion 1990: Papers on Greek and Hellenistic Legal History* (Cologne 1991), 18–20.

[36] J. B. Pritchard, *Ancient Near Eastern Texts*[3] (Princeton 1969), 331–34. Cf. e.g. O. R. Gurney, *Some Aspects of Hittite Religion* (Oxford 1977), 31: 'in the festival texts the performance of the ceremonies is described in great detail so that a whole tablet is usually assigned to the rites of a single day'.

fundamental distinctions, such as that between sacrifices burnt whole and those eaten by the participants, are in fact indicated. But it is clear that much traditional usage remains unexpressed in the early calendars, and must have been left to collective memory or the memory of priests. (It may be relevant that the commonest title for religious administrators in the classical period was 'sacred remembrancers', ἱερομνήμονες, though their functions had ceased by then to bear much relation to their name.[37]) One has only to translate mentally what we know of any Attic festival into the form in which it would appear in a calendar of Solonian type to appreciate how much is left out. Hellenistic sacred laws are often notably more discursive than their predecessors, because they no longer rely on oral memory to fill in the details of the ceremonies. And where innovation occurred, as in the sacrificial programme of the *Lesser Panathenaea* in the 330s, a decree of some length and detail was required to regulate the new procedure.[38]

It is somewhat more plausible to argue that a main function of the calendar was to define the division of ritual privileges and responsibilities. Such matters could certainly be controversial,[39] and the surviving portions of the revised code treat them quite extensively: the long extract from the tribe-kings' list, for instance, has much to say of their perquisites at the festival of *Synoikia*, while a set of offerings to Eleusinian gods and heroes is to be 'sacrificed by the Eumolpids'.[40] But the deme calendars are extremely irregular in providing information of this kind, that from Thorikos, the earliest, being entirely silent on the subject. This function should doubtless be seen as ancillary, not fundamental.

The irreducible minimum of a calendar entry, as we have seen, is the name of a deity and the specification of a victim: a specification that implies a cost, even where this is not explicitly stated. When the old code was revised, the controversy that led to the prosecution of Nicomachus in 399 had much to do with questions of finance; and in

[37] See *RE* s.v. *Hieromnemones* (Hepding): the most important new texts are *SEG* XXX 380, Tiryns, (?) late seventh cent. (the earliest instance), and the actual archive of the *hieromnemones* from the temple of Zeus Olympios at Locri, which shows them busy with financial administration—A. de Franciscis, *Stato e società in Locri Epizefiri* (Naples 1972), *passim*. Attic *hieromnemones*: Ar. *Nub.* 624, *Dem.* 18.148 (dispatched to the Delphic Amphictyony) and (belonging in each case to subgroups such as demes or *gene*) *IG* II².1232.18, 1247–48, 1299.80, 1596; and Whitehead, *Demes*, 183–84. It is not certain that the memory of the *hieromnemones* had originally been applied, as the ancient lexica explained, to 'the rites' (Hepding, col. 1495) rather than e.g. to questions of ownership and contract (cf. with Hepding the parallel secular office of μνήμονες) relating to the shrine.

[38] Hellenistic sacred laws: see *LSCG* 96 (Mykonos) and particularly the Coan calendar *LSCG* 151 (where A 1–46 treat a single sacrifice). Panathenaic law: *LSCG* 33 (= Schwenk 17; but the extent of novelty here is controversial: Ch. 11, n. 98).

[39] See e.g. [Dem.] 59.116.   [40] *LSS* 10 A 33 ff., 60 ff.

the fourth century the deme calendar of Erchia was divided into five mini-calendars carefully balanced to be all but equal in cost. (As a result, to understand the text as a religious rather than a financial document one has to reassemble the five sections into one.) In 363/2, the two branches of the *genos* of the *Salaminioi* resolved to inscribe their sacrificial calendar on stone 'so that the *archontes* on both sides may know what money is to be contributed by each party for all the sacrifices'.[41] A prime function of the sixth-century code was surely to define what monies of the Athenian people were to be expended on what gods. To say this is not to deny the religious importance of the code, as if it were an administrative document the interest of which for the religious historian is incidental to its main purpose. On the contrary, we saw in the introduction that the most important Greek equivalent to the concept of 'public' religion lay in the adjective δημοτελής, 'paid for by the people', applicable to rites, shrines, and even gods. The modalities of such public funding escape us at this date (and complicating cases must be recognized of popular festivals, such as the *Anthesteria* or *Diasia*, to which the contribution of the *demos* was in fact small); but to define the festivals that were δημοτελεῖς was in a sense to define the pantheon of the city.

Two negative observations follow. On the one hand, the sixth-century codification was far from containing the whole corpus of tradition concerning ritual that existed at that date. As we have already noted, detailed prescriptions for the conduct of rites were not written out; nor is it clear that, for instance, rules of purity for priests and worshippers were ever encoded.[42] We hear of 'the unwritten laws, according to which the Eumolpids expound [ἐξηγοῦνται]'; during the fourth century, such traditional knowledge began to become public, with the composition of *Exegetika*, do-it-yourself guides to various forms of ritual.[43] The legal status of these unwritten *nomima* is very uncertain. It is conceivable that, before 403, an offence

[41] Erchia: see S. Dow, *BCH* 89 (1965), 180–213; id. *BCH* 92 (1968), 170–86. *Salaminioi*: *LSS* 19.82–83. Nicomachus: see Ch. 11, n. 2.

[42] Elsewhere, rules of purity seem often to have been first published in the fourth cent. or later: see e.g. *LSS* 115 (ancient material, but an inscription of the fourth cent.); *LSCG* 154, 156. But there are some earlier instances, associated particularly with murder pollution and funerals: *LSCG* 56, 97, and now Jameson et al., *Selinous*, A and B, *passim*. No such text survives from Athens (Parker, *Miasma*, 37, n. 17). Proclamations on such topics were perhaps not rare (for the Eleusinian proclamation see Foucart, *Mystères d'Éleusis*, 311; and cf. very generally Eur. *IT* 1226–30 [with *LSS* 115 B 55], *Med.* 1053–55; Callim. *Dem.* 128–32) and oaths could be administered ([Dem.] 59.78).

[43] Eumolpids: [Lys.] 6.10, on which see M. Ostwald in E. N. Lee, A. P. D. Mourelatos, and R. M. Rorty eds., *Exegesis and Argument. Studies in Greek Philosophy Presented to Gregory Vlastos* (*Phronesis* Suppl. 1, 1973), 89–91; cf. App. 2A s.v. *Eumolpidai*. *Exegetika*: Jacoby, *Atthis*, 16; Tresp, *Kultschriftsteller*, 40–53. Jacoby, *Atthis*, 19, stresses that such material may earlier have existed in written but not published form.

against the laws of the Eumolpids concerning the Eleusinian shrine could be very severely punished. But violations of unwritten laws of purity were presumably left to the gods to deal with.[44]

The second negative observation concerns the relation between writing and religion in Greece. What is striking is surely the circumscribed area within which contact between the two was confined.[45] As everyone knows, Greek religion was not a 'religion of the book'. No doubt it acquired its distinctive stamp before writing was thought of. But it persisted as a religion 'not of the book' through something like a millennium of literacy. (And it had passed through an earlier literate phase in the Mycenaean period.) In this area, it seems, social factors prevented the 'technology of communication' from exercising a really decisive influence.[46]

The city used writing to record publicly its commitment, financial and so moral, to the cult of particular gods. What mattered about this declaration was that it could be seen to have been made, even if not all Athenians had the skill, and fewer still the interest, to read the dry and difficult inscriptions. Writing was not, by contrast, used to build up a complicated specialized corpus of ritual knowledge. We stressed earlier the crucial importance of the fact that 'sacred laws' (not a Greek term) are a subsection of the whole law-code of a community, not an independent category resting on a different authority. They are so, of course, because of the indissoluble unity of 'church and state' in Greece, powers that could never be at odds because they could never be clearly distinguished. A crucial aspect of this integration of religion in Greece is the ordinariness of the priests; they were ordinary in many ways, but above all in lacking all pretension to distinctive learning. Elaborate ritual texts are the hallmark of a more specialized priesthood and a more autonomous religious order than those of Greece.[47]

The amateur status of the Greek priesthood was not affected in any way by the advent of the art of writing. One does not picture the priestess of an Athenian public cult with a book in her hand. The famous sixth-century marble sculptures of 'seated scribes' from the acropolis are generally held to represent not priests but,

[44] This was often the case even when such rules were in fact inscribed (Parker, *Miasma*, 253 n. 105). 'Before 403': see App. 2A s.v. *Eumolpidai*.

[45] A fuller discussion would of course have to consider the extent to which writing restrained the traditional fluidity of myth: see e.g. F. Graf, *Griechische Mythologie* (Munich 1987), 147–48; and on the slowness of such change as occurred M. Detienne, *L'invention de la mythologie* (Paris 1981), ch. 2 (who follows works of E. A. Havelock).

[46] On this issue contrast J. Goody, *The Interface between the Written and the Oral* (Cambridge 1987), 59–77, and G. E. R. Lloyd, *The Revolutions of Wisdom* (Berkeley 1987), 70–78.

[47] Cf. Goody, *Logic of Writing*, 16–22.

significantly, 'treasurers' or similar officials, bound to give account of the sacred monies in their care. When the religious book begins to appear, it is rather the mark of marginal figures, the wandering initiators and purifiers and prophets, who in the phrase of the Derveni papyrus 'make a craft out of rites'.[48] Lacking a position in the civic religious structure, they naturally need to display credentials of other kinds. The association between bookishness and irregularity is at its clearest in Orphism.[49] Both in social and religious terms Orphism is profoundly unorthodox; and it displays several characteristics of a 'religion of the book', being indeed transmitted through a 'hubbub of books'.[50] The only books of public cult, by contrast, are the calendars inscribed for all to view (though few to read) on wood or stone.[51]

[48] Col. xvi 3–4 (*ZPE* 47, 1982, after p. 300). On such books see Burkert, *Mystery Cults*, 70–72, who cites *inter alia* Dem. 18.259 (street mysteries) and Ar. *Av.* 974–89 (an oracle-monger); add Isoc. 19.5–6, books on prophecy used by wandering seers (cf. e.g. the pseudo-Hesiodic prophetic works, R. Merkelbach and M. L. West, *Fragmenta Hesiodea*, Oxford 1967, p. 157); note too Plut. *Arist.* 27.4 on a πινάκιον ὀνειροκριτικόν .

[49] Cf. M. Detienne, *L' écriture d'Orphée* (Paris 1989), 101–15.

[50] Characteristics: e.g. a universal, non-local perspective; asceticism; ritual formulas that aspired to be standard throughout the Greek world (cf. R. Janko, *CQ* NS 34, 1984, 89–100). Cf. Goody, *Logic of Writing*, 1–44, esp. 10–16. 'Hubbub of books': Pl. *Resp.* 364e; cf. West, *Orphic Poems*, ch. 1.

[51] On the sense in which books are alien to the ethos of the democracy see Loraux in Detienne ed., *Les savoirs de l'écriture*, 126–29.

5

Archaic Priesthood: The Problem of the Gene

In the last chapter, we looked at the religious content of Solon's code. It may be, however, that his political reforms more profoundly affected the structure of traditional religious life. We must consider more closely the nature of the archaic Attic *genos*, and with it the relation between priesthood and political power. On one interpretation of this mysterious institution, Solon's political reforms wrought here a decisive change. And on any view, the *gene* are a fundamental part of the religious order of archaic Attica.

Since there is almost no evidence for the archaic period, it is best to start with the *gene* as they are known later and to work back.[1] In the fourth century, a *genos* was a recognizable legal entity. The *archon basileus* probably knew how many of them there were in all, and the membership of each was recorded; in the Hellenistic period, antiquarian monographs were written about 'the *gene* at Athens'. If there were 60 *gene* with an average roll of 100 (both figures are mere guesses), perhaps about one Athenian in five will have been a *gennetes*. In structure, they were hereditary groups based on descent in the male line, all legitimate children (or perhaps all sons) of a father who belonged to a *genos* being in principle admitted shortly after birth. An individual was enrolled, therefore, in one *genos* at most.[2] In this respect the *gene* were exactly analogous to the patrilinear descent groups to which all Athenians belonged, the phratries. A certain social cachet attached to membership, particularly in some

[1] For a much more detailed history of the institution, which makes much finer chronological distinctions, see Humphreys' important 'Genos' (for access to which in advance of publication I am most grateful).

[2] But the patrilineal principle was blurred in the Hellenistic period: see App. 2, n. 7. *Archon basileus*: cf. Arist. *Ath. Pol.* 57.2. Enrolment: Andoc. 1.127; Isae. 7.15–16; [Dem.] 59.59–61. Records: *LSS* 19.57–58. Monographs: *FGrH* 344–45. For further organizational details (*archontes, tamiai, hieromnemones*, etc.) see e.g. U. Kahrstedt, *Staatsgebiet und Staatsangehörige in Athen* (Stuttgart 1934), 264–68; Bourriot, *Génos*, 544–47. App. 2 below lists the attested *gene* and discusses the evidence for the activities of each.

prestigious *gene* such as the *Eteoboutadai*, and doubtless *gennetai* were on average more prosperous than the rest of the population; but one can easily find individual *gennetai*, and perhaps whole *gene*, of rather shabby aspect. Though a substantial number of prominent figures were *gennetai*, there is no sign (the doubtful case of the Alcmaeonids aside) that these organizations had any political importance.[3]

The names of *gene*, it is usual to claim, typically have the form of a 'heroic' personal name combined with the suffix -*idai*—producing, for instance, *Eumolpidai*, 'persons associated with Eumolpus', 'descendants of Eumolpus'. But -*idai* also appears added to names that are not, so far as we know, borne by heroes (as in *Amynandridai*), and even to words that primarily evoke rites (*Theoinidai*) or gods (*Kynnidai*, from Apollo Kynneios) rather than people; several formations (*Brytidai*, *Kollidai*, *Selladai*) defy interpretation in any of these ways.[4] There are also functional names such as Heralds, Wind-Calmers (?), Ox-Yokers (*Kerykes*, *Heudanemoi*, *Bouzygai*), and ones taken from places, such as *Salaminioi* and perhaps *Kolieis* (of cape Kolias) and 'Inlanders' (*Mesogeioi*).[5] Exceptions are in fact so numerous that it is better to abandon the notion of a typical *genos*-name.

Much the fullest picture of the activities of a *genos* comes from a long fourth-century inscription concerning 'the Salaminians'. We learn that they appointed officials, kept records, and owned property. Most of their revenue, however, was spent on sacrificial victims; and it is as a body concerned above all with cult that the inscription reveals them. These religious activities are of two kinds. On the one hand, they appointed from their number no less than four priests or priestesses to serve (as it seems) public cults; and they were closely associated with a state festival, the *Oschophoria* (or, as

---

[3] For prestigious *gene* see App. 2 A s.v. *Bouzygai*, *Eteoboutadai*; also [Dem.] 59.116 (*Eumolpidai*). For prosperous *gennetai* see s.v. *Brytidai*, *Kerykes*, *Lykomidai* (Lycomedes son of Aischraios), *Salaminioi* (p. 311), and Isae. 7, esp. 15–16 (cf. Davies, *Propertied Families*, 43–47: *genos* unknown); for obscure or impoverished *gennetai* the speaker of Dem. 57 (his membership of an unknown *genos* is mentioned in Dem. 57.22–24 and 67); six of the seven *Brytidai* mentioned in [Dem.] 59.59–61; Dem. 21.182 (a failed Eteoboutad). Known *gennetai* of political prominence were: Demostratos and Demainetos (*Bouzygai*); Harmodius and Aristogeiton (*Gephyraioi*, if these were a *genos*); Lycurgus the orator and forebears perhaps stretching back to the sixth cent. (*Eteoboutadai*); Kallias Lakkoploutos and his grandson (*Kerykes*); supposedly Themistocles (*Lykomidai*); probably Alcibiades (*genos* uncertain, perhaps *Salaminioi*: see App. 2, n. 94); probably the family of Miltiades (*Philaidai*). J. K. Davies, *Gnomon* 47 (1975), 376, remarks that the archon-list of the 470s and 460s is still 'dotted with recognisably gennete names (Akestorides, Praxiergos, Demotion)'.

[4] Cf. Kearns, *Heroes of Attica*, 65–72, and App. 2 below.

[5] Note too *Gephyraioi*, and the toponymic form of *Kephisieis*.

they called it, *Oskophoria*). Animals 'provided by the city' for such
rites are duly listed in their calendar.[6] On the other, they had a fairly
extensive programme of sacrifices, conducted at not less than three
different sites in Attica, which were financed by the *genos* from its
own revenue. Some of these apparently coincided with public festivals, but even here the *Salaminioi* presumably consumed their own
victims together as a group. Thus the *Salaminioi* served public cults,
but also had an independent corporate existence.

No *genos*, it seems safe to say, existed that did not engage in ritual
activity of one of these two kinds. Many associations between *gene*
and public priesthoods are recorded: famous instances include those
of the hierophant of the Eleusinian Mysteries, recruited from the
Eumolpidai, or the priestess of Athena Polias, always an Eteoboutad,
but other, much more obscure priesthoods such as that of Kranaos
(filled from the *Charidai*) were transmitted in the same way. Indeed,
disputes between *gene* over entitlement to particular priesthoods
sometimes ended in the courts.[7] Public priesthoods vested in the
gene were held for life and in principle, it seems, were filled by lot; in
practice, particular families within a *genos* often succeeded in reserving particular priesthoods to their members.[8] The link between
genos and public cult was not always restricted, and perhaps not
ever, to providing the priest: at one of Athena's festivals, for
instance, 'Pallas' was escorted to the sea 'by the *gennetai*' (probably
Praxiergidai), and certain sacrifices in the revised Solonian calendar
are said to be performed 'by the *Eumolpidai*', not just the officials
drawn from them.[9]

For cults confined to the *gennetai* there is (not surprisingly) much
less evidence; but Herodotus speaks of the private rites of two
groups that sound very much like *gene* (the Gephyraeans and the
'kinsmen of Isagoras'), and it may be that a full calendar such as that
of the Salaminians was the norm.[10] Whether we can go on to say that
every *genos* was involved (as were the Salaminians) with both public

---

[6] *LSS* 19.86, cf. 20. For a full discussion see App. 2 A s.v. *Salaminioi*. Of the four 'public'
cults, one was perhaps of a deme rather than of the city.

[7] See Arist. *Ath. Pol.* 57.2, and App. 2 A s.v. *Krokonidai, Phoinikes*. In general, on the tendency to associate *gene* with religion in the fourth cent., see Arist. *Ath. Pol.* 42.5; Aeschin.
3.18. For details of their priesthoods see App. 2 or, in brief, Kearns, *Heroes of Attica*, 78–79.

[8] See App. 2, n. 21.

[9] See App. 2 A s.v. *Praxiergidai*, and *LSS* 10 A 73–74.

[10] See App. 2 A s.v. *Gephyraioi* (where the question whether the *Gephyraioi* were in fact a
genos is discussed). Isagoras: Hdt. 5.66.1—Ἰσαγόρης Τισάνδρου οἰκίης μὲν ἐὼν δοκίμου,
ἀτὰρ τὰ ἀνέκαθεν οὐκ ἔχω φράσαι· θύουσι δὲ οἱ συγγενέες αὐτοῦ Διὶ Καρίῳ. Isaeus apparently uses συγγενεῖς for γεννῆται in 7.1, 27 (see A. Andrewes, *JHS* 81, 1961, 5, n. 19); this is
not decisive for Herodotus' expression (Isaeus is doubtless distorting normal usage in order to
suggest that his speaker has been accepted by the testator's kin; and cf. Bourriot, *Génos*,
1184–87), but organized rites of γεννῆται are well attested, while those of συγγενεῖς are not.

and private rites is less clear. There is indeed a temptation to take
association with a public priesthood as the defining mark of a *genos*,
given that it is so common;[11] but in the case of the Gephyraeans it is
their private and exclusive rites that Herodotus takes as a key to their
identity and origin. The implication (not, certainly, inescapable) is
that a *genos* could exist turned in upon itself.

As custodians of cult, *gene* could also be custodians of myth. The
attempt to trace details of myth to particular interest-groups has
often been taken to speculative extremes. But Attic tradition offers
instances for which any other explanation is much further-fetched.
Why is Theseus credited by Philochorus with a pilot Nausithoos
and a look-out Phaiax who are said to be from Salamis, even though
their names associate them with that nautical people the Phaeacians?
We know from their calendar that offerings were made to Phaiax and
'Nauseiros' by the *genos* of *Salaminioi*. . . And that is only one of several virtually incontestable examples.[12]

It is sometimes suggested that entities of very different type came
to share the label '*genos*'.[13] The *Eumolpidai*, for instance, whose very
essence seems to lie in association with the famous mystery-cult,
would be fundamentally distinct from 'the Salaminians', a local and
indeed an expatriate association the prime function of which was to
preserve a sense of distinctive Salaminian identity and origin. Most
of the cults with which the Salaminians are involved, both publicly
and privately, are clearly associated with the cults and myths of
Salamis itself. (Herodotus' Gephyraeans too are, in his view, an
immigrant group, though one long settled in Attica.) But precisely
the case of the Salaminians works against this thesis in its strongest
form: far from merely celebrating 'Salaminian' rites among themselves, they have, as we have seen, a place of honour in the public
religion of Athens. The specific evidence which by chance survives
reveals a much more privileged and more integrated group than
could reasonably have been predicted on the basis of the name alone.

What had these *gene* been in the archaic period? The only explicit
statement in an ancient source is of little help. According to a fragment of the *Constitution of the Athenians*, the whole citizen-body had
once (in the distant past, no doubt) been divided into 360 *gene* (of
30 men each), one for every day of the year. Thirty *gene* together
formed a *trittys* or phratry, which thus corresponded to a month.
This calendarian vision of early society is generally dismissed

[11] See App. 2 A *passim*. An *argumentum ex Hesychii silentio* in cases where he names a *genos*
but not a priesthood would be invalid, since *gene* demonstrably possessed priesthoods unmen-
tioned by him (see s.v. *Hesychidai, Phoinikes*).

[12] See p. 315; also App. 2 A s.v. (e.g.) *Krokonidai, Philaidai*.   [13] See n. 18 below.

without more ado. But is there an importantly unorthodox underlying assumption to be saved: that the *gene* were not constituted by an élite alone?[14] On the contrary, the fragment dovetails neatly with orthodoxy: if only 60, say, of the 360 *gene* survived, and the vacancies had been filled from less ancient stock, the survivors would indeed constitute a blue-blooded élite. Seen thus, the fragment merely confirms that there existed in the historic period an unspecified number of *gene* that claimed to be 'of straight descent'.

According to the most widespread modern interpretation, the *gene* were the aristocracy of the archaic state.[15] A *genos* was not indeed itself a true family, since its supposed common ancestor was fictitious;[16] but it was through this broader pseudo-familial association that groups of true families (one perhaps dominant) exercised their power. Such *gene* held property in common and had a common burying-place. The cults controlled by a *genos* were in origin nothing other than the private observances of that aristocratic club; they centred typically on the cult of the group's eponymous ancestor. In its most potent form, the theory identifies the *gennetai* with the *Eupatridai*, that charmed circle of the 'well-born' from whom alone the magistrates were supposedly recruited before Solon. (Some, however, distinguish the *gennetai* as a kind of 'mere gentry' from the true nobility, the Eupatrids.[17])

The crucial transition, on this view, came with Solon. He transformed the qualification for office from one of birth to one of wealth, with the result that a monopoly of political power was no longer vested in the *Eupatridai/gennetai*. Membership of a *genos* accordingly became less important, and the *gene* faded into the primarily cultic organizations which we know from the classical period. The original link between religious authority and political power was broken.

A fierce and effective attack has lately been launched against this

---

[14] So Bourriot, *Génos*, 460–91, 691–92; Roussel, *Tribu et cité* , 79–88, on fr. 3 Kenyon.

[15] For a detailed doxography see Roussel, *Tribu et cité* , 17–25; Bourriot, *Génos*, 52–195; for a broader perspective also S. C. Humphreys, 'Fustel de Coulanges and the Greek *Genos*', *Sociologia del diritto* 8 (1983), 35–44 (issue ed. by R. Treves and entitled *Alle origini della sociologia del diritto*, Milan).

[16] As was already noted in antiquity: lexicographers (Harp., *Etym. Magn.*, Suda, s.v. γεννῆται, etc.) stress that *gennetai* are not true kinsmen, but either (Harp.) descendants of the original *gene* (of Arist. *Ath. Pol.* fr. 3 Kenyon), or participants συγγενικῶν ὀργίων ἢ θεῶν, or a mixture of the two, ἀπ᾽ ἀρχῆς κοινὰ ἱερὰ ἔχοντες (*Etym. Magn.*).

[17] So H. T. Wade-Gery, *CQ* 25 (1931), 4 = id., *Essays in Greek History* (Oxford 1958), 90; cf. Rhodes, *Commentary Ath. Pol.*, 67, 76. Most potent form: so e.g. A. Andrewes , *CAH²* III.3 (1982), 367 f.

traditional conception.[18] The central criticism is that (in effect if not in protestation) two quite different entities have been confounded; and the political power really wielded by a more restricted group, the aristocratic extended family or *oikos* based on real kinship, has been falsely ascribed to the *genos*, which resembles it only in the deceptively similar patronymic form of its name. And yet the two things are quite distinct: a *genos* has rites of admission and a clearly defined membership, an *oikos* lacks both; entry to a *genos* is strictly through the father, association with an *oikos* can occur on both sides; an *oikos* is based on real, a *genos* on fictive kinship; the eponymous hero of a *genos* is normally a mythological, of an *oikos* a historical personage.[19] It is pointed out that no case is known of an acknowledged *genos* such as the Eumolpids taking concerted political action, and even individual members of *gene* who rose to prominence are hard to find; the Alcmaeonids, by contrast, the model of an aristocratic extended family of real power, controlled no priesthoods to our knowledge and are described in sources before the late fourth century not as a *genos* but as an *oikos*. The powerful family of Miltiades too, that '*genos* of the Philaidae' of many modern accounts, is for Herodotus a 'house'.[20]

As for the religious functions of the *gene*, it can, as we have seen, be absurd to derive the priesthoods that they held (such as that of Athena of the City) from the private cult of a restricted group.[21] The very names of certain *gene* evoke sacral functions; what is more important, the *gene* regularly associate themselves in myth with heroes of a specific type, founders of cults and mysteries.[22] They

[18] By Roussel, *Tribu et cité*, pt. 1, esp. 65–78; Bourriot, *Génos, passim*. In their criticisms the works overlap; of their positive interpretations, which differ, it is Roussel's which is discussed here. Bourriot (followed by Lambert, *Phratries*, 59–64) seeks to dissociate the original *genos* from the aristocracy entirely, arguing that to two early types of *genos* (a) religious guilds, made up of humble cult-functionaries, and (b) local associations, like the later demes, there was added, only in the fourth cent. and afterwards, (c) the aristocratic *oikos* such as the Alcmaeonids which became 'gentified' (see e.g. 1347–66). But he is reduced to some special pleading to purge the *gene* of noble and powerful members, and neglects the common association in Greece between priesthood and privilege; and the case for acknowledging distinctive *gene* of type (b) is, as was argued above, very much weakened by the undeniable association of the *Salaminioi*, the paradigm instance, with the cults of the city. It is admittedly surprising to learn that the members of a *genos* were apparently called not γεννῆται but ὁμογάλακτες in the fifth cent. (Philochorus *FGrH* 328 F 35); but the context of the word's only other substantive appearance is ambiguous (Arist. *Pol.* 1252ᵇ17–18), and it is not clear that Aristotle interprets it as a locality group, κώμη, rather than as a blood group, παῖδές τε καὶ παίδων παῖδες. (On other such terms see Jameson et al., *Selinous*, 20.) My debt to this book is none the less very great.

[19] Cf. Wade-Gery, *Essays in Greek History*, 107; Humphreys, 'Fustel de Coulanges', 41. The argument from a supposedly typical *genos*-name, however, is invalid, as we saw above.

[20] See App. 2 B s.v. *Alkmaionidai*, A s.v. *Philaidai*.   [21] See p. 24 above.

[22] See Kearns, *Heroes of Attica*, 68–70, on Boutes, Bouzyges, Lykos, Phytalos, and many others.

present their own relation to religion, therefore, not as contingent but as fundamental. The Eleusinian Mysteries are a particularly intractable case for the old theory, because five distinct *gene* had a role in them.[23] We obviously cannot unravel the complex sacral web to recover the private rites of five separate families. Rather, the *gene* had always been what they still were in the fourth century: colleges entrusted with performing certain rites and filling certain priest-hoods. They doubtless had an aristocratic coloration, because when such a college was formed (in the eighth century, say) an aristocratic family or group of families would naturally have put itself forward for the honorific (and perhaps expensive) duty. But such a *genos* had not existed as a social group before it was assembled to officiate at particular rites.[24] (The *Salaminioi*, and perhaps a few other local groups, are recognized as exceptions.) As artificial, not natural groups, the *gene* did not, in fact, have communal property (except a little which provided revenue for cult) or common tombs, and only occasionally worshipped an eponymous ancestor. The *Eupatridai*, an order of aristocratic *oikoi*, were something quite distinct.

Can any resistance be mounted to this fierce attack? In the matter of tombs, property, and eponymous ancestors, it does not seem so.[25] And perhaps we should not press the point, noted above, that Herodotus does not seem to endorse the view that a *genos* was defined by a relation to public cult; nor yet that the powerful *Philaidai* and *Alkmaionidai* were possibly *gene* after all. But in its central claim about the relation between the *gene* and political power the new theory is exposed to two objections. No amount of evidence that the *gene* were politically impotent in the fourth or fifth or even sixth centuries can refute the view that they had been influential bodies before the reforms of Solon. And even if one allows that *gene* and *oikoi* were distinct, and that direct power had always belonged to the smaller groups, the *oikoi*, the role of the *genos* was none the less structurally crucial if it is true that membership of one was the patent of nobility, the qualification for office. (From Pindar's Aeginetan odes, we see the conjoint importance that the *oikos* and a

---

[23] *Eumolpidai, Kerykes, Philleidai, Krokonidai, Koironidai.*

[24] Similarly already L. Ziehen, *RE* s.v. *Hiereis*, 1413–14, and N. Forsberg, *Une forme élémentaire d'organisation cérémoniale* (Uppsala 1943); the latter's particular concern, in a comparative perspective, was with 'organisations cérémoniales bipartites', of which he saw the partnership of *Eumolpidai* and *Kerykes* as an instance.

[25] On property see Bourriot, *Génos*, 727–828; on tombs ibid. 831–1042 and S. C. Humphreys, *JHS* 100 (1980), 96–126 = ead., *The Family, Women and Death* (London 1983), 79–130 (note esp. the distinction between *gennetai* and sharers of tombs in Dem. 57.67); on the cult of the eponymous ancestor, Kearns, *Heroes of Attica*, 65–72, who modifies the extreme reductive position of Bourriot, *Génos*, 1077–1115, while accepting the main point that the cult of the eponym is not the nub of the *genos*' religious life.

larger group, in this case the '*patra*', could have in an archaic aristocracy.[26]) Indeed it has been suggested that the system of *gene* was
created, in the eighth or early seventh century, precisely as a way of
formalizing (and so restricting) entitlement to office.[27]

Here indeed we reach the heart of the matter, and the crucial
uncertainties. Was political power in pre-Solonian Athens formally
confined to an oligarchy of birth, that of the *Eupatridai*? So says a
tradition which is never contradicted, but which cannot be traced
back beyond the Aristotelian *Constitution of the Athenians* and can
certainly be suspected of translating a much more fluid reality into
unduly fixed and schematic terms. (The claim of an Athenian who
died late in the sixth century to have been 'one of the Eupatrids'
proves that he was proud of his origins, not that he belonged to a
strictly defined order.[28]) But if one believes in a defined Eupatrid
class, there are certainly attractions in supposing that it consisted,
precisely, of the collectivity of the *gene*. (The essential point would
be unaltered if only certain *gene* had Eupatrid status; what matters is
that there should have been no access to the Eupatrid order except
through the *gene*.) Two late sources state explicitly that the
Eupatrids had charge of religion, the area *par excellence* of the *gene*'s
activities. And since priesthood in Greece was a mark of honour, it
would be odd if the system whereby such honours were allocated
were independent of any other formal structure of privilege that may
have existed. It looks as if in the second century BC, when the *gene*
enjoyed a revival, an identification between some or all of them and

[26] Pindar often slips easily from praise of the *oikos*, including maternal kin, to praise of the
πάτρα: so e.g. *Pyth.* 8.35–38, *Isth.* 6.62–63 (cf. Roussel, *Tribu et cité*, 52 f.). For Aeginetan
πάτραι see (?) *Ol.* 8.75 (*Blepsiadai*: possibly an *oikos*); *Pyth.* 8.38 (*Meidylidai*); *Nem.* 4.73–79
(*Theandridai*), 6.31–38 (*Bassidai*—in 35b a *patra*, despite *oikos*, 25), 7.70 (*Euxenidai*), 8.46
(*Chariadai*); *Isth.* 6.63 (*Psalychiadai*). Past victories of members of the *patra* are mentioned in
Ol. 8 and *Nem.* 6; the *patra* will apparently perform the victory ode in *Nem.* 4, and is regularly
assumed to rejoice in the victory. For cultic emplacements of the (?) *patra* of *Prossaridai*, and
of other nameless groups, see G. Welter, *AA* 1932, 162–63; *AA* 1938, 494 (*SEG* XI 5–6). The
exact nature of these *patrai* is unknown: they are indifferently interpreted as phratries (cf. the
mark φρα on a ritual object published by Welter) and *phylai* by the scholia, and are evidently
patrilineal groups; but one wonders whether they are not more exclusive than Attic phratries
or tribes. (See further H. Winterscheidt, *Aigina*, Würzburg 1938, 42–46, whose discussion is
fuller than that in T. J. Figueira, *Aegina*, Salem Mass. 1981, 312–13). Patronymic groups
from other states mentioned by Pindar are normally *oikoi* (*Emmenidai*, *Ol.* 3.38, *Pyth.* 6.5,
where cf. *Σ*; *Timodemidai*, *Nem.* 2.18; *Kleonymidai*, *Isth.* 3/4.22, cf. 15; *Alkmaionidai*, *Pyth.*
7.2); the *Aigeidai* (*Pyth.* 5.75, *Isth.* 7.15) and *Iamidai* (*Ol.* 6.71) are of *genos* type, the case of
the *Eratidai* (*Ol.* 7.93) and *Oligaithidai* (*Ol.* 13.97) is unclear.

[27] By Humphreys, 'Fustel de Coulanges'. She compares other Greek oligarchies where one
or more 'families' restricted office to themselves: those of the Corinthian Bacchiads, and (as
late as the third cent. BC) the Thessalian Basaids (*BCH* 94, 1970, 161–89 = Moretti, II.97: but
on this text contrast now A. Bresson and P. Debord, *REA* 87, 1985, 191–211).

[28] See App. 2 B s.v. *Eupatridai*.

the 'straight-born', the Eupatrids, was accepted.[29] Indeed, if the *gennetai* were not the Eupatrids, one may wonder who were; the identification has the advantage of showing how they could have been, what *ex hypothesi* they were, a clearly defined group.

Again, such an origin would explain, some argue, a special relation that continued to exist between the *gene* and the phratries. A phratry could be closely associated with a *genos*, to the point of sharing its altars; registration in the two bodies was often performed at the same time, and a person accepted in a *genos* was apparently accepted without further scrutiny in a phratry of which it formed part. One can therefore imagine the phratry members as humble clients of the lordly *gennetai*, and see this pair of institutions (through which access to citizenship was controlled) as a principal structure of domination in the archaic state. We see the old relation still effective, it is argued, in the 'Demotionid decrees' of 396/5 BC, on one plausible interpretation of which controversies over the right of membership of a phratry are taken on appeal to a board of higher instance which, it is said, must be an associated *genos*. This single example of significant power exercised by a *genos* would, if allowed, be sufficient to refute all attempts by scholars to depoliticize the institution. A particular application of the general relation here postulated is that concerning 'ancestral Apollo'. Every candidate for a magistracy had to be able to lay claim to 'an Apollo Patroos'. The *gene* certainly sometimes honoured this god. Perhaps originally they alone did so (and so were alone qualified for office); and later allowed phratry members access to him only on a 'grace and favour' basis.[30]

It is, however, far from certain that the appeal-board of the Demotionid decrees is in fact a *genos*. And though *gene* certainly honoured Apollo Patroos, the god who gave access to political office, so certainly did at least one phratry; it is not established that the one did so by ancestral right, the other only by grace and favour or appropriation.[31]

---

[29] Late sources: Plut. *Thes.* 25.2; *Anecd. Bekk.* I.257.7–11. Second cent. BC: on Hesychius' use of the term ἰθαγενεῖς and its origin see p. 284; but what are Εὐπατρίδαι if not ἰθαγενεῖς? And the relation of 'Eupatrids' to named *gene* in the *Pythais* inscriptions of the late second cent. BC is probably best seen as one of whole and parts (see App. 2 B s.v. *Eupatridai*).

[30] See the very important study by Andrewes, *JHS* 81 (1961), 3–9. Shared altars: Aeschin. 2.147, Isae. 7.15–17. Simultaneous registration in *genos* and phratry: Isae. ibid.; probably [Dem.] 59.59–61; Philochorus *FGrH* 328 F 35 as interpreted by Andrewes (Andoc. 1.126–27 is less clear). On the relation of *genos* to phratry see further p. 108. For Lambert's suggestion that a phratry could contain more than one *genos* see App. 2 B s.v. *Glaukidai*; since many more phratry names are known than *genos* names, this is likely in principle (though Andrewes seeks to explain away the discrepancy in numbers of known names).

[31] See App. 2 B s.v. Δημοτιωνίδαι. The theory that each phratry was dominated by a *genos* nesting within it finds only weak support in Dem. 57.24, where the implication that every

Our uncertainties remain. The most that can be said is that we have no absolute reason to deny that a closed Eupatrid order once existed (the counter-argument being largely *ex silentio*[32]); that if such an order existed, it must have been defined; and that no structure of definition can be readily identified (for the *oikos* was not a legal entity[33]) other than that of the system of *gene*. The intermixing of socio-political and religious functions that the *gene* acquire on this account is not an argument against the identification but much in its favour, given the normal relation of religious authority and political power in archaic Greece.[34] The kings of Sparta held priesthoods *ex officio*, and large power in archaic Miletus seems to have fallen to the sacro-political college of Molpoi.[35] If such an intermixing did indeed exist at Athens, it came to an end when Solon opened office to those who lay outside the class of Eupatrids, which was also the priestly class.

A different conclusion can, however, be cast in less hypothetical form; and it is of the greatest importance for our whole study. The cults for which the *gene* provided priests were public, as we have seen; and there is no sign that in the archaic period any public priesthood was filled in any other way than from among the members of a designated *genos*. Whatever else it may have been, the system of *gene* was therefore certainly the structure through which the allocation of priesthoods was organized in archaic Attica—the only such structure, in fact, known from archaic Greece as a whole. And, as we have seen, not just the priesthoods but considerable responsibilities for the organization and conduct of public festivals were entrusted to the *gene*. Much about the system remains, of course, obscure. Are we to suppose that in, say, the eighth century there existed a religious 'enterprise culture', whereby individuals might group together to found and run a new cult? (For a cult could be open to outsiders, as

---

juror has been scrutinized by *gennetai* is rhetorically exaggerated, and *Lex. Patm.* s.v. γεννῆται (*BCH* 1, 1877, 152), perhaps just careless. The role of Kallias the daduch in phratry admissions (Andoc. *Myst.* 126, drawn to my attention by Christiane Sourvinou-Inwood) is interesting but inconclusive; he had perhaps been chosen phratriarch. The main support for a special relation between *gene* and Apollo Patroos (denied by Bourriot, *Génos*, 1046–71 and Roussel, *Tribu et cité*, 72–74) remains Dem. 57.67, Ἀπόλλωνος Πατρῴου καὶ Διὸς Ἑρκείου γεννῆται; for the other evidence on his relation to *gene* and phratries see Andrewes, *JHS* 81 (1961), 7; App. 2 B s.v. *Elasidai*.

[32] See e.g. Welwei, *Athen*, 108 f. For believers in a Eupatrid order see e.g. n. 17 above.

[33] See D. M. MacDowell, *CQ* NS 39 (1989), 10–21.

[34] Does it follow that on this view all *gene* must have been associated with public cults? Not necessarily, given that the system of *gene* now has an independent *raison d'être* (to define the Eupatrid order).

[35] Hdt. 6.56; F. Poland, in *RE* Suppl. vol. VI.512.

we have argued that those of the *gene* were,[36] even if initially private in finance and organization.) Might Attica's other Mysteries, those administered by the *genos* of *Lykomidai* at Phlya, be such a case? Two points about the system are rather less speculative. On the one hand, priesthood and sacral privilege are treated as a natural inheritance, passing down within a 'family' (*genos*) that often claims descent from the founder of the rite. On the other, this principle of transmission within fixed groups ensures a certain crude distribution of privilege within the élite, no individual being associated by birth with more than a fixed number of cults. The system of *gene* brought a large number of citizens (by the standards of Greek oligarchies) into a modest proprietarial relation with the cults of the state.

[36] But one might allow that, in origin, the cults of groups such as the Salaminians may indeed have been confined to the group: a cult of Athena Skiras confined to the Salaminians is intelligible in a way that a cult of Athena Polias confined to the Eteoboutads is not.

6

The Sixth Century: New Splendours

Architecturally, the sixth century was an age of transformation for Athens. Indeed, in a certain sense, it was then that she became a *polis*. 'From Chaeronea it is 20 stades to Panopeus, a *polis* of the Phocians, if one can give the name of *polis* to people who lack magistrates' offices and gymnasia, who have no theatre, no *agora*, no water brought to a fountain,' grumbles Pausanias. In Athens, every one of these amenities (if we neglect the 'old *agora*') is first attested in the sixth century.[1] Fine temples too began to arise, of which we can still see substantial remains. This new architectural magnificence is accompanied by a proliferation of festivals of a new type, urban and spectacular.

It is obviously tempting to associate the transformation with Pisistratus and his sons, who ruled the city on and off from 561 to 510. Programmes of public works were, to later Greek eyes, a typical device by which despots could keep their subjects 'busy' (and so docile) and 'poor'. Though that attribution of motive is unconvincingly cynical, there seems in fact to have been lively building-activity under the tyrannies both at Corinth and Samos, designed no doubt to promote civic pride as well as to display the personal magnificence of the ruler.[2] That Pisistratus and his sons had an ample share in the sixth-century transformation of Athens is beyond doubt. But we should not emphasize their importance too much,

---

[1] Paus. 10.4.1; cf. in general Boersma, *Building Policy*, 11–27 (on which P. H. Young, *Building Projects and Archaic Greek Tyrants*, Diss. Pennsylvania 1980, 106–90, largely depends). Old *agora*: see Ch. 1, n. 30.

[2] See Arist. *Pol.* 1313^{b}21–25 (instancing the Pisistratid Olympieum *inter alia*); Hdt. 2.124–28 (the Pyramids). For a more positive view see *Pol.* 1314^{b}37–38, where the 'good' tyrant is advised to adorn the city. In defence of cynicism, however, see W. L. Newman's striking parallel from Burma in his note on Arist. *Pol.* 1313^{b}18. Cf. R. Martin, *L'urbanisme dans la Grèce antique*^{2} (Paris 1974), 84–89 (who also mentions the fountain-house of Theagenes tyrant of Megara, Paus. 1.40.1); J. Salmon, *Wealthy Corinth* (Oxford 1984), 180 (but Young, *Building Projects*, 18–53, is sceptical); Shipley, *Samos*, 72–73, 76–80.

except as agents of a broader tendency of the age.[3] Large temples and large festivals continued to be founded (with some interruption, of course, through the Persian invasions) in increasing numbers under the subsequent democracy. And, what is perhaps more important, the transformation was probably already under way before Pisistratus first seized the acropolis. It is common to stress the advance that the Pisistratean 'initiation-building' at Eleusis (perhaps of around 540) marked over its 'Solonian' predecessor. But one should equally note the advance that the 'Solonian' building had marked over its own predecessor (if indeed it had one). The colossal unfinished temple of Zeus Olympios was, for later antiquity, a symbol of arrogant Pisistratid display. Beneath it have been found the massive foundations of (very possibly) an earlier temple, which may itself have been unusually grandiose for its time. The *agora* was developed perhaps by the tyrants, but had apparently acquired its present function as a political centre around 600.[4] Uncertainty surrounds two very important innovations, the transformation of the *Panathenaea* into an international festival, and the construction of a first stone temple of Athena on the acropolis. Both demanded ambition, organizational energy, and the ability to supply or levy resources; both fall very close in time to Pisistratus' seizure of power. One might, on independent grounds (source-critical in the one case, archaeological in the other), incline to put the festival before 561 and the temple after it; but either could easily cross that line.

[3] Cf. Boersma, *Building Policy*, 11–27; T. L. Shear Jr., 'Tyrants and Buildings in Archaic Athens', in *Athens Comes of Age* (Princeton 1978), 1–19 (both seek to contrast the more civic policy of Pisistratus with the personal ostentation of his sons); Kolb, 'Baupolitik'. For the qualification cf. Shipley, *Samos*, 89: 'There is no essential link between the tyrannies and the apparent cultural and economic apogee [in Samos] of c. 570–530.' J. Blok has suggested, *Babesch* 65 (1990), 17–28, that the modern habit of crediting the Pisistratids with a broadly conceived cultural policy is a *vitiosa hereditas* from F. Schachermeyer's *RE* article, of 1937, on Pisistratus' *Führertum*. But they had a policy in the sense that as holders of power they inevitably made decisions. I have not seen S. Angiolillo, *Ο ΕΠΙ ΚΡΟΝΟΥ ΒΙΟΣ: Appunti sulla politica culturale nell'Atene di Pisistrato e dei Pisistratidi* (Cagliari 1992).

[4] Eleusis: see J. Boardman, *JHS* 95 (1975), 4–5 [+]; Travlos, *Bildlexikon*, 92–94; the 'Solonian' building was *c.*24 × 14 m., within a finely built *peribolos*. On its (?) predecessor see above, Ch. 2, n. 37. Zeus Olympios: see G. Welter, *AM* 47 (1922), 66–67, and Boersma, *Building Policy*, 199 [+]; Travlos, *Pictorial Dictionary*, 403. On this building Dr J. J. Coulton kindly advises me that: 'There is no doubt that an M-shaped foundation 2.5 m. thick runs beneath the Olympieion with distance of 30.5 m. from corner to corner. The size in the other direction must be over 15 m. or so, but the c. 60 m. [of several reconstructions] is a (not impossible) guess. It is not unreasonable to suppose that a foundation so thick, lying under a temple, in a sanctuary with an extensive history, does itself belong to a temple—at least in some fairly loose sense. It *could* be the foundation for the colonnade of a peripteral temple, as suggested, but one really needs more of the plan to be sure of that . . . Such a large, and thick-walled, building would be surprising before 600 B.C., very surprising before 700. But surprises do happen...' *Agora*: see esp. Shear, 'Tyrants and Buildings', 4–7.

At the bottom end of the period, it is uncertain whether the Pisistratids were in their last years, or had already been expelled, when a great temple of Athena was either built or elaborately redecorated, and a cycle of deeds of Theseus was created; a similar doubt attaches to the foundation or refoundation of the *City Dionysia*. The religious chronology of the period is thus a concertina, which if squeezed brings all the relevant events within the Pisistratid period, if stretched puts almost all outside. In the name of caution—and perhaps even of truth—one should speak more generally of 'the sixth century expansion' rather than more specifically of 'Pisistratean religious policy'.[5]

The evidence for architectural history begins to be abundant from about this time. It is not necessary or practicable to trace the history of every shrine down through the classical period.[6] But it seems worth while to give some account of the early stages of this transformation of Athens from a city of brick to one of limestone and marble.

> Our city will never be destroyed by the destiny of Zeus
> or the intent of the blessed immortal gods.
> Such a great-spirited protectress, child of a mighty father,
> Pallas Athena, holds her hands out over it.

So sung Solon at the beginning of the century, expressing for the first time in our records (though scarcely in history) a fundamental tenet of civic piety at Athens.[7] A little later, Athena's presence above the city on the acropolis at last begins to leave monumental traces. In or near the second quarter of the sixth century, a ramp was constructed to allow processions to approach the acropolis with ease.[8] At about the same time, Athena at last received a large limestone[9] temple of (in the main) familiar classical form: decorated with relief sculpture, and (almost certainly) ringed with a colonnade. Probably (but nothing could be more controversial) it stood on the foundations still visible beside the present Erechtheum. One of the surviving monumental reliefs (which show animal-fights, a mysterious three-bodied being, and Heracles struggling with Triton) stands out stylistically from the rest. Some scholars accordingly suppose that an earlier large temple bore this more archaic work, while others

---

[5] So rightly Welwei, *Athen*, 237; *aliter* Stahl, *Aristokraten und Tyrannen*, 234, n. 21, whose 'who but Pisistratus?' approach (to paraphrase crudely) leads to circularity. For details on the disputed datings see below.

[6] For this see Boersma, *Building Policy, passim*.   [7] Fr. 4.1–4 West.

[8] See E. Vanderpool in D. W. Bradeen and M. F. McGregor eds., *ΦΟΡΟΣ: Tribute to B. J. Meritt* (Locust Valley 1974), 156–60.

[9] The material is usually said to be *poros*; but on the imprecision of this term (unknown to geologists) see R. E. Wycherley in *ΦΟΡΟΣ*, 179–87.

recognize the collaboration of craftsmen from different generations on the one building. On the latter view, that building, Athena's first stone temple, can perhaps just be credited to Pisistratus; on the former, the earlier building, at least, will probably antedate him.[10]

In about 550 (perhaps) an inscribed altar was dedicated to Athena Nike, on the site by the entrance to the acropolis where her fifth-century temple still stands.[11] Fragments of limestone reliefs also survive from several smaller constructions, possibly to be associated with the 'buildings' under charge of the Treasurers of Athena known from the archaic Hekatompedon inscription. (But for treasuries of the type known from Delphi and Olympia there was no possible place on the Athenian acropolis.) The reliefs are the first mythological sculptures from Attica; and, parts of public monuments though they are, they show the same indifference as the early vase-paintings to distinctively Athenian subjects. Heracles is the hero of the three certainly identifiable scenes. Only very conjecturally can one, enigmatic, relief be associated with the cults of the acropolis.[12] By the end of the Pisistratid period, however, or a little

[10] For the extensive bibliog. see Boersma, *Building Policy*, 13 (with notes); Floren, *Griechische Plastik I*, 238 f. The main controversies are surveyed by S. Bancroft, *Problems Concerning the Archaic Acropolis at Athens* (Diss. Princeton 1979), chs. 1–3, and, very lucidly, by J. M. Hurwit, *The Art and Culture of Early Greece* (Ithaca, NY 1985), 236–48; that about the temple's site briefly by Wycherley, *Stones of Athens*, 144–45. τὸ ἑκατόμπεδον in *IG* I³. 5 B 10, 18 is a region, not a building (see F. Preisshofen, *AA* 1977, 74–84); there is thus no documentary evidence for a second temple, the Hekatompedon, distinct from the Ancient Temple of Athena. (For an interesting explanation in terms of continuity of function—storage of treasures—of the word's later application to the *cella* of the Parthenon see R. Tölle-Kastenbein, *JdI* 108, 1993, 43–75.) The large reliefs are all assigned to one building by W. B. Dinsmoor, *AJA* 51 (1947), 146, followed e.g. by Harrison, *Agora* XI.32 f.; Ridgway, *Archaic Style*, 199 f.; *contra* still I. Beyer, *AA* 1977, 67; Floren, *Griechische Plastik I*, 239–42; H. Knell, *Mythos und Polis* (Darmstadt 1990), 1–9; Boardman, *Greek Sculpture: Archaic*, 154, with an important low dating for the 'later' pieces (*c*.550, favoured also by D. Williams, *AA* 1982, 62–63; *c*.580–570 is more normal).

[11] *IG* I³.596 ('c. 550?'). See now the full republication by Mark, *Athena Nike*. He boldly proposes (125–28) that a cult statue and perhaps a temple were erected, as well as the altar, in the period 580–560, on a site probably not hitherto used for cult (contrast the lower chronology of Shapiro, *Art and Cult*, 24).

[12] Smaller buildings: see Robertson, *History*, 90–93; Floren, *Griechische Plastik I*, 242–43; Ridgway, *Archaic Style*, 201–205. (Bancroft, *Archaic Acropolis*, 67–69, refutes the theory of Beyer, *AA* 1974, 639–51, favoured by Shapiro, *Art and Cult*, 21–24, that the 'small' pedimental sculptures can be combined with the large rather than assigned to separate buildings. She notes, 72, that the 'Introduction' pediment implies a building of some size.) Hekatompedon: *IG* I³.3 B 17–18; cf. Tölle-Kastenbein, *JdI* 108 (1993), 63. One enigmatic scene: the 'Olive-tree' pediment, on which contrast R. Heberdey, *Altattische Porosskulptur* (Vienna 1919), 26–28 (an Attic interpretation); Robertson, *History*, 92 f. and 629, n. 48 (myth of Troilus). The triple-bodied figure on the large limestone pediment (e.g. Boardman, *Greek Sculpture: Archaic*, fig. 193) has also received a very speculative Attic interpretation, as the Tritopatores (see the refs. in B. Kiilerich, *OpAth* 17, 1988, 125, n. 17, who himself pleads for Geryon, and a date *c*.575). As a way of glorifying Athena (so Knell, *Mythos und Polis*, 5–6), glorification of Heracles, whom she protected, was at best very indirect.

later, there is a hint of change. Fragments dating to the last twenty years of the century survive from large marble pediments, perhaps a replacement for the earlier limestone decoration of the temple of Athena. At one end of the building, animal still devours animal, but at the other a majestic Athena vanquishes the Giants.[13] Vases depicting this scene had in fact been judged a particularly pleasing offering to bring to Athena on the acropolis since about the middle of the century.[14]

The sculptor's arts were also available to individual piety. The acropolis had been a place of dedication since the eighth century, but it is in the sixth that the great series of marble offerings begins that makes the site perhaps the most impressive monument in Greece to the 'votive religion'[15] of the wealthier classes. The practice itself of dedicating marble statues in sanctuaries is first attested, in Attica, at Sunium, with four *kouroi* (of about 590?) that are among the earliest from anywhere in Greece. The evidence from the acropolis does not begin for another generation or so: as it happens, what may be the first such offering, the lovely 'Calf-bearer' dedicated by [Rh]ombos, has been ascribed to the same sculptor who carved the limestone pediments of the temple of Athena.[16] Can any conclusion be drawn from this slight delay? A festival is refashioned, a stone temple is built, a convenient approach is laid out, individuals begin to dedicate expensive statues, all within a decade or so: it is certainly tempting to infer that the acropolis achieved its familiar status as the sacred place *par excellence*, that, in an attractive formulation, fortress was transformed into sanctuary, quite suddenly, in the second quarter of the sixth century.[17] But if that is so, Athens had lacked a major sanctuary altogether in the seventh century, since no plausible

[13] See Robertson, *History*, 159 f.; Floren, *Griechische Plastik I*, 246 f.; Ridgway, *Archaic Style*, 205–10. Note that, on a different view about the site of the earlier temple with the limestone pediments (nn. 10 and 12), those in marble adorned an entirely new building. They are normally dated *c*.520, but for a lower dating see K. Stähler in R. Stiehl and G. A. Lehmann eds., *Antike und Universalgeschichte: Festschrift Hans Erich Stier* (Münster 1972), 101–12, and Welwei, *Athen*, 217, n. 204 [+]. Athena again fights a giant on a late archaic dedication, Schrader, *Marmorbildwerke*, no. 413 (Floren, *Griechische Plastik I*, 277, n. 2).*

[14] See Shapiro, *Art and Cult*, 38, who speaks of 'a remarkable correlation of subject-matter and findspot'.

[15] Cf. Burkert, *Mystery Cults*, 12–17.

[16] See e.g. Robertson, *History*, 45 and 620, n. 32, Floren, *Griechische Plastik I*, 252 f. (Sunium *kouroi*); Robertson, *History*, 94, Floren, *Griechische Plastik I*, 276 (calf-bearer = *IG* I³.593).

[17] So W. Zschietzschmann, *Klio* 27 (1934), 209–17; Ridgway, *Archaic Style*, 197. Fortress: Vanderpool in *ΦΟΡΟΣ*. But Floren, *Griechische Plastik I*, 264, ascribes the fr. Athens Acr. Mus. 3552 to a *kore* of *c*.600. Note too the eds.' tentative early dates for the dedications *IG* I³.584, 589–93 (but H. R. Immerwahr, *Attic Script*, Oxford 1990, 23, is sceptical); n. 47 below on the 'Treasurers of Athena'; Ch. 2, n. 35, and Ch. 3, n. 44 above on earlier acropolis dedications (and Immerwahr, *Attic Script*, 21–22 on fine vase dedications from *c*.600 –580).

alternative can be identified. And dedications in materials other than marble were of course made in good number on the acropolis long before the 560s. More probably, the apparent delayed start of offerings in stone is simply due to chances of preservation. As the sixth century proceeds, the dedications become more and more abundant. The acropolis sacked by the Persians must have been an enchanted forest of fair marble maidens.[18]

There were at least two further major religious building-projects. At Eleusis, the sanctuary was reshaped, and within it was built a fine, square 'initiation-building', the first of what was to become the canonical form. The sons of Pisistratus, emulous no doubt of the monumental works of Polycrates and Croesus, began but could not finish a colossal double-colonnaded temple of Olympian Zeus. They were perhaps also responsible for redecorating Athena's temple on the acropolis with new marble pediments; or possibly for constructing a whole new temple.[19] An earlier attempt by Pisistratus to honour Apollo Pythios with a temple had fallen foul of the populace—if we believe the explanation offered by lexicographers of the proverb 'it would have been better to shit in the Python'. Only thus, it is said, could the impotent people express their odium for the tyrant. He responded by threatening offenders with death, and indeed carrying out the penalty in one obdurate case: whence the proverb, used of those 'suffering through their own fault'. How much actual history may lie behind the story we can scarcely say. The younger Pisistratus, at all events, later dedicated an altar in the sanctuary,

---

[18] The surviving abundance is due to the invasion, which caused statues to be toppled and then buried and so sealed. For other particularly rich collections of *kouroi* and *korai* (almost all sanctuaries have yielded some) see J. Ducat, *Kouroi du Ptoion* (Paris 1971)—remains of perhaps 120 survive (p. 451); B. Freyer-Schauenburg, *Samos* 11 (Bonn 1974), 13–105 (mostly from the Heraeum). For the debate about their function see B. S. Ridgway in *Studies in Athenian Architecture, Sculpture and Topography Presented to Homer A. Thompson* (*Hesperia* Suppl. 20, Princeton 1982), 118–27. A supposed deficiency in dedications from the Pisistratean period has sometimes been linked with the tyrant's supposed residence on the acropolis (see n. 70 below), which would have closed it to private piety: E. Langlotz in Schrader, *Marmorbildwerke*, 9, followed e.g. by Raubitschek, *Dedications*, 456 (cf. Kolb, 'Baupolitik', 104). The theory is incoherent: major dedications virtually only begin under the tyranny (see n. 17), and the sharp rise in numbers occurs before 510 (see Langlotz, in Schrader, *Marmorbildwerke*, 41–42), even though the Pisistratids had as much reason to live on the acropolis as their father. [Arist.] *Oecon.* 2.2.2, 1346[b]7–12, sometimes supposed to show that tyrants discouraged the practice of private dedication, in fact attests the practice under a tyranny.

[19] Eleusis: above, n. 4. I have, however, been told that Dr J. Binder questions the conventional Pisistratean dating of these works (Shapiro, *Art and Cult*, 68, also appears doubtful). Olympian Zeus: see Boersma, *Building Policy*, 199; Travlos, *Pictorial Dictionary*, 402–11 (both +); D. M. Lewis in *CAH*[2] IV.2 (1988), 296 (who favours Vitruvius' attribution to Pisistratus over Aristotle's to the Pisistratids); for the monumental precedents cf. Shipley, *Samos*, 73. Pediments: above, n. 13.*

which still survives.[20] And a monumental temple must have been built somewhere in the *agora*, unless the fragment found there of a large limestone pediment has strayed down from the acropolis.[21]

On a lesser scale, the growing *agora* perhaps received small shrines of Apollo Patroos and Zeus;[22] more interestingly, the younger Pisistratus founded there an 'Altar of the Twelve Gods' which was henceforth the 'navel' of Attica, from which distances were measured.[23] By the end of the century, Athenian 'branch-offices' had perhaps been opened of the two most celebrated country cults: there was probably an Eleusinion in the *agora*, and perhaps (but the dating is perilously fragile) a precinct of Artemis Brauronia on the acropolis.[24] Below the acropolis, Dionysus was probably installed in a first temple, which sported a rather uninhibited pediment; and traces of minor shrines begin to dot the city.[25] An

[20] The most circumstantial testimonium (for others see J. P. Lynch in *Studies Presented to Sterling Dow*, GRBM 10, 1984, 177–79) is *Paroem. Graec.* I.406–407, no. 66 (from the Bodleian codex, on the value of which see W. Bühler, *Zenobii Athoi Proverbia*, Göttingen 1987, 126): the victim was a metic, the people hated Pisistratus because of the 10% tax (a learned detail, cf. Arist. *Ath. Pol.* 16.4–5). Suda, Photius s.v. Πύθιον say merely that Pisistratus founded the sanctuary (a reflection of the more elaborate story, or its origin?); a 'temple' in the sanctuary is mentioned only by the sources for the excretion story, and has not been traced archaeologically (L. H. Jeffery's reference, *Archaic Greece*, London 1976, 97, to 'the traces of a little temple in the precinct' is obscure to me). Cf. Judeich, *Topographie*, 386, n. 5 (who suspects that the whole tradition is merely spun out of the younger Pisistratus' dedication); Travlos, *Pictorial Dictionary*, 100–103. The altar: Thuc. 6.54.6; *IG* I³.948 (M/L 11, CEG 305).

[21] See Harrison, *Agora* XI. 31–33, no. 94; cf. ibid. 36–37, no. 96 for a smaller later fr.

[22] Apollo Patroos: H. A. Thompson, *Hesperia* 6 (1937), 79–84; Thompson/Wycherley, *Agora*, 136–37—a small (?) apsidal structure (with a *terminus post quem* given by pottery of *c.*575) and a limestone base below the fourth-cent. temple of Apollo Patroos. But C. W. Hedrick Jr., *AJA* 92 (1988), 185–91, effectively questions, from the intrusion of other structures in the fifth cent., whether the site can already have been sacred in the sixth, and points out that the adjacent sixth-cent. foundry was not necessarily constructed *ad hoc* to cast the cult image. Zeus: Thompson, *Hesperia* 6 (1937), 8–12; Thompson/Wycherley, *Agora*, 96—below the Stoa of Zeus Eleutherios, 'remains of a small archaic structure (6th c. B.C.) surrounding a rectangular base appropriate for a statue. To the east are slight traces of what appears to have been the altar' (*Agora Guide*, 79). No precise dating is possible. The importance of all this should not be exaggerated. These gods had certainly already been honoured elsewhere, and were now (if the identifications are correct) introduced to the *agora* on a small scale. On the sixth-cent. *agora* cf. H. van Steuben, in G. W. Weber ed., *Idee, Gestalt, Geschichte: Festschrift Klaus von See* (Odense 1988), 31–58 (who stresses its role in the *Panathenaea*).*

[23] Thuc. 6.54.6; cf. Wycherley, *Testimonia*, 119–21; Shapiro, *Art and Cult*, 133–41; the speculations of S. Angiolillo, *Ostraka* 1 (1992), 171–76; and on the precinct's later history L. M. Gadbery, *Hesperia* 61 (1992), 447–89. On the herms of Hipparchus (surely a related project) see below.

[24] Eleusinion: a precinct wall has been identified which is now said to be of the mid-sixth cent. See Travlos, *Pictorial Dictionary*, 198, with fig. 260; *Agora Guide*, 145 (a modification from *Hesperia* 29, 1960, 338; Thompson/Wycherley, *Agora*, 152). Brauronion: see Osborne, *Demos*, 154–57 [+]; Shapiro, *Art and Cult*, 65.*

[25] Dionysus: see n. 111 below. A sixth-cent. Tritopatreion may be attested by the archaic *horos IG* I³.1067 (but '500–480', eds.) − Travlos, *Pictorial Dictionary*, fig. 395. The Amyneion is said to go back to the sixth cent.: Kutsch, *Heilheroen*, 12 f.; Judeich, *Topographie*,

intimate of the tyrants, Charmus the polemarch, founded a famous altar of Eros at 'the shady limit of the gymnasium' of the Academy.[26] Finally, the sanctuaries at Rhamnus, Sunium, and Brauron all seem to have received their first modest temples in the sixth century; that at Brauron is explicitly associated with Pisistratus by one recently discovered source.[27] (There was also probably a temple of Dionysus at Icaria, where parts of a colossal image of the god have been found; but for that the Icarians themselves may have been responsible, as indeed the Rhamnusians perhaps were for theirs.[28]) And near the presumptive site of the temple of Athena Pallenis, the most important unexcavated sanctuary in the Attic countryside, a sixth-century capital has been found.[29]

289. A small late sixth-cent. shrine at Poulopoulou Street 29 has yielded figurines and a small marble herm-head dated to *c*.500: *ArchDelt* 33 1978 (1984–5)/*Mel.* 342–53 and *Chron.* 10–12; *BCH* 109 (1985), 765; 110 (1986), 677. On a similar shrine at Odos Vassilis 18–20 see *ArchDelt* 34 1979 (1987)/*Chron.* 26–27.

[26] Clidemus *FGrH* 323 F 15; Paus. 1.30.1 (mistakenly ascribed to Pisistratus by Plut. *Sol.* 1.7). For other refs. (in Platonist writings) see Frazer's note on Paus. 1.30.1; and on the homosexual *eros* of the gymnasium see Shapiro, *Art and Cult*, 119 f., 123.

[27] Rhamnus: *BCH* 108 (1984), 751; B. C. Petrakos, in Φίλια ἔπη εἰς Γεώργιον E. Μυλωνᾶν II (Athens 1987), 299–305; id., *ΡΑΜΝΟΥΣ* (Athens 1991), 20—two temples, one early, one late in the sixth cent. Sunium: the small temple of Athena, Boersma, *Building Policy*, 183 (? *c*.550). Brauron: Photii Patriarchae *Lexicon*, ed. Chr. Theodoridis, I (Berlin 1982), s.v. Βραυρωνία (β 264) · ἦν τὸ ἱερὸν πρὸς τῷ Ἐρασίνῳ ποταμῷ, κατασκευασθὲν ὑπὸ Πεισιστράτου, with S. Angiolillo, *PP* 212 (1983), 351–54. On the evidence of sixth-cent. vases see R. Osborne in *Placing the Gods*, 151. That the rhapsodic recitations of Homer attested for the site (Hesych. β 1067) were a Pisistratid introduction is an obvious further possibility.

[28] See I. B. Romano, *Hesperia* 51 (1982), 398–409; Floren, *Griechische Plastik I*, 260, n. 44. The identification of Ath. Mus. Nat. 3711 (= *LIMC* s.v. *Dionysus*, 437, no. 135) as another sixth-cent. seated statue of the god is more questionable.

[29] See H. Möbius, *AM* 52 (1927), 162–63 (cf. 167–71, an Ionic capital from the same region). Other archaeological evidence for new religious sites in Attica in the sixth cent. is very slight. Proposed cases (collected with the help of M. Petropoulakou and E. Pentazos, *Ancient Greek Cities 21: Attica*, Athens 1973, fig. 22; Morris, *Burial*, 222–28) are: (1) two smallish temples at Profitis Elias above Koropi on Mt. Hymettus, dated architecturally by their discoverer N. Kotzias to the sixth cent. (see Ch. 3, n. 3); (2) remains of a 'shrine, perhaps of the archaic period', seen by J. Papademetriou on the hill Hagios Demetrios at Pyrgos near Brauron (Γέρας Ἀντ. Κεραμοπούλλου, Athens 1953, 142, n. 3); (3) a large, supposedly archaic, polygonal *peribolos* at Plasi near Marathon (*AAA* 3, 1970, 16, 66), associated by E. Vanderpool (*ap.* J. S. Traill, *Demos and Trittys*, Toronto 1986, 148) with the Dionysion known from *Anecd. Bekk.* I.262.17; (4) the cave of the Nymphs at Vari—but the only clearly pre-fifth-cent. item, the epitaph *IG* I³.1247, must be a stray; (5) the temple of Apollo Zoster at Vouliagmeni, late sixth/early fifth cent. (*ArchDelt* 11, 1927–8, 49 and Travlos, *Bildlexikon*, 477); (6) the temple of Artemis Tauropolos and associated buildings at Halai Araphenides (Loutsa) (Travlos, *Bildlexikon*, 211–15); the temple is of uncertain date (M. B. Hollinshead, *AJA* 89, 1985, 436), and no sixth-cent. material appears to have been pub.; (7) the Herakleion at Limni Zophra (*BCH* 84, 1960, 655–66); again no sixth-cent. material; (8) the small temple of Dionysus in the theatre at Thorikos has been down-dated to the fifth cent. with the theatre (see Kolb, *Agora und Theater*, 64–65); (9) the 'Herakleion' at Point Zeza in the Sunium region (J. H. Young, *Hesperia* 10, 1941, 169–74; Young offers no dates, but the limestone members perhaps point to sixth-cent. sacred buildings); (10) healing-shrines at Rhamnus and Thorikos (see Ch. 9, n. 80); (11) a small shrine at Ano Voula, *ArchDelt* 34, 1979 (1987)/*Chron.* 77–78.

Unless they were associated with new festivals, or new gods, new temples, however magnificent, had no direct effect on the pattern of religious life. They can be classed with other urban improvements of the period: the laying-out of gymnasia and the provision of a fine new water-system. It is not clear that the Pisistratid tyranny expanded the actual pantheon of Athens very much.[30] But it is widely believed that, in the sixth century, public religion was in some sense made more open to all. In its cruder form, according to which the tyrants promoted the cults of 'the people's gods', this doctrine cannot stand, for several reasons. The supposed 'people's gods', Demeter and Dionysus, enjoyed much honour at Athens even before the tyranny; the tyrants also glorified Athena, Zeus, and Apollo; and, above all, the ancient sources give only faint and ambiguous support to any attempt to distinguish between popular and aristocratic gods.[31] Such a distinction is, in fact, probably incompatible with the nature of Greek polytheism. An aristocrat might despise the coarse revelry of peasants, but he could not despise Dionysus unless he was prepared to deny that he was a son of Zeus (and thus much better-born than himself[32]). In a more sophisticated and plausible form the theory speaks not of popular gods but of popular festivals or forms of cult. According to Aristotle, the democratic reformer should concentrate religious practice around 'few and public' cults.[33] Democrats and tyrants have something in common, in that both may be opposed to aristocrats. Can Aristotle's formula be transferred back to the sixth century?

The history of the festival calendar in the sixth century is full of uncertainties, and a detailed discussion would divert the main argument too far.[34] In brief, the *Panathenaea* was certainly transformed into an athletic festival of Panhellenic appeal in or near the 560s. The *City Dionysia* was deliberately founded or refounded as another 'Panathenaic' festival, to provide a forum for dithyramb or tragedy, by—at latest—the last decade of the sixth century. (Note that

[30] *Aliter* Shapiro, *Art and Cult*, 164–66. The collective cult of the twelve gods was almost certainly new, and perhaps the worship of Dionysus as Eleuthereus, of Athena as Nike (see n. 11, esp. I. S. Mark as cited there), and of Eros (see n. 26); in other cases, it is far from clear that new altar or new shrine meant new cult.

[31] For an attempt see R. A. Neil's note on Ar. *Eq.* 551 (Poseidon an oligarch: note esp. Ar. *Av.* 1570); and cf. e.g. Eur. *Bacch.* 430–31. But many aspects of the cult of the gods concerned defy such categorization.

[32] Cf. Philoctetes' comment on Achilles' death at Apollo's hands, Soph. *Phil.* 336: ἀλλ' εὐγενὴς μὲν ὁ κτανών τε χὠ θανών (and perhaps Aesch. *Eum.* 435).

[33] *Pol.* 1319ᵇ24. Cf. e.g. A. Andrewes, *CAH*² III.3 (1982), 415: 'The general tendency [under Pisistratus] is certainly towards the development of public cults in which the ordinary man could take part with pride.' For dissent see above all Kolb, 'Baupolitik' (with the reservations of A. Aloni, *QS* 19, 1984, 136, n 13).

[34] See the annexe to this chapter.

neither event definitely falls within the Pisistratid period.) It is likely in varying degrees that each of the *Thargelia, Olympieia, Eleusinia, Herakleia* at Marathon, *Brauronia*, and Eleusinian Mysteries were reshaped and expanded in the second half of the sixth century. Many other festivals, of course, went their way in the period, completely outside our vision.

Can we conclude that public religion became less exclusive? The masses were certainly not the only gainers. Through the reform of the *Panathenaea*, Athens acquired a place in the world of Panhellenic athletics. Whatever qualifications may be required to the traditional conception of athletics as an exclusively aristocratic preserve, however significant it may be that at the *Panathenaea*— very unusually—competition was for extremely valuable prizes, the beneficiaries of the reform certainly included the horse-rearing gymnasium-haunting rich, the chariot set.[35] It is scarcely plausible to see any populist intent in the foundation or reform of the *City Dionysia*: the aim was to provide a forum for new forms of enter- tainment, to the benefit of all. The god himself had long been embedded in public religion through his other rites, the *Anthesteria* and *Lenaea*. And 'choruses', we should remember, were, along with gymnastics, a central component of traditional upper-class educa- tion.[36] Festivals were opened up in the sense, perhaps, that élite practices were given a more popular setting, which may have encouraged broader participation; but a revolution against the actual forms of aristocratic culture certainly did not occur.

Above all, we need to take a broader view of the history of popu- lar festivals in Attica. Beyond a doubt, there were very many of these before Pisistratus. There is nothing aristocratic or exclusive, for

---

[35] Note for instance the dedication made at the Ptoion in Boeotia by the blue-blooded Alcmeonides, son of Alcmeon, for a chariot victory won ὅτ' ἐν Ἀθάναις Παλάδος πανέ{γ}υρις, *IG* I³.1469 (*CEG* 302). Ultra-snobs might see gymnastic events, in contrast to horse-racing, as potentially a little common (Isoc. 16.33), but this was in reaction against a more common association between gymnasia and good breeding (Ar. *Ran.* 729; [Xen.] *Ath. Pol.* 1.13). Qualifications: see D. C. Young, *The Olympic Myth of Greek Athletics* (Chicago 1984), with M. Poliakoff's review, *AJP* 110 (1989), 166–71; but the study of known Athenian athletes by Kyle, *Athletics in Athens*, 102–23, confirms aristocratic predominance until well into the fifth cent. And if funerary games for private individuals took place in Athens in the sixth cent., despite Solon's legislation, they were not eliminated by competition from the public *Panathenaea*; since the problematic stone discuses inscribed ἐχ τῶν ἐρίον vel. sim. that *ex hypothesi* attest such games (see Ch. 8, n. 47) are dated late in the sixth cent.

[36] See Ar. *Ran.* 729 on the τραφέντες ἐν παλαίστραις καὶ χοροῖς καὶ μουσικῇ. The rela- tion between large tribal choruses and democracy (cf. J. Winkler in id. and F. I. Zeitlin eds., *Nothing to Do with Dionysus?*, Princeton 1990, 48–58; Aloni, *QS* 19, 1984, 114–16) is therefore complex. Even if competitions and competitiveness (perhaps over-general concepts) instilled certain civic virtues (see R. Osborne in A. H. Sommerstein et al. eds., *Tragedy, Comedy and the Polis*, Bari 1993, 21–38), they did so perhaps only within a restricted social stratum, ini- tially at least.

instance, about the twelve or so known old Ionian rites.[37] The only doubt concerns the size of the group that assembled for them. If they were characteristically celebrated by villages or groups of villages only, then Pisistratus will indeed have wrought a transformation if he introduced 'Panathenaic' rites. But we should not assume that a festival held forty or so miles away was beyond the purview of a seventh-century Attic countryman. In more recent times, peasants have readily travelled such distances for a party. The *panegyris* or 'all-assembly' is in fact as ancient a Greek institution as any that we know of. If, as is likely, the system of tribal competition in Attic cults is archaic, there must always have been some pan-Attic festivals.[38] Some old favourites (the *Pandia* for instance, the 'all-Zeus' festival, or the *Dipolieia*) perhaps gradually faded away in the classical period.

This is not to deny that the Pisistratids may have promoted festivals of Panathenaic appeal. They were keen, modern historians plausibly suppose, to encourage allegiance to an 'Athens' (state and place) the splendours of which were largely in their own control.[39] But if such was their aim, their method was perhaps the opposite of the crude religious populism with which they are often credited. To understand the change, we need to evoke a typical ancient *panegyris*.[40] It occurred in a rustic setting; the participants picknicked on layers of foliage (*stibades*), and for long rites camped overnight in makeshift huts (*skenai*). (Attic women were to continue to do this at the *Thesmophoria*.) The entertainments and competitions were perhaps semi-spontaneous, the abundant food was brought by the participants themselves or donated by the munificent rich. Probably only a small proportion of the total of meat that was consumed came from public sacrifices performed by the priest. The *Diasia* is the best

[37] See Ch. 2, n. 65 above.

[38] Peasants: on *panegyreis* in modern Greece see B. Schmidt, *Das Volksleben der Neugriechen*, I (Leipzig 1871), 83–88; M. Hamilton, *Greek Saints and their Festivals* (Edinburgh 1910), 73–92 (on the Festival of the Annunciation at Tenos); in Italy, N. Douglas, *Old Calabria* (London 1915), ch. 20. Antiquity of *panegyreis*: note the early Amphictyonic festivals, and the ethnic festivals (*Panionia, Pamboiotia*), with esp. Thuc. 3.104. Tribal competitions: see p. 113 below.

[39] So recently Millett, *Lending and Borrowing*, 51; Stahl, *Aristokraten und Tyrannen*, 243–55 (on the *Panathenaea*); Welwei, *Athen*, 240; E. Stein-Hölkeskamp, *Adelskultur und Polisgesellschaft* (Stuttgart 1989), 150–52, who speaks of 'religiöse Integration der Bürgerschaft, Legitimierung der Vorherrschaft des Tyrannenhauses und Selbs-darstellung der Tyrannen als Herrscher über Athen'.

[40] See L. Gernet, 'Frairies antiques', *REG* 41 (1928), 318–59 (= id., *Anthropologie de la Grèce antique*, Paris 1968, 21–61), whence derives id., *Le génie grec dans la religion* (Paris 1932/1970), 35–67; Nilsson, *Geschichte*, 826–31; and the feasts in Plato's 'pig-city', *Resp.* 372b. For a much later period see R. MacMullen, *Paganism in the Roman Empire* (New Haven 1981), 18–34; also e.g. Ovid, *Fasti* 3.523–42.

Attic instance of such old-fashioned festivity. It was celebrated '*pan-demei*','*en masse*', at Agrae outside the city, and certainly drew participants from much of Attica. There was much eating and much hospitality; there were probably booths selling toys for children; but we have no evidence that the state provided any entertainment or sacrificial meat whatsoever.[41]

New festivals founded in the fifth and fourth centuries were normally of very different type. They took place in the city; they were built around performances by highly trained choruses, or competitions between the finest athletes of Greece, or spectacular displays of other kinds; and whole hecatombs of meat were often provided at public expense.[42] The description at the start of the *Republic* of the new festival of the new god Bendis is a lovely evocation of this new urban religion. Socrates has gone down to the Piraeus to pray to the goddess and to 'watch' the first performance. Having admired two elegant processions, he is about to depart; but doesn't he realize, protests Adimantus, that there is to be a torch-relay on horseback for the goddess in the evening? 'On horseback? That *is* something new.' 'Yes, and they'll perform an all-night rite [παννυχίς] which will be worth seeing.' 'Watch', 'new', 'worth seeing': the vocabulary tells its own story. From another source we learn that the *Bendideia* was also the occasion of mass sacrifices.[43] Such occasions required elaborate preparation and supervision, and the many boards of officials charged with organizing the individual festivals are duly listed by Aristotle.[44]

This surely is the transformation to which the Pisistratids contributed. (It was probably already under way.) It is not a process that can be traced in detail, when the history of so many festivals is unknown. In particular, we do not know when the crucial development occurred (truly demotic, this) whereby at major festivals the city undertook to distribute large quantities of meat to the citizens free of charge.[45] But we find in the cults of this period a stress on the city,[46] on spectacle, on entertainment provided, so to speak, profes-

[41] On the festival see M. Jameson, *BCH* 89 (1965), 159–66; Hornblower's note on Thuc. 1.126.6. Some meat was provided by participating demes: *LSCG* 18 A 37–42; *SEG* XXXIII 147.35. Eating, hospitality, booths: Ar. *Nub.* 408–11, 864; Deubner, *Attische Feste*, 156. The country festival at Skillous founded and financed by Xenophon (*Anab.* 5.3.7–13) is another lovely case; indeed it would be hard to find a passage more instinct with Greek religious feeling than Xenophon's warm and graceful description of it.

[42] On mass sacrifices *IG* II².1496 is the central text; cf. Rosivach, *Public Sacrifice*, 48–67.

[43] *IG* II².1496.86, 1496.117.   [44] *Ath. Pol.* 54.6–7, 56.4, 57.1, 60.

[45] See Ch. 8, n. 25. About the funding of cult in the period nothing is known; Thuc. 6.54.5 assumes that the tyrants met the costs from general revenue.

[46] Note, however, that according to Arist. *Ath. Pol.* 16.2–6 it was Pisistratus' design literally to 'depoliticize' life by diverting people to the country and to farming (cf. Rhodes's

sionally. The 'performers of rites', ἱροποιοί, entrusted with the *Panathenaea* herald the era of elaborate organization, and the board of 'Treasurers of Athena' soon also appears in our sources.[47] Several factors only partially dependent on the will of the tyrants seem to lie behind the change: increasing prosperity, including the increasing wealth of sanctuaries; increasing population; the rapid development of Athens itself as an urban centre; and the growing pretensions of the state to organize and provide. *Panegyreis* were not invented, or even popularized; they were urbanized, made more regulated and professional—gentrified, as it were.

Spectacular festivals: but are they religion? Has not piety yielded to barren show?[48] So judging, some eminent students of Greek religion have said as little as possible about such desecrated rites. As a result, their picture of the highlights of the festival year doubtless differs a little from that of a Dicaeopolis or a Strepsiades.[49] But it is too easy to sneer at these distinguished (and candid) Protestant[50] scholars. We should rather ask whether their reaction is anticipated at all by Greek thought about the nature of true piety. The bodies which organized the splendid festivals, obviously, did not acknowledge that they were guilty of any derogation of religious duty. Putting on a show in a way 'worthy of the god' was an act of piety, as we see from many a vote of thanks recorded on stone. It was pious to promote even the *Dionysia*, that secularized festival as it has so often been called.[51] So speaks the city, predictably. But even such a critic of traditional religion as Plato directed his attack elsewhere. There would still be elegant processions in his Magnesia.[52] The 'Orphic' reaction may have been in part provoked by these developments, but they were not its explicit target. We come closest to the Protestant

parallels on 16.3). But he had other concerns too, as the building-programme shows. 'Ils mènent une politique à la fois agraire et urbaine,' says Martin, *L'urbanisme dans la Grèce antique*[2], 84, of tyrants.

[47] See *IG* I[3].507–508, 510, 590 (Raubitschek, *Dedications*, 330). The board of Treasurers in fact is said to go back at least to Solon (Arist. *Ath. Pol.* 8.1, 47.1).

[48] 'Die Religion aber im öden Prunk erstickte': M. P. Nilsson, *Arch. Jahrb.* 31 (1916), 311 = id., *Op. Sel.* I.169; cf. e.g. F. Bömer in *RE* s.v. *Pompe*, 1894. Contrast Veyne, *Pain et cirque*, 364, n. 304.

[49] Note the limitation in the title of M. P. Nilsson, *Griechische Feste von religiöser Bedeutung*, a work which excludes agonistic and literary festivals. For Deubner see e.g. n. 120 below.

[50] Cf. Nilsson, *Geschichte*, 827: a warning against Protestant prejudice surely addressed in part to his own (? younger) self. (But note the late page on which the important phenomenon still appears!)

[51] See e.g. *IG* II[2].410.20, 649.27, 1186.16; Ar. *Nub.* 311–13; Dem. 21 (*Against Midias*) 126 *et passim*.

[52] *Leg.* 796c5–6.

position perhaps in the insistence of certain fourth-century texts that the 'character of the sacrificer' and not the 'number of the victims' is the touchstone of piety.[53] A Magnesian from Asia who 'led a hecatomb to Apollo in procession and honoured him with great magnificence' was told by the Pythia that in all the world the truest worshipper of the gods was one Clearchus of Methydrion in Arcadia, who garlanded his Herm and Hecate each month and made modest offerings at all the public festivals. But the thrust of such stories is to vindicate the piety of honest (usually Greek) poverty against the presumptions of individual (usually semi-barbarian) wealth. It is not to pass a judgement on the magnificent rites organized by cities. The distinction between 'religious' and 'secular' aspects of festivals which comes so naturally to modern observers was not one drawn by the Greeks.

Piety seems to have survived the sixth-century transformation; but perhaps there was a different loss. It is a commonplace that Greek women enjoyed a kind of 'cultic citizenship', which granted them at a different level the recognition that they were denied in the political sphere. And this is broadly true of Attica as of other Greek states. But where are the tribal choirs of maidens, competing publicly like the equivalent choruses of boys? Athenian girls certainly did dance at festivals, but only within the less-organized penumbra, at 'all-night ceremonies' and the like. They were never allowed into the limelight to compete. Perhaps it had always been so in Attica (in contrast to Sparta); but it may have been when the festivals were made more formal in the archaic period that maidens were banished to the fringes.

Another intriguing development perhaps has some bearing on the Pisistratids' attitude to 'popular' religion. Several ancient authors saw the herm as a distinctively Attic form of monument.[54] It is so familiar, and seemingly so primitive, that one may be surprised to learn that the first clearly datable example is of the last quarter of the sixth century. At about that time, Pisistratus' son Hipparchus had marble herms set as half-way markers on the roads between Athens and the Attic townships. The one that survives announces itself in a hexameter: 'Midway between Kephale and the city, splendid Hermes'. A lost pentameter, according to another source, would have contained an advertisement, 'This is a monument of Hipparchus', and a moral maxim 'Think just thoughts as you jour-

---

[53] See the texts cited in Porph. *Abst.* 2. 15–19 (for fifth-cent. anticipations see Parker, *Miasma*, 323, n. 8).

[54] Hdt. 2.51.2; Thuc. 6.27.1; Paus. 1.24.3, 4.33.3. Cf. in general H. Wrede, *Die antike Herme* (Mainz 1986); G. Siebert, *LIMC* s.v. *Hermes* [both +].

ney' or 'Do not deceive a friend'.[55] Hipparchus' undertaking can be seen as a way of stressing the unity of an Attica that has Athens, and in particular the altar of the Twelve Gods founded by the younger Pisistratus, as its centre. But herms and herm-makers quickly begin to appear on vases in other contexts, and the city was soon flooded with them.[56] By the late fifth century the doorstep herm, that cheerfully shameless figure, must have been much the most familiar divine presence in the streets of Athens. On vases they can seem so animate that one would scarcely be surprised to see one wink.[57] Perhaps because Hermes was god of the *agora*, the herm became a regular form for dedications made there by the people and its representatives, magistrates and generals. The practice seems to have started by the end of the century, and 'the Herms' grew into a familiar area, with strong political associations.[58] The conspirators who mutilated 'almost all the herms' in Athens in 415 were thus attacking both public monuments of the Athenians, and familiar friends.[59]

It was long customary to seek aniconic or semi-iconic precursors of the herm. The god began as a shaft set in a heap of stones, a *herma*, according to a once popular but untenable etymology (for that is not what *herma* means). Or perhaps one should think of a pillar or board topped with a mask, an assemblage known from the cult of Dionysus. More recently, the view has gained ground that the god's pillar-body is not, after all, a primitive relic: the trunk was used by Hipparchus as a surface to receive inscriptions, and as such a convenient surface it must have been designed. The divine messenger was, of course, well suited by nature to become a vehicle for communications in the

---

[55] *IG* I³.1023 = *CEG* 304; Pl. *Hipparch.* 228b–229b. The original number of Hipparchan herms is unknown (cf. B. M. Lavelle, *EchCl* NS 4, 1985, 411–20, at 417); the figure often quoted, *c*.135, is anachronistically based on the later Clisthenic demes. Lavelle stresses the value for Hipparchus individually of this 'name publicity', which presented him as a voice of moral guidance on every main road of Attica.

[56] Cf. most recently Shapiro, *Art and Cult*, 126–32; *LIMC* s.v. *Hermes*, nos. 9–19 (early marble herms), 92–187 (vases).

[57] See e.g. the group of three herms on a pelike fragment by the Pan painter, Louvre [Campana] 10793, *PCPS* 211 (1985), 63, pl. 3, Thompson/Wycherley, *Agora*, pl. 50b (*LIMC* s.v. *Hermes*, no. 141); or the herm with a turned head on a BF oinochoe in Frankfurt (*LIMC* s.v. *Hermes*, no. 105; P. Zanker, *Wandel der Hermesgestalt in der attischen Vasenmalerei*, Bonn 1965, 93). J. D. Beazley, *The Pan Painter* (Mainz 1974), 5, speaks of 'a monstrously vivid humanity'. On doorstep herms note however the reservation of M. Jameson in Murray/Price, *Greek City*, 194: 'an ideal pattern which not all houses could accommodate or afford'.

[58] See Wrede, *Die antike Herme*, 8–12 [+]; note esp. the new herm-head from the *agora* (*Hesperia* 53, 1984, 42, with pl. 10), dated 510–500 (cf. perhaps *SEG* XXII 87, n. 61 below). Hermes Agoraios: so A. v. Domaszewski, *Die Hermen der Agora zu Athen* (*SBHeid* 1914, 10), 7; but see the comments of Harrison, *Agora* XI.112.

[59] Thuc. 6.27.1; cf. R. Osborne, *PCPS* 211 (1985), 47–73. Cratippus *FGrH* 64 F 3 *ap.* [*Plut.*] *X Orat.* 834d, confines the attack to the 'Herms around the *agora*', in which case it was more directly political.

new written form. If the herm is seen thus, as a *stele* with a head, it can be accepted as an invention of the period in which it first appears. And thus it was Hipparchus, elegant patron of Simonides and Anacreon, who gave to the world this most potent image of the ithyphallic.[60]

This boldly positivist proposal is not without its difficulties. As it happens, herms have recently been discovered at Sunium and Rhamnus for which an origin in the first half of the sixth century has been claimed.[61] But it might be wrong to insist on this dating of rough and weathered works. It is not, however, true that the herm is simply a *stele* with a head. On the sides of the shaft near the top there are always two projecting stubs, the 'laterals' or 'arms', of which the theory gives no account. But what is really embarrassing is the phallus. Hermes is not in general portrayed as ithyphallic, and if the herms do not derive from a tradition, it is mysterious why he should have become so now. The phallus is not an organic part of Hermes, we are told; it was put on the first herms, which were milestones, as a good luck charm for travellers; or perhaps as a fertility symbol dear to passing farmers.[62] It then got stuck: for herms soon entered the city as images to which cult was paid, but retained the gross appendage. Seldom can a tyrant's whim have transformed the nature of a god so rudely. And the hypothesis in fact implies even more than this: the whole domestic cult of Hermes, centred on the herm,[63] will seem to derive from Hipparchus' initiative.

The matter is very uncertain; but the best view may be that Hipparchus (or a predecessor) found Hermes wooden and left him

[60] Semi-iconic: see R. Lullies, *Die Typen der griechischen Herme* (Königsberg 1931), 34–42 [+]; *WürzJbb* 4 (1949–50), 126–39; Nilsson, *Geschichte*, 205–207. Etymology: see *contra* A. J. Windekens, *RhM* 104 (1961), 289 f.; P. Devambez, *RA* 1968, 139–54, at 140–44. The god was none the less associated with rocks and stony outcrops (Devambez). Board with mask: H. Goldman, *AJA* 46 (1942), 58–67 (who explains the laterals as pegs for drapery; cf. Simon, *Götter*, 312). Herm as *stele*: first J. F. Crome, *AM* 60–61 (1935–6), 300–14, strongly supported by Devambez, *RA* 1968, 139–54, accepted by Osborne, *PCPS* 211 (1985); dissent in Shapiro, *Art and Cult*, 127, an intermediate position in G. Siebert, *LIMC* s.v. *Hermes*, 375–76. For another approach (which still regards the pillar-herm as essentially a new creation) see F. Frontisi-Ducroux, *Le dieu-masque* (Paris 1991), 217–18: she suggests that the suppression of the body of the pillar-herm, as of the mask Dionysus, served to recall the otherness of a god who could seem too familiar.

[61] *ArchDelt* 32 A 1977 (1982) 119, pls. 47–49; *Ergon* 1983 (1984), 54, fig. 69; cf. Floren, *Griechische Plastik I*, 261–62. Note too Jeffery, *Local Scripts*, 78, no. 33, with *SEG* XXII 87. Another new herm from Rhamnus ('2nd half of 6th c.', ed.) carries, unusually, a verse dedication which alludes to a different function of Hermes: [ ] καὶ βοτὸν ἐπίσκοπον/[ ] Λάχες μ'ἱδρύσατο (B. C. Petrakos, *Prakt* 1990 [1993], 30, no. 13).

[62] So respectively Devambez (*RA* 1968) and Crome (*AM* 60–61, 1935–6). The laterals do not look to me like arms, at least as a sophisticated sculptor of the 520s unconstrained by tradition would have portrayed them. Were they handles to lift wooden herms by? (For another view see n. 60 above.)

[63] Best-known from the vases (above, n. 56).

marble. Perhaps we see the prototype in the 'herms', sometimes of quite irregular form, that several vases show set on a rock or heap of stones in the country; certainly, wooden ithyphallic figures continued to be made throughout antiquity (most commonly as 'Priapus').[64] The old form may have been substantially remodelled when it was transferred to marble, acquiring, for instance, the large flat surface ready to receive inscriptions.[65] The sudden explosion of evidence certainly suggests that Hipparchus' example made the herm immensely more fashionable.[66] Was it, then, a populist gesture on his part to promote the ithyphallic god? But for the job in hand, the care of roads, there was no rival candidate. One might rather stress the modern elegance of the marble dress in which (with some concessions to his special nature) the old reprobate was confined. For though the Hipparchan herms are consciously archaic in some regards, they are none the less refined works that claim a place in the history of sculpture.[67] Hermes too was gentrified.

With the Pisistratids we have almost left the prehistoric period. Several other religious phenomena of the period are known and should be mentioned, even if they cannot quite be brought together into a unified picture.

The most intriguing incident is Pisistratus' ceremonial first return from exile, sharing a chariot with a fine tall girl armed like Athena. 'Athenians, receive Pisistratus with a good heart; Athena honours him most of all men, and is escorting him back in person to her own acropolis,' declared Pisistratus' supporters; and according to an amazed Herodotus, the Athenians believed them, and received him back. On any interpretation of this remarkable tradition, there could scarcely be a more plastic illustration of Athena's power in the sixth century to embody the identity of her people. Beyond this point we

---

[64] Prototype: see Metzger, *Recherches*, 78–79. The importance of the type was seen by H. Herter, *De Dis Atticis Priapi Similibus* (Diss. Bonn 1926), 16–19; *RE* s.v. *Phallos* 1692 f.; but the stony setting surely shows, against him, that Hermes (cf. n. 60 above) rather than other ithyphallic Attic gods is intended. Wooden ithyphallic figures: see H. Herter, *De Priapo* (Giessen 1932), 163–201; the herm on Epiktetos' cup (below) must be of wood (Jameson, in Murray/Price, *Greek City*, 194); for wooden Pans see (?) Cratinus fr. 75 K/A.

[65] But cf. Goldman's interesting suggestion, above, n. 60.

[66] Cf. n. 56 above. (But Zanker, *Wandel der Hermesgestalt*, 92, ascribes the appearance of herms on vases merely to a new interest in everyday scenes, perhaps rightly in the main.) The virtual fixity of the type in the fifth cent. also argues the influence of a dominant model, as has often been noted. But the inscription Ἵπαρχος καλός on a cup by Epiktetos which shows a hermoglyph at work (Boardman, *Red Figure: Archaic*, pl. 74: *LIMC* s.v. *Hermes*, no. 170) is scarcely of significance, given that some dozen vases of various theme by the painter are so inscribed (*aliter* Shapiro, *Art and Cult*, 126).

[67] Cf. Harrison, *Agora* XI.129–34; D. Willers, *Zu den Anfängen der archaistischen Plastik in Griechenland* (*AM-BH* 4, 1975), 33–47.

can only speculate. On one attractive view, the Athenians were less callow than Herodotus supposed. Pisistratus' entry was not a trick but a piece of theatre; Phye was, as it were, an actress playing Athena, and the spectators, not deceived, went along with the fiction as an expression of the truth that Pisistratus was the man of the hour for Athena's city. If this is so, we gain a lovely insight into the symbolic resources through which events of high importance might be expressed, in this, the 'histrionic' age of Greek culture.[68]

Both on this occasion and when he first seized power, Pisistratus' target was the acropolis, the mystic centre of the city as well, of course, as its fortress. Many scholars suppose that, having arrived there, Pisistratus will have stayed; and though the chief attraction of the place would doubtless have been security, he would also have been maintaining a claim, by so abnormal a residence, to a very special relationship with the goddess. The development of Athena's citadel in the sixth century must certainly take on a new significance, if it also harboured Pisistratus.[69] In its strong form, that Pisistratus and his sons lived permanently on the acropolis, this thesis cannot be proved; all we know for certain is that he 'secured the acropolis' initially, as anyone attempting a *coup* at Athens had necessarily to do. But the family unquestionably kept firm control of it as a place of potential refuge. In a revealing phrase in the *Constitution of the Athenians*, the Pisistratids' final departure is spoken of as 'surrendering the acropolis to the Athenians'. Some Athenians must, before that, have had complicated feelings about the growing splendours of a citadel that was not wholly their own.[70]

Another form of symbolic manipulation with which Pisistratus has been credited concerns myth. His influence has been seen behind the great popularity of certain themes in the vase-painting of the period; in particular, it is suggested that the pair 'Heracles aided by Athena' dominates the iconography of the age because Pisistratus presented himself as a second Heracles, no less dear to the goddess

---

[68] Hdt. 1.60; cf. Arist. *Ath. Pol.* 14.4; Clidemus *FGrH* 323 F 15. For a full discussion, and the interpretation mentioned here, see W. R. Connor, *JHS* 107 (1987), 42–47 (who cites the phrase 'histrionic period' from G. F. Else); so too R. H. Sinos, 'Divine Selection', in C. Dougherty and L. Kurke eds., *Cultural Poetics in Ancient Greece* (Cambridge 1993), 73–91, at 86: Pisistratus 'created a heroic model that the Athenians willingly accepted'.

[69] Cf. n. 18 above.

[70] The relevant texts are Hdt. 1.59–60, Arist. *Ath. Pol.* 14.1 ('securing'); Hdt. 5.90 (oracles left on the acropolis by the Pisistratids when expelled); Arist. *Ath. Pol.* 15.4 (Pisistratus addresses the people from near the entrance to the acropolis) and 19.6 ('surrendering')—cf. Kolb, 'Baupolitik', 104–106 [+]. The Pisistratids were in fact blockaded in the acropolis just before their final departure, but in its rhetorical context 'surrendering the acropolis' refers to more than this.

than the first. But the theory appears to work neither chronologically, nor in terms of the logic of communication: the relevant scenes begin too early and end too late, and they do not force the viewer to look beyond Heracles to Pisistratus in the way that effective propaganda would need to do. A broader background of wistful aristocratic imagining lies behind the sixth-century fame of Heracles, that hero who through the exercise of virtue won godhead and union with Youth.[71] It is much more plausible to detect a particular design behind a different phenomenon, Theseus' rise to new glory. Theseus was, it is true, already clearly the most heroic of Attic heroes on the François vase early in the century,[72] but near its end he is suddenly credited by vase-painters with a whole cycle of hitherto unattested labours, a match for those of Heracles. An obvious supposition is that the hero came in with the democracy, whose champion and founder he was later supposed to be, and he duly shares with Heracles the metopes of the Athenian treasury at Delphi, the first monumental work certainly to be dated after the tyranny. But most art historians feel that the first illustrations of the new cycle on vases begin just too early, during the last Pisistratid years, and it is rather artificial to suggest that they represent a first signal of ideological revolt by the tyrants' exiled opponents.[73] It was perhaps rather through the patronage of the cultivated Hipparchus that an epic *Theseis* came into existence, which in turn inspired the vase-painters. Tyrants could be concerned to see their states adorned with suitable heroes, as the activities of Clisthenes of

[71] For the theory (of John Boardman) and its critics (particularly W. G. Moon and R. Osborne) see J. M. Cook, *JHS* 107 (1987), 167–69 [+]; add now Boardman's answer, *JHS* 109 (1989), 158–59, and Blok's further critique, *BABesch* 65 (1990), 17–28 (for bibliog. see too *LIMC* V.1, 1990, 189). For a less political view of Heracles' apotheosis see A. Verbanck-Piérard in C. Bérard, C. Bron, and A. Pomari eds., *Images et société en Grèce ancienne* (Lausanne 1987), 187–99. Political explanations do not seem necessary either for the developments in Dionysiac imagery in this period, which are discussed, sometimes in these terms, by S. Angiolillo, *DialArch* NS 3 (1981), 13–22; L. Gasparri in *LIMC* s.v. *Dionysos*, 499–503; T. H. Carpenter, *Dionysian Imagery in Archaic Greek Art* (Oxford 1986); contrast W. R. Connor, *ClMed* 40 (1989), 14, n. 24, and, on one detail, G. M. Hedreen, *Silens in Attic Black-Figure Vase-Painting* (Michigan 1992), 88 f.

[72] Cf. Robertson, *History*, 125–26, and following note.

[73] For a good *mise au point* see C. Sourvinou-Inwood, *JHS* 91 (1971), 97–99 [+]; cf. most recently J. Neils, *The Youthful Deeds of Theseus* (Rome 1987), 143–51; but against the Alcmaeonid hypothesis see Vidal-Naquet, *Black Hunter*, 322, n. 77 (402, n. 87 in the French edn.). The older view that associates the promotion of Theseus with Pisistratus is still supported by Herter, 'Theseus', 1046 f. and Shapiro, *Art and Cult*, 146 (and cf. n. 75 below). One can, of course, deny Pisistratus' responsibility for the postulated *Theseis* and still acknowledge that he may have taken some interest in the hero (why should he not?). He tampered with texts to improve the hero's reputation, according to Hereas of Megara (*FGrH* 486 F 1 *ap.* Plut. *Thes.* 20, citing Hes. fr. 298 Merkelbach/West), whom, however, we are not obliged to believe (Sourvinou-Inwood, *JHS* 91, 1971, 98). Aristotle's reference to a Pisistratean Theseum in *Ath. Pol.* 15.4 is probably an anachronism (see Rhodes ad loc.).

Sicyon, who expelled the Argive hero Adrastus from the *agora*,[74] notoriously show. If this is so, it is of course striking that Theseus' fresh laurels were not blasted by the revolution that followed so soon. But this is a problem only if one assumes that the Theseus of the *Theseis* was manifestly a hero of party rather than of country, a Pisistratus retrojected.[75] A truly Athenian hero, as valorous as Heracles but more useful to society[76]—there was no reason for tyranny to cherish such a vision more than democracy, or democracy more than tyranny. It was probably in the same late Pisistratid period that the famous coin-type showing Athena and her owl, another potent national symbol, was struck for the first time.[77]

Beyond a doubt, the perpetual reshaping of mythology, that process without beginning or end, had many further consequences in the period. The problem is to identify them. The complaints of the deserted Thracian princess Phyllis to Theseus' son Demophon, recorded in one of Ovid's most desperate *Heroides*, probably owe their ultimate origin to Athens' colonizing activities in the Thracian Chersonese, which began in the sixth century with the expedition of Miltiades.[78] Similarly, other places with which Athens was involved politically at this time, such as Delos and Megara and Salamis, were also associated with her mythologically. But, as Athenian preoccupation with Thrace continued for the next two centuries, we cannot pin down a moment when the myth of Demophon's Thracian visit must have emerged; and a similar doubt affects the other cases.[79] These stories have, perhaps, a political context, but not a date.

[74] Hdt. 5.67. Epic *Theseis*: a mere hypothesis, of course, rejected e.g. by Neils, *Youthful Deeds*, 11–12 (with an argument from the silence of Pherecydes).

[75] For this view see still M. P. Nilsson, *Cults, Myths, Oracles and Politics in Ancient Greece* (Lund 1951), 51–56; W. R. Connor in A. G. Ward ed., *The Quest for Theseus* (London 1970), 143–74; contrast Calame, *Thésée*, 403–406, 424: 'probablement indépendamment de la volonté politique d'un parti singulier, le récit de l'adolescence de Thésée véhicule les aspirations d'Athènes à contrôler, en y introduisant sa civilisation, le territoire de l'Attique et celui de ses voisins'.

[76] So Isoc. *Hel*. 23–25.

[77] See Kraay, *Greek Coins*, 60–61; J. H. Kroll, *ANSMN* 26 (1981), 24; Kroll and N. M. Waggoner, *AJA* 88 (1984), 331–33; and Lewis in *CAH*² IV.2 (1988), 290 f. Kroll stresses the commercial reasons for which a standard type was essential.

[78] Cf. Robert, *Heldensage*, 1484–87; Kron, *Phylenheroen*, 142–45; Kearns, *Heroes of Attica*, 88–89. The first hint of the myth is in Aeschin. 2.31 (where, as often, the relevant Theseid is Akamas), but Kron rightly stresses that the non-Athenian Stesichorus took Demophon to Egypt on the way from Troy (*PMG* 193); she wonders about epic *nostoi*.

[79] K. Friis Johansen's case that Theseus' association with Delos is not attested by a scene on the François vase (*LIMC* III.1, 1056, no. 48) but was first created by Pisistratus (*Thésée et la danse à Délos*, Copenhagen 1945, esp. 58–61) remains controversial: see e.g. H. Gallet de Santerre, *Délos primitive et archaïque* (Paris 1958), 182 f. and discussions cited by Herter, 'Theseus', 1143; Shapiro, *Art and Cult*, 146; Smarczyk, *Religionspolitik*, 470, n. 181 (Calame, *Thésée*, 428, down-dates the association even to the fifth cent.). The interpenetration of Megarian and Attic genealogy (see esp. Soph. fr. 24 Radt), often taken to reflect their

Floating oracles and oracle-mongers, so familiar a feature of later Athenian life, are first attested at the Pisistratid court. The tyrants were evidently enthusiasts. Pisistratus' nickname 'Bakis' must reflect his devotion to the prophecies of that ancient seer, and even when Onomacritus, 'arranger' of the oracles of Musaeus, was detected in a forgery, the estrangement between him and the Pisistratids that ensued was only temporary. When the tyranny fell, a clutch of oracles was found which Hippias had stowed away on the acropolis.[80] By contrast, no public consultation of Delphi is attested throughout the Pisistratid period; and it was the hostility of the Pythia, spurred on by the exiled Alcmaeonids, that, according to Herodotus, brought the dynasty down in the end. The inference that the Pisistratids shunned and mistrusted Delphi has often been drawn.[81]

The foreign religious centre with which the Pisistratids were associated was not Delphi but Delos.[82] According to Herodotus, Pisistratus 'purified the island in accordance with the oracles', by removing all graves from within view of the precinct. It is likely that he also commissioned a small sixth-century limestone temple, of Attic materials and construction.[83] The Athenians, inhabitants of 'the most ancient land of Ionia', in Solon's phrase, had probably been sending official representatives to the ancient *panegyreis* of the

sixth-cent. conflicts, is seen as a Mycenaean memory by Kron, *Phylenheroen*, 107–109 (doubts too in Kearns, *Heroes of Attica*, 115–17). The myths associating Athenians (Teucer, the Theseids) with Cyprus (Robert, *Heldensage*, 1478–84; Kron, *Phylenheroen*, 144; Kearns, *Heroes of Attica*, 88–89) raise similar problems. All these instances are ascribed to sixth-cent. myth-making by Nilsson *Cults, Myths, Oracles*, 49–59. On the myths concerning Salamis see Shapiro, *Art and Cult*, 154–57.

[80] Suda β 47: Βάκις· ἐπίθετον Πεισιστράτου; Hdt. 7.6.3–4, 5.90.2 (cf. 93); cf. Lewis in *CAH*² IV.2 (1988), 294. Other passages linking the Pisistratids with prophecy or prophetic dreams (Hdt. 1.62.4; 5.56; 6.107) are of a kind that can attach, in Herodotus, to any powerful figure.

[81] Hdt. 5.62–63; cf. e.g. J. Bousquet, *BCH* 80 (1956), 570; J. Boardman, *RA* 1978, 234; W. G. Forrest in *CAH*² III.3 (1982), 316—'Pisistratus resigned the Delphic whip' (!). But C. W. Hedrick Jr., *AJA* 92 (1988), 206, observes that this evidence, such as it is, only relates to the final Pisistratid years; and cf. Lewis in *CAH*² IV.2 (1988), 294. The rumour reported in Σ Pind. *Pyth.* 7.9b that the Pisistratids set fire to the temple at Delphi was invented, I conceive, by a reader of Hdt. 5.62–63. For a possible allusion to Delphi (via the hero Delphos) on a hemidrachm, perhaps of the first year of the democracy, see Kroll, *ANSMN* 26 (1981), 25–26.

[82] Cf. Gallet de Santerre, *Délos primitive*, 297–311; Forrest in *CAH*² III.3 (1982), 257–59 (cf. J. Boardman in III.1, 769 f.); Smarczyk, *Religionspolitik*, 466–71.

[83] Hdt. 1.64.2 (the source of the oracles is unknown); cf. Thuc. 3.104. On the temple see Bruneau/Ducat, *Guide de Délos*, 128, no. 11 [+] (where a late sixth-cent. date is not excluded); it is less important than used to be believed, now that it is no longer thought (cf. ibid. 120–23) to be the first temple of all on the site.

Ionians on Delos since at least Solon's time.[84] We can still recover something of the context of Pisistratus' more direct intervention. The Delians probably always had to rely on foreign patrons to adorn their sacred island in a way worthy of the god. In the immediately preceding period, the dominant influence, to judge from dedications, had been that of powerful Naxos. Since Pisistratus had recently 'subdued Naxos by force and entrusted it to Lygdamis'[85] (his Naxian associate), it was not unnatural that he should now stand forth as a chief patron of the shrine. Piety towards the Delian Apollo seems indeed to have become a competitive sport, among those who sought to control the waters in which his birthplace lay. (Even Datis the Mede was later to join in.) Polycrates of Samos 'dedicated' the nearby island of Rheneia to the god, attaching it to Delos by a chain; and he had supposedly only recently celebrated an opulent Delian festival when he died.[86] The sacred place served as a showcase for the pious magnificence of Ionian tyrants. In form, no doubt, their benefactions were gifts and services received with gratitude by the Delian people (or by 'the Amphictyons', if such a body existed[87]). But one suspects that, in the event of resistance, the tyrants might have put their duty to Apollo above the particular wishes of the Delians.

With pious magnificence we have come back to our starting-point, the construction of fine new temples. In archaic Greece, religion was

[84] See Polemon fr. 78 Preller *ap.* Ath. 234e–f (= Solon fr. 88 Ruschenbusch): ἐν δὲ τοῖς κύρβεσι τοῖς περὶ τῶν Δηλιαστῶν οὕτως γέγραπται· 'καὶ τὼ κήρυκε ἐκ τοῦ γένους τῶν Κηρύκων τοῦ τῆς μυστηριώτιδος. τούτους δὲ παρασιτεῖν ἐν τῷ Δηλίῳ ἐνιαυτόν'. 'Solon's phrase': fr. 4a 2 West, and on Ion's association with Athens see now Hesiod fr. 10a 20–23 in the edn. of F. Solmsen, R. Merkelbach, and M. L. West (2nd edn., Oxford 1983), 227. On the very complicated issue of the development of Athens' claim to be mother city of Ionia see the excellent account of Smarczyk, *Religionspolitik*, 328–84. According to Mimnermus (fr. 9 West), Colophon was settled by emigrants from 'Neleian Pylos': Smarczyk stresses, 339 f., that the tradition whereby Neleids also settled in Athens (a precondition for the key divergence whereby the Neleids of Ionia came not directly from Pylos but via Athens: see first Pherecydes *FGrH* 3 F 155) is already implied by the genealogical claims of individual Athenian families around 600 BC (see esp. Hdt. 5.65.3–4). He also argues forcefully from Hdt. 1.145–46 that pure Athenian origin was claimed as a title of nobility by Ionian cities themselves in the late sixth cent. (and perhaps earlier).

[85] Hdt. 1.64.2.

[86] Thuc. 1.13.6, 3.104.2; Suda τ 175, π 3128, s.vv. ταὐτά σοι καὶ Πύθια καὶ Δήλια and Πύθια καὶ Δήλια; cf. H. W. Parke, *CQ* 40 (1946), 105–108, and, on the festival as perhaps the occasion for *Hymn Hom. Ap.*, W. Burkert in *Papers on the Amasis Painter and his World* (Malibu 1987), 53–54 [+]. Datis: Hdt. 6.97.

[87] Delian 'Amphictyons' first appear in the late fifth cent. (*IG* I³.1459–61: 1460 is Tod, *GHI* I.85), when Delian administrative documents first appear. They are always Athenian, except for a brief period in the fourth century when Andrians are also found (cf. Rhodes, *Commentary Ath. Pol.*, on 62.2). A body of 'Amphictyons' recruited from a single state is a monstrosity: it seems more likely that these false Amphictyons are descendants of true ones (cf. Thuc. 3. 104, περικτιόνων) than that the title was created in the fifth century as a cloak for Athenian domination (cf. Smarczyk, *Religionspolitik*, 476, n. 193 [+]).

the sphere of public activity *par excellence*, and the ceremonials through which status was put on display were almost all associated with worship. One could scarcely, therefore, be magnificent without also being pious. It is a characteristic detail that the assassination of Hipparchus occurred while he and Hippias were engaged in marshalling the Panathenaic procession,[88] a duty they must have undertaken by choice. The reason was surely not merely that power needs to clothe itself in pomp. The opportunity of organizing the Panathenaic procession, of presiding authoritatively over the city's display of its own magnificence, was itself one of the sweetest fruits of power.

ANNEXE: NEW AND UPDATED FESTIVALS IN THE SIXTH CENTURY

The *Panathenaea* were, beyond all question, remodelled in the second quarter of the sixth century. One late source gives the credit to Pisistratus, while others incompatibly mention a particular year, 566/5, or a particular archonship, that of Hippoclides, which is otherwise undated but could certainly coincide with 566/5.[89] Vexatious discrepancy: but the specific date seems less likely to be an invention than the association with the famous Pisistratus. Whoever was responsible for it, the central element in the reform was the establishment of the *'Greater' Panathenaea*, held every four years, as an athletic festival of Panhellenic appeal. Important musical competitions too were introduced, either at the time of the main reform or not long afterwards, as vases reveal; somewhat later, Hipparchus is said to have either introduced or regulated performances of Homer by rhapsodes.[90] The new athletic programme was probably built round an existing nucleus of local games, in particular the hazardous

[88] Thuc. 1.20.2, 6.57; Arist. *Ath. Pol.* 18.3.

[89] Pisistratus: *Σ* Ael. Arist. *Panath.* 189, p. 323.29 Dindorf, also printed under Aristotle fr. 637 Rose. Introduction of the *agon gymnicus* in 566/5: Jerome/Eusebius 01.53.3 p.102b 4–5 Helm. Hippoclides: Vit. Marcellinus Thuc.3 = Pherecydes *FGrH* 3 F 2; cf. Jacoby on Istrus *FGrH* 334 F 4 (who, n. 1, dismisses the *Σ*'s attribution to Pisistratus as an 'autoschediasm'); J. A. Davison, *From Archilochus to Pindar* (London 1968), 28–69 (from *JHS* 78, 1958, 23–42; 82, 1962, 141–42). Further proofs of the change are the dedication by the [ἱεροποιοί] who τὸν δρόμον [ἐποίεσαν] and τὸν ἀ]γῶ[να θέσ]αν πρῶτοι γλαυκόπιδι κόρει: *IG* I³.507, *CEG* 434 (cf. *IG* I³.508–509); and the emergence of the prize amphorae. For bibliog. on the *Panathenaea* see N. Robertson, *RhM* 128 (1985), 232, n. 2, adding now J. Neils ed., *Goddess and Polis* (Hanover 1992) and S. V. Tracy, 'The Panathenaic Festival and Games: An Epigraphic Enquiry', *Nikephoros* 4 (1991), 133–53; best factually are L. Ziehen, *RE* s.v. *Panathenaia*, 457–89 (1949), and Tracy, 'Panathenaic Festival'.

[90] [Pl.] *Hipparch.* 228b; cf. H. A. Shapiro, 'Mousikoi agones: Music and Poetry at the Panathenaea', in Neils ed., *Goddess and Polis*, 53–75.

competition of *apobatai*, who jumped on or off moving chariots.[91] In its new form the festival was evidently modelled on other Panhellenic biennial or quadrennial festivals—the *Pythia*, *Isthmia*, and *Nemea*—that had been founded or refounded in the 580s or 570s. But the prize offered to the Panathenaic competitors was, no doubt deliberately, ostentatiously Athenian. 'In earth burnt in fire . . . the fruit of the olive-tree . . . in the richly decorated walls of jars', Pindar calls it: olive-oil pressed from the sacred olive-trees of Athena, contained in choice products of the newly dominant Attic ceramic-industry (this too subject to Athena's care), the famous Panathenaic prize amphorae. By the fourth century, at least 1,400 such amphorae were awarded at each celebration, the victor in the chariot-race receiving no less than 140.[92] Was it as patroness of the games that Athena received her title of Athena Nike, first attested and perhaps first created at about this time?[93] It has been objected that Athena Nike confers victory in war and not in sport.[94] If the objection is correct, a point of some theoretical interest emerges: within the composite figure Athena Nike, Athena, the goddess of war, remains dominant over Nike, patroness of victory in every sphere. Thus a competitor in Athena's games would not have felt able to pray for victory to Athena Victory. The conclusion is a little bizarre,[95] though it is true that actual dedications by grateful victors have not been found. But whether or not competitions were theoretically within Athena Nike's purview, one may wonder whether a public cult established to celebrate the great new games would have given her just this title (rather than say 'Panathenaic' Athena). Success in war, by contrast, was the commonest occasion for the foundation of cults of every kind: the likelihood must be that the cult of Athena Nike was created or expanded in commemoration of such a victory.

[91] Cf. P. E. Corbett, *JHS* 80 (1960), 58; note the 'Horse-head' amphorae (early sixth cent.), possibly prizes in proto-*Panathenaea* (Boardman, *Black Figure*, 17 f.). Possible *apobatai* in LG art: *AA* 78 (1963), 224; K. Fittschen, *Untersuchungen zum Beginn der Sagendarstellungen bei den Griechen* (Berlin 1969), 27 f.; E. Simon, *Die griechischen Vasen* (Munich 1976), 39 [+]; cf. in general Kyle, *Athletics in Athens*, 22–24, and note G. Ferrari, *JHS* 107 (1987), 182 (? seventh-cent. evidence).

[92] Pind. *Nem.* 10.35–36; cf. A. W. Johnston, '*IG* II².2311 and the Number of Panathenaic Amphorae', *BSA* 82 (1987), 125–30 (for Athena's care cf. *LIMC* s.v. *Athena*, 962, nos. 40–42); on the collection of the oil, Arist. *Ath. Pol.* 60, with Rhodes. (Were the sacred trees first identified, and taxed, now?) For some events, by contrast, there were large cash-prizes.

[93] See n. 11 above; for the suggested link with the games see Raubitschek, *Dedications*, 359.

[94] See C. J. Herington, *Athena Parthenos and Athena Polias* (Manchester 1955), 41, n. 2; Graf, *Nordionische Kulte*, 214–17; Mark, *Athena Nike*, 125–28; and in general on Athena Nike, R. Lonis, *Guerre et religion en Grèce à l'époque classique* (Paris 1979), 234–38.

[95] In Ar. *Eq.* 581–94 Athena is asked to 'bring with her' the Nike of poetic competitions. (Dedications to Athena by victors are in fact quite numerous—*IG* I³.597, ? 598, 823, 880, 893—but none addresses her specifically as Athena Nike.)

The *Greater Panathenaea* contained other elements besides the games, including tribal competitions and, of course, the procession, sacrifice, and presentation of a robe so familiar from the Parthenon frieze. The procession is the supreme example in the Greek world of civic pageantry, of a society on display before itself and the rest of Greece. And that society displayed itself comprehensively, since this was the 'all-Athenian' festival. (According to legend, the original name *Athenaea* was changed to *Panathenaea* by Theseus at the time of the synoecism.[96]) In the fifth century, all sections of society and representatives from all Attica took part. What is quite unknown is the extent to which the sixth-century reform affected, or was responsible for, these civic aspects of the festival.[97] The Panathenaic procession in its familiar form is obviously unthinkable outside the context of the developed *polis*, with its civic consciousness and pride. But processions of some kind had probably always existed, as a way of involving a whole group (a village, for instance) in a rite. Such homespun events had certainly begun to be transformed into a form of elaborate display by the mid-sixth century, as we see from a cheerful band-cup showing a sacrificial procession approaching an altar of Athena: hoplites march as hoplites, cavalrymen ride, musicians walk ahead. . .[98] Here are the beginnings of 'pomp' (a word that derives directly, of course, from *pompe*, 'procession'). It is very likely that the *Panathenaea* became more pompous in 566 (as it must certainly have continued to do throughout the fifth century), since Athens was now on display before the rest of Greece.[99] Perhaps the processional route through the *agora* dates from this time.[100] But it is also very likely that a Panathenaic procession of some kind, not necessarily lacking in pomp, antedated 566. What a picture of the Athenians' changing sense of themselves the history of

[96] Paus. 8.2.1; cf. Istrus *FGrH* 334 F 4, with Jacoby.

[97] On the festival before the reform see in particular A. Brelich, *Paides e Parthenoi* (Rome 1969), 312–48; and also (much more speculative) Robertson, *RhM* 128 (1985), 231–95; id., *Festivals and Legends*, 90–119.

[98] *Pompai* and *polis*: see F. Bömer in *RE* s.v. *Pompe*, 1892–94; and in general R. Lane Fox, *Pagans and Christians* (Harmondsworth 1986), 66–68, 80–82; Price, *Rituals and Power*, 100–102. Primitive *pompai*: see e.g. above, Ch. 3, n. 13, on mountain cults; and esp. Ar. *Ach.* 237–79 (though admittedly there may have been some imitation of civic *pompai* at humbler levels). Band-cup (private collection, Basle): see e.g. Simon, *Götter*, 193; ead., *Festivals*, pls. 16.2, 17.2; *LIMC* s.v. *Athena*, 1010, no. 574; cf. Shapiro, *Art and Cult*, 29–31, with pl. 9, and in general K. Lehnstaedt, *Prozessionsdarstellungen auf attischen Vasen* (Diss. Munich 1970).

[99] Cf. James Boswell on the Lord Mayor's dinner of 1772: 'It was truly a superb entertainment, and made the metropolis of Great Britain appear in a respectable light' (Journal for 20 Apr. 1772). For one change in the fifth cent. see Arist. *Ath. Pol.* 18.4.

[100] See Travlos, *Pictorial Dictionary*, 422–27, 477–81. On topographical questions see the studies of Robertson, *RhM* 128 (1985) and *Festivals and Legends*; note too van Steuben, in Weber ed., *Idee, Gestalt, Geschichte* (n. 22).

the Panathenaic procession would reveal—if only it could be written.[101]

The *City Dionysia* was, by the fifth century, the other civic festival *par excellence*, it too the occasion of a spectacular procession.[102] It was, of course, the showcase for tragedy.[103] Was it also created for tragedy, or was an existing festival adapted to accommodate tragedy? No source offers an explicit statement, though Thucydides and the Aristotelian *Constitution of the Athenians* treat it as a relatively young festival.[104] It declares by its name that it is a city equivalent to the *Rural Dionysia* of the Attic demes (as the only such case, it has a special interest in any study of religious centralization); and some of the ritual elements that it contains—the phallic procession and perhaps the revel (*komos*)—have parallels in the country ceremonies.[105] But it was celebrated three months after them, in March, and was thus not just one local celebration among many but a pan-Attic festival which countrymen could enjoy without being obliged to forsake the *Dionysia* of their own deme. March is an ideal month in Greece for open-air performances, and one can argue that it was to accommodate these that a city equivalent to the old country festival was newly created on an artificial date. On the other side, it may be said that inhabitants of the city are likely always to have had their own *Dionysia*; and that the city festival contains one element, a ritual introduction and reception of Dionysus, which has no attested rustic equivalent but reflects a fundamental ritual and mythical perception of Dionysus as a god who comes from afar, a god of advents.[106] One might wish to see here a trace of a *City Dionysia* that antedated tragedy; it seems probable at all events that more was added to the *Rural Dionysia* than just the new genre when the *City Dionysia* was created.

Most histories of Attic drama assure us that Pisistratus gave the festival its familiar form, in the year 534. But this traditional assumption has recently been shown to be very weakly founded. The

---

[101] Cf. e.g. D. Cannadine, 'The Transformation of Civic Ritual in Modern Britain: The Colchester Oyster Feast', *Past and Present* 94 (1982), 107–30.

[102] See Pickard-Cambridge, *Dramatic Festivals*², 57–70; on its civic character, 58–59. On the growth of literary festivals in Attica in the sixth cent. see C. J. Herington, *Poetry into Drama* (Berkeley 1985), 79–99.

[103] And also for dithyramb; but C. Sourvinou-Inwood, 'Something to Do with Athens: Tragedy and Ritual', in *Ritual, Finance, Politics*, 269–90, at 276–77, argues strongly from the rectangular shape of the earliest theatres that tragedy came first.

[104] Thuc. 2.15.4 (by implication); Arist. *Ath. Pol.* 56.5, with 3.3. and 57.1.

[105] See e.g. Deubner, *Attische Feste*, 134–38. For a recent but unconvincing revival of the view that the *City Dionysia* is calqued not on the *Rural Dionysia* but on the *Lenaea* see Kolb, *Agora und Theater*, 75–78 [+].

[106] See Sourvinou-Inwood's important study 'Something to Do with Athens', esp. 274.

official record of victories at the festival apparently began in the last decade of the century, or at most a few years earlier.[107] It is true that, according to the Parian marble, 'Thespis first won a prize' in 534 or thereabouts; but the apparent precision of this and other such dates offered for early dramatic performances is a product of Hellenistic calculation, not archival research,[108] and we do not know at what festival Thespis might have been competing.[109] As far as direct testimony goes, therefore, the young democracy has more claim to the credit of bringing tragedy to the city than does Pisistratus.[110] The first archaeological remains in the precinct of Dionysus beside the theatre appear to date from somewhere in the period 550–500, perhaps closer to its beginning than its end.[111] But even if the dating could be made more secure, we would have no compelling reason to believe that precinct and festival were founded at the same date.

But what of Eleutherae? The image of the god that was at the centre of the ritual had supposedly been brought to Athens from this settlement in the frontier-zone between Athens and Boeotia; and it is very widely believed that the festival was established after the incorporation of Eleutherae into the Attic state and in a sense in celebration of it.[112] The source of this belief is a passage in Pausanias:

The boundary [of Boeotia] with Attica used to be at Eleutherae. But the people of Eleutherae came over to the Athenians, and so Cithaeron is now the boundary of Boeotia. It was not because of military pressure that they came over, but out of desire for Athenian citizenship and hatred for the Thebans. In the plain there is a shrine of Dionysus, and the ancient image

---

[107] See Pickard-Cambridge, *Dramatic Festivals*², 102, and M. L. West, *CQ* NS 39 (1989), 251, n. 1, on *IG* II².2318.

[108] See West, *CQ* NS 39 (1989), 251–54.

[109] So already Pickard-Cambridge, *Dramatic Festivals*², 72; W. R. Connor, 'City Dionysia and Athenian Democracy', *ClMed* 40 (1989), 7–32 (also available in Connor *et al.*, *Aspects of Athenian Democracy*, Copenhagen 1990) adds (26–32) that the supposed specification that Thespis won 'in the city' rests on a completely unreliable 'reading' in *Marmor Parium FGrH* 239 A 43.

[110] A case strongly urged by Connor, 'City Dionysia'. But Sourvinou-Inwood ('Something to Do with Athens') argues from the elements in the festival that are not tribally organized that it should antedate Clisthenes.

[111] See A. W. Pickard-Cambridge, *The Theatre of Dionysus in Athens* (Oxford 1946), 3–4; Boersma, *Building Policy*, 137, 189; Travlos, *Pictorial Dictionary*, 537. On the ill-preserved pediment fragment, showing an ithyphallic satyr and a maenad, which may come from this building see Floren, *Griechische Plastik I*, 243, n. 37 [+], and esp. E. Coche de la Ferté, in *Mélanges Charles Picard*, II (= *RA*, 6th ser., 29–30, 1948 [1949]), 196–206 (date ? *c.*540); for a lower date see Connor, 'City Dionysia', 24–26.

[112] But Pickard-Cambridge, *Dramatic Festivals*², 57–58, is yet again an exception, as is Sourvinou-Inwood, 'Something to Do with Athens', 273–75, whom I follow.

was brought to Athens from there. The image now at Eleutherae is a copy of that one.[113]

Not surprisingly, Pausanias has been taken to be saying that the image was brought to Athens only after Eleutherae had become Athenian. But there also existed a story telling how a missionary, Pegasus of Eleutherae, brought an image of Dionysus to Athens but was spurned; the god punished the Athenians by afflicting them with a disease of the genitals that was only cured, on Apollo's advice, by preparing phalli 'publicly and privately' 'in commemoration of the affliction'. That, of course, is in large part a characteristic myth of resistance to the advent of Dionysus, which one would naturally ascribe to the mythological period. And Pegasus is also set in the distant past by the most obvious interpretation of another passage of Pausanias.[114] No source, by contrast, explicitly places the bringing of the image in the historical period. It looks as if first appearances were misleading and Pausanias implied no chronological relation between this introduction and the accession of Eleutherae itself to Athens. It would in fact have been a uniquely graceless response on the part of the Athenians to carry off their new dependants' most precious relic to Athens.[115]

No source connects these events: but should we? Is any aspect of the myth or festival of Dionysus Eleuthereus, is the very fact that they existed, hard to explain other than on the hypothesis that Eleutherae had only recently come under Athenian control? But it is not in these terms that other Athenian cults of gods with local epithets—Apollo Pythios or Delios, Athena Itonia and the rest—are to be interpreted. Eleutherae claimed to be the birthplace of Dionysus, and a second celebrated cult of the god, as Melanaigis, was perhaps located there.[116] For the Athenians, Dionysus Eleuthereus was

---

[113] 1.38.8; cf. 1.20.3 for the location of this image in the old sanctuary beside the theatre. On the site of Eleutherae (probably modern Gyphtokastro) see most recently J. Ober, *Fortress Attica* (Leiden 1985), 223.

[114] Σ Ar. *Ach.* 243a (it is scarcely a counter-case to the location in the mythological period that something similar appears in the Archilochus legend, *SEG* XV 517 A col. iii); Paus. 1.2.5 (which should set Pegasus before Amphictyon).

[115] To judge at any rate from the remarks on statue seizure in Paus. 8.46: the topic needs more investigation.

[116] Birthplace: Diod. 3.66.1. (Or Dionysus founded Eleutherae: ibid. 4.2.6.) Note too the reference in fr. 203 Nauck of Eur. *Antiope*, a play set in or near Eleutherae, to a στῦλος εὐίου θεοῦ; perhaps the 'pillar-Dionysus' was associated with the region (Simon, *Festivals*, 103). The numerous finds of fifth-cent. Boeotian kantharoi in the region have been associated with the cult (*SEG* XXX 36). Melanaigis: our reports about this cult almost all come as a subsidiary *aition* within the aetiological myth, set in north-west Attica, of the *Apatouria* (cf. Vidal-Naquet, *Black Hunter*, 109 f.; the sources are conveniently printed in F. J. Fernandez Nieto, *Los acuerdos bélicos en la antigua Grecia* II, Santiago de Compostela, 1975, 15–18). The uncertainty is whether the cult belongs to the *Apatouria* (as e.g. *Anecd. Bekk.* I.417.32 states,

surely above all Dionysus in a peculiarly potent and authentic form. (Does the analogy hold? Is Dionysus 'Eleuthereus' as potent as 'Pythian' Apollo? These things are hard to measure. . .) The myth and associated ritual have no features that demand a special, historical explanation; the introduction of a cult by an intermediary bearing a statue is an unusual motif, particularly in the case of Dionysus, but not unique.[117] Some difficulties perhaps arise from our earlier argument that the *City Dionysia* is a wholly new festival created in the sixth century. Why should a new foundation at just this time choose to associate itself with the god of Eleutherae (who hitherto had *ex hypothesi* not been honoured at Athens)? Where indeed did the founders come by the ancient image supposedly introduced by Pegasus in mythological time? But these difficulties might be met on the view that a cult of Dionysus Eleuthereus in some form existed at Athens before the foundation of the *City Dionysia* in its familiar shape.

None of this discussion, we can now note, affects the narrow chronological question about the date of the first tragic festival; for even if the accession of Eleutherae were relevant, we do not know when that event in fact occurred.[118] So the question about tragedy's first patrons must remain tantalizingly unresolved.

The *Thargelia* is well known to modern scholars as the festival at which scapegoats were expelled. An Athenian of the fifth century would probably have thought first of dithyrambic choruses. As a festival of the arts it was perhaps second only to the *City Dionysia* in importance. As far as testimony is concerned, its history at Athens is

perhaps through confusion) or to north-west Attica; the partially independent tradition in Suda s.v. Μελαναίγιδα Διόνυσον, which associates the cult with Eleuther and his daughters, supports the latter view (so Wilamowitz, *AM* 33, 1908, 142; and cf. W. R. Halliday, *CR* 40, 1926, 179–81. Kolb, 'Baupolitik', 124, identifies the Dionysuses Eleuthereus and Melanaigis). Cf. in general Schachter, *Cults*, I.175.

[117] Sourvinou-Inwood, 'Something to Do with Athens', 274–75, cites the introduction of the cult of Artemis Tauropolos via her image (Eur. *IT* 1450–57), and the introduction of Dionysos Lysios to Sicyon by Phanes of Thebes (Paus. 2.7.6) in the mythological period. The extent to which the image's arrival from Eleutherae was evoked in the ritual is controversial: in Pausanias' day (1.29.2) the statue was taken out to the Academy (on the road thither), but Sourvinou-Inwood, 'Something to Do with Athens', 281–85, argues that the *eschara* from which the ephebes 'brought Dionysus in' in earlier texts (e.g. *SEG* XV. 104.15, of 127/6 BC; cf. Pickard-Cambridge, *Dramatic Festivals*², 60) was in the *agora*. The issue does not affect our argument here.

[118] A *terminus ante quem* is given by *IG* I³.1162.96–7 (M/L 48) of (?) 447 BC, where one 'Semichides Ἐλευθερᾶθεν' appears in a list of Athenian casualties. There was Atheno-Theban tension in 519 (Hdt. 6.108, Thuc. 3.68.5, to emend which is *petitio principii*, as Hornblower shows ad loc. [but D. Hennig, *Chiron* 22, 1992, 13–24, treats the whole tradition as a late construct]) and conflict in 506 (Hdt. 5.77; *IG* I³ 501 A); but earlier dates are not excluded. It is not decisive that Eleutherae was not a Clisthenic deme; no more was Salamis, though Athens certainly controlled it in 508 (so C. Ehrhardt, *Ancient History Bulletin*, 4/2, 1990, 23).

a blank, but as the artistic dithyramb is generally believed to be a creation of the sixth century, a reform must be postulated[119] by which such choruses were added to the ancient festival (possibly replacing choral performances of a different type). A case can then be made for dating the reform to the Pisistratid period: for the festival appears to have honoured Apollo Pythios, and it was in the Pythion—a sanctuary in which, as we have seen, Pisistratus and his family took an interest—that victors at the *Thargelia* dedicated their prize tripods.[120] If, however, the first performance of dithyramb at the *City Dionysia*, which honoured the genre's patronal god, Dionysus, was at some time between 510 and 500,[121] there is some awkwardness in supposing that it already formed a part of a festival of a different god a decade or more earlier. Possibly the reform belongs to the early years of the democracy.

Another god patronized by the Pisistratids, Zeus Olympios, had a festival of some magnificence, the *Olympieia*.[122] It is not attested until the fourth century, but may possibly have been founded by the tyrants in the sixth. We should at least consider the possibility that it was the tyrants who first introduced to Athens the formal worship of Zeus as Olympios and of Apollo as Pythios. These are very general titles of honour, well suited for gods intended to exercise, from their new precincts, a very general appeal. Having considered the possibility, we should probably reject it: for Thucydides believed both sanctuaries to be very ancient.[123]

Three further competitive festivals can be mentioned here, though they are, again, without directly recorded history: the *Eleusinia*, a musical and athletic competition (to be distinguished from the Mysteries) held at Eleusis; the *Herakleia*, a similar compe-

---

[119] See Hdt. 1.23 on Arion; cf. Pickard-Cambridge, *Dithyramb*, 19–21. Note too p. 8, on the role of the eponymous archon at the festival.

[120] Suda π 3130 s.v. Πύθιον (Deubner, *Attische Feste*, 198, n. 2); cf. *LSS* 14; Travlos, *Pictorial Dictionary*, figs. 131, 135–37; P. Amandry, 'Trépieds d'Athènes. II: Thargélies', *BCH* 101 (1977), 165–202. I cannot explain why Theophrastus, περὶ μέθης fr. 119 Wimmer (fr. 576 Fortenbaugh) *ap*. Ath. 424e–f, associates the festival with Apollo Delios. On the choruses (which earn but one sentence in nineteen pages on the festival in Deubner, *Attische Feste*) see Pickard-Cambridge, *Dithyramb*, 9–10 ('the development of the *Thargelia* as a popular festival may possibly have been due' to Pisistratus: cf. G. Ieranò, *QS* 36, 1992, 174), 51–53.

[121] See *Marmor Parium FGrH* 239 A 46; Connor, 'City Dionysia', 13; B. Zimmermann, *Dithyrambos* (Göttingen 1992), 36. So late a date for the first dithyramic competitions in any context, however, sits uneasily with Simonides' fifty-six victories (if that figure is reliable: see Page's discussion in *FGE*, 241–43), and cannot be counted secure—the genre could have moved to the *City Dionysia* from another festival of Dionysus.

[122] See Deubner, *Attische Feste*, 177. Attested elements are (?) an equestrian *pompe* and competitions, and large sacrifices. A Pisistratean origin for the festival is widely assumed (see the refs. in Robertson, *Festivals and Legends*, 139, n. 20: Robertson believes it to be older).

[123] Thuc. 2.15; cf. p. 8 above.

tition at Marathon; and from the city itself the little-known *Anakeia*. The two former were attended by good men from the rest of Greece, Pindar's clients, by the 60s of the fifth century; while a bronze vessel survives which was apparently offered as a prize at the *Anakeia* early in the century. The meeting at Marathon was perhaps promoted as a commemoration of the great victory of 490, in which Heracles had lent his aid. It was certainly reorganized not long after that, as we learn from an inscription; but it might already have risen to some prominence during the athletic boom of the sixth century. That claim can be made rather more confidently for the *Eleusinia*: the 'lovely running-course' which 'Alciphron as *archon* of the people of Athens' built 'for the sake of Demeter and long-robed Persephone', probably around the middle of the century, must surely have been intended for the festival.[124]

As we have seen, there was building-activity at the country sanctuaries in the Pisistratid period. The sixth century has in fact very regularly been viewed as a crucial epoch in the history of the cults at Brauron and Eleusis, which brought their incorporation for the first time into the religious system of Athens itself.[125] But we saw in Chapter 2 that there is no compelling reason to believe (nor, one must allow, to deny) that either cult had ever been independent, or had served a merely local clientele. The attentions bestowed by Pisistratus on Artemis Brauronia, at her home and perhaps on the acropolis, strictly prove no more than the popularity that the cult had achieved.

About Eleusis there is more to be said, though with no more certain outcome. In general terms, this is one cult which we can feel confident must have undergone very significant reforms at some point in its early history.[126] To say nothing of the mutation which

---

[124] See most recently on the *Eleusinia* R. M. Simms, *GRBS* 16 (1975), 269–79 (and K. Clinton, *AJP* 100, 1979, 1–12 on *IG* I³.5); on the *Herakleia*, E. Vanderpool in *Studies Presented to Sterling Dow* (*GRBM* 10, 1984), 295 f. (on *IG* I³.3), and on the link with Marathon, id., *Hesperia* 11 (1942), 336. A citharodic competition at this festival is unexpectedly attested by an inscription recording a victory there on *ARV*² 1044.9. Alciphron: *IG* I³.991 (= *CEG* 301); *IG* I³.988, 992 (*CEG* 299 f.), and 989 are probably dedications by sixth-cent. victors. Pindar's clients: *Ol.* 9.99, 13.110; *Isth.* 1.57; *Ol.* 9.89 with Σ, 13.110; *Pyth.* 8.79. *Anakeia*: for an (?) early fifth-cent. bronze *kalpe* of unknown provenance inscribed ἐχς Ἀνακίο ἆθλον and another (from the Pontic Chersonnese: ? *c.*400) inscribed ἆθλον ἐξ Ἀνακίων see P. Amandry, *BCH* 95 (1971), 615; a horse-race is also attested by Lysias fr. 75.3 Thalheim, xvii 2.3 Gernet/Bizos. Note too the sixth-cent. marble disc inscribed Ὀεθεν ἆθλα, *IG* I³.1396. For a useful review of Attic competitive festivals see Osborne in Sommerstein et al. eds., *Tragedy, Comedy and the Polis*, 21–38; add now the *Nemesia* (cf. Ch. 11, n. 126).

[125] So recently e.g. F. J. Frost, 'Peisistratos, the Cults and the Unification of Attica', *The Ancient World* 21 (1990), 3–9. Contrast pp. 24 ff. above. Building-activity: n. 27 above (where the cases of Sunium and Rhamnus are also mentioned).

[126] Sourvinou-Inwood's 'Reconstructing Change: Ritual and Ideology at Eleusis', in P. Toohey and M. Golden eds., *Inventing Ancient Culture?* (London forthcoming) will doubtless be an important contribution; I have not seen it.*

perhaps first created eschatological Mysteries, it is questionable whether the unparalleled link between two distinct cults, the 'lesser' Mysteries of Agrae and the 'greater' of Eleusis, had always existed, and very unlikely surely that the mystic promise had always extended, as it did in the classical period, to the whole Greek world. The singularity of these arrangements in Greek eyes is reflected by certain expansions of the myth of Heracles, greatest of initiates. The hero arrived at Eleusis polluted with the blood of the Centaurs, and was a foreigner; he had therefore too be purified by Eumolpus, and then adopted by an Athenian (one Pylios), before undergoing initiation.[127] Perhaps the Lesser Mysteries were founded specially in order to purify him, or to permit him to be initiated, foreigner though he was.[128] These stories explain the paradoxical coexistence of Lesser and Greater Mysteries (as well as alluding perhaps to rites of purification associated with one or the other); they also postulate a time when the Mysteries had been open to Athenians alone, in a way more characteristic of Greek cult in general than the later openness. One might in fact have expected the first foreigner's initiation to serve as a charter for the later, more hospitable stance; the myth does not, however, claim explicitly that Heracles' privilege became posterity's right. Is there any history to be extracted from these myths? That is possible only if one supposes that they 'preserve a memory of' (rather than 'postulate') a time when initiation had been restricted to Athenians. But even if they do, there is no knowing when they were first told or the change occurred.[129]

More specifically, a major building-programme took place at Eleusis in (it is normally supposed) the Pisistratean period; and it is certainly at this time that two of the most important Eleusinian myths are first attested. In the *Homeric Hymn to Demeter*, the great gift bestowed on Athens and mankind by the goddess at the time of her visit to Eleusis had been the Mysteries. In later tradition, it was, above all, corn and the art of cultivating it. The foundation of the Mysteries received less emphasis, and in some conceptions was perhaps not ascribed to the goddess at all; for we begin to hear of human founders, Eumolpus or Orpheus, who were perhaps thought of as having instituted the rites a little after Demeter's visit, in 'com-

---

[127] Apollod. 2.5.12; adoption by Pylios also in Plut. *Thes.* 33.2. Boardman, *JHS* 95 (1975), 6, associates Pylios with the Pylian (Hdt. 5.65.3–4) Pisistratus. For Diodorus 4.25.1 Musaeus was hierophant; many claimed that Theseus organized the initiation, according to Plut. *Thes.* 30.5.

[128] Diod. 4.14.3, *Σ* Ar. *Plut.* 846 (= 1013) respectively. Cf. refs. in Parker, *Miasma*, 285, n. 1. The link with Agra also in Steph. Byz. s.v. Ἄγρα.

[129] But Christiane Sourvinou-Inwood suggests to me the possibility that the greatly increased size of the 'Pisistratean' *telesterion* is a consequence of the change.

memoration' of it.[130] In the old myth, corn had always existed, but might be temporarily 'hidden' by the goddess in anger. The new myth told of the first emergence of corn, a crucial step in the progress of human civilization, and, very conveniently for Athenian sentiment, located it in Attica. Agriculture was a gift (the first of many, perhaps) from Athens to the Greek world.[131] Triptolemus, who in the *Hymn* had been merely one of several Eleusinian princes, rises to unexpected prominence in this account as the hero chosen by Demeter to be missionary of the new technique. His world-wide mission, on a winged throne on wheels, first appears in literature in the fragments of Sophocles' *Triptolemos* (probably of 468), but vase-paintings show beyond doubt that it had been familiar since about 540. In the late sixth and early fifth century it is one of the most popular of scenes.[132]

It was important also for the prestige of Eleusis that, soon after their foundation, the Mysteries attracted distinguished initiates from abroad: none other than Heracles (as we have seen) and the Dioscuri, in religious terms much the greatest of the heroes. Heracles' visit is attested earlier and in more detail.[133] It was motivated by an ingenious adaptation of an older story: he sought initiation before descending to the Underworld to fetch Cerberus, in order no doubt to win Persephone's favour before entering her domain.[134] It has been suggested that the new myth is reflected on certain sixth-century vases which represent Heracles receiving Cerberus peaceably (even the dog seems mellowed) rather than seizing him by force.[135] However that may be, Heracles must be an ini-

[130] Eumolpus: e.g. *Marmor Parium FGrH* 239 A 15; cf. the sources cited in schol. Soph. *OC* 1053; F. Jacoby, *Das Marmor Parium* (Berlin 1904), 72–75, and already Eur. *Erechtheus* fr. 65.100 Austin. Orpheus: [Eur.] *Rhes.* 943 f., [Dem.] 25.11, (?) Ar. *Ran.* 1032, cf. Graf, *Orphische Dichtung*, 22–39. Even Triptolemus could perform a similar role: Xen. *Hell.* 6.3.6. For the two stages see *Marmor Parium* A 12–15. But Demeter still bestows both gifts in Isoc. *Paneg.* 28.   [131] Cf. Ch. 8, n. 85.

[132] See Schwarz, *Triptolemos*, *passim* [+], who lists 154 representations on vases (and others on reliefs), the vast majority Attic; cf. now Shapiro, *Art and Cult*, 76–77, and K. Clinton, *Myth and Cult* (Stockholm 1992), 41–47.

[133] The Dioscuri are mentioned in Xen. *Hell.* 6.3.6, along with Heracles, as the first foreign initiates (Triptolemus was hierophant), and appear as initiates on three fourth-cent. vases (Schwarz, *Triptolemos*, nos. V 125, ? 131, 132). The only narrative account is Plut. *Thes.* 33: having invaded Attica, to recover Helen, they asked to be initiated, as Heracles had been, and were for this purpose adopted by an Athenian, as Heracles had been. The initiation of Heracles is no doubt in fact primary, as it is better motivated.

[134] See Eur. *HF* 610–13; [Pl.] *Axioch.* 371e; Diod. 4.25.1, 26.1; Apollod. 2.5.12. For a different view see N. Robertson, *Hermes* 108 (1980), 296–99; on 'Herakles Mystes' see in general J. Boardman in *LIMC* IV.1 (1988), 805–806.

[135] See Boardman, 'Herakles, Peisistratos and Eleusis', *JHS* 95 (1975), 1–12, at 7–9, who also illustrates, pl. 1a, the Exekias sherd (= Schwarz, *Triptolemos*, no. V 1; *LIMC* IV.1 (1988), 806, no. 1405; cf. Shapiro, *Art and Cult*, 78–80, who locates the scene at Agrai, not Eleusis). Appropriately, Heracles and Cerberus appear on a shoulder frieze on the sherd.

tiate on a sherd perhaps by Exekias of about 530 which shows him amid various Eleusinian gods and heroes; and a fragment of (almost certainly) Pindar seems to identify Eumolpus as the officiating hierophant. Pindar's source may have been an epic 'Descent of Heracles', which took the hero to the Underworld via Eleusis.[136]

Perhaps then the Eleusinian cult underwent a drastic overhaul in the second half of the sixth century, the central myths being modernized at the same time as the sanctuary was rebuilt.[137] The matter is not established beyond doubt, however. It is not the case that Triptolemus and Heracles intrude around 540 upon an established tradition of Eleusinian iconography: the vases that show Triptolemus are the first with Eleusinian themes. What is new therefore is the adoption by vase-painters of such subjects—an index perhaps of the cult's growing popularity—not necessarily any individual myth that is first attested at this date. The *Homeric Hymn to Demeter* says nothing of Triptolemus' mission, which is in fact incompatible with its own narrative. Possibly then, the myth postdates the *Hymn*;[138] but that possibility is no great help when estimates of the date of the *Hymn* vary between about 650 and 550 BC. For the origin of the story of the initiation of Heracles no *terminus post quem* at all is available.[139] Proud though the Eleusinians were of their distinguished visitor,[140] we cannot even be sure that the story was devised on Attic soil. Once the cult had achieved fame, a hero could be sent to Eleusis by a non-Eleusinian poet, as to Delphi by a non-Delphian.

The magic ingredient of 'Orphism' is sometimes brought into the discussion. By the fourth century, at the latest, Orpheus could be seen as founder of the Eleusinian Mysteries; the Pisistratids had contacts with an 'Orphic' poet, Onomacritus; and an Orphic poem is attested on the theme of 'The rape of Kore and Demeter's search and ... the many people who received the corn' (sc. from Triptolemus). An Orphic reinterpretation of the Eleusinian cult in the sixth century can therefore be postulated, responsible, for

[136] See H. Lloyd-Jones, 'Heracles at Eleusis: P. Oxy. 2622 and P.S.I. 1391', *Maia* 19 (1967), 206–29 = id., *Greek Epic, Lyric and Tragedy* (Oxford 1990), 167–87 (on Pindar fr. dub. 346 Snell/Maehler), who tentatively suggests 'Musaeus' as author of the epic *Katabasis* (date ? 600–550) that he infers; cf. Graf, *Orphische Dichtung*, 142–50, and (speculative) Robertson, *Hermes* 108 (1980), 274–99.

[137] See esp. Boardman, *JHS* 95 (1975).

[138] But cf. *GaR* 38 (1991), 12 and 17, n. 46.

[139] For Boardman's arguments in favour of a Pisistratid date see ns. 127 and 135 above; they are plausible but far from certain.

[140] See Schwarz, *Triptolemos*, nos. V 1, 85, (?) 124, 125, 131–32, 134, 149, (?) 150; and, in sculpture, the presumptive Attic original of the 'Lovatelli urn' and the 'Torre Nova sarcophagus' (cf. Richardson, *Hymn to Demeter*, 211–13).

instance, for the sudden rise of Triptolemus to prominence. But the hypothesis finds no support in the little that we know of the Orphic poet's account of Demeter's coming to Eleusis. The poem was apparently set in a primeval twilight, and portrayed the rough conditions of pre-agricultural life. Demeter was not received (as in the *Homeric Hymn*) by King Celeus but by 'Hard Home' (Dysaules), with his vulgar wife, Baubo. Their sons, Triptolemus and the swineherd Eubouleus, gave information to Demeter about the rape of Kore (which had occurred at Eleusis), and Triptolemus was entrusted with his great mission as a reward. Certain aetiological details absent from the *Hymn* seem to have been worked into the narrative.[141] But this speculative and intellectual version (of unknown date) can scarcely have inspired the vases, which show no knowledge of Hard Home and his inelegant household. The painters more probably considered Triptolemos a son of Celeus, as he was in the dominant later tradition.[142] To conclude: the sixth century BC is very likely, indeed, to have been a time of most significant innovation in the Eleusinian cult; but no single change at any level other than the architectural can be certainly identified.

[141] Orpheus as founder: above, n. 130. Onomacritus: Hdt. 7.6.3. Orphic poem: see Kern, *Orph. Frag.* T 221 (= *Marmor Parium FGrH* 239 A 14), frs. 49–53; cf. above all Graf, *Orphische Dichtung*, 151–81. For advocates of a sixth-cent. date see Graf, *Orphische Dichtung*, 178, n. 105 (and still e.g. Kolb, 'Baupolitik', 114–15); Graf favours the late fifth cent., because of the poem's apparent dependence on sophistic/proto-sophistic theories of cultural development ('Hard Home', and fr. 292, which, however, need not belong to this poem). A *terminus ante quem* in the late fourth cent. is apparently given by Asclepiades *FGrH* 12 F 4; cf. Graf, *Orphische Dichtung*, 159 f. Aetiology: Baubo's gesture, fr. 52; the rite of μεγαρίζειν at the Thesmophoria, fr. 50.

[142] He appears with Celeus (and Hippothoon), all identified by inscriptions, on a bell-krater by the Oreithyia painter, Palermo V 779 (Schwarz, *Triptolemos*, no. V 61). Other identifications of Celeus are speculative (see Schwarz, *Triptolemos*, 254, index s.v. *Keleos*). But note that other traditions about Triptolemos are found even in Athenian authors of the fifth cent.: son of Ocean and Earth in Pherecydes (*FGrH* 3 F 53), of Rharos in Choerilus (*TrGF* 2 F 1): cf. Richardson, *Hymn to Demeter*, 195 f.

7

Before and after Clisthenes

The Pisistratid Hipparchus, we have noted, was struck down while marshalling the Panathenaic procession. After the fall of the tyranny, the privilege of organizing the great procession would presumably have passed to a magistrate drawn from a restricted group of 300 aristocrats, if the oligarchic scheme of Isagoras had prevailed. It fell instead, with great symbolic propriety, to the 'demarchs', the executive heads of the 139 or so demes (or villages) that were the foundation upon which Clisthenes erected his restored democracy.[1]

To reshape the political life of Athens, Clisthenes had also to reshape its society. These social changes meant a transformation of the structures within which religious life took place. Thus Attic religion in its familiar shape is a creation of Clisthenes no less than is the democracy.[2] We need to review these structures of religious life, in both their pre- and post-Clisthenic form. The exposition may unfortunately be a little dry; the underlying subject, however, is not administration, but the forms of communal life.

After Clisthenes (it is natural to begin here, with what is much better known), any Athenian necessarily belonged to four organizations—deme, *trittys*, tribe, and phratry—apart from the city itself. The first three were units of a single structure, a group of demes forming a *trittys*, three *trittyes* a tribe (and ten tribes the city). The phratry was distinct.

In religious life, much the most important of the organizations was the deme. It was, as it were, the *polis* writ small; it had its own sanctuaries, priests, and programme of sacrifices running throughout the year. A large proportion of the innumerable local cults of Attica must have been in the care of the demes.[3]

[1] Suda δ 421 s.v. δήμαρχοι; Σ Ar. *Nub.* 37 (cf. *LSCG* 33 B 24).

[2] An exhaustive treatment would therefore need to consider the possible influence of the reforms on every single festival (note for instance C. Sourvinou-Inwood, *Studies in Girls' Transitions*, Athens 1988, 111–17, on the *Brauronia*).

[3] See esp. Whitehead, *Demes*, ch. 7 [+]; also my 'Festivals of the Attic Demes', in *Gifts to the Gods*, 137–47, and now Rosivach, *Public Sacrifice*, 14–34.

A *trittys* contained between one and seven demes, depending on their size. Of the three *trittyes* in each tribe, one came from each of three regions, 'city', 'coast', and 'plain', into which Attica was for this purpose divided. The *trittys* system is at the moment controversial in almost all its aspects. For our purpose, the important issue is whether such a unit might be a social group as well as a mechanism of political and military organization. Two inscriptions mention rites which were possibly celebrated by a *trittys*; on the other hand, the constituent demes were not necessarily neighbours, and could even be a long way apart; and nowhere in Attic literature do we find so much as a word for 'fellow *trittys* member', still less an indication that this could be a tie of any real emotional force. Nor apparently did the *trittyes* commonly own property, or shrines. Any social aspirations they may have had do not seem to have proved very successful.[4]

Through the *trittyes*, each of the ten tribes contained a mix of demes from the three regions of Attica; this mixing was, on any view, one of the system's fundamental aims, and the Clisthenic tribe was, above all, a centralizing institution. Its main functions were political and military, but it was also involved in religious life in several ways. The teams and choirs that competed at the great festivals were normally recruited tribe by tribe; and on at least two such occasions, *Panathenaea* and *City Dionysia*, rich members were required, as a public liturgy, to provide a 'tribal dinner' for their humbler fellows.[5] A single tribe could also represent the whole city in religion: the public offering made annually to the 'Sphragitic Nymphs' in commemoration of the battle of Plataea was brought by members of Aiantis, supposedly in recognition of the exceptional valour shown by Ajax's men on that great day. Perhaps more surprisingly, late in the fourth century the *prytaneis* of the tribe Akamantis were put in charge of an annual sacrifice 'in commemoration of the good news reported during the prytany of Akamantis'. That can remind us that

---

[4] Controversial: see e.g. P. J. Rhodes, *JHS* 103 (1983), 203–204; D. M. Lewis, *Gnomon* 55 (1983), 431–36; G. R. Stanton, ibid. 63 (1991), 25–30; M. H. Hansen, *The Athenian Democracy in the Age of Demosthenes* (Oxford 1991), 48. Two inscriptions: (*a*) *IG* I³.258.30 (cf. *IG* I³, addenda, p. 958); on this see, however, p. 330 below (*b*) a sacred calendar of uncertain origin contains the word τριττύϊ in a fragmentary context (*IG* I³.255.9: cf. Jameson's notes). Even if this is a post- and not (cf. *LSS* 10 A 35–37) a pre-Clisthenic *trittys*, the dative does not support the view that the whole calendar is that of a *trittys*. *Trittys* property seems to be attested only by the fragmentary lease *IG* II².2490.

[5] See Jones, *Public Organization*, 48–51, and on *hestiasis* Schmitt Pantel, *Cité au banquet*, 121–25. Tribal teams competed at the *Hephaisteia*, *Greater* and *Lesser Panathenaea*, *Prometheia*, *Theseia*, and, it seems (cf. Ch. 11, n. 126), *Nemesia*: tribal choruses at all the choral festivals (though dramatic choruses were non-tribal); cf. J. K. Davies, *JHS* 87 (1967), 33–40. Representatives of the tribes had an irrecoverable function at the *Bendideia* (*IG* I³.136.4–5).

in a different sense each tribe in turn represented the city in religion as a matter of routine, since presidency of the council rotated between the tribes, and various religious functions fell to the representatives of the presiding tribe.[6]

The tribes also, surely, sacrificed each to their own eponymous hero (even though direct evidence is rather scanty[7]). When and how often they did so is unknown, but these patronal banquets are likely to have occurred, as are tribal assemblies, on the occasion of a larger public festival. Individual tribes perhaps associated themselves with the festival that seemed most relevant to their patron-hero: it has been noted that the only tribal assembly the date of which is known,[8] one of the tribe Pandionis, was held 'on the day after' the similarly named (though etymologically, of course, quite unrelated) *Pandia*. Tribal rites and activities would therefore have been set firmly within the framework of the broader religion of the state. The religious functions of the tribe, important though they were, were also strictly circumscribed. It was through the mediation of the tribe that the individual participated in certain public festivals; but the distinctive sacrificial calendar of each tribe appears to have contained but one name, that of the eponymous hero.

Every male Athenian citizen almost certainly belonged to one of the hereditary associations known as phratries; and in the classical period the scrutiny of candidates for admission to membership, and thus in effect to citizenship, was apparently not merely one of the functions that the phratry exercised but its principal *raison d'être*. Of more than twenty distinct passages in Attic comedy and oratory that refer to the institution, all but one (a passing metaphor) concern questions of disputed legitimacy or citizenship.[9] The registration

[6] Nymphs: Plut. *Qu. Conv.* 628e–f, *Aristid.* 19.5–6, this latter close to a citation of Clidemus (*FGrH* 323 F 22; but note Schachter, *Cults*, II.55–56, 185–86). Akamantis: Ch. 12, n. 11. Council: Rhodes, *Boule*, 132–34.

[7] Only *IG* II².1165.6 (Erechtheis); *AM* 51 (1926), 36, no. 5 (Pandionis: cf. Ch. 8, n. 93). Indirect evidence comes from the sometimes substantial revenues of the tribes (cf. R. Schlaifer, *HSCP* 51, 1940, 252, n. 1, on, esp., *Agora* XIX P26.504–30, which shows that Aiantis had income of 2,000 drachmas; also *SEG* XXIII 78), and the existence of the 'priest of the eponymous' hero (p. 118 below).

[8] *IG* II².1140 (in *IG* II².1165.8 the vital specification is restored): cf. Kron, *Phylenheroen*, 112; Kearns, 'Continuity and Change', 193; ead., *Heroes of Attica*, 81, n. 6. But possibly Pandionis was merely imitating the civic practice of assembling μετὰ Πάνδια (Dem. 21.9; cf. Aeschin. 2.61, 3.68; Mikalson, *Calendar*, 137).

[9] The exception is Ar. *Eq.* 255 ὦ γέροντες ἡλιασταί, φράτερες τριωβόλου. The invariable appeal to phratry membership in these contexts implies that *de facto* it remained a precondition for citizenship even after Clisthenes (so Lambert, *Phratries*, ch. 1); the postulated citizen who is not a *phrater* (see refs. in ibid., 26, n. 6) is a wholly theoretical being. And why could individual phratries fine and ὁ βουλόμενος prosecute supposititious *phratores* (*IG* II².1237; Craterus *FGrH* 342 F 4), unless the phratry was 'un organisme de droit public' (Roussel, *Tribu et cité*, 146)? If, however, one believes that bastards, certainly excluded from phratries,

normally occurred at the great ancestral festival *Apatouria* (which was thus, uniquely, a kind of 'working festival'), celebrated at their different altars throughout Attica,[10] but at the same time, by the individual phratries. Let us note in passing that, distributed thus throughout Attica, the phratries to a considerable extent had the character of local associations, most members of a given phratry belonging to the deme in which its altar lay.[11]

The introduction of new members was accompanied by a sacrifice, the animal being presented by the father, who swore to the child's legitimacy; with fine archaic symbolism, to 'take a portion of meat' signified acceptance of the new *phrator*, while it was possible to protest by 'leading the victim away from the altar'. (Voting is also mentioned; even here, the voting-token was 'fetched from the altar of Zeus Phratrios while the sacrifice was burning'.) The newly married also brought 'wedding-offerings' for their brides, the prospective mothers of future *phratores*. A happy consequence of these forms of bureaucracy was an abundance of free meat for all. The *Apatouria* lasted three days, and included homespun competitions among the children, as well as enough festivity to make the name of the day after it, *Epibda*, into the normal term for 'hangover'. The other *raison d'être* of the phratries, therefore, was to celebrate this cheerful old-fashioned festival, one of the longest and most important in the year.[12]

could be citizens, phratry membership becomes the mark of legitimacy and right of inheritance rather than of citizenship (cf. S. G. Cole, *ZPE* 55, 1984, 234). Daughters were probably not admitted (cf. *LSS* 48, Tenos) except in special circumstances (see most recently Lambert, *Phratries*, 178–81 [+], who stresses that the practice of individual phratries may have varied). On the complicated issue of the age of phratry admission see M. Golden, *Children and Childhood in Classical Athens* (Baltimore 1990), 25–28; Lambert, *Phratries*, 161–69. I do not discuss the phratry subdivisions sometimes known as *thiasoi* (Lambert, *Phratries*, ch. 2), since it is not clear that they had religious functions.

[10] See *IG* II².1237. 52–54, 67 (but not *IG* II².1299.29 f., a mere supplement); cf. Hedrick, 'Phratry Shrines', 252–55, 259–62 (but note the reservation of Lambert, *Phratries*, 158–59).

[11] See above all Hedrick, 'Phratry Shrines', 262–66. The evidence of phratry catalogues in which members of the local deme may be listed without demotics is particularly important, if controversial (*IG* II².2344–45; on the latter cf. S. C. Humphreys, *ZPE* 83, 1990, 243–48: the counter-argument of Lambert, *Phratries*, 369–70, that persons listed here without demotics demonstrably come from different demes relies on a questionable interpretation of line 72 and on the fallible assumption that homonymous father–son pairs separately attested must be identical [contrast C. Habicht, *Hesperia* 59, 1990, 459–62; id., *ZPE* 103, 1994, 117–27]; cf. App. 2, n. 86). But it is true that several *gene* have members widely spread among the demes (see App. 2, s.v. *Amynandridai, Brytidai, Salaminioi*), as does probably the phratry *Medontidai* (Lambert, *Phratries*, 319–20).

[12] Oath: Dem. 57.54; Isae. 8.19 (contrast Andoc. 1.126). ἀπάγειν τὸ ἱερεῖον: Isae. 6.22; [Dem.] 43.14, 82. μερίδα λαμβάνειν: [Dem.] 43.82. Vote: [Dem.] 43.14, 82; cf. *IG* II².1237.16–18, 29, 82–84. ἡ γαμηλία: see W. Wyse's note on Isae. 3.76.1 in his edn. (Cambridge 1904), Lambert, *Phratries*, 181–85, and cf. *LSS* 48, Tenos. Competitions: Pl. *Tim.* 21b. See in general Lambert, *Phratries*, ch. 4, and Schmitt Pantel, *Cité au banquet*, 82–90.

At the centre of all accounts of phratry-registration is an altar, that
of Zeus Phratrios when it is identified. From inscriptions we see that
he was normally paired with Athena Phratria; and a phratry centre
at its simplest was probably just an open-air precinct around such a
joint altar.[13] Thus the main gods of the subgroup, the phratry, were
none other than the main civic gods of the city itself (which may
indeed have maintained its own cult of Zeus and Athena of phratries).[14] Individual phratries might have other precincts too: from
their boundary-markers (the source incidentally of four of the six
phratry names that are known for certain) we learn that the
Therrikleidai honoured Apollo Patroos, the Thymaitian phratry
Zeus Xenios, the Gleontian phratry Cephisus, the *Achniadai* Apollo
Hebdomeios, and the *Demokleidai* (if they are indeed a phratry)
Artemis Orthosia; the *Demotionidai* too perhaps had a shrine of
Leto, and two further groups of uncertain character that had their
own precincts of the Tritopatores, the *Euergidai* and *Zakyadai*, were
perhaps phratries.[15] We may guess that such phratries with special
gods of their own none the less did not neglect Zeus Phratrios and
Athena Phratria, though the physical arrangements (one sanctuary
with two altars? more than one sanctuary?) are not known.[16] There
is no sure evidence that any phratry honoured more than one such
special god; but it is possible that the *Therrikleidai* had a shrine of a
hero Theriklos in addition to that of Apollo Patroos (the only
instance of an eponymous phratry-hero receiving cult, if so), the
Thymaitian phratry of '*x* and Heracles' as well as of Zeus Xenios.[17]

[13] Zeus Phratrios and Athena Phratria: see Lambert, *Phratries*, 208–209 (with reference to
the inscriptions, which are reproduced in his long app. 1); note too the appearance of these
gods outside phratries in *LSS* 10 A 48–49; ibid. 19.91. Precinct: see esp. Hedrick, 'Phratry
Shrines', 256–59 on *Hesperia* 7 (1938), 612–19 (Travlos, *Pictorial Dictionary*, 573–5), a
temenos with inscribed altar of Zeus Phratrios and Athena Phratria from north central Athens.
SEG III 121 (cf. XXXIX 150: = T 17 Lambert), a phratry decree from Liopesi, is unique in
mentioning a ναός of the two gods.

[14] Cf. Sourvinou-Inwood, 'Polis Religion' (1), 316–20. It is unclear whether the altar of
Zeus Phratrios and Athena Phratria found in the *agora* (*Hesperia* 6, 1937, 104–106: T 24
Lambert) belongs to an individual phratry or to a state cult: see Lambert, *Phratries*, 357.

[15] *IG* II².4973; *IG* I³.1057; *Agora* XIX H9; n. 16 below; *IG* I³.1083; *IG* II².1237.124–25
(cf. *IG* II².1242 = Lambert, *Phratries*, T 4, and App. 2 B s.v. *Demotionidai*); App. 2 B s.v.
Euergidai and *Zakyadai* (cf. Kearns, *Heroes of Attica*, 76–77); for a further possible phratry-
cult of Apollo Patroos see App. 2 B s.v. *Elasidai*. Other certain phratry-names are *Dyaleis* (*IG*
II².1241) and *Medontidai* (q.v. in App. 2 B); many further possibilities appear in App. 2 B, and
Lambert, *Phratries*, 363–68, also considers *Philieis* (p. 303 below) and *Miltieis* (*IG* II².1596.2).

[16] Contrast, however, C. W. Hedrick, *CQ* NS 39 (1989), 129. It is not clear whether the
'boundary of the phratry of the *Achniadai*' and the 'shrine of Apollo Hebdomeios of the phratry of the *Achniadai*', both from Keratea (*IG* II².2621 and 4974: Lambert, *Phratries*, 281–84),
refer to one plot of land or two.

[17] *IG* I³.243.30 attests a Θερικλεῖον, probably in Melite; but there is no evidence that the
Therrikleidai were associated with it (if indeed it is a shrine); for some speculations see
Lambert, *Phratries*, 321–26. Thymaitian phratry: see the text rightly ascribed to this phratry

Theophrastus' 'Mean' Character exhibits his grasping ways even when 'feasting his *phratores*' (in what circumstances we are not told).[18] That is almost the only explicit indication that an individual might normally have met his *phratores* (several hundred perhaps—but the size of these bodies is very unclear[19]) or a group of them often, if at all, except at the *Apatouria*. It is not decisive, indeed, that no sacrificial calendar of a phratry has been found, when our knowledge of the busy ritual life that a *genos* might conduct depends on a single document. A stronger argument may be that, to judge from comedy, it was less common to invoke the bond that united members of the same phratry than that between members of the same deme or even tribe.[20]

Phratries were, one must allow, active in various directions. They owned and might lease property, could become involved in litigation, passed honorary decrees, and needed officials (phratriarchs and phratry-priests) to order their affairs; groups of *phratores* or whole phratries made loans, very probably to other members of the same phratry; an individual might judge the phratry shrine a worthy object of his munificence.[21] If leases and loans within the phratry were common, there were solid practical advantages, of a type characteristic of this society of networks, to be derived from membership. But in its formal aspects such business could perhaps normally all have been conducted at a single annual meeting.[22] We know that one phratry, presumably one based in Athens itself, did once meet to admit a new member during the *Thargelia*, a state festival held in the

by C. W. Hedrick, *Hesperia* 81 (1988), 81–85 (= *SEG* XXXVIII 172; *Agora* XIX H131); but he may be wrong to restore it as a sanctuary *horos* (cf. Lambert, *Phratries*, 330–31). On the eponymous heroes of phratries (obscure figures) see Lambert, *Phratries*, 222.

[18] Theophr. *Char.* 30.16; the setting is the *aischrokerdes*' home, according to most commentators; but R. G. Ussher may be right to think of the *Apatouria*.

[19] Contrast M. A. Flower, *CQ* NS 35 (1985), 232–35 [+] and Hedrick, ibid. 39 (1989), 126–35, on *IG* II².2344. Lambert, *Phratries*, 20, puts the outside limits at 30–140 phratries in total, 140–1,000 members per average phratry.

[20] Comedy: for the deme see Whitehead, *Demes*, 337–38 (and for abundant prose evidence, ibid. 223–34); for the phratry, above n. 9; for the tribe, Ar. *Ach.* 568, *Av.* 368, cf. Dem. 29.23. For the *genos* as social bond, I know only Men. *Kolax* fr. 5 Sandbach. Sacred calendar: neither of the two scraps of sacred law perhaps to be associated with phratries that Lambert, *Phratries*, adduces (*IG* II².1240, 1242 = his T 20, T 4) need allude to more than the cult of one or two 'special gods'.

[21] Property and leases: see Hedrick, 'Phratry Shrines', 243–48 (main text *IG* II².1241: the lessee is probably a member of the phratry). Litigation and honorary decrees: id., *AJP* 109 (1988), 111–17 (*SEG* XXXVIII 128); *IG* II².1238–39, (?) 1233. Loans: Lambert, *Phratries*, 196–98, on his T 10 and T 21 (*Agora* XIX P5.17 ff. and *IG* II².2723). Munificence: *SEG* III 121 (cf. XXXIX 150). See in general Lambert, *Phratries*, ch. 5 'Property and Finances' (and his app. 1 for all the texts here cited). Officials: see Hedrick, *Demotionidai*, 21–30; Lambert, *Phratries*, 225–35.

[22] But for possible counter-indications see Lambert, *Phratries*, 202.

city. But this additional meeting still only served the central purpose of registration.[23] Even if they were in fact not rare, such assemblies of the phratries during public festivals are still to be distinguished from rites that they celebrated in their own name.

It has been suggested that rural phratries might in some cases also have a kind of *pied-à-terre* in town.[24] But it is not certain that such ex-phratriate meeting-places—suggestive evidence, if they existed, for the body's social importance—did exist in fact. Obviously phratries that owned subsidiary precincts of the type discussed above must have put them to some use. But even in these they seem to have honoured gods associated with their own main concerns: Apollo Patroos (and by association Hebdomeios) and Zeus Xenios with questions of citizenship; Cephisus, Leto, and Artemis Orthosia with the birth and safe growth of future *phratores*. The Tritopatores too, 'fathers in the third generation' and thus symbols of the continuity of the line, fit neatly in the same context.[25] No phratry to our knowledge had a true pantheon.

From these associations to which all citizens belonged, we turn to others confined to a minority. One of these, the *genos*, has already been considered in Chapter 5. We saw there that the *genos*, like the phratry, was a hereditary group to which fathers formally introduced their sons. Indeed, *gene* and phratries sometimes shared altars, and introduction to the two groups could form part of the same process. The principle even seems to have been legally enacted that those who had passed the severer scrutiny of a *genos* should be automatically admitted by the relevant phratry. Appropriately,

[23] Isae. 7.15 (but Lambert, *Phratries*, 216–17, inclines to think that some phratries may have met regularly at this festival of Apollo Patroos). No evidence associates the phratries with the crowning of children at the *Anthesteria* (a possibility raised by M. Guarducci, 'L'istituzione della fratria', *MemLinc*, 6th ser., 6, 1937, 37); they may have had a role at the *Synoikia*, cf. *LSS* 10 A 48–49 (with ns. 38 and 43 below, and Robertson, *Festivals and Legends*, ch. 2).

[24] See Hedrick, 'Phratry Shrines', 261; Lambert, *Phratries*, 13, n. 47. '*Medontidai*' had property (an *agora*?) near the acropolis but, it seems, a *hieron* at Keratea, while an honorary decree associated with them has been found in yet another place (*IG* I³.1062, 1383; *IG* II².1233); more ownership is attested by the sales record *Agora* XIX P5.17–18. If all these documents relate to a single body (cf. App. 2 B s.v. *Medontidai*), they are the prime example of a rich phratry with ramifying affairs, membership in which must have been important. The Thymaitian phratry, which had an altar or altars near the Areopagus (see above), evokes by its name the deme Thymaitadai on the coast west of Athens. The famous allusion to a 'barbershop where the Deceleans go' (Lys. 23.3, cf. *IG* II².1237. 63–64) refers in my view to demesmen, not *phratores*.

[25] Apollo Patroos: cf. Ch. 5, n. 31 above. Zeus Xenios: *xenoi* seeking incorporation required a phratry (for a myth associating Thymoites himself, indirectly, with 'hospitality' see Demon *FGrH* 327 F 1); cf. Aesch. *Eum.* 656, on the polluted Orestes, ποία δὲ χέρνιψ φρατέρων προσδέξεται. Leto and Cephisus: see e.g. *IG* II².4547. Artemis Orthosia: cf. Σ Pind. *Ol.* 3.54, Callim. *Dian.* 128. Tritopatores: see Kearns, *Heroes of Attica*, 76–77; Jameson et al., *Selinous*, 107–14.

therefore, *gennetai* celebrated the *Apatouria* as a group; and a *genos* was probably, in a sense, a subdivision of a phratry.[26]

Another form of hereditary association confined to a minority was that of the group of *orgeones* (a collective noun is inconveniently lacking). Etymologically, *orgeones* are celebrants of *orgia*, rites. Various kinds of group of *orgeones* are known, only one of which concerns us here. This is a hereditary society that was probably, like a *genos*, a subdivision of a phratry; the law that apparently required phratries automatically to admit *gene* conferred the same privilege on this class of *orgeones*.[27] Of the various types of orgeonic club known from inscriptions, several groups of citizen '*orgeones* of [a hero]' are perhaps examples of the hereditary associations originally linked to phratries.[28] The identification is not certain, because it cannot be shown that these groups (which first appear epigraphically in the fourth century) were recruited on strict hereditary principles;[29] but the form of association that they represent, a small society honouring a local hero, does not look like a late creation, and if these were not the orgeonic groups associated with phratries, we certainly do not know what were. The sole document (of 306/5) from which we hear of 'the hero Egretes' and his worshippers is characteristic:

The *orgeones* have leased the sanctuary of Egretes to Diognetos son of Arkesilos of Melite for ten years at 200 drachmas per year. He should treat the sanctuary and the buildings built in it as a sanctuary. Diognetos shall

---

[26] See p. 64 and p. 316; and cf. Lambert, *Phratries*, 17–18.

[27] See Philochorus *FGrH* 328 F 35, with A. Andrewes, *JHS* 81 (1961), 1–3, 8–9 (whom Lambert follows, *Phratries*, 74–77). The point is, admittedly, controversial (contrast Ferguson, 'Attic Orgeones', 70); Andrewes' interpretation of Philochorus must be made to override the prima-facie implication of Isae. 2.14 (the only relevant text) that registration among the *orgeones* was a distinct process from phratry registration.

[28] The discussion by Ferguson, 'Attic Orgeones', is fundamental (cf. Kearns, *Heroes of Attica*, 73–75); the group relevant here are his class A, the 'orgeones of heroes'. He finds traces of twelve representatives of the class in all: the main texts are *LSS* 20 (Echelos and the heroines; third cent., containing also a decree of ? the fifth cent.); *IG* II².2499 (*LSCG* 47, *SIG*³ 1097: Egretes), 2501 (late fourth cent., Hypodektes), 1252 (fourth cent., Amynos, Asklepios, and Dexion; cf. 1253, 1259); and (unknown to Ferguson) Πραγματεῖαι Ἀκαδ. Ἀθηνῶν 13 (1948), no. 2 = H. W. Pleket, *Epigraphica*, I (Leiden 1964), no. 43 (333/2, perhaps the 'hero doctor', as A. Papagiannopoulos-Palaios suggests, *Polemon* 3, 1947–8, 128, by comparison with the find-spot of *IG* II².839, 840: but note Wycherley, *Testimonia*, 115). For the inscribed cult-table of a group of *orgeones* perhaps of this type see S. Dow, D. H. Gill, *AJA* 69 (1965), 103–114.*

[29] Those of Ferguson's class B, 'the orgeones of gods and goddesses mostly alien', were certainly not so recruited (cf. p. 337), and the question must be whether the wall of division between the two classes is firm. It is interesting but inconclusive (cf. Kearns, *Heroes of Attica*, 73) that sixteen *orgeones* from Prospalta who made a dedication to Asclepius in the third cent. (*IG* II².2355; Ferguson, 'Attic Orgeones', 91) demonstrably belong to a small number of families. Not much can be done with the reference to *orgeones* in the interpolated 'Solonian' law, *Solon* frs. 76a–b Ruschenbusch.

stucco [?] such walls as need it, and do any other building or fitting he may wish. When the term of the ten years is out, he shall take with him the beams and the roof-tiles and the doors, but shall remove nothing else. He shall look after the trees growing in the sanctuary and replace any that die and pass on the same total . . . When the *orgeones* sacrifice to the hero in [the month] Boedromion, Diognetos must make available the building where the shrine is, open, and the hut and the oven and dining-couches and tables for two *triclinia*. (*SIG*³ 1097)

A group of buildings in a field; in one of them, a shrine (or sacred image) at which, once a year, a small group of *orgeones* assembles to sacrifice and feast in honour of a hero; for the rest of the year the shrine closed, the *orgeones* absent, the field and building put to secular use (and earning rent for the *orgeones*, no doubt to finance the feast): this seems to have been a typical pattern of orgeonic piety. It is very likely, in this old boys' world, that the lessee was himself a member of the society. We know of two other associations that honoured their hero once a year;[30] one of them prolonged the festival for two days, and, surprisingly, assigned portions of the meat to be taken home for wives and children.

In contrast to the cults for which the *gene* provided priests, these look at first view like wholly private concerns.[31] The shrine of Egretes was evidently owned by his *orgeones*, and no outsider perhaps would ever be able to enter it. And yet it is hard to see why a private association should have been formed to worship, say, Egretes, or why such a group should perhaps have enjoyed privileged access to a phratry.[32] Might such *orgeones* have been perceived as having a more public role? That hypothesis finds a little support. It can be argued that the job of the *orgeones* of Hypodektes, 'Receiver', was to 'receive' the sacred objects that were brought to Athens from Eleusis before the Mysteries, on the very day of the hero's annual sacrifice; the healing-heroes Amynos and (probably) 'hero-doctor' had their *orgeones*, though they certainly also attracted a wider clientele; and *orgeones*, though of a different type, were

[30] Those of Hypodektes and Echelos (see the previous note). Leasing within the group: see M. Jameson's excellent remarks, *Vanderpool Studies*, 73–74, based esp. on V. N. Andreyev, *Eirene* 12 (1974), 43–44; cf. Rosivach, *Public Sacrifice*, 141–42. Lambert, *Phratries*, 75, n. 71, rightly stresses that *orgeones* engaged in the same kinds of financial transactions as phratries.

[31] Cf. Suda o 511 s.v. ὀργεῶνες· οἱ τοῖς ἰδίᾳ ἀφιδρυμένοις θεοῖς ὀργιάζοντες (other definitions follow). For the rest of the lexicographical evidence see Ferguson, 'Attic Orgeones', 62–64; the most interesting detail is in Pollux, 8.107: οἱ κατὰ δήμους ἐν τακταῖς ἡμέραις θύοντες θυσίας τινάς (note κατὰ δήμους).

[32] This argument is fallible, as we have seen (ns. 27 and 29 above). But we must clearly reject either the association between *orgeones* and the phratry, or the view (Ferguson, 'Attic Orgeones', 72) that a group of such *orgeones* could come into being merely by the decision of a group of would-be *orgeones*, without external authorization.

responsible for the fine processions in the public cult of Bendis.[33] Even if we concede that Egretes, say, was inaccessible to ordinary persons and that his *orgeones* participated in no public rite, does it follow that the association was seen as no more than a hereditary dining-club in thin religious disguise? Perhaps the presence of Egretes had, by whatever means, been detected in the locality, and an association had been formed to propitiate the potentially dangerous hero by regular worship. The *orgeones* feasted in private for the public good.

Yet one final form of hereditary association needs to be mentioned, the local league uniting several demes. The best-known example is that of the Marathonian Tetrapolis, made up of the four 'cities', or Clisthenic demes as they later became, Marathon, Tricorynthus, Oinoe, Probalinthus. A large fragment survives of their calendar, which seems to have listed both individual sacrifices of the four demes and also, separately, their communal rites. Thus (in the post-Clisthenic period at least) the league was an extra level of association fitted over the normal structure of deme religion, which it left intact: the participating demes had their own rites—to which there is no sign that members of the other three cities were invited—but also took their place in a broader group. How often the Tetrapolitans did in fact assemble *en masse* is uncertain. In the fragment of the calendar that seems to treat communal rites, numerous sacrifices are listed, but with one, and perhaps two, exceptions, the offering seems scarcely large enough to feed more than the '*archon* of the Tetrapolis', the four demarchs, and a few friends. There must, of course, have been at least one plenary festival in the year. In the case of another such association (about six are known in all) we can give the festival a name, and a famous one: 'the demes around about used to come together in Hekale [the place] to sacrifice to Hekaleian Zeus, and pay honour to Hekale [the future suffering heroine of Callimachus]'. A very recent discovery has shown that a pair of smallish demes, Kydantidai and Ionidai, celebrated two hitherto unknown festivals of Heracles in common.[34]

These were the principal hereditary structures of religious life after Clisthenes. (We hear also of 'bands' (*thiasoi*) of Heracles in which

---

[33] Hypodektes: cf. Kearns, *Heroes of Attica*, 75. Bendis: below, Ch. 9, n. 63. In its earliest appearances (*Hymn Hom. Ap.* 389, Aesch. fr. 144 Radt) the word ὀργεών simply means 'celebrant, priest'.

[34] Hekale: Plut. *Thes.* 14.2. For the Tetrapolis (*IG* II².1358 = *LSCG* 20), the demes Kydantidai and Ionidai (*SEG* XXXIX 148), and other local associations, see App. 3; and on the Tetrapolis calendar, Rosivach, *Public Sacrifice*, 36–40.

fathers registered sons, but of their doings little is known.[35]) What had they been before? The differences can be quickly stated. Rather than ten tribes, there had hitherto been four, the old Ionian set that traditionally (and perhaps in reality) antedated the colonization of Ionia (where they are sometimes also found). As a local administrative unit, there had existed not demes but 'naukraries'. In contrast to these innovations, however, Clisthenes 'let everyone retain their *gene* and phratries [and, doubtless, groups of *orgeones*] and priesthoods according to ancestral tradition'.[36]

New tribes; a new administrative unit, the deme; an approach to certain traditional religious structures that was, at least superficially, conservative: these are the reforms and the failures to reform which we must try to understand. Behind these particular topics lies the broader issue of traditional aristocratic predominance in religious life.

If a tribe was felt to have an ideal maximum size, ten could accommodate the expanded population of Attica[37] much more adequately than four. And the new *trittys* system ensured that each tribe contained a mix from all Attica, so that each was in effect interchangeable in political outlook with all the others. The comparison cannot be pushed much further, when we know so little of the old tribes. It is impossible to say, for instance, whether they were mutually equivalent in the same sense as their successors, or displayed instead any regional or other bias. The most important item of evidence about them is an entry in the revised sacrificial calendar of Nicomachus: the *trittys* of the White-Fillet Men (τριττὺς Λευκοταινίων) of the tribe Gleontis was to receive a sheep on the 15th of Hekatombaion, and on the following day the tribe itself was to receive two cattle, to be offered to Zeus Phratrios and Athena Phratria; at both ceremonies, which were evidently closely related, the 'tribe-kings' presided (and the authority cited for the sacrifice is the 'tribe-kings' list).[38]

From this we learn, first, that the old tribes lived on as religious entities even after Clisthenes. There must presumably still have been old tribes even in the late fourth century, to appoint the 'tribe-kings' whose residual functions in homicide jurisdiction are mentioned in the *Constitution of the Athenians*.[39] But the complete absence of 'old tribe' decrees suggests that, deprived of political functions, theirs was a rather spectral survival. We learn also that the

---

[35] See p. 333 below.   [36] Arist. *Ath. Pol.* 21.6.

[37] See Morris, *Burial*, 99–101. The demography of the late sixth and fifth cents. seems to me a topic that needs more attention from archaeologists.

[38] *LSS* 10 A 31–58; cf. W. S. Ferguson in *Classical Studies Presented to Edward Capps* (Princeton 1936), 151–58; Ch. 2, n. 17 (for the association with the *Synoikia*) and Ch. 4 for the 'tribe-kings' list'.

[39] Arist. *Ath. Pol.* 57.4, with Rhodes's note.

old tribes, like their successors, contained *trittyes*, about the functions of which, however, the one attested name, 'the White-Fillet
Men', reveals absolutely nothing.[40] The 16th of Hekatombaion, the
day of the large sacrifice of Gleontis, is also that of the *Synoikia*, of
which the tribal rite evidently formed a part. It seems to follow that
one religious function of the old tribes, as of the new, was as a structure within which individuals participated in the festivals of the
whole city. (In the particular case, however, the tribe's role in the
public rite is not quite that which was typical later.[41]) About rites
and gods and shrines confined to the individual tribes we know
nothing (though there are likely to have been some); and it may be
that most of the entries in the tribe-kings' lists of sacrifices in the
Solonian code, like this one associated with the *Synoikia*, concerned
festivals of the city that were organized tribe by tribe. Were there
already inter-tribal competitions at public festivals before
Clisthenes? However that may be, the old tribes, like their successors, were surely designed to bring Athenians together rather than to
keep them apart; for their heads, the tribe-kings, acted together as a
group (the pre-Clisthenic board of Treasurers of Athena too perhaps consisted of eight members, two from each tribe[42]), and it is
precisely with the festival of Attic unity, the *Synoikia*, that the calendar shows one tribe to have been involved.

The substitution of new tribes for old affected the phratries.
These were, in all appearance, subdivisions of the old tribes,[43] and
probably had had some role in such public festivals as were tribally
organized. Within the new tribe the minimum unit was the deme,
through several of which the members of a single phratry will normally have been dispersed. Henceforth, therefore, it will have been
by private arrangement only that *phratores* met together during festivals of the city.

[40] The argument that a body so named cannot have had a local basis may underestimate the
senses in which names can be arbitrary. On the old *trittyes* see Ferguson, in *Studies Presented
to Capps*, 151–58, and Rhodes, *Commentary Ath. Pol.*, 68–69 (both argue, surely rightly, that
Arist. *Ath. Pol.* fr. 3 Kenyon is wrong to identify old *trittyes* and phratries).

[41] Both the singling-out of one tribe, and the assignation of sacrificial victims by tribe, seem
untypical of later practice. But in general for the role of tribes at city festivals see *LSCG* 151
A (Cos); and for a comparable phenomenon, Hom. *Od.* 3.4–8 (on which see C. Sourvinou-
Inwood in N. Marinatos and R. Hägg eds., *Greek Sanctuaries*, London 1993, 3).

[42] *IG* I³.510.

[43] The vital evidence, in support of Arist. *Ath. Pol.* fr. 3 Kenyon (unreliable in itself), is the
fact noted in the text that the old tribe Gleontis sacrificed to Zeus Phratrios and Athena
Phratria (cf. the works cited in n. 40 above). A reader for the Oxford Press rightly notes the
possibility that an earlier descent-group might 'pick up the interests of the members of a later
group', since most individuals would belong to groups of both types (similar doubts in
Lambert, *Phratries*, 16). But would a cult quite as specific as that of Zeus Phratrios be likely
to cross boundaries thus?

The deme did not exist as an administrative unit before Clisthenes. Local rites, however, there must certainly have been, the predecessors of those listed on the elaborate deme-calendars. How were they organized? To this important question there seem to be three possible answers.

One can think of the *gene*. There is no reason why they should not have furnished priests for local cults, as they did for those of the city. But if we press the analogy, a difficulty emerges. The central cults which the *gene* served were not theirs, but the city's: whose then were the local cults which they would hypothetically have served? Unless we suppose that at this level the *gene* were acting as wholly autonomous bodies,[44] we have still to find a local organizing authority.

Another candidate is the phratry, a group which, though not local by definition, seems often, as we have seen, to have had a strong local basis in fact. The phratry was an archaic institution. In its classical form, it was a kind of corridor leading to the city; there is great intuitive appeal in supposing that it had once itself been the hall in which life outside the narrow family-circle was lived. And this does to some degree appear to have been the function of the 'phratry' of the *Labyadae* at Delphi.[45] But we must distinguish here. The phratry was in effect weakened by dissociation from the new tribal structure, as we have just noted. Against such debilitating isolation it could not protect itself; but against the surrender of its shrines (that is to say valuable property) and rites and priesthoods and privileges to the newly created demes, it surely could and would have done, unless constrained by law. As we have seen, the classical phratries probably had few, if any, communal rites other than the *Apatouria*, and did not own and administer shrines, except one or two of specialized type. And yet we are told explicitly by the *Constitution of the Athenians* that Clisthenes left the phratries in their traditional state. Only if we reject that statement[46] can we believe that the religious

---

[44] This is not inconceivable, at least in a few cases: cf. App. 2 A s.v. *Lykomidai*.

[45] From the great inscription (now *Corpus des inscriptions de Delphes*, I: *Lois sacrées et règlements religieux*, ed. G. Rougemont, Paris 1977, no. 9) we learn of their concern with funerals; column D, desperately obscure, treats θοῖναι and festivals, most of them apparently festivals of Delphi during which the *Labyadai* probably also met for feasts, a few perhaps exclusive to the phratry (43–49): see Rougemont's extensive commentary, and Schmitt Pantel, *Cité au banquet*, 91–93. Other helpful parallels are sparse: on the Aeginetan *patrai* see Ch. 5, n. 26; the Clytiads of Chios appear to be contrasted with a phratry, not identified with one, in *LSCG* 118.27–28 (*SIG*³ 987; aliter Graf, *Nordionische Kulte*, 37). In Attica, Drakon gave them a role in cases of homicide (*IG* I³.104.18, 23 = M/L 86); and note *IG* I³.247 (Spata), the inheritance rules of a group ending in ντιδôν. Lambert, *Phratries*, ch. 8, argues that the archaic phratry did not have notably larger functions than its post-Clisthenic successor. See in general on early phratries Roussel, *Tribu et cité*, 117–32.

[46] As does most recently O. Murray in Murray/Price, *Greek City*, 14–15.

functions performed in the fifth century by the demes had belonged in the sixth century (whatever might have been true of the more distant past) to the phratries.

As a final possibility we are left with 'proto-demes'. It is widely accepted that 'demes' existed as social groups before Clisthenes; the innovation of this cautious reformer was merely to give them a place in the administrative structure of the state.[47] The easy solution to our difficulty is surely to suppose that these social groups which pre-existed Clisthenes had also, as one might expect, been religious groups. The Marathonian Tetrapolis, which is obviously of ancient origin, is a locally based religious association; and it is almost inconceivable that a proud ancient *polis* such as Thorikos did not celebrate communal rites in the sixth century. (A dedication apparently made collectively by 'the Sunians' has in fact been ascribed on high authority to the mid-sixth century; but on this it would be rash to insist.) How this religious life of the proto-demes might have been organized—and in particular what part the *gene* might have taken in it[48]—of course we cannot know.

This does not mean that there was nothing new about the religious life of the true demes. On the contrary, the self-consciousness created by their new political status is very likely to have been a powerful stimulus. The new official, the demarch, is soon at the centre of local religious life. A deme such as Atene, sited in a region that seems scarcely even to have been inhabited before the fifth century, is an intriguing special case: it will evidently have had to assemble its pantheon from scratch.[49] And it can scarcely be coincidence that evidence for both the religious and political life of the demes fades away at about the same time in the third century BC. But normally it was by growth rather than revolution that the classical demes became such flourishing religious centres.

[47] See Whitehead, *Demes*, 16–30; and, on 'proto-demes' and cult, Kearns, 'Continuity and Change', 200.

[48] Interesting consequences follow on any view. If the *gene* did supply priests to the proto-demes, they should, given Clisthenes' general policy, have continued to do so to the true demes. This is, in fact, very possible, even though in the only explicitly attested case a deme priesthood was filled from the demesmen (Dem. 57.46–47, 62). (A role for *gene* in the practice of the Marathonian Tetrapolis is implied by Philochorus *FGrH* 328 F 75; and for the possible association of the Salaminians with deme cult see App. 2, n. 73.) On the other view, the proto-demes had emancipated themselves from the *gene* before the city did. About the possible religious function of naukraries (cf. Rhodes, *Commentary Ath. Pol.*, 151–53; Lambert, *Phratries*, 252–61) it is not worth speculating. The Sunians: *IG* I³.1024, cf. Jeffery, *Local Scripts*, 78, no. 27. The next-oldest deme-dedication is probably *IG* I³.1013 (Halai Aixonides, ? c.475), now that *IG* I³.522 bis has been down-dated.

[49] See Lohmann, 'Country Life', 35. It is less clear that Piraeus, which Lohmann also mentions, started from nothing, given the existence of the Tetrakomia (see App. 3).

Was there, then, no Clisthenic revolution? On this issue two plausible arguments confront one another. That Clisthenes constructed a new political order is not in doubt; the debate is whether he was also actively concerned to demolish the old. On one view, he was a vigorous (if devious) subverter of the social structures of the *ancien régime*. This approach takes its start from Aristotle's famous remark that the extreme democratic reformer should follow the example of Clisthenes and the democrats of Cyrene:

He should create new tribes and phratries, in greater number, and combine private shrines [or 'rites'] into a few public ones, and do everything to ensure that all the citizens are as intermingled as possible, and earlier associations are dissolved.[50]

It is conceded, of course, that Clisthenes did not abolish any existing organization, not even the phratries or old tribes. But, it is argued, he diverted the main flow of political life elsewhere, so that what had been main channels stagnated into backwaters. Similarly, Clisthenes did not destroy old local associations such as the Marathonian Tetrapolis or the Tetrakomoi of Phaleron; but at a different level he dissolved their unity by distributing them for political and military purposes between different tribes. And the cults of the *trittyes* were created, artificially, to compete with them and with other traditional religious structures.[51]

But, it has been well countered of late, one has only to shift the perspective a little to appreciate this reformer's extreme conservatism.[52] Even though, for his own positive purposes, he had to create certain new political structures, he pointedly refrained from attacking the old (even the now quite redundant old tribes). The cornerstone of the new democracy was to be a popular council that would represent the *demos* of the whole of Attica.[53] As the smallest sub-unit in the new system, only the deme would serve; for there were probably too few phratries for a system based on them to have guaranteed adequate local representation. But no attempt was made to replace the phratry by the deme as a recorder of title to citizenship;[54] rather, the two rode on in cheerful tandem.

As for the argument that the old religious associations were delib-

---

[50] *Politics* 1319[b] 23–27.

[51] The argument about phratries is widespread (see e.g. M. Ostwald, *CAH*[2] IV [1988], 310: on *trittyes* see ibid. 315), that about religious associations was first advanced by D. M. Lewis, *Historia* 12 (1963), 22–40.

[52] By Kearns, 'Continuity and Change', to which I am much indebted; cf. Roussel, *Tribu et cité*, 269–89.

[53] See C. Meier, *Die Entstehung des Politischen bei den Griechen* (Frankfurt 1980), 91–143.

[54] See Manville, *Citizenship*, 24–25 and n. 9 above.

erately weakened by unnatural distribution between different tribes, the rationale of the new tribal division is in many ways obscure; and we do not in fact know that the Tetrapolites, say, had belonged to a single tribe even before Clisthenes. It is very uncertain that the postulated rival cults of the *trittyes* ever existed.[55] And there is an important general consideration: the members of the old associations, the hoplite farmers on whose support Clisthenes depended, will surely not have regarded them as rotten boroughs ripe for reform. Their attitude is much more likely to have been one of affectionate pride.[56] An attack on them could only be covert; and it is not very satisfactory to assign much of Clisthenes' programme to a secret agenda kept hidden from his own supporters. A democratic reformer could not but be conservative in dealing with social groupings which all men loved because they had grown up with them. Would Clisthenes ever so much have dreamt of a world without phratries?

This is no easy dispute to resolve. To the conservatives it must be granted that many social structures of the *ancien régime*—phratries and local associations of the Tetrapolis type, if not in full vigour the old tribes—survived throughout the great centuries of the radical democracy. But we can scarcely deny to the Aristotelians that when attachments are multiplied, the strength of any individual bond is liable to be weakened; in speaking of the 'dissolution' of existing associations Aristotle is too emphatic, but new friendships might certainly tend to cause old acquaintance to be forgot.

However that may be, Clisthenes' central policy was not destructive but positive: he created new tribes. We should pause a little over this intriguing process. In one sense, the new Clisthenic order was rational, abstract, 'geometric', and secular. No tribe was effectively different from any other; every Athenian from every corner of Attica was distributed among these ten homogeneous tribes, and even time was henceforth divided for civic purposes not by months but by the ten 'prytanies', the divisions that arose as the presidency of the *boule* rotated between the ten tribes.[57] But in another sense the Clisthenic

[55] See n. 4 above.

[56] Cf. Kearns, 'Continuity and Change', 192: 'group consciousness, and only secondarily aristocratic influence, was the salient fact about the old groups'; on Clisthenes' declared aims see A. Andrewes, *CQ* NS 27 (1977), 241–48 (who, however, believes that Clisthenes must inevitably have justified his *trittys* reform by an appeal to the desirability of 'mixing', i.e. breaking of old associations).

[57] For this interpretation of Clisthenes see Lévêque/Vidal-Naquet, *Clisthène*. esp. ch. 2; the prytany system is, however, perhaps post-Clisthenic (Rhodes, *Boule*, 17–19). W. R. Connor, ' "Sacred" and "Secular": ἱερὰ καὶ ὅσια and the Classical Athenian Concept of the State', *Ancient Society* 19 (1988), 161–88, well shows that the two terms of his title remained complementary aspects of public life even under the radical democracy.

tribes are deeply embedded in traditional religious assumptions. Each was associated with an 'eponymous' hero, by an 'artificial' process than which, at this date, perhaps nothing could have been more natural. The final choice of the 10 heroes was apparently made, from a short list of 100, by Apollo of Delphi.[58] Thus the new order was not really artificial because not really man-made.

It seems likely that Apollo's choice was shaped by one of those forms of innocent manipulation in which oracular practice abounds. (Possibly, for instance, the 100 candidates were arranged by Clisthenes in an order of preference, and the Pythia sought Apollo's yea or nay for each in turn until 10 names were approved.) It has often been felt that a wholly random selection out of 100 would have produced a much less distinguished list than the 10 names actually chosen, who include four Attic kings (Cecrops, Erechtheus, Pandion, and Aegeus), a son of Theseus (Akamas), a hero associated with a famous monument (Leos and the Leokoreion), a token Eleusinian (Hippothoon), and glamorous Salaminian Ajax (added to the natives as a neighbour and a valiant ally, according to Herodotus, and a particularly happy choice at a time when Athens had still to assert her title to Salamis). On the other hand, we perhaps know the name of three failed candidates, Araphen, Cephalus, and Polyxenos; and though Araphen, eponym of a coastal village, would obviously have been much less suitable as the figurehead of a centralizing institution than any of the eight just listed, the eminent east-Attic hero Cephalus might have done better than the two obscurer figures who made up the successful ten, Oeneus, a son of Pandion or Dionysus, and a little-known son of Heracles, Antiochus.[59]

The cult of these heroes was not whistled into being by Clisthenes out of nothing; not, at least, in every case. A particular argument puts this all but beyond doubt. Each tribe had a 'priest of the eponymous' (hero), and three surprisingly recruited their priest from outside their own members. The anomaly can be neatly explained by the hypothesis that the cult of the hero was left with the *genos* which had traditionally had it in charge; and in two cases it is now all but certain that this did occur.[60] We have, it is true, no such proof that

[58] Arist. *Ath. Pol.* 21.6 (the only source).

[59] The heroes are well studied in detail by Kron, *Phylenheroen*; for the case for selection see ibid. 29–32 and esp. Kearns, *Heroes of Attica*, 87–90 (who suggests several further ways in which particular heroes were relevant). Ajax: Hdt. 5.66.2. Araphen was εἶς τῶν ἑκατὸν ἡρώων, according to Herodian Gr. π. μον. λεξ. 17.8, p. 923 Lenz; plausible corrections in Σ Eur. *Hipp.* 455 and Hesych. π 2896 give the same description of the other two (see P. J. Bicknell *ap.* Kearns, *Heroes of Attica*, 90, n. 57). But it is not stated that the 'hundred heroes' of this classification are those of Clisthenes' list; nor is it clear how authentic tradition could possibly have been preserved.

[60] See App. 2 A s.v. *Amynandridai* and (Hippothoontis) ibid., n. 21.

an existing cult was adopted by those tribes that (when our evidence begins, rather late) chose the 'priest of the eponymous' internally; and it is possible that in these cases the relevant hero had lacked a priest of his own before Clisthenes.[61] But appeal can be made to a different factor: the siting of the 'tribal sanctuaries' at which the tribes assembled and displayed their decrees. These were dotted throughout Athens, not necessarily within the territory of the tribe itself; one, that of Hippothoontis, was even at Hippothoon's home, Eleusis.[62] An obvious explanation for this diversity is that use was made of existing sanctuaries. The exception who supports the rule is the eponym of Aiantis, Ajax. As a Salaminian hero, he probably lacked a shrine on Attic soil; but his son Eurysakes chanced to have one in Melite, and instead of constructing a new Aianteion, Aiantis displayed its decrees in the Eurysakeion. (Ajax may indeed already have been introduced there before Clisthenes.) Thus the new order made conservative use of existing religious structures, and even in this special area left the *gene* their privileges. Even if in fact a few of these sanctuaries had to be newly founded, they were not bunched together artificially. As a result, the uniformly created tribes immediately acquired a pleasing, natural-seeming diversity.

In their new role, however, the ten heroes certainly acquired new lustre. Not surprisingly, their cult retained a public character, and dedications to them were made, with rare exceptions, by officials of the tribes. We even find the *boule*, the body representative of all the tribes, making a collective dedication of ten vessels to 'the *eponymoi*'.[63] But even if an ordinary individual only approached them

[61] As Schlaifer supposed, *HSCP* 51 (1940), 251–57; but Kearns, 'Continuity and Change', 193–94, suggests that the priesthoods were originally all gentilician, but in some cases passed to the tribes through the extinction of the relevant *gene*.

[62] Those of Erechtheis, Kekropis, and Pandionis were on the acropolis; Antiochis had its shrine in the Kynosarges region, perhaps in the precinct of Antiochus' father Heracles, Akamantis probably in the modern Kallithea region (*IG* II².4983 will scarcely belong to the tribal shrine), Leontis probably in or near the *agora* (and cf. the following note); for Aiantis and Hippothoontis see the text and (Ajax) p. 311 below (the Αἰάντειον known from *IG* II².1008.87 and *Hesperia* 24, 1955, 228–32, line 141, is not relevant, being on Salamis: G. R. Culley, *Hesperia* 46, 1977, 295); for Oeneis (though cf. Meyer, *Urkundenreliefs*, 188–89) and Aegeis there is no conclusive evidence. See Kron, *Phylenheroen, passim*, and Kearns, *Heroes of Attica*, 81, n. 3 and App. 1; cf. briefly S. Rotroff, *Hesperia* 47 (1978), 205–206.

[63] For dedications by tribal officers see Jones, *Public Organization*, 48–51; *Hesperia* 9 (1940), 56–66, no. 8; *IG* II².1742; *SEG* XXX 69.19. For other traces of worship of the *eponymoi* see Kearns, 'Continuity and Change', 195 (or *Heroes of Attica*, 86). She notes: one private dedication from the acropolis to an eponymous hero, Erechtheus, by members of the relevant tribe (*IG* I³.873); probably one sacrifice by a city deme, Skambonidai, to the hero of its tribe, Leos (*IG* I³.244 C 4); one altar probably dedicated to, *inter alios*, an eponymous hero (Akamas), found in a city deme of the relevant tribe (*IG* II².4983). She stresses that worship of the eponyms seems scarcely to have spread outside the city itself (but a dedication to Leos, by officials of Leontis, from the Daphni region has now been joined by another such to Hermes, which strengthens the possibility that the tribe had a subsidiary sanctuary there,

from within the group, at the ceremony of his tribe, every Athenian must in course of time have become very familiar with them. Most or all of them were portrayed in a famous group dedicated at Delphi, supposedly as a thank-offering for Marathon; and whether or not the tribal heroes are the figures who look down from the east frieze of the Parthenon, 'the *eponymoi*' in the *agora* (a statue-group) was universally familiar as the place where official notices of all kinds were displayed. We would much like to know when this important monument, a symbol of the new order, was first erected.[64] On a humbler level, there are vases of the late fifth century that defy mythological probabilities by showing two or more of the eponymous heroes together, clearly because of their role in Athenian life.[65]

The hero was also sometimes, and perhaps originally, known as the *archegetes* or *archegos* of the tribe,[66] a term of potent ambiguity that unites the ideas of origin (*arche*) and leadership (*hegeomai*). (Several demes too honoured 'archegete heroes':[67] a parallel Clisthenic creation, or one of his models?) The Clisthenic heroes were perhaps originally envisaged as 'leaders', by analogy, for instance, with Athena, *archegetis* of the whole city; but the male archegete of a group was never secured against slipping into parenthood, and in time we find the members of the tribe Antiochis, for

doubtless of Leos: *IG* II².2818 and *SEG* XXXVI 269). *Boule* and the *eponymoi*: see Rotroff, *Hesperia* 47 (1978), 207 f. on lines 13–17 of the text she publishes (*SEG* XXVIII 53); whether an established cult of the *eponymoi* as a group is to be inferred is uncertain.

[64] Cf. Kron, *Phylenheroen*, 202–36 [+]; and for the debate on the east frieze, Castriota, *Myth, Ethos, Actuality*, 218, n. 106; on the problems of the Marathon monument, Kearns, *Heroes of Attica*, 81, n. 8 (reporting a theory of A. H. Griffiths). On the surviving fourth-cent. monument of the *eponymoi* see Thompson/Wycherley, *Agora*, 38–41 [+]; Travlos, *Pictorial Dictionary*, 210–12; J. M. Camp, *The Athenian Agora* (London 1986), 97–100. The site of its predecessor is disputed, see H. Thompson, *Gnomon* 54 (1982), 391–92. For the testimonia see Wycherley, *Testimonia*, 85–90; the group is first attested in Ar. *Pax* 1183–84, that is to say very soon after relevant evidence becomes available, and could therefore be much older: Lévêque/Vidal-Naquet, *Clisthène*, 72–73 attractively see it as Clisthenes' counter to Hipparchus' altar of the twelve gods.

[65] See Kearns, 'Continuity and Change', 197 (or *Heroes of Attica*, 91); L. Burn, *The Meidias Painter* (Oxford 1987), 18; and more generally Kron, *Phylenheroen*, 116–18, 166–69, 237–42 (eponymous heroes represented on honorary decrees, etc.; cf. Meyer, *Urkundenreliefs*, 187–91).

[66] First in Ar. Γῆρας fr. 135 K/A, ὁ δὲ μεθύων ἥμει παρὰ τοὺς ἀρχηγέτας (a reference to the statue-group, perhaps not yet so called, of 'the *eponymoi*').

[67] See Lévêque/Vidal-Naquet, *Clisthène*, 70, on *IG* I³.1019 (cf. *Ergon* 1991 [1992], 6 on a new fr.), *IG* II².2849 (both from Rhamnus: add now the *horos*, *Ergon* 1991 [1992], 6 and 1993 [1994], 1); Soph. *OC* 60; Pl. *Lys.* 205d. They point out that the deme archegetes could be seen like the well-known archegetes of colonies as 'founders' (cf. Arist. *Ath. Pol.* 21.5). *IG* I³.1024 is restored as a dedication to Zeus Archegetes by the Sunians. For the word cf. W. Leschhorn, '*Gründer der Stadt*' (Stuttgart 1984), 180–84 and 364, no. 30 (Athena: add *SEG* XXVIII 60.65); I. Malkin, *Religion and Colonization in Ancient Greece* (Leiden 1987), 241–48.

instance, occasionally described as Antiochids, descendants of Antiochus.[68] This is not to say that anyone 'really believed' that a social unit first constituted in the late sixth century in fact carried on the line of Heracles, but that no difficulty was experienced in applying to it the idiom of fictional kinship in which phratries too, for instance, were traditionally conceived. The artificial creation had become no less natural than its predecessors.

[68] See [Dem.] 58.18; Clidemus *FGrH* 323 F 22; [Plut.] *X Orat.* 851a; *SEG* III 116, XXXVII 100.10 (= XXXIX 145 and *Agora* XIX L8); *IG* II².1163.15, 1165.17 (but not 27), 2670; *Hesperia* 15 (1946), 189, no. 35.8; and (verse) *IG* II².1141 (*CEG* 890). Conversely, we hear of the Θυμαιτίς or Γλεοντίς φρατρία (n. 15 above) where a patronymic might be expected.

8

The Fifth Century: Democracy and Empire

In the fifth century, the history of religion overlaps to a rare degree, at least in its externals, with the history of events. In Greek eyes, the supreme offence of the Persian invaders who ravaged Attica in 480 was that they 'burnt the temples of the gods'. To commemorate the crime, the Athenians built a number of the desecrated members into a conspicuous position high in the restored north bastion of the acropolis, where they can still be seen. Several of these temples, in fact, had only recently been built or were still incomplete when the barbarian came;[1] the most ambitious, the 'pre-Parthenon', was perhaps an offering of gratitude for the repulse of the earlier invasion at Marathon in 490. According to tradition, the Greek allies vowed before the battle of Plataea in 479 to leave the ravaged temples unrestored, as a 'memorial of the sacrilege of the barbarians'. However that may be, a lull in temple-building activities of some thirty years apparently ensued,[2] until peace occurred and—aided, if to a degree that is controversial,[3] by the involuntary contributions of their now subjected allies—the Athenians were free to raise those matchless temples at which we still marvel. With the spoils of empire, however, there also came to Athens the sophists and progressive thought. The threat to traditional order that they posed evoked (it is often said) a conservative reaction, which reached a tragic culmination in the execution of Socrates for impiety in 399.

This is a familiar story; and much of it can be passed over briefly here. We need not struggle with the many controversial particulars of the temple-building programme: the main point is clear, that the

---

[1] Cf. n. 4 below.

[2] See Meiggs, *Athenian Empire*, 504–507 (with the reservations ibid. 597), where the authenticity of the 'Plataea oath' is defended against Theopompus' condemnation, *FGrH* 115 F 153.

[3] See L. Kallet-Marx, 'Did Tribute Fund the Parthenon?', *ClAnt* 8 (1989), 252–66; A. Giovannini, *Historia* 39 (1990), 129–48.

democracy was no less ambitious to honour the gods with monumental buildings than the tyranny had been, and this not only in the
later Periclean years, when democratic Athens had become in turn,
for its allies, the 'tyrant city', but already in the decades before
Salamis; then it was, apparently, that the first Parthenon and the first
temple of Poseidon at Sunium were built, both almost as ample as
their surviving successors.[4]

We may consider other issues instead. The new democracy developed ideologically with startling speed, and assumed an aggressive,
'militant'[5] stance towards many traditional values. Harmodius and
Aristogeiton, reputed destroyers of the old order, were to receive
'honours equal to those of the gods' under the new.[6] Athens also, of
course, acquired an empire; and we must look at the religious implications both of radical democracy and of imperialism. This is also a
period in which evidence for the introduction of new cults, of various types, is unusually abundant and instructive. And, finally, we
must certainly touch on the religious background to the trial of
Socrates.

We begin with the new constitution, and its implications for religious life. For Herodotus, the brilliant military successes of the
young democracy prove the transformation wrought by Clisthenes'
reform.[7] For us, the political revolution is revealed no less clearly by
two archaeological phenomena: the shaping of the Pnyx as a place of
public assembly, and the sudden outburst of decrees passed by the
demos which assembled there. Whereas no single decree of the sixth
century survives in its original form,[8] those of the fifth fill a stately
volume. Many deal with religious topics (six, for instance, of the earliest surviving eight), and we are reminded that ordinary meetings of
the assembly had a divided agenda, at which sacred matters (*hiera*)
preceded profane (*hosia*).[9] A fourth-century rhetorical handbook

[4] See on the pre-Parthenon, Boersma, *Building Policy*, 38–39, 176; Castriota, *Myth, Ethos,
Actuality*, 279, n. 4 [+]; R. Tölle-Kastenbein, *JdI* 108 (1993), 61, n. 57; on Poseidon at
Sunium, Boersma, *Building Policy*, 36–37, 195. The 'pre-Propylaia' were apparently begun
then too: W. B. Dinsmoor Jr., *The Propylaia to the Athenian Acropolis*, I: *The Predecessors*
(Princeton 1980), pp. xvii–xviii; and if T. L. Shear is right the supposed 'Cimonian' works at
Eleusis in fact belong here (in *Studies in Athenian Architecture, Sculpture and Topography
Presented to Homer A. Thompson*, *Hesperia* Suppl. 20, 1982, 128–40).

[5] Cf. P. Veyne *ap.* C. Meier, *Introduction à l'anthropologie politique de l'antiquité classique*
(Paris 1984), 9.

[6] See n. 55 below.   [7] 5.78. The Pnyx: see Travlos, *Pictorial Dictionary*, 466–75.

[8] Except conceivably (cf. *IG* I³ ad loc., and F. Preisshofen, *AA* 1977, 76–77; *contra*,
G. Németh, *JdI* 108, 1993, 76–81) *IG* I³.4, which treats religious matters; the content is yet
older, according to B. Jordan, *Servants of the Gods* (Göttingen 1979), 37–38.

[9] See Arist. *Ath. Pol.* 43.6, with Rhodes; on the ἱερά/ὅσια distinction, which any translation
inevitably distorts, see W. R. Connor, *Ancient Society* 19 (1988), 161–88. Since ὅσια are

identifies seven themes on which the aspirant politician must be able to 'speak before the people': the first, said to be especially important, is 'rites'.[10] Religious authority now lay with the council and the assembly, and this not just ultimately but to a large extent on a practical, day-to-day level. The relation is nicely symbolized by the practice whereby public priests made 'reports' to the council of the good omens that they had secured in their sacrifices 'on behalf of the Athenian people'; the council in turn formally resolved to 'accept the benefits arising from the sacrifice' on behalf of the state. Though that institution is first attested in the second half of the fourth century, the structure of authority that it implies is already clearly present early in the fifth.[11] The nerve-centre of the city's religion was now the democratic council.

This, certainly, is a change; but of what kind? This is not the place to discuss the role of religious arguments, and advisers, in a democratic assembly, except to stress that the transition to democracy did not, of course, entail secularization of any overt kind.[12] We will look rather at the effect of popular control on the traditional structures of religious life. A typical example of the early decrees is one of (probably) the second quarter of the century, concerning the cult at Eleusis. It regulates such matters as the 'sacred truce' and the fees that the officials of the cult may charge to initiates. In this and other such cases, it has often been argued, the *demos* was intruding its authority into untraditional areas.[13] But there is in this proposition a crucial ambiguity. That the affairs of the two goddesses had not traditionally been regulated in a democratic assembly is certainly true. But it is almost certainly false that they had hitherto been subject to no form of public, Athenian supervision. Control by the *demos* succeeded, not independence, but control by the previous organs of state, above all the archons. Even if we concede (what in this book has been denied) that the cults administered by the *gene*

'things which may be freely discussed or disposed of without offence to the gods' (cf. Parker, *Miasma*, 330), even the 'profane' is defined by direct reference to the sacred.

[10] [Arist.] *Rh. Al.* 3.1423ª20–1424ª8. Cf. [Lys.] 6.33 on the religious concerns of the *boule*— 'Sacrifices, processions, prayers, and oracles'.

[11] Cf. R. Garland, *BSA* 79 (1984), 78–80; Rhodes, *Boule*, 43, n. 6, and 132; below, Ch. 11, n. 102. The 'reporting' priest then normally received honours, for which the report constituted a request (Gauthier, *Bienfaiteurs*, 117). On the role of the *boule* in regard to the Eleusinian Mysteries see K. Clinton, *Hesperia* 49 (1980), 280.

[12] Cf. Connor, *Ancient Society*, 19 (1988).

[13] *IG* I³.6 = *LSS* 3; cf. e.g. D. M. Lewis, *BSA* 55 (1960), 193 (who speaks of 'all the fifth century Athenian decrees where a private cult is taken over and regulated by the state'); Ostwald, *Popular Sovereignty*, 137–71; and for the general approach, J. K. Davies, *CAH²* IV (1988), 368–88. The decree concerning the Praxiergids (*IG* I³.7 = *LSCG* 15) is often invoked in this context (see e.g. D. M. Lewis, *BSA* 49, 1954, 17–21; J. K. Davies, *Democracy in Classical Greece*, Hemel Hempstead 1978, 69–70).*

had once been their private fiefs, it is rather unlikely that they had remained so down to the early fifth century. In the case of Eleusis it is actually impossible, unless we suppose that the relevant *gene* were rich enough to finance the extensive building-programme of the sixth century. None of the fifth-century decrees contains anything to show that it concerns the nationalization of an independent, long-established cult. We can, of course, concede that the *demos* may have proved in practice a more rigorous and intrusive master than an aristocratic *archon* had been. By the fourth century, priests and priestesses recruited from the *gene* were subject to a form of public audit, εὔθυνα, like any other officers of the state.[14]

Several decrees treat the financing of cults, a dark subject from which the veil is at last lifted a little. We find landing-taxes paid by shipowners and merchants put to the profit of unknown gods at Sunium, of (perhaps) Apollo Delios at Phaleron, and of the Dioscuri, appropriately maritime gods, at Athens; while the military are probably required to support Apollo Lykeios, in whose gymnasium they exercised.[15] We see here, it is sometimes supposed, the transformation of private cults supported by voluntary contributions into state cults supported by taxation: originally, the shipowners had freely offered their mite to the protecting god. One may wonder, however, how many taxes in history have had such a spontaneous origin. It can scarcely be coincidence that three of the four decrees relate to shipowners and merchants, who at Athens were normally foreigners, and what they illustrate above all is surely the characteristic eagerness of Greek states to place as much of the tax burden as possible on non-citizen shoulders. The gods could thus profit from the great boom in commercial activity that Athens in the fifth century must certainly have experienced.

In different ways, however, the old order did change, and the fifth century saw the partial supersession of the *gene*. Our picture of the history of priesthood at Athens has to be almost recklessly impressionistic, for lack of precise evidence; but the one surviving document which records the establishment of a priesthood is probably of the 440s, and certainly attests, even if it does not introduce, a radical change. The new priestess of Athena Nike, we learn, is to be

---

[14] Aeschin. 3.18.

[15] *IG* I³.8, 130, 133, 138; cf. R. Schlaifer, *HSCP* 51 (1940), 233–41; Lewis, *BSA* 55 (1960), 190–94 (but cf. H. B. Mattingly, *ZPE* 83, 1990, 112–13); M. Jameson, *Archaiognosia* 1 (1980), 213–36; also *LSS* 85 (Lindos, fifth cent.); F. Sokolowski, *HThR* 47 (1954), 161–64; for the view here contested see Lewis, *BSA* 55 (1960), and C. Preaux *ap.* J. Velissaropoulos, *Les naucléres grecs* (Paris 1980), 229. On taxes and endowments for the funding of cults in Athens see Faraguna, *Atene nell'età di Alessandro*, 341–46, with information about the unpub. *Ag. Inv.* 1.7495; on *epidosis* see n. 23 below.

recruited by lot, not from a *genos*, but from 'all the Athenian women'.[16] And henceforth no new priesthood seems to have been assigned to a *genos*; at least, no such case is known, and of two that were established subsequently, for the new gods Bendis and Asclepius, one was certainly, and one very probably, open to all citizens.[17] According to the orator Apollodorus in the fourth century, persons who seek to arrogate to themselves the right of offering political advice are behaving 'as if this were a private priesthood of their own', when in fact in a democracy it is open to 'anyone who chooses'.[18] The old restricted priesthoods are thus seen as an exception, if not a very threatening one, to democratic egalitarianism.

Whether the priestess of Athena Nike was the first to be chosen in the new unrestricted way is much less clear. If priesthoods had to be established to serve any of the heroes who became 'eponymous' in 506, the new system in some form may have come straight in with the democracy; and there is no refuting even the view that it goes back still earlier, more plausible though it may seem that the tyrants would have preferred to reward complaisant *gene*.[19] However that may be, an 'open' priesthood founded in the first half of the century would probably still have been restricted, like the archonship, to the upper two property classes. To the priesthood of Athena Nike, by contrast, two of the three characteristics of office-holding under the more radical democracy applied: she was chosen by lot, and from the whole citizen body. About the third democratic characteristic, restricted tenure, the decree leaves us uninformed.[20] Priests drawn

---

[16] *IG* I³.35 = M/L 44 (cf. *IG* I³.36 = M/L 71, of 424/3, and for the first priestess's epitaph *IG* I³.1330 = *CEG* 93). On the acute associated chronological problems see Meiggs, *Athenian Empire*, 497–503; B. Wesenberg, *JdI* 96 (1981), 28–54; M/L, addenda, p. 311. For evidence on priesthoods (not quite complete) see D. D. Feaver, *YCS* 15 (1957), 123–58; Garland, *BSA* 79 (1984), 83–111; Maass, *Prohedrie*, 99–143; J. A. Turner, *Hiereiai* (Diss. Santa Barbara, 1983). S. Aleshire promises a much-needed monograph.

[17] Bendis: *IG* I³.136.29–31, cf. Ch. 9 below. The term of office is unknown. Asclepius: see Ch. 9, n. 100 below. From *c*.355 this priesthood was certainly annual, and probably (as certainly later) rotated by tribe. The situation from 421 to *c*.355 is unclear; but even if the priesthood was hereditary in the family of Telemachus for a period, the *demos* imposed a new system once it assumed control. Two unusual cases should, however, be noted. The priesthood of Asclepius in the Piraeus, which would naturally have been treated in the same way as that in the city, went in the first half of the fourth cent. to the specialist Euthydemus of Eleusis (Ch. 9, n. 104); and a priesthood of Asclepius was specially granted by decree (presumably for a year) to Demon of Paeania (Ch. 11, n. 112).

[18] [Dem.] 51.19, ὥσπερ ἱερωσύνην ἰδίαν τινὰ ταύτην ἔχοντες.

[19] Eponymous heroes: see Ch. 7, n. 61 above. The terms on which priesthoods established in the sixth cent. may have been held are simply unknown; the role of magistrates in related festivals (Feaver, *YCS* 15 (1957), 132) is a quite separate matter.

[20] Restricted tenure: cf. Eur. *Supp.* 406–407. For Athena's priestess, life-tenure is widely assumed, without argument; but no source attests it, and Ziehen's suppl. which introduces it in *IG* I³.35.4–5 is certainly wrong (see B. D. Meritt and H. T. Wade-Gery, *JHS* 83, 1963, 110; Schlaifer, *HSCP* 51, 1940, 259, n. 3). One Myrrhine boasts in her epitaph (n. 16 above) that

from the *gene* served for life, while the later established priesthood of Asclepius rotated annually, as did some others of uncertain origin.[21] In the case of Athena Nike's priestess, it is impossible to say a priori whether, in these years of transition, the Athenians would have chosen the more traditional or more radical alternative.

In another respect too the *gene* were superseded. Boards of 'supervisors' and 'treasurers' and 'performers of rites', appointed by the people, play an ever-increasing part in religious life, of a kind that very well might have fallen to members of appropriate *gene* in earlier times. Even at Eleusis they intrude. But this is, perhaps, not so much a matter of public control supplanting private, as of a newer form of public organization supplanting another that was now felt to be outmoded. This change certainly had begun well back in the sixth century. The 'Treasurers of Athena' had originally to be drawn, 'according to the law of Solon', from the highest property-class, but the restriction came in time to be purely nominal.[22]

Not the *gene* but the rich were affected by a different reform, one that probably was a genuine product of the democracy. Religious life, requiring as it did smart choruses and fat sacrificial victims, must always have been a favoured arena for the exercise of ambitious beneficence. Herodotus tells how the Alcmaeonids, who had contracted to build a new temple for Apollo at Delphi of *poros*-stone,

she was the first to tend the shrine of Athena Nike, i.e. doubtless (though cf. Garland, *BSA* 79, 1984, 91) first priestess; but primacy was a ground of pride (cf. *IG* I³.507 = *CEG* 434), as was even tenure of an annual sortitive office (see S. C. Humphreys, *JHS* 100, 1980, 116, on Dem. 43.42–43). The consensus is challenged by Turner, *Hiereiai*, 77–96 (cf. Parker, *Miasma*, 89, n. 60), who, however, goes too far in insisting that selection by lot implies annual tenure: contrast the Salaminians' law, *LSS* 19.12–14. For the possibility that the marble grave *lekythos* Ath. Nat. Mus. 4485 = *IG* I³.1285 commemorates the same Myrrhine see most recently C. W. Clairmont, *Classical Attic Tombstones* (Kilchberg 1993), IV.160–66 (his no. 5.150); the eds. of *IG* I³ are unconvinced.*

[21] Asclepius: n. 17 above. Priests of the eponymous hero drawn from within a tribe served for a year (*SEG* III 117, Antiochis, 303/2). Other annual priesthoods are those of (Artemis) Kalliste (*IG* II².788–89, *SEG* XVIII 87, third cent.), Artemis Soteira (*IG* II².1343.24–25, first cent.), and probably Theseus (*IG* II².2865, second cent.: for the dedicatory formula ἱερεὺς γενόμενος applied to an annual priesthood cf. *SEG* XVIII 87). The practice of dating dedications by reference to a priest might seem to imply annual tenure (so e.g. in *IG* II².1297.44, 4427–28), in which event we could add Artemis at Melite (*SEG* XXII 116, fourth cent.), Nemesis and Themis at Rhamnus (*IG* II².3109, 4638, fourth/third cent.), Aphrodite Pandemos (*IG* II².659, dated 283/2), Demos and Charites (*IG* II².2798, late third) to the list; but from the second cent. BC (or late third?: D. M. Lewis, *BSA* 50, 1955, 9) we find dedications dated by priests who served for life (ibid.; Clinton, *Sacred Officials*, 76), and the practice could be older.*

[22] Cf. Ch. 6, n. 47. On the boards cf. Garland, *BSA* 79 (1984), 116–18; Rhodes, *Commentary Ath. Pol.*, on 54.6–7. On Eleusis see esp. *IG* I³.32, with B. D. Meritt and H. T. Wade-Gery, *JHS* 85 (1963), 111–14; R. Meiggs, *JHS* 86 (1966), 96; and *SEG* XXX 61 (Ch. 11, n. 9 below). On the 'ox-buyers' (βοῶναι) see Rosivach, *Public Sacrifice*, 108–20. Treasurers of Athena: Arist. *Ath. Pol.* 47.1.

displayed their piety and magnificence by making the front parts of Parian marble instead. Demes and private associations continued to depend to a significant extent on individual generosity; and Xenophon still assumes that a rich individual will have to make 'many large sacrifices' to maintain the favour 'both of gods and men'. The sums required were larger than ever under Pericles, when, according to Plutarch, the people were treated to a constant succession of 'spectacles, festivals, feasts, and processions'. But in public cult the new system of compulsory liturgies (apparently established in the first years of the democracy) transformed generosity, for the rich, into an obligation. Of course, liturgies differ from taxes in very significant ways. No tax-payer, one imagines, expects to be thanked, or pays more than the bare minimum that the law requires. Liturgists felt that the people owed them gratitude; they knew that the more opulently they discharged the task, the more credit they would win; and some, such as Nicias, eagerly seized the opportunity to display their magnificence. Even instances of liturgies voluntarily undertaken are not hard to find. The liturgical system was in a sense simply an institutionalization of old patronal practices.[23] None the less, a real change had occurred. Whatever they may have hoped, liturgists must in fact have received much less 'gratitude' than when their gifts appeared spontaneous, and were directed to objects of their own choice. For the recipient, the real benefactor might now seem to be the political system which forced the liturgist to be generous.[24] And of course in the heyday of the empire the scale of the funds that were publicly available was such that no private individual, however opulent, could effectively compete. 'As for sacrifices and shrines and festivals and precincts, the people realize that it is impossible for each of the poor individually to sacrifice and feast and own shrines and inhabit a fine large city,

[23] Hdt. 5.62.2–3; Xen. *Oec.* 2.5; Plut. *Per.* 11.4. Demes: Whitehead, *Demes*, 172, n. 145. Private associations: e.g. *IG* II².1271.10–11, 1277.11. In several demes cults are also financed by forms of liturgy (M. Jameson in *Vanderpool Studies*, 73; Whitehead, *Demes*, 171–75), whether voluntary or compulsory we do not know (cf. now Rosivach, *Public Sacrifice*, 128–35). On state liturgies see J. K. Davies, *JHS* 87 (1967), 33–40. On 'gratitude' for them id., *Propertied Families*, pp. xviii; P. Millett, 'The Rhetoric of Reciprocity', in C. Gill, R. Seaford, and N. Postlethwaite eds., *Reciprocity in Greek Society* (Oxford forthcoming); J. Trevett, *Apollodoros the Son of Pasion* (Oxford 1992), 171–73. And on their archaic, patronal (and agonistic) aspect, Veyne, *Pain et cirque*, 186–200 (on voluntary, and spectacular, liturgies, ibid. 195). The financing of a public sacrifice by 'contributions' (*epidosis*), a related practice, is attested once only (Plut. *Phoc.* 9.1). On patronage (admittedly not an identical phenomenon with the 'euergetism' which concerns us here) before and after Clisthenes see M. I. Finley, *Politics in the Ancient World* (Cambridge 1983), 35–49; P. Millett, 'Patronage and its Avoidance in Classical Athens', in A. Wallace-Hadrill ed., *Patronage in Ancient Society* (London 1989), 15–47.

[24] Cf. the complaint of Isoc. 8.13.

but they have found a way of achieving all this. The city sacrifices a large number of victims at public expense, and it is the people that feasts and portions out the victims' is the analysis of one contemporary, the so-called Old Oligarch. It has been calculated that in the 330s at least sixteen festivals were occasions for such banquets, which every citizen was entitled to attend. Thucydides' Pericles hints at the same phenomenon when he speaks of the 'year-round competitions and sacrifices' that provide a 'relief from labour'. The great patron, which arrogated the gratitude traditionally due to individuals, was now the democracy itself.[25]

Yet another change was the substitution of the lot for the vote in the selection of magistrates (in 487), and, eventually, the opening of office to all classes of society. Three magistrates had substantial religious responsibilities, and one, the *basileus*, was in a sense the head of the religion of the city. That position was now open to all.[26]

Several of these reforms had, it seems, the same tendency: to reduce yet further the religious authority of individual mortals. Of the reverence that is so fundamental a mood of Greek religion, no great part had ever been bestowed on reverend priests; but even their few marks of distinctiveness—high birth, access to ancient tradition, long service, the test of election—were now stripped away. Priesthood was reduced, as it were, to a minor magistracy. That of Asclepius rotated year by year among the tribes, as did, for instance, the post of 'secretary to the *boule*'. Indeed, the study that first recognized this phenomenon bears the splendidly revealing title *The Priests of Asklepios: A New Method of Dating Athenian Archons*.[27] According to Isocrates, most people consider that 'priesthood is for anybody'. (Under the Romans, rather characteristically, a reversion to life priesthood can be observed.[28]) Those religious specialists who did have influence in the assembly—the seers—did not derive it from established office, and to judge from the comic poets' many jibes were in no sense reverend.

[25] [Xen.] *Ath. Pol.* 2.9 and (abundance of festivals) 3.8; Thuc. 2.38.1. The *Greater Panathenaea* of 410/9 cost more than 6 talents (*IG* I³.375 = M/L 84, 5–7; cf. ibid. 378.14–18). For the charge that Pericles or his successors used sacrifices and festivals as a bribe to the people see e.g. Plut. *Per.* 11.4, *Aristid.* 24.5 (texts much influenced by later euergetism: see Veyne, *Pain et cirque*, 297–98); and cf. Ch. 11, n. 8 on the theoric fund. The 330s: see Rosivach, *Public Sacrifice*, 64.

[26] See Arist. *Ath. Pol.* 22.5 (lot), 7.4, 26.2 (admission of lower income-groups to archonship), 56–58 (religious duties). What happened in 487 was a restoration of the lot, first introduced by Solon, if we believe *Ath. Pol.* 8.1.

[27] By W. S. Ferguson, Berkeley, 1906 (*Univ. Cal. Publ. Class. Phil.* 1, no. 5, 131–73).

[28] Isoc. 2.6; similarly Dem. *Proem.* 55.2. These disparaging comments doubtless refer to the democratic priesthoods allocated by lot (cf. Diodorus comicus fr. 2.23 ff. K/A). Reversion: see *Hesperia* 10 (1941), 242, no. 42 (after AD 125) for a life priest of Artemis Kalliste (contrast n. 21 above); *IG* II².4481 and *Hesperia* 16 (1947), 264, no. 17 for Asclepius (first cent. AD).

These tendencies, certainly, never reached complete fulfilment. Since no priesthood was ever forcibly transferred from a *genos* to the people, the majority continued to be filled in the old way. Dominant families within the *gene* in practice were sometimes able, by whatever means, to arrogate the succession to prestigious priesthoods to themselves. And in the only instance where the means of election to a local priesthood is recorded, we hear that it was filled by sortition from a short list consisting, according to a speaker, of the 'best born' men of the deme. As for magistracies, various kinds of filter operated to catch candidates who might be deemed undesirable. There still existed (or was soon to be created) a board of exegetes, to offer specialized advice on issues of pollution.[29] And the council of the Areopagus continued to be a kind of citadel of reverent fear. It was still spoken of with the highest respect even after the reforms of Ephialtes in 462 had deprived it, on the common view, of its traditional political authority, and possibly also of a much broader religious competence.[30] The powers that it retained related, in imaginatively powerful ways, to the fundamental security of the state. In one instance, it supposedly intervened discreetly against a magistrate whose wife it judged unfit to perform traditional religious duties; as the court in murder trials, it guarded the citizens from pollution; it protected the sacred olives of Athena, those symbols of Athena's care for her state, talismans of the city's eternal existence; and it also knew the location of the 'secret deposits' (or, by a plausible conjecture, 'secret tombs'), 'on which the safety of the city depends'.[31] But even the case of the Areopagus only partly violates the principle that religious reverence was dissociated from reverend mortals. The ex-archons who composed it were not in theory, under

---

[29] Dominant families: App. 2, n. 21 below. Deme priesthood: Dem. 57.46–48, 62 (on 'parasites of Heracles' in the demes see Ch. 11, n. 109). Filters: 'pre-selection' again (Arist. *Ath. Pol.* 22.5), *dokimasia* (ibid. 55), perhaps the supervision of the Areopagus (n. 31 below). Exegetes: cf. Ch. 11, n. 10.

[30] Fear: Aesch. *Eum.* 700–706; cf. C. W. Macleod, *JHS* 102 (1982), 127–29 = id., *Collected Essays* (Oxford 1983), 23–25. For the continuing reverence with which it was spoken of see e.g. Soph. *OC* 947–49; Din. 1.9; D. M. MacDowell, *Athenian Homicide Law* (Manchester 1963), 42. The character of its pre-Ephialtean authority is, of course, highly controversial: see most recently G. L. Cawkwell, *JHS* 108 (1988), 1–12 (*censura morum*); P. J. Rhodes, *CAH*² V.2 (1992), 71–73; and Wallace, *Areopagos Council, passim* (who allows it little role).

[31] Magistrate: [Dem.] 59.79–83 (but the speaker must acknowledge the limited extent of its powers, and C. Carey, *Apollodoros against Neaira*, Warminster 1992, note ad loc., considers the whole episode a fiction). Pollution: note esp. Soph. *OC* 947–49. Olives: Lys. 7 *passim*; Arist. *Ath. Pol.* 60.2. 'Secret deposits/tombs': Din. 1.9. The Areopagus was also granted a share in the supervision of sacred precincts, including the *hiera orgas*, by *IG* II².204.19, of 352, and according to Σ Dem. 21.115 chose the *hieropoioi* of the Semnai: cf. Wallace, *Areopagos Council*, 106–12 (who is rightly sceptical of later anecdotal evidence that implies a general competence against impiety, but perhaps underestimates the symbolic importance of the functions attested; there will have been others comparable).

the democracy, an élite; and the respect that it evoked was for an institution that transmitted corporate traditions. The Areopagus was the citizen body, at its most solemn;[32] and its authority in a sense confirms the principle that the only object of reverence, apart from the gods themselves, was the city.

That principle would certainly have been endorsed by the speakers of the Funeral Oration for the war-dead of each year. To this most characteristic democratic institution we must now turn; but as it has been much and well studied of late, we can be brief.[33] The public funeral is relevant to the theme of this book in two particular ways: as a focus for the development of patriotic mythology, and as a religious ceremony in its own right. More generally, one can scarcely understand the democracy without paying some attention to the one context in which it gave formal (if very partial) expression to its own values.

The basic facts are known from a famous passage of Thucydides:[34]

During the same winter, the Athenians buried the first victims of the war in the following manner, as is traditional. Two days in advance they lay out the bones of the dead in a tent which has been erected; everyone brings whatever offerings they wish to their own kin. On the day of the funeral-procession, coffins made of cypress-wood, one for each tribe, are carried on wagons; these contain the bones of the victims, tribe by tribe. One bier with coverings is carried out empty for the bodies which could not be found for removal. Any citizen or non-citizen who wishes participates in the funeral-procession, and female kin come and lament at the tomb. Then they deposit the bones in the public cemetery, which is in the city's most attractive suburb. They bury all those who die in battle here, with the exception of the dead of Marathon, whom they considered so outstanding in heroism that they buried them on the battlefield. After the burial, a man chosen by the city, of proven intelligence and high prestige, makes the appropriate speech of praise over them. Then they depart.

The democratic or 'isonomic' ('equally-sharing') character of the institution is clear from Thucydides' account, although he does not stress it. The dead are buried (as they were also listed on stone, on the characteristic casualty-lists) without differentiation of status, tribe by tribe. In the early years of the century a patriotic death was

---

[32] Aesch. *Eum.* 487–88.

[33] By Stupperich, *Staatsbegräbnis*, and Loraux, *L'invention*; see too Pritchett, *Greek State at War*, IV. 106–24, 249–51. C. W. Clairmont, *Patrios Nomos* (Oxford 1983) is largely a study of individual monuments (cf. R. Stupperich, *Gnomon* 56, 1984, 637–47).*

[34] 2.34.

a privilege reserved for cavalry and hoplites, but later the oarsmen of the fleet too must have been included, although, revealingly, we cannot distinguish them.[35] Thucydides, however, does not reveal the full extent of the honours that were paid. From the fourth-century funerary speeches, we hear of competitions in music and athletics and horse-racing held in honour of the dead; and three bronze vessels, from the period 480–440 or so, have duly been discovered, inscribed 'The Athenians [gave as] prizes in honour of those who died in war.'[36] These are remarkable splendours. In epic poetry, funerary games belonged to men of the stamp of Achilles. Thersites too could now have his share in them, if he only succeeded in being killed in battle. 'Dying in war seems to be a splendid thing in all sorts of ways. Even if a man is poor, he receives a magnificent burial, and even if he is a low fellow, he is praised' is the acid comment of Plato's Socrates.[37]

The origin of the public funeral is notoriously controversial. Any account has to admit exceptions, as Thucydides already had to do, when he said that the dead of Marathon were buried on the field of battle, and not brought home, as an exceptional mark of honour. It seems he was wrong in this, and until after the Persian wars the Athenians normally, like other Greeks, interred their dead on the field[38] (though one exceptional case of bringing home, in 491 or thereabouts, has to be acknowledged). Thus those who died beside the Euripos in 506 received 'public' burial where they fell; the same

[35] See Stupperich, *Staatsbegräbnis*, 4–12; Loraux, *L'invention*, 32–37; and on the early hoplite army, Vidal-Naquet, *Black Hunter*, 85–105 (125–49 in the French edn.).

[36] See Lys. 2.80; Dem. 60.36, cf. 13; Arist. *Ath. Pol.* 58.1. The vases: E. Vanderpool, *ArchDelt* 24, 1969 (1970), 1–5; *IG* I³.523–25; cf. P. Amandry, *BCH* 95 (1971), 602–25, whose suggestion that these prizes were donated by the Athenians to an (unattested) funerary contest away from the city itself is, however, rightly rejected in *IG* I³ (on 523). On the vases, as often in the funerary speeches, 'war' takes the definite article; but in some instances a reference, even a fossilized reference, to a particular war is very unlikely (e.g. Dem. 60.2), and it looks as if πόλεμος is simply being treated as a semi-abstract noun. The relation of the *agon* to the funeral has been much discussed, since the *agon* was (in the fourth cent.) annual, and so, one would expect, fixed in the calendar, the public funeral occasional and doubtless of variable date (cf. Loraux, *L'invention*, 37–39). But it is surely easier to renounce either the fixity of the *agon* or the variability of the funeral than to allow, as many have done, that both could occur separately in a single year, funeral games apart from funeral (cf. F. Jacoby, *JHS* 64, 1944, 59, n. 99, and 61, n. 114; Stupperich, *Staatsbegräbnis*, 56 [+]; Pritchett, *Greek State at War*, IV.118–20, who disputes the apparent implication of Pl. *Menex.* 249b that the *agon* was annual).

[37] *Menex.* 234e: the μνημεῖον (figurative) of those who die for their country is fairer than that available to the richest citizen, according to Thrasybulus in Xen. *Hell.* 2.4.17.

[38] See Jacoby, *JHS* 64 (1944), 44–45; Pritchett, *Greek State at War*, IV.249–50: this point can probably survive the criticisms of A. W. Gomme in his long note on Thuc. 2.34.1, where Jacoby's precise dating of the public funeral's origin to 465/4 is attacked. One exceptional case: Paus. 1.29.7, from nearby Aegina (see Stupperich, *Staatsbegräbnis*, 2.116 n. 7; Pritchett, *Greek State at War*, IV.166).

instance shows that the idea of an honorific 'public' burial antedated the practice of bringing home the remains, on which the Athenian institution in its familiar form of course depended.[39] Of the many collective tombs seen by Pausanias in the public cemetery, only one, the exceptional case from 491 mentioned earlier, dates from before about 470.[40] And two sources state explicitly that it was only after the Persian wars that the games and the oration were introduced, as yet another means of commemorating the valour of those who died resisting the Mede.[41] Possibly that dating is still a little too early, and it was only in the 470s or 460s that the Athenians began regularly as a public duty to bring remains home, in response to the resentments created by persistent foreign campaigning—and dying—on a hitherto unprecedented scale. The first memorial which Pausanias saw of the period after the Persian wars was that for the dead of Eurymedon, of about 470.[42]

A complication must now be mentioned. Among the finest ornaments of sixth-century Attica are the sculpted grave-monuments, often inscribed with majestic verse. Perhaps it was Solon's limitation on the scale of the actual funeral that encouraged 'pride mixed with grief' to vent itself instead in the lasting memorial.[43] The great archaic sequence of these monuments comes to an end about 500. (But some would put a few survivors as late as 480.) This cessation

[39] 'Simonides' ii in *FGE*, 191, as interpreted by Pritchett, *Greek State at War*, IV.164 rather than by Page himself. The reference by Herodotus' Solon (1.30) to an Athenian who received public burial at Eleusis is less helpful: only an individual is concerned, and the language might anyway be anachronistic. The two sixth-cent. Attic epitaphs for individual citizens who had died in unspecified battles ought also to be considered (*IG* I³.1194 bis, 1240 = *CEG* 13, 27). Possibly it was already a regular or occasional practice for bones to be brought home privately, as continued to be done by the relatives of those who had died on campaign but not in battle (Isae. 4.19, 26; 9.4). In that case Aesch. *Ag.* 437–44 becomes less drastically anachronistic.

[40] The exception: n. 38 above. But Stupperich, *Staatsbegräbnis*, 222, can also point to apparent earlier instances of public burials of individuals in the Ceramicus (Clisthenes, Paus. 1.29.6, and the tyrannicides, ibid. § 15), and reasonably concludes that the region was in some sense a public cemetery from about 500 (the point is not addressed by Clairmont, as Stupperich notes in his review: n. 33).

[41] Dion. Hal. *Ant. Rom.* 5.17.4 (479 or 490); Diod. 11.33.3 (479); on these sources' authority see Pritchett, *Greek State at War*, IV.116, n. 67. Paus. 1.29.4 provides a divergent date of 465/4 (accepted by Jacoby and Pritchett: see n. 38) only if πρῶτοι ἐτάφησαν in his usage must mean 'the first to be buried were . . .' rather than 'the first burials you meet on entering the cemetery are . . .' (cf. Stupperich, *Staatsbegräbnis*, 235–36 [+]); both renderings appear linguistically possible (the same chapter contains other apparent instances of ἐτάφησαν as a stylistic variation on κεῖνται, which L. Weber, *RhM* 75, 1926, 300–302 scarcely succeeds in invalidating), the latter is contextually far superior.

[42] Paus. 1.29.14.

[43] Statius, *Thebaid* 6.68 'gloria mixta malis adflictaeque ambitus aulae'; cf. Seaford, *Reciprocity and Ritual*, 84, n. 36. Against such an emphasis on aristocratic display see, however, C. Sourvinou-Inwood's very important *'Reading' Greek Death* (Oxford 1995), esp. 279–94.

has long and plausibly been explained by reference to Cicero's report that 'some time after Solon' restrictions were imposed by law on the scale of grave monuments.[44] (But another difficulty must be admitted: though 'monumental' mound graves become much rarer in the fifth century, they do not disappear completely.) Perhaps the ban on private funerary monuments and the institution of the public funeral for the war-dead should be seen as two sides of the same coin.[45] If he wanted an epigram by Simonides, even an aristocrat had now to die for his country. Henceforth, therefore, Athens was to resemble Sparta, where only those who had died in war were allowed to lie in a marked grave.[46] The transformation is even more pronounced if we accept, what is however very doubtful, that certain marble discuses inscribed 'I am from the tombs' (ἐχ τôν ἐριôν εἰμι) or something similar are prizes won in games still celebrated, despite all Solon's legislative efforts, at private aristocratic funerals in the late sixth century.[47]

But this elegant theory meets chronological difficulties, since the private monuments seem to disappear a little before the Ceramicus was brought into regular use for public burial. The hypothesis must therefore be that the 'ancestral custom' developed by stages.[48] Originally, perhaps, 'public' burial, on the field of battle, was accorded to individuals of outstanding valour; the young democracy extended the honour to all the battle-dead without distinction

---

[44] *Leg.* 2.64–65; on the chronology see Stupperich, *Staatsbegräbnis*, 71–86 (and now the individual dates in *IG* I³); cf. Humphreys, *JHS* 100 (1980), 101–102. In three largely overlapping discussions (*Death-Ritual and Social Structure in Classical Antiquity*, Cambridge 1992, ch. 5; *Hephaistos* 11/12, 1992–3, 35–50; A. L. Boegehold and A. C. Scafuro eds., *Athenian Identity and Civic Ideology*, Baltimore 1994, 67–101), Ian Morris has recently argued that the change is a product of fashion, not law. He highlights the chronological hard cases and exceptions that had already been recognized. His main new argument is that 'restraint' in funerary display in the fifth cent. is a Panhellenic, not merely an Attic phenomenon (but is the change elsewhere in Greece quite so abrupt and drastic?).

[45] This important suggestion is the central thesis of Stupperich, *Staatsbegräbnis*. More generally, Seaford, *Reciprocity and Ritual*, 74–86, stresses the common aims of all funerary legislation from Solon onwards.

[46] Plut. *Lyc.* 27.3, *Mor.* 238d, and inscriptions (see e.g. Pritchett, *Greek State at War*, IV.244–46).

[47] *IG* I³.1394–95, 1397 [+]; note esp. L. E. Roller, *Stadion* 7 (1981), 3–5. But there is force in L. H. Jeffery's objection (*BSA* 57, 1962, 147) that ' "out of the grave-mound(s)" seems an odd expression for "from the funeral games" ' (note too the failure to name the deceased in 1395 and 1397: contrast esp. the prizes from seventh-cent. Boeotian funeral games, *IG* I³.584–88; also the parallels in Amandry, *BCH* 95, 1971, 615–18). She suggests that the discs were tomb-ornaments (an attested function for similar discs), inscribed to deter souvenir-hunters.

[48] So roughly Stupperich, *Staatsbegräbnis*, 206–38 (who, however, perhaps retrojects too many details; the battlefield burials during the Persian wars are hard to explain on his theory); cf. F. Jacoby, *Hesperia* 14 (1945), 176–77 = id., *Kleine Philologische Schriften*, I (Berlin 1961), 479–81.

(probably for the first time after the battle at the Euripos in 506[49]), and simultaneously restricted private funerary ostentation; only after the defeat of the Persians (and in some sense in commemoration of it) was the process brought to its culmination, with the establishment of a public cemetery in Athens,[50] the foundation of games, and the 'addition of a speech' in which the ideological implications of the public funeral could be worked out in words. This reconstruction is credible, but not irresistible; it depends rather heavily on the guess that the 'public' burial granted to the dead at the Euripos represents a novel practice introduced by the young democracy. Perhaps the decline of private display should not, after all, be brought into close association with the growth of the public institution. Private grave-monuments and monumental tombs reappear in the last quarter of the fifth century, at a time when the collectivist ideology of the funeral speeches had lost none of its vitality.[51] It remains striking, however, that the sculpted monument, that potent device of élite display, should disappear as it did just in the early years of the democracy. If this was Clisthenes' work, it was his most direct attack upon the symbols of the old order.

From the origins of the institution we revert to its functioning. What was the status of the dead buried in the public monument? A paradox has been noted.[52] On the one hand, the speakers of the Funeral Orations never apply the term 'hero' to the patriotic dead; the immortality which they repeatedly predict for them is that of renown; and it is only tentatively, by ratiocination and appeal to 'probability', that stronger claims are occasionally advanced. Thus Pericles supposedly argued that those who died at Samos in 440 'had become immortal like the gods. For even the gods we do not actually see, but we infer that they are immortal from the honours they receive and the benefits they confer. But just these things are true of those who have died for their country.' Demosthenes urges similarly that 'one could reasonably describe them [the war-dead] as associates [πάρεδροι] of the gods below, granted the same position as the good men of old in the islands of the blessed. For in that case too our belief is not based on report by an eyewitness but on inference: we suppose that those who are honoured by the living on earth receive the same honours in the underworld.' Hyperides too declares it only

---

[49] See n. 39 above. [50] But cf. n. 40 above.
[51] Cf. Stupperich, *Staatsbegräbnis*, 243 ff.: he stresses that in the new phase commemorative display was common enough no longer to seem offensively élitist, but still feels the need for an *ad hoc* hypothesis (an oracle consequent on the plague) to explain the repeal of the postulated Clisthenic ban.
[52] See Loraux, *L'invention*, 39–42 (an excellent discussion, which I follow).

'plausible' ($\epsilon i \kappa \acute{o} s$) that the patriotic dead should experience special
favour from the gods for their piety.[53] On the other hand, there is no
form of cultic honour customarily granted to heroes that the war-
dead do not receive. Annual commemorative games, in particular,
were the clearest of all markers of heroic status.[54] No less paradoxically, the tyrannicides Harmodius and Aristogeiton were granted by
the grateful democracy statues in the *agora*—a unique honour at that
date—a 'share in libations at sacrifices in every shrine', and public
funeral cult in perpetuity, and yet never receive the actual title
'hero'.[55] We must reject as an explanation any 'two-tier' hypothesis,
whereby the authors of the Funeral Speeches, resolutely intellectual, ignored the more religious emotions of their simpler auditors.
On the contrary, as good Greek rhetoricians they would certainly
have exploited such emotions; and we have seen that they do what
they can to establish a 'probability' that the war-dead are getting
their just reward. It is more helpful to wonder about the process by
which men could become heroes, by which, that is, the recently dead
could join a group that was traditionally distant in time, exceptional
in nature. Could the assembly make heroes by decree? It hardly
seems so. Oracular gods certainly could, but may have been as slow

[53] Stesimbrotos *FGrH* 107 F 9 *ap*. Plut. *Per*. 8.9 (which, if pressed, shows that the patriotic dead were believed still—note the present tense—to 'confer benefits': so Loraux, *L'invention*, 40, n. 95); Dem. 60.34; Hyperides, *Epitaph*. 43 (cf. 35–39, on the reception to be expected
from past heroes); on these passages cf. H. S. Versnel in J. W. van Henten ed., *Die Entstehung
der jüdischen Martyrologie* (Leiden 1989), 168–71. The war-dead of Plato's *Republic*, by contrast, are unquestionably to be treated as *daimones*, by a procedure to be sanctioned by Delphi
(468e–469a; distinct from 'heroization', according to O. Reverdin, *La religion de la cité pla-
tonicienne*, Paris 1945, 125 ff.).

[54] See e.g. Hdt. 1.167.2, 6.38.1 (Miltiades); Diod. 16.90.1 (Timoleon), 20.102.3
(Demetrius Poliorcetes); cf. Hornblower, *Mausolus*, 257–58. The war-dead receive 'the same
honours as the gods', Lys. 2.80. For similar expressions see Dem. 60.36; Isoc. *Paneg*. 84 ('like
the demi-gods'). These parallels surely support the traditional view that the *agon* was annual,
against Pritchett's doubts (n. 36). Slaves buried in the public cemetery (Paus. 1.29.7; *IG*
I³.1144.139, $\theta\epsilon\rho\acute{a}\pi o\nu\tau\epsilon s$) presumably in theory shared in these honours; the point is noted by
K. W. Welwei (in G. Binder, and B. Effe eds., *Tod und Jenseits im Altertum*, Trier 1991,
62–63), but he seems wrong to conclude that the Athenians cannot therefore have heroized the
war-dead because this would have meant heroizing the small number of slaves among them.
For occasional burial of the war-dead of other states in the *agora* (as protecting heroes?) see
Stupperich, *Staatsbegräbnis*, 66.

[55] See Wycherley, *Testimonia*, 93–98 (statues); Arist. *Ath. Pol*. 58.1 (*enagismata*—a term
not confined to heroic cult, cf. Isae. 2.46—by the polemarch); Dem. 19.280 (libations: I am
unclear what is meant exactly). Dem. ibid. speaks of honours 'equal to those of gods and
heroes', just as Lysias says the war-dead 'receive the same honours as the immortals' (2.80).
(The eponymous heroes of the tribes too enjoy $i\sigma\acute{o}\theta\epsilon o\iota$ $\tau\iota\mu\alpha\acute{\iota}$, according to Lycurg. *Leoc*. 88.)
Thus the widespread assumption that the tyrannicides, in contrast to the war-dead, were
indisputable heroes appears ill-founded. The word 'cult' in the title of studies of the tyrannicides by A. J. Podlecki, *Historia* 15 (1966), 129–41, and C. Fornara, *Philologus* 114 (1970),
155–80, is metaphorical. M. W. Taylor, *The Tyrant Slayers*², (Salem Mass. 1991), 5–8,
stresses the Athenian tendency to assimilate tyrannicides to war-dead.

and cautious about doing so as modern popes are in making saints.[56] What could readily be done, of course, was to pay the war-dead honours indistinguishable from those of heroes, since no sharp divide separated funerary from heroic cult. They might then grow fully into the heroic mould; and later ages at a greater cultural remove duly applied the term 'hero' to the dead of the Persian wars.[57] The classical Athenians, we might say, heroized their benefactors as best they could.

We should not, however, suppose that, in this ritual of communal fortification in response to death, the dead were really allowed to carry away the honours. The Funeral Speeches in practice praised the city as a whole; and through them the Athenians were presented with a most distinctive image of their own characteristics and achievements. It is this self-congratulation that is the main target of Socrates' irony in the dialogue that introduces Plato's mock Funeral Speech in *Menexenus*. No surviving example except that put in Pericles' mouth by Thucydides antedates the fourth century; but in what concerns us here—the creation of a political mythology—allusions in Herodotus and tragedy prove that the later speeches perpetuate a remarkably fixed tradition.[58] One can wonder at most whether a period of experimentation preceded the establishment of a definitive canon of 'labours of the Athenians'. In the epigram commemorating Cimon's capture of Eion in 475, it was still optimistically argued that Homer's lukewarm praise of Menestheus testified to Athens' ancient military renown. That unpromising theme was later prudently abandoned. It was wiser to depreciate Homer and his overvalued war, and stick to exclusively Athenian achievements.[59]

---

[56] On such issues cf. S. R. F. Price, *JHS* 104 (1984), 79–85. An oecist could perhaps be fully assimilated into the heroic class at once (Thuc. 5.11.1), because he fell into an established category. But even in such cases one can observe a tendency to avoid the word 'hero': see the almost verbatim report of the Syracusans' decree in favour of Timoleon in Diod. 16.90 and Plut. *Tim.* 39.5.

[57] Paus. 1.32.4 (on reverence of 'the Marathonians' for the dead at Marathon, 'whom they call heroes'; for cult paid to them see—only—*IG* II².1006.69, offerings by ephebes, in the second cent. BC); Heliodorus, *Aithiopica* 1.17 on 'the pit in the Academy where the polemarchs make offerings to the heroes'. Note that heroic cult at the tombs of the dead at Marathon (on which see J. Whitley, *AJA* 98, 1994, 213–30) and Plataea is not attested early; and the showy Panhellenic festival of *Eleutheria* at Plataea (Plut. *Aristid.* 21) is proven to be post-classical by comparison with the simpler rites, performed by the Plataeans alone, of Thuc. 3.58.4–5 (cf. Isoc. 14.60–61); see R. Étienne and M. Piérart, *BCH* 99 (1975), 51–75 [+].

[58] Hdt. 9.27; cf. Euripides *Erechtheus, Heraclidae, Supplices*. For attempts to determine the political context in which the canon was formed see Loraux, *L'invention*, 64–72; Stupperich, *Staatsbegräbnis*, 230–34.

[59] Eion: 'Simonides' xl in *FGE* [+] *ap.* Aeschin. 3.183; cf. still Hdt. 9.27.4 (also 5.94.2, 7.161.3), and W. Kierdorf, *Erlebnis und Darstellung der Perserkriege* (Göttingen 1966), 98–99. A monumental bronze dedicated on the acropolis late in the fifth cent. assigned a privileged place to 'Menestheus, Teucer and the sons of Theseus' among the Greek warriors in the

Of what stuff, then, were these Athenians?[60] They were, first, as *autochthones*, each and every one of them spectacularly well-born. The claim to autochthony was traditionally associated with the myths of the two literally earth-born kings, Cecrops and Ericthonius/Erechtheus. The surviving Funeral Speeches, however, except the late example of Hyperides, shun almost every reference to individual Athenians, present or past; and it is the Athenians *en masse* who are now born, not from a mother and father, but from a mother (Earth) who is also a fatherland.[61] (In other contexts too, heroic ancestry as a source of individual prestige seems to have been put out of fashion by the democracy.[62]) As every mother naturally produces sustenance for her offspring, so Earth brought forth crops for the young Athenians, who then magnanimously distributed them to the rest of mankind.[63] The old myth of Demeter's gift of corn to the Eleusinians is here deftly redeployed, as a 'proof' that the Athenians are true children of Earth. The quintessential virtues of this noble race (a race dear also to the gods, as the contest of Athena and Poseidon for possession of Attica proved[64]) were already displayed in four great achievements of the mythical period. They repelled from their homeland the invasions both of Eumolpus with his Thracian hordes and of the man-hating Amazons; and they intervened twice in defence of suppliants, forcing the Thebans to grant burial to the famous Seven, the Peloponnesians to receive home the much-wandering Heraclidae. The original form of these legends is largely a matter of curious conjecture.[65] But we cannot

Wooden Horse: Paus. 1.23.8, cf. Castriota, *Myth, Ethos and Actuality*, 167. (The tendency to compare Trojan and Persian wars is attested anew by Simonides fr. 11 in West².) Depreciation: Pericles *ap*. Plut. *Per*. 28.7, Dem. 60.10, Hyperides, *Epitaph*. 35–36. Cf. Thuc. 2.41.4; Loraux, *L'invention*, 70.

[60] Cf. H. Strasburger, *Hermes* 86 (1958), 22–28; Stupperich, *Staatsbegräbnis*, 40–53; K. R. Walters, 'Rhetoric as Ritual: The Semiotics of the Attic Funeral Oration', *Florilegium* 2 (1980), 1–27; Loraux, *L'invention, passim*, esp. 147–56; 'Myths', 193–95, 201–204 [+]; V. J. Rosivach, 'Autochthony and the Athenians', *CQ* NS 37 (1987), 294–306.

[61] The ingenious expression of Lys. 2.17 (cf. Isoc. *Paneg*. 25); this nationalization of *eugeneia* is noted by Rosivach, 'Autochthony and the Athenians', *CQ* NS 37 (1987), 303–304; W. R. Connor in Boegehold/Scafuro eds., *Athenian Identity*, 38; Ober, *Mass and Elite*, 261–63.

[62] Exceptions of course exist (see Ch. 9, n. 54 on Cimon; App. 2, n. 94 on Alcibiades; and Hellanicus *FGrH* 323a F 24 on Andocides), but it is instructive to compare Pl. *Lys*. 205c–d, where stories of ancestral association with Heracles and descent from Zeus are treated as comically old-fashioned—ἅπερ αἱ γραῖαι ᾄδουσι—with such earlier or non-Attic evidence as Hdt. 5.65.3–4, 7.204; Pind., *Nem*. 10.49–51.

[63] Pl. *Menex*. 237e–238a; Dem. 60.5.

[64] So Pl. *Menex*. 237c–d, alone among surviving *epitaphioi*. Other themes exclusive to Plato are the emergence of olives in Attica, and the role of the early Athenians as the first people to whom the gods taught τέχναι (238a–b).

[65] On the Seven see Ch. 3, n. 25 above, and Walters, 'Rhetoric as Ritual', 10–14 (who stresses the implication of the orators' preference—cf. Plut. *Thes*. 29.4–5—for the version whereby Athens secured the burial by armed intervention, not persuasion). On Eumolpus,

mistake how the patriotic tradition has shaped them into paradigms of valour as just as it is heroic, exercised both against the barbarian invader and, within Greece, in defence of sacred rights.[66] They form a seamless web with the more recent exploits, above all those of the Persian wars, that are also celebrated. Such heroism was, of course, only to be expected from an autochthonous people who in fighting for their country were fighting for a literally native land—the different themes of praise confirm one another's validity, in this magic world. *Autochthones* are, after all, the genuine article, predisposed by birth to liberty, equality, fraternity.[67] The modern reader of the *epitaphioi*, wearied by vapid self-congratulation endlessly repeated, will gladly suppose that the ancient hearer too found them meaninglessly formulaic. Did not Thucydides' Pericles wisely tread a more individual path? For Plato, however, the *epitaphios* of traditional form presented a challenge precisely because it gave such pleasure.[68] If we take them seriously, the *epitaphioi* provoke sombre reflections about patriotic enthusiasm and its underpinning, even in a city of the highest cultural achievement. They helped Athenians not to understand the sense in which theirs had become, in the famous Thucydidean phrase, a 'tyrant city'.[69] There were Athenian casualties in the campaign that culminated in the annihilation of the Melians, and we must assume that a Funeral Speech was delivered in that year.

'Myths', 201–204 (where the role of the *epitaphioi* themselves in shaping the story into one of a barbarian invasion should have been more considered: cf. Stupperich, *Staatsbegräbnis*, 47). On the introduction of Theseus into the Amazon legend, via the rape of Antiope (a typically Thesean *geste*), by about 510, and the transference of the subsequent war from near the river Thermodon to Attica (a version first unambiguously attested in Aesch. *Eum.* 685–89) see J. Boardman in D. Kurtz and B. Sparkes eds., *The Eye of Greece* (Cambridge 1982), 1–28 (though some of the precise political correspondences claimed are unconvincing); Castriota, *Myth, Ethos, Actuality*, 43–49. The reception of the Heraclidae in Attica, first attested in Pherecydes *FGrH* 3 F 84 (not verbatim), (?) Aesch. *Heraclidae*, Hdt. 9.27.2, Eur. *Heraclid.* (their persecution already in Hecataeus *FGrH* 1 F 30), is obviously related in some way to the many east-Attic cults of the Heraclidae (*ZPE* 57, 1984, 59): cf. Prinz, *Gründungsmythen*, 233–43; M. Schmidt in *LIMC* IV.1 (1988), 723–25. The myth of autochthony itself is essentially a fifth-cent. construct, according to Rosivach, 'Autochthony and the Athenians', *CQ* 37 (1987).

[66] Cf. Isocrates' division in *Panegyricus* into, 54 ff., ἱκετεῖαι, and, 66 ff., τὰ πρὸς τοὺς βαρβάρους.

[67] Cf. 'Myths', 195, n. 36, on Lys. 2.17, Pl. *Menex.* 239a, Dem. 60.4. On liberty see Dem. 19.261; 'genuine' e.g. Lys. 2.43. The primary differentiation stressed by the myth is that between Athens and other cities (so Hdt. 7.161.3; Eur. *Erechtheus* fr. 50.8–12 Austin; Lys. 2.17; Dem. 60.4; Isoc. *Paneg.* 63), but it could also provide a ground for looking down on non-citizens at Athens (Lycurg. *Leoc.* 41).

[68] *Menex.* 235a–b. In Xen. *Mem.* 3.5.9–13, by contrast, 'Socrates' summarizes the typical themes of the *epitaphioi* and argues that they are an incentive to present virtue.

[69] 1.122.3, where see Hornblower's refs. Cf. Walters, 'Rhetoric and Ritual', and the classic study of Strasburger, *Hermes* 86 (1958), 17–40.

It is, of course, obvious that not many Athenians actually lived their lives in the atmosphere diffused by these highly ideological documents. Even the city could scarcely live up to its own high standards and—however often the orators in the Ceramicus might imply that the supreme excellence lay in patriotic valour—continued to treat Athenians who won victories in the Panhellenic games to public hospitality in the Prytaneum.[70] (Indeed, the ideology of the Funeral Oration, narrowly conceived, is deconstructed by the Funeral Games themselves, at which the city offers prizes for individual excellence in traditional aristocratic pursuits.) The point is nicely illustrated by the emergence, at the end of the great democratic century, of a new form of religious image, of noticeably unegalitarian stamp. 'Hero-reliefs'[71] typically show a male figure reclining on a couch, with a wine-jug grasped in one hand, a table of foodstuffs beside him. He is attended by a woman and sometimes a boy, and often approached by a file of smaller worshippers who bear offerings. The inscribed examples are dedicated to heroes of, it seems, no particular type. Thus the banqueting figure must have represented very generally the idea 'hero'. These reliefs first appear around 500 (a related form occurs earlier in Laconia), enter Attica around 400, and are thenceforth extremely common throughout the Greek world.[72] (As always with votive reliefs, the surviving marble examples are likely to have had wooden or terracotta precursors. In that event, the argument presented here will concern the persistence rather than the emergence of an aristocratic image of the hero.) Why is the hero so portrayed? The 'reclining banquet', it has been argued, is an ancient image of royal privilege, eastern in origin, which could be readily naturalized in Greece to evoke the relaxed and enviable life-style of the aristocracy.[73] A detail often added to the Attic examples supports this interpretation very strongly against its rivals (the view, for instance, that a feast in the afterlife is depicted). At the top of the relief a horse's head commonly appears, anti-naturalistically, within a frame. Though much miscellaneous information used to be assembled to establish an association between the horse and the

---

[70] *IG* I³.131.12.

[71] See esp. R. N. Thönges-Stringaris, *AM* 80 (1965), 1–99; Dentzer, *Banquet couché*, esp. 453–527. For the inscriptions see Thönges-Stringaris, 49; Dentzer, 453–55; for the horse's head, Dentzer, 490–93.

[72] See in brief Thönges-Stringaris, *AM* 80 (1965), 3–4, 13–15, 60.

[73] The central thesis of Dentzer, *Banquet couché* : see e.g. 481, 'l'idéal aristocratique, qui fait la cohérence de cette imagerie'. B. Fehr in his review, *Gnomon* 56 (1984), 335–42, stresses that this is the ideal in its most hedonistic form; shields and helmets, seen on early specimens (cf. Dentzer, *Banquet couché*, 252), fade away. It is likely that worshippers will also have seen, in the hero's meal, an allusion to offerings brought to him in ritual (as so often on votive reliefs: note esp. those to the Dioscuri); but the two evocations are not incompatible.*

Underworld, what the noble beast in fact symbolized for an Athenian, as any reader of Athenian popular literature knows, was the wealth required to buy and feed it. A horse was conspicuous consumption, luxury on four legs. (The analogy with cars is obvious; Athenian horses too were insured, and lost value year by year.) Lysias can even bluntly identify chariot-races as 'contests in wealth'.[74] The very ambivalent attitudes of the Athenians to the *hippeis*, the cavalry élite, are displayed at length in Aristophanes' *Knights*. At the end of the fifth century, Athenians still imagined the heroes, the protectors of the land, in the image of that symposium-haunting horse-owning class which they so democratically mistrusted, so undemocratically envied and admired.[75]

We ought, perhaps, to turn from the *epitaphioi* to the ideological messages carried by the temples of the fifth century, the Parthenon above all. Something, doubtless, remains to be said on the subject even after it has been acknowledged that few Greeks are likely to have spent much time peering up at awkwardly positioned architectural sculptures (for the great message communicated by a building such as the Parthenon is 'I exist, and it was power that built me', and does not reside in the details of the decoration).[76] Like the *epitaphioi*, the sculptures sing a hymn of praise to force triumphant;[77] they preclude moral uncertainties by showing images of violence turned only against unexceptionable targets—barbarians and Centaurs and Amazons—and setting them in parallel with the great just war of the gods themselves against the Giants. But they are much less concerned than the speeches with differentiating Athens from all other Greek states; the Panhellenic expedition against Troy, for instance, abandoned by the Athenian orators, remains a common theme of monumental art. The allusions on the Parthenon to Attic myth and cult are not typical of architectural sculpture, and even these exalt the city without depreciating others. It would lead too far from our theme to study these presentations of general Greek values

[74] Lys. 2.80, cf. e.g. Aesch. *PV* 466 ἵππους, ἄγαλμα τῆς ὑπερπλούτου χλιδῆς, with M. Griffiths' note; Ar. *Nub.* 1–125; Thuc. 6.15.3, with 16.2; Dem. 18.320. Insured: see G. R. Bugh, *The Horsemen of Athens* (Princeton 1988), 57–58.

[75] Cf. N. R. E. Fisher in P. Cartledge, P. Millett, and S. Todd eds., *Nomos* (Cambridge 1990), 137 'the contradictory attitudes to the rich on the part of the *demos* included some vicarious admiration for their "goings on" '; Ober, *Mass and Elite*, ch. 6.

[76] See P. Veyne, *La société romaine* (Paris 1992), 311–42, esp. 326. Of course, the citizens of a participatory democracy may have taken more interest in such matters than the subjects of Trajan... (and cf. e.g. Eur. *Ion* 184 ff.)

[77] So R. G. Osborne, 'Framing the Centaur: Reading Fifth Century Architectural Sculpture', in S. Goldhill and R. G. Osborne eds., *Art and Text in Ancient Greek Culture* (Cambridge 1994), 52–84 (who reaches, however, an opposite conclusion).

here.[78] (So too would an account of tragedy, relevant in all sorts of ways though of course this is.) We turn instead to the empire.[79]

Two aspects of the Athenians' religious relations with their 'allies' are commonly recognized: on the one hand, it is said, the Athenians introduced some of their own cults to subject territory; conversely, they required subject cities to participate in the most important festivals at Athens itself. The second of these points is uncontroversial. From, perhaps, the 440s, the allies were required to send 'a cow and a panoply' to the *Greater Panathenaea*, which they were to escort in the procession (if a supplement is sound) 'like' or 'as' 'colonists'.[80] The requirement is certainly likely to have been justified by the traditional ritual obligations of colonies to mother-cities: the settlers at Brea, true and recent colonists these, were asked to send home both the cow and panoply, and also a phallus for the *Dionysia*. In regard to the allies, this appeal to an established model was partly justified, more largely tendentious. Many Ionian cities did, indeed, freely acknowledge that they had been founded from Athens;[81] but we have no evidence that before the establishment of the empire they dispatched the cow of gratitude to their mother-city (in the fourth century, however, a few voluntary instances must be allowed[82]); and many subject states were in no sense Athenian colonies. Athens' self-presentation as the 'mother-city' of the whole empire was a

[78] Castriota, *Myth, Ethos, Actuality*, is a thorough recent study (though too prone to see very specific historical allusions); cf. Smarczyk, *Religionspolitik*, 298–317, on 'Die Bauten der Akropolis und die politische Selbstdarstellung Athens'.

[79] Cf. Meiggs, *Athenian Empire*, 291–305; and now the thoughtful and immensely thorough study of Smarczyk, *Religionspolitik*, *passim*. I discuss a further set of questions, concerning the religious life of Athenian settlements within the empire, in 'Athenian Religion Abroad', in *Ritual, Finance, Politics*, 339–46.

[80] See *IG* I³.34 (M/L 46) 41–42 ('?447–446': M/L); *IG* I³.71 (M/L 69) 56–58; *IG* I³.46.15–17 (M/L 49.11–13) (Brea); Σ Ar. *Nub.* 386 (where the obligation is specifically referred to colonists); in a text of the 370s (*SEG* XXXI 67: cf. Ch. 11, n. 13) the Parians are similarly required to send offerings 'as colonists'. In *IG* I³.14 (M/L 40) 3–5 the Erythraeans are required to send (?) corn to the *Greater Panathenaea*; it is commonly inferred from this specific requirement that at this date (? 453/2) the general obligation did not yet exist. Cf. B. D. Meritt and H. T. Wade-Gery, *JHS* 82 (1962), 69–71 (the basic discussion); Meiggs, *Athenian Empire*, 292–94; Smarczyk, *Religionspolitik*, 525–91, who revives the case (cf. M/L, p. 121) for a dating of the Kleinias decree *IG* I³.34 = M/L 46 ('?447–6': M/L), and thus of the institution in its general form, to 425/4. There is no sign that the request for a phallus for the *Dionysia* (made to the new foundation Brea, and later to Paros) was ever extended to the empire at large: see Smarczyk, *Religionspolitik*, 158–61. For a supposed archaic instance of religious tribute paid to Athena Polias, for different reasons, see Hdt. 5.82–83.

[81] See e.g. Pindar, fr. 52b = *Paean* II.29–30 Snell/Maehler; Hdt. 1.146–47, 5.97.2; Thuc. 1.95.1, 6.82.3, 7.57.4; Ar. *Lys.* 582 (the Athenians' own view). Cf. J. P. Barron, *JHS* 82 (1962), 6, n. 40; id., *JHS* 84 (1964), 46; Meiggs, *Athenian Empire*, 294; Smarczyk, *Religionspolitik*, 318–84, who discusses the relevant colonization myths (cf. Ch. 6, n. 84).

[82] See Ch. 11, n. 14.

potent imperial fiction.[83] Through the offerings, the *Panathenaea* was transformed into an imperial festival, which displayed the splendours of empire not just to the Athenians and the Greeks at large but also to the allies. About the reactions of these 'colonists' themselves we can only speculate. As they escorted the tributary beasts, they may have been impressed by a festival and a city and a complex of temples so much more magnificent than their own, in which they had none the less some share. But it was under compulsion that they sent the expensive offerings; and the suit of armour that Athena received from each allied city could have served as a bitter symbol of the Athenian military might which created that compulsion.[84]

We find a similar extension of tradition in the cause of Athenian magnificence in the famous decree (perhaps of the 420s) in which the Athenians require their allies, and invite the Greek cities at large, to dispatch 'first fruits' of corn and barley each year to Eleusis, in gratitude, we must understand, for the city's ancient gift of corn to mankind.[85] The myth of Triptolemus' mission on which this claim was based had existed since the sixth century; and the decree insists three times that the dispatch of such offerings will be 'in accord with ancestral tradition and the oracle' (of date and content unknown) 'from Delphi'. It may well have been traditional for a tithe of crops to be sent to Eleusis by the Attic demes, who remain prominent in the decree;[86] but it was doubtless only at the height of her political and cultic hegemony that Athens, with the support of the Delphic oracle, could press her claims on the rest of the Greek world—and,

---

[83] Cf. W. Schuller, *Die Herrschaft der Athener im ersten Attischen Seebund* (Berlin 1974), 112–17; Smarczyk, *Religionspolitik*, 590–91; S. Hornblower, *HSCP* 94 (1992), 197.

[84] See Smarczyk, *Religionspolitik*, 549–69, for a good discussion of the *Panathenaea* as 'Reichsfest'; ibid. 592–611 on possible allied reactions.

[85] *IG* I³.78 = M/L 73. For the justification see p. 99 above and e.g. Pl. *Menex.* 237e–238a; Dem. 60.5; Xen. *Hell.* 6.3.6; and above all Isoc. *Paneg.* 28–31. Note too the presence of Triptolemus scenes on fourth-cent. Panathenaic vases (Schwarz, *Triptolemos*, nos. V 23–30). M/L favour '? c. 422' for the decree, while keeping open the possibility of dates throughout the period c.435–415; Smarczyk, *Religionspolitik*, 224–52, argues for 416/5. The identity of the Eleusinian festival with which the *aparchai* must have been associated is discussed by Smarczyk, *Religionspolitik*, 184–216 [+]. He dismisses as a secondary elaboration the link with the *Proerosia* found in lexicographers (Suda ει 184, εἰρεσιώνη, with Adler's parallels), since the primary justification for the tribute must have lain not in these pre-ploughing sacrifices offered 'on behalf of the Greeks' by the Athenians, but in the mission of Triptolemus. Accordingly he links the tribute with the Mysteries. Note, however, that a *lex sacra* of the deme Paeania, probably prior to the first-fruits decree (*IG* I³.250: '450–430' *IG* I³), refers (A 22, B 4), darkly, to πρεροσιάδον κριθόν; note too the association of *Proerosia* with 'first corn' in Eur. *Suppl.* 29–31.*

[86] For a possible trace of this institution see the previous note, *ad fin.*

it seems, find a hearing.[87] At the same meeting of the assembly that passed the 'first-fruits' decree, the seer Lampon was invited—or at least allowed—to report to the council on a scheme for a similar tithe on olive-oil (the olive being another Athenian gift to mankind).[88] That proposal came to nothing, apparently, but it is revealing that it was made.

Thus tribute was certainly summoned inwards to the gods of the city. We should remember indeed that a sixtieth part of the tribute in the literal sense was claimed for Athena, and had to be paid even when the main sum was remitted.[89] In the 440s or 430s, a community on the little island of Carpathus even won political privileges by providing cypress-wood—probably a single magnificent tree—'for the temple of Athena who rules Athens' (which temple is unclear) on the acropolis.[90] It is less clear that Athenian cults were propagated outwards, neatly though the one process would balance the other. (Nor is there any specific evidence that 'Theseus the Ionian' was exploited as a unifying symbol.[91]) The argument that they were is based on a group of boundary-markers of sacred precincts, found in subject states but inscribed in Attic script or dialect or both (sometimes with some admixture of local forms). A group from Samos marks precincts of 'Athena who rules Athens', 'the eponymous heroes at Athens', and 'Ion at Athens'; Aeginetan examples are of 'Apollo and Poseidon' and 'Athena'; and specimens from Chalkis and Cos are of 'Athena' and 'Athena who rules Athens'.[92] The question has of course been asked whether the cults apparently attested by these stones were introduced by natives or Athenians. But a prior

[87] Isoc. *Paneg.* 31 claims that 'most' cities send the tribute, and that defaulters are reminded by the Pythia of their ancient duty. Cf. Smarczyk, *Religionspolitik*, 266–98; and on the further fortunes of the *aparche*, Ch. 11, n. 16 below. The Athenian pretension to be the source of corn was, however, rejected by many states: F. Jacoby, *Das Marmor Parium* (Berlin 1904), 62. C. Auffarth thus suggests that the ridicule of the Mysteries by Diagoras of Melos (Ch. 10, n. 37) can be seen as a political protest against ideological, and actual, imperialism (in W. Eder ed., *Die athenische Demokratie im vierten Jahrhundert*, Stuttgart 1994; approved by J. N. Bremmer, 'Religious Secrets and Secrecy in Classical Greece', in H. G. Kippenberg and G. Stroumsa eds., *Secrecy and Concealment*, Leiden 1995, 59–78).

[88] *IG* I³.78 = M/L 73.59–61; a reader for the Oxford Press points out, however, that passing a proposal to a further body for consideration is not necessarily a way of expressing enthusiasm for it. On the olive see e.g. Hdt. 5.82.2, Soph. *OC* 694–706, Pl. *Menex.* 238a, with M. Detienne, *RHR* 178 (1970), 5–11 = M. Finley, *Problèmes de la terre en Grèce ancienne* (Paris 1973), 293–97; Smarczyk, *Religionspolitik*, 216–24.

[89] See *IG* I³.61 (M/L 65) 5–9, with M/L p. 179.

[90] *IG* I³.1454 [+]; the tree was to become 'a splendid ridge-beam for the main *cella* of the Parthenon', suggests Meiggs as there cited.

[91] As K. Tausend suggests, *RhM* 132 (1989), 225–35.

[92] See the fundamental studies of J. P. Barron, *JHS* 84 (1964), 35–48; 103 (1983), 1–12; cf. Meiggs, *Athenian Empire*, 295–98; Shipley, *Samos*, 114–16; T. J. Figueira, *Athens and Aigina in the Age of Imperial Colonization* (Baltimore 1991), 115–20 (who all in broad outline follow Barron). The texts are now *IG* I³.1481–99, 1502.

question must be whether the markers in fact have anything to do with locally celebrated cults at all. The term *temenos*, sacred precinct, is ambiguous in Greek: it is used indifferently both for the actual temple-precinct and also for revenue-earning estates, which could be at a great distance from the temple itself. Athenian gods and heroes are known to have owned *temene* of the second type outside Attica.[93] Perhaps then these stones attest no conciliatory attempt to create a spirit of unity within the empire by the propagation of common cults; they may rather record the most abhorred of all imperial practices, appropriation of allied land for the benefit of absentee landlords, in this case the gods and heroes of Athens.[94] All are found in territories where land-seizures are known, or are very likely, to have occurred.

But what about Ion? Surely this, if any, was a cult which the Athenians had good reason to propagate within the empire; for it was of course on the myth of Ion and his descendants that their claim to be motherland of their Ionian colonies in good part depended.[95] But the exaltation of the hero was still timely, even if it occurred in Athens itself; and this is surely the more ready interpretation of a 'boundary-marker of the sacred precinct belonging to Ion at Athens'.[96] There would have been a grim propriety in dedicating land that had been punitively confiscated from rebellious 'colonists' to the hero who symbolized their duties to the native city. Seizure of allied land is an attested practice; so too is the ownership by Athenian cults of revenue-earning land abroad. The practice of exporting 'unifying' cults is by contrast wholly hypothetical. The burden of proof must lie with those who suppose that it occurred.[97]

[93] See *IG* I³.386.147; 394 B 7, 10; 418; (?) Thuc. 3.50.2; *SEG* III 117 (303–302: = Moretti 8). *AM* 51 (1926), 36, no. 5 attests a tribe (Athenian? or a local branch within the cleruchy?—see *Ritual, Finance, Politics*, 343, n. 19) with funds on loan in Samos.

[94] For a thorough argument for this conclusion (which I had reached independently, but on skimpier grounds) see Smarczyk, *Religionspolitik*, 58–153 (who contests several high datings, based on epigraphical arguments, that are fundamental to Barron's case). The 'eponymous heroes from Athens' will therefore not be the four sons of Ion (so Barron, *JHS* 1964, 39–40), but the Clisthenic ten. The pair 'Apollo and Poseidon' is a puzzle, since they had no important joint cult in Athens; their presumptive patronage of the Delian league while this was still based on Delos (see Barron, *JHS* 1983, 11) will scarcely help, on the view of the *horoi* taken here. Smarczyk, 126–29, thinks of an Aeginetan cult taken over by Athenian cleruchs.

[95] Cf. 'Myths', 205–207; Smarczyk, *Religionspolitik*, 360–71, 615–18. On the initially surprising absence of Ion from the *epitaphioi* cf. Loraux, *L'invention*, 84.

[96] ὅρος τεμένος Ἴονος Ἀθένεθεν *IG* I³.1496. For Ἀθένεθεν (similarly in *IG* I³.1497–99) cf. e.g. *IG* II².2604, ὅρος τεμένους Ἀφροδίτης Κεφαλῆθεν (= 'at Cephale'); the suggestion sometimes made that in our case it indicates the cult's origin ('Ion ⟨imported to Samos⟩ from Athens') neglects ordinary usage.

[97] This point retains its force even if one allows that many chronological and thus historical problems concerning these stones remain open, because of the continuing controversies concerning dating by letter-forms.

We can mention here an intriguing but mysterious cult-foundation that seems to have taken place in the second half of the fifth century, in territory under Athenian control.[98] Oropus, the coastal region, facing Euboea, that divides north-east Attica from Boeotia, was first settled by Eretria, from just across the water in Euboea. In the fourth century it suffered the familiar fate of a tactically important enclave perched between powerful neighbours, and repeatedly changed hands. The first firm date in its history is 430, at which time it was, in Thucydides' rather vague phrase, 'subject to Athens'. An earlier period of Boeotian domination has often been postulated, but on the basis of no positive evidence except an imprecise claim in Pausanias; Oropus had perhaps remained Eretrian in allegiance, as it did in dialect, until it was swallowed up by Athens, at a date not later than her thrust into Euboea in the mid-fifth century.[99]

In later antiquity, Oropus was, of course, famous for the incubation-shrine of Amphiaraus that it contained, a few miles from the town itself. This was much the most celebrated of the five or so cult places of Amphiaraus that can be named in all, and Pausanias says that 'it was the Oropians who first honoured Amphiaraus as a god. Subsequently the rest of the Greeks have come to consider him so too.'[100] Traces of earlier use of the site, however, are so slight that archaeologists agree, it seems, that the present sanctuary was not founded until the last quarter of the fifth century or thereabouts. (Aristophanes' *Amphiaraus* gives a *terminus ante quem* of 414, and two reliefs apparently commemorating victory in the *apobates* competition attest games around 400, unless they have been misdated by a long way.) That puts the foundation squarely into the Athenian period; and it will remain there, if less squarely, even if a herm found at the site and recently ascribed to '470–450' is allowed to raise the date by twenty-five years or so.[101] Little though we know of the

---

[98] On the foundation see esp. C. Bearzot, 'Problemi del confine attico-beotico: La rivendicazione tebana di Oropo', in M. Sordi ed., *Il confine nel mondo classico* (Milan 1987), 80–99 (and on the political context, ead. in H. Beister and J. Buckler eds., *Boiotika*, Munich 1989, 113–22); on the cult in general, Petrakos, Ἱερὸν τοῦ Ἀμφιαράου (and id., Ἐπιγραφικὰ τοῦ Ὠρωποῦ, Athens 1980 = *SEG* XXXI 424–92), and the refs. in Schachter, *Cults*, I.19–21.

[99] Thuc. 2.23.3; Paus. 1.34.1 τὴν γῆν τὴν Ὠρωπίαν . . . Βοιωτίαν τὸ ἐξ ἀρχῆς οὖσαν— but this yields to the statement of Nicocrates in his *On Boeotia* that Oropus was an Eretrian foundation (*FGrH* 376 F 1: this testimonium was rescued from neglect by D. Knoepfler, 'Oropos, Colonie d'Érétrie', *Les Dossiers: Histoire et archéologie* 94, 1985, 50–55). *IG* I³.41.67–71, a tariff for ferry fees, seems to provide *c.*446/5 as a *terminus ante quem* for Athenian control; Knoepfler thinks of *c.*470, and earlier dates can scarcely be excluded.

[100] Paus. 1.34.2; on cults elsewhere see E. Bethe in *RE* s.v. *Amphiaraos*, cols. 1887–88, or L. R. Farnell, *Greek Hero Cults and Ideas of Immortality* (Oxford 1921), 406, no. 31.

[101] Petrakos, Ἱερὸν τοῦ Ἀμφιαράου, 18, 22, 66–67; Travlos, *Bildlexikon*, 301. The frs. of Aristophanes' play (frs. 17–40 K/A, where Bergk's bold speculations are rightly not endorsed) reveal little, but it seems safe to assume that the Amphiareion envisaged in the Athenian play

mechanisms of Athenian control of Oropus, it seems obvious that the sovereign power would have taken an interest in such an event,[102] and probably in fact lay behind it. But what were the circumstances?

Strabo says that the cult of Amphiaraus was 'transferred to Oropus from Knopia' (an unidentified place, probably near Thebes) 'in accordance with an oracle'. He does not say when, and he might of course be reporting a myth, not a historical occurrence. But two well-known passages of Herodotus attest an oracular shrine of Amphiaraus, apparently at Thebes, famous enough in the sixth century to be consulted by Croesus and in 479 by Mardonius' agent Mys; and Aeschylus too probably alludes to it. This shrine had one remarkable characteristic: 'Amphiaraus instructed the Thebans', says Herodotus, 'by an oracular message to choose whichever they pleased of two things, to make use of him either as an ally or as a prophet, but to refrain from the other.' The Thebans chose an ally, and were accordingly debarred from consulting their own oracle. Subsequently—perhaps because of this restriction—nothing is reported of the Theban shrine, and it had conceivably gone into decline by the time of Herodotus: for he says that the offerings sent by Croesus to Amphiaraus were still visible not in the hero's own precinct but in that of Ismenian Apollo.[103]

An obvious hypothesis to account for almost all these data is that the shrine of Amphiaraus was transferred from near Thebes to Oropus in the second half of the fifth century.[104] Difficulties arise at once, however. We should, perhaps, not insist too strongly on the oddity of Amphiaraus being moved from Thebes, the site of his death, to Oropus, a place with which he had no mythical association:

is not that of Thebes. A herm: Petrakos, Ἱερὸν τοῦ Ἀμφιαράου, 121, no. 15; *IG* I³.1476; before *IG* I³ this was commonly dated to the sixth cent. and judged a stray. There appears to be very little precise archaeological evidence for use even in the late fifth cent.: two small altars and the adjacent 'theatre' are conventionally so dated (Petrakos, Ἱερὸν τοῦ Ἀμφιαράου, 67–68). The dedication to an unidentified god in Attic script of '? c. 550' recently found at Skala Oropou (*IG* I³.1475) introduces another uncertainty. *Apobatai* dedications (uninscribed but so identified iconographically): E. Berlin ex Saburoff 725 (Petrakos, Ἱερὸν τοῦ Ἀμφιαράου, 121, no. 16, *LIMC* s.v. *Amphiaraos*, 702, no. 67), 'early 4th c.'; Ath. Nat. Mus. 1391 (Petrakos no. 17), 'c. 400'. One would prefer to date them to a period of Athenian control, since the *apobates* competition may have been distinctively Attic (Harpocration's reference s.v. ἀποβάτης to Boeotia may refer precisely to Oropus): see N. B. Crowther, *JHS* 111 (1991), 174–76.

[102] This point is not considered by Bearzot, 'Problemi del confine attico-beotico', who ascribes the introduction to a Theban desire to 'Boeotianize' Oropus. But Oropus had an Attic garrison (Thuc. 8.60) and archon of some kind (Lys. 20.6).

[103] Strabo 9.2.10 (404); Hdt. 1.46–52 (esp. 52), 8.133–34; Aesch. *Sept*. 587–88 (cf. Soph. fr. 958 Radt). On all this see Bearzot, 'Problemi del confine attico-beotico', 89–93.

[104] So e.g. Petrakos, Ἱερὸν τοῦ Ἀμφιαράου, 66–67; Bearzot, 'Problemi del confine attico-beotico'; D. Musti and L. Beschi in their note on Paus. 1.34.1.

a myth arose that, though he vanished into the earth at Thebes, he re-emerged from the sacred spring at Oropus, and the parallel case of Asclepius anyway shows how a mythical healer could shake off the geographical restrictions normally set on a hero and acquire, in effect, the ubiquitous powers of a god. In due course he also appears in Attica proper, and in the Peloponnese.[105] But it was certainly not normal for a cult, as it were, to hang a notice on the door and 'transfer to new premises', when the premises were in territory controlled by a different state. It would be much easier to ascribe the foundation to a period when Thebes controlled Oropus; but chronologically that is difficult, if not impossible.[106] This is one reason why many have urged that Herodotus does not explicitly locate his Amphiaraus in Thebes, and suppose that he is referring instead to the famous shrine at Oropus.[107] Just possibly they are right; but theirs is not the easiest way to read Herodotus, and, as we have seen, the archaic cult at Oropus which they postulate has quite failed to leave archaeological traces.

Perhaps we should abandon the idea of a cult 'transfer', and suppose that Amphiaraus was introduced to Oropus, as was Asclepius to Athens, without any expectation that the original cult would then cease. But can we guess the motives for the introduction? If it occurred about 425, the great plague might have provided an impulse. But it is hard not to wonder also about factors of imperial policy. In 411 Athens lost control of Oropus to Thebes; when she recovered it, by at the latest 374, we soon find (as we learn from a recently redated decree) the Athenian assembly actively involved with the affairs of the shrine, and an Athenian holding the priest-

---

[105] Sacred spring: Paus. 1.34.4. Peloponnese: n. 100 above. Attica: for Rhamnus see Ch. 9, n. 83. A cult at Athens itself is commonly taken to be attested by *IG* II².171 and its associated relief (Ath. Nat. Mus. 1396), which shows Amphiaraus and Hygieia honouring one Artikleides; but since the relief is now dated by art historians to 'after 330' (see *LIMC* s.v. *Amphiaraos*, 702, no. 65), Artikleides' services might have concerned the cult at Oropus. The first firm evidence is therefore *Hesperia* 51 (1982), 53, no. 10 from the *agora* (cf. *Bull. Ép.* 1982, no. 138 for a correction; *SEG* XXXII 110), which honours the priest in 273/2 (cf. *IG* II².4441, a dedication by the priest later in the century). *IG* II².1282 (262/1, Piraeus) is a resolution by a college of worshippers of Ammon that honours for a member be proclaimed 'at the [sacrifice] of Amphiaraus'. This perhaps does not prove an association between the college and Amphiaraus (cf. Aeschin. 3.41), but probably implies a festival of Amphiaraus in the Piraeus. An unexplained small payment 'to Amphiaraus' appears in the Eleusinian accounts of 329/8 (*IG* II².1672.305). (Note too *IG* II².1344, near Acharnae, AD 28.)

[106] It becomes just possible if we both raise the foundation to the early part of the century on the basis of *IG* I³.1476 and postulate a period of Theban control before the Attic take-over: see ns. 99 and 101 above.

[107] See Schachter, *Cults*, I.22, n. 2. But Aeschylus too (*Sept.* 588) seems to point to the vicinity of Thebes.

hood;[108] when it was reassigned to her, after another loss in 366, by Philip or Alexander in the 330s, numerous decrees attest intense interest at the highest level, expressed most notably in the reorganization of the *Amphiaraea* as a prestigious penteteric festival.[109] In the fourth century, therefore, the Athenians celebrated their recovery of the eagerly desired territory by heaping attentions on the god of the shrine; it may be that in the fifth they had founded a shrine partly in order to assert their presence in a territory which they had recently acquired or (on a lower chronology) their grip on which was threatened by the Peloponnesian war. If this is so, the decision to introduce not an Attic but a Theban cult is, perhaps, a little surprising. But originally, of course, Amphiaraus had been an enemy of Thebes.[110]

All this is speculation; and all would be changed if evidence emerged (as it easily might) that Amphiaraus had been worshipped in Oropus earlier, at a different site.[111] For a clearer instance of the imperial city's religious policy we must look elsewhere. Athens had become 'the tyrant-city'; and her treatment of Delos curiously echoes that by the actual tyrant Pisistratus in the sixth century.[112] Where, however, under Pisistratus the fiction of Delian independence was perhaps preserved, the sacred island is now quite unmistakably under partial

---

[108] See D. Knoepfler, *Chiron* 16 (1986), 71–98 (summarized in *SEG* XXXVI 442), on *ArchEph* 1923, 36–42, no. 123. This brilliant study is now fundamental for Oropus' history in the fourth cent. The two surviving sacred laws (*LSS* 35 and *LSCG* 69) date from non-Attic periods: see A. Petropoulou, *GRBS* 22 (1981), 39–63 (= *SEG* XXXI 415–16; but on the order of these texts contrast Knoepfler, *Chiron* 16, 1986, 96, n. 116).

[109] *IG* VII.3499 (cf. C. Habicht, *ZPE* 77, 1989, 83–87), 4252–54 (= Schwenk 28, 40–41, 50), 4255 (*SIG³* 973); Schwenk 56 and *Michel* 1704 (= Reinmuth, *Ephebic Inscriptions*, no. 15); probably Arist. *Ath. Pol.* 54.7 (see Rhodes's note ad loc., Knoepfler as cited below, and Ch. 11, n. 100). Cf. Petrakos, Ἱερὸν τοῦ Ἀμφιαράου, 26–29; Mitchel, 'Lykourgan Athens', 208–209; Humphreys, 'Lycurgus', 224, n. 16. For dedications by individual Athenians in the Lycurgan period see *SEG* XV 284–85, (?) 291. D. Knoepfler in M. Piérart ed., *Aristote et Athènes* (Paris 1993), 279–302, argues wholly convincingly that the penteteric games were proposed in 331 (see Schwenk 41.13) but first celebrated only in 329, by the illustrious board attested in Schwenk 50 (much too distinguished to be in charge of 'lesser' Amphiaraic games, as has often been supposed merely because the insignificant musical competition is not explicitly mentioned); to this celebration, or less probably that of 325, belongs the victory list *ArchEph* 1923, 46, no. 125 = Petrakos, Ἱερὸν τοῦ Ἀμφιαράου, 196, no. 47 (certainly from the Athenian period, despite the 'Panhellenic' identification of Athenian victors by *ethnikon*, not *demotikon*). On earlier games see n. 101.

[110] Note his own prophecy in Aesch. *Sept.* 588 that he will lie in Thebes μάντις κεκευθὼς πολεμίας ὑπὸ χθονός. On the 'enemy hero' cf. Ch. 9, n. 18.

[111] But even so, a reorganization or extension of the cult under Athenian auspices in the fifth cent. would remain plausible. Schachter, *Cults*, I.23, notes that it might have been at this stage that the cult came to specialize in healing (in the two Herodotean refs. it seems to provide 'general purpose incubation').

[112] Cf. Meiggs, *Athenian Empire*, 300–302; Smarczyk, *Religionspolitik*, 504–25; Hornblower, *Commentary*, 517–25 and *HSCP* 94 (1992), 186–97; on Pisistratus, Ch. 6 above.

control by Athenian functionaries. A large new temple begun for Apollo in the mid-century was probably planned and paid for by the Delian League, under the auspices of Athens.[113] The league treasury was removed and the temple was not completed, but Athenian interest in the island was not at an end. The Athena Parthenos of Phidias, it has been suggested, was conceived as an Attic equivalent to the famous sixth-century cult statue of Apollo on Delos, which in scale, materials, and certain details of iconography, it recalls. The assembly apparently also voted in the 430s to build Apollo Delios a modest new temple in Phaleron.[114] In the 420s, probably in response, as Diodorus says, to the plague—but the novel presence of Spartan ships in Aegean waters has also been noted—interest in the island itself became intense. 'In accord with a certain oracle', the Athenians now transformed it, a home of men as well as a birthplace of gods though it was, into an uncomfortably sacred place. Where Pisistratus had purified only the region in sight of the temple, all graves were now dug up, and no birth or death was henceforth to be permitted anywhere on the island (with the consequence, it was noted, that no Delian henceforth had a native land).[115]

At the same time, in yet another example of very untraditional imperial traditionalism, the Ionian *panegyris* on Delos, an ancient but faded institution, was revived with novel splendour as a quinquennial festival. The surviving core of the festival—competition between choruses sent by the participating states—was retained, the athletic competitions known from the *Homeric Hymn to Apollo* were restored, and horse-racing was added for the first time. In this form the *Delia* could be an Ionian substitute for the great Panhellenic games, which cannot have been very attractive to the Athenians and their allies during the war, even if they were not formally excluded from them. Before the allies, private munificence could be usefully exploited, and the opulence and good discipline of the Attic chorus

---

[113] See Bruneau/Ducat, *Guide de Délos*, 130–31; Boersma, *Building Policy*, 170. Functionaries: *IG* I³.402 = M/L 62, with their notes; ibid. 1457–61 (on 'Amphictyons' cf. Ch. 6, n. 87 above).

[114] Athena Parthenos: so B. Fehr, *Hephaistos* 1 (1979), 71–91. Temple in Phaleron: Lewis, n. 15 above on *IG* I³.130 (who suspects a connection with the Delian earthquake, Thuc. 2.8.3).

[115] Link with plague: Diod. 12.58.6–7 (cf. Thuc. 3.87; Smarczyk, *Religionspolitik*, 506, n. 17; Hornblower, *Commentary*, 519). Diodorus' explanation receives strong support from Lewis's redating to the fifth cent. of *IG* I³.1468 bis = *CEG* 742, an altar on the island dedicated by 'Athens' (*sic*) to Apollo Paion and Athena. Spartan ships: so Smarczyk, *Religionspolitik*, 508–12. Purification and oracle: Thuc. 3.104, with Hornblower's discussion of the source of the oracle (respectable enough to motivate public action, but probably not, given Thucydides' silence, fresh from Delphi); for a scrap of an Athenian decree perhaps of this date, proposed by Cleonymus and concerning Delos, see D. M. Lewis, *ZPE* 60 (1985), 108, on *Inscr. Dél.* 80 = *IG* I³.1454 bis, with Hornblower, *Commentary*, 518. No native land: Plut. *Apophth. Lac.* 230c–d.

trained by that great gentleman Nicias made a sensation. Another early delegation to the festival was led by the immensely rich Kallias. A new temple of Attic decoration and design, small but fine, dates from this period.[116]

But the most startling intervention was the wholesale expulsion of the islanders from their home in 422, followed by their restoration a year later. According to Thucydides the motive was religious in both cases: the Athenians drove the Delians out 'in the belief that they had been consecrated although they were impure because of an ancient offence, and that this was an omission in their former purification of the island', and restored them later because they 'took to heart their set-backs in the war, and because the god of Delphi so instructed them'. According to Diodorus, by contrast, it was believed that the islanders were engaged in secret negotiations with the Spartans (a fear that would of course have been removed by the signing of the Treaty of Nicias in 421).[117] Either Diodorus' (i.e. Ephorus' account) is a rationalizing invention, or Thucydides has been culpably economical with the truth. However that may be, modern scholars have suggested an underlying urge distinct from either of these motives: the desire to have unfettered control (not that the fetters that the Delians could impose were at all tight) of the sacred place.[118] Certainly, the Oropians met a very similar fate when their territory, home of Amphiaraus' oracle, fell back into Athenian hands in the fourth century.[119] Shrines and festivals and gods were among the most precious spoils of empire.

[116] Restored festival: Thuc. 3.104; *IG* I³.1468 is a dedication by the ἀρχεθέωροι of the first πεντετηρίς. Ionian substitute: Hornblower, *Commentary*, 521–22 (though note with him that some Dorian islanders frequented Delos) and (no formal exclusion) 390; id., *HSCP* 94 (1992), 191–94. Nicias: Plut. *Nic.* 3.5–8, cf. *IG* I³.1474 (for the debate about the date see Smarczyk, *Religionspolitik*, 517, n. 54; Hornblower, *Commentary*, 518). Kallias: dedications associated with his delegation are mentioned in (e.g.). *Inscr. Dél.* 104.115–16 (cf. J. Coupry's note ad loc. in *Inscr. Dél.*, 43, 45, and Smarczyk, *Religionspolitik*, 519, n. 59 on other Athenian dedications). Small Delian temple (the 'temple of the Athenians' of inscriptions): see Bruneau/Ducat, *Guide de Délos*, 129–30; Boersma, *Building Policy*, 171. An up-to-date study of the *Delia* is a desideratum (Deubner, *Attische Feste*, is inadequate on this): see still T. Homolle in DarSag s.v. *Delia* (1892), with the modification of Nilsson, *Griechische Feste*, 144–49, itself modified by Bruneau, *Recherches*, 85–86. *Inscr. Dél.* 98.31–40 (= Tod II.125) attests the scale: 109 sacrificial oxen. On the festival before 426 see Smarczyk, *Religionspolitik*, 472, n. 184, who cites the poems of Bacchylides (17: note line 130) and Pindar (several *paeans*, and cf. *Isth.* 1.4–8) probably written for it.

[117] Thuc. 5.1, 5.32.1; Diod. 12.73.1 (accepted by Meiggs, *Athenian Empire*, 302, who, however, notes that 'Ephorus is quite capable of adding such an explanation from his own imagination'). On the 'ancient offence' see Ch. 11, n. 31 below.

[118] So Homolle in DarSag 56, followed by Smarczyk, *Religionspolitik*, 521. Fetters: cf. M/L, p. 170, Smarczyk, *Religionspolitik*, 521–25.

[119] See Knoepfler, *Chiron* 16 (1986), 71–98. For the Delians' resentment of Athenian control in the fourth cent. see Ch. 11 below.

9

The Fifth Century: New Gods

We turn now to another conspicuous phenomenon of the century: religious innovation, and in particular the introduction of new cults.[1] A good starting-point will be the misfortunes of Nicomachus, one of the men entrusted with codifying and republishing the sacrificial calendar of Athens at the end of the fifth century. He ended by being prosecuted for abuse of his office, and the charge brought against him was that—o horror!—he had perpetrated change: by admitting expensive new sacrifices he had caused other, older rites to be neglected. And yet:

Our ancestors, who only made the sacrifices prescribed in Solon's code, bequeathed to us a city which was the greatest and happiest in all Greece; and so we ought to perform the same sacrifices as them, if for no other reason, for the good fortune that they brought.[2]

This is a revealingly double-edged little incident. The prosecutor is certainly affirming what few Athenians would deny when he insists that, in religion, old ways are best.[3] Many continued to believe that they could distinguish between 'ancestral sacrifices', those of especial sanctity, as they always insisted, and a regrettable but, evidently, highly popular category of 'additional' rites. And yet Nicomachus, the man with a practical job to do, could not ignore the many changes that had occurred in Athenian practice; and not even the prosecutor can deny the legitimacy of certain sacrifices, not established by Solon, which 'the people had decreed' over the years. If the prosecutor truly represents the ideology of Greek religion, or at least an important strand of it, it is Nicomachus who represents the practice. 'Traditional' polytheisms are subject to constant change; that is

---

[1] On most of the topics here treated see too now Garland, *New Gods*.

[2] Lys. 30.18; on Nicomachus' revision cf. Ch. 11 below.

[3] See above all Isoc. *Areop*. 29–30; cf. Mikalson, *Athenian Popular Religion*, 96–97. For the πάτριος/ἐπίθετος distinction see Isoc., *Areop*. 29–30, and Ch. 1, n. 25.

one of their traditions.[4] And the change characteristically occurs in exactly the fashion described in the speech against Nicomachus: existing rites are not formally abolished, but, with the coming of new gods, old gods simply fade away. The innovations that occurred in the fifth century are not a sign that a hitherto stable religious order was now in crisis. The interest in studying them is not this; it is rather that they allow us to observe, with unusual clarity and precision, a quite normal operation of polytheism. We will begin by surveying some of the different forms that innovation and adaptation might take (in particular the reception of 'foreign gods'), before turning more specifically to four cults that came to Athens in circumstances that can be described in some detail.

One common form of change was the elevation of a minor cult to new prominence. There had been an altar of Athena Nike on the Acropolis since the mid-sixth century; but it was not until the second half of the fifth that, doubtless to celebrate the Delian League's defeat of Persia, a priestess was appointed and the lovely small temple was constructed that still stands on the bastion of the acropolis. Before the great battle, the Athenians encamped in a precinct of Heracles at Marathon. The pan-Attic games, the *Herakleia* at Marathon, were surely either created or expanded to celebrate the hero's aid. Xenophon tells us that, again before Marathon, the Athenians vowed to sacrifice to Artemis Agrotera one goat for every Persian slain. So vast was the slaughter that, for want of goats, they commuted the vow to an annual offering of 500, but in that form it was still carried out in Xenophon's day, and the procession to Artemis' shrine survived in Plutarch's. (A cult of Zeus Tropaios at the site of the battle also commemorated the victory more directly.[5]) This spectacular rite—the earliest attested instance, incidentally, of the great democratic institution of the 'public feast', δημοθοινία— must have enhanced the fame of Artemis Agrotera, and it was perhaps she who was honoured (in the 440s?) with the elegant Ionic temple beside the Ilissus which Stuart and Revett were still able to capture in a drawing in the 1750s. Similarly, Ajax of Salamis was invoked (among others) before the battle in the straits in 480, and a commemorative festival, the *Aianteia*, was established on the island

---

[4] See above all J. North, 'Conservatism and Change in Roman Religion', *BSR* 44 (1976), 1–12; cf. Goody, *Logic of Writing*, 8, on the inevitable 'obsolescence' of cults that promise practical goods which they cannot provide (cf. id. in *Africa* 27, 1957, 356–65); Burkert, *Greek Religion*, 176: 'Polytheism is an open system'.

[5] See *IG* I³.255.11, with Jameson's notes ad loc., where the possibility that the cult rather concerns Salamis is noted.

perhaps not long afterwards (though the first allusions are Hellenistic).[6]

In the period *c*.450 to 430 (at the limit 460 to 420) were built a series of temples of medium size and fine workmanship: of Poseidon at Sunium, of Nemesis at Rhamnus, of (possibly) Ares at (possibly) Acharnae, and that of Hephaestus above the *agora* in Athens (the 'Theseum') which survives almost intact. Through this programme (which it is attractive to see as coherent, though recent datings raise new doubts) the marks of Athens' magnificence, in the form of fine temples, were taken right out into the recesses of Attica; and the message was proclaimed that Athens was a city of craft and of military might by both land and sea, which had inflicted on the Persians a bitter nemesis. In the process unusual honour was bestowed on a local goddess, Nemesis of Rhamnus, and on (?) Ares and Hephaestus, habitually the least esteemed of the twelve Olympians. Hephaestus' festival was even reorganized, in 421/0, on an elaborate and extravagant scale, to include a team torch-race, large sacrifices, a procession and (apparently) a musical competition—a distinction for the limping god for which one in vain seeks a parallel. A yet more spectacular elevation was that of Theseus, when his bones were brought home and lodged in a new shrine in Athens in the 470s. More modestly, Delian Apollo, who had never lacked honour in Athens, was apparently voted a new shrine at Phaleron around 430, in consequence perhaps of the Athenians' many anxieties in respect of Apollo and Delos at that period.[7]

Another common form of change was the application to a long-established god of a new epithet. As it happens, the clearest instance

[6] Athena Nike: see Meiggs, *Athenian Empire*, 495–503 (chronological problems can be left aside here: for radical new proposals see Mark, *Athena Nike*, 129 ff.). *Herakleia*: above, Ch. 6, n. 124. Artemis Agrotera: Xen. *Anab.* 3.2.12; cf. Ar. *Eq.* 660–63, (?) *Lys.* 1262 (NB context); Arist. *Ath. Pol.* 58.1, with Rhodes; Deubner, *Attische Feste*, 209 (who cites the later evidence); and M. H. Jameson in V. D. Hanson ed., *Hoplites* (London 1991), 210–11. Temple by the Ilissus: Travlos, *Pictorial Dictionary*, 112–20 (who supports this identification against the commoner one as the temple of the 'Mother at Agrai'), and most recently W. P. Childs, *AM* 100 (1985), 207–51 [+]. Ajax: Hdt. 8.64 and (for the dedication of a captured trireme to him) 121; cf. Deubner, *Attische Feste*, 228; Pritchett, *Greek State at War*, III.175–76 and now *Hesperia* 48 (1979), 174–75, lines 17–22 (of 214/3).

[7] 'Series of temples': Boersma, *Building Policy*, 76–80, cf. Hornblower, *Greek World*, 113, who speaks of 'a huge fourfold piece of political iconography'; but on the chronology see now M. M. Miles, *Hesperia* 58 (1989), 221–35, and on Ares and Acharnae the justified doubts of K. J. Hartswick, *RA* 1990, 258–72 (*SEG* XL 126). Hephaisteia: *IG* I³.82, with J. K. Davies, *JHS* 87 (1967), 35–36 (but against his denial of musical competitions note *IG* I³.82.14); Rosivach, *Public Sacrifice*, 154, now suggests, however, that the rites prescribed in this text were to be performed once only. On the neglect of Hephaestus outside Athens see Nilsson, *Griechische Feste*, 428–29. A payment of some kind to Athena and Hephaestus was prescribed in the famous 'coinage decree' of (?) 449 (*IG* I³.1453 C17). Theseus: see below. Delian Apollo: see Ch. 8, n. 15.

of this in the period is of a singular kind. Plutarch tells us that, after the Persian wars, Themistocles made himself unpopular by founding in Melite (a deme of the city) a shrine of Artemis 'whom he named Aristoboule' (best-planner) 'as having himself formed the best plans for the city and the Greeks'. (A little shrine of Artemis, of the right period, has now in fact been uncovered at Melite.[8]) This is one of three shrines said to have been founded by Themistocles in connection with the Persian wars (but neither of the other two accounts can bear much weight),[9] and the question arises of the authority by which he acted; 'why Artemis?', one may also wonder.[10] But what concerns us now is the epithet Aristoboule. Here Themistocles' offence lay only in the personal vainglory; it was entirely normal to invent or import new epithets, and in particular to unite a goddess with an abstract noun to create a combination such as Athena Victory or Athena Health. Another new foundation of comparable type, made according to Pausanias from the spoils of Marathon, was the shrine of Eukleia, 'Fair Fame'. Any personification was, one might say, a potential goddess (and this particular one probably already received cult in some Greek states, in her common combination with Artemis as Artemis Eukleia); the 'Fair Fame' won at Marathon changed Eukleia at Athens from a familiar if unworshipped force to a divinity of fixed abode. The cult of Pheme, 'Rumour', was said to have been instituted only a little later, to

[8] Plut. *Them.* 22.2; for the shrine see Travlos, *Pictorial Dictionary*, 121–23 [+]. In it was found *SEG* XXII 116, which shows that in the late fourth cent. it served as deme-shrine of Melite. P. Amandry in *Charisterion eis Anastasion K. Orlandon* (Athens 1967), IV.265–79, is sceptical of Plutarch's account and of the excavators' argument that the shrine was demonstrably founded in the first half of the fifth cent.; but see A. J. Podlecki, *The Life of Themistocles* (Montreal 1975), 175.

[9] See Ch. 11, n. 73 for his supposed association (perhaps a mere error) with the famous Aphrodisium of the Piraeus. And *IG* II².1035.45 (? first cent. AD) mentions, apparently in the Piraeus, a [ἱερὸν Ἀθηνᾶς Ἑ]ρκάνης (so Culley, *Sacred Monuments*, 151–56, cf. id., *Hesperia* 44, 1975, 214 = *SEG* XXVI 121; P. Funke, *ZPE* 53, 1983, 184–86) 'which Themistocles founded before the battle of Salamis'. Other problems aside, the ascription to Themistocles in a text of this character has little authority.

[10] Authority: cf. pp. 215–16. Artemis: the same problem is raised by the link between Artemis Mounichia and Salamis twice attested by Plutarch (see n. 124 below; Amandry, *Charisterion*, 274, n. 15; Pritchett, *Greek State at War*, III.177). The moonshine during (*sic*) the battle mentioned by Plutarch (*De Glor. Ath.* 349f) but not Aeschylus or Herodotus looks like aetiological fiction (the possible relevance of the crescent moons on tetradrachms is unclear: Kraay, *Greek Coins*, 61–62; Pritchett, *Greek State at War*, III.174, n. 70); but might the battle's important nocturnal prelude of itself evoke Artemis? Amandry wonders whether a temple of the goddess might already have existed in Melite. Vernant argues that wild Artemis was distinctively associated with, in P. Ellinger's phrase, 'les guerres d'anéantissement total' (*Figures, idoles, masques*, Paris 1990, 165–66). More simply, note that the goddess was associated with the land on both sides of the straits of Salamis (Hdt. 8.77, with commentators, and esp. G. Roux, *BCH* 98, 1974, 69); her presence here may have seemed the more significant given that an important earlier phase of the campaign took place at Artemisium (Plut. *Them.* 8.3–5).

commemorate a miraculous report of the Greeks' great victory at
Eurymedon in the 460s.[11]

In the same way, innumerable powers known from mythology
were potential gods. Herodotus tells us how the Persian wars, yet
again, led to one of them receiving actual worship. When the Persian
fleet was anchored in 480 at the beach Sepeia above Thermopylae, it
was struck and devastated by a 'Hellespontine' wind. Herodotus catalogues the vast losses, and goes on:

The story is told that the Athenians invoked Boreas because of a prophecy,
since a further oracle had come to them telling them to call on their son-in-
law as ally. According to Greek tradition Boreas has an Attic wife,
Oreithuia the daughter of Erechtheus. The Athenians inferred, the story
goes, that because of this marriage-tie Boreas was their son-in-law, and
when they realized as they lay at anchor at Chalkis in Euboea that the storm
was growing even stronger, they made sacrifice and called on Boreas and
Oreithuia to avenge them and destroy the ships of the barbarians, as they
had done earlier at Athos. I cannot say if that is the reason why Boreas fell
upon the barbarians as they lay at anchor. But the Athenians certainly claim
that Boreas had aided them before, and was also responsible in this case;
and on their return they founded a shrine of Boreas beside the river
Ilissus.[12]

This account of the Athenians' beliefs and actions is wholly credible. Boreas' earlier intervention had been directed against
Mardonius' expeditionary force of 492, when it lay off the god's own
Thracian homeland.[13] That was probably the incident that put the
Athenians and the oracle in mind of their powerful kinsman. Greeks
often paid cult to winds, though normally perhaps only when particular need arose, to start or stop them blowing.[14] It is scarcely surprising if in the crisis of 480 (when Apollo advised the Greeks in

[11] Eukleia and Marathon: Paus. 1.14.5, admittedly not wholly reliable (see W. Gauer,
Weihgeschenke aus den Perserkriegen (Tübingen 1968), 26, 70); on the goddess see R. Hampe,
RhM 62 (1955), 110–23; A. Kossatz-Deissmann, *LIMC* s.v. *Eukleia*, 48–51 [+]. E. B.
Harrison, *AJA* 81 (1977), 139, n. 14, identifies the 'Theseum' as the shrine of Eukleia. But it
is much too large for a minor cult. Pheme: see p. 233 below (where the special issues raised by
such deified personifications are discussed).

[12] Hdt. 7.189; cf. A. R. Burn, *Persia and the Greeks*[2] (London 1984), 389 f.

[13] Hdt. 6.44.2; cf. Burn, *Persia and the Greeks*, 222 f.

[14] See R. Hampe, 'Kult der Winde in Athen und Kreta', *SBHeid* 1967, 1, 7–17, who cites
e.g. Hom. *Il.* 23.193–95; Ar. *Ran.* 847, Xen. *Anab.* 4.5.4. 'Divine men' too, such as
Empedocles, claimed control over winds. Hampe observes that cult of the winds is likely to
have been practised in some form in Athens even before 480: cf. App. 2 A s.v. *Heudanemoi*,
Paus. 1.37.2 (an altar of Zephyrus beside the Cephisus), Hesych. β 819 Βορεασμοί (Βορεασταί
Pearson)· Ἀθήνησιν οἱ ἄγοντες τῷ Βορέᾳ ἑορτὰς καὶ θοίνας, ἵνα ἄνεμοι πνέωσιν. ἐκαλοῦντο
δὲ Βορεασμοί (though this may reflect arrangements made after Artemisium). He associates
the 'stone-curbed pit' in the *agora* (above, Ch. 3, n. 20) with the *Heudanemoi* (pp. 18–22).

general to 'pray to the Winds'[15]) the Athenians remembered that divine helper on whom they had a particular claim. And several signs appear of a new interest in Boreas and Oreithuia in the years following the victory. The first literary allusion to the myth is in Simonides' poem celebrating 'the sea-battle at Artemisium'; Aeschylus wrote an *Oreithuia*, and possibly Sophocles did so too; and in the half-century after the battle the seizing of Oreithuia, a theme hitherto untouched, appears on a good fifty Attic vases. It even entered the repertoire of divine rapes that served so neatly to adorn the acroteria of temples.[16]

Within the great reservoir of potential gods were also those of other Greek states. A Panhellenic deity could be introduced, in the form in which he or she was worshipped outside Attica. Long, doubtless, before the fifth century, Zeus Kenaios of Euboea, Poseidon Kalaureiates of Kalaureia and Athena Itonia of Thessaly and Boeotia had been brought thus to Attica. Late in the Periclean period, a large stoa, one of the *agora*'s finest monuments, was erected in honour of Zeus Eleutherios, that liberator from (in particular) foreign oppression to whom the Greeks had made a famous sacrifice after the victory at Plataea.[17] (But the phenomenon in this case was not one of simple borrowing from outside Attica; for the cult of Eleutherios was probably grafted on an existing one of Zeus Soter, at Athens as elsewhere.) Lesser gods or heroes could also be introduced from other Greek states. Early in the century Pan came from Arcadia, towards its end Asclepius from Epidaurus. A less well-known case is that of the Aeginetan hero Aeacus. Long before bribing the enemy had become an important technique in Greek warfare, the importance of suborning the enemy's heroes had been recognized. While planning hostilities against Aegina (in 505 perhaps), the Athenians accordingly, on the advice of Delphi, built a shrine for the enemy hero Aeacus in a place of honour in their own *agora*.[18]

---

[15] Hdt. 7.178.1.

[16] Simonid. fr. 534 *PMG* (and cf. now *P. Oxy.* 3965 fr. 20 = Simonides fr. eleg. 3 West²); Aesch. fr. 281 Radt; *TrGF* IV.496; S. Kaempf-Dimitriadou, *LIMC* s.v. *Boreas*, 133–42 [+] (one sixth-cent. example—139, no. 76—is very questionable).

[17] Thuc. 2.71.2. See esp. K. Raaflaub, *Die Entdeckung der Freiheit* (Munich 1985), 125–47, and cf. Ch. 11, n. 76 below. Zeus Kenaios et al.: Ch. 2, n. 64 above.

[18] Pan and Asclepius: see below. Aeacus: Hdt. 5.89. An inscription to be pub. by R. S. Stroud (presented by him at a lecture in Oxford in July 1993) proves the Athenian Aiakeion to have been much larger than hitherto supposed; Stroud very interestingly suggests that the form of the original Aeginetan shrine (Paus. 2.29.6–7) may have been reproduced. On the (controversial) chronology and circumstances see e.g. H. W. Parke and D. E. W. Wormell, *The Delphic Oracle* (Oxford 1956) I.150; N. G. L. Hammond, *Historia* 4 (1955), 406–11; W. G. Forrest, *CR* NS 8 (1958), 123; J. P. Barron, *JHS* 103 (1983), 10, n. 28. On the religious issues (enemy heroes), M. Visser, *HThR* 75 (1982), 403–28; A. Mastrocinque in M. Sordi ed., *Religione e politica nel mondo antico* (Milan 1981), 8–9; Kearns, *Heroes of Attica*, 47, 50.

There were, finally, 'foreign gods'. Scholars used sometimes to react to the Greeks' interest in foreign gods much as did Moses to the Israelites' interest in the Golden Calf. We read, for instance, that:

The invasion of the western mind by eastern religious ideas is not something which happened once in ancient history. It is a recurrent phenomenon, something which reappears like the plague whenever the conditions favour its emergence—that is to say, roughly, whenever immigration from the East has been sufficiently intense and prolonged, and at the same time the western mind is sufficiently discouraged to be receptive. These conditions coexisted at Athens during the later years of the Peloponnesian war . . .

Thus far the enemy without; there follows the enemy within:

Those foreigners down in the Piraeus, not content to practise their mysteries in the twilight of their licensed chapels, had started to proselytize. Probably at first they had little success with the men—in time of war, men have other things to think about—but the infection was spreading among the wives and daughters of the Athenian citizens.[19]

Here, by contrast, the subject of foreign gods has deliberately been introduced not as an aberration but amid the many changes that Greek religion constantly underwent.

Perhaps it might be best to abandon the concept of 'foreign' gods altogether. The Athenians themselves did, it is true, speak of *xenikoi theoi*. The comic poet Apollophanes offers a little list of them, and Aristophanes in a lost play showed 'Sabazius and other foreign gods' put on trial and expelled from the city. Such passages paradoxically earned the city a reputation in later antiquity for 'hospitality' to divine as well as mortal immigrants.[20] But the *xenikoi theoi* are not identical with 'foreign gods'. Just as an Epidaurian was a *xenos* for an Athenian, so was the Epidaurian hero Asclepius for Apollophanes a *xenikos theos*, son of Apollo though he was. The essential distinction is not between Greek and non-Greek gods, but between those tradi-

---

[19] The most remarkable feature of this passage is the name of its author: E. R. Dodds, *HThR* 33 (1940), 171–76. Contrast A. D. Nock's much-quoted claim that it was as natural to import Bendis to Athens from Thrace as to introduce the potato to England from the New World (*Conversion*, Oxford 1933, 18), and e.g. Burkert, *Greek Religion*, 176–80.

[20] Apollophanes fr. 6 K/A (from Hesych. θ 275 s.v. θεοὶ ξενικοί + Phot. α 3404): Ἀσκληπιὸς, Κύννειος (? : Κίννιος cod.), Ἀφρόδιτος, Τύχων (cf. Ar. frs. 325, 908 K/A); Cic. *Leg.* 2.37: 'novos vero deos et in his colendis nocturnas pervigilationes sic Aristophanes . . . vexat, ut apud eum Sabazius et quidam alii dei peregrini iudicati e civitate eiciantur' (in reference perhaps to Ὥραι: see K/A, p. 296). Hospitality: Strabo 10.3.18 (471). On the meaning of ξένος see P. Gauthier, *Ancient Society* 4 (1973), 1–13, who argues that in the fifth cent. it is applied to Greeks rather than barbarians. Herodotus has a striking account of the expulsion of ξεινικοὶ θεοί by the Kaunians, 1. 172.

tionally honoured in Athenian public cult and all others.[21] ('Traditional honour' is a crucial determinant, since mythologically Asclepius is no more a *xenos* than Hermes or, indeed, Athena.) There was, in fact, a strong tendency to blur the distinction between Greek and barbarian among gods. Among children of Zeus, Dionysus had arrived from the Orient, Aphrodite spent much of her time there; conversely, Phoenician Adonis was courted by three Greek goddesses, and 'Kybebe' makes her first appearance in Greek literature as 'daughter of Zeus'.[22] Herodotus, of course, tends to suppose that Greek and foreign gods can be translated into one another, like Greek and foreign words. Indeed it seems that for him the gods themselves are the same everywhere; the differences that exist between nations relate merely to the names by which they are identified, the customs by which they are honoured.[23]

The 'foreign gods', therefore, are not a group recognized as such by the Greeks. They are assembled by modern scholars, in the belief that they were in fact first worshipped outside Greece. But even if certain elements of a cult, such as a god's name, are genuinely of eastern origin, it does not follow that the cult as a whole was imported without alteration. We should learn caution from recent studies of the 'Oriental Religions' of the Roman empire, which have shown that these may be less 'oriental' than 'orientalizing', Greco-Roman products stamped 'made in Egypt' or 'Persia'.[24] The 'initiations and purifications' known to us from a famous passage in Demosthenes look like an Athenian instance of the same phenomenon: the cries and some of the symbolism evoke Sabazius, but the officiating priestess, Aeschines' mother, is Greek, the whole ceremony remarkably resembles indigenous Dionysiac and Orphic rites, and the initiate's acclamation 'I have escaped from evil, I have found what is better' even seems to be borrowed from the Athenian marriage-ceremony.[25]

Many complications have to be recognized. A cult such as that of the Great Mother probably came to Athens not direct from Phrygia but via Ionia, where it had long been naturalized. In such a case, were the Athenians receiving a Greek or an oriental cult? The

[21] Cf. Pl. *Leg.* 738c: the wise legislator will not tamper with established cults, *whatever their place of origin*, Greek or foreign.

[22] Hipponax fr. 127 West.

[23] See J. Rudhardt, *RHR* 209 (1992), 219–38; for similar assumptions in earlier texts see W. Burkert in *Hérodote et les peuples non-grecs* (*EntrHardt* 35, Geneva 1990), 5–8.

[24] See R. L. Gordon, in J. R. Hinnells ed., *Mithraic Studies* (Manchester 1975), I.242–45, and M. Beard, J. North, and S. Price, *Religions of Rome* (Cambridge forthcoming), ch. 6.

[25] Dem. 18.259–60; for details see the commentary of H. Wankel (Heidelberg 1976), ad loc.; Graf, *Nordionische Kulte*, 322–23. The interest of the passage in this regard was pointed out to me by J. Bremmer.

meaning of an imported element may be transformed in a new setting.[26] 'Foreignness' can be a metaphor, a way of indicating the
strangeness of the experience associated with the god. Greeks
believed that the cult of the Magna Mater entered Greece from Asia,
amid the swirling of ecstatic dancers and the harsh clash of cymbals;
and archaeological evidence proves that they were right. Greeks
believed much the same about the cult of Dionysus; but here archaeological evidence appears to prove them wrong.[27] One can scarcely
insist enough on the paradox that ecstatic dancing, the mark *par
excellence* of an 'eastern' cult, was, in all seeming, indigenous in
Greece. For Athenians, the 'Mother' and her associates the Kory-
bantes are linked with madness, which they both send and heal. In
Greek symbolism, it is their status as outsiders, intruders from
abroad and from the wilds, which appears to qualify them for the
role.[28] One may wonder whether they had fulfilled it in quite the
same way in Phrygia, where they were in fact at home.

Again, the contribution of actual foreigners to the diffusion of
'foreign' cults is far from clear. If Aeschines' mother could conduct
initiations of an oriental stamp, it is not self-evident that a 'collector
for Cybele' could not have been Greek. Any non-Greek worshippers
of Sabazius or the Mother of the Gods there may have been in
Athens in the fifth and fourth centuries have left no certain trace;
while non-Greek votaries of Adonis are first attested a century after
Aristophanes' complaints about the laments for him performed by
Greek women. Egyptian worshippers of Isis, Phoenician worshippers of Aphrodite Ourania there certainly were; in 333, the 'merchants of Kition' were granted permission to found a shrine to
Aphrodite, on the motion of the famous Lycurgus, 'as the Egyptians
have founded a shrine of Isis'. But Isis seems not to have been taken
up by the Athenians until much later, while they were probably
already honouring Aphrodite Ourania, at a different shrine, when
the merchants of Kition founded theirs.[29] Only in the cult of Bendis

---

[26] For a fearless application of this principle see M. Detienne, *The Gardens of Adonis* (tr.
J. Lloyd, Hassocks 1977), *passim*.

[27] See esp. the new Linear B tablet from Khania, KH Gq 5, *Kadmos* 31 (1992), 76.

[28] Cf. Parker, *Miasma*, 244–48.

[29] No non-Greek votaries: note however that on the Ferrara krater (below, n. 142) the male
dancers wear oriental dress. And Manes the dedicator of *IG* II².4609 is perhaps a Phrygian
(slave?). 'Collector for Cybele': the first reference to an ἀγερσικύβηλις is in Cratinus fr. 66
K/A. Non-Greek worshippers of Adonis: cf. what follows. Merchants of Kition: *IG* II².337,
cf. 4636 (Piraeus: supposedly found, puzzlingly, during the excavation of the Piraeus
Metroon), a dedication to Aphrodite Ourania by 'Aristoklea of Kition', and, probably, *IG*
II².1261 (*SIG*³ 1098: Piraeus), three decrees of 302/1–300/299 of *thiasotai* of Aphrodite in
honour of Stephanos son of Mylothros, a breastplate-maker, for *inter alia* leading the 'proces-
sion of the *Adonia*'; a link between this text and the expatriate Cypriot cult is suggested by *IG*
II².1290 (Piraeus, mid-third cent.), honours decreed by 'the Salaminians' (doubtless of

do we find Athenians and foreigners certainly co-operating. Of course the argument from silence is not to be pressed, when the many thousands of metics we know that there were at Athens have left so few traces of their presence, and the still more numerous slaves are still less visible.[30] The point is that the role of non-Athenians and non-Greeks in such cults needs to be treated as a problem, not taken for granted. And if, in fact, we lack the materials to study what were probably complex interactions with any precision, that lack needs to be recognized explicitly.

Many of the 'foreign' cults do, it must be allowed, differ from the commonest native type in a highly significant way. In traditional Greek religion, the only groups within which the individual worships are those into which he is born. The *thiasos* of Sabazius, by contrast, is a group which is entered by choice.[31] Native gods too, however, could be worshipped within similar elective, non-established structures. 'If anyone had summoned them to a Bacchic rite, or to Pan's shrine, or to Cape Kolias, or to Aphrodite Genetyllis, you wouldn't have been able to get through for the mass of cymbals', says Lysistrata about the women of Athens in the opening lines of her play: the reference seems to be to informal festivals of women, like the mourning for Adonis, but held in this case not in a house but at public shrines. The deme Piraeus had to pass a law

Cyprus) for the work of their *epimeletes* in regard to Aphrodite and the *Adonia* (cf. M.-F. Baslez, 'Cultes et dévotions des Phéniciens en Grèce', in C. Bonnet, E. Lipiński, and P. Marchetti eds., *Studia Phoenicia*, IV. *Religio Phoenicia*, Namur 1986, 289–305, at 293: at 303 she contrasts the forms of worship of Adonis found in this society—sacrifice and procession—with those practised by Greek women). On the temples of Aphrodite/Astarte and Astarte at Kition (a town ruled in the fourth cent. by a Phoenician dynasty) see K. Nicolaou, *The Historical Topography of Kition* (Göteborg 1976), 105–107; *pace* Nicolaou (326), the Kitians of the Attic texts were doubtless Phoenicians wholly or in good part, as some of the Attic epitaphs (*IG* II².9031–36; cf. for Salamis 10216–18) are bilingual. Apparently Greek names should not deceive: Phoenicians often 'translated' their names into Greek—see F. Millar, *PCPS* 29 (1983), 61, where the temple of Baal built at Athens by Sidonians (*IG* II².2946; cf. App. 4, n. 48 below) is also mentioned. Isis: see S. Dow, *HThR* 30 (1937), 184–232 and Ch. 12, n. 71; the citizen 'Isigenes' born *c*.400 (*IG* II².1927.50) is isolated. Athenian cult of Aphrodite Ourania: see n. 159 below. Of course the Kitians (perhaps present in Athens from the fifth cent., to judge from the epitaphs) had probably honoured Aphrodite and Adonis in houses even before acquiring a temple: a metic named Adonis is attested in the fifth cent., *IG* I³.476.294–95, 301–302. On foreign associations see in general M.-F. Baslez in R. Lonis ed., *L'étranger dans le monde grec* (Nancy 1988), 139–58.*

[30] In the late fourth cent., Demetrius of Phaleron's census revealed a citizen–metic ratio of 2 : 1 (Athen. 272c: cf. M. H. Hansen, *Three Studies in Athenian Demography*, Copenhagen 1988, 10–11); a still-larger proportion of metics in the fifth cent. is advocated by R. P. Duncan-Jones, *Chiron* 10 (1980), 101–109, but contrast T. J. Figueira, *Athens and Aigina in the Age of Imperial Colonization* (Baltimore 1991), 209–12 (Thuc. 2.13.6–7 is a key text). On slaves see Hansen, *Three Studies*, 11–13. On Athens as the trading capital of Greece see P. McKechnie, *Outsiders in the Greek Cities in the Fourth Century B.C.* (London 1989), 185 88.

[31] Paul Veyne has distinguished 'set menu' and 'à la carte' religion: *Writing History*, 113.

forbidding unauthorized persons to 'assemble *thiasoi*' in its Thesmophorion. Begging-priests, the surest mark of a non-established cult, are occasionally found in the service of Greek as well as foreign gods; the disguised Hera, for instance, appears as an old woman begging for the local Nymphs in Aeschylus' *Xantriai*. Perhaps it was in this kind of milieu that various louche ithyphallic deities were honoured who, we know, were worshipped in Athens, in contexts unspecified.[32] The Bacchic rites conducted by 'Orpheus-initiators' provide the clearest of all instances of non-established rites; like many of the foreign cults, they have an ecstatic element, and like them they are liable to be stigmatized—despite their claim to treat matters of high importance—as self-indulgent play. (Moderns are most struck by the wild irrationality of ecstatic cults; but in the ancient world the charges characteristically brought against them by outsiders were of frivolity and luxuriousness.[33]) The suspicion and hostility that unestablished cults could evoke led in the fourth century to the prosecution of three 'priestesses', of whom two were actually executed; the third, the courtesan Phryne, is said to have escaped only by baring her breasts to the jury after all the eloquence of her lover Hyperides had failed. The details of the charges in the first two cases are uncertain, and an extract from the prosecutor's speech against Phryne may be our best guide to the kind of objection that was made:

I have demonstrated that Phryne is impious; she has led most shameless revels, she is the introducer of a new god, she has assembled illicit *thiasoi* of men and women.

By good fortune we know the name of Phryne's 'new god': he was Isodaites, 'equal divider' or, perhaps, 'equal diner'. In this case, very

---

[32] *IG* II².1177.3–4 (*LSCG* 36: but it is possible that the *thiasoi* here envisaged honoured Magna Mater, a 'foreign' goddess); Aesch. fr. 168.16–17 Radt. (But in the Hellenistic period 'collections' entered even established cults: see *SIG*³ 1015; M. Segré, *Iscrizioni di Cos*, Rome 1993, ED 178.29, 215.23, 236.7; Nilsson, *Op. Sel.* III. 246, n. 22.) Phallic gods: Strabo 13.1.12 (587–88), [Πρίαπος] ἔοικε τοῖς Ἀττικοῖς Ὀρθάνῃ καὶ Κονισάλῳ καὶ Τύχωνι καὶ τοῖς τοιούτοις; cf. Ar. *Lys.* 982; Plato Comicus fr. 188.12 ff. K/A. *ap.* Ath. 441E; the play-titles *Orthanes* (Eubulus) and *Konisalos* (Timocles); Apollophanes fr. 6 K/A (n. 20 above); and in general H. Herter, *De Dis atticis Priapi similibus* (Diss. Bonn 1926). Phallic gods were not confined to marginal social contexts (see Ar. *Ach.* 263–79: *IG* XII.8.52), but for a case of one in such see Dem. 54.13–17, esp. 17—οἱ τελοῦντες ἀλλήλους τῷ Ἰθυφάλλῳ (obscenely ambiguous).

[33] Orpheus-initiators (and 'play'): Pl. *Resp.* 364e, cf. Theophr. *Char.* 16.12. Cf. Ar. *Lys.* 387 (τρυφή) and Men. *Sam.* 41 (παιδιά), both of the *Adonia*; Pl. *Euthyd.* 277d (παιδιά), of Corybantic initiations; Posidippus fr. 28.22 K/A, where Κορύβαντες = 'temulenti comis-satores' (Meineke). That the Orphic rites were communal is not attested, but, given their Bacchic character, highly likely. Ancient criticisms of non-established cults are repeated, and endorsed, by P. Foucart, *Des associations religieuses chez les Grecs* (Paris 1873), 153–77.

clearly, it is not a new foreign god who evokes a *thiasos*; it is a new informal *thiasos* that evokes a god with, as it happens, a Greek name.[34] Conversely, foreign gods could be adopted within the pantheon of the state. The crucial distinction is not between foreign and native but between established and non-established cults; native or foreign, the unlicensed god is exposed to suspicion, hostility, contempt, and the threat of actual repressive action.

We have surveyed various forms of enhancement of old cults and introduction of new ones. The arrival of 'foreign' cults, it has been urged, should be seen in this context of perpetual change, rather than as an isolated and aberrant phenomenon. The dividing-line between indigenous and foreign gods is blurred in various ways; and the Annexe to this chapter will argue that foreign gods arrive earlier and in greater number than is sometimes recognized, and are more variously received. We can now turn to four particular cults, which we have the rare opportunity of observing as they are introduced or transformed. They are of various types: Pan and Asclepius are non-Attic Greeks, Bendis is a barbarian, and Theseus is a native whose cult was raised to new prominence. The first to arrive was Pan; and we learn the circumstances from a famous passage in Herodotus.[35]

On learning that the Persians had landed at Marathon, the Athenian generals sent Philippides, a trained all-day runner, as messenger to Sparta.

And, as Philippides himself claimed and reported to the Athenians, when he was near the Maiden mountain above Tegea, he was met by Pan. Pan called out Philippides' name, and told him to tell the Athenians that they neglected him although he was well disposed to them and had often been helpful to them, and would be so again. The Athenians accepted that his

---

[34] Phryne: see Hyperides frs. 171–80 Jensen; A. Raubitschek in *RE* s.v. *Phryne*, 903–907; G. Bartolini, *Iperide* (Padua 1977), 116–19 [+]; and now esp. Versnel, *Ter Unus*, 118–19; the fr. for the prosecution appears in L. Spengel, *Rhetores Graeci*, I (Leipzig 1853), 455.8–11 (390.12 ff. in C. Hammer's rev. of I, pt. 2, 1894). Harp. s.v. ʾΙσοδαίτης (= Hyperides fr. 177) gives the god's name; in later antiquity (cf. *RE* s.v. *Isodaites*) he was variously identified (e.g. with the ecstatic Dionysus by Plutarch, *E Delph.* 389a), but it is not clear that anything independent was in fact known about him, or that he pre-existed Phryne's *thiasos*; for the various significances Athenians might have found in a name of this form see the etymological dictionaries s.v. δαίομαι. The executed priestesses were: Nino, guilty of 'assembling *thiasoi*' (Dem. 19.281: one of the prosecutors was Menekles, Dem. 39.2, 40.9) or making love-potions (Σ 495a Dilts on Dem. 19.281) or mocking the Mysteries (Σ 495b ibid.), or, probably, initiating in rites of foreign gods (see Joseph. *Ap.* 2.267 in Naber's edn., where a conjecture of H. Weil introducing Nino's name is accepted); and Theoris, put to death with her whole family for dealing in drugs and charms ([Dem.] 25.79–80, who calls her a Lemnian), or for various offences, including inciting slaves against masters (Plut. *Dem.* 14.6, 'the priestess Theoris': Demosthenes is said to have prosecuted) or for 'impiety' (Philoch. *FGrH* 328 F 60: '*mantis*').

[35] 6.105.

story was true, and when the crisis was over established a shrine of Pan below the acropolis, and propitiate him with annual sacrifices and a torch-race because of this message.

The god did not reveal the exact form which his aid to the Athenians had taken and would take (though suggestions have been made since antiquity);[36] perhaps he sent his own 'panic' fear against their enemies. The 'torch-race' may have been chosen in commemoration of Philippides' own so significant run.

Archaeology appears to confirm, with rare and pleasing clarity, that the cult of Pan was introduced to Athens shortly after Marathon. Pan himself was probably known (though not worshipped) a little before this, as indeed one would expect if Herodotus' account is true: the god whom Philippides met and recognized was one of whom he had already heard. In the sixth century, there is no trace of Pan's presence in Attica, nor indeed anywhere in Greece except in his homeland Arcadia and in neighbouring Peloponnesian regions. He first appears on an Athenian vase around 500. In the fifth century, depictions and allusions become much more common, and one drinking-cup from about 475 which shows him running with a torch seems to reflect the ritual which Herodotus says was set up in his honour.[37] The really compelling confirmation for Herodotus' account, however, comes from the many caves scattered through Attica which have been securely identified, from finds, as belonging to 'the Nymphs and Pan'. Though the actual 'shrine below the acropolis' (in fact a cave) of Herodotus is archaeologically bare, no fewer than six further such caves, of various sizes, have been investigated; and in every case the earliest finds (Helladic material apart) date from early in the fifth century.[38] It looks as if the

---

[36] See Borgeaud, *Pan*, 146–47, 202; Garland, *New Gods*, 51–54 (who also discusses the circumstances that may have made Philippides receptive to a vision, 48–51). R. Lonis, *Guerre et religion en Grèce à l'époque classique* (Paris 1979), 182–83, unconvincingly revives E. Harrison's attempt to dissociate Panic from Pan (*CR* 40, 1926, 6–8).

[37] See F. Brommer, *RE* Suppl. vol. VIII.953 ff. [+]; J. Boardman and M. Pope, *Greek Vases in Cape Town* (Cape Town 1961), 7–8 (first appearance); E. Simon, *AntK* 19 (1976), 19–25 (torch-race); cf. Borgeaud, *Pan*, 81–84, 197. Pan also enters other parts of the Greek world in the fifth cent.; that the Athenians' hospitality set the fashion is possible, but no more.

[38] At Oinoe near Marathon, on Penteli, on Parnes above Phyle, at Eleusis, at Daphni, at Vari: see P. Zoridis, *ArchEph* 1977 (1979)/*Chron*, 4–11, with 4, n. 3 [+]; and on the Vari cave now W. R. Connor, *ClAnt* 7 (1988), 179–89; on the Marathon cave the *lex sacra* of the first cent. BC, *SEG* XXXVI 267. For a survey of finds see P. Amandry, in *L'antre corycien II* (*BCH* Suppl. 9, Paris 1984), 404–406; and for pictures, Travlos, *Bildlexikon*, 90, 151, 186, 246, 325–26, 332–34, 462–65, and id., *Pictorial Dictionary*, 142, 294, 417–21. The solitary Geometric vessel found in the Parnes cave (*ArchEph* 1906, 100) scarcely disturbs the chronological pattern. For other cult-places known from literature or to be inferred from finds of reliefs see *RE* s.v. *Nymphai*, 1558–60; Suppl. vol. VIII.993–94; for an unexplored cave at Rapedosa see F. Muthmann, *Mutter und Quelle* (Mainz 1975), 90, n. 39; cf. too E. Vanderpool, 'Pan at Paiania', *AJA* 71 (1967), 309–11. See in general Map II.

Athenians did indeed introduce Pan to Athens in the aftermath of Marathon because they believed that the god himself had ordered them to do so.

And yet the new cult was not a simple re-creation in Attica of what had been practised in Arcadia hitherto. Attic Pan was invariably (except possibly in his own cave below the acropolis) worshipped in association with the Nymphs; and the location of the joint cult was invariably a cave. Arcadian Pan appears to have had no dealings with the Nymphs, and no single cave of Pan in Arcadia is known.[39] The two differences are surely connected: the Nymphs are regular denizens of caves from Homer onwards,[40] and it must have been through taking up with them that Pan too adopted this habitat. (No cave dedicated to Pan alone is known, whereas outside Arcadia joint cave-cults of Pan and the Nymphs are widespread.) Indeed, it often seems that the true owners of the Attic caves are the Nymphs, while Pan is, as it were, a lodger or a neighbour. In the 'Cave of Pan' at Vari, for instance, an image of the god occupied a prominent niche in what was in fact, as we learn quite clearly from an inscription, a 'cave built for the Nymphs'. And in the important votive reliefs which are so characteristic a product of this joint Attic cult, the Nymphs regularly sit or dance within a cave, which worshippers perhaps enter, while a smaller Pan pipes amid his goats on the mountain above it.[41] When such reliefs bear inscriptions, we learn that they are offered 'to the Nymphs' or to 'Pan and the Nymphs', never to Pan alone.[42] In the prologue to Menander's *Dyskolos*, finally, Pan himself describes the shrine which he haunts as 'the Nymphaion of the Phylasians'.

An obvious hypothesis presents itself: it was through annexation to an older form of worship that the new cult was assimilated, and acquired genuine popular appeal. In one non-Attic instance, the Corycian cave at Delphi, Pan perhaps simply entered a cave which had previously belonged exclusively to the Nymphs.[43] In Attica, we cannot trace so straightforward a development, since, as we have seen, none of the country caves seems to have harboured cult of any

---

[39] See Borgeaud, *Pan*, 80; M. Jost, *Sanctuaires et cultes d'Arcadie* (Paris 1985), 476.

[40] *Od*. 13.103–12; cf. Amandry, *L'antre corycien II*, 407–408; *RE* s.v. *Nymphai*, 1538.

[41] Vari: see *IG* I³.974–81. Reliefs: see R. Feubel, *Die attische Nymphenreliefs und ihre Vorbilder* (Heidelberg 1935); W. Fuchs, *AM* 77 (1962), 242–49; C. Edwards, *Greek Votive Reliefs to Pan and the Nymphs* (Diss. New York 1985); for pictures, Travlos, *Bildlexikon*, 90, 151, 186, 246, 325–26, 332–34, 462–65, and id., *Pictorial Dictionary*, 142, 294, 417–21.

[42] Nymphs: *IG* II².4565, 4592, 4647, 4650–52; *SEG* XII 166, XXIX 195; and cf. *IG* I³.974 (and *IG* I².798), Pan and Nymphs: *IG* II².4545, 4646, 4875; (?) *AM* 67 (1942), 68, no. 116b; *SEG* XXXVI 267. The only candidate for a sole dedication to Pan is the obscure scrap *IG* II².4672 (*SEG* XVII 88).

[43] See Amandry, *L'antre corycien II*, 398; (?) also at Lera in Crete (cf. ibid. 407).

kind before the fifth century. But the famous cave of Pan below the acropolis has no archaeological history, and we are free to suppose that it or one of its several neighbours had once been a cave of the Nymphs.[44] However that may be, there had certainly been Nymphs in Attica before the coming of Pan, whether or not they had been worshipped in caves. And the votive reliefs bear abundant witness that it was his association with these older residents that helped to secure Pan an entreé into Attic society.

The cult that spread throughout Attica so rapidly in the aftermath of Marathon was, therefore, not wholly new. It was, as it were, an existing cult reissued in revised and expanded form, with the added commendation of topical interest. Simply in cult-practice, the change brought by the addition of Pan to the Nymphs was perhaps rather slight. Rituals proper to him alone are hard to identify, except of course for his official torch-race in Athens. The rustic banquet with which *Dyskolos* concludes would doubtless have been not much less cheerful even if it had honoured the Nymphs alone.[45] The novelty that Pan brought was rather a kind of imaginative expansion. To illustrate this point we need to contemplate for a moment the figure of the god.

Traditionally, he has often been felt to be easy to understand. His home was Arcadia, a land of herds and mountains; and he can seem a transparent embodiment of Arcadian concerns, being himself half goatherd, half that billy-goat on whose beneficent lusts the future of the herd depends. But it has been well argued that, whether or not that simple formula catches Pan's significance for his Arcadian worshippers, it certainly cannot explain the diffusion of the cult beyond its ancient home.[46] On leaving Arcadia, Pan ceased in the main to be a herdsman's god. He entered Attica not informally, over the mountains with the flocks, but through a decision of the Athenian assembly; and it was surely in imitation of the city's example that the new

[44] See Travlos, *Pictorial Dictionary*, 91–94, 417–21. Edwards, however, *Greek Votive Reliefs* (23–27), makes a good case for identifying cave A (equally bare) rather than D as Pan's cave. For the suggestion that there was an ancient cult of the Nymphs at the nearby Klepsydra (cf. Hesych. s.v. Κλεψύδρα· κρήνη ἥτις πρότερον Ἐμπεδὼ προσηγορεύετο; see *LIMC* s.v. *Empedo* for a companion of Theseus so named on a cup of *c*.540), whence might derive several Nymph-reliefs found on the northern slope and *IG* I³.1063 (= *Agora* XIX H3) Νυνφαίο hιερô hορός, see A. W. Parsons, *Hesperia* 12 (1943), 201–204, 232–33 (cf. Travlos, *Pictorial Dictionary*, 323–31). For the cult of the Nymphs on the 'Hill of the Nymphs' see U. Kron, *AM* 94 (1979), 63–75, on *IG* I³.1065. On a cave probably of the Nymphs on the northern side of Kastela-i-Spilia near Anavyssos, which has yielded material going back to the sixth or seventh cent., see H. Lohmann, *Atene* (2 vols., Cologne 1993), I.230, II.494 (on his site AN1); cf. M. Küpper, *MarbWPr* 1989 (1990), 18–19. I have not seen J. M. Wickens, *The Archaeology and History of Cave Use in Attica* ([Diss.?] Ann Arbor 1986).

[45] Cf. the famous Pitsa plaque, *EAA* VI, s.v. *Pitsa*, opp. 202.

[46] See Borgeaud, *Pan* (an important study), *passim*.

cult spread so rapidly through the countryside. Indeed it may have been taken up and propagated by the young and self-confident Clisthenic demes.[47] Neoptolemus of Melite, who dedicated a recently discovered relief of Pan and the Nymphs, was one of the richest Athenians in the late fourth century, and lived no closer to mountain pastures than did those *bons bourgeois* whose dealings with the god are portrayed in Menander's *Dyskolos*. (Of course even in Attica, Pan and the Nymphs also had humble worshippers, including goatherds, and may even have been especially attractive to them.[48] But the familiar notion that certain 'country' gods such as Pan were honoured only by countrymen, and countrymen honoured none but them, appears to be part of the pastoral dream.) For a long tradition of writers and painters, Pan has represented the life of wild nature not as it is experienced, day to day, by those who live close to it, but as it is imagined from afar.[49] That tradition has its beginnings in the Attic cult. Like the Satyrs and Silens, not 'country gods' these, but wholly mythological beings, Pan lives on the imaginative boundary between man and beast. His caves were symbolically set away from human habitation (and sometimes in genuinely remote spots) not because this was where his worshippers typically spent their days, but because it was not. Philippides himself surely met Pan precisely because, amid the mountains of Arcadia, he felt himself far and frighteningly removed from his own familiar home.

This representation of wild Pan has two aspects. Fear and danger are certainly in it; but so too are liberation and desire. He is associated, by Pindar and in votive reliefs, with Cybele, another dangerous figure of the wild whose cult is, none the less, ecstatic and delightful.[50] Dancing, noise, clapping, laughter characterize his worship;[51] and it was perhaps an added touch of licensed abandon

[47] Ibid. 235–37, and note Men. *Dysc.* 2–3, where the Nymphaion belongs to the Phylasians. The Vari cave (above, n. 38) was adorned by the foreigner Archedemos; but was it he who first put it to cultic use?

[48] See *IG* I³.974 (a goatherd), *IG* II².4833 ('the shepherds'), and collective dedications by groups of slaves (*IG* II².2934, 'the launderers'; 4650). The seventeen (?) citizens who clubbed together to dedicate one relief (*IG* II².4832) were probably also poor. But the finest Nymph-reliefs were expensive works; and for the classlessness of the Nymphs see e.g. Eur. *El.* 783–86. Neoptolemus: see T. L. Shear Jr. *OpRom* 9 (1973), 183–92; *Agora Guide*, 193 f.

[49] See P. Merivale, *Pan the Goat-God: His Myth in Modern Times* (Cambridge, Mass. 1969).

[50] See Pindar fr. 95 Snell/Maehler; Vermaseren, *Corpus Cultus Cybelae*, II, nos. 182, 309, 339 (= 318, no. 190 in Naumann, *Die Ikonographie der Kybele*, and (Hadrianic) 180 (= *IG* II².4773, *SIG*³ 1153); Cybeles were also found in the 'caves of Pan' at Marathon (Vermaseren, *Corpus Cultus Cybelae*, II.119, no. 394) and Phyle (Borgeaud, *Pan*, 216, n. 112), while the large seated figure in the Vari cave is often identified as a Cybele (cf. however Connor, *ClAnt* 7, 1988, 185–87). On Pan and Bendis see n. 72 below.

[51] See Borgeaud, *Pan*, 217–21, on e.g. *Hymn Hom. Pan*, *PMG* 936 *passim* (noise, dancing, laughter); Soph. *Aj.* 694–701 (joyful dancing); Men. *Dysc.* 433–34, Lucian, *Bis. Acc.* 9–10

that he brought to the cults with which he was associated. (Often he seems less a power than a mood.) Inhibitions could not but be relaxed in the presence of the jaunty, laughter-loving, lustful god.

A few years after Pan arrived in Athens, Theseus returned. The Athenians under Cimon had now taken the offensive, and carried war into the Aegean. In or near the year 476/5,[52] they captured and colonized Skyros. This hitherto barbarian island was also, according to legend (a 'legend' possibly invented at precisely this moment), the scene of Theseus' death; and Cimon, instructed by an oracle to 'bring home the bones of Theseus', made search for the precious relics. Guided by an eagle, he eventually found them, and on his return the hero's bones were welcomed 'with splendid processions and sacrifices, as if Theseus himself were coming home'. According to Pausanias, the Theseum, an important but still unlocated shrine, was now built to receive the honoured bones.[53]

The eagle's helpful collaboration suggests that this story has been elaborated; but there is no reason to doubt the core. Many Athenians would have heard of the advantage that the Spartans had acquired in the previous century by 'bringing home the bones' of their hero Orestes. For the last forty years Theseus' popularity and prestige had been soaring; at about this time, he was portrayed as an intensely glamorous figure in Dithyrambs 17 and 18 of Bacchylides, one of them not even written for Athens; and he was believed to have brought aid to the Greeks at Marathon, a patriotic intervention that was soon to be commemorated in a famous painting in the Stoa Poikile. At that battle, of course, Cimon's father had been general; and there is reason to think that the family even laid claim to descent from the hero.[54] We would like to know more of the oracle that

(noise). Pan's jauntiness appears on the reliefs (above, n. 41); his lusts, on the vases (see F. Brommer, *Marb. Jahrb. Kunstwiss.* 15, 1949–50, 5–42).

[52] See J. P. Barron, *JHS* 92 (1972), 21, n. 7.

[53] Plut. *Cim.* 8.5–7; *Thes.* 36.1–4; Paus. 1.17.2–6, 3.3.7. In Diod. 4.62.4 andΣ Ar. *Plut.* 627 the bones are seemingly brought home in the mythological period; this is carelessness, not independent tradition. For the Theseum see Wycherley, *Testimonia*, 113–19; Castriota, *Myth, Ethos, Actuality*, 33–63 [+]. Legend invented: cf. Herter, 'Theseus', 1201 [+], who dissents. Wilamowitz's attractive suggestion that the bringing home of Theseus was a 'charter' for the new practice of bringing home ordinary Athenian dead cannot be substantiated (see Stupperich, *Staatsbegräbnis*, 235–36); nor can Tausend's that Theseus was intended as a unifying symbol for the Delian league (see Ch. 8, n. 91).

[54] Marathon and Stoa Poikile: Plut. *Thes.* 35.8; Paus. 1.15.3. He also appeared on the problematic Marathon monument at Delphi, Paus. 10.10.1. Theseus' popularity: above, p. 85. But for the view that his reputation ebbed and flowed see Vidal-Naquet, *Black Hunter*, 312–15; Loraux, *L'invention*, 65–66. Descent: see J. P. Barron, *BICS* 27 (1980), 2, on Plut. *Thes.* 29.1 and Pherecydes *FGrH* 3 F 153, Istrus 334 F 10. But the allusions to Cimon's affairs seen by Barron in Bacchylides 17 seem self-defeatingly oblique, as well as poetically undesirable.

instructed the Athenians to bring home the hero's bones. If it was indeed, as Plutarch says,[55] freshly issued by Apollo, the god showed himself alert and sensitive to the mood of the day.

Henceforth Theseus towered over all other Athenian heroes in cult as well as in story. He eventually owned three shrines in addition to the great one founded by Cimon, and was honoured by a sacrificial and athletic festival on the grand scale, the *Theseia*, which was perhaps established on this occasion. To finance his cult, a special tax was levied, the 'five drachmas for Theseus', possibly on the supposed descendants of the boys and girls whom he had rescued from the Minotaur. And yet the Athenians still felt that these honours did not fully match his merits. There were, they observed, many more shrines in Attica of Dorian Heracles: they must once have belonged to Theseus, and have been surrendered by him, with typical magnanimity, to his much-suffering colleague. And a whole series of existing festivals underwent an *interpretatio Theseana*: the *Synoikia*, the *Hekalesia*, the *Kybernesia*, the *Oschophoria*, the *Pyanopsia*, a procession to the Delphinion, all became in some way commemorations of events in his career. By the fourth century, the great source of ritual meaning was Theseus.[56]

If possession of Theseus' bones was a precondition for his worship, all this must have grown up after 476/5. But a *genos*, the Phytalids, seems to have had some role in his cult, and one would not in general expect such a body to acquire new privileges at so late a date. Possibly, however, a special explanation is available in this case: the Phytalids may have owed their promotion to the influence of the great man of their deme Lakiadai, none other than Cimon.[57] However that may be, it is still perhaps more probable that an existing cult was greatly expanded to celebrate the hero's return.[58] In the absence of literary evidence, many details of Theseus' fortunes in the mid-century remain tantalizingly vague. As a son of Poseidon, he could become a symbol of Athenian heroism by sea as well as by

[55] On what occasion? Possibly (cf. Paus. 3.3.7) the Athenians had sought Delphi's advice about the coming campaign. If it were not for Plutarch's statement one might suppose that an older 'sleeping' oracle had been revived by Cimon. On the other hand it is conceivable that the oracle is a narrative device attached to the transfer of the bones *post eventum*, as the 'plague' that provokes the enquiry in the latest sources (Herter, 'Theseus', 1200) certainly is.

[56] Philochorus *FGrH* 328 F 18 (four shrines); Ar. *Plut.* 627–28 (first reference to *Theseia*); Eur. *HF* 1328–31 and Philoch. *FGrH* 328 F 18 (surrender of shrines to Heracles); below, App. 2 A s.v. *Phytalidai* (tax). On *interpretatio* briefly H. Herter, *RhM* 88 (1939), 304–305, more fully Kearns, *Heroes of Attica*, 120–24; and above all Calame, *Thésée*, ch. 3. See in general on Theseus' cult Herter, 'Theseus', 1223–29 [+].

[57] Paus. 1.37.2; cf. App. 2 A s.v. *Phytalidai*, and, for Cimon's exercise of local patronage, Arist. *Ath. Pol.* 27.3. The suggestion is made by Humphreys, 'Genos'.

[58] Cf. Herter, *RhM* 88 (1939), 285–86, 289–91 (but on the Pisistratean Theseum see Ch. 6, n. 73 above).

land, and it was with a great sacrifice at Rhion to him and his father (duly commemorated by an inscription at Delphi) that Phormion's fleet celebrated its victories in the Corinthian gulf in 429.[59] More startlingly, by the time of the *Supplices* of Euripides, perhaps of the 420s, Theseus has already acquired his paradoxical role as the democratic king—a role that demonstrates, by its exquisite anachronism, the continuing vitality of mythological thought in the late fifth century. In becoming a democrat, Theseus did not cease to be a national hero, at a time when loyalty to the democracy was among the most valued virtues. Earlier in the century, emphasis lay rather on hating the barbarian enemy. That virtue Theseus displays as leader in the many desperate defensive battles against invading Amazons that decorate the vases of the mid-century.[60] This graceful but doughty fighter was doubtless Cimon's Theseus.

The most puzzling coming of a god to Athens is that of Thracian Bendis.[61] 'To the Thracians alone of all foreign peoples (*ethne*) has the Athenian people granted the right to acquire land and found a shrine, in accord with the response from Dodona, and to conduct a procession from the prytaneum-hearth': so they proudly proclaim in the mid-third century, with reference apparently to events of almost two centuries before. The boast is not quite accurate, since 'the Egyptians' and 'the merchants of Kition' were also to be allowed to buy land to found shrines of their native gods in the fourth century; but what is indeed unique is that the Thracians' shrine, the Bendideion in the Piraeus, should have become the centre of an Athenian public cult in which they themselves had a privileged role. They were even allowed to lead their procession 'from the prytaneum-hearth', the symbolic centre of the city.[62]

Our picture of how this came to be is a jigsaw with missing pieces. The text just quoted is one of a series of decrees of the late fourth and third centuries passed by a group of *orgeones* of Bendis, based at the Bendideion.[63] According to the explicit statement in that text, they

[59] Paus. 10.11.6 (prima-facie evidence for Athenian access to Delphi in 429); cf. Thuc. 2.83–92, M/L 25, and for the shrine of Poseidon at Rhion, Strabo 8.2.3 (336).

[60] See J. Boardman in D. Kurtz and B. Sparkes eds., *The Eye of Greece* (Cambridge 1982), 1–28.

[61] For a good survey see R. R. Simms, 'The Cult of the Thracian Goddess Bendis in Athens and Attica', *AncW* 18 (1988), 59–76 [+]. I have profited at a late stage from conversation with Prof. Mariko Sakurai of Tokyo Gakugei University, who is preparing a paper on the subject.

[62] *IG* II².1283; for the other grants see *IG* II².337, and for the Bendideion (familiar enough to be a landmark) Xen. *Hell.* 2.4.11.

[63] In rough chronological order: *IG* II².1361 ('post med. s.iv', Kirchner; for the association with Bendis see Kirchner's note in *IG* II² ad loc.), 1255 (337/6, not certainly Bendidean), 1256

or some of them ought to be Thracians, even though the names that they bear are Greek. Their officials organized the great procession, and they themselves presumably marched at the centre of it. Like other groups of *orgeones*, they owned their own shrine, and outsiders wishing to sacrifice had to pay a modest fee.[64] The role of non-citizens in the cult thus remained extremely marked. Indeed no single dedication certainly made to the goddess by an Athenian survives. (It is commonly accepted that some of the decrees were issued by a distinct group of native Athenian *orgeones*, also based at the Bendideion, who organized the procession of the 'locals' of which we hear from Plato.[65] But from the inscriptions it is not certain that such an Athenian group continued to exist.) By the middle of the third century there was also a group of *orgeones* (nationality unknown) with their own shrine in Athens itself, and also a club (*koinon*) of *thiasotai* of Bendis on Salamis, many of whose members sound from their names like slaves or ex-slaves.[66]

An earlier cluster of texts takes us back near to the cult's foundation. The most famous is the opening scene of *Republic*, a dialogue with a dramatic date of about 410 BC. We find the first celebration of an elaborate new festival in honour of the goddess in progress: two processions, one by the Thracians and one by the natives, have been equally splendid, while a novel torch-race on horseback (doubtless to be performed by the 'horse-loving' Thracians, as Sophocles called them) and an 'all-night rite' are still to come. Victory in a torch-race of some kind must be commemorated by a fourth-

---

(329/8, identified as Bendidean by the relief), 1324 (? late fourth cent., see Dow, *HThR* 30, 1937, 197, n. 54), 1283 and 1284 (archonships of Polystratos and Lykeas, somewhere in the third cent.: Habicht, *Untersuchungen*, 121, n. 33). Names and nationality: see Ferguson, 'Orgeonika', 162–63; he thinks of Greek settlers in Thrace.

[64] *IG* II².1361, cf. 1324.3–4. For this combination of private ownership and public responsibility in other orgeonic groups see pp. 192–3 below. It is probably their public role that earns them the remarkable title of *orgeones*: cf. Ferguson, 'Attic Orgeones', 104.

[65] See A. Wilhelm, *ÖJh* 5 (1902), 127–39; Kirchner's note on *IG* II².1361; Ferguson, 'Attic Orgeones', 98. But once the Salaminian group of texts (following note) is separated off, the differences noted by Wilhelm can be explained chronologically. The strongest evidence for citizen *orgeones* comes from *IG* II².1255, a decree probably issued by *orgeones* of Bendis in honour of citizen *hieropoioi* who were presumably (despite the reservations of Ferguson, 'Orgeonika', 155) members of the association (since large sums are spent on honouring them, and the comparable *hieropoioi* of 1361 are apparently subject to instructions from the *orgeones*).

[66] Athens: *IG* II².1283, perhaps founded because the city and the Piraeus had often been divided in the preceding years (P. Gauthier, *REG* 29, 1979, 396–97). Thence may derive the scrap *Hesperia* 29 (1960), 21, no. 27, which mentions Bendis, Deloptes, and Thracians (now dated by M. B. Walbank, *Agora* XIX L16, to the late second/early first cent.: much the latest attestation of the cult if so). Salamis: *IG* II².1317, 1317b (p. 673); *SEG* II 9, 10, with Nilsson, 'Bendis', 73, and the comment of Ferguson, 'Attic Orgeones', 160, n. 85; these texts range from 272 to *c*.240.

century relief which shows eight naked youths led up to Bendis by two older men, perhaps their trainers, one of whom holds a torch. A very recently published dedication confirms that Thracians (or at least non-Athenians) continued to compete in events of this type. Indeed it juxtaposes an archetypal slave-name with the most characteristic exercise of the well-born Athenian young with startling bluntness: 'To Bendis by Daos, who had won in a torch-race.'[67]

Details of the cult are regulated in a decree of the assembly which appears to be roughly contemporary with the dramatic date of the *Republic*. Only fragments remain, but we hear, as in Plato, of a *pannychis*, and of an enquiry to be made to an oracle about the selection of a priestess: 'Should she be Athenian or Thracian?' was perhaps the question. There is also mention of a tax or levy ($\dot{\epsilon}\pi\alpha\rho\chi\dot{\eta}$), doubtless used to support the cult. These two texts might naturally be thought to refer to the foundation of the new cult or its adoption by the state. But they can scarcely both antedate 429, by when, as we shall see, the modest joint funds of Bendis and Adrasteia were already controlled by magistrates of the state.[68] So the decree seems after all to concern an expansion of the cult, reflected in Plato, and not its creation. A skyphos in Tübingen which shows Bendis and Themis together (both identified by inscriptions) confirms that the goddess had in some sense entered the establishment at the date of its manufacture, around 425 or somewhat later. A similar message may be conveyed a little earlier by the tondos of a pair of interrelated cups by the Phiale painter, of which one shows a running Bendis and the other a tranquil Greek figure (woman or goddess?) at an altar.[69]

It is hard to assemble these fragments into a coherent whole. Was the cult first practised by the Thracians of Attica (but how? on what premises?) before being taken up by the Athenian state? Or was it in fact the Athenians who founded the cult, entrusting it then or subsequently to the Thracian association's care?[70] Again, it is unclear whether or not the oracle which the Athenians decide to seek is iden-

---

[67] Pl. *Resp.* 327a–328a; Soph. fr. 582 Radt; London, BM 2155 = *LIMC* s.v. *Bendis*, 96, no. 3 (Garland, *New Gods*, pl. 26); P. G. Themelis, *Horos* 7 (1989), 23–29 = *SEG* XXXIX 210 (cf. n. 74), fourth/third cent.—*Λαμπάδι νικήσας Δᾶος Βενδῖδι ἀνέθηκεν*. On torch-races see Ch. 11, n. 127. But *LGPN* II countenances the possibility that our man is a citizen.

[68] *IG* I³.136 (where see Jameson's excellent commentary), and 383.142–43; cf. 369.68 (cf. p. 195). The decree was dated *c*.430 when first pub., to make it precede *IG* I³.383.142–43, but a lower date appears preferable (no more) epigraphically: see J. Bingen, *RBPhil* 37 (1959), 31–44, for 413/2 (accepted in *IG* I³), and cf. Pečírka, *Enktesis*, 122–30.

[69] See *LIMC* s.v. *Bendis*, 96, nos. 1–2; J. H. Oakley, *The Phiale Painter* (Mainz 1990), 34–35, 90, and pls. 122, 124 ([+]; he dates the cups 435–430).

[70] So Ferguson, 'Orgeonika', 156–57. This is scarcely what the Thracians themselves imply in *IG* II².1283; but their version at the least conflates events, unless we suppose that more than one oracular consultation was involved; for that mentioned in *IG* I³.136 post-dates the foundation of the shrine.

tical with that 'from Dodona' to which the Thracians themselves much later make appeal.

On any view, the decision to celebrate the *Bendideia* so elaborately was the Athenians'. It was perhaps the oldest of several large festivals that served the needs of the Piraeus, that boom-town of the fifth and fourth centuries. In the 330s it was still being celebrated sumptuously, with at least 100 head of cattle slaughtered.[71] Thus, as spectators and consumers of meat, at least, large numbers of Athenians came into association with the goddess. The other great festivals in the Piraeus, however, honoured more familiar gods, Zeus Soter and Dionysus; an explanation for the choice of Bendis is still required.

Several have been offered, none wholly convincing. (They relate, inevitably but regrettably, to the 'introduction of a Thracian goddess' rather than 'of Bendis', of whose specific attributes we know little. She was portrayed as a huntress, in Thraco-Phrygian garb, and entered into cultic relations with the Nymphs and Pan; perhaps she had some of the wild fascination of the Mountain Mother.[72]) To appeal to the influence of the oracle at Dodona is only to relocate the problem, since Zeus must have had some reason for promoting the cult of a goddess unrelated to himself. As Bendis was not, to our knowledge, a healing-goddess, there was no obvious reason for seeking her protection against the ravages of the plague. A political approach is more promising, but still incomplete.[73] At just this date the Athenians were wooing Sitalces, king of the Odrysian Thracians, in hope of military aid. His son Sadokos was actually enrolled as a citizen of Athens in 431, perhaps the first barbarian to be so honoured, two years before Bendis appears enrolled among the Athenian gods. The connection appears irresistible. And yet Bendis may in fact have been naturalized years before; and by the dramatic date of the *Republic*, when the great festival was instituted, all immediate hope of Thracian aid had dissolved. One may wonder too how impressed a Thracian king would really be by the news that Bendis now enjoyed honourable lodgement in Athens. The more immediate beneficiaries were the Thracians of Athens, a mysterious group

[71] *IG* II².1496.86–87, 117; cf. Garland, *Piraeus*, 120.

[72] See Z. Gočeva and D. Popov, *LIMC* s.v. *Bendis* [+] and *Deloptes* (of this associated hero, who is portrayed in reliefs in the iconography of Asclepius, nothing is known). Nymphs and Pan: the Copenhagen relief Glypt. Ny Carlsberg 462 = *LIMC* s.v. *Bendis*, 96, no. 4 (= Garland, *New Gods*, pl. 25); *IG* II².1283.18; and the carving on Paros dedicated by a Thracian, D. Berranger, *REA* 85 (1983), 235–39 = *LIMC* s.v. *Bendis*, no. 2a; note too the association with Cybele in Hipponax fr. 127 West (the first ref.), and with Adrasteia (n. 153). Late sources (Strabo 10.3.16 [470], cf. Proclus in Pl. *Ti*. 20e, 1.85 Diehl) claim that her worship was of orgiastic, 'eastern' type; but that was scarcely true of the Athenian public cult.

[73] Oracle: P. Foucart, *Mélanges Perrot* (Paris 1903), 95–102. Plague: Ferguson, 'Orgeonica', 157–62. Politics: Nilsson, 'Bendis'.

about whose identity, interests, and aspirations we are bafflingly uninformed.[74] There are signs that Bendis became popular in the mining region of Laurion, where Thracian slaves were doubtless numerous. But the Athenians are very unlikely to have chosen to honour the goddess merely because their slaves did. A troop of mercenaries could no doubt have acquitted itself well in the torch-race, and we happen to know that one from Thrace was briefly present in Athens in 413, around the dramatic date of the *Republic*—the one that went on to perpetrate the massacre at Mycalessus. But can the lasting cult be explained by reference to such birds of passage? If it was the Thracians who provided horses for the famous mounted torch-relay, they must in fact have been extremely prosperous metics.[75]

Perhaps a broader approach is needed. In the fifth century, two barbarian countries were constantly in the thoughts of any alert Athenian. There was no question, of course, of adopting the gods of Persia, the ancient enemy. The status of Thrace was much more ambiguous: a savage country and home of a savage people, but one with which it was indispensable for economic and strategic reasons constantly to grapple. Since Miltiades' first colonizing venture in the sixth century, Thrace had been for Athenians what America long was for Europeans, a land of promise and peril. Colonists had been sent to Brea in 440, to Amphipolis for a second time in 437. Many Athenians will now have had connections who had lived or served or died in the 'Thraceward regions'. Ideologically too, Thrace had made an important contribution or capture in the figure of Orpheus. The grim tale of Athenian Procne's marriage to Thracian Tereus became, it seems, the bizarre justification for a claim that there existed kinship, συγγένεια, between the two peoples.[76] For an Athenian, Thrace was a phenomenon that loomed; there was no get-

---

[74] Sadokos: Thuc. 2.29.5, Ar. *Ach.* 138–50; cf. Osborne, *Naturalization*, III/IV. 12, 26, 188–89. Thracians at Athens: I have traced only a mining-contractor (Xen. *Poroi* 4.14), a περσικοποιός (*IG* II².11689), and mercenaries (*IG* II².1956); the many 'Thracians' (occupation unspecified) known from epitaphs (*IG* II².8896–8928, 11686–88) are likely to be slaves. Perhaps Bendiphanes, a metic who helped in the restoration of the democrats in 403 (*IG* II².10; cf. Tod, *GHI* II.100), was a Thracian. Two women named Bendidora are also attested at Athens: one, nationality unknown, made a dedication 'to the goddess' (Bendis?), the second is clearly Thracian (*IG* II².4866 and 9223, with O. Masson, *MH* 45, 1988, 7). Laurion: see Themelis, *Horos* 7 (1989), 23–29, on three statues of the goddess (*LIMC* s.v. *Bendis*, 97, nos. 7 and 8, and one unpub., all of late fourth–third cent. BC) which he says were found in the region, as was the new dedication by Daos which he publishes (perhaps to be joined in fact to the statue *LIMC* s.v. *Bendis*, n. 8). Mycalessus: Thuc. 7.27–30.

[75] I owe this point to Prof. Sakurai (n. 61). She also points out that the departure of the Thracian mercenaries, and subsequent massacre by them, is likely to precede by a little the passing of *IG* I³.136; she wonders about a causal connection.

[76] See Xen. *Anab.* 7.2.31 and 7.3.39 with Thuc. 2.29.1–3 (a connection perhaps first made by K. W. Krüger, *De Authentia et Integritate Anabaseos Xenophonteae*, Halis Saxonum 1824,

ting around it. That, at bottom, seems to be the truth that was acknowledged by the admission of Bendis, whatever particular circumstances may also have played a part.

The coming of Asclepius to Athens was in a way a routine occurrence, just one stage in the progress of a rapidly expanding cult. But for us it is surrounded by rare and fascinating details. The very day of his arrival is known: 18th Boedromion, 420/19. We infer this from a monument set up by the private individual who introduced the hero, and founded his sanctuary on the sunny south slope of the acropolis, one Telemachus. A different source tells us that the divine newcomer was hosted for a period by the poet Sophocles. A second sanctuary was soon founded in the Piraeus (or possibly this came first), and curious documents survive that illuminate the early history of this cult too. First, however, we must look briefly at the earlier divine healers of Attica,[77] and at Asclepius' own earlier career.

Before Asclepius, Apollo Paion had had a sanctuary in Athens; and both Apollo and Heracles are mentioned with the title Alexikakos in connection with the great plague. 'Health', Hygieia, who became a close associate of Asclepius, had before this combined with Athena to form the composite Athena Hygieia. Not all of these were necessarily 'healing-cults' in the familiar sense; one can imagine, for instance, that Athena Hygieia's role was essentially prophylactic, and directed to the health of the community as a whole, not of individuals. But Apollo Paion at least had doubtless been approached by individuals in sickness, before Asclepius took away his clientele.[78] And votive breasts and genitals continue to be found in the shrines of goddesses, both Artemis and Aphrodite, as well as of Asclepius.[79]

---

33); there was another marriage-connnection through Boreas (above). Orpheus: see e.g. Strabo 10.3.17 (471); and generally Parker, 'Myths', 203–205. In 2.95–102 Thucydides digresses, unusually (see Hornblower's introductory comment), to instruct his Athenian audience in Thracian ethnography. On the tensions in Greco-Thracian relations in Thrace itself see N. Ehrhardt, *Eos* 76 (1988), 289–304, and the important new fourth-cent. text, *BCH* 118 (1994), 1–15.*

[77] Cf. Kutsch, *Heilheroen, passim*; Kearns, *Heroes of Attica*, 14–21, 171, and for the votives representing healed limbs, van Straten, 'Gifts', 105–21.

[78] Apollo Paion: *IG* I³.383.163–64 (his treasury: for the only other refs. see Ch. 8, n. 115, Delos, and Paus. 1.34.3, Oropus). The Alexikakoi: see n. 121. Athena Hygieia: attested in the first half of the fifth cent. by the graffito Graef/Langlotz, *Vasen von der Akropolis*, II.119, no. 1367, pl. 91 (*ARV²* 1556), then by the base *IG* I³.506 and an associated anecdote concerning Pericles (see e.g. Plut. *Per.* 13.12–13, and notes on *IG* I³.506); later at Acharnae by Paus. 1.31.6. There was also Athena Paionia: Paus. 1.2.5, 1.34.3. Prophylactic: but the Pericles anecdote (above) implies a healing-cult of familiar type.

[79] See van Straten, 'Gifts', 105 ff., nos. 4 (Aphrodite, on the northern and southern slopes of the acropolis), 5 and 6 (Artemis Kalliste, near the Ceramicus, and late evidence for Artemis

There were also 'doctor heroes', who may always have had greater appeal than doctor gods; certainly they succeeded rather better in resisting the new competitor. A figure commonly known just as that, 'doctor hero' (*heros iatros*), is found at four different places; at Eleusis he was identified as 'Oresinios', at Marathon and Rhamnus as 'Aristomachus', while at Athens he apparently remained simply 'the hero-doctor in the city'.[80] At Athens, there was also a named healing-hero, Amynos, whose cult west of the acropolis was in the charge of a group of prosperous and respectable *orgeones*. Through an exceptionally rewarding excavation, we can follow the history of the modest shrine from the sixth century to the Roman period.[81] Even a non-specialist hero, such as Herakles Pankrates, might, it seems, turn his hand to healing.[82]

These older figures were liable to be intruded upon by the younger heroes of broader fame. Asclepius entered the precinct of Amynos, without, however, effacing its first occupant completely; but at Rhamnus a comparable figure, Amphiaraus, after first moving alongside Aristomachus, did in the end, it seems, succeed in supplanting him. The 'doctor hero' at Athens is still so described in the second century BC, but seems eventually to have become 'the doctor hero Amphilochus' by identification with a son of Amphiaraus.[83]

What of Asclepius? He was as yet far from being that pre-eminent

Kolainis in Athens), 11 (Aphrodite at Daphni). Cf. Travlos, *Pictorial Dictionary*, 231; id., *Bildlexikon*, 185. The overlap between the goddesses and Asclepius remains significant even if Aleshire, *Asklepieion*, 41, is right that such offerings relate to functions of the organs shown (e.g. lactation), not diseases. Travlos, *Pictorial Dictionary*, 569–72, is wrong to retroject the late healing-cult of Zeus Hypsistos on the disued Pnyx to the classical period: see B. Forsen, *Hesperia* 62 (1993), 507–21.

[80] Eleusis: *Anecd. Bekk.* I.263.11, (?) cf. *IG* I³.393.3, 395.3 (or is this the Athenian?). Marathon: *Anecd. Bekk.* I.262.16, and (very doubtful) *LSCG* 20 B 19–20. Rhamnus: *SEG* XXXIII 200 [+]. Athens: Dem. 19.249, *IG* II².839–40 (on which see S. Dow, *Bull. Am. Soc. Papyrologists* 22, 1985, 33–47); *Hesperia* 17 (1948), 39, no. 26; and see Ch. 7, n. 28 above and n. 83 below (on *IG* II².7175). The Σ on Dem. 19.249 identifies the Athenian as Aristomachus, perhaps unreliably. The cult at Rhamnus appears to go back to the sixth cent. (cf. the head, Pouilloux, *Rhamnonte*, pl. xliii.1 and 2 = Ath. Nat. Mus. Sculpt. 2337). At Thorikos, a two-roomed shrine of a healing power, located in the 'industrial sector', is said to go back to the late sixth cent.; nearby was found a fourth-cent. dedication to (?) ['Υγι]είᾳ (H. F. Mussche *et al.*, *Thorikos* 1968, Brussels 1971, 103–50; Travlos, *Bildlexikon*, 441; but the identification as a shrine is doubted by Lauter, *Landgemeinden*, 135, n. 426).

[81] See A. Körte, *AM* 21 (1896), 287–332; Kutsch, *Heilheroen*, 12–16, 54–59, 124–27; Ferguson, 'Attic Orgeones', 85, n. 33, 86–91; Travlos, *Pictorial Dictionary*, 76–78; W. Graham *ap*. Wycherley, *Stones of Athens*, 196; Aleshire, *Asklepios*, 223–39 (prosopography). The inscriptions are *IG* II².1252–53, 1259, 4365, 4385–86, 4422, 4424, 4435, 4457, and the graffito Kutsch, *Heilheroen*, 55, no. 9.

[82] See van Straten, 'Gifts', 116, no. 7; Travlos, *Pictorial Dictionary*, 279.

[83] Amynos: Asclepius receives dedications from the fourth cent., but the latest of all (*IG* II².4457) still mentions both heroes separately. Rhamnus: Amphiaraus first appears in the late fourth cent.; when a society of *Amphieraistai* is formed, after 229, to revive the cult, Aristomachus is forgotten (*IG* II².1322; cf. Pouilloux, *Rhamnonte*, 97–98, on his nos. 30–34,

god familiar from late antiquity. As healers in myth, indeed, he and his sons had been familiar throughout Greece since Homer, and by the sixth century, doctors were known generically as 'Asclepiadae'. But his own cult as a healing-hero is first attested at Epidaurus only around 500, and seems to have spread through the Peloponnese during the fifth century. From an allusion in *Wasps*, of 422, we learn that there was by then an Asclepieum in Aegina to which Athenians had recourse. What Telemachus introduced to Athens, therefore, was a comparatively young, rapidly expanding cult. His arrival in Athens, perhaps the first important city outside the Peloponnese in which he gained a foothold, was in turn an important step in Asclepius' career.[84]

Telemachus—we assume that he was responsible—built a remarkable monument, an elaborate double-sided sculpted relief supported by a column on which was inscribed a brief year-by-year chronicle of the early history of the shrine.[85] There survive fragments of the entries for eight years. Most concern building and planting and adornment, performed by Telemachus 'at his own expense'; we also hear that, in the year following the foundation, difficulties arose when the great Eleusinian *genos* of *Kerykes* 'laid claim to the site'. (Did the *Kerykes* profess to be standing out in defence of traditional religion against the 'new god'?[86] But according to Telemachus the point at issue was merely the site; and other evidence rather suggests a hospitable attitude to Asclepius on the part of the Eleusinian priesthood.) The vital entry comes under the first surviving year, 420/19, and we must pause over it, fragmentary though it is. The passage begins in mid-sentence, and the subject of the verb is unknown (a corrected or partially supplemented word is followed by a question mark):

coming up from Zea (?) during the Great Mysteries he lodged (?) [in the Eleusinion] and summoning a snake (?) from home brought it here on [a

---

pp. 143–47, with B. Petrakos, *Prakt* 1981 (1983), 126 f. = *SEG* XXXII 261; XXXIII 200–202). Amphilochus: *IG* II².7175 ('s. II/III'), cf. Schachter, *Cults*, I.27 (Oropus); contrast still *IG* II².840.

[84] See e.g. Edelstein, *Asclepius* II.1–22, 54–55, 242–46; *LIMC* s.v. *Asklepios*, 864–65; Ar. *Vesp.* 122–23.

[85] Brilliantly reconstructed by L. Beschi, *ASAtene* NS 29–30 (1967–8), 381–436; id., *AAA* 15 (1982), 31–43 (note too *SEG* XXXVI 275). On the order of the frs. of the inscription see now Beschi's text (= *SEG* XXV 226, XXXII 266); for the various suppls. see the app. crit. to *IG* II².4960 [+]. For a general view of the complicated iconography of the monument see *ASAtene* NS 29–30 (1967–8), 411, with the description *AAA* 15 (1982), 31–32 and the modification to the top level (missed in Garland, *New Gods*, 119, fig. 12) ibid. figs. 8 and 9.*

[86] There is a tempting but perhaps delusive parallel concerning the fortunes of Sarapis on Delos: see Ch. 10, n. 68; cf. too n. 99 below.

wagon] [*a reference to Telemachus in an uncertain case follows immediately, as part of the same sentence*] At the same time came Health (?). And so this whole shrine was founded in the archonship of Astyphilos.

As this incident has become famous, a warning is needed about its central character. What is here described is, it is generally supposed, the bringing to Athens of a sacred snake, closely associated with, or even representing, Asclepius. But the stone-cutter actually described the creature brought on—if a supplement is correct—a wagon as a *ΔIA*[. . . . ., which admits the epigraphically perfect reading *ΔIAKONON*, 'attendant'. The objection to this obvious supplement is that it gives an absurd prominence, in a sacred narrative every detail of which should bear meaning, to a mere ancillary. Snakes, by contrast, regularly feature in accounts of the introduction of Asclepius;[87] and one can be brought in here if we suppose that *ΔPA*[*KONTA* is what the stone-cutter intended to inscribe. Bold though it is, the change appears necessary. But who 'summoned' and 'brought' the snake? By analogy with similar accounts, the mortal should be subject of the verb, not the god;[88] and this suits the first half of the sentence better too, since it is hard to see in what form Asclepius would have 'arrived' and 'lodged' before the fetching of the snake. An unexpected consequence seems to follow. Telemachus, who is unidentified in the inscription, has regularly been taken to be the grandfather of Telemachus of Acharnae, a prosperous figure who took part in public life and became a butt of comic poets in the 330s.[89] But if the snake came, as it surely did, from the great sanctuary at Epidaurus, and Telemachus summoned it 'from home', he was probably himself an Epidaurian. The name is in fact regularly borne by members of one dominant Epidaurian family.[90]

Asclepius was in general an 'imported' god, one brought in by states that had heard of his fame; but in this case, if we are right, the

[87] Körte, *AM* 21 (1896), 316–17, refers to Paus. 2.10.3, 3.23.6–7, Epidaurian cure 33 (= T 748, 757, 423 in Edelstein, *Asclepius*, I), to the well-known bringing of Asclepius to Rome (ibid. T 845–57), and, for the wagon, to *SIG*³ 697 L 3.

[88] Cf. the previous note. For the alternative (most ingeniously defended by Wilamowitz, *Glaube* II.221, n. 1), see the app. crit. to *IG* II².4960.8–9, and still Ferguson, 'Attic Orgeones', 88.

[89] On him see R. Osborne, *Liverpool Classical Monthly* 8 (1983), 11; id., *Demos*, 5. The identification goes back to U. Koehler, on *IG* II².1649. On the base of it, several further connections between Telemachus of Acharnae and his supposed grandfather's activities have been postulated (Osborne, *Liverpool Classical Monthly* 8, 1983; the suppl. in *IG* II².4963; R. Schlaifer, *HSCP* 51, 1940, 240); they are plausible in varying degrees if the identification is correct, inadequate to establish it. It has now also been questioned by Aleshire, *Asklepieion*, 7, n. 4.

[90] See *IG* IV².I, p. xxv; and cf. the snake of Asclepius brought οἴκοθεν by the people of what became Epidauros Limera, Paus. 3.23.7. We cannot, however, altogether reject the possibility that οἴκοθεν refers to the snake's home, not Telemachus'.

other form of diffusion operated, 'export' by a proud fellow-citizen of a local god of exceptional powers.[91] Of course, the fortunes even of an exported god depended ultimately on the attitude of the city in which he arrived. Brought in perhaps by an Epidaurian resident in Athens, Asclepius was taken up by the native Athenians with passion. The first Athenian Asklepiodoros was born, probably, in the late fifth century; and the inventories and the abundant votive reliefs (systematically mutilated alas, presumably by Christian hands) still vividly evoke centuries of devotion. And though it is sometimes supposed that the cult depended on the credulity of the vulgar, we find numerous devotees among the cultural and social élite of the fifth and fourth centuries—the tragic poet Aristarchus, the comic poet Theopompus, Sophocles, of course, and the politician Demon of Paiania.[92]

The coming of Asclepius occurred 'during the Great Mysteries'. In commemoration, one of his two main festivals, the *'Epidauria'*, was celebrated for ever after on 18th Boedromion, an empty day within the week-long programme of the Mysteries; and eventually it was said that Asclepius himself had been specially initiated on that day.[93] Was this timely arrival, seen in the pious legend as a significant coincidence, in fact designed? Was the healer deliberately associated with two 'saviours' of older type? The incident can be seen as a rare illustration of the down-to-earth politics of polytheism, the way in which the advent of a new god could be made possible through the interest of the priesthood of an old.[94] But if this was

[91] Asclepius imported: so e.g. to Sicyon and Rome, T 748, 845 ff. in Edelstein, *Asclepius*, I and cf. Garland, *New Gods*, 122. But on the cult at Epidauros Limera see the previous note; and for 'export' of other cults see e.g. Possis of Magnesia, *FGrH* 480 F 1 (cults introduced by the exiled Themistocles), Alexis of Samos, *FGrH* 539 F 1 (not very reliable: but cf. V. Pirenne, *AntCl* 57, 1988, 150), and M. Totti, *Ausgewählte Texte der Isis- und Sarapis-Religion* (Hildesheim 1985), nos. 11 and 71.

[92] See Aleshire, *Asklepieion*, 113–369 (a re-edition of the inventories); *IG* II².4351–4544; *CEG* 755, 763–66, 772 (dedications). Cf. U. Hausmann, *Kunst und Heiltum* (Potsdam 1948); van Straten, 'Gifts', 105–13; Aleshire, *Asklepieion*, 37–51 (and on the architectural history 7–36). For Aristarchus and Theopompus see Suda under these names (α 3893 and J 171 = Aelian frs. 101 and 99 Hercher). On Demon, who donated a property to the god in return for the priesthood (in, presumably, the city cult)—a transaction that required the approval of Delphi—see *IG* II².4969, with R. Schlaifer, *CP* 38 (1943), 39–43; Davies, *Propertied Families*, 117–18; and Aleshire, *Asklepieion*, 163–64. Aeschines too was a devotee of Asclepius, though at Epidaurus (*CEG* 776); note too [Plut.] *X Orat.* 845b on Demosthenes. Asklepiodoros: *IG* II².12888 (cf. 4619); on this and other Asklepi- names at Athens see M. B. Walbank, *AJAH* 4 (1979), 186–91, and now *LGPN* II.

[93] Arist. *Ath. Pol.* 56.4; Paus. 2.26.8; Philostr. *Vit. Ap. Ty.* 4.18 (T 564–65, 567 in Edelstein, *Asclepius*, I); cf. Deubner, *Attische Feste*, 72–73, and a reference to 'the arrival of the god', *IG* II².1019.8 (second cent. BC).

[94] So Garland, *New Gods*, 20, 124. A fr. of Nicomachus' calendar to be published by K. Clinton (in R. Hägg ed., *Ancient Greek Cult Practice from the Epigraphic Evidence*, Stockholm) may show that Eleusinian officials were involved in the *Epidauria* in the late fifth

not so, the commemoration of a coincidence is no less remarkable. Where a god passes, all around becomes hyper-charged with meaning: even the contingencies of his coming prove profoundly significant.[95] A relief found in the Asclepieum can accordingly show Asclepius and the two goddesses together, approached by a file of worshippers.[96]

Was there a specific motive for the introduction of Asclepius in 420? The great plague had broken out in 430, and continued on and off until 426. Asclepius arrived, not indeed immediately, but almost as soon as free association between Athens and Epidaurus was restored by the Peace of Nicias in 421. It is an obvious and plausible conjecture that the two events were connected.[97] An upwardly mobile hero such as Asclepius, however, would doubtless have reached Athens in the end, even without this particular incentive.

Telemachus' shrine was certainly in one sense a private foundation: he met the expenses himself, and had to resist the *Kerykes'* claim to the site; and some suppose that the priesthood passed like a personal fief to his son.[98] But no one introduces a healing-god for his own use alone, and that venerable establishment-figure Sophocles was involved in some way in 'receiving' the eminent guest. One may wonder too whether an individual (particularly, if we are right, a non-citizen) could appropriate a sizeable area of what was presumably common land without the consent of the 'council and the people'.[99] Possibly Telemachus had sought and received permission to

cent. (Aleshire, *Asklepieion*, 8). Note too n. 99 on the conflict of Telemachus and the *Kerykes*; also, perhaps, the role of Euthydemus of Eleusis in the Piraeus cult, and the early emergence of a cult of Asclepius in the deme Eleusis itself (*IG* II².4366).*

[95] Cf. J. Z. Smith, *Imagining Religion* (Chicago 1982), 53–54.

[96] *IG* II².4359 = *LIMC* s.v. *Asklepios*, 886, no. 313 ('mid 4th c.', Aleshire). The relief is commonly supposed to commemorate honours conferred on public doctors at the '*Epidauria*' (perhaps still at this date just called *Asklepieia*): see the commentary to *IG* II².4359; but contrast Aleshire, *Asklepieion*, 8, esp. n. 7, and 94–95. C. Benedum, 'Asklepios und Demeter', *JdI* 101 (1986), 137–57, argues that the association (for which see the later evidence in Edelstein, *Asclepius*, II.127–29) antedates Asclepius' arrival in Athens; but the case is not conclusive. Garland's list of parallels between the two cults, *New Gods*, 124, is exaggerated.

[97] See e.g. J. D. Mikalson in *Studies Presented to Sterling Dow* (*GRBM* 10, 1984), 220.

[98] See the note to *IG* II².4963; but contrast n. 89 above.

[99] Cf. Schlaifer, *HSCP* 51 (1940), 240, n. 2; Wilamowitz, *Glaube* II.229. The evidence of Lampon's rider to the Eleusinian first-fruits decree (*IG* I³.78.54–56; M/L 73) is double-edged, since it both attests and forbids the practice of founding altars without permission in the Pelargikon, where (see Beschi, *ASAtene* NS 29–30 (1967–8), 386–97) the Asclepieum was, and may itself either precede (so, tentatively, M/L) or follow (so Smarczyk, *Religionspolitik*, 224 ff.) Telemachus' act. (Telemachus, of course, founded more than an altar.) The claim of the *Kerykes* to the land is a further complication, since we now know that the Eleusinion was well away from the shrine; some suppose that they had originally hoped to incorporate the new cult under their own control (cf. the apparent reference to an original reception within the Eleusinion), and were seeking to thwart Telemachus' bid for independence (see e.g. Smarczyk, *Religionspolitik*, 249, n. 268); but it is best to admit ignorance.

'summon' the new god to a sanctuary to be built, at his own expense, on a piece of public land below the acropolis. There are even uncertain signs that the new god's festival, the '*Epidauria*', may already have found a place in the state sacrificial calendar as revised by Nicomachus at the end of the fifth century. However that may be, the cult had certainly become public in the normal sense by about 350,[100] and by the second half of the fourth century was among the most prominent, equipped with a priest, an income, and at least two festivals on the grand scale.

The other main Asclepieum, in the Piraeus, is already public when first we meet it in, probably, the second quarter of the fourth century. For the relation between the two shrines, no direct evidence is available. Since Telemachus apparently claimed to have 'come up from Zea' (in the Piraeus) to found the Asclepieum in the city, it is often thought that the Piraean was the earlier foundation, though by a few years only;[101] and if, as is plausible at first sight, the famous incubation-scene in Aristophanes' *Plutus* is imagined as taking place near the sea,[102] the shrine in the Piraeus and not the one below the acropolis was still for the Athenians in 388 the Asclepieum *par excellence*. But when we first meet it, the cult at the Piraeus is still being set in order: the sacrificial rules are being drafted, the shrine has yet to be built; though this might in principle be a reorganization (in consequence possibly of the adoption by the people of a hitherto private sanctuary), there is little objection to the simpler view that the

---

[100] A firm *terminus ante quem* of 343/2 is given by *Agora* XIX P26.487–88, a fee of 'a drachma for Asclepius': see Aleshire, *Asklepieion*, 15 on this and other less securely datable items. Aleshire denies that the cult can have come under state control much earlier, on the not absolutely decisive ground that there is no previous trace of the annual priesthood (on which see her pp. 72–85; in later periods it rotated between the tribes, but she regards the case as not proven for the fourth cent.). Income: from the 'drachma for Asclepius' (above: but Aleshire, *Asklepieion*, 98–99, drastically reduces its yield), and property (see n. 92 above on Demon). Festivals: cf. *IG* II².1496.78, 109, 133 (with Kirchner's note), 142; Deubner, *Attische Feste*, 72–73, 142 (a third, the *Heroa*, is only later attested). The relevant decrees are re-edited (or listed, p. 169, n. 3), by R. O. Hubbe, *Hesperia* 28 (1959), 169–201 (= *SEG* XVIII 11–33). Though primarily of local appeal, the shrine was well enough known to attract the patronage of Alexander's mother, Olympias; Hyperides, *Eux.* 19, 26. *Epidauria*: n. 94 above.

[101] So e.g. Garland, *Piraeus*, 115; the ship's prow perhaps visible on the Telemachus monument (n. 85) is also sometimes held to allude to Asclepius' arrival at Zea. But for doubts about the reading Ζεόθεν see E. Meyer in *RE* s.v. *Zea*. Would Telemachus have stressed this dependence when the city cult's main affiliation was with Epidaurus? The shrine in the Piraeus can scarcely have enjoyed much reputation in 422 (cf. Ar. *Vesp.* 122–23), if it existed by then. On other Attic cults of Asclepius see S. Solders, *Die ausserstädtischen Kulte und die Einigung Attikas* (Lund 1931), 57 f.

[102] Cf. θάλασσα, lines 656–58, where the rendering 'basin' is only weakly supported by the 'sea' of Poseidon on the acropolis, a special case (though see too M/L, p. 171 on their 62.24). On the other hand, it is hard to suppose that the thirty-year-old shrine within a stone's throw of the theatre (for which Σ Ar. *Plut.* 621 plumps) could be simply ignored. Cf. R. Ginouvès, *Balaneutikè* (Paris 1962), 355–57 [+].

cult had been but lately founded. Most unusually, we see ritual rules in process of creation, and we can even name their author, the priest of 'Asclepius in the Piraeus',[103] Euthydemus of Eleusis. In one text, we learn that he has 'expounded' the preliminary offerings that are to precede an elaborate public festival; in another, where Euthydemus is again mentioned, the 'preliminary offerings' are actually listed which, it seems, an individual had to offer prior to incubation.[104]

In certain respects the list is remarkable. Three cakes, we learn, are owed to each of the following: Maleatas, Apollo, Hermes, Iaso, Akeso, Panakeia, Dogs, and Hunters-with-Dogs ($\kappa\upsilon\nu\eta\gamma\acute{\epsilon}\tau\alpha\iota$). It is no surprise to find Asclepius associated, as often, with his daughters 'Curer', 'Healer', and 'All-Heal'; and in a cult of incubation we can readily understand the role of Hermes, bringer of dreams. But it is normally as a single figure that Apollo Maleatas is associated with Asclepius,[105] while the dogs and hunters are quite mysterious. The eccentric rules are often thought to provide precious late testimony to antique traditions, soon to be obliterated. But it is hard to see why these should emerge in a cult newly established in the Piraeus in the early fourth century. Perhaps, to give the recent foundation a distinctive mark, Euthydemus was innovating; a lewd burlesque of, possibly, this very law in a contemporary comic poet may be a parody of this unfamiliar fussy elaborateness.[106] According to a myth first attested in the Hellenistic period, the baby Asclepius was exposed by his mother (often in the region of Epidaurus), suckled or guarded by an animal which is sometimes a dog, and discovered, in the commonest version, by a group of 'hunters-with-dogs'.[107] A

---

[103] So Schlaifer, *HSCP* 51 (1940), 243; as it happens, the title is not attested here or elsewhere, but it is implied by *IG* II².354.33, 'priest of Asclepius in the city'.

[104] See *IG* II².47 = *LSS* 11 (the festival is apparently unregistered in the handbooks); *IG* II².4962 = *LSCG* 21 (on which see L. Ziehen's commentary, *Leges Graecorum Sacrae*, no. 18). On the date of Euthydemus' activities ('ca. 370–350'), see the prosopographical analyses of Aleshire, *Asklepios*, 244–46. The list of property belonging to the shrine in *IG* II².47 is perhaps the strongest argument that it had been in existence for some time; note too M. Meyer's argument, *AM* 102 (1987), 213–24, that the relief Ny Carlsberg 1430, supposedly from the Piraeus, depicts Asclepius and Hygieia and dates from 420–410. On finds associable with the Piraeus shrine see B. Forsen, *ZPE* 87 (1991), 173–75.

[105] See the refs. in Edelstein, *Asclepius*, II.186, n. 9 and in Sokolowski ad loc. (*LSCG* 21), also *Der Kleine Pauly* s.v. *Maleatas*. No certain case of an independent Maleatas is cited (*IG* V.1.927, 929, and *Schwyzer* 12.57 are indecisive: cf. *IG* V.1.929c, and Graf, *Nordionische Kulte*, 37–39); the composite Apollo Maleatas is first attested apparently in Isyllus and is very common thereafter at Epidaurus.

[106] Plato Comicus fr. 188 K/A; cf. L. R. Farnell, *CQ* 14 (1920), 144.

[107] Apollodorus of Athens, *FGrH* 244 F 138. Cf. Paus. 2.26.3–5; Edelstein, *Asclepius*, II.72–73, 227. A connection between Apollodorus' version and sacred laws such as that of the Piraeus must surely exist, even if the influence in fact went the other way from that is suggested here.

recently published plate by the Midias painter, which shows the baby Asclepius with 'Epidauros', suggests that a form of this myth was known in Athens by the late fifth century; indeed, it looks as if the plate commemorates a victory won by a poet with a dithyramb on this theme.[108] Was Euthydemus inspired by the myth to give cultic honours to the preservers of the miraculous child?

The Meidias painter's plate is one of several new documents that expand our picture of Asclepius as he was when he came to Athens. The grave elderly doctor so familiar to us from art had once, we see, been, like Heracles, a sacred, perhaps a wonder-working child; and as such he appears to be portrayed on a relief found in the Asclepieum, on which a minuscule worshipper draws near to an enormous baby. The newly reconstituted Telemachus-monument presents a contrasting image: it showed Asclepius, as now seems certain, surrounded by the symbols not of a god but of a hero, in particular the characteristic horse's head. In one sense, therefore, Asclepius was just one more healing-hero added to the many that Athens already had. Yet another new document is one of the earliest votive reliefs, freshly reassembled. We see (typically) the god and his family, approached (untypically) by a muleteer in a cap with his humble cart. Through the inscription, he perhaps gave thanks for rescue from a fall of 'mighty rocks'. If so, Asclepius was already not just a healer but a saviour and helper of much broader power.[109]

From these diverse documents, no single image of the hero appears. We are left to ask—perhaps in vain, since the 'epidemiology

---

[108] See D. Cramers, *AA* 1978, 67–73; *LIMC* s.v. *Asklepios*, 868, no. 1; L. Burn, *The Meidias Painter* (Oxford 1987), 71, with pl. 46. For the same myth see perhaps the votive relief Ath. Nat. Mus. 1351, *LIMC* s.v. *Asklepios*, 868, no. 5 (but cf. F. van Straten, *BABesch* 51, 1976, 8), and the 'eroe cacciatore circondato da cani' of the Telemachus monument (Beschi, *AAA* 15, 1982, 32). Of course, Euthydemus may also have been influenced by the existing role of dogs (but not hunters) in the cult (cf. F. R. Walton, *HSCP* 46, 1935, 176–78; there are several on the Telemachus monument). For a different approach see W. Burkert, *The Orientalizing Revolution* (tr. M. E. Pinder and W. Burkert, Cambridge, Mass. 1992), 77: a link with the dogs of the Babylonian healing-goddess Gula of Isin; and cf. F. Graf, in *Le sanctuaire grec* (*EntrHardt* 37, Geneva 1992), 184–85.

[109] Child: Ath. Nat. Mus. 1424, *LIMC* s.v. *Asklepios*, 869, no. 6; cf. Paus. 2.26.5. Hero: see *AAA* 15 (1982), 31–43, figs. 7 and 9. This new evidence comes close to finally proving that the 'banqueting hero' reliefs found in the Asclepieum were offerings to Asclepius himself (see Hausmann, *Kunst und Heiltum*, 111–24; Dentzer, *Banquet couché*, 463); such reliefs were also found in the Amyneion, the Piraeus Asclepieum, and the Amphiareum of Oropus (nos. R 206, 226, 242 in Dentzer's catalogue), while two (one from Attica) bear dedications 'to the doctor (hero)' (R 267, 503). Muleteer: Ath. Nat. Mus. 1341 + EM 8754 + Acr. Mus. 7988 = *LIMC* s.v. *Asklepios*, 890, no. 395 (see L. Beschi, *ASAtene* NS 31–32 (1969–70), 85–93; not noted in *CEG* 764). Saviour: see *IG* II².4357, a dedication by a man 'rescued from the wars and ransomed and freed' ('ante med. s. iv a.'); *CEG* 755 ('? 400–350')—Hegemachos δεινὰ παθὼν καὶ πολλὰ [ἰ]δὼν σωθεὶς ἀνέθηκεν ('ecce Ulixes Atheniensis', Hansen: cf. Hom. *Od.* 1.3–4); *CEG* 772.4 (= *IG* II².4368.4), μέγας σωτήρ; and much later *IG* II².4499. See in general Edelstein, *Asclepius*, II.101–108.

of representations' is no exact science[110]—why he outdid his competitors. Over the older Attic healing-heroes he had the advantage of pre-eminent mythological fame. It is attractive to suppose that he introduced to Attica, in incubation, a new technique of great psychological appeal; but this is uncertain, as we know nothing at all of the healing-methods of the indigenous heroes. Another feature is certainly characteristic of his cult, though again we cannot insist that it is unique. Divine healer though he was, Asclepius had the wisdom never to resist the developing secular 'art' of medicine. On the contrary, he appropriated it: not its substance perhaps, but its symbols, its aura, its prestige. We already find various medicinal instruments listed in an early inventory of the Asclepieum in the Piraeus, and represented behind the god on Telemachus' monument; and the public physicians of Athens actually sacrificed twice annually in the hero's shrine.[111] The truest explanation for the rise of Asclepius may be that he was, as it were, in partnership with Hippocrates.

With Asclepius' doctorly professionalism went his extraordinary 'friendliness to man'. This is perhaps his most remarkable trait. All gods and heroes, of course, traditionally had a friendly side; the novelty of Asclepius was to have no other. The note of eager and grateful praise, so familiar from later antiquity, is already struck in Aristophanes' *Plutus*, where Asclepius is acclaimed 'a great light to mortals'. Even earlier, 'Happiness' had been present on the plate by Meidias that showed the young god.[112] His childhood may, according to myth, have been passed in wild places, but no less than his teacher Chiron, a true denizen of the wilds, he had 'a mind friendly to men'.[113] Asclepius is the precursor of the softened deities of the fourth century—Zeus of Friendship and Good Luck and Peace—who made to man the novel promise of good without evil. Like Zeus of Friendship, he is commonly imagined as a comfortable family-man.[114]

We may turn at this point, finally, to Sophocles. According to late sources, Sophocles 'received Asclepius in his house and founded an altar'; and for this reason the Athenians, eager to honour the poet, built a hero-shrine for him after his death and named him 'Dexion',

---

[110] See D. Sperber, *Man* NS 20 (1985), 73–89.

[111] Inventory: *IG* II².47. Public physicians: *IG* II².772; cf. 483. *IG* II².4359 is a dedication to Asclepius by a group of men with strong medical associations, even if Aleshire, *Asklepieion*, 94–95 is right to deny that they are public physicians. Cf. in general the refs. in Parker, *Miasma*, 249.

[112] Ar. *Plut.* 640; above, n. 108; cf. Edelstein, *Asclepius* II.113–14.

[113] Pind. *Pyth.* 3.5. For a brilliant attempt to detect broader traits of marginality in Asclepius' cult see Graf in *Le sanctuaire grec*, 159–99.

[114] Ar. *Plut.* 639; *IG* II².4962; and the votive reliefs, *passim*.

'receiver'. These reports acquired new actuality when two decrees were discovered, issued in the fourth century by an association of '*Orgeones* of Amynos and Asclepius and Dexion', who controlled a 'shrine of Amynos and Asclepius' and another of 'Dexion'. The cult of Sophocles/Dexion was, therefore, a reality, and it was administered by an association, to which the poet himself had possibly belonged, originally founded to worship one of the pre-Asclepiean healing-heroes Amynos. (Sophocles, as we learn from a separate source, was certainly priest of a hero associated with Asclepius; but the manuscript gives the name Halon, not Amynos.[115]) We do not know how Sophocles came to host the hero whom Telemachus had introduced;[116] but combination of the two accounts creates the memorable (if, it must be allowed, scarcely dependable) image of the dramatist entertaining a sacred serpent in his house. As an emblem of the old-fashioned piety of the poet, so unravaged (as Matthew Arnold once said of Oxford) by the fierce intellectual life of the century, this image has been much admired.[117] And yet the snake whom Sophocles harboured was a 'new', a 'foreign' god, one destined, according to some, to undermine true Greek religion, indeed the 'nation' itself.[118] Against Euripides the charge of destroying the spirit of tragedy has often been laid. But it was Sophocles, in his works 'the last great exponent of the archaic world-view',[119] who received this harbinger of the Hellenistic age in his house.

Two general issues are suggested by these various cases. The first is the role of the individual. The individual mortal is a habitual absentee from studies of Greek religion; and yet here we have heard of Philippides, of Cimon, of Telemachus and Sophocles and

---

[115] *Etym. Magn.* 256.6 s.v. *Dexion*, etc. (cf. 67–73a in *TrGF* IV). For reception 'in the house' cf. Garland, *New Gods*, 125, n. 4, and the myths and practices of Theoxeny. The decrees: *IG* II².1252, 1253, cf. 1259. Halon: *Vit. Soph.* 11 = T 1 Radt; cf. Radt ad loc. [+]; see esp., in support of the change to 'Amynos', Ferguson, 'Attic Orgeones', 86, n. 34; *contra*, Wilamowitz, *Glaube* II.222; with the transmitted reading, the priest of one healing-hero becomes heroized by the *orgeones* of another. Dexion's shrine must have been well away from Amynos' (in Sophocles' own house?), since separate *stelai* are inscribed for display in each (*IG* II².1252; cf. O. Walter, *Geras A. Keramopoullou*, Athens 1953, 469–79); some have located it in the Asclepieum, supposing that 'Halon' had previously been worshipped there (so Walter, *Geras*, 469–79; Beschi, *ASAtene* NS 29–30, 1967–8, 423–28); but there is no firm evidence for independent heroic cult on the site before or after Asclepius' coming (cf. n. 109 above).

[116] Hausmann, *Kunst und Heiltum*, 22, is rightly cautious. Beschi, *ASAtene* NS 29–30 (1967–8), 422–28, tentatively detects Sophocles/Dexion depicted on the Telemachus monument; contrast Aleshire, *Asklepieion*, 10, n. 4, who also questions, 10–11, whether Sophocles was in reality associated with the cult of the city Asclepium at all, though soon linked with it in legend.*

[117] See Lloyd-Jones, *Justice of Zeus*, 212, n. 13.

[118] See the passages of Wilamowitz and Kern cited in Edelstein, *Asclepius*, II.109, n. 2.

[119] Dodds, *Greeks and the Irrational*, 49.

Euthydemus of Eleusis, introducing or welcoming or shaping new cults. Their importance should not be exaggerated, however. None of the individuals changed the direction of religious thought or founded a sect; they merely introduced cults, or wrote religious rules, as many others had done before them. And it is very unlikely that any of them brought new gods, as do the introducers of cults in myths, to a wholly unsuspecting city. In each case, there is good evidence that the Athenians already knew something of the god or hero concerned. If a phenomenon such as the spread of the cult of Asclepius or Pan is considered not case by case but as a whole, a Philippides or a Telemachus comes to appear as an agent rather than as an instigator of change. In the foundation of cults, one sees both the scope available, even within Greek polytheism, for individual action, and the narrow and traditional limits within which it is confined.

The second topic is that of motivation. If one asks why a particular cult has been introduced, explanations of very various types can, of course, be offered. At one level, the influence of oracles and visions and dreams will be important, as our examples have shown.[120] The most interesting question is perhaps whether those who introduced or received cults hoped to secure defined practical goods thereby, as a particular pragmatic view of pagan religion might cause one to predict. Only in a few cases does this prove to be true. Asclepius was introduced to bring health to the Athenians, Aeacus to help them to conquer Aegina, Theseus (possibly) to aid them against Skyros; but there the list ends. (Ancient sources also claim that shrines or statues of both Apollo and Heracles with the epithet Alexikakos were consecrated during the great plague; but in both cases the sculptors named appear to have worked much earlier.[121]) More commonly, the cult was instituted after the benefit had been received: sometimes in fulfilment of a vow made in time of danger, sometimes apparently as a spontaneous expression of gratitude. A conditional vow made before a battle was, of course, in one sense a way of seeking a practical good from the gods; but psychologically such 'thank-offering' cults (whether pledged in advance or not) were also, above all, celebrations of the great event. Of these commemorative cults, some probably remained just that, and faded away in time, while others cut loose from the occasion of the foun-

---

[120] Note too that two subsidiary altars were founded in Asclepius' precinct, one perhaps by Telemachus himself, 'by divine command' (*IG* II².4355, 4358: *CEG* 763, 765).

[121] See Paus. 1.3.4, with commentaries; Σ Ar. *Ran.* 501, with S. Woodford, 'Herakles Alexikakos Reviewed', *AJA* 80 (1976), 291–94; Tagalidou, *Herakles*, 9–19. On responses to the plague see Ch. 10, n. 7.

dation, acquired new functions, and survived: Boreas' shrine perhaps fell into neglect,[122] while Pan, as we have seen, found a new niche with the Nymphs and lived on. What is truly striking is the extent to which the new foundations of the fifth century reflect in one way or another its great historical centrepiece, the struggle against Persia. The cults of Artemis Agrotera, Zeus Tropaios, Pan, Boreas, Artemis Aristoboule, Eukleia, Theseus (probably), Nemesis, Zeus Eleutherios, Athena Nike, and (eventually at least) Ajax on Salamis all in different degrees testify to the unique intensity with which the national crisis and triumph were experienced. The Parthenon itself was seen in the fourth century as a kind of memorial to the victory.[123] Existing festivals, too, could be reinterpreted or reorganized: the *Herakleia* at Marathon doubtless acquired new splendour, and it came to be believed that the festival of Artemis Mounichia commemorated the exact day of the victory of Salamis won nearby.[124] Possibly a connection even exists between the hero Eurymedon, known from a single dedication in the fourth century, and the famous victory over the Persians won by Cimon at the mouth of the river Eurymedon in 467.[125] In this perspective Greek religion does not appear as a mechanism for controlling the world; it is rather a celebration of achievement—that achievement in the face of Persian hordes which for the Greeks was almost heroic in the literal sense—an affirmation of value.

[122] Note, however, that commemorative cults of Boreas were founded in similar circumstances (doubtless on the Attic model, but possibly mediated through Herodotus) in Thurii, where the wind was granted citizenship and a *kleros*, and Megalopolis (Aelian, *VH* 12.61; Paus. 8.27.14, 8.36.6): Pritchett, *Greek State at War*, III.205. A sacrifice to Boreas is also mentioned in Menander, *Carchedonius*, fr. 1 Sandbach.

[123] See Castriota, *Myth, Ethos, Actuality*, 135, with notes [+], on Dem. 22.13.

[124] Plut. *Glor. Ath.* 349 f., *Lys.* 15.1 (doubtless unhistorical: cf. n. 10). The passage of *Glor. Ath.* just cited comes in a list of Athenian sacrifices which Plutarch interprets as χαριστήρια and ἐπινίκια—cf. Ch. 7, n. 6, and n. 10 above; Pritchett, *Greek State at War*, III.172–83; and on the commemorative festivals of other states Gauer, *Weihgeschenke* (n. 11), 16 (and ibid. *passim* for the rich dedicatory material). Even the day of Athena's victory over Poseidon was commemorated (Pritchett, *Greek State at War*, III.168). Note too the synchronization of various Persian-war battles with the first day of the *Thargelia*, Aelian *VH* 2.25. Cf. F. Gearing, 'Preliminary Notes on Ritual in Village Greece', in J. G. Peristiany ed., *Contributions to Mediterranean Sociology* (Paris 1968), 65–72, at 70: 'Independence day and the Annunciation are the same day . . . men say the day marks the beginnings of freedom from sin and freedom from the Turks.'

[125] *IG* II².4567 (Piraeus); the connection is made by Garland, *Piraeus*, 22.

ANNEXE: 'FOREIGN' GODS

It was argued above that there is no point in trying to generalize about foreign cults.[126] They need to be considered one by one, with close attention to the social framework in which each occurs. There come into consideration some nine.[127]

With the first, the 'Mother of the Gods', we encounter a great puzzle and great paradox at the heart of religious and civic life. By, at latest, the end of the fifth century, there was a shrine of the Mother, the Metroon, next to, or even within, a symbolic centre of Athenian political life, the Council House; the practice of depositing in it objects of public significance, documents above all, is attested in the fourth century.[128] By the 460s, the Lesser Mysteries honouring the 'Mother at Agrai' had been associated, as a preliminary, with the Greater Mysteries of Demeter at Eleusis.[129] But who was this 'Mother' who watched over state documents and prepared Athenians for the most sacred of all their rites? By the late fifth century the Mother at the Metroon was certainly in some sense the great Mother of the Gods, the Phrygian Mountain Mother, the figure sometimes known as Cybele who nurses lions on her lap and loves 'the boom of kettle-drums and castanets and blazing torches'. A famous cult-image in the Metroon, a work of Phidias or his pupil Agoracritus, showed her with drum and lions.[130] The Mother subsequently worshipped elsewhere in Attica was the same.[131] About 'Mother at Agrai' very little is known except her name, but her shrine too could be called a 'Metroon'.[132] Possibly the original

---

[126] Cf. Burkert's protest, *Mystery Cults*, 2–3.

[127] I omit 'Herakles Pankrates' (mentioned by Baslez, 'Cultes et dévotions' (n. 29), 293, n. 29), since a serious judgement of that cult must await the imminent publication by E. Vikelas (cf. Tagalidou, *Herakles*, 159–65).*

[128] The strict *terminus ante* for the Metroon's existence is provided by the statue of Agoracritus/Phidias. According to a probable restoration in *IG* I³.138.11–12, the *boule* already appointed its *tamiai* in the 430s. Its familiar use as an archive is first reliably attested in Dem. 19.129 of 343 (Rhodes, *Boule*, 31, n. 6) but goes back, some suppose, to the first establishment of a public archive *c*.405 (A. L. Boegehold, *AJA* 76, 1972, 23–30; Thomas, *Oral Tradition*, 39–40); for related functions see *SEG* XXVI 72.12, with R. S. Stroud, *Hesperia* 43 (1974), 177, n. 77 (consecration to Mother of counterfeit coins: 375/4, and perhaps earlier); A. M. Woodward, ibid. 25 (1956), 98–100 (storage of sacred objects: by *c*.392).

[129] Robertson's proposal, *Festivals and Legends*, 27, to dissociate the Lesser Mysteries from Mother at Agrai is puzzling: where were they held if not in the Metroon there?

[130] Arrian, *Peripl. M. Eux.* 9.1; for further sources see Naumann, *Die Ikonographie der Kybele*, 159. 'Kettle drums': Pind. *Dith.* II. 9–11 Snell/Maehler, cf. *Hymn. Hom.* 14; other Pindaric refs. are *Pyth.* 3.77 f., frs. 80, 95, 96 Snell/Maehler, and cf. *Isth.* 7.3.

[131] See Vermaseren, *Corpus Cultus Cybelae*, II.3–67 (Athens), 68–97 (Piraeus), 110–20 (Attica: there are also figurines of Cybele in the museum at Brauron). On the Piraeus see also now J. Petrocheilou, *ArchEph* 131, 1992 [1993], 21–65.

[132] Clidemus *FGrH* 323 F 1.

Mother had been differently and more demurely imagined, as Rhea or more probably as Earth or as Earth/Demeter.[133] Certainly it was henceforth very common for old Greek goddesses such as Ge or Demeter or Rhea to be identified with Cybele by poets and theologians; syncretism was here a means of assimilating and domesticating the potentially disquieting foreign power.[134] In that case it may be too simple to say that the Mother of the Metroon simply 'is' the wild Mountain Mother. But she certainly did not spurn comparison with her. By whatever process, a goddess linked with ecstasy, or assimilable to one who was, came to occupy a position of considerable symbolic importance in Athenian life. Cybele in charge of the state documents is an image no less startling than that of Dionysus wedded to the *archon basileus*' wife.[135]

The origin of the singular cult was explained in a story much repeated by the lexicographers of late antiquity, but not reliably attested before the emperor Julian. The Athenians had executed, by 'hurling him into the pit', a Phrygian who 'initiated women to the Mother'; plague or crop-failure followed, and on the advice of an oracle they levelled the pit and built a council-chamber and shrine of the Mother on the site (perhaps) of the actual killing. According to one remarkable variant, the Phrygian had preached that the Mother was returning to Attica in search of her daughter; thus Mother was assimilated to Demeter bereft of Persephone, just as she is in a

---

[133] See E. Will in *Éléments orientaux dans la religion grecque ancienne: Colloque de Strasbourg 1958* (Paris 1960), 95–112, esp. 103, 111. He shows that the true indigenous παμμήτωρ is Earth (Aesch. *PV* 90, etc.), not Rhea; but stresses how faint is the evidence for actual cult of a 'Mother' prior to Magna Mater in Greece. 'Mother at Agrai' retains an identity distinct from Magna Mater, but only because she is identified via the Mysteries with Demeter (Hesych., Suda, *Anecd. Bekk.* I.334. 11, s.v. Ἄγραι).

[134] Mother is identified with Demeter (Eur. *Hel.* 1301–68; cf. Melanippides *PMG* 764 and perhaps already Pind. *Isth.* 7.3), Earth (Soph. *Phil.* 391–402, fr. 269a51 Radt), and Rhea (Eur. *Bacch.* 128), and closely associated with Dionysus (Eur. *Palam.* fr. 586 Nauck; *Bacch.* 78–79, 120–34; and already Pind. *Dith.* II.9 ff.; *Isth.* 7.3 ff.). Cf. (with later evidence) R. Kannicht, *Euripides, Helena*, II (Heidelberg 1969), 328–32; A. Henrichs, *HSCP* 80 (1976), 253, n. 3; G. Sfameni Gasparro in *Hommages à M. J. Vermaseren*, III (Leiden 1978), 1148–87. Rather heterogeneous archaeological evidence for an association between the Metroon or Cybele and the Eleusinian cult is offered by H. Thompson, *Hesperia* 6 (1937), 206–208; the strongest item is *IG* II².140, an Eleusinian law to be displayed outside (not kept within) the Metroon. The presence of Cybele votives in precincts of Demeter is indecisive, as they also appear e.g. in Artemis' precinct at Brauron (cf. in general B. Alroth in *Gifts to the Gods*, 9–19); more interesting is *ABV* 705, 39 quater (Metzger, *Recherches*, 22, no. 43), a BF olpe showing Demeter, Kore, and a lion. For non-Attic evidence, and the concept of 'domestication', see Versnel, *Ter Unus*, 108–109.

[135] The paradox is rightly stressed by N. Loraux, *Les mères en deuil* (Paris 1990), 101–19; she seeks to explain it in terms of Greek attitudes to mothers. Mother had somewhat similar functions in Smyrna and Colophon (Graf, *Nordionische Kulte*, 317)—an argument against the view that an indigenous mother had preceded her in the role at Athens?

famous ode of Euripides' *Helen*.[136] The story presents a religious world that is thrillingly volatile, in which dramatic conversions occur. (A similar volatility is presupposed by those moderns who argue that Cybele 'came to Athens' suddenly, perhaps in 430, and was granted political functions not associated hitherto with any god or goddess.) The account is obviously not true (to speak dogmatically)—or rather, even if it were true, we could not know it to be so, so closely would reality on this view have imitated an aetiological legend of familiar type. And we may doubt whether it is ancient enough even to provide evidence for Athenian perceptions of the cult.[137] This myth having been effaced, the history of Cybele's arrival in Attica (that is to say, perhaps, of her superimposition on an earlier cult) becomes almost a blank page.[138] The evidence of the *agora* excavations cannot be decisive, because even if the 'small temple of the Mother of *c*.525–500'[139] beside the Council House complex could be so identified with complete security, we would still be

[136] Julian *Orat.* 5.159a; Σ Aeschin. 3.187; Photius β 61 and p. 422 Naber (the latter = Suda μ 1003 and some paroemiographers); the variant Σ Ar. *Plut.* 431, whence Suda β 99. On the *Helen* chorus (1301–68) in this regard see esp. G. Cerri, *QS* 18 (1983), 155–60, 179–82.

[137] For the other view see esp. Cerri, *QS* 18 (1983), 155–95. He argues that Σ Aeschin. 3.187, where the close association of the Metroon with the *bouleuterion* 'because of that Phrygian' is said to be mentioned ἐν τοῖς Φιλιππικοῖς, proves the story to have been told in a fourth-cent. historian of Philip, either Theopompus or Anaximenes. But that phrase without citation of an author can surely only refer, as regularly in these and other scholia, to the *Philippics* of Demosthenes as read with a commentary; and since Demosthenes does not tell the story, we are back with a late antique commentary (possibly on 8.45 = 10.16 βαράθρῳ or 10.53 βουλευτήρια, unless indeed the ref. should have been to 19.129). The argument that the story is based on a good knowledge of Attic *Realien* appears to founder on the claim in Photius that the Metroon was built on the spot where 'they killed' (ἀνεῖλον) the *metragyrtes*, sc. over the quondam pit: Cerri's suggestion that the verb here, in a Byzantine lexicographer, has the old technical sense of 'take up for burial' is unconvincing.

[138] N. Frapiccini, 'L'arrivo di Cibele in Attica', *PP* 42 (1987), 12–26, is a useful survey.

[139] See Thompson, *Hesperia* 6 (1937), 135–40; Thompson/Wycherley, *Agora*, 30–31. For alternative identifications, not very compelling, see Boersma, *Building Policy*, 31–32 (Zeus); Cerri, *QS* 18 (1983), 173 (Demeter); Frapiccini, 'L'arrivo di Cibele', 19 (Zeus Eleutherios); E. D. Francis, *Idea and Image in Fifth-Century Greece* (London 1990), 118–20 (built *c*.460 as an archive: but against this chronology see T. L. Shear Jr., *Hesperia* 62, 1993, 418–29). It is generally accepted that after the destruction of the archaic temple in the Persian wars Meter was rehoused in the adjacent Council House (or that this was her first home), and was left in sole possession of it when the new *bouleuterion* was built *c*.405. She would thus have been uncomfortably perched in an unidentified corner of a secular building, whose acknowledged gods were not her (Antiphon 6.45), from 479 to *c*.405. It would be more attractive to suppose, unless there is a decisive archaeological objection, that the archaic temple was put back in use, the old *bouleuterion* being perhaps annexed to it after 405. (No text before Σ Aeschin. 3.187 states that the Metroon was actually inside a *bouleuterion*, whether functioning or disused. But it must have been if the development whereby storage of documents 'in the *bouleuterion*' gives way *c*.350 to storage 'in the Metroon' is a mere change in nomenclature [so Rhodes, *Boule*, 31, n. 6]; in other contexts, however, the name Metroon certainly occurs earlier—see e.g. *IG* II².1445.24 and even a *horos*, *Agora* XIX H14.) The Metroon was the centre of an active cult (see n. 143 below; and for a votive, *Hesperia* 6, 1937, 204), though this required no more at the minimum than the outdoor altar (Aeschin. 1.60–61).

left to ask whether this archaic Mother was identical with the Magna Mater of the East. There is, however, no difficulty of principle in supposing that she was, as the great Mother was certainly honoured in the sixth century in other parts of Greece. Allusions to her in Attic texts begin about 430, but so too, Aeschylus aside, does Athenian literature; the earlier silence counts for very little.[140] The cult-statue by Phidias or Agoracritus proves that she was publicly accepted in the last quarter of the fifth century, not necessarily that she became so only then. A small marble votive of about 500 from the acropolis which probably depicts her[141] should perhaps tip the balance towards an early date—but one must certainly allow that it does not prove that she was very widely known, still less that she received public cult.

The Greek sense of order, it has often been said, curbed the ugliest excesses of the oriental devotion. It was a portent, not the start of a movement, when, according to Plutarch, one unfortunate unmanned himself on the altar of the Twelve Gods just before the departure of the great expedition to Sicily. Hellenic restraint is not very apparent, however, on a superb krater of about 440 now in Ferrara.[142] A goddess who holds a lion, and a god with snakes in his hair sit tranquilly side by side in a temple; they are approached by worshippers in procession, the foremost holding a winnowing-fan. Behind, ecstatic dancing takes place to the music of flute and castanet. Here everything is disorder: snake-handling men and women,

[140] On Cybele's coming to Greece see W. Burkert, *Structure and History in Greek Mythology and Ritual* (Berkeley 1979), 102–104; Graf, *Nordionische Kulte*, 107–15 [+]. She was apparently established in Ionia by about 600, familiar perhaps in the Peloponnese in the sixth cent. (J. de la Genière, *CRAI* 1986, 29–46; ead., *ArchDelt* 43 1988 [1993]/*Chron.* 113–15), and well known to Pindar (see Henrichs, *HSCP* 80, 1976, 253–57). She is named (as Kybala) on a graffito from Locri Epizephyrii of 600–550 (Jeffery, *Local Scripts*, 464 A, pl. 78.2) and by Hipponax (fr. 127 West, Kybebe), but has recently vanished from the Siphnian frieze (V. Brinkmann, *BCH* 109, 1985, 123). For the first Attic literary allusions see previous note, and Cratinus frs. 66 K/A ἀγερσικύβηλις, 87 κύβηβον; Eur. *Hipp.* 144, *Cretans* fr. 79.13 Austin (Mountain Mother); Ar. *Av.* 746, 876 f. Cf. in general Nilsson, *Geschichte*, 725–27.

[141] Akr. Mus. no. 655, cf. Naumann, *Die Ikonographie der Kybele*, 145, and 308, no. 111; there are also a few small terracottas (ibid. 145, no. 140, and Vermaseren, *Corpus Cultus Cybelae*, II.107, no. 359). But the 'Cybele in a temple' identified on a BF amphora of *c.*530 in the British Museum (*ABV* 326 London B 49; Naumann, *Die Ikonographie der Kybele*, 117) has rightly been discounted by Shapiro, *Art and Cult*, 59 f. and Frapiccini, 'L'arrivo di Cibele', 20–21.

[142] Excesses: so e.g. Wilamowitz, *Hermes* 14 (1879), 194–95. Plutarch: *Nic.* 13.3–4. Krater: from Spina, now in Ferrara (Mus. Nat. Arch. T 128); cf. Naumann, *Die Ikonographie der Kybele*, 171–75, and 312, no. 134 [+]. E. Simon, *Opfernde Götter* (Berlin 1953), 79–87 identifies the deities as Cybele and Sabazius, whose cults are, however, usually seen as distinct even if (Ar. *Av.* 876; Strabo 10.3.15, 18 [470–71]) related; perhaps the male is rather Attis? (cf. n. 165). For other views see Naumann, *Die Ikonographie der Kybele*; App. 2, n. 59 below; and for principled agnosticism, C. Bérard in *A City of Images*, tr. D. Lyons (Princeton 1989), 23–29.

Greeks and Orientals, even adults and children are all tumbled together in the dance. But what realities other than those of the imagination the splendid scene may reflect is scarcely possible to say. The many surviving votives tell us much about the popularity of the Mother, nothing about the forms in which she was worshipped. At the Metroon she had a public priest, and a public festival, the *Galaxia*,[143] in which, because of her civic functions, officials such as members of the *boule* took part; but it seems to have been a tranquil and somewhat unimportant affair, which took its name, like many an old Attic festival, from a homely festival-food. This γαλαξία, a barley porridge cooked in milk, is perhaps the strongest clue that at the Metroon, Cybele was superimposed on an older, indigenous goddess with traditions of her own.

It was perhaps only at the ceremonies of private associations that the boom of kettle-drums was to be heard. The sanctuary of one such association was excavated in 1855 by French soldiers stationed in the Piraeus during the Franco-Russian war. The material uncovered by the soldiers does not pre-date about 300, but the Mother was doubtless worshipped in the Piraeus earlier, at this site or another; we have from the port a fourth-century epitaph of a citizen woman whom her husband describes as 'attendant and solemn matron of the all-bearing Mother'.[144] There is a problem about the early history of the excavated shrine, since two distinct cult-societies, one of citizens and one of metics, both appear to have control of it at about the same time, in the early third century. A votive of about 300 (?) was dedicated by Manes and Mika, who sound like non-Greeks.[145] But all later texts show the citizen group in charge.

The shrine continued in use until the high Roman empire, and attracted dedications to an expanding range of powers; an offering was apparently made to Men Tyrannos here in 213/2, as if there

[143] See Deubner, *Attische Feste*, 216; the first attestation is a certain conjecture by Wilamowitz in Theophr. *Char.* 21.11. Priest: *IG* II².4595 (328/7). The non-Attic month-name Galaxion does not necessarily have any relation to the Attic festival: see *RE* s.v. *Galaxios, Galaxion.**

[144] *IG* II².6288 = *CEG* 566: μητρὸς παντοτέκνου πρόπολος σεμνή τε γέραιρα; *IG* II².4563 ('400–350') is a dedication from the Piraeus, by an unknown donor, to 'Mother of the Gods'.*

[145] *IG* II².1316, almost certainly of 272/1 (*Hesperia* 26, 1957, 54–57), was issued by citizens and strongly resembles an interrelated group of texts, one of which (*IG* II².1327) was found during the Metroon excavations of 1855; *IG* II².1273, of a year following the archonship of a Nicias (thus 281/0 or *c*.265/4), was issued by metics and also derives from the excavation. Thus Ferguson's suggestion ('Attic Orgeones', 137–40) that citizens took the shrine over from metics is still just possible on the earlier dating of *IG* II².1273 (recently advocated by L. Arnaoutoglou, *ZPE* 104, 1994, 103–106, against e.g. M. J. Osborne, *ZPE* 78, 1989, 230, n. 97). Manes and Mika: *IG* II².4609, Vermaseren, *Corpus Cultus Cybelae*, II.82, no. 267 (but cf. *LGPN* II s.h. vv.).*

were a kind of fellowship between all foreign gods. The annually appointed priestess seems to have collected money for the goddess from non-members, who, in turn, could probably make dedications in the shrine and, no doubt, watch some of the rites. (Of these, the only ones known to us by name are 'both the *Attideia*'.[146]) In that case, of course, the 'private' shrine does not differ so greatly in function from one that was publicly financed.

Another sanctuary of Cybele, recently discovered at Moschato, again in the Piraeus region, and dated by its excavators to the early fourth century, may have belonged to a similar association. Cybele and her lion were both found, side by side, on separate bases in a small temple.[147] Permanent private associations are perhaps the formalized descendants of earlier revel-bands that existed only for the duration of a particular rite. Such temporary *thiasoi* are attested in other cults, and it may have been by assembling them that *Metragyrtai*, 'Collectors for the Mother', promoted the worship of their goddess.[148]

If we have traced the relation between public and private cult aright, it is most revealing.[149] The Mother of the Metroon assumes some of the traits of Cybele, not unnaturally given the Greek perception that the gods of all nations are all at bottom the same. But she continues to be honoured in the traditional way. More exotic rites are reserved for private associations—whose practices are, however,

[146] See Ferguson, 'Attic Orgeones', 107–15, 137–40 (the fundamental discussion: 108, n. 52 gives bibliog. on the excavation history); Vermaseren, *Corpus Cultus Cybelae*, II.68–97 (where, however, new evidence on archon dates is neglected). There are some twenty decrees and inscribed dedications (for the latter see Ferguson, 'Attic Orgeones', 108, n. 52: on *IG* II².4714 cf. *SEG* XXXV 143). Men: L. Robert, *BCH* 60 (1936), 206–207 (= Robert, *OMS* II.913–14) on *IG* II².4687a, addenda, p. 353. (For other dedications to Men in Attica—never made by citizens—see S. Lauffer, *Die Bergwerkssklaven von Laureion²*, Wiesbaden 1979, 178–86; E. N. Lane, *Corpus Monumentorum Religionis Dei Menis*, III, Leiden 1976, 1–16; the oldest is probably *IG* II².4684, of ? c.300, but a date c.340 has been claimed for the fine votive relief M. B. Comstock and C. C. Vermeule, *Sculpture in Stone*, Boston 1976, 53, no. 78, and there is already a slave Manodoros in Ar. *Av.* 657 [Masson, *MH* 45, 1988, 6].) Collections: *IG* II².1328.11, 1329.15; *Attideia*: *IG* II².1315.10; relation to non-members: see *IG* II².1329.13. For a problem see n. 29 above.

[147] See Travlos, *Bildlexikon*, 288–97 [+]. We now see that the small 'Cybeles in a *naiskos*', a most common form of votive, have a large-scale equivalent. Travlos plausibly suggests that the adjacent buildings form part of a single complex.

[148] The first attestation is Cratinus fr. 66 K/A, ἀγερσικύβηλις (used contemptuously, as is μητραγύρτης in Arist. *Rhet.* 1405ᵃ20). Antiphanes and Menander both wrote a *Menagyrtes* or *Metragyrtes* (fr. 152 K/A of the former describes a magical cure), Philemon an *Agyrtes*. The term θίασον συνάγειν was applied to the recruitment both of temporary (Dem. 19.281; *IG* II².1177.4) and permanent (*IG* II².1297.4) *thiasoi*.

[149] Cf. Versnel, *Ter Unus*, 110, on Mother's 'double identity'. See too P. Borgeaud, 'Comment lui trouver un nom?', in *Les mères* (= *Nouvelle revue de psychanalyse* 45, spring 1992), 173–93, who speaks (189) of 'un procès visant à intégrer l'autochthone à l'intérieur d'une scène exotique'.

in a sense licensed by the assimilation of their goddess to the venerable native at the middle of the *agora*. It is conceivable (all evidence
being lacking) that the ceremonies of Mother at Agrai also took an
ecstatic turn.[150] In that event, it was the status of the cult as an 'initiation' into 'Mysteries' that provided a suitable frame for the
Mother's wilder manifestations.

Closely associated with the Mother are her attendants, the
Corybantes. They are attested (first in Aristophanes' *Wasps* of 422)
as patrons of a homoeopathic ritual in which madness is cured by
music and ecstatic dancing, of just the type associated with the
Mother herself. But these Corybantic initiations, as they were
called, were not confined to the mad, as the Platonic Socrates can
suggest that a sane and respectable interlocutor may have experienced them. They must have much resembled the kind of informal
rites in honour of the Mother which we have just postulated.[151]

With Sabazius and Adonis we are still in the world of informal
rites. To mourn Adonis, a group of women came together at the
house of one of their number. Nothing is said of priests or priestesses, and it may be that no formal structure existed at all, but individuals simply made arrangements with their friends year by year.
The festival was, notoriously, popular with courtesans, but there is
every reason to think that many married women celebrated it too.
An old man's complaint in Aristophanes about 'the luxury of the
women, their cymbal-beating and constant Sabazius rites, and all
this worship of Adonis on the roofs' suggests that they may have
assembled to dance for Phrygian Sabazius in much the same informal way. But there were also 'initiations for Sabazius', for which a
priest or priestess assembled a temporary *thiasos* (perhaps consisting
predominantly of men), as in the Corybantic initiations. Sabazius
too was a god who possessed his worshippers, and the rituals of the
two cults were perhaps not dissimilar. An allusion in Aristophanes
suggests that participation by slaves was conceivable, and perhaps
even characteristic. And a mysterious text possibly shows that there
existed a society of *Sabaziastai* (of unknown civic status) in the
Piraeus in 342/1.[152]

---

[150] So Frapiccini, 'L'arrivo di Cibele'. Cf. ns. 132–33 above.

[151] See Dodds, *Greeks and the Irrational*, 75–80 [+]. Sane interlocutor: Pl. *Euthyd.* 277d, on
which cf. Dodds, *Greeks and the Irrational*, 99 n. 104. On the association with Cybele see ibid.
96, n. 90 (but contrast Graf, *Nordionische Kulte*, 331); Pl. *Leg.* 790d, however, attests female
Corybantic initiators, while *Metragyrtai* are normally conceived as male.

[152] *Adonia*: Men. *Sam.* 38–46, with N. Weill, *BCH* 94 (1970), 591–93; Ar. *Lys.* 387–89
(with rites of Sabazius). Initiations of Sabazius: Dem. 18.259–60 (cf. 19.199, 249, 281) and
Theophr. *Char.* 27.8. Sociology of the *Adonia*: J. J. Winkler, *The Constraints of Desire*
(London 1990), 199–202. Possession in the cult of Sabazius: Ar. *Vesp.* 9; Iambl. *Myst.* 3.9–10,
and the term Σαβοί (Harp. s.v. Σαβοί) applied to worshippers; for the sparse literary

Two further foreign gods appear in the Accounts of the Treasurers of the Other Gods ('other' than Athena) in 429/8. (We also meet there a figure known simply as *Xenikos Theos*; but a parallel in Plato suggests that he is 'God of Strangers' rather than 'Stranger God'.) With a similar text of 423/2 this document gives us a unique (though still fragmentary) panorama of cults the monies of which were under public control.[153] The two foreign gods who appear, therefore, had in contrast to Adonis and Sabazius been formally adopted in Athens. They are Bendis of Thrace and Adrasteia, and they seem to have shared a treasury or accounts. This Adrasteia is a puzzling figure, but when she first appears, in an epic fragment and in Aeschylus, she is located on Mount Ida in Phrygia, and is thus an appropriate associate for Thracian Bendis.[154] Of her cult we hear no more. Bendis, as we have seen, came to receive prominent public worship, without, however, leaving the world of private associations entirely. Her shrine in the Piraeus remained the property of a society of Thracians; at least one other *thiasos* that honoured her is attested; and we even hear that people 'made collections for the goddess'.[155] About another Thracian goddess, Cotyto, we can say only, on the evidence of Eupolis' play *Baptai*, that Athenians knew of her and of Greeks who worshipped her, and could be invited by comedy to despise both. If she had worshippers in Athens itself, nothing is known of their doings.[156]

There remains one foreign god, and perhaps another. Egyptian Ammon was receiving costly dedications by the 370s, and by the 330s at the very latest had a public priest and shrine and (occasionally at least) a festival. Many of the dedications were made by public *theoroi* who had gone to his Libyan home to take him gold offerings and, no doubt, to consult the oracle about the welfare of Athens;

testimonia, see E. Lane, *Corpus Cultus Iovis Sabazii*, II: *The Other Monuments and Literary Evidence* (Leiden 1985), 46–51; cf. R. Fellmann in M. J. Vermaseren ed., *Die orientalischen Religionen im Römerreich* (Leiden 1981), 316–40. Male initiates of Sabazius are unmistakably present in Dem. and Theophr., cited above (cf. Dem. 18.265, ἐτελούμην); Dem. 18.260 also mentions 'old women' (initiates, or assistants?). Slaves: Ar. *Vesp.* 9. Sabaziasts: p. 335 below. The oracle which supposedly forced the Athenians to abandon their initial hostility to Sabazius is a transparent scholiast's invention to explain a supposed contradiction in the text (ΣDem. 19.281).

153 *IG* I³.383 and 369.55–97. 'God of Strangers': *IG* I³.383.308, cf. *Leg.* 879e.

154 *Phoronis* fr. 2.4 in M. Davies, *Epicorum Graecorum Fragmenta* (Göttingen 1988); Aesch. fr. 158.2 Radt.

155 Other *thiasos*: n. 66 above. Collections: Photius β 126 s.v. Βενδῖς· Θρᾳκία δαίμων, ὀπαδὸς Ἀρτέμιδος. διὸ καὶ οἱ ἀγείροντες αὐτῇ [Theodoridis: ἐγείροντες αὐτὴν cod.] διλογχιδίῳ [διλογχιαίῳ cod.] ἐχρῶντο; but the correction is not quite certain, as in Photius δ 590 s.v. δίλογχον Βενδῖν we hear that it is Ἀθήνησι πομπεύοντες . . . τοῖς Βενδιδείοις who carry two spears.

156 See Eupolis frs. 76–98 K/A; Jameson et al., *Selinous*, 23–25.

such missions are doubtless the reason why a sacred trireme was eventually named *Ammonias*. But in the *Birds* of 415, Aristophanes already seems to take the idea of consulting Ammon for granted.[157] We should finally mention 'Heavenly Aphrodite'. She was perhaps oriental in origin, and was certainly the form of Aphrodite who was felt by Greeks most to resemble the comparable figures they encountered in the east.[158] If the identification of a recently discovered altar is correct, she received public cult in Athens by about 500 BC. A yet more recent discovery is an offering box ($\theta\eta\sigma\alpha\nu\rho\delta$) of the early fourth century found near the acropolis and designed to accommodate 'pre-marriage offerings [$\pi\rho o\tau\epsilon\lambda\epsilon\iota\alpha$ $\gamma\dot{\alpha}\mu o$] to Aphrodite Ourania' of a drachma. The recipient of such tribute must have been Aphrodite in her most respectable guise.[159] The forms of her worship, unfortunately, are otherwise quite unknown.

One easy conclusion emerges from this survey. The common supposition that the last quarter of the fifth century saw a sudden outburst of interest in barbarian gods is simply false. What really changes in the last quarter of the century is the character of our evidence. Sabazius has to wait until 422 to appear in literature, because before 425 nothing is left of the one genre in which he is at all likely

---

[157] On the fourth-cent. evidence see the brilliant study of A. M. Woodward, *BSA* 57 (1962), 5–13 (cf. *SEG* XXI 241, 562), who argues that the shrine was built in the 360s; this shrine of Ammon or another was apparently in private hands in the third cent., *IG* II².1282. On Ammon in Greece see C. J. Classen, *Historia* 8 (1959), 349–55, and on the Ammonias, Rhodes on Arist. *Ath. Pol.* 61.7. *Av.*: 619, 716; Plut. *Cim.* 18.7 and *Nic.* 13.2 are less straightforward.*

[158] Paus. 1.14.7 derives the cult from Assyria, via intermediate stages. Otherwise, the evidence adduced for oriental origin appears to be the coincidence of her epithet with Astarte's title 'Queen of Heaven' (Jer. 7: 18, 44: 17–19: so e.g. Burkert, *Greek Religion*, 155; the epithet is perhaps presupposed by Hes. *Theog.* 154–210), and the geographical diffusion of the cult (cf. E. Wüst in *RE* s.v. *Urania*, 935–41). Herodotus' regular application of the name Aphrodite Ourania to foreign gods, however (e.g. 1.105.2, 1.131.3), reflects his normal assimilating practice, and suggests that for him she is a familiar Greek goddess; what is significant is merely his choice of 'Aphrodite Ourania' rather than plain 'Aphrodite'. The same may be said of the tendency of Phoenicians, when speaking Greek, to identify their goddess as 'Aphrodite Ourania' (*IG* II².4636, cf. n. 29 above; *Inscr. Dél.* 1719, 2305). Her special characteristics in cult largely elude us (cf. S. Settis, *XEΛΩNH, Saggio sull'Afrodite Urania di Fidia*, Pisa 1966, 95–159; and cf. J. Rudhardt in *Chypre des origines au moyen-âge*, Geneva 1975, 131–33; V. Pirenne in E. Lipiński ed., *Studia Phoenicia* 5, Louvain 1987, 145–56 and in *AntCl* 57, 1988, 142–57); on iconography see most recently C. M. Edwards and E. B. Harrison, *Hesperia* 53 (1984), 59–72; 379–88. On Aphrodite's antecedents in general see D. Boedeker, *Aphrodite's Entry into Greek Epic* (Leiden 1974), 1–17.

[159] Altar: T. L. Shear Jr., *Hesperia* 53 (1984), 24–40, and Paus. 1.14.7 (cf. Wycherley, *Testimonia*, 49); but the reanalysis of the faunal remains by D. S. Reese, *Hesperia* 58 (1989), 63–70, appears to weaken the identification. Offering-box: K. Tsakos, *Horos* 8–9 (1990–1), 17–28 (*SEG* XLI 182). He associates it with the precinct of Eros and Aphrodite on the north slope of the acropolis (Travlos, *Pictorial Dictionary*, 228–32).*

to be mentioned, Old Comedy.[160] Of the foreign gods admitted to public cult, Bendis and Adrasteia had already been adopted by 429, Mother and Heavenly Aphrodite perhaps long before that. In the last quarter of the century, by contrast, no foreign god seems to have been officially received. All that can be cited is the expansion of Bendis' cult that probably occurred in or near 413. These details of chronology have their importance. It remains plausible that Athens became more open to foreign gods in the fifth century, because she became in every sense a city with wider horizons;[161] but we cannot argue that she yielded to eastern temptations only when demoralized by plague and a weary war. Scenes of oriental cult perhaps first appear on vases around 450,[162] and possibly we should recognize a special influx of foreign gods around the middle of the century, a little-acknowledged if, on reflection, quite comprehensible aspect of those golden Periclean years. But here too there may be an evidence-trap to be avoided: for it is well known that 'scenes from the life of women', of which scenes of cult are just a form, gained greatly in popularity in vase-painting in the second half of the century.[163]

A second easy conclusion is that the 'foreign gods' were indeed diverse, in nature and in their reception in Athens. Ammon, clearly, is a case apart: unlike the others, he was not, as it were, brought to Athens for the use of the citizens; like other oracular gods, he had still to be consulted in his distant home, and the cult accorded him at Athens was primarily an acknowledgement that the Athenian state did now seek to tap this potent source of prophecy. Of the other foreigners, some were officially adopted by the Athenians, while others remained in the shadows, which, however, they shared with various Greek gods of doubtful repute; Mother's position was ambiguous. Bendis, uniquely, apparently remained, even when adopted, a kind of national symbol for the Thracian community in Athens.[164]

Foreign gods who actually fit the ancient and modern stereotype, orgiastic gods of the kind that Aristophanes depicted being tried and

---

[160] Ar. *Vesp.* 9–10.

[161] Cf. Garland, *New Gods*, 11, 'the comparative lack of religious choice was a feature of conservative and culturally backward communities'. Whence the Athenian reputation in later antiquity for an especial σπουδὴ ἐς τὰ θεῖα (Paus. 1.17.1, 1.24.3; Aelian, *VH* 5.17; Acts 17: 22–23).

[162] Ath. Nat. Mus. 19522, *Paralipomena* 400 (= *LIMC* s.v. *Adonis*, 227, no. 45, cf. 46) of 'c. 450', has usually been interpreted as depicting a ritual associated with Adonis; but cf. Edwards, *Hesperia* 53 (1984), 63–66 (wedding scene). The krater from Ferrara (n. 142) is dated '440–420'. On Bendis see n. 69.

[163] So e.g. J. Boardman, *Athenian Red Figure Vases: The Classical Period* (London 1989), 97.

[164] See above.

expelled from the state, represent therefore only one possible type among many. What it was like for an Athenian to be an adherent of a cult of this type, a worshipper of Adonis or Sabazius, is a question we can barely answer. Of the myths told at this date about Cybele and Sabazius and even Adonis, little is known.[165] We have Demosthenes' portrayal of the supposed antics of Aeschines' mother, not the credo of an actual 'attendant and solemn matron of all-bearing Mother'. Were the ecstatic cults places of sectarian, missionary enthusiasm (like that displayed by the chorus of Euripides' *Bacchae*)?[166] Did a turning to Sabazius or Mother entail in any degree a turning away from other gods? The questions rest. According to men, then and now, such cults appealed especially to the superstitious and sensual sex.[167] But except in the case of the *Adonia*, the evidence available to us scarcely confirms that women predominated. We can only guess whether other forms of social restriction—the barriers between men and women and citizen and non-citizen—were to some extent lowered within the elective cults.[168] On a more mundane level, they would obviously have had some appeal to the many inhabitants of Attica who lived at a distance from their ancestral cults: not just metics but also, for instance, Athenians registered in demes throughout Attica but resident in the Piraeus. (Many 'foreign cults' are first and best attested in the Piraeus; but the 'Piraeus factor' is not reducible simply to the number of foreigners who lived in the port.) Not until the third century BC, however, does it begin to be possible to write a sociological account of the elective cults.[169]

---

[165] A dedication of (?) 350–325 from the Piraeus, with relief, is made to Angdistis (a name borne by the Mother in Phrygia) and Attis; for Agdistis/Angdistis cf. Men. *Theophoroumene* fr. dub. p. 146 Sandbach line 20, and Ch. 10, n. 68; for Attis, n. 146, (?) a fourth-cent. terracotta (H. Thompson, *Hesperia* 20, 1951, 53) and Theopompus Comicus ('saec. V/IV') fr. 28 K/A κολάσομαί σ᾽ ἐγώ/καὶ τὸν σὸν Ἄττιν. Other votive reliefs (Vermaseren, *Corpus Cultus Cybelae*, II.270, 309, 310) hint at mythological associations but defy close interpretation. The Piraeus relief (*IG* II².4671 = Vermaseren, *Corpus Cultus Cybelae*, II.92, no. 308; *LIMC* s.v. *Attis*, 41, no. 416) is discussed by L. E. Roller, 'Attis on Greek Votive Monuments', *Hesperia* 63 (1994), 245–62; she argues strikingly that 'Attis' first becomes a god in Greece, 'Ates' vel sim. being in Phrygia a personal name and also a title borne by chief priests of the Mother.

[166] See Versnel's striking study of *Bacchae* from this perspective in *Ter Unus*, esp. 181–89.*

[167] Ibid. 121, n. 101.

[168] Critics (Demosthenes on Aeschines' mother, and the prosecutors of Phryne) of course insinuated that they were. For the later evidence on membership of such groups see App. 4.

[169] See ibid.

The Trial of Socrates: And a Religious Crisis?

In 399 BC, Socrates was condemned and put to death on a charge of impiety, having declined to suggest that counter-penalty of exile which the jury would doubtless have preferred to impose. Around that bizarre and tragic event cluster a series of quite fundamental questions about the character of Athenian society, and the historical development of Greek religion. Perhaps no execution has been as much discussed as Socrates',[1] except that of Jesus; and a detailed discussion of the related issues would spring the bounds of this book by far. All that can be offered is a sketch-map of the terrain. We will begin with the condemnation of Socrates, pass to other acts of repression against religious unorthodoxy, and ask whether and in what sense it is legitimate to speak of a religious crisis in the late fifth century. And we must raise again from a new perspective the issue of 'new gods'; for a charge of 'introducing new gods'—a standard practice of the Athenian people, as we saw in Chapter 9—figured none the less in the formal indictment against Socrates. An underlying issue that still evokes strong feelings is that of intellectual dissent and the Athenian democracy's response to it. To what extent was there in fact freedom of thought or freedom of religion or freedom of the intellectual (revealingly anachronistic terms) in the vaunted home of *parrhesia* and *isegoria*, political free speech?

But, it may be objected, is it not anachronistic, in a study of the religion of a people, for a chapter to take its start from the trial of one eccentric individual? Would not a contemporary of Socrates have named quite different events as the 'religious crises' of his experience? The second part of the objection, at least, must be allowed. In a sense, Socrates was just one trouble-maker or bad citizen among many put to death by the Athenians.[2] The truly spectacular religious

---

[1] There is an extensive bibliog. in Brickhouse/Smith, *Socrates on Trial*.

[2] So R. W. Wallace, 'Private Lives and Public Enemies: Freedom of Thought in Classical Athens', in A. L. Boegehold and A. C. Scafuro eds., *Athenian Identity and Civic Ideology* (Baltimore 1994), 144.

trials of the period related to the mutilation of the Herms and profa-
nation of the Mysteries in 415, a pair of crimes that stunned all
Athens.[3] And Thucydides tells how the great plague that began in
430, against which all religious remedies proved vain, drove men to
nihilism and despair (just as the Lisbon earthquake of 1755 caused
Voltaire to renounce the optimistic doctrine of Leibniz and Pope
that 'whatever is, is good'[4]). About the effects of both events in the
longer term we can only speculate. Did the experience of 415 make
many Athenians more prone to lash out against persons of suspect
piety, including perhaps Socrates? Had the trauma of the plague, by
contrast, left a residue of disbelief? The two influences in combination might have tended to create a polarization of attitudes.

On the surface, however, civic religion very soon picked itself up
from the plague, any interruption in celebration of the festivals
being very temporary;[5] from the cheerful piety of an Aristophanes
one would never guess that such an event had ever occurred.
Believing societies seem in fact normally to respond to huge natural
catastrophes not by loss of faith but with such reactions as anger
against 'the authorities', search for scapegoats, and, above all, forms
of self-blame and mutual accusation that confirm existing religious
assumptions: the Black Death brought the Church, the Jews, and, of
course, man's sinfulness into disrepute, not God himself. 'Only this
antidote apply | Cease vexing heaven and cease to die', advised
Thomas Dekker in the early seventeenth century.[6] In a sense the
plague strengthened the faith of the Athenians, if it is right to see, for
instance, the purification of Delos and the introduction of Asclepius
as responses to it.[7] As for the impious citizens of 415, a surprising
number were permitted to return to Athens in due course. To sur-

---

[3] So Todd, *Athenian Law*, 312; on the crisis cf. Parker, *Miasma*, 168–70; Ostwald, *Popular Sovereignty*, 537–59; O. Murray in id. ed., *Sympotica* (Oxford 1990), 149–61.

[4] W. Breidert ed., *Die Erschütterung der vollkommenen Welt* (Darmstadt 1994) is a collec-
tion of contemporary responses to the tragedy (also discussed by T. D. Kendrick, *The Lisbon Earthquake*, London 1956).

[5] See J. Mikalson in *Studies Presented to Sterling Dow* (*GRBS* 10, 1984), 423–31.

[6] Cited by P. Slack, *The Impact of PLAGUE in Tudor and Stuart England* (London 1985),
39–40—a superb study which charts the gradual and partial supersession of such attitudes, but
not in favour of explicit atheism; bibliog. on 'Disaster Studies' ibid. 344–45, and cf. P. Ziegler,
The Black Death (London, 1969), chs. 5 and 17. On the plague as *flagellum dei* see the sections
on Cyprian and Gregory in J. Grimm, *Die literarische Darstellung der Pest in der Antike und in der Romania* (Munich 1965).

[7] Cf. Ch. 8, n. 115, and Ch. 9, n. 97; for other responses that have been suggested in ancient
and modern times see Ch. 8, n. 51, and Ch. 9, n. 121; and note too Thuc. 1.118.3 on Apollo's
involvement. Thucydides, 2.64.1, makes Pericles say he was 'hated' because of the plague: cf.
M. Marshall in E. M. Craik ed., *Owls to Athens* (Oxford 1990), 169, who suggests that it was
blamed on Pericles' pollution (Thuc. 1.126–27). Impious citizens: cf. Parker, *Miasma*, 170,
n. 148.

mount these two crises nothing perhaps was required but time. A deeper readjustment may have been needed to cope with the issues raised by supposed impieties of thought such as those of Socrates. And the ground for singling out Socrates is that we happen to know more about the popular prejudice against him than against any other impious intellectual—Diagoras, as it might be, or Anaxagoras. He owes his prominence here to Aristophanes' attacks, not to anachronistic reverence for the pagan saint.

The official charge ran: 'Socrates does wrong by not acknowledging the gods the city acknowledges, and introducing other, new powers [*daimonia*]. He also does wrong by corrupting the young.'8 The exact legal position is unclear, but fortunately little hangs by it; most probably, the practices in the charge were not formally forbidden by a specific law, but were cited as evidence that Socrates was guilty of the broad and undefined offence of 'impiety'.9 A much more serious difficulty is that we know the arguments of Socrates' accusers only as they are refracted through his various defenders. Very broadly, we have to choose between two main interpretations; or rather, since both surely contain some truth, where to place the emphasis between two extremes. According to one, the jurors condemned Socrates because they mistook him for an embodiment of all that was worst in the type of the impious intellectual or sophist. For the other, the general charge of 'corrupting the young' concealed one much more specific: that it was Socrates' teaching which had produced the two men who had harmed the city most, Alcibiades and Critias. And since the memory of the tyrant Critias was the fresher and more bitter of the two, Socrates was particularly liable to be thought, like Critias, a 'hater of the people'. As Aeschines was to tell a jury half a century later, with memorable lack of nuance, 'You [i.e. the Athenian people] put the sophist Socrates to death because he was shown to have educated Critias.'10 On this latter view the issue was fundamentally one of politics rather than of religion. In either case, the decision to prosecute an old man for saying and doing what he had been saying and doing unmolested for so many years must

---

8 Favorinus *ap.* D.L. 2.40. In the phrase νομίζειν θεούς the verb is poised between a reference to 'custom, customary [worship]' (so e.g. Hdt. 4.59.19) and 'belief' (so e.g. Eur. *Supp.* 732, rightly so taken by C. Collard ad loc.): see W. Fahr, *ΘΕΟΥΣ ΝΟΜΙΖΕΙΝ* (*Spudasmata* 26, Hildesheim 1969); Yunis, *A New Creed*, 62–66.

9 See below, n. 63.

10 1.173. For doxography see Brickhouse/Smith, *Socrates on Trial*, 70, n. 29; they cite R. Hackforth, *The Composition of Plato's Apology* (Cambridge 1933), 73–79, as unique to their knowledge in denying the importance of political factors (which they too doubt, 69–87; and cf. M. I. Finley, *Aspects of Antiquity*, London 1968, 58–72).

have been a response to the wounds of recent history:[11] a lost war, a lost empire, an oligarchic *coup*. The problem is to decide whether the Athenians' diagnosis was more specific—'Socrates taught subversives'—or more general—'Socrates embodies the moral malaise that has brought Athens low'.

Before addressing that problem, let us note that the interweaving of religious and political factors is far from being unique to this case. On the contrary, it may be that an accusation of impiety was almost never brought before an Athenian court without political anxiety or hatred being present in the background.[12] But the relation between the two kinds of motivation is not a simple or single one. One possibility is the accusation of 'impiety' or something similar brought against persons whose political attitudes were widely resented, but who had unfortunately failed to commit any other identifiable offence. The attacks at the end of the fourth century on various antidemocratic philosophers were doubtless primarily of this type.[13] Here the formal charge was a screen not just for the prosecutors but for the jurors. But those who supposedly brought similar charges against 'the friends of Pericles' in the 430s had no such reserve of general hostility to draw on. If they were to achieve their own political aims, they had to convince the jurors that the associates of the brightest political star of the day were indeed impious and dangerous men. Different again was the crisis of 415, where a conspiracy to mock the gods was taken as proof of a conspiracy against the state, and the two terrors stoked each other's fires. It will not do, therefore, to deny a given incident all religious content simply because political factors also intrude.

We return to Socrates. The apolitical interpretation of course gains in strength if the accusation of impiety had a foundation in reality. Was Socrates prosecuted, as has lately been suggested, because of a true perception that his teaching subverted the basis of traditional religion? One feature of the historical Socrates certainly

[11] Finley, *Aspects of Antiquity*, stresses that the trauma was not just that of the tyranny of the 30.

[12] As Robin Lane Fox suggests to me. The hierophant Archias, condemned for a technical offence of impiety ([Dem.] 59.116), warned the Theban oligarchs of Pelopidas' impending *coup* in 379/8 (Plut. *Pelop.* 10.3, cf. 14.1), an act that must have been unpopular, however complicated the Athenians' public attitude to the *coup* had to be (R. J. Buck, *Boiotia and the Boiotian League*, Alberta 1994, 72–78; Hornblower, *Greek World*, 209). The political record of the speaker of Lys. 7 was perhaps poor (Todd, *Athenian Law*, 308). About the cases known from Dem. 57.8 and Lys. 5 we know little. See in general Todd, *Athenian Law*, 307–10. The use of charges under the 'Statutes of Recusancy' against persons suspected of treason in sixteenth-cent. England has been compared (see 'Statutes, of Recusancy', in the index to G. R. Elton, *England under the Tudors*[2], London 1974).

[13] Discussed in Ch. 12 below; on the friends of Pericles see later in this chapter.

was exploited by his accusers: for the charge that he 'introduced new powers [*daimonia*]' must, as Plato and Xenophon recognize, allude to his 'divine sign', *daimonion*, though seeking also to implicate him in further innovations left threateningly vague.[14] But stereotype and distortion intrude even here. The prosecution must have argued that Socrates had abandoned the gods of the city in favour of his personal divine voice; but no one who knew anything of the real character of Socrates' sign could suppose that it was in any kind of rivalry with the traditional gods.[15] Possibly a prosecutor could have exploited the kind of sharp remark about revered Athenian myths with which Socrates is credited in Plato's *Euthyphro*;[16] but this too would have been most unjust, criticism of myth being an accepted, and indeed in some ways a pious, practice. Socrates was unorthodox, it has been suggested, in declaring justice, not sacrifice, the key to divine favour, or in postulating gods who were wholly benevolent to mankind.[17] But it is strange to suppose that the fellow-countrymen of Solon would have been stirred to outrage by sentiments such as these. Socrates' actual religious position would never, surely, have caused him to be singled out as a target for attack.

Religious resentment against Socrates was, however, not necessarily the less acute for being misdirected. The portrait of 'Socrates' in Aristophanes' *Clouds* becomes, therefore, a document of prime importance. For our purpose, it does not matter at all whether 'Socrates' bears much relation to the historical figure. What is important is that the play is treated in Plato's *Apology*[18] as a typical expression of the popular prejudices against him. For many jurors, therefore, 'Socrates' was, in caricature, Socrates. And the portrait of Socrates in *Clouds* has an intrinsic interest for our theme which makes it worth pausing over here. Popular fears of impiety are here displayed, much more fully and clearly than in any other source.

'Socrates' is head of a school. He is, in fact, literature's first don. This very obvious fact is also very important. Traditionally, young

---

[14] Pl. *Euthyphr.* 3b; Xen. *Mem.* 1.1.2 etc. Cf. Versnel, *Ter Unus*, 126 [+].

[15] Contrast Garland, *New Gods*, 149 (with an interesting citation of Kierkegaard). That Socrates participated in civic rituals in the usual way cannot strictly be proved. But to doubt it we must reject both Xenophon's explicit statement that he did (*Mem.* 1.1.2) and the whole presentation in all the works of both Xenophon and Plato of Socrates' attitude to Delphi and to cult more generally; we must also discount the biographical fact that pious Xenophon admired him.

[16] 6a; but the remark has much too clear a place in Plato's strategy in that dialogue (see n. 48 below) to be good evidence for the historical Socrates.

[17] See W. R. Connor, 'The Other 399: Religion and the Trial of Socrates', in *Georgica: Greek Studies in Honour of George Cawkwell* (*BICS* Suppl. 58, 1991), 49–56; G. Vlastos, *Socrates* (Cambridge 1991), ch. 6.

[18] 19b–c; note too Xen. *Symp.* 6.6–8.

men had been 'trained in virtue'—that is, 'the ability to manage one's own affairs and those of the city'—by informal association with older men: relations, family friends, and lovers. The sophists, by contrast, are the founding fathers of Higher Education, formal instruction purveyed by an outsider; and it has rightly been argued that this educational revolution, which of course undermined traditional familial authority in some degree, is at the root of the Athenians' profoundly ambiguous attitudes to philosophers and sophists and Socrates. Though Socrates was unique in being condemned by an Athenian court 'for words' (as Hyperides put it) not actions, the point was that he was a teacher and his were action-inspiring words.[19]

In 'Socrates' ' school are taught both strange doctrines about the heavens, and also the art of 'making the worse appear the better cause' (94–99, 112–15). His prospective pupil Strepsiades assumes that, as one who 'contemplates the sun', he will 'look down on the gods' (225–26). And indeed Socrates declares that the conventional gods 'aren't currency with us' (247–48), and undertakes to introduce Strepsiades to 'our gods', the Clouds, and to reveal 'the true nature of things divine' (250–53). He argues in some detail that rain, thunder, and lightning, the phenomena that cause Strepsiades to fear Zeus, have natural causes; and points out that lightning, far from picking on Zeus' enemies, spares perjurers and strikes inanimate objects, even Zeus' own temple (366–411). Socrates' tone is light, but the arguments he uses remained, throughout antiquity, fundamental to the case against gods who intervene in the world.[20] (Interestingly, his atheism is wholly based on scientific arguments of this kind. He seems unaffected in this area by Protagorean scepticism, and by sophistic speculations about the origin of belief in the gods.) His own gods, we soon learn, are Chaos, Clouds, and Tongue (424), and these novel deities recur as a comic leitmotif throughout the play (627, 814, 1150). The strength of his reverence for the new gods does not excuse but underlines his turning away from the old;

---

[19] Educational revolution: cf. the portrayal of Anytus' attitude in Pl. *Meno.* 91c–92b, and E. Havelock, 'Why Was Socrates Tried?', in M. White ed., *Studies in Honor of Gilbert Norwood* (*Phoenix* Suppl. 1, Toronto 1952), 95–109. Mrs Thatcher was quoted in the 1980s as being distressed at the way in which 'young people who were absolutely thrilled at getting a place at university have every decent value drubbed out of them when they get there' (I quote from memory but am sure of 'drub'). That Socrates was in this broad sense a true sophist is rightly stressed by M. Nussbaum in J. Henderson ed., *Aristophanes: Essays in Interpretation* (= *YCS* 26, 1980), 43–97; G. B. Kerferd, *The Sophistic Movement* (Cambridge 1981), 55–57. Hyperides: fr. 55 Jensen, cited by Hansen, 'Trial of Sokrates'. Note too, with Wallace, 'Freedom of Thought' [n. 2], the ostracism of Damon, another teacher (Arist. *Ath. Pol.* 27.4).

[20] See e.g. Lucretius 6.379–422, with C. Bailey's notes in his commentary ad loc. (Oxford 1947).

'kainotheism' is not an alternative to atheism but the form it takes. Similarly, admission to his school is portrayed as a form of initiation into Mysteries (255 ff.),[21] but the effect is much less to present Socrates as a man of strong if misguided piety than to stress the secret, élitist, anti-social character of his teaching.

But what harm is there in atheism? That it angers the gods, a factor often stressed in modern accounts, is not stated in the play. What is stressed instead is how, allied with rhetoric, it subverts social morality. Strepsiades laughs in the face of a creditor who reminds him of his oath to make repayment (1228–41). 'Those are not at all to be tolerated who deny the being of God. Promises, covenants and oaths, which are the bonds of human society, can have no hold upon an atheist. The taking away of God, though but even in thought, dissolves all': the words are John Locke's,[22] but the thought is also Aristophanes'. The overthrow of morality reaches its climax when Strepsiades' son Pheidippides, also initiated in the mysteries of the school, begins to beat his father, scorning, of course, his pathetic appeals to 'Zeus of Fathers' (1468).[23] Strepsiades now repents (it is in fact the comi-tragic motif of Strepsiades' delusion and repentance that gives the play its coherence and bite[24]), and realizes 'how mad I was to renounce the gods because of Socrates' (1477). He leads a violent attack on the school, designed to eradicate it from the community and expel (though not destroy) its occupants.[25] Strepsiades speaks the final words of the play: 'Well, why did you insult the gods, and inspect the seat of the moon? Chase them, hit them, pelt them, for a hundred reasons, but most of all remembering how they wronged the gods.' The obscene pun on 'inspecting the seat of the moon' only slightly mitigates the grim violence of this ending.

Clearly, the Socrates of the play and the Socrates of the indictment are the same man. Both are atheists; both corrupt the young. And these are the prejudices that, very largely, the *Apologies* of both Plato and Xenophon seek to dispel.[26] According to Plato,[27] Socrates was hated because he exposed the ignorance of older men in the

---

[21] Cf. A. M. Bowie, *Aristophanes* (Cambridge 1993), 112–24.

[22] In *A Letter Concerning Toleration*.

[23] For the importance of the father-beating theme see the probable allusion to this play in Ar. *Vesp.* 1037–42.

[24] See C. W. Macleod, *Phoenix* 35 (1981), 142–44 = id., *Collected Essays* (Oxford 1983), 49–51.

[25] See M. Davies, *Hermes* 118 (1990), 237–42.

[26] As did that of Socrates himself, if Hansen, 'Trial of Sokrates', is right to revive the view that coincidences between Plato and Xenophon derive from this common source rather than from imitation.

[27] e.g. *Apol.* 23c–d; cf. Xen. *Apol.* 20, *Mem.* 1.2.49; B.S. Strauss, *Fathers and Sons in Athens* (London 1993), 199–209.

presence of his younger followers: the same charge of setting the
younger generation against the old is translated into comic fantasy in
the father-beating scene in *Clouds*.

We hear of the political charges not from Plato but from the point-
by-point rebuttal of an unnamed 'accuser' in the first two chapters
of Xenophon's *Memorabilia*. According to a long-accepted view,
Xenophon is there responding not to any of the actual speeches for
the prosecution but to an *Accusation of Socrates* published by the
rhetorician Polycrates at least six years after the trial. That consensus has recently been strongly challenged; but even if the challenge
is correct, we still have in Xenophon not a faithful transcript of the
arguments actually employed by the prosecution, but a re-creation
of them made after an uncertain interval of time during which the
celebrated case had been repeatedly discussed.[28] Xenophon's
'accuser' emphasized (among many others) the charges that Socrates
had educated Critias and Alcibiades, that he constantly ridiculed the
use of that key democratic device, the lot, and was in general hostile
to the 'people and the poor'.[29]

Can any of these resentments be declared irrelevant to the actual
condemnation? The ancient prejudice against sophists as atheists
and teachers of unjust arguments is surely not to be dismissed: such
was, as we know from Aristophanes, the popular perception of
Socrates, and the prosecution had no reason at all not to exploit it to
the full, even if they also wished to appeal to political anger. We see
from the trials of 415 how ready Athenians were to suspect the same
individuals of impiety and of treacherous disloyalty to the constitution; indeed, since five of the persons convicted in 415 were associates of Socrates,[30] some responsibility for the earlier impious
outrage may well have been laid at his door in 399. And we have, as
it happens, in Lysias 6 a spectacular demonstration of the virulence
with which religious arguments could still be deployed in this same
year of Socrates' trial.[31] Are the political factors similarly unelim-

[28] For Polycrates: A. H. Chroust, *ClMed* 16 (1955), 1–77 [+], reworked in his *Socrates,
Man and Myth* (London 1957), 69–100; against, Hansen, 'Trial of Sokrates', and independently N. Livingstone of Christ Church, Oxford, in a doctoral diss. in preparation on
Isocrates. A coincidence of detail (citation of *Il.* 2.188 ff.) between Xen. *Mem.* 1.2.58 and
Polycrates *apud* Σ Ael. Arist. III, p. 480.30 Dindorf is one of the indications usually held to
prove their interdependence; on the other view it attests, on this point, fidelity on the part of
both to the actual prosecutor.

[29] *Mem.* 1.2.9–11, 12, 58.

[30] For a prosopography see most recently Ostwald, *Popular Sovereignty*, 537–50; he
stresses that most of the persons accused were youngish men, of an age to be seen as products
of the new education.

[31] J. Burnet (note on Pl. *Euthyphr.* 2b9) described Lys. 6 as 'almost the only monument of
religious fanaticism that has come down to us from antiquity'. For the possibility that the
Meletuses involved in the prosecutions of Socrates and Andocides are the same see

inable? It has been suggested that they were first brought into the debate by Polycrates,[32] several years after Socrates' death. But, even if the influence of Polycrates on subsequent tradition is allowed, there are no strong reasons to doubt that political arguments were already used in 399. Because of the Amnesty of 403, Socrates could not be charged with spreading anti-democratic sentiments before that date; but there was no bar to the argument that, having corrupted Alcibiades and Critias in the past, he was liable to go on corrupting the present generation.[33] Plato's *Apology*, of course, does not imply that political factors had any importance (except perhaps in one passing aside[34]). But we have no reason to take Plato's defence any more seriously as a historical record than whatever accusation underlies the 'accuser' of Xenophon.[35] It is, therefore, hard to doubt that the names Critias and Alcibiades, the word 'hater of the people', were spoken at the trial. Beyond this point we can scarcely go. Different arguments will have had different weight with different jurors; and the motives of most individual jurors were surely also mixed. It is pointless to attempt to clarify that complex mess of human resentment, and declare religious or social or political factors decisive.

We turn to the other instances of repression. It was believed in later antiquity that Socrates was not alone: his death was only the culmination of a series of trials and other attacks on intellectuals dotted through the second half of the fifth century. But the evidence is extraordinarily difficult and untrustworthy.[36] Only in one case is it

H. Blumenthal, *Philologus* 117 (1973), 169–78 [+]; cf. Brickhouse/Smith, *Socrates on Trial*, 27–28. Note too Lys. 30, a milder instance from the same year.

[32] So, tentatively, Brickhouse/Smith, *Socrates on Trial*, 80. Ar. *Av.* 1281–83 is sometimes cited to prove that Socrates was already renowned for philolaconism in the fifth cent., but also makes sense on the view that he merely symbolized austerity (as we know that he did).

[33] So Hansen, 'Trial of Sokrates', who stresses how implausible it is that the prosecution should have failed to raise political issues.

[34] The reference in 33a4–5 to 'those who people slandering me claim are my students', which is often taken as an allusion to Critias and Alcibiades: see Brickhouse/Smith, *Socrates on Trial*, 194–97. Note too the admission in 23c that he associates with rich young men.

[35] Contrast Brickhouse/Smith, *Socrates on Trial*, 2–10. The recent publication (*P. Köln* 205, in M. Gronewald, K. Maresch, and W. Schäfer, *Kölner Papyri* 5, Opladen 1985, 33–53) of a fr. of a Socratic dialogue in which the philosopher, conversing on his deathbed as in *Phaedo*, demonstrates that 'pleasure is the goal', ought to serve as a caution (admittedly in a not quite comparable context) to those who believe in the historicity of any Socratic literature.

[36] The basic discussion is now K. J. Dover, *Talanta* 7 (1975), 24–54 = id., *The Greeks and their Legacy* (Oxford 1988), 135–58; Kerferd, *The Sophistic Movement*, 21, n. 7, judges it 'excessively sceptical'; but the case for less scepticism would need to be made out point by point. Note, however, with Kerferd, Arist. *Rhet.* 1397ᵇ25–27, where Aristotle appears to say that 'sophists' are often put to death (I do not understand Dover's view of the passage, *Greeks and their Legacy*, 148, n. 25). For another sceptical discussion see now Wallace, in 'Freedom

contemporary; and here it appears that it was for mocking the Eleusinian Mysteries, not for preaching atheism, that the Melian poet Diagoras was outlawed from Athens with a price on his head. (It looks as if he had been notorious for impiety for some years but was only indicted in 415/4, just when sensitivity to any slight to the Mysteries was at its height.[37]) We have early fourth-century evidence that Pericles' mistress Aspasia was prosecuted (unsuccessfully) for impiety, but no indication of the details of the charge.[38] Protagoras was supposedly condemned to death for writing his sceptical *On the Gods*, while the book itself was burnt in the marketplace; but these reports begin in the Hellenistic period, and appear simply incompatible with a remark in Plato that Protagoras had lived out his life in high repute throughout Greece.[39] For the most striking claim of all, that shortly before the Peloponnesian war the well-known seer Diopeithes proposed a decree which was to make 'those who do not acknowledge the divine' or who 'teach about things in the air' liable to prosecution, we have only the testimony of Plutarch; apart from the lack of supporting evidence, there is no very strong reason to be suspicious.[40] There is fourth-century testimony

of Thought', who recognizes only the ostracism of Damon and possibly (Pl. *Theaet.* 171d) a prudent withdrawal by Protagoras.

[37] See Ar. *Av.* 1071–73, Lys. 6.17–18; Melanthius, *FGrH* 326 F 3; Craterus *FGrH* 342 F 16 (both in *Σ* Ar. *Av.* 1073). A book containing explicitly atheistic doctrines appears first in Aristoxenus fr. 45.I Wehrli² (superseded text) *ap.* Philodemus *P. Herc.* 1428 col. xi.5 ff. (*CronErcol* 4, 1974, 21–22; cf. ibid. 18, 1988, 122), who apparently doubts its authenticity (*aliter* A. Henrichs, *CronErcol* 4, 1974, 28; but both ἐπεμφέρω and the following contrast with 'his only genuine writings' suggest that spurious writings are alluded to: read perhaps [ἀληθὲ]ς in line 10, cf. D.L. 2.39.12). For an excellent brief account of the problems concerning Diagoras see F. Wehrli, *Gnomon* 33 (1961), 123–26, followed in the essentials in the full studies by M. Winiarczyk, *Eos* 67 (1979), 191–213; 68 (1980), 51–75 [+]; cf. id., *Diagorae Melii et Theodori Cyrenaei Reliquiae* (Leipzig 1981), and Smarczyk, *Religionspolitik*, 278 ff. As to chronology, the natural inference from Ar. *Av.* 1071–73 that his banishment was recent has ancient support (*Σ* Ar. *Av.* 1073; Diod. 13.6.7; and the Mubassir life, T 10 Winiarczyk), which is, however, itself likely to be based on inference from the *Birds* passage (cf. F. Jacoby, *Diagoras* Ὁ Ἄθεος, *AbhBerl* 1959, no. 3, 20, who sets the banishment much earlier); but there is already an allusion to his notorious impiety in *Clouds* (Ar. *Nub.* 830; the relevance of Hermippus fr. 43 K/A, of 430, is less certain), even the rev. version of which is generally and probably rightly held (see Ar. *Nub.* 551–59; E. C. Kopff disagrees, *AJP* 111, 1990, 318–29) to antedate the ostracism of Hyperbolus in 416. See further J. N. Bremmer's study, 'Religious Secrets and Secrecy in Classical Greece', in H. G. Kippenberg and G. Stroumsa eds., *Secrecy and Concealment* (Leiden 1995), 59–78 (with a fresh translation of the Mubassir life).

[38] Antisthenes fr. 35 in the edn. of F. D. Caizzi (Milan 1966) *ap.* Ath. 589e; but cf. Wallace, 'Freedom of Thought', 132.

[39] *Meno* 91e; the growth of the book-burning legend can be traced with much plausibility step by step: see Dover, *Greeks and their Legacy*, 142–45, 158; and for another sceptical treatment of the tradition, C. W. Müller, *Hermes* 95 (1967), 148–59; cf., however, n. 36 above.

[40] Plut. *Per.* 32.2; note, however, Dover, *Greeks and their Legacy*, 146–47, who points out that the verbal formulation in Plutarch is unlikely to be original. That the decree was remembered though never passed is a rather remote possibility. Ostwald, *Popular Sovereignty*, 528–32, argues that it was in fact the first Athenian law against impiety.

that Anaxagoras was 'prosecuted for impiety' by the enemies of Pericles (but the later accounts that give details of the actual trial are mutually contradictory in a very suspicious way), and that Diogenes of Apollonia 'came close to danger'.[41] Finally, we have further fifth-century evidence that natural philosophers were resented (though not necessarily attacked): 'who, seeing this, does not recognize a god, and does not hurl far from him the crooked deceits of talkers about the heavens [*meteorologoi*], whose mad tongue makes random throws about what is hidden, devoid of understanding?', enquires a chorus in Euripides.[42] It was to sentiments such as these that those who attacked the great scientist Anaxagoras (if such indeed there were) must have appealed, however political their own motivation may have been.[43]

Clearly, enough uncertainties remain (and doubtless will always remain) to prevent any confident conclusion. If Anaxagoras was never tried, if the decree of Diopeithes was passed only on the comic stage, if it was for political crimes that Socrates was executed, we are left with little more than resentful talk, as heard in Aristophanes and Euripides. (No argument, however, can remove the charge of atheism from the formal indictment against Socrates.) On a less sceptical view, talk became action more than once, though still not with great frequency. One general observation can perhaps escape these specific uncertainties.[44] We are not considering the extent to which the Athenians in practice restricted a liberty which in principle they allowed. On the contrary, no Greek surely would have supposed that an impious opinion should be permitted to circulate out of respect for freedom of speech. In practice, no doubt, the Athenians very rarely moved against verbal impiety. A wide variety of opinions

---

[41] Anaxagoras: Ephorus *FGrH* 70 F 196 *ap.* Diod. Sic. 12.39.2; cf. Dover, *Greeks and their Legacy*, 140–41 (who doubts even this); Yunis, *A New Creed*, 66–68 (who, however, makes too much of an ordinary narrative imperfect in Ephorus); attempts are still made to sort out the later tradition, and believe parts of it, by J. Mansfeld, *Mnemosyne*, 4th ser., 33 (1980), 17–95; L. Woodbury, *Phoenix* 35 (1981), 295–315; cf. M. Ostwald, *CAH*² V.2 (1992), 339. Diogenes: Demetrius of Phaleron *ap.* D. L. 9.57 (fr. 91 Wehrli); but on Demetrius' motivation and reliability see Dover, *Greeks and their Legacy*, 145–46.

[42] Fr. 913 Nauck; see too Cratinus fr. 167 K/A = D/K 38 A 2, a supposed attack (not verbatim) on Hippon for impiety; and Eupolis fr. 157 K/A, ἔνδον μέν ἐστι Πρωταγόρας ὁ Τήϊος | ὃς ἀλαζονεύεται μὲν ἀλιτήριος | περὶ τῶν μετεώρων. A whole tradition of attacks by poets (in various genres) on philosophers is attested by Pl. *Resp.* 607b–c, with *Leg.* 967c–d (cf. Pindar fr. 209 Snell/Maehler). For the popular association of astronomy with atheism see Pl. *Apol.* 18b–c, 26d, and *Leg.* 967a; Plut. *Nic.* 23.3–4.

[43] So rightly Derenne, *Procès d'impiété*, 41.

[44] Cf. the conclusion to Derenne, ibid. 254–67; P. Decharme, *La critique des traditions religieuses chez les grecs* (Paris 1904), 179—'la loi sans doute a été sévère pour les libertés de la pensée, mais, dans la pratique, l'esprit public le fut rarement'; D. Cohen, *Law, Sexuality and Society* (Cambridge 1991), 210–17 (the work by P. Garnsey that he cites appears in W. J. Sheils ed., *Persecution and Toleration* [*Studies in Church History* 21, 1984], 1–28).

about the gods could be comfortably accommodated, in a religion that lacked dogma and revelation; and it is easy to think of intellectuals, such as Hippon, whose views would doubtless under investigation have seemed impious to some, and who none the less went unmolested. But in such cases we are dealing not with principled tolerance but with a failure to live up to intolerant principles. Fortunately such failures seem to have been very regular.

Was there, as has often been supposed, a 'religious crisis' in the second half of the fifth century? In the sense that traditional religion was seriously undermined, certainly not; there is any amount of evidence, from inscriptions, dedications, oratory, and comedy, that it continued to flourish in the fourth century just as before. But in the sense that speculative thought was perceived by some as a threat, perhaps for the first time, a kind of crisis did arise (though its extent is partly veiled by the various uncertainties that we have just discussed).

Several difficult problems arise in connection with this crisis. Late fifth-century opinions about the divine can sound, to a modern ear, like a babel of unorthodox and critical voices. We hear scientific determinists; critics of myth, or of divine morality, or of divine justice, or of divination; various kinds of allegorist; speculative theologians prepared to declare, for instance, that 'Earth and Mother and Rhea and Hera are the same'; thinkers of another stamp who offer explanations of how men first came to form a conception of the divine.[45] We need to ask what in all this was truly threatening or 'impious'; what constituted an attack from without rather than from within the traditional religious framework, that loose and accommodating structure within which certain forms of doubt, criticism, and revision were, in fact, traditional.[46]

From the contemporary evidence, beginning with *Clouds* and ending with Plato's important discussion of atheism in *Laws*, it emerges that one position above all was feared: that of the 'atheist' scientist, who substitutes chance and necessity for the gods as an explanation of celestial phenomena—and so deprives Zeus of his

[45] See in general Burkert, *Greek Religion*, 311–17. On allegorists see N. J. Richardson, *PCPS* 21 (1975), 65–81. Speculative theologian: see the Derveni papyrus, *ZPE* 47, 1982, after p. 300, col. XVIII 7, tentatively ascribed to Stesimbrotus by W. Burkert, *ZPE* 62 (1986), 1–5.

[46] In particular, the criticisms of divine justice and morality aired in the plays of Euripides have numerous antecedents (cf. A. B. Drachmann, *Atheism in Pagan Antiquity*, London 1922, 52, cf. 16: 'in so far . . . he is still entirely on the ground of popular belief'), though Euripides presses them unusually hard. For recent discussions which stress the traditional aspects of Euripides' theology see M. Heath, *The Poetics of Greek Tragedy* (London 1987), 49–64; M. R. Lefkowitz, *CQ* NS 39 (1989), 70–82; for the unusual pressure see Yunis, *A New Creed*, pt. 2.

thunderbolt.[47] (Scepticism about divination certainly also created unease, but we hear nothing of repression of sceptics. And Socrates is scarcely to be taken seriously when, in *Euthyphro*, he moots the possibility that a critic of certain myths of divine conflict might be prosecuted for impiety.[48]) Now, in a certain illuminist perspective, science and religion may appear as natural enemies, destined to come into conflict. But in Greece they were able, as a rule, to maintain good neighbourly relations. Provided science stayed clear of militant atheism (as it did[49]), there was no obvious need for hostilities between it and the undogmatic, ever-changing Greek theology, protected by no Holy Office. Scientists could even borrow the characteristic argument 'from within' of the religious reformer, and reveal that their new position was, behold, actually more pious than its traditional precursor: thus the Hippocratic author of *On the Sacred Disease* urges that it is impious to suppose (as most people in this case did) that gods, the source of good, can inflict disease.[50] Hippocratic medicine is in fact a prime example of a science that lived in easy harmony with traditional religion.

Conflict, therefore, was scarcely inevitable. But, it may be countered, the particular point in dispute between, say, Anaxagoras and the Athenian people was too fundamental to admit of compromise: it was the very power of Zeus, or any other god, to intervene in the world. It was no use merely acknowledging 'the divine', if this 'divine' had no purchase on the affairs of men. 'Who ever refrained from wrongdoing from fear of Air or Aither?', as a critic of Stoic theology was later to enquire.[51] Yet even if this is conceded, we have still to ask why the conflict arose when and where it did. Ionian philosophers had been offering such mechanistic explanations of the

---

[47] See n. 42 above, and Pl. *Leg.* 886d–e, 889b–890a, 967a–d.

[48] Divination: cf. the defensive or threatened tone of Hdt. 8.77; Soph. *OT* 897–910; Xen. *Eq. Mag.* 9.7–9, *Cyr.* 1.6.46; for an attack, Eur. *Hel.* 744–60 (of, perhaps significantly, the year after the Sicilian disaster: cf. Thuc. 8.1). Myths: Pl. *Euthyph.* 6a. Socrates is merely 'teasing' Euthyphro with this whimsical suggestion, according to W. K. C. Guthrie, *A History of Greek Philosophy*, IV (Cambridge 1975), 110, n. 1; rather, the issue is raised, in a way characteristic of a dialogue that is in part a *retorsio criminis impietatis*, to stress the division between true Socratic piety and the traditional version, in fact impious, that has presumed to arraign him. The attack on the Panathenaic robe (of all things) in 6b–c sharply separates Socrates from civic piety. Note too the hint contained in the reference to secret doctrines (of Orphic type?) in 6c that the truly dangerous innovators in religion (cf. the charge made against Socrates of καινοτομεῖν, 16a) are soi-disant experts such as Euthyphro.

[49] Indeed, most pre-Socratic philosophers are demonstrably theists, if of a quite untraditional type: see e.g. C. H. Kahn, *Anaximander and the Origins of Greek Cosmology* (New York 1960), 155–59; J. Barnes, *The Presocratic Philosophers* (London 1979), I. 94–99; II. 156–59, 279–80.

[50] Loeb Hippocrates, ed. W. H. S. Jones, vol. 2, p. 144 § 3. For the type of argument cf. e.g. Pind. *Ol.* 1.35 ff.; Xen. *Apol.* 13.

[51] Philodemus *De Pietate* in *P. Herc.* 1428 col. xiii.8 ff. (*CronErcol* 4, 1974, 23).

natural order since the sixth century, without, to our knowledge, arousing protest. And at no other time or place in the Greek world were philosophers put on trial for the impiety of their physical theories.[52] Why did Athens fear what Miletus had applauded, what Megara was to tolerate?

Part of the answer must be that, even if the natural philosopher was not a new phenomenon in the fifth century, he enjoyed a new prominence. Scientists were rare enough in the sixth century to be admired and patronized, brilliant eccentrics ever in danger of tumbling down wells. By the fifth they were common, and influential, enough to be felt as a threat.[53] It is obviously tempting to add that it was through association with the threatening intellectual movement *par excellence*, that of the sophists, that natural philosophy acquired a taint. Earlier philosophers, it can be argued, attacked religious tradition constructively and from within: the sophists advanced much more radical criticisms and drew more radical conclusions; or at the least such radical criticism first emerged in the sophistic period. Protagoras denied that secure knowledge is possible about the existence of the gods; Prodicus argued that early man had acquired his gods by deifying natural products and the inventors of techniques; a character in a play by Critias declared that the gods were an invention of a 'wise lawgiver' eager to discourage secret wrongdoing.[54] If theories such as these were put about in association with mechanistic accounts of the workings of the universe, the ugly atheistic implications of the latter would be starkly revealed. The 'atheism' of Socrates in *Clouds* is so dangerous because he is also a sophist and a moral relativist. And Plato too says that the typical atheist combines 'scientific' belief in a mechanistic universe with the characteristic 'sophistic' commitment to a life led according to nature, not convention.[55]

In broad outline this explanation is likely to be correct: natural philosophy became offensive only once it was felt to be combined with moral relativism or antinomianism. But it is very uncertain whether prominent sophists did in fact make provocative attacks on

[52] Expulsions of philosophers, usually Epicureans, are, however, attested from a few Greek states (in the Hellenistic period when datable): see C. Habicht, 'Hellenistic Athens and her Philosophers' (David Magie Lecture 1988, Princeton), reprinted in his *Athen in hellenistischer Zeit* (Munich 1994), 237. On later Athenian impiety trials see Ch. 12 below.

[53] I owe this point to Edward Hussey.

[54] D/K 80 B 4; D/K 84 B 5 + *P. Herc.* 1428 fr. 19 (n. 56 below); D/K 88 B 25 = *TrGF* I.43 Critias F 19 (on which see most recently M. Winiarczyk, *WS* 100, 1987, 35–45 and M. Davies, *BICS* 36, 1989, 16–32).

[55] *Leg.* 889b–890a. Sophists did sometimes, it seems, discuss scientific topics (see Pl. *Prot.* 318e and Kerferd, *The Sophistic Movement*, 38–40); at all events, the man in the street was convinced that they did, as we see from *Clouds* (cf. Ar. *Av.* 692 and n. 18 above.)

traditional belief. In later antiquity, the theological positions of Protagoras and Prodicus, taken perhaps out of context, were certainly adjudged impious; no such charge is brought against them in Aristophanes or Plato, for whom, as we have seen, the archetypal atheistic position is primarily scientific rather than sophistic.[56] We have no more than uncertain hints that some of Protagoras' *Overthrowing Arguments* may have been designed to overthrow 'ancestral traditions, coeval with time' in the matter of religion, such as belief in divination.[57] It is impossible, therefore, to fill in the details of the alliance between a scientific determinism that was pushed to an atheistic extreme and sophistic antinomianism. We are left with Plato's unsubstantiated testimony that such an alliance occurred[58] (perhaps among hearers of philosophers and sophists rather than the thinkers themselves), and the general likelihood that this was the source of public fear of the impious scientist.

If a kind of religious crisis did indeed occur in the late fifth century, one may reasonably ask how it was resolved. 'By Stoicism' is doubtless the answer in the long term; in a shorter perspective we would need to consider how key elements in the Stoic solution were already being developed in the fourth century: the argument from design; the 'double determination' theory of causality (whereby god works through natural process); that other compromise, best known from Roman sources, by which traditional forms of cult (*theologia civilis*) are accepted by the educated as the proper way to honour a divine principle that is intellectually quite differently conceived

---

[56] For the atheists recognized in later antiquity see M. Winiarczyk, *Philologus* 128 (1984), 157–83. That Protagoras' attitude was not polemical is argued by Müller, *Hermes* 95 (1967), 140–48; Lloyd-Jones, *Justice of Zeus*, 130–31; Kerferd, *The Sophistic Movement*, 164–68; that Prodicus was a 'modernist', not an atheist, by e.g. Drachmann, *Atheism in Pagan Antiquity*, 42–44, and E. R. Dodds in his note on Eur. *Bacch.* 274–85. The 'modernist' view of Prodicus is confuted by the new evidence of *P. Herc.* 1428 fr. 19, where he is credited with explicit atheism (A. Henrichs, *HSCP* 79, 1975, 107; id. *CronErcol* 6, 1976, 15–21), only if the doxographer is directly reporting rather than, as is perhaps more plausible, interpreting his views; it is, however, hard to see what ground Prodicus could have had for believing that gods of traditional form existed, once the origin of men's belief in them had been explained away. On Prodicus' contemporary reputation see C. W. Willink, *CQ* NS 33 (1983), 25–33, who detects an allusion to his impiety in the comparison with Tantalus in Pl. *Prot.* 315b–c; this is possible, no more. Epicurus certainly treats him as an atheist, fr. 27.2 Arrighetti.

[57] Namely, the language of Hdt. 8.77, χρησμοῖσι δὲ οὐκ ἔχω ἀντιλέγειν ὡς οὐκ εἰσὶ ἀληθέες, οὐ βουλόμενος ἐναργέως λέγοντας πειρᾶσθαι καταβάλλειν ... (the word ἀντιλογία recurs later) and Eur. *Bacch.* 199–203, esp. πατρίους παραδοχὰς ... οὐδεὶς καταβαλεῖ λόγος (see L. Radermacher, *RhM* 53, 1898, 501–502).

[58] *Leg.* 889a-890a. The evidence of this text is more slippery than it at first appears. No philosopher can be identified who held the amalgam of views that Plato here attacks and describes as common (see Guthrie, *History of Greek Philosophy*, III, Cambridge 1969, 115–16). It is probably Plato's own synthesis of tendencies he perceived as threatening (so W. de Mahieu, *RBPhil* 41, 1964, 16–47); but Plato was too imaginative and too emotional to be a very careful reporter of other people's views.

(*theologia physica*). Plato in old age could already claim that actual atheism was in decline.[59] These issues in religious philosophy cannot be discussed here: let us merely note that traditional religion surrendered none of its rights, explicitly at least. Plutarch indeed describes how, as early as 430, Pericles allayed his troops' religious fears by explaining the physical causes of a terrifying eclipse. But the incident is chronologically impossible;[60] and everything we know of the permissible tone of public life in the fourth century suggests that politicians and generals still paid respect to divination, still acknowledged the traditional divine signs as signs. It is possible that a preference for natural over theological explanations of certain phenomena made a creeping advance, plausible certainly that such was now the preference of some of the educated. But scientific determinism neither sought nor won any victories in the open field. According to Plutarch again, an eclipse of the moon in 357 left Dion and his entourage, graduates of Plato's Academy, unalarmed; but one of them, the seer Miltas, offered a heartening interpretation in religious terms to the frightened troops. The formal victor was certainly traditional religion.[61]

We revert to 'new gods'. At first sight Socrates has little in common with the great courtesan Phryne. Yet they shared the fate of being accused of 'introducing a new god'; Socrates, however, too proud to supplicate the jury, was condemned, while a novel and most impressive appeal secured the acquittal of fair-breasted Phryne. Was 'kainotheism' therefore formally proscribed by law (as two unreliable late

---

[59] Pl. *Leg.* 967a-b. Design: see e.g. Henrichs, *HSCP* 79 (1975), 105, n. 53; W. Jaeger, *The Theology of the Early Greek Philosophers* (Oxford 1947), 167–71; Parker in *Apodosis: Essays Presented to Dr W. W. Cruickshank* (London 1992), 84–94. Double determination: Plut. *Per.* 6 is the classic illustration (cf. D. Babut, *Plutarque et le Stoïcisme*, Paris 1969, 521). *Ratio civilis* and *physica*: Jaeger, *Theology*, 2–4, with notes; G. Lieberg, *RhM* 125 (1982), 25–32 [+]. On the whole issue see Burkert, *Greek Religion*, 317–37; L. P. Gerson, *God and Greek Philosophy* (London 1990). Of course questions about the social role of schools of philosophy are also relevant.

[60] Plut. *Per.* 35.2 (a story repeated in philosophical schools, Plutarch notes); cf. Dover, *Greeks and their Legacy*, 47, 141. Plutarch also claims that Demosthenes forbade the Athenians to attend to oracles, and reminded them that Pericles and Epaminondas had regarded such things as mere pretexts for cowardice (*Dem.* 20.1). But his story is probably spun out of Demosthenes' denunciation of the philippizing Pythia (Aeschin. 3.130), a specific and not a general attack, no more a sign of theoretical scepticism than pious Hector's attack on Poulydamas in *Il.* 12.231–50. For appeals by Demosthenes to oracles see 18.253, 19.297–99, 21.51. About Pericles' own religious attitude (discussed by F. Schachermeyer, 'Religionspolitik und Religiosität bei Pericles', *SBWien* 258, 1968) little can be learnt from scraps of his public speeches (Plut. *Per.* 8.9; Lys. 6.10) and questionable anecdotes (Plut. *Per.* 8.6, 13.12–13, 35.2, 38.2), the only sources.

[61] Cf. Burkert, *Greek Religion*, 305. Dion: Plut. *Dion* 22.6, 24.1–3; Pritchett, *Greek State at War*, III.111.

sources declare[62])? A broader question is whether Athenian law identified specific forms of impiety, such as kainotheism, or merely laid down penalties and procedures for use against an offence, 'impiety', the content of which it was left to jurors and tradition to decide. Not only Socrates and Phryne but also Demades and Aristotle were charged with 'introducing new gods', in their case by deifying mortals: the recurrent complaint implies, it has been urged, a formal prohibition.[63] But it remains possible that a charge of introducing new gods was simply one of the accepted ways in which one could seek to persuade a jury that an individual was guilty of impiety, not part of a formal definition of the offence.

But how could a prejudice (whether codified or not) against kainotheism coexist with the Athenians' famous 'hospitality' towards foreign gods? This is a much more serious problem than that concerning the exact terms of the law. A simple solution to the paradox is available: new gods could be introduced by the city (Pan, Bendis, and others),[64] perhaps in consultation with the gods themselves via an oracle, but ultimately by the city alone; though individuals or groups could establish new cults at their own expense, they could do so only with the authorization of the people. All religious practice undertaken on Attic soil occurs therefore by gracious permission of the assembly.

At the deepest level this simple solution is probably correct.[65] The principle that the individual should worship no gods other than those approved by the state would doubtless not have been controversial. In practice, however, things seem to have run on in a less regulated way. It is not clear, for instance, that individuals ever did approach the assembly with a request for permission to 'introduce a new god'. Was it with authorization that Themistocles founded his

---

[62] Joseph. *Ap.* 2.267; Serv. on Virg. *Aen.* 8.187; cf. A. Hausrath ed., *Corpus Fabularum Aesopicarum*, I.i² (Leipzig 1970), no. 56.

[63] So Derenne, *Procès d'impiété*, 223–36, and J. Rudhardt, *MusHelv* 17 (1960), 87–105; for Demades and Aristotle see below Ch. 12, ns. 5 and 87, for Demades esp. Ath. 251b, 'the Athenians penalized him ὅτι θεὸν εἰσηγήσατο Ἀλέξανδρον'. But for the view that the law against impiety was non-specific see D. Macdowell, *The Law in Classical Athens* (London 1978), 197–202; Ostwald, *Popular Sovereignty*, 535; Cohen, *Law, Sexuality and Society*, 207–10; for the view that Athenian law was typically procedural, not substantive, see Todd, *Athenian Law*, 61, n. 14, 64–67.

[64] Such a formal civic recognition of the divinity of heavenly bodies ('foreign gods' though they are) is what the author of the Platonic *Epinomis* recommends, according to A. J. Festugière, *Études de religion grecque et hellénistique* (Paris 1972), 129–37. The text is remarkable in containing an explicit proposal to 'introduce new gods'. The author therefore stresses that existing cults should not be tampered with (καινοτομεῖν, 985c–d) and that the barbarian worship will be much improved by the cultured and experienced Greeks, aided by the Delphic oracle (987d–988a).

[65] Cf. Sourvinou-Inwood, 'Polis Religion' (2), 270–73.

offensively vainglorious shrine to 'Artemis Aristoboule'? Perhaps
the case is not relevant, since Themistocles did not introduce a new
god but applied a new epithet to an old one.[66] Our key example
ought therefore to be Asclepius, unquestionably a new god[67]
imported by private initiative; alas, on the point that concerns us
nothing explicit is recorded. It would no doubt have been bold for
Telemachus to build a sizeable sanctuary just below the acropolis
without authorization; but the subsequent claim to the site lodged
by the *Kerykes* might be taken as evidence that he did just that. (If
so, the claim also suggests that his procedure was hazardous. The
grandson of the Egyptian priest who introduced Sarapis to Delos in
the third century was prosecuted when he built a fixed shrine for the
god, who had hitherto lived unmolested in rented accommodation.[68]
In such a case a court that decided in favour of the new god provided
a kind of retrospective authorization.)

Asclepius had a precinct; other foreign gods such as Sabazius and
Adonis lacked one, and it is surely out of the question that their disreputable rites had ever received the authorization of the people. An
immigrant community, wishing to found a shrine in Athens to its
native god, had to apply to the assembly, since otherwise it could not
buy land on which to build it;[69] but what was sought was right of
ownership, not of worship, and the cults in question may have been
carried on in rented accommodation before the shrine was thought
of. Plato in a famous passage of *Laws* both attests and proscribes the
practice of founding private shrines, often no doubt to 'new gods'.[70]
In practice, therefore, individuals seem to have 'introduced new
gods' with some freedom (though it may have been uncommon, and
for non-citizens was certainly illegal, to lodge such a god in a substantial shrine without approval). They were called to account only
if they or their religious associations proved objectionable on other
grounds. The accusation brought against Socrates of 'acknowledging new powers' is only a counterpoise to that other and much more

[66] Contrast Garland, *New Gods*, 115, 151; on Themistocles see Ch. 9 above.

[67] Unless indeed the Zea foundation (of which we know nothing) is prior: on all this see
pp. 175–185 above.

[68] *IG* XI.4.1299 (= M. Totti, *Ausgewählte Texte der Isis- und Sarapis-Religion* (Hildesheim
1985), no. 11; an extract in *SIG*³ 663, commentary in H. Engelmann, *The Delian Aretalogy of
Sarapis*, Leiden 1975). The legal ground for the charge is uncertain: 'introducing new gods'?;
or failure to seek the special permission required by a non-citizen to own land? (see C. Vial,
Délos indépendante, Paris 1984, 155–56). Pouilloux, *Rhamnonte*, no. 24 (first cent. BC) has been
compared: an Antiochene has appealed (successfully) to the *boule* against the attempts of 'certain persons' (Rhamnusians?) to debar him from celebrating rites of Agdistis.

[69] Permission to own land: cf. pp. 170, 243, and 337–38; and for a Delian instance, *Inscr.
Dél.* 1519.11–16. Wilamowitz, *Antigonos*, 273, 277, points out that the Athenians had no
choice but to allow foreigners to worship their own gods if they allowed them to reside at all.

[70] *Leg.* 909d–910d; cf. Festugière, *Études de religion grecque*, 136.

damning one of 'not acknowledging the gods the city believes in'. And it was as a priestess in what we have called an 'elective' cult, a 'leader of lawless revel-bands of men and women', that Phryne was attacked. Against such revel bands—centres, as they saw them, of social subversion and crime—the Athenians were indeed always ready to strike.[71] And in charging their leaders with, among other things, 'introducing new gods', they were affirming their right of ultimate control over all the religious practices of Attica. But Phryne would scarcely have been spared even if she had dedicated her troupe to an honest Attic god. When such groups were suppressed, as when the *Bacchanalia* were suppressed at Rome, the issue was not fundamentally one of theological orthodoxy.

[71] Cf. Ch. 9, n. 34 above.

11

The Fourth Century

From about 401, the Athenians performed their public sacrifices according to a new calendar drawn up by the secretary Nicomachus. The decision to revise the document on which the whole religion of the state depended was probably taken almost incidentally, as a by-product of the urgent need, created by the oligarchic *coups* of 411 and 403, for a general revision of the laws. Nicomachus apparently tackled the sacrificial code twice, at some time between 410 and 404 and again after 403. For his pains, he was, as we have already noted, brought to court in 399 on, as it seems, a capital charge.[1] The speech of the prosecutor survives (Lysias 30), and is potentially a precious document of Athenian religious history. We would much like to know what task precisely the Athenians set this reviser of their sacred traditions, and how, if at all, he deviated from it. But it is impossible to extract clear information from this outraged but evasive speaker, who cloaks what appears to be his real motive, resentment of the influence exercised by such figures as Nicomachus, under the guise of the most traditional piety.[2]

According to the prosecutor, Nicomachus' task had been to

[1] Cf. p. 152, and for the two revs. Ch. 4, n. 3. Noel Robertson, however, argues, *JHS* 110 (1990), 43–75, that (*a*) Nicomachus revised the sacred code once only, in 410–404 and (*b*) the later of the two surviving inscriptions is therefore the work of Nicomachus' opponents after his downfall. But (*a*) involves a hard interpretation of Lys. 30.3–6, and (*b*) requires the postulate that the weak case presented in Lys. 30 was, in fact, successful. Capital: § 23, 27. On the speech see now S. C. Todd, 'Lysias *Against Nikomakhos*: The Fate of the Expert in Athenian Law', in L. Foxhall and A. Lewis eds *Ancient Greek Law and Society* (Oxford forthcoming).

[2] For such resentment of Nicomachus as an expert and a specialist in written documents in an amateur and oral political culture see Todd, 'Fate of the Expert', and F. Ruze in M. Detienne ed., *Les savoirs de l'écriture en Grèce ancienne* (Lille n.d.), 89–91, who notes the restrictions imposed in some *poleis* (H. Engelmann and R. Merkelbach, *Die Inschriften von Erythrai und Klazomenai*, Bonn 1972, I, no. 1 = *Schwyzer* 702; Lys. 30.29) on the iteration or duplication of the office of 'secretary'. Robertson, *JHS* 110 (1990), 72–75, sees the prosecutor's main motive as a concern for economy (see e.g. §19, 22 and Nicomachus' reply that the prosecutor ἀσεβεῖ καταλύων τὰς θυσίας), but the very instructive survey of how to argue for and against new sacrifices in [Arist.] *Rh. Al.* 3.1423ᵃ30–1424ᵃ8 suggests that these and other considerations adduced were conventional.

ensure that the city should 'make the sacrifices from the *kurbeis* and the *stelai* in accord with the drafts' (17); he had, that is, to combine the old Solonian code with other sacrifices established later by popular decree.[3] In fact, he claims, Nicomachus 'inscribed more sacrifices than he was instructed' to an extent of 6 talents a year, and as a result the treasury was drained and 'last year 3 talents' worth of traditional sacrifices went unsacrificed' (19–20). One point seems to emerge from that formulation: Nicomachus did not abolish any traditional sacrifices, or the prosecutor would surely have said so, with high indignation.[4] The lapse of the older rites was merely a by-product of the excessive scale of the whole calendar. Nor does the prosecutor quite say—though he certainly seeks to imply—that any of the 'excess' sacrifices were simply invented by Nicomachus; it is indeed hard to see what motive Nicomachus could have had for innovating in such a dangerous and pointless way. Either, then, Nicomachus erred by including certain sacrifices that, though traditional, should none the less have been left out—but what category of established rites might the Athenians have decided in principle to exclude?[5]—or he simply failed to stay within financial limits that had been suggested or required. The adaptation of an ancient calendar to modern prices would certainly have been a puzzling task, and we do not know how Nicomachus went about it. His answer to his critics, according to the prosecutor, was that he was legislating 'for piety, not for economy' (21). Or perhaps he did not err at all, and the prosecutor's implication that matters of finance were Nicomachus' concern is just a lie. The critic says nothing of the independent scrutiny that the code must, surely, have faced and passed before entering into use.[6]

If this analysis is correct, the commission that Nicomachus received was thoroughly conservative. He was not required to cut the dead wood out of the old Solonian calendar, to limit, for instance, the anachronistic privileges of the *gene*. The surviving portions of what is almost certainly his code in fact abound in archaic-seeming offerings: as we saw in an earlier chapter, it is through his

[3] Cf. Ch. 4, n. 6 above.

[4] *Aliter* S. Dow, *Historia* 9 (1960), 291, who believes that Nicomachus expanded festivals of the *polis* at the expense of the *gene*. His ingenious reconstruction of the successive stages of Nicomachus' work largely hangs by this assumption.

[5] Robertson, *JHS* 110 (1990), 73–75, suggests rites deriving from the period between Solon's legislation and the emergence of the practice (? around the middle of the fifth cent.) of adopting laws κατὰ συγγραφάς. That suits the letter of Lysias.' text (§ 17) perfectly: but what could have been the rationale for such a policy? (Indeed, Robertson supposes that the prosecutor is disingenuous in suggesting that the assembly intended such a restriction.)

[6] See Dow, *Historia* 9 (1960), 275, on Andoc. 1.83–84 (though it is not clear that the procedure specified there would have applied in Nicomachus' case).

work that we can look back to that of Solon. And yet, if we believe
the prosecutor, 3 talents' worth of traditional sacrifices went
unsacrificed under the new dispensation. That is to say, when
specific decisions about expenditure had to be made (perhaps by the
boule), the old-fashioned rites tended to seem more dispensable. The
incident reminds us that written calendars, which look like the
solidest of all evidence for ritual practice, in fact merely represent
aspirations and ideals.

Financial difficulties, a thoroughly conservative 'modernization'—
these are fit introductions to a century in which the basic structures
of religious life remained unaltered, though the temple-building
splendours of the age of 'the Propylaea' (a more famous monument,
surprisingly, than the Parthenon)[7] were just a memory. To the dis-
gust of the liturgical class, Athens remained a city of frequent and
sumptuous festivals; and the Periclean conception of the festival as a
public utility was extended when the controversial theoric fund was
established, to subsidize attendance at the *Dionysia* and
Panathenaea, and even on occasion to pay, it seems, for additional
rites.[8] No important reform can be identified (although the quite
complex arrangements for the administration of sanctuaries and festivals continued, as always, to be adjusted[9]). Some have supposed
that the office of exegete, official adviser on problems of pollution
and purification, was first established in the legislative programme
of 403.[10] But this is merely an unreliable inference from the silence
of earlier sources. In the second half of the century, the Areopagus

[7] Dem. 13.28, 22.13, 76; 23.207; Aeschin. 2.74, and esp. the threat of Epaminondas cited
ibid. 105; Lycurgus fr. 58 Blass, IX.2 Conomis; cf. already Thuc. 2.13.3.

[8] See esp. Harp. s.v. θεωρικά, with J. J. Buchanan, *Theorika* (Locust Valley 1962), 48–74;
cf. Rhodes, *Commentary Ath. Pol.*, 514–15. *Panathenaea* and *Dionysia*: so Hesych. θ 442
θεωρικὰ χρήματα (for *Panathenaea* cf. Dem. 44.37); Dem. 3.31 speaks of the provision of a
procession at the *Boedromia* (though not necessarily from the fund). On the enormous dole
which Demades (he who described the *theorikon* as the 'glue of the democracy', Plut. *Quaest.
Plat.* 1011b = Demades fr. xxxvi De Falco) supposedly once proposed to distribute at the
Chytroi (Plut. *Praec. Reip. Ger.* 818e-f) see Mitchel, 'Lykourgan Athens', 179, n. 55; it can
scarcely have anything directly to do with the theoric fund, though it reflects the same political values. Liturgists: see Isoc. 8.13, 128; 7.53. According to Theopompus (*FGrH* 115 F 213)
the Athenians 'spent more on public banquets and meat-distributions (τὰς κοινὰς ἑστιάσεις
καὶ κρεανομίας) than on the whole administration of the city'.

[9] Note esp. the Eleusinian law ('367–348 B.C.?'), pub. by K. Clinton, *Hesperia* 49 (1980),
258–88 = SEG XXX 61.

[10] So J. H. Oliver, *The Athenian Expounders of the Sacred and Ancestral Law* (Baltimore
1950), 24–52, followed e.g. by R. J. S. Garland, *BSA* 79 (1984), 114–15; for the other view,
Jacoby, *Atthis*, 8–51. It is surely not decisive that the quite separate institution of Eumolpid
exegesis was apparently reformed at about this time (p. 295 below). Exegetes are first attested
in Pl. *Euthyphr.* 4c (dramatic date 399). Humphreys, 'Genos', questions whether a board of
exegetai pythochrestoi existed at all in the classical period (though individual Delphians may
sometimes have served, and all religious specialists could provide exegesis within their own
speciality). But refs. to *the* exegete/s seem to presuppose an institution.

acquired new powers, but not to our knowledge in the religious sphere.[11] In a text of the Lycurgan period, 'the generals' appear, rather unexpectedly, in charge of a series of large public sacrifices;[12] slight shifts thus constantly took place in the allocation of ritual dignity within the state. But no fundamental structure or principle was affected.

No single great story confronts us. Instead, this chapter will treat disparate themes: the religious policy of Athens as a 'post-imperial' power, and in particular her continuing dealings with Delos; the new introductions to the city's pantheon in the fourth century; and finally the religious programme associated with Lycurgus (which brings with it the reform of the ephebate). We begin with the post-imperial power.

With the loss of the empire, the great Athenian festivals were no longer thronged with allies, attending voluntarily or perforce. The *Panathenaea* and *Dionysia* ceased to be occasions of imperial display. Only occasionally can faint echoes of motifs from the fifth century be heard. By the terms of an 'agreement between the allies' (i.e. the Second Athenian Confederacy) 'and the Parians' of 372, it is laid down that the Parians should bring a 'cow and a panoply to the *Panathenaea* and a cow and phallus to the *Dionysia* . . . as being [colonists] of the people of Athens'.[13] That looks like a first attempt to restore the conditions of the fifth century; but it led to nothing if so, and it is not until after the collapse of the Second Confederacy that we again find cities of Asia Minor sending cattle and panoply to the *Panathenaea*, of their own accord in this case, to express solidarity with their 'mother-city'.[14]

Temple-inventories do, however, from time to time show gold crowns sent to the goddess by allied and even unconnected cities,

---

[11] So Wallace, *Areopagus Council*, 210–11 (*aliter*, tentatively, 111); on the actual new powers see ibid. 175–84, 198–201. The Areopagus' concern with 'impiety' possibly increased later, under Demetrius of Phaleron (see Ch. 12, n. 94).

[12] *IG* II².1496; cf. ns. 72 and 108.

[13] *SEG* XXXI 67, which is the perhaps over-optimistic interpretation of a very worn stone by S. Accame, *La lega ateniese del sec. iv a.c.* (Rome 1941), 230 (whose argument that the Parians had rebelled, but are none the less treated with some mildness, is accepted by e.g. J. Cargill, *The Second Athenian League*, Berkeley 1981, 163–64). On the 'colonial' status of the Parians see Hornblower, *Mausolus*, 193; cf. Smarczyk, *Religionspolitik*, 158 f.

[14] See B. D. Meritt and H. T. Wade-Gery, *JHS* 82 (1962), 69–71, for the dispatch of πομπὴ καὶ πανοπλία as a μνημεῖον τῆς ἐξ ἀρχῆς συγγενείας καὶ φιλίας by Priene somewhere between 334 and 322 (*Inscr. Priene* 5: cf. ibid. 6; cf. Hornblower, *Mausolus*, 325 n. 264; Osborne, *Naturalization*, III/IV.129), of crown and panoply 'as an *aristeion* for Athena' by the Colophonians 'as colonists' upon the liberation of Athens in 307/6 (*IG* II².456: cf. 470 for Colophonian friendship); the Tenians too perhaps promised to dispatch a *bous* in 307/6 (*IG* II².466 23–24). For a second-cent. instance see *Inscr. Priene* 45, and C. Habicht, *Chiron* 21 (1991), 329.

probably as 'excellence awards' (*aristeia*) on the occasion of the
Panathenaea (for at competitive festivals the presiding god was commonly awarded first prize *ex officio*). Such voluntary tributes to the
state's goddess were in effect expressions of loyalty or friendship,
virtually indistinguishable in meaning from the gold crowns which
from time to time cities sent to 'the Athenian council' or 'people'.
When the Macedonian domination was temporarily overthrown in
307, Athens duly received a flurry of expressions of support of all
these types.[15] Any first-fruits that continued to come to the goddesses of Eleusis from foreign states (as Isocrates around 380 still
claims that they did[16]) will likewise have been voluntarily offered, as
a tribute in this case less to Athens than to the genuine religious
prestige of the Eleusinian cult.

Upon Delos, however, Athens' religious pretensions weighed
scarcely less heavily in the fourth century than they had in the fifth.
The island had, it is true, become independent after the battle of
Aegospotami, and the Spartans Lysander and Pharax had seized the
opportunity to make dedications in the temple, in a gesture doubtless of symbolic taking-possession like that by which, at the end of
the Peloponnesian war, Lysander forced a gift on the very Athena of
the Athenian acropolis.[17] But the 'Athenian Amphictyons' were
back shortly after the battle of Cnidus in 394, and did not depart,
except probably for a short break in the 380s when the King's Peace
supposedly inaugurated a period of general independence, until
314/3 or thereabouts.[18] The Delians survived as a *polis*, with their
own shrines and festivals and even, to a limited extent, their own foreign relations; but the jewel in their crown, the sanctuary of Apollo
and Artemis with all its properties, was effectively under Athenian
control; and numerous, apparently, were the Athenians who actually
lived on the sacred island.[19] The great quadrennial festival first
instituted in 427 was revived, and is certainly likely to have become
an important attraction within the world of the islands; unfortunately, the visitors, wherever they may have come from, have left
few traces. Athenian choirs, Xenophon assures us a little ingenu-

[15] See *IG* II².1485 A (cf. previous note). Crowns for *boule* and *demos*: *IG* II².1425.221–31;
1441, 1443.89–122, 1485 A, 1491.14; Dem. 22.72. On Panathenaic and other such *aristeia* see
the refs. in L. Robert, *BCH* 109 (1985), 472.

[16] *Paneg.* 31; but by 329/8 offerings seem to come from Attica and Attic possessions alone
(*IG* II².1672.263–88; *SEG* XXX 61 B fr. a 13 and *IG* II².140 are unrevealing on this point).*

[17] *Inscr. Dél.* 104.82, 120, with Coupry's note ad loc. (p. 42). Lysander on the acropolis: e.g.
IG II².1388.32.

[18] See Coupry on *Inscr. Dél.* 97, 98, 104 (pp. 13, 21, 43); Rhodes, *Commentary Ath. Pol.*, on
ch. 62.2. For a complication see Hornblower, *Mausolus*, 190.

[19] See J. Coupry in *Atti del terzo congresso internazionale di epigrafia greca e latina* (Rome
1959), 55–69; for Athenian residents see ibid. 64.

ously, always outstrip their competitors on these occasions with ease.[20] From 359, we find a commission of *Naopoioi*, temple-builders, busily and expensively at work—set up in rivalry, it has been suggested, with the *Naopoioi* who were engaged at just that time in rebuilding the great temple at Delphi. Certainly, it seems to have been a large temple of—a little paradoxically—the Pythian Apollo that the Delian *Naopoioi* were having built.[21]

Many Delians bitterly resented the Athenian domination.[22] In 376/5, eight islanders, some of them influential men, were sentenced to large fines and 'permanent exile' (on a charge of 'impiety') for 'driving the Amphictyons out of the temple and beating them up'; the appearance of Andrian Amphictyons alongside the Athenians for a brief period after 374/3 may represent a concession caused by this incident.[23] A great enemy of Athens perhaps tried to woo the islanders during his Aegean cruise of 364, to judge from 'a crown coming from Epaminondas' that appears in the inventories. In the 40s or 30s a pro-Athenian Delian had to flee to Athens for his life.[24] And in the 340s the point in dispute came into the open in a formal debate between the Delians and the Athenians as to 'which should control the sanctuary'. The Delians had apparently seized their chance and appealed for arbitration to the Delphic Amphictyony, once this fell under the control of Athens' enemy Philip.[25] Out of respect, presumably, for Greek opinion, the Athenians accepted the

[20] Inscriptions give some indication of the scale and costs of the festival—see *Inscr. Dél.* 98.32–40 (Tod, *GHI* II.125) (109 sacrificial oxen), 100.40–43; 93 and 95 are less clear—but not of the identity of the *archetheoroi* for whom a mysteriously large sum, a talent, was set aside (98.34). For the crown that attests the regular performance of the festival see *Inscr. Dél.* 101, with Coupry's commentary ad loc. (p. 32; also pp. 42–43). For Delos' associations in the period cf. the cities which borrowed from the shrine (*Inscr. Dél.* 98 A 11–15; B 1–10); for dedications, see 104, with Coupry's list, p. 43, bottom. Xenophon: *Mem.* 3.3.12.

[21] See *Inscr. Dél.* 104-4, 104-5, 104-24; Coupry, *Terzo congresso*; and on the building in question Bruneau/Ducat, *Guide de Délos*, 150–51 [+]; it had a frieze depicting deeds of Theseus, according to J. Marcadé cited by Coupry on *Inscr. Dél.* 104-24 (p. 94).

[22] See esp. M. J. Osborne, *Eranos* 72 (1974), 168–84.

[23] *Inscr. Dél.* 98 B 24–30 = Tod, *GHI* II.125.134–42: two of the culprits may be attested as Delian archons (Tod, *GHI* II.81; W. Laidlaw, *A History of Delos*, Oxford 1933, 80). Andrian Amphictyons: see e.g. Rhodes, *Commentary Ath. Pol.*, on 62.2; for other ripples from the affair cf. Osborne, *Eranos* 72 (1974), 171–74.

[24] On the cruise see Osborne, *Eranos* 72 (1974), 173–74 (who associates with it the Athenians' need to renew ties with their Delian supporters, shown by *Inscr. Dél.* 88 = *SIG*³ 158); for the στέφανος χρυσοῦς δάφνης ὁ παρ' Ἀμεινώνδα (or Ἐπαμεινώνδα) ἀπελθών see *IG* XI.2.161 B 46 (and other refs. cited ad loc.). Why ἀπελθών (a unique qualification in these lists)? Had Epaminondas piously 'sent back' to the god a crown the islanders had sent to honour him? Pro-Athenian Delian: Osborne, *Eranos* 72 (1974), 175–84, on *IG* II².222, which he dates to c.334.

[25] For this (universally accepted) reconstruction from our very scrappy sources see H. Wankel, *Demosthenes Rede für Ktesiphon über den Kranz* (Heidelberg 1976), 727–30 (on Dem. 18.134); on the date (between 345 and 343), Osborne, *Eranos* 72 (1974), 176, n. 19.

legitimacy of the appeal, and dispatched the graceful Hyperides (wisely substituted by the Areopagus for their first choice, Aeschines) to plead their case.

The *Delian Speech* that he delivered was one of his most famous in antiquity.[26] If it survived, it would of course be the starting-point for any account of Athens' claim to the island. It would also be an almost matchless specimen of the application of mythological arguments in political debate: 'he makes abundant use of myth', says one ancient critic, 'to show that the sanctuary had belonged to Athens from ancient times'.[27] It is worth pausing even over the fragments (and over those of some related traditions), in order to get the feel of a certain mode of discourse.

A rare word indicating 'the writings in accord with which colonists set out' is cited from the speech (fr. 73); Hyperides doubtless used it in connection with the claim, which is already attested in Pindar, that Delos was in origin an Athenian colony. A yet earlier connection between the two places may also have been exploited (no fragment attests it, but the tradition appears in the almost contemporary *Atthis* of Phanodemus): the first pilgrimage to the sacred island had been led by Cecrops' son Erysichthon, who had even, some said, founded the first temple of Apollo.[28] But Hyperides went back yet further, to the very birth of the god. That the sacred event had occurred on Delos could scarcely be denied; it would indeed have been ridiculous to do so, and so strip the island of the especial sanctity which made it a prize worth competing for. But the great event was put, as it were, under Attic patronage: it was at Cape Zoster near Athens that Leto, her hour near at hand, had loosed her girdle (*zoster*), and it was Athena Foresight (*Pronoia*) who then guided the suffering mother to Delos—that Athena Foresight whose temple stood at Prasiae in east Attica, starting-point of one of the ancient pilgrimage-routes to Delos.[29]

[26] Hyperides XIII, frs. 67–75 Jensen, *FGrH* 401b; cf. A. Boeckh, *Kleine Schriften*, V (Leipzig 1871), 447–52 (from *Abh. Preuss. Ak.* 1834). Delian antiquities were also treated extensively in the same period in Lycurgus' speech of prosecution 'Against Menesaechmus, Concerning the Sacrifice on Delos' (frs. 82–90 Blass, XIV Conomis, *FGrH* 401c).

[27] See the testimonia to fr. 67 Jensen. The text pub. by J. Bosquet, *REG* 101 (1988), 12–53 (*SEG* XXXVIII 1476) is a spectacular instance from the late third cent. of an argument designed to demonstrate συγγενεία ἀπό τε τῶν θεῶν καὶ τῶν ἡρώων between two distant cities.

[28] Pindar fr. 52e = *Paean* 5.35–40 Snell/Maehler, with Σ; *FGrH* 325 F 2.

[29] Hyperid. fr. 67; actual birth of Apollo at C. Zoster is mentioned only (among other unorthodox claims) by Semos of Delos, *FGrH* 396 F 20. For Athena Pronoia at Prasiae see *Anecd. Bekk.* 1.299.6–7 (a cult on Delos itself is mentioned only by Macr. *Sat.* 1.17.55, whom Bruneau, *Recherches*, 249, disbelieves). Erysichthon supposedly died at Prasiae on his way back from Delos, Paus. 1.31.2 (cf. Kron, *Phylenheroen*, 94); it is not, however, clear that the Athenian state *theoria* to Delos started from there (G. M. and M. E. Hirst, *CR* 41, 1927, 113 f.).

Prasiae appears in another tradition which Hyperides in all probability exploited, so closely does it display the same concerns as his own. Herodotus tells how mysterious offerings, wrapped in a wheat-sheaf, were sent to Apollo of Delos stage by stage from the sacred land of Apollo beyond the North Wind. But according to Pausanias these offerings, which for Herodotus on reaching Greece passed from Dodona to Euboea to Carystus to Tenos to Delos, made the last stage of their journey via Prasiae instead, under Attic escort. The report gained a new interest when Delian inscriptions of the fourth century were published in which 'offerings from the Hyperboreans' are duly mentioned, in contexts which suggest that they still arrived from time to time, perhaps in connection with the great festival.[30] If so, the Athenians had apparently kidnapped not just a myth (which is certain), but also a practice—completely mysterious though the identity of the 'Hyperboreans' who set the offering-relay in motion must remain.

Panhellenic themes apparently had a place in Hyperides' speech, and one of his claims was doubtless that the Athenians administered Delos in the best interests of all Greece. One fragment (69) runs 'the Greeks in common mix the Panionian mixing-bowl' (an object known from the temple-inventories); and he mentioned the Attic festival of *Proerosia* (fr. 75), which, according to a myth that was given new emphasis in the fourth century, had its origin in a sacrifice offered in a time of famine by the Athenians 'on behalf of all the Greeks'. Hyperides' handling of the myths was, according to 'Longinus', graceful and poetical; he will have adopted a grimmer tone in describing (fr. 70) the ugly massacre of Aeolian pilgrims which (as the Athenians had probably already argued in 425) rendered the Delians unfit to manage a sacred place.[31] And yet, as has often been noted, it was doubtless neither the orator's elegance nor his earnestness that won the cause, but rather Philip's desire to make a conciliatory concession to Athens at no cost to himself.

Philip had been subjected to another lecture on ancient history by an Athenian orator in 346, when Aeschines explained to the king

[30] So J. Tréheux in *Studies Presented to D. M. Robinson*, II (Saint Louis 1953), 758–74, commenting on Hdt. 4.33, Paus. 1.31.2, and *Inscr. Dél.* 100.49, 104-3 A 8. Bruneau, *Recherches*, 38–48 (followed by Smarczyk, *Religionspolitik*, 515, n. 53), uses the presence of Sinope in Pausanias' route to associate the change with Pericles' Pontic expedition (H. Gallet de Santerre, *Délos primitive et archaïque*, Paris 1958, 168, n. 7, had thought of the Pisistratids). H. W. Parke, however, *The Oracles of Zeus* (Oxford 1967), 285 f., ascribes Pausanias' version to the later period of Attic domination of Delos, beginning in 166 BC.

[31] Panionian krater: *Inscr. Dél.* 104.129. *Proerosia*: cf. Lycurgus frs. 84–85 Blass, XIV.4–5 Conomis, also in a Delian context (and in general Smarczyk, *Religionspolitik*, 190–93)—were the 'Hyperborean offerings' explained as originating in a quid pro quo in gratitude for the *Proerosia*? 'Longinus': *De Subl.* 34.2. Massacre: cf. Ch. 8, n. 117 above.

how the site of Amphipolis belonged to the Athenians by ancient right, having been granted to Akamas the son of Theseus as a dowry. Three years later, at a most delicate moment in the relation between Philip and Greek public opinion, a Thessalian historian 'discovered' various myths which proved that, lo, the various disputed cities in the Thraceward region, and also a seat on the Amphictyonic council, belonged to Philip by ancient right. To his great disgrace (unless he is victim of a misascription) Plato's nephew Speusippus commended the work to the king, adding on his own account that Philip was in fact a fellow citizen of the Athenians: had not his ancestor Heracles been adopted by an Athenian in order to be initiated at Eleusis?[32]

How seriously were such appeals to remote antiquity taken, at this date? Numerous complex issues lie beneath the surface of the apparently simple question. Here we might merely note the status of myth in Atthidography, a literary genre that seems to reflect very accurately the outlook of the speech-making classes (to which several Atthidographers in fact belonged) in the fourth century. Every *Atthis* begins, as a matter of course, in the mythical period; that is where the *summa* of worthwhile knowledge about Attica starts. But every *Atthis* also of course continues with the intervening centuries, the history of which it recounts in ever-increasing detail.[33] A Greek of the fourth century, in contrast to one, say, of the seventh, was separated from the heroes by a thick wedge of history. And of course any Atthidographer would acknowledge that the earlier sections of his work depended more on uncertain tradition, on 'what is said', than the later. Myth has become 'ancient', as we see, for instance, from a passage where Aeschines describes to an Athenian jury the speech he had made to Philip about Amphipolis. 'On that occasion it was appropriate to speak about the original acquisition of the territory and the place called Ennea Hodoi and the sons of Theseus, of whom Akamas is said to have received the country as dowry for his wife; and I spoke with all the precision that was possible. But now I probably ought to abbreviate. I also mentioned the proofs that derive not from ancient myths but from events that occurred in our

---

[32] Aeschin. 2.31; E. J. Bickerman and J. Sykutris, *Speusipps Brief an König Philipp* (*SBLeip* 80, 1928, 3), with Bickerman's masterly commentary (where the other fourth-cent. instances used here are quoted), 22–24, 42–44. The frs. quoted from the Thessalian, Antipater the Magnesian, appear as *FGrH* 69 F 1–2; for the debate about the letter's authenticity see H. Flashar ed., *Ältere Akademie* (= vol. III of the rev. of F. Ueberweg, *Grundriss der Geschichte der Philosophie*, Basle 1983), 22 [+]. Speusippus wanted to be appointed tutor to Alexander, according to M. M. Markle III, *JHS* 96 (1976), 92–99. Isocrates' *Philippos* repeatedly stresses the king's supposed descent from Heracles.

[33] This is not to deny that the relation between 'archaeology' and 'history' varied from *Atthis* to *Atthis*: Jacoby, *Atthis*, 111–19.

own time . . .' and these he goes on to recount to the jury.[34] 'Akamas is said', 'all the precision that was possible', 'ancient myths': myth is fading, for Aeschines, into the mists of antiquity.

Was his appeal to it then, when addressing Philip, mere ceremonial flimflam, one of the obsolete elegancies of a diplomatic encounter?[35] Hyperides' *Deliakos* was certainly ceremonial in style, and it was certainly in interstate encounters that such arguments tended to be adduced: the daduch Kallias, for instance, on the occasion of the peace of 371, pompously reminded the Spartans of the ancient friendship between their peoples created by the initiation of Heracles and the Dioscuri at Eleusis; and Callistratus in the 360s warned the Arcadians not to ally themselves with Thebes and Argos, the cities of polluted Oedipus and Orestes (but where did those heroes end their lives, Epaminondas pointedly asked in reply). The formulation is none the less too extreme. Greeks felt that land properly belonged to its 'original' owners (unless wrenched from them by way of reprisal in a just war):[36] thus in debates about territory they adduced myths of origin, although of course these normally proved inconclusive, because of their intrinsic uncertainty and because such issues are normally settled in the end by considerations of power and interest. And it was not for diplomatic or ceremonial purposes that Atthidographers recorded the traditions of their city. We live by traditions, they might have said, even if we cannot wholly believe in them.

The fourth-century history of Athens' other extra-Attic religious centre, that at Oropus, was touched on in another chapter.[37] We turn instead, once again, to new cults; but the new cults of the fourth century raise quite different questions from those of the fifth. No 'foreign' god is imported except Ammon, a special case; rather, we find sacrifices being made to a series of (as we would call them) personified abstract nouns. The great public festivals of the late 330s are illuminated for us, brilliantly and unexpectedly, by the chance that

[34] Aeschin. 2.31. On the 'antiquity' of myth cf. e.g. Isoc. *Paneg.* 30, 68; Lycurg. *Leoc.* 83. For 'mythical/heroic' time contrasted to 'what is more recent', 'what we ourselves are witnesses to' vel sim. see Thuc. 1.73.2; Dem. 23.65, 60.8–9; Isoc. *Archid.* 24, 42. .

[35] See Veyne, *Les Grecs ont-ils cru à leurs mythes?*, 89 ff. 'Le mythe employé comme "langue de bois" '.

[36] Cf. Bickerman/Sykutris, *Speusipps Brief*, and Bickerman, *Revue internationale des droits de l'antiquité* 4 (1950), 123–24 (German version in F. Gschnitzer, *Zur griechischen Staatskunde*, Darmstadt 1969, 498–500), adduced by Smarczyk, *Religionspolitik*, 323–25. Callias and Epaminondas: Xen *Hell.* 6.3.6; Nepos, *Epaminondas* 6.1–3 (cf. Plut. *Reg. Apophth.* 193c–d etc.). On appeals to mythical συγγένεια see the new text from Xanthos, n. 27 above, and the works of L. Robert cited by the ed., p. 38, n. 47.

[37] See Ch. 8 above.

Lycurgus treated the proceeds from the sale of the skins of the victims as a separate item of public revenue, partial records of which
survive;[38] and of the sixteen powers to whom sacrifices are listed,
three are personified abstractions, Democracy, Peace, and Agathe
Tyche. We will look at them individually, before turning to the more
general issues raised by the deification of such powers. Evidence for
the worship of abstractions in other Greek states post-dates that
from Athens, though not necessarily by very long;[39] so the phenomenon can best be studied in the Attic context.

'Democracy' had been known as a figure, as well as a constitution,
at least since she had been shown on the tomb of Critias at the end of
the fifth century, receiving a drubbing at the hands of oligarchy.
Even before that, as we learn from Antiphon, the *boule* was making
sacrifices 'for the Democracy'. In the fourth century, triremes were
named after her, and Euphranor grouped her with Theseus and
Demos in a famous painting. She aroused a particular flurry of interest in the 330s, a time when, as we see from Eucrates' 'law against
tyranny' of 337/6, she was felt by some to be under renewed threat:
Eucrates' law itself was topped by a relief which apparently shows
Demos crowned by Democracy; and in 333/2 a statue of her was
dedicated in the *agora* by the *boule*, very probably the giant statue of
which the torso was discovered in 1970.[40]

In the skin-sale records of 332/1, under the month Boedromion,
appears a sacrifice 'to Democracy'. About the origins of her cult
(which is first attested by that entry) two plausible accounts confront
one another. It has often been suggested[41] that this sacrifice to
Democracy in Boedromion is identical with a 'thanksgiving for free-

---

[38] *IG* II².1496.68–151 (= *SIG*³ 1029). S. C. Humphreys in S. N. Eisenstadt ed., *The Origins and Diversity of Axial Age Civilizations* (Albany NY 1986), 102–103, briefly discusses the list, stressing that most of the largest festivals are not of archaic type; cf. now Rosivach, *Public Sacrifice*, 48–67. The value of an oxhide, and thus the number of animals sacrificed in each case, is uncertain: after a careful calculation, M. H. Jameson suggests 6–7 drachmas per hide (in C. R. Whittaker ed., *Pastoral Economies in Classical Antiquity*, *PCPS* Suppl. 14, 1988, 107–12; similarly now Rosivach, *Public Sacrifice*, 95–96, 155–57, though he regards only the outer limits of 'between 4 and 10' drachmas as certain). Ammon: see Ch. 9, n. 157.

[39] Note esp. the remarkable new 'Decree on Concord' from Mytilene (*SEG* XXXVI 750: of the 330s?), which records a *votum publicum* to Zeus Heraios and Basileus and Homonoios (all titles of Zeus) and Homonoia and Dike and Ἐπιτέλεια εια τῶν ἀγαθῶν.

[40] For details see A. E. Raubitschek, *Hesperia* 31 (1962), 238–43 (the main study, which identified the *boule*'s dedication of 333/2); O. Palagia, *Hesperia* 51 (1982), 111–13 (the giant torso); and for a summary, O. Alexandri-Tzahou, *LIMC* III.1 (1986), 372–74; add (on Antiphon 6.45) M. H. Hansen, *Liverpool Classical Monthly* 11 (1986), 35–36.*

[41] First apparently by A. R. van der Loeff, *De Ludis Eleusiniis* (Leiden 1903), 78 f., citing Plut. *De Glor. Ath.* 7.349f, followed e.g. by Deubner, *Attische Feste*, 39. On attitudes to 'the heroes of Phyle' soon after the event see Tod, *GHI* II.100, with Tod's commentary; Loraux, *L'invention*, 201–204. Sacrifice to Democracy: *IG* II².1496.131–32 (year 332/1: sacrificed by the generals; the skins fetched 414½ drachmas), ibid. 140–41 (following year, sums lost).

dom' which is said by Plutarch to have been offered on the twelfth of the same month, the day on which the democrats returned from exile at Phyle in 403. In that case, it might have been instituted quite soon after 403; and, what is more important, the cult of the abstraction would have had its origin in a particular great event, the memory of which it preserved. We saw in an earlier chapter that many of the new cults of the fifth century were in a sense war-memorials, in lightly disguised form.

Alternatively, it may be that the cult only began when the *boule* of 333/2 dedicated what would, therefore, have been the cult-statue.[42] On this view, it was in part anxiety about her future that made Democracy into a goddess. (The two views are not strictly incompatible, since even a cult founded in the 330s could have harked back to heroic earlier events; but it would be somewhat odd to describe a sacrifice first offered in the 330s as a 'thanksgiving for the freedom' recovered in 403.) At all events, the cult survived (or perhaps revived) in the late third century, when a priest of Democracy, and apparently a procession in her honour, are found.[43]

About Peace we can be more definite. She is already personified as one of the Hours in Hesiod, and appears in art by the late fifth century; Aristophanes can play with the idea of making sacrifice to her in his *Peace* of 421 (and she is a 'child-nurturing goddess' in Euripides' *Bacchae*):[44] but our more reliable sources agree that she first in fact received cult in celebration of the eagerly greeted though short-lived peace that followed Timotheus' victory over the Spartans near Corcyra in 375. Here then the association of the abstract cult with a specific event is explicitly attested. What is more, the character of that event sets the idea of 'Peace' in a particular light which is not that of a nascent pacifism. Of course, the cult must

[42] So e.g. Mitchel, 'Lykourgan Athens', 206. The silence of *IG* II².1496 about sacrifices to Democracy in earlier years allows no argument: the relevant entry for 333/2 is lost, while receipts for 334/3 (the first year of the surviving record) only begin in mid-year, after the presumptive date of the sacrifice (presumably because the *dermatikon* fund was only set up halfway through this year). Loraux, *L'invention*, 286–87 is rightly cautious.

[43] See Maass, *Prohedrie*, 108–13, on *IG* II².5029a, where a priest appears, closely associated with the priest of the Demos and Graces and of Ptolemy Euergetes; and an ephebic decree of 214/3 (*Hesperia* 48, 1979, 174–78, no. 1 = *SEG* XXIX 116) which mentions (18), in a fragmentary context, Δημοκρατίαι τὴν πομπήν. Even if the reference is to a separate statue of Democracy on Salamis (cf. line 17, and *IG* II².1011.62, which, given the parallels cited by Pélékidis, *Éphébie*, 201, n. 7, may well refer to a Salaminian monument), one might *a fortiori* expect similar attentions to the Democracy of the *agora*.

[44] *Theog.* 901–902; *Peace* 1017–19; *Bacchae* 419–20. For the many other literary references, and the artistic evidence, see E. Simon in *LIMC* III.1 (1986), 700–705; Shapiro, *Personifications*, 45–50. She consorts on an equal footing with Olympians on a recently pub. altar from Brauron, *IG* I³.1407 bis ('c. a. 420–410' *IG* I³, where, however, a lower dating is countenanced).

also have been a celebration of 'the blessings of peace': a famous statue by Cephisodotus, perhaps the cult statue itself, showed the cheerful goddess with the boy Wealth in her arms. But Isocrates, our earliest witness, explains that Timotheus' victory had forced the Spartans to make terms which destroyed their power, 'in consequence of which from that day on we have sacrificed to Peace every year, in the belief that no other peace has brought such benefits to the city'. Is it a coincidence that a new Gold Victory, the first of the century, appears in the inventories of the Treasurers of Athena in 374/3? The cult began and was for some time remembered as one of Glorious Peace, in a century in which Athens had to accept so many peaces that were bitter humiliations. It too was a kind of war-memorial.[45]

The sacrifice to Peace took place on the same day as the old festival of *Synoikia*. The explanation may be in part contingent, this being perhaps the actual day on which the peace was made; but one might also suspect a desire to revitalize the ancient ceremony by introducing a contemporary note. The old festival of civic unity— the original source of Athens' power—became in addition a celebration of a peace that, it was hoped, confirmed Athens' primacy among the Greek states. A fragmentary inscription, which was to be set up 'beside the *stele* concerning the Peace' and lays down regulations for a new musical and athletic festival, possibly shows how eagerly the new goddess was honoured, in the early years. She was still receiving large sacrifices in the 330s, but disappears thereafter from our view.[46]

The cult of Peace and Democracy seems to have been, not sur-

---

[45] Foundation in 375: Isoc. 15.109–10 (whence the passage quoted); Philoch. *FGrH* 328 F 151 (cf. Jacoby ad loc. on Plut. *Cim.* 13.5, which wrongly speaks of the Peace of Callias); Nepos, *Timotheus* 2.2: 'quae victoria tantae fuit Atticis laetitiae ut tum primum arae Paci publice sint factae eique deae pulvinar sit institutum'. On the peace see G. L. Cawkwell, *Historia* 12 (1963), 84–95. Timotheus was honoured with a statue in the *agora*, which kept the memory of his victory alive: Aeschin. 3.243. Cephisodotus' statue: Robertson, *History*, 384; H. Jung, *JdI* 91 (1976), 97–134 (who pleads for a date in the 360s); E. Simon, *LIMC* s.v. *Eirene*, 702, no. 6 (on the recently discovered Panathenaic amphorae of 360/59 which depict the statue); see e.g. Parke, *Festivals*, pl. 3. New Gold Victory: e.g. *IG* II².1424.31 ff., cf. A. M. Woodward, *ArchEph* 1937, 167–68; but see Ferguson, *Treasurers*, 118, n. 1, 137, for the view that it had been planned since 378/7.

[46] *Synoikia*: Σ Ar. *Pax* 1019: cf. Mikalson, *Calendar*, 31. Date of the peace: so Cawkwell, *Historia* 12 (1963), 90, n. 56. Festival: P. Roussel, *RA* 18 (1941), 215 f. and L. Robert, *ArchEph* 1977, 211–16 (Robert, *OMS* VII.781–86), on *Hesperia* 7 (1938), 295, no. 20; but, unless we think of a reinscription, their argument, from the introductory formula, for an early date can scarcely outweigh the consensus of Attic epigraphists that the letter forms are Lycurgan (so the first ed., E. Schweigert; A. M. Woodward, *BSA* 51, 1956, 3–5, whence *SEG* XVI 55; M. B. Walbank, *Vanderpool Studies*, 173–82, who ascribes this and the new text he publishes to the same cutter). Sacrifice: *IG* II².1496.95 (year 333/2; sacrificed by the generals; skin-yield 874 drachmas), ibid. 127–28 (next year, 710½ drachmas).

prisingly, exclusively public. The third of the new abstractions, Agathe Tyche (the form in which Athens honoured 'luck'), also had an important public aspect: in 304/3, for instance, the Athenians resolved to sacrifice to Athena Nike, Agathe Tyche, and 'the Saviours' for the protection of their troops on campaign.[47] But unlike the other two she was also of importance to individuals; and her wider popularity is reflected in the much more varied evidence that there is for her cult (two sacred precincts are mentioned, for instance[48]). Several dedications and votive reliefs of the fourth century survive;[49] and, though two of these were made by persons active in politics and point back indirectly to the public sphere, a remarkable relief in Copenhagen sets her in a quite different context. Here three worshippers, a man and two women, approach a banqueting god and goddess: the inscription reads 'Dedicated by Aristomache, Theoris, and Olympiodorus to Zeus Fulfiller, of Friendship [*Epiteleios, Philios*], to the god's mother Friendship, to the god's wife Good Luck.' The three mortals, it has been suggested,[50] formed a trio of mother, son, and daughter-in-law like the divine family which they approached and which they had, on this hypothesis, fashioned in their own image (no tension between in-laws here!); however that may be, Zeus the son of Friendship and husband of Good Luck certainly looks like a product of that unusual phenomenon, individual invention within polytheism. A more normal associate of Agathe Tyche is Agathos Daimon, the power who received libations at the end of a meal. More immediately, perhaps, than other gods, Agathe Tyche is a product of language, a

---

[47] See Ch. 12, n. 28. Possibly the deme Kollytos made a similar decision in similar circumstances a little earlier: see line 29 of the text reconstituted by M. B. Walbank, *Hesperia* 63 (1994), 234–35, with the comments of S. V. Tracy, ibid. 241–42. But a parallel is desirable for the postulated use of ὑπάρχειν for the performance of a sacrifice.

[48] *IG* II².1035.44 (apparently Piraeus), 48 (site unknown): cf. Culley, *Sacred Monuments*, 146–48. Lycurgus' law *IG* II².333 (= Schwenk 21) speaks of her shrine, its *epistatai* and [*tamiai*]; the public sacrifice to her, however, was on a smallish scale (*IG* II².1496.76, 107–108, ? 148–49: the largest skin-sale yield is 160 drachmas). For Agathe Tyche in a public context see Din. 1.29, 98; it was Demosthenes' shield blazon, Plut. *Dem.* 20.2. Her associate Agathos Daimon received a dedication from prytaneis in (?) 343/2, *Agora* XV 35.

[49] See *IG* II².4564, a dedication to the Twelve Gods and Agathe Tyche by a trierarch of the 360s; 4610 (by Kalaides Lytidou, proposer of a decree in 303/2: *SEG* XXXVI 165); (?) 4644 (cf. n. 52 below); 4761 ('I/II p.'). A. Greifenhagen (*RhM* 52, 1937, 238–39) associated with Agathe Tyche *IG* II².4589 (Piraeus, (?) late fourth cent., from the supposed Asclepieum region: van Straten, 'Gifts', 120 10.2), a healing-relief dedicated to 'Agathe theos', who is shown holding a cornucopia, as is Agathe Tyche in *IG* II².4644 (n. 52 below); but there is no other firm evidence that Agathe Tyche is a healer (ἀγαθῇ τύχῃ is doubtless a heading, not a dedication, in the late healing-votive *ZPE* 87, 1991, 173–74, also from the Piraeus). On extra-Attic evidence for Agathe Tyche see Graf, *Nordionische Kulte*, 163.

[50] By C. Blinkenberg, as cited in *IG* II².4627: cf. Dentzer, *Banquet couché*, 503–505, 594 R 228 [+], Nilsson, *Geschichte*, pl. 28.2.

translation from word into form of the fixed appeal for good luck that was made at the start of decrees of the assembly and in many other contexts. Indeed it has been noted that the 'with good luck' formula, used spasmodically hitherto, becomes a cliché of decrees in just the same period (the second half of the fourth century) as evidence for actual worship of Agathe Tyche first appears.[51] None the less, like the other personified deities of the fourth century, this product of language became subject of an important work of art, in this case a statue, probably by Praxiteles, in a symbolic centre of public life, the Prytaneum; perhaps she was shown holding a cornucopia, as in one inscribed relief.[52] The date of her formal consecration is unknown; Tyche had of course long been known to literature as a supernatural power.[53]

Of the cult of various other personified abstractions worshipped at Athens, we know regrettably little. The shrine of Eukleia was built, according to Pausanias, with spoils from the Persian wars; the goddess re-emerges in the Roman period, when she shares a priest and a precinct—as she may have done from the start—with Eunomia.[54] Modesty (*aidos*) and simplicity (*apheleia*)—the two nurses, according to an otherwise unattested myth, of Athena—supposedly had altars on the acropolis; and in discussing the famous 'Altar of Pity' at Athens (which seems in fact to have been a late creation) Pausanias also mentions an altar of Impulse, *Horme*; abundance too, *Euporia*,

[51] By S. V. Tracy, '*IG* II² 1195 and Agathe Tyche in Attica', *Hesperia* 63 (1994), 241–44, at 243.

[52] Praxiteles: Aelian, *VH* 9.39, Pliny *HN* 36.23 (who also mentions a 'bonus eventus', commonly taken to represent 'agathos daimon'); cf. Palagia, *Hesperia* 51 (1982), 110, n. 62 (who also—109, n. 61—discusses the iconography of Agathe Tyche). Inscribed relief: *IG* II².4644, v. Straten, 'Gifts', 120 10.2 (who apparently rejects the view of Walter, *Akropolismuseum*, 186, that it is not a votive but comes from a document: it is not discussed in Meyer, *Urkundenreliefs*). Agathos Daimon: see F. Dunand, *LIMC* s.v. *Agathodaimon*, 277–82: her no. 4 (= Acropolis Museum no. 4069: Walter, *Acropolismuseum*, 184, no. 391; not in *IG* II²) is a votive relief showing Agathos Daimon and Agathe Tyche (both identified) with another female, perhaps Philia. Note too the graffito (M. Lang, *The Athenian Agora*, XXI, Princeton 1976, 54, G9) inscribed for Philia, Dionysus, Zeus Soter, Agathos Daimon, Agathe Tyche. For the formula ἀγαθῇ τύχῃ (normally used with imperatives) see e.g. Ar. *Av.* 436, 675; *Thesm.* 283; *Eccl.* 131; for the epigraphical uses see Tracy, '*IG* II² 1195 and Agathe Tyche', 243, ns. 27–28.

[53] The 'Agathe Tyche' identified on a Panathenaic amphora of 392/1 (Berlin Antiquarium 3980) can now be ignored: the figure is masculine (N. Eschbach, *Statuen auf panathenäischen Preisamphoren*, Mainz 1986, 23). For Tyche in literature see esp. Pind. *Ol.* 12; cf. G. Herzog-Hauser, *RE* s.v. *Tyche*; H. Strohm, *Tyche* (Stuttgart 1944); n. 67 below.

[54] Paus. 1.14.5 (cf. Ch. 9, n. 11 above); *IG* II².1035.53, 3738, 4193, 4874, 5059 (cf. Maass, *Prohedrie*, 127). Eukleia and Eunomia are already associated by Bacch. 13.183–89, and both appear in fifth-cent. vase-painting (see e.g. *LIMC* IV.1 (1988), 48–51, 62–65; Shapiro, *Personifications*, 70–85); [Dem.] 25.35 claims that there are altars of Eunomia, as of Dike and Aidos, 'among all men' (cf. the praise of Eunomia ibid. §11).

receives a dedication in the Roman period.[55] A rock-cut inscription in letters of the fifth century appears to attest a 'Shrine of Nymphs ⟨and⟩ Demos' on the Hill of the Nymphs (which is named from it) west of the acropolis;[56] but the combination 'Nymphs and Demos' is very strange, and some suspicion must remain that this was in fact a shrine not 'of' but owned by the people. We should also, of course, remember the various personifications who are sufficiently well integrated into Olympian mythology, or closely associated with particular Olympians, for it to be easy to think of them rather as ordinary gods: Peitho, Ploutos, Eros, Nemesis, and Themis. We know, finally, a little of the cult of Pheme, in consequence of an entertaining exchange between Aeschines and Demosthenes. 'The city and our ancestors founded an altar of Pheme, as being a great goddess,' says Aeschines in his speech against Timarchus; and he goes on to quote several poets' witness to her power. But the universal *pheme* of the city, he goes on, declares Timarchus to be a prostitute. 'If I had presented witnesses about an individual, you would have believed me. Will you then disbelieve me, if I cite the goddess as witness?' Aeschines is here interpreting the divine *pheme* as 'general repute, what men say'; the goddess' testimony thus proves a useful way of evading the need for actual evidence. But, when Demosthenes counters that, after all, men say that Aeschines has taken bribes from Philip, a distinction has to be introduced: it is *pheme* when 'the whole city spontaneously, for no reason, says that a thing has happened'; it is not *pheme* when cheap slanders are put about by a Demosthenes. On this second account, the divine *pheme* sounds less like 'what men say', more like a rumour of mysterious accuracy. Such was the *pheme* which brought word to the Greeks fighting at Mycale in 479, with supernatural speed, of their compatriots' victory at Plataea—a clear

---

[55] *Aidos* and *Apheleia*: Istrus *FGrH* 334 F 25, and the sources cited ad loc. by Jacoby; *IG* II².5147 (priest of *Aidos*). *Sophrosyne*, daughter of *Aidos*, is invoked in *CEG* 102 (= *IG* II².6859). (See too, for *Aidos* and *Dike*, [Dem.] 25.35, n. 54 above.) *Horme*: Paus. 1.17.1 (cf. the small marble votive altar of the Roman period dedicated to her, *IG* II².4734). *Euporia*: *SEG* XIX 224. On the 'altar of pity' see G. Zuntz, *ClMed* 14 (1953), 71–85; R. E. Wycherley, *CQ* NS 4 (1954), 143–50: unless we allow an allusion in Callim. fr. 51 (see A. S. Hollis, *ZPE* 93, 1992, 6), the first, ambiguous attestation is a passage deriving from Carneades/Clitomachus *ap.* Sext. Emp. *Adv. Math.* 9.187, which speaks of altars of pity at Athens. The 'altars' of Hybris and Anaideia found in some sources are a misunderstanding of the stones so named on the Areopagus (Paus. 1.28.5: see Jacoby on Istrus F 11). I am suspicious too of the supposed Ἀρᾶς ἱερόν, mentioned without any details in Hesych. α 6978 = Ar. fr. 585 K/A.

[56] *IG* I³.1065; see esp. U. Kron, *AM* 94 (1979), 63–75, who discusses the abundant iconographic evidence for a personified Demos (cf. in brief O. Alexandri-Tzahou in *LIMC* III.1 (1986), 375–82; and Meyer, *Urkundenreliefs*, 177–87). The much later cult of 'Demos and the Graces' is scarcely an adequate parallel, given its special meaning (Ch. 12 below). Possibly (?) 'Nymphs of the People': cf. *IG* I³.58.36 θεοὶ τὸ δέ⌊μο τὸ Ἀθεναίον.

proof for Herodotus of 'the divine element in events'. The ancient
commentator on Aeschines in fact claims that the cult was founded
when, in just the same way, news of Cimon's victory at Eurymedon
in the 460s reached Athens 'the same day'. But a cult so founded
would also, of course, have served as a commemoration of the victory itself.[57]

For a reason that will emerge, it is important to ask whether the
altars of these personifications were independent, or were sited
within the precinct of a different god. Aeschines says nothing of any
cult-associate Pheme may have had; but it is surely likely that her
altar lay close to one of the god of communication, Hermes.[58] We
might compare the case of Peitho. Isocrates complains that, though
the Athenians make sacrifice to Peitho each year, they view with suspicion all those persons, professors of rhetoric such as himself, who
seek to share the goddess's powers. One might infer that there
existed an independent cult of a Persuasion that was interpreted in
political or rhetorical terms. But Peitho had a place in the precinct of
Aphrodite Pandemos; and it is surely easier to suppose that Isocrates
is referring to this well-known cult than to postulate two distinct
public sacrifices to the same minor power. Most worshippers no
doubt supposed that the persuasion exercised by a Peitho who was
associated with Aphrodite—as so often in poetry—would be erotic;
but all persuasion is persuasion, and Isocrates was free to highlight
the opposite end of the broad spectrum of the goddess's powers.[59]
What of Eukleia? Her temple, according to Pausanias, was her own;
but in the rest of Greece she was regularly associated with Artemis,
as Artemis Eukleia, and it may be that this conception, which
Sophocles knew, was also informally present in Attica.[60] The altars

---

[57] Aeschin. 1.128–30 (with Σ); Dem. 19.243; Aeschin. 2.145; Hdt. 9.100.1 (such *phemai*
bringing word of victories are a *topos*: see Plut. *Aem.* 24.4–25). Hes. *Op.* 760–64 does, however, support Aeschines' interpretation of the divine *pheme* as 'what men say' (and see Pl. *Leg.*
838c–d on its morally coercive power). Bacch. 2 and 10 open with appeals to Pheme, as a messenger; oracular responses too are immortal *phemai* (Soph. *OT* 158; Eur. *Hel.* 820), as are
significant chance utterances of the kind also known as κληδόνες (Hom. *Od.* 20.100, 105, cf.
120). See M. Detienne, 'La rumeur, elle aussi, est une déesse', in id., *L'écriture d'Orphée* (Paris
1989), 135–45.   [58] Cf. Hdt. 9.100.

[59] Isoc. *Antid.* 249; Paus. 1.22.3. On the 'broad spectrum', and its underlying unity, see
R. G. A. Buxton, *Persuasion in Greek Tragedy* (Cambridge 1982), 29–48, 111, noting esp.
Aesch. *Eum.* 885, 970; Ar. *Lys.* 203; Men. *Epitrep.* 555 (379) (therefore the postulate, 34, of a
separate cult to which Isoc. and Dem. *Proem.* 54 [sacrifice by *prytaneis*] would refer appears
unnecessary). See too now V. Pirenne-Delforge, *RHR* 208 (1991), 395–413. For a priestess of
Peitho (Roman period), see *IG* II².5131. Amid the many prose dedications to 'Aphrodite'
found in her precinct at Daphni (*IG* II².4574–85: cf. Travlos, *Bildlexikon*, 184–85) is one, in
verse, addressed to 'Peitho' (*IG* II².4583: not in *CEG*).

[60] See Plut. *Arist.* 20.6, with F. W. Hamdorf, *Griechische Kultpersonifikationen der vorhel-
lenistischen Zeit* (Mainz 1964), 111, no. 442; Soph. *OT* 161, cited by D. C. Braund, *JHS* 100
(1980), 184.

of *aidos* and *apheleia* were on the acropolis, close to the temples of Athena; about *horme* we can only guess.

What can be said historically about the worship of 'personifications' in Attica? And, in particular, do the three fourth-century instances from which we started represent in any way a new phenomenon, as has often been supposed?[61] Any such claim needs to be hedged round with reservations. The deification or daimonization (better terms than personification) of abstract forces, it has been pointed out,[62] is a fundamental mode of archaic Greek religious thought. The Olympian gods themselves are powers as much as they are persons; it is not hard, therefore, for powers—the invisible powers that shape men's lives in mysterious ways—to be seen as divine. 'No *pheme* disappears altogether, which many men speak; *pheme* is a goddess, in fact', says Hesiod, in a passage duly cited by Aeschines in the interchange with Demosthenes we noted earlier. The easy transition from a description of Pheme's power to an inference that she is divine perfectly illustrates this mode of thought. And the nature of an Olympian god is defined by the powers that form his or her entourage: Dike sits beside Zeus, Peitho attends on Aphrodite. There are hundreds of such goddesses in the *Theogony*; the odes of Pindar and Bacchylides are thickly populated with them too, as are vases of the late fifth century; and Euripides is certainly continuing, though perhaps extending, the old usage when he makes characters say such things as 'recognizing one's friends is a god'.[63] The cultic deification of abstractions clearly continues this tradition; often, the very abstractions honoured in cult had previously been deified in poetry or art. If one is to detect, none the less, a rupture here, a significant change of direction, very strong stress has to be laid on the difference between deification in word or figure and that through acts of cult. It is one thing, the argument must run, to speak, momentarily, of Peace as a 'child-nurturing goddess'; quite another to assign to this instantaneous goddess a permanent altar, on which one will sacrifice a cow.

But it is not in fact the case that cultic deification of abstractions is unknown in the archaic period. To save the argument, a further and

---

[61] See esp. Nilsson, 'Kultische Personifikationen', *Eranos* 50 (1952), 31–40 = id., *Op. Sel.* III.233–42 (summarized in Nilsson, *Geschichte*, 812–15). Hamdorf (previous note) is a useful collection of material, marred by slapdash treatment of the important epigraphic evidence.

[62] By K. Reinhardt, 'Personifikation und Allegorie', in id., *Vermächtnis der Antike*[2] (Göttingen 1966), 7–40: a very important study. Better terms: for, as Reinhardt points out, abstract nouns are never personified without also becoming divine.

[63] Vases: see Shapiro, *Personifications, passim* and e.g. L. Burn, *The Meidias Painter* (Oxford 1987), 32–40. Pheme: Hes. *Op.* 763–64. On Euripides' usage see e.g. R. Kannicht's note on Eur. *Hel.* 559 f. Note too Hdt. 7.111 on the rebuff of Themistocles' 'two great gods', Persuasion and Compulsion, by the Poverty and Incapacity of the Andrians.

perhaps more important principle has therefore to be introduced:[64] in the early period, it is claimed, abstractions can only enter cult through what might be called 'Olympianization'. They must either infiltrate the genealogical and mythological world, as does Nemesis, or they must coalesce with an Olympian to form a couple such as Athena Nike or Artemis Eukleia, or at the least be closely associated with an Olympian, as is Peitho with Aphrodite. Worship of Peace— not Peace the daughter of Zeus or Aphrodite Peace—would therefore remain a new phenomenon.

What is new, therefore, is not the deification, in word or form, of abstractions, nor yet the cultic worship of them; the novelty lies rather in worshipping an abstraction which is at the same time allowed a certain autonomy from the world of the Olympians, in whose train such powers were traditionally found.[65] In this form, the proposition has considerable plausibility. But to sustain it—or at least to sustain the view that the change occurred in the fourth century—we must suppose that Pheme was indeed linked to Hermes and that Eukleia was indeed informally identified with Artemis;[66] for otherwise these are clear examples, in the fifth century, of the supposedly fourth-century type of the 'autonomous cultic abstraction'.

Clearer perhaps than an absolute difference between the centuries is a difference in the number and prominence of cults of this type. The worship of Pheme was, to our knowledge, on no great scale, whereas, as we have seen, in the 330s the new abstractions were claiming a substantial share of the public ritual budget. And of course new tendencies may well be revealed in the selection of particular abstractions for worship that the Athenians made. 'Luck' and 'the gods' were not opposed in traditional thought; on the contrary, what appeared to mortals as luck was, on a deeper level, the will of the gods. The natural addressee for a prayer for good luck was therefore a divinity. The deification of Agathe Tyche gave her a new autonomy, although there was still far from being an opposition between her and the gods: a rich Athenian of the fourth century, for instance, made a dedication 'to the 12 gods and to good luck'.[67]

It does not need demonstration that Democracy (one could not

---

[64] So Nilsson, 'Kultische Personifikationen'; and cf. A. Raubitschek, *Hesperia* 35 (1966), 242.

[65] Compare Menander's use of such figures as $T\acute{v}\chi\eta$ (*Aspis*) and $\mathring{A}\gamma\nu o\iota a$ (*Perikeiromene*) as prologue-speaking deities.

[66] See p. 234 above.

[67] *IG* II².4564; and cf. 'Athena Nike and Good Luck' in *SEG* XXX 69. On luck and the gods see G. W. Bond's note on Eur. *HF* 1393 [+], and e.g. G. Herzog-Hauser, *RE* s.v. *Tyche*, 1652, 1654; in Pind. *Ol*. 12, Saviour Tyche is daughter of Zeus Eleutherios.

say the same for Peace) is a young goddess. This indeed is the cult which moderns may find hardest to reconcile with their own understanding of the nature of religion.[68] Let us grant that powers such as Pheme—uncontrollable, eternal, inescapable—are divine: but how can one treat Democracy as such a divine power when, everyone knew, it was created by men at a particular historical moment, was always in danger of suppression, and was notoriously absent from most parts of the inhabited world? These objections are unanswerable, but irrelevant; for a worshipper of Democracy, at the moments when he thought of her as a goddess, was doubtless thinking along quite other lines. The gods are 'givers of blessings': and can one name, can one imagine, a power that brings greater blessings to ordinary Athenians than Democracy? It is easy to see from the orators that 'democracy' is in a sense a sacred word.[69]

This unusual goddess is likely to bring to mind the deities of the French Revolution, Reason and the Supreme Being. But it is quite wrong to interpret the deified abstractions of Athens in the light of the revolutionaries' hostility to established religion. As we have seen, they derive from an ancient tradition of Greek religious thought, without which they would certainly not have come into being; it is not at all clear that Hesiod or Aeschylus or Pindar would have found them shocking. Often these cults were instituted, in a very traditional way, in commemoration of a particular event. In a sense they represent an end rather than a beginning; perhaps the 'new' deifications of the fourth century came too late, at a time when the old instinct for translating powers into gods and back again was dying out.[70] That might be why Eirene, in contrast, say, to Nemesis, failed to be 'Olympianized'. (But we noted earlier the marriage between Zeus and Good Luck, arranged by a dedicator; and an Athena Demokratia eventually emerged, though not until the first century BC.[71]) In his remarks on Pheme, Aeschines was still thinking in the old way. But he had contemporaries to whom the proposition 'Pheme is a goddess' would doubtless have seemed as conceptually incoherent, if taken literally, as much a 'figure of speech', as it does to a modern philosopher.

[68] See e.g. Burkert, *Greek Religion*, 186 'more propaganda than religion' (in the original, 288, 'mehr Demonstration als Religion': but in other writings Burkert sees 'Demonstration' as fundamental to ritual!).

[69] See e.g. Lycurg. *Leoc.* 3 (democracy and ἡ τῆς πόλεως εὐδαιμονία associated), 20, 79, 138. Democracy is 'protected by the gods and the laws', according to Aeschin. 3.196.

[70] So Reinhardt, 'Personifikation und Allegorie', 32–33, on what he sees as a new self-consciousness in Agathon's praise of Eros in Plat. *Symp.* or in Lysippus' sculpture of Kairos. But note by contrast how easily abstractions (Hygieia, Iaso, etc.) continued to be associated with a god in the cults of Asclepius.

[71] *IG* II².4992.

Alongside the new abstractions, it should be stressed, the cult of the Olympians continued to diversify and proliferate in the traditional way. We learn of 'Hermes Hegemonios'—possibly a new cult, since the generals were in charge of it—only from an entry in Lycurgus' skin-tax record; it may commemorate some now forgotten military adventure.[72] A fine temple of Aphrodite Euploia, a landmark of the Piraeus, was built, if we believe Pausanias, by Conon to recall his great victory of 394 off Knidos, that Aphrodisian place. (But there are chronological complications, as an Aphrodision seems already to have existed in the Piraeus, and Aphrodite could certainly have been worshipped in a harbour without inspiration from the east.[73]) In commemoration of Chabrias' victory of 376 off Naxos, a kind of wine-festival was added to the jollities of 16th Boedromion, day of the victory but also traditional occasion for the ritual trip of 'initiates to the sea' before the Mysteries.[74] Two cults of Zeus gain new prominence in the fourth century; both, as it happens, illustrate the complexity of reference of many divine epithets. Zeus 'the Saviour' had long received the third libation at symposia; and it may seem odd to discuss, in a chapter treating the fourth cen-

[72] *IG* II².1494.84–85, 115–16 (sum lost in both cases). Humphreys, 'Lycurgus', 231, n. 49, wonders about a connection with the great return of 403; but the attested commemorations (n. 41) and miracles (Graf, *Nordionische Kulte*, 230) associated with that event are different. Hermes is already Hegemonios in Ar. *Plut.* 1159. The generals: cf. n. 108; but U. Kahrstedt, *Untersuchungen zur Magistratur in Athen* (Stuttgart 1936), 288–90, notes that in this text different boards can have responsibility for the same rite in different years, and the generals occasionally appear in charge even of long-established festivals such as the *Lenaea*.

[73] Aphrodite and harbours: see Graf, *Nordionische Kulte*, 261. Knidos: see *RE* s.v. *Aphrodite*, 2755. As regards Conon's temple, the essence of the problem is: (*a*) temples of Aphrodite in the Piraeus are ascribed to both Themistocles (Ammonios of Lamptrae, *FGrH* 361 F 5) and Conon (Paus. 1.1.3: (?) Aphrodite Euploia); neither is precisely located, but Conon's is said to be a conspicuous landmark; (*b*) an Aphrodision is thrice mentioned as a landmark of the Piraeus (*IG* II².1657.5; *FGrH* 370 F 1; *IG* II².1035.46); the first reference demands a location on the peninsula Eetioneia, the other two are best suited by it (Culley, *Sacred Monuments*, 162–63; P. Funke, *ZPE* 53, 1983, 175–89, at 181); (*c*) a dedication to Aphrodite Euploia was found at a different site in the Piraeus (*IG* II².2872)—but this matters little, as stones in the Piraeus often roll; (*d*) *IG* II².1657, the first of the references to the Aphrodision, is a building-account referring to work on the Piraeus fortifications undertaken in the archonship of Euboulides (394/3)—Conon's return to Athens, the presumptive *terminus post quem* for the foundation, apparently occurred in the penultimate prytany of that year (Funke, *ZPE* 53, 1983, 163, using new evidence). Topographically therefore it is easiest to believe that there was just one Aphrodision in the Piraeus, a conspicuous landmark on Eetioneia. But (*d*) tends to imply that an Aphrodision on this site pre-existed Conon's return: for otherwise we must suppose that within a month or so of his return the planning of the temple was already far enough advanced for it to serve as a landmark in a building-contract. A radical solution would be to reject the association between Conon and the temple; more often, scholars have supposed that Conon extended Themistocles' foundation (for a full discussion see Funke, *ZPE* 53, 1983; he believes the chronological difficulty of (*d*) can be met).

[74] Plut. *De Glor. Ath.* 349e–f, *Phoc.* 6.7; cf. Ephorus *FGrH* 70 F 80; Polyaenus 3.11.2 (cf. Pritchett, *Greek State at War*, III.171); and for the new rite's popularity, Menander fr. 454 Koerte. Chabrias met the cost himself.

tury, a cult title of Zeus to which repeated reference is made in Aeschylus' *Oresteia*.[75] But in the early period Soter seems to have had neither a festival nor a shrine, except perhaps for an altar at the site in the *agora* on which the stoa of Zeus Eleutherios was built, around 430. By the early fourth century, we find him located in two distinct places, each associated to some extent with a different aspect of his powers. He certainly now had a place in the *agora*, where the statue in front of the stoa of Zeus Eleutherios was spoken of indifferently as representing either Zeus Eleutherios or Zeus Soter.[76] Clearly the 'rescue' offered by this saviour/liberator was primarily public; after his great victory of 394, for instance, which first broke the Spartan domination of the Aegean, Conon was granted a statue 'beside Zeus Soter'.[77] But in *Plutus* of 388 Aristophanes introduces a priest of Zeus Soter who lists a series of circumstances in which individuals would turn to the god: safe completion of a voyage, success in a court case, or 'when one has to get good omens' (to establish, presumably, that a particular project is safe). He complains that his hitherto thriving sacral business has been destroyed by the new conditions (in the fiction of the play) of universal wealth. It seems to follow, from Aristophanes' choice of precisely this priest to voice this complaint, that the cult was already one of the most popular; and this surprising implication is confirmed by the skin-sale records, in which the *Diisoteria* yields a larger return than does any other

---

[75] Cf. Aesch. *Ag.* 1386–87, with Fraenkel's note; *Eum.* 759–60, with Sommerstein's note (and for the libation custom, the graffito *SEG* XXXI 268). The oath by Zeus Soter, common in New Comedy, already occurs in Ar. *Ran.* 738, 1433 (cf. *Thesm.* 1009). Various deities are described as 'Soter' or 'Soteira' in Pindar (see W. Slater's *Lexicon to Pindar*, Berlin 1969). Note too the fifth-cent. strigil (provenance unknown) which portrays a (Zeus) Soter (identified by an inscription) of archaic iconographic type: *AntK* 22 (1979), 72 ff.

[76] The statue of Conon, said by Isocrates to be beside Zeus Soter (9.57), is for Pausanias—as doubtless for the assembly that decreed the honour (cf. Dem. 20.69)—beside Zeus Eleutherios (1.3.2); and lexicographers identify the two explicitly (e.g. Harp. s.v. Ἐλευθέριος Ζεύς). The stoa, which is dated architecturally to *c.*430–420 (Thompson/Wycherley, *Agora*, 96–103), is always 'of Zeus' or 'of Zeus Eleutherios'; public inscriptions of the fourth cent. vary between 'Soter' and 'Eleutherios' for the statue (see Wycherley, *Testimonia*, 29). Neither name is securely attested in the fifth cent., but note already the market-place altar of Zeus Soter in Eur. *HF* 48, the public vow supposedly made to him before the battle of Arginusae (Diod. 13.102.1), and the *horos* from the *agora* of *c.*450 supplemented as Διὸς Ἐ[λευθερίο] (*Agora* XIX H7 = *IG* I³.1056). Perhaps the earlier altar on the site of the stoa (Thompson/Wycherley, *Agora*, 96) belonged to Soter (cf. Judeich, *Topographie*, 340, n. 1); K. Raaflaub, *Die Entdeckung der Freiheit* (Munich 1985), 136, argues strongly that Zeus Eleutherios is a specialization of one function of Zeus Soter.

[77] See previous note; similarly symbolic are e.g. the display there of the decree carrying the charter of the Second Athenian confederacy (*IG* II².43.65–66) and that honouring Euphron of Sikyon, the liberator (*IG* II².448.69–70): see V. J. Rosivach, 'The Cult of Zeus Eleutherios at Athens', *PP* 42 (1987), 262–85; and for extra-Attic parallels, Graf, *Nordionische Kulte*, 182, n. 165.

festival.[78] The centrepiece of the *Diisoteria* was a procession through the Piraeus to a large shrine, shared by Zeus Soter and Athena Soteira, which, according to Pausanias, was 'the thing most worth seeing' in the port;[79] and the audience would doubtless have understood Aristophanes' priest to come from this precinct, since there is little sign of worship by individuals at the altar in the *agora*. It was probably the establishment of the shrine in the Piraeus, that 'new town' hungry for cults, that made the Rescuer so popular so suddenly. (The date of foundation can only be guessed, unfortunately; the argument from silence might point to the late fifth century or early fourth, but there is no refuting those who suppose that Zeus Soter was installed, say, in the 470s, as a kind of patronal deity of the new port.[80]) The joint cult of Zeus Soter and Athena Soteira spread widely in Attica (it was particularly attractive to soldiers, not surprisingly), and Athenians continued to look to the pair for rescue both public and private.[81] The Olympians retreated from earth, it is sometimes said, in the fourth century; they became too distant to

[78] Ar. *Plut.* 1171 ff.; *IG* II².1496.88–89 (334/3, 1050 drachmas), 118–19 (333/2, 2610½ drachmas). Zeus Soter is the χρησιμώτατος of gods to man, according to a speaker in Alexis fr. 234 K/A. On the festival see Deubner, *Attische Feste*, 174–75, and the following note; the sacrifice to Zeus Soter on Skirophorion 30 known from Lys. 26.6 is surely distinct, and perhaps happened at the *agora* altar as Deubner suggests (but he is not certainly right in identifying it with the entry sacrifices of Lys. 26.8, despite *IG* II².689–90, since these prima facie occurred the following day).

[79] Paus. 1.1.3. There has been doubt about where the *pompe* occurred (see Rosivach, 'Cult of Zeus Eleutherios', 279): that this large festival (see Arist. *Ath. Pol.* 56.5) was originally associated with the large Piraeus shrine is certain (see *IG* II².380.20–21, 30–31; 1006.30), and the difficulties disappear if we suppose that in the 270s, when the Piraeus was separated from the city (cf. Ch. 9, n. 66), a version of the *pompe* was also held in connection with the *agora* shrine, which perhaps only then acquired a priest (see Meritt, *Hesperia* 26, 1957, 54–55 no. 11 = *SEG* XVI 63; *IG* II².676, cf. 689–90 for the priest; the Piraeus priest is explicitly described as that in a later text, *IG* II².783, as not before, *IG* II².410.18).

[80] So e.g. Garland, *Piraeus*, 137 (but the supposed fifth-cent. attestation of the cult in *IG* I².128 = *IG* I³.130 is very questionable: see Ch. 8, n. 15). Major works were still in progress in the shrine in the fourth cent. (*IG* II².1669), and Cephisodotus designed an altar (Pliny *HN* 34.74), which was 'adorned' before festivals (Plut. *Dem.* 27.8, [*X Orat.*] 846d). There are two supposedly fourth-cent. dedications to Zeus Soter from Piraeus (and none later, surprisingly), one of them in combination with Hermes (*IG* II².4603, 4972).

[81] See *SEG* XXIV 156, an honorary decree from Eleusis issued by *thiasotai/eranistai* during the Demetrian war (239–229), which mentions offerings made μετὰ τῶν δεκαδαρχῶν, i.e. petty officers of the garrison (L. Robert, *ArchEph* 1969, 14–23 [Robert, *OMS* VII.720–29]: cf. *Bull. Ép.* 1970, no. 260), to Zeus Soter and Hygieia; *SEG* XXVIII 107, honours for their general from the Athenian *hypaithroi* stationed at Rhamnus *c.*229 for, *inter alia*, sacrifices to Zeus Soter and Athena Soteira (perhaps in connection with the recent 'recovery of the ancestral freedom', mentioned in line 8); *SEG* XV 111 (*c.*229), which is similar and mentions a torch-race; Moretti 29, of 225/4, honours from the Rhamnusians and his crew for a trierarch who had sacrificed to Zeus Soter and Athena Soteira 'for the health and safety and harmony' of the crew; *Prakt* 1989 (1992), 17–19, nos. 1–4 (of which 1 = *IG* II².2869), *Ergon* 1991 (1992), 5, dedications by generals, at Rhamnus, *c.*100 BC, perhaps in connection with torch-races; also (?) *IG* II².1954. On the military cult of Zeus Soter see M. Launey, *Recherches sur les armées hellénistiques* (Paris 1951), II.914–16, who cites *inter alia* Xen. *Anab.* 1.8.16, 3.2.9.*

meet the needs or touch the hearts of ordinary worshippers. But Zeus had perhaps never been so generally popular in Attica as when he became Soter.

Zeus Philios lacks the public face of Soter. He probably first appears in Aristophanes' *Acharnians* of 425, in the form of an oath, which was subsequently very common, 'by (Zeus) Philios'. A god who is alluded to so casually in the first surviving comedy is likely to have been long familiar; and the distinctive form of worship that he received—a rite of *lectisternium* in private houses—would have left no trace archaeologically.[82] The justification—if justification there is—for treating him as a 'new god' of the fourth century is that this is when dedications to him first appear, in Athens and the Piraeus.[83] Thus he certainly now had sacred places outside the household, though details remain frustratingly vague (he apparently shared an informal shrine in the Piraeus with Zeus Meilichios), and neither a public priest[84] nor a festival is attested. He is, obviously, much concerned with Philia, the affection that binds not only fellow revellers—witness a dedication to him by a group of *eranistai* in 324—but also families: Helen, for instance, is said in Euripides' *Andromache* to have 'abandoned' Menelaus' 'Philios' by deserting him.[85] Is this then, in effect, nothing but another cult of a personified abstraction? Is not the same power being celebrated as by that unknown individual who, we learn from an elegy by Aristotle, founded an altar to 'the sacred friendship of Plato'?[86] But a deified

[82] Ar. *Ach*. 730, the Megarian's greeting to the Athenian *agora*: ἐπόθευν τυ ναὶ τὸν Φίλιον ἇπερ ματέρα, where the idea of affection is present as probably in all uses of the oath or the related appeal πρὸς Διὸς Φιλίου (for instances see LSJ s.v. φίλιος or more fully Cook, *Zeus*, II.1175–77). From the same period are Pherecrates fr. 102.4 K/A, the oath again, and Eur. *Andr*. 602 f. Lectisternium: Diodorus comicus fr. 2 K/A, from Ath. 6.239a–f.

[83] Athens: *IG* II².4555 ('a. 400–350'), 2935 (by a group of unnamed eranistai, 324/3 BC); *Horos* 8–9 (1990–1), 59, a fragmentary dedication by two citizens from the acropolis slopes (fourth cent.). Piraeus: *IG* II².4623–25 (all ascribed to the fourth cent.), 4845–46. *IG* II².4627 (Aristomache's dedication: above, n. 50) lacks a precise provenance.

[84] Until the late theatre-seat, *IG* II².5066. Joint cult with Zeus Meilichios?: Judeich, *Topographie*, 435, n. 1; Nilsson, *Geschichte*, 413 (dedications to both have been found in the same area, near to votive-niches, and a worked grotto). As two of the Athenian dedications come from the south side of the acropolis, Zeus Philios may well have had a shrine in that region, but by no means necessarily in the Asclepieum, as G. Welter suggests, *AM* 50 (1925), 165 f., on the basis of an equally undemonstrated association in the Piraeus.

[85] Eranistai: n. 83 above (cf. *philia* in the graffito n. 52 above, and Nilsson, *Geschichte*, 809: but for a slightly different possibility see p. 337 below); Eur. *Andr*. 602–603, τὸν σὸν λιποῦσα Φίλιον ἐξεκώμασε (where the verb is taken by Nilsson to confirm the sympotic connotations of *Philios*: but one might rather see a contrast). Aristomache's dedication (n. 50 above) also shows the domestic aspect of the god, as Nilsson notes.

[86] Aristotle fr. 673 Rose (same number in West, *Iambi et Elegi Graeci*, II): cf. W. Jaeger, *CQ* 21 (1927), 14; I. Düring, *Aristotle in the Ancient Biographical Tradition* (Göteborg 1957), 315–18. Another personification: cf. Nilsson, *Geschichte*, 809.

abstraction is just what Zeus Philios is not: he is the greatest of the gods, the god of the social order, seen in relation to a central value of social life. The importance assigned to *philia* is perhaps new, the method of incorporating it in the Olympian system entirely traditional. And it has long been noted that for some worshippers Zeus, as it were, prevailed over Philia. The decisive evidence here comes from votive reliefs, which show him in exactly the iconographical forms that are characteristic of Zeus Meilichios: banqueting, cornucopia in hand, as he is approached by worshippers, or even, remarkably, in snake form.[87] Whatever his origins, he seems to have been assimilated to other domestic Zeuses, as a bringer of prosperity to the *philoi* united under one roof.

One individual is of outstanding interest for the study of civic religion in the fourth century: not Plato or Aristotle, of course, but Lycurgus, the orator who restored Athens' finances, dominated her domestic policy, and adorned her with buildings in the years following the catastrophe of Chaeronea. Lycurgus was one of the few members of a priestly *genos* to make a mark in political life, and himself held a priesthood of the most ancient dignity: no less than that of Poseidon Erechtheus, first occupied by Boutes the brother of Erechtheus. Within the *genos*, the priesthood seems traditionally to have belonged to a member of Lycurgus' own family, and some of his earliest memories were doubtless of the solemn ceremonies of the acropolis. (But to forestall too facile an association, let us remember a figure who was prominent in public life late in the fifth century, Kallias son of Hipponicus, patron of advanced thought, profligate, and daduch of the Eleusinian Mysteries.) In the case of Lycurgus, as of almost no other Athenian politician, one can speak of a religious policy.[88] But it would be wrong to stress his singularity too strongly, as if he had been led by personal temperament to divert political life into wholly new channels. On the contrary, the structure of Athenian society was such that any politician had necessarily to consider questions of cult to a greater or lesser degree (Androtion, for

---

[87] See Cook, *Zeus*, II.1160–78, on the reliefs attached to many of the inscriptions cited n. 83 above. Cook speaks, 1160, of Zeus Philios as an updated form of Zeus Meilichios. Graf accordingly suggests, *Nordionische Kulte*, 205, that Zeus Philios was understood not just as god of *philia* but also as Ζεὺς ὃς φιλεῖ, friendly Zeus. But the evidence (n. 82) of the oath (more important than explicit statements such as Phryn. *Praep. Soph.*, p. 123.11 de Borries, φίλιος· ὁ ⟨τῆς⟩ φιλίας ἔφορος θεός) suggests that in usage a reference to φιλία was heard.

[88] See esp. Humphreys, 'Lycurgus', and Faraguna, *Atene nell'età di Alessandro*, chs. 4, 7–9; also Mitchel, 'Lykourgan Athens'; W. Will, *Athen und Alexander* (Munich 1983), 79–93 (Lycurgan buildings); A. B. Bosworth, *Conquest and Empire* (Cambridge 1988), 204–15. On the *genos* see App. 2 A.

instance, had busied himself with the treasures of Athena[89]); and in particular, any programme of national restoration, in a period of peace after long wars, could not but involve the restoration of shrines and cults. Lycurgus' singularity is only one of emphasis.

Again, it is hard to define his religious policy more precisely than as one of encouraging the worship of the gods to flourish as the centre of a flourishing state. He was not seeking to move religious life in a new direction: not forwards, certainly, but not backwards either, unless by his very insistence on the prime importance of cult and myth in the life of the city. The fragments of his speeches do, it is true, display a detailed and, one might say, Atthidographic interest in the myths and procedures of quite minor cults; in his several speeches on ritual topics, he evidently treated the jurors to disquisitions on religious antiquities of a type seldom heard in an Attic court.[90] The Atthidographer Phanodemus was, it seems, a close associate. But Lycurgus' political and cultural ideal appears to have been the age of Pericles,[91] and there is no trace of a desire to replace the splendid festivals of the fifth century with the roughshod piety of ancient days. He was not, however, hostile to cults that arose after the great age, such as that of Agathe Tyche. It was even on the motion of Lycurgus, as we learn by chance from an inscription, that the merchants of Kition were granted permission to buy land on which to found a shrine of their Aphrodite, 'just as the Egyptians have founded the shrine of Isis'; to make Athens attractive to revenue-producing metics was, it seems, more important than to protect the citizens from contamination by foreign gods.[92] (It was, however, in the Lycurgan period that a law seems to have been passed to exclude foreigners who had been granted citizenship from membership of certain phratries, presumably on religious grounds.[93]) In the festival programme of his years of predominance,

[89] Cf. D. M. Lewis, *BSA* 49 (1954), 39–49, on *IG* II².216–17 (who associates the similar concern shown in *IG* II².120, of 352/3 [E. Schweigert, *Hesperia* 7, 1938, 286], with Eubulus).

[90] εἶπε δὲ καὶ περὶ ἱερῶν πολλάκις: [Plut.] *X Orat.* 843d (§ 42 Conomis, p. 11): see esp. the frs. of speeches VI, VII, X/XI, XIII, XIV Conomis.

[91] See fr. 58 Blass, IX.2 Conomis; Humphreys, 'Lycurgus', 199.

[92] Agathe Tyche: see Lycurgus fr. 23 Blass, V.6 Conomis. Merchants of Citium: *IG* II².337 (Tod, *GHI* II.189; Schwenk 27); Xenophon's advice to attract metics by allowing them to buy building-land has often been compared (*Poroi* 2.6); in both cases something more restricted than a generalized right to buy land is in question (cf. Pečírka, *Enktesis*, 59–61). (The idea by contrast that Lycurgus had inherited a sympathy for Egypt from his grandfather, the 'Ibis' of comedy [see K/A on Cratinus fr. 32], is fanciful: see R. R. Simms, 'Isis in Classical Athens', *CJ* 84, 1989, 216–21.)

[93] See Osborne, *Naturalization*, III/IV.176–81; Schwenk, *Age of Alexander*, 170 (who agree on a date of 334/3); Lambert, *Phratries*, 53. The restriction first appears in *IG* II².405 + *SEG* XXI 275 = Schwenk 24 (Osborne, *Naturalization*, I, D 21); contrast *IG* II².336 + addenda, p. 659 = Schwenk 31 (Osborne, *Naturalization*, I, D 23).

Democracy rubs shoulders with such a venerable relic as the Eleusinian Daeira. The battered fragments that survive of an important religious law—perhaps the centrepiece of his programme—show him making provision to improve the *kosmos*, the cult equipment, of a catholic range of gods: Athena, no doubt, Zeus Soter, Zeus Olympios, Dionysus, Athena Itonia, Agathe Tyche, Amphiaraus, Asclepius, Artemis Brauronia, Demeter, and Kore.[94]

Such *kosmos* was a central interest of Lycurgus. In 307/6, when a decree was passed granting him posthumous honours, Stratocles the proposer stressed his unswerving democratic sympathies, his financial management, his defensive provisions, his many building-works, and the fact that 'when chosen by the people he assembled much property on the acropolis and, as adornment for the goddess, he provided solid gold Victories and gold and silver procession-vessels and gold ornaments for a hundred basket-bearers'. Financial measures, building, *kosmos* for the goddess: all are seen as parts of a single programme of restoration, without the religious expenditure being singled out under a separate heading of 'piety'. No clear division can in fact be made between the religious and the financial aims of measures of this kind. The Periclean Golden Victories, which Lycurgus at last succeeded in replacing—potent symbolic act—had been melted into coin in 407/6 or thereabouts, and everyone knew that in the last resort the same could be done with their successors. (Such seems indeed to have been their fate, at the hands of the 'tyrant' Lachares in 295, who even 'stripped Athena' to pay his mercenaries.[95]) It was, of course, always hoped that the last resort would not be reached; it is anachronistic to see dedications, which were meant to be seen and admired, simply as public funds in a deposit account. But, psychologically, rich gods symbolized a rich state.[96]

This was a major project, and a new board of officials was created to administer it. Lycurgus took other measures too to swell the flow of precious metals into sacred places. Liturgists on discharge of their

---

[94] Festival programme: *IG* II².1496 A. Religious law: *IG* II².333 (better read as Schwenk 21; note too D. M. Lewis's readings in 20–21 *ap.* Conomis, 21, which add Artemis Mounichia and the Twelve Gods).

[95] See *FGrH* 257a F 4, with Jacoby. Demetrius Poliorcetes may have made earlier depredations in 304 (D. M. Lewis in *Comptes et inventaires dans la cité grecque: Colloque en l'honneur de Jacques Tréheux*, Geneva 1988, 305).

[96] Stratocles' decree: *IG* II².457 = (with variants) [Plut.] *X Orat.* 851f–852e (cf. already Din. 1.96). On the phrase 'assembled much property' cf. Ferguson, *Treasurers*, 126. Hyperides, fr. 118 Jensen, mentions revenue and buildings only. Gold victories: see Woodward, 'The Golden Nikai of Athena', *ArchEph* 1937, 159–70; Rhodes, *Commentary Ath. Pol.*, on 47.1 (and on their appearance D. B. Thompson, *Hesperia* 13, 1944, 173–209). The law providing for the restoration of a statue of Athena Nike (*IG* II².403) may also be Lycurgan. Anachronistic: cf. T. Linders, in *Gifts to the Gods*, 115–22; but for the permanent possibility of melting see Dem. 22.48; Din. 1. 69.

liturgies, freedmen and women at the moment of their liberation, were required to dedicate a silver vessel on the acropolis. Or private munificence could be exploited, in this as in other areas. Neoptolemus of Melite undertook to 'gild the altar of Apollo in the *agora* in accord with the oracle of the god'—and was duly rewarded when Lycurgus proposed that a statue of him be dedicated, *quid pro quo*. The gilding was to be performed, we note, 'in accord with the oracle of the god'—a common ground of action in the Lycurgan period. To judge from the analogous cases, this will mean that, the project having been conceived, Apollo was asked for his approval. A characteristic Greek piety is expressed in thus checking that a god is indeed happy with a change which seems so obviously to his advantage. (In similar circumstances we once find a propitiatory sacrifice offered, on Lycurgus' own motion.) But such a consultation might also have encouraged a benefactor to come forward to undertake the project which a god had explicitly approved.[97]

Most obviously, therefore, Lycurgus' religious policy was one of ways and means, of shrewd financial management directed to maintaining and enhancing traditional cults. Particular revenues, some of them newly contrived, are carefully earmarked for particular cultic purposes: a decree proposed in the late 330s, for instance, by an associate of Lycurgus, defines how a large sacrifice at the *Lesser Panathenaea* is to be financed from the rental income produced by a particular 'new' territory (probably that of Oropus). In the Eleusinian accounts Lycurgus is mentioned as having made a proposal about a revealingly trivial administrative matter.[98] The religious building-projects of the period are mostly restorations or extensions of existing temples, or, revealingly, the continuation of

---

[97] New board: *IG* II².1493. Liturgists: D. M. Lewis, *Hesperia* 37 (1968), 374–80. Freedmen: D. M. Lewis, *Hesperia* 28 (1959), 208–37 (237 for the date); 37 (1968), 368–74, and 376, n. 22. (A further extension is now suggested by a decree of the deme Acharnae of 315/4, *ArchEph* 131, 1992, 179 A 7, which praises a ταμίας for dedicating a silver phiale κατὰ [τὸν νόμον]; the ed., G. Steinhauer, suggests a percentage of the revenue collected in the year was set aside for it, comparing *SEG* XXXVIII 138 of 320/19, a gold cup made by the Treasurers of Athena as a ἑκατοστή of monies collected ? by the archon.) Neoptolemus: [Plut.] *X Orat.* 843f. 'In accord with the oracle': cf. *IG* II².1933, and the provision for confirmatory oracular consultation in Lycurgus' major religious law *IG* II².333 (above n. 94), lost portions of which might indeed have treated Apollo's altar in the *agora*. 'Propitiatory sacrifice': *IG* II².1672.302–303 (cf. *IG* II².403.18).

[98] *Lesser Panathenaea*: D. M. Lewis, *Hesperia* 28 (1959), 239–47, on Schwenk 17; cf. the careful funding provisions in *IG* II².333 (Schwenk 21); but note n. 102 below. On the common view, new revenue is here deployed to fund an existing sacrifice; but for the view that the sacrifice itself is new see V. J. Rosivach, *PP* 261 (1991), 430–42. On the territory concerned see most recently M. Langdon, *Hesperia* 56 (1987), 55–58 (who proposes the island Nea near Lemnos; but on his own showing 'Neai' is the usual form); O. Hansen, *Eranos* 87 (1989), 70–72 = *SEG* XXXIX 88 (Halonnesos: an unconvincing redating of the inscription has therefore to be proposed). Eleusis: *IG* II².1672.302–303.

earlier undertakings that had foundered for lack of funds: the great portico to the *telesterion* at Eleusis, for instance, which had been talked of since the 350s, at last got under way.[99] The only changes in the festival programme that are ascribed to Lycurgus in the ancient life are the addition of new musical and dramatic competitions to existing festivals. A similar addition (of a horse-race, in this case) to the *Eleusinia* occurred in the period; and it is to the reorganization or extension of existing festivals that a group of frustratingly fragmentary texts possibly point.[100] It may well have been now that the practice of issuing commemorative coins at the *Eleusinia*, a competition of growing importance, was initiated. We should also allow the possibility that the agonistic *Nemesia* at Rhamnus, which seem first to be attested in this period, were also a creation of it. They would have had an obvious appeal to those stationed at the fortress, in particular the ephebes.[101]

[99] Definitely of the Lycurgan period are: the building of the smallish temple of Apollo Patroos in his existing precinct in the *agora* (cf. Travlos, *Pictorial Dictionary*, 96; J. Engels, *Ancient Society* 23, 1992, 19, n. 27: the Lycurgan date is virtually assured by Neoptolemus of Melite's involvement with the altar, discussed above); the completion of the Plutonium (*IG* II².1672.168–69 etc.), and active work on the great portico, at Eleusis (see K. Clinton, *ArchEph* 1971, 107–13, on *IG* II².1670–71, 1675, and esp. 1673, to which he adds a fr. [*SEG* XXXIV 122]); a porch for the city Eleusinion (Travlos, *Pictorial Dictionary*, 198–99; *IG* II².1672.166); restoration by Neoptolemus of Melite of the small temple of Artemis in his deme (Travlos, *Pictorial Dictionary*, 121). On the form of the temple of Apollo Patroos see now H. Knell, *JdI* 109 (1994), 217–37; he associates with it the neighbouring small shrine of (?) Zeus Phratrios and the new monument of the Eponymous heroes (date uncertain) as parts of a coherent Lycurgan programme. A Lycurgan date is merely possible for the stoa and temple of the Asclepieum (Travlos, *Pictorial Dictionary*, 127). The Eleusinian portico, the largest of these projects, was not in fact completed until the period of Demetrius of Phaleron, unless Vitruvius errs (preface to bk. 7); for the earlier plans see *IG* II².204, 1666. See in general Will, *Athen und Alexander*, 79–93.

[100] New competitions: [Plut.] *X Orat.* 841f (§ 14 Conomis: comic competitions at the *Anthesteria*), and 842a (§ 17), where the unattested and implausible festival offered by the manuscripts τοῦ Ποσειδῶνος ἀγῶνα . . . ἐν Πειραιεῖ κυκλίων χορῶν is removed by A. Koerte's palmary Ποσειδεῶνος (*RhM* 57, 1902, 625–27), the month of the Piraeus *Dionysia*. Horse-race at the *Eleusinia*: *IG* II².1672.261, a payment in 329/8 εἰς τὴν ἱπποδρομίαν τὴν προστεθεῖσαν κατὰ ψήφισμα (though it is perhaps not quite certain that the 'addition by *psephisma*' had only just occurred). Fragmentary texts: the *Hephaisteia* became a *penteteris*, according to the papyrologically most easy reading in Arist. *Ath. Pol.* 54.7; but the historical case for reading *Amphiaraea* is almost overwhelming (see Ch. 8, n. 109 above, and, on the difficulties raised by the reading *Hephaisteia*, Faraguna, *Atene nell'età di Alessandro*, 366, n. 48). (For interest in the cult of Hephaestus and Athena Hephaestea earlier in the century—but perhaps to be associated rather with the *Chalkeia*—see Ag. Inv. 7495, a tax of 354/3 [see Faraguna, *Atene nell'età di Alessandro*, 345]; *IG* II².223 of 343/2; Phanodemus *FGrH* 325 F 18, with Jacoby.) The sacrifice to Peace was perhaps extended into a festival (see n. 46 above). Walbank's new festival text (*Vanderpool Studies*, 173–82 = *SEG* XXXII 86), which refers to a hippodrome, the polemarch, tribes, and a sacrifice to Athena, is associated by him with the *Amphiaraea*; Humphreys, 'Lycurgus', 227, n. 33, thinks, better, of the *Epitaphia*, a long-established festival (Ch. 8, n. 36 above). The case for a Lycurgan date for this text is based on letter-forms only (*pace* the unacceptable restoration *SEG* XXXV 73).

[101] *Eleusinia*: so M. Thompson, 'Coins for the Eleusinia', *Hesperia* 11 (1942), 213–29, at

Circumstances might of course make innovation necessary. When the much-longed-for Oropus was recovered in the 330s, it was almost inevitable that the Amphiareum should be brought into the Athenian festival orbit. The Amphiaraic games now entered the Athenian calendar as an elaborate penteteric festival. What is characteristic of the period is perhaps the energy with which Lycurgus and his associates, chief among them Phanodemus, cultivated the god. Amphiaraus even became the only immortal (perhaps) to be voted a gold crown worth 1,000 drachmas by the Athenian assembly; the proposer of the decree was Phanodemus, the grounds given were that 'the god takes good care of the Athenians and other persons who visit the shrine, for the health and protection of all those in the country' (and the same assembly went on to vote a like honour, *mutatis mutandis*, to Phanodemus). The same high-level enthusiasm for religious matters is seen in the decision to dispatch a *Pythais* or sacred embassy to Delphi, probably in 326, for the first time, to our knowledge, since 355. A characteristic institution first attested in this period is that whereby a priest reports to the *boule* the successful performance of sacrifices 'on behalf of the Athenian people'; the *boule* resolves to 'accept the benefits arising from the sacrifice'; and the priest is then commended by decree for his services. The *boule* takes note of the outcome of the sacrifices, the priest is brought into the orbit of civic commendation: here too we seem to see a Lycurgan stress on the importance of religion for the state. There are some signs that the demes too were affected by the Lycurgan ethos of piety based upon sound finance.[102]

We saw earlier that in the fifth century, public religion had largely ceased to be an arena for the display of private wealth. The rich contributed not at their own pleasure, but through the system of liturgies, which was itself controlled by the state. The few instances of

---

218–19. *Nemesia*: see n. 126 below, and Moretti 25.28 (236/5). I suggest that the *Nemes[e]ia* at which offerings are made to dead parents apparently attested by Dem. 41.11—and always an embarrassment to heortologists—are an early textual corruption for *Genesia* (cf. Ch. 4, n. 27); the various lexicographical notices (Deubner, *Attische Feste*, 230, n. 2) are simply guesses based on this single passage.*

[102] Amphiareum: above, Ch. 8, n. 109: the decrees mentioned are *IG* VII.4252–53 = Schwenk 40–41 (the second is *SIG*³ 287). *Pythais*: *SIG*³ 296, cf. D. M. Lewis, *BSA* 50 (1955), 34, and *Hesperia* 37 (1968), 377, n. 29; also E. Voutiras, *AJA* 86 (1982), 229–33. Reports: cf. Ch. 8, n. 11 above; the first such text seems to be *IG* II².354 = Schwenk 54, and cf. *IG* II².410. Demes: cf. Mitchel *ap.* Schwenk, p. 218–19, on the decrees of the deme Eleusis, *REG* 91 (1978), 289–306 = *SEG* XXVIII 103 = Schwenk 43; for such specific funding of sacrifices, however, cf. perhaps already *IG* II².47. The practice of sending first fruits to Eleusis (*IG* II².1672.263 ff., of 329/8; cf. Mitchel, 'Lykourgan Athens', 207) is attested in the period, and the revival of it would be another typical specimen of the Lycurgan enthusiasm; but the expenditure of 70 drachmas on the repair of a storage tower (*IG* II².1672.292) is scarcely proof that it had lapsed.

extra-liturgical magnificence that are known from the late fifth and early fourth centuries are all, arguably, special cases. Ion gave a jug of Chian wine to every Athenian after winning with a tragedy; but Ion was a foreigner, not liable to liturgies. Chabrias endowed a wine-festival, Conon sacrificed a literal hecatomb and (perhaps) built a temple in commemoration of their respective victories; but the distinctions granted to victorious generals were in all respects unique.[103] Lycurgus supposedly passed a law forbidding women to attend the Eleusinian Mysteries on a carriage, 'so that women of the people would not be outdone by the rich', and would doubtless have applauded the principle that religious occasions should not serve as a pretext for the rich to display their magnificence.[104] None the less, it is in the Lycurgan period and just after it that notable patrons of religion rise into view, for the first time almost since the sixth century. Neoptolemus of Melite rebuilt the small temple of Artemis Aristoboule and made numerous dedications, in addition to gilding Apollo's altar; Xenokles of Sphettos (a year or two after the death of Alexander, it is true) built a bridge on the road to Eleusis for the mystic procession, and was duly acclaimed in an epigram which has been seen as one of the earliest expressions of Hellenistic taste; such benefactors have, of course, themselves a Proto-Hellenistic feel to them. Lycurgus himself was a skilled solicitor of donations for all his projects.[105] Should we conclude that he was led into contradiction, forced in practice, by his desire to embellish the city, to allow the rich a prominence in religious affairs that he would in principle have deprecated? But, it might be countered, ought not any good democrat to applaud the expenditure of private wealth for the public good?[106] If an individual had offered to gild an altar in the age of

[103] Fifth cent.: Ch. 8 above. Ion and Conon: Athen. 1.3e–f (where a comparable gesture by Alcibiades, but at Olympia, is mentioned). Conon's temple: n. 73 above. Chabrias: n. 74. Note too Douris of Samos, *FGrH* 76 F 35, and Heraclides comicus fr. 1 K/A on a public banquet provided by Chares. Nicias endowed a sacrifice, but on Delos: Plut. *Nic.* 3.7. Generals: see Gauthier, *Bienfaiteurs*, 95–103; they alone were honoured with statues in the *agora*.

[104] Lycurgus' law: [Plut.] *X Orat.* 842a (§ 18 Conomis); for the offensiveness of a carriage in this context, Dem. 21.158.

[105] Neoptolemus: to the evidence in Davies, *Propertied Families*, 399 f., add now his dedication to the Nymphs and Pan, Ch. 9, n. 48 above (also the possibility of supplementing him in *IG* II².1231, mentioned by R. Develin, *Athenian Officials*, Cambridge 1989, 416). Xenokles (see esp. C. Habicht, *Hesperia* 57, 1988, 323–27): he also served as *epimeletes* of the Mysteries (*IG* II².1191, 2840–41), and was honoured by the genos *Kerykes*, *Hesperia* 29 (1960), 2, no. 3; on the epigram (*Anth. Pal.* 9.147 = Antagoras II Gow and Page) see G. O. Hutchinson, *Hellenistic Poetry* (Oxford 1988), 22. Solicitation of benefactions by Lycurgus: see further examples in Humphreys, 'Lycurgus', 205, and cf. Faraguna, *Atene nell'età di Alessandro*, ch. 9. This 'Proto-Hellenistic' view of Lycurgus is, however, opposed by J. Engels, *Ancient Society* 23 (1992), 5–29.

[106] See e.g. Dem. 13.28–31, 20.10, 22.76.

Pericles, would the assembly, grandly, have refused the benefaction? As it happens, an inscription of the 440s or 430s possibly allows us to give that question the answer it does not expect: for we read in connection with the provision of a fountain-house at Eleusis that the assembly resolved to 'praise [Pericles and] Paralos and Xanthippos and . . . [and/but to meet the expenses from the money] which is paid into the Athenian tribute'.[107] Fundamentally, however, the change is likely to be less one of value than of circumstance. In the 430s, private wealth was nugatory by comparison with what was available publicly; for the post-imperial Athens it was very significant.

A related development does, however, seem to subvert the principle of religious egalitarianism. In the fifth century, even prominent public figures might, perhaps, never have the chance to occupy positions of religious dignity: how many cows did Cleon, for instance, sacrifice 'on behalf of the city and people of Athens'? (The question is unanswerable not least because we do not in fact know when the board of generals was first entrusted with the performance of certain sacrifices.) In the fourth century, we seem to see a recovery by the rich and powerful of ceremonial privilege. Much of the responsibility for important festivals such as the *Dionysia* appears in practice to have been diverted from the lot-appointed archons to the generals and the hipparchs and the taxiarchs, the most important elected officers of the state.[108] For those without military skills, too, new opportunities arose. When a board of 'supervisors of the Mysteries' was appointed in the middle of the century, it was decided that appointment should be by election, not lot; and in due course we find figures such as Midias and Xenocles of Sphettos holding the office. Similarly, the post of '*hieropoios* of the Semnai Theai' turns out to have been filled by appointment in the same period (though

---

[107] *IG* I³.49, adduced by P. A. Stadter in his commentary (Chapel Hill, NC 1989) on the apocryphal story of Pericles' offer to meet the costs of the Parthenon, Plut. *Per.* 14.1.

[108] No word of this in Arist. *Ath. Pol.*; but for the involvement of the military officers with processions see Xen. *Hipparch.* 3 *passim*; Dem. 4.26, 21.174; *Hesperia* 9 (1940), 104–105, no. 20 (praise for the taxiarchs of 302/1 for preserving *eukosmia* at rites of Demeter); and note the remarkable range of sacrifices, skin-sale receipts from which are marked as coming (in some years at least) παρὰ στρατηγῶν in *IG* II².1496—the sacrifices to Hermes Hegemonios, Peace, Ammon, Democracy, Agathe Tyche, and probably all three *Dionysia* (city, Piraeus, Lenaea). Exactly what level of involvement that implies is uncertain; but for the actual performance of (unspecified) traditional sacrifices by generals and officers, when not on campaign, see *IG* II².649.23–27; Moretti 18 (both early third cent.) (for hipparchs also *SEG* XXI 435, of 187/6, and 526, *c*.160); (?) cf. *IG* II².673. It also became normal for generals on garrison duty to preside not only over rites confined to their troops but also over the public festivals of neighbouring shrines: see *IG* II².1287, 1299.9 (*Haloa* at Eleusis), 1304.24–26 (*Greater Eleusinia*), 1309b; *Prakt* 1990 (1993), 21, no. 1.10–16. For involvement of the generals in care of temple treasures see *IG* II².839.28, 840.12 (*LSCG* 41–42); *SEG* XXXIV 95.27 (all second cent.).

here we know nothing of the board's history), and to have been held by none other than Demosthenes. Such positions were probably in effect disguised liturgies, the holders being expected to subsidize the rites.[109] The development that we are considering, therefore, pre-dates Lycurgus; and the movement was not in fact all in one direction: the ten supervisors of the *Dionysia*, the *Athenaion Politeia* tells us, 'used to be elected by the people, and they met the expenses of the procession from their own resources, but now one is chosen by lot from each tribe' and a state allowance is made to them.[110] But it is certainly plausible that one mechanism and consequence of the Lycurgan religious enthusiasm was a further intertwining of cere-monial and political life. The ten 'supervisors' elected for the Amphiaraic games in 329/8, the ten leaders of the *Pythais* of 326, read, it has often been noted, like a roll-call of the Lycurgan estab-lishment. Not politicians, but ten very prosperous citizens form the list of those whom 'the hierophant picked out' (ἐπιώψατο) 'to strew the couch and adorn the table for Plouton in accord with the oracle of the god' at some time in this period. (This text is all the more indicative if, as has been suggested, this was a newly introduced rite[111]—given an archaic patina by the ancient hieratic verb ἐπιώψατο.) It has been reasonably asked whether the priests who now began to receive crowns and commendations had, therefore, also begun to make contributions to the costs of the cult. And it was very possibly in this period that, as we learn from a striking inscrip-tion, 'the god decreed to the people of Athens that it should conse-crate Demon's house and the garden next to it to Asclepius, and that Demon should be his priest'; in other words, the politician Demon of Paeania, Demosthenes' kinsman, had, with the approval of Apollo, in effect purchased (though perhaps for a year only) an important priesthood.[112]

---

[109] Semnai Theai: Dem. 21.115, cf. App. 2, n. 41. Mysteries: *SEG* XXX 61 A fr. a+b 29–32 (cf. n. 9). Midias: Dem. 21.171. Xenokles: *IG* II².1191, cf. n. 105—for later incumbents, their duties and their contributions see *IG* II².661, 683, 807, 847. Disguised liturgy: cf. Arist. *Ath. Pol.* 56.4, cited in the text. Perhaps the *epimeletai* of Zeus Soter (*IG* II².676, *SEG* XVI 63) were similarly expected in normal circumstances to adorn the altar (cf. n. 80). In the third cent. we hear that the 'parasites of Heracles' in the demes were chosen not by lot but from the ἔχοντες οὐσίας, καλῶς βεβιωκότες (Diodorus comicus fr. 2.23–30 K/A), but nothing is known of the institution's history (on the parasites of Athena Pallenis see App. 3, n. 9).

[110] 56.4. The change was apparently very recent when this was written: cf. Rhodes ad loc. Note too that the nominal principle that the Treasurers of Athena should be rich was not enforced (Arist. *Ath. Pol.* 47.1).

[111] Humphreys, 'Lycurgus', 226, n. 28, on *IG* II².1933. For the verb see *IG* I³.3.4, Pl. *Leg.* 947C, Suda s.v. ἐπιώψατο, where it is said to be Attic, with appeal to Plato and the phrase ὁ βασιλεὺς ἐπιώψατο ἀρρηφόρους. Amphiaraists and Pythaists: see Lewis, *BSA* 50 (1955), 34–36, and e.g. Schwenk, *Age of Alexander*, 243–48.

[112] Priests: so Humphreys, 'Lycurgus', 213; I know no honorary decree for a priest in a public cult which says so explicitly at this date, however, though there was no inhibition about

But what was it all for? Why was Lycurgus so eager to enhance the cults of the city and to involve the citizenry in them? Almost our only evidence comes from his one surviving speech, in which this 'Athenian grand-inquisitor'[113] urged the death-penalty against the wretched Leocrates, seven years after the event, for fleeing the city after the battle of Chaeronea. In a speech, of course, the subtler reasonings, if such there were, of this erstwhile pupil of Plato are unlikely to be revealed;[114] we hear only the politician's public voice. Religious arguments turn out, not surprisingly, to be extremely prominent; indeed, Leocrates is repeatedly taxed with 'treachery' against the gods of the city which he abandoned, against his forefathers' tombs, and also (a little inconsistently) against his own 'ancestral shrines' which he exported when he took up residence abroad.[115] In denouncing this sacrilege, Lycurgus strikes a Roman note: the Athenians excel other men in piety towards the gods, the gods accordingly feel especial affection for the Athenians—but Leocrates has sought, for his part, to 'export the favour of the gods'.[116] Fortunately, the gods reward the good and punish the bad; into the minds of the wicked they put a madness that leads to their downfall—the old doctrine of *ate* or 'quem deus vult perdere, prius dementat' is here given an explicitly moral twist—as now, by returning to Athens, Leocrates has exposed himself to a richly deserved punishment.[117]

Lycurgus' tendency to digress was noted by ancient critics. He made use, it seems, of his unique prestige with the jurors in order to turn the courtroom speech into a textbook in civic virtue.[118] In the central part of *Against Leocrates*, numerous ancient and modern examples are cited to demonstrate the rewards of piety, the wretched fate of the wicked, the supreme value of patriotic self-sacrifice. This last theme is illustrated (predictably) by two Attic myths, those of King Codrus and of the daughters of Erechtheus (Lycurgus' own kinswomen). Such a use of myth as a pattern-book of patriotic conduct was much in fashion at just this period. In the *Epitaphios* spoken for the victims of Chaeronea in 337/6, Demosthenes showed, with all the ingenuity that the task required, how the members of

---

mentioning such matters. Demon: see *IG* II².4969, with R. Schlaifer, *CP* 38 (1943), 39–43 and Davies, *Propertied Families*, 117–18 (who favours a Lycurgan date against Schlaifer's preference for the Eubulan period: Aleshire, *Asklepieion*, 163–64, is agnostic).

[113] So J. Beloch, *Die attische Politik seit Perikles* (Leipzig 1884), 237.

[114] For an indirect approach, via Phanodemus, see Humphreys, 'Lycurgus', 214–16.

[115] So e.g. 1, 2, 8, 17, 25–26, 35, 97, 143.

[116] 15, 82, 25–26; for the Roman note cf. e.g. Dem. 3.26.   [117] 90–97.

[118] Hermogenes π. ἰδεῶν, p. 402 Rabe (cited in Conomis, 31); for his prestige, [Plut.] *X Orat.* 841f (§ 13 Conomis).

each tribe had found inspiration in the example of the tribal hero. And when, after the revolt of Thebes in 335, Alexander demanded the surrender of ten anti-Macedonian politicians, Demosthenes and Lycurgus of course among them, the good Phocion urged that 'the men who were asked for should imitate the daughters of Leos and the daughters of Hyacinthus, and willingly accept death in order to save their native land from disaster'.[119]

Once again the question of the status of such arguments is posed. A Sicilian story is introduced by Lycurgus with the *apologia* 'even if the story is somewhat far-fetched [*mythodes*], it is suitable that all you younger people should hear it'. Should we conclude that Lycurgus shared the ugly view of some of his contemporaries that a story or myth is not the less useful for not being true?[120] But it would be eccentric to admit to such a belief in public, if one wished to act on it in its most cynical form. He might rather have wished to say that within the whole set of such stories some are true—because the moral lessons they embody are true—even if some doubt is always necessary in the individual case.

Tragedy, for Lycurgus, was a precious part of the city's educational heritage; and often he brings to mind a speech by a tragic hero, another grim patriot, the Eteocles of Aeschylus. Eteocles tells the Thebans that each of them must

protect your city and the altars of the gods of the land, that their honours may not be wiped out, and your children and your mother earth, dearest of nurses. For as you crawled as babies on her friendly soil she nursed you, readily accepting the whole labour of rearing, to be shield-bearing citizens, so that you could prove loyal in this time of need.[121]

Patriotism is here seen—as sometimes in the Funerary Speeches— as an obligation created by an organic, parent–child relationship between the citizen and his 'native' earth. But since that earth is also a goddess and a home of gods and goddesses, patriotic devotion is also a form of piety. Such a conflation of obligation to parents, country, and gods seems also to be the central core of Lycurgus' religion.

I pray to Athena and the other gods and heroes established in the city and country, if I have acted justly in denouncing and bringing to trial Leocrates, who betrayed their temples and images and precincts and the sacrifices laid down by law and handed down by your forefathers, make me today a fit prosecutor of Leocrates' crimes . . . What most separates you

---

[119] Dem. 60.27–31; Diod. 17.15.2; cf. Plut. *Phoc*. 17.2–3 (which however lacks this detail).
[120] So M. Vielberg, *RhM* 134 (1991), 49–68, on *Leoc*. 95, which he compares with Isoc. *Paneg*. 28.
[121] *Sept*. 14–20.

Athenians from other men is piety to the gods, respect for parents, pride in the city . . . He was not content just to deposit his body and his property abroad; he summoned to Megara and removed from the country his ancestral shrines [ἱερὰ πατρῷα], which his ancestors had established and bequeathed to him, in accord with your laws and ancestral custom. He was not deterred by their name 'ancestral' [πατρῷα], but removed them from his ancestral land [πατρίς] and forced them to share his exile, leaving behind the temples and land which they had occupied, and to be established in a foreign land, where they were alien to the country and the customs observed in Megara.[122]

Native city, gods of the city, ancestral gods, ancestors, ancestral traditions: the emotional charge attached to these terms is equal and interchangeable. Here surely are the strong wells of feeling that fed the Lycurgan religious enthusiasm.

It is an easy transition from the *patris*-religion of Eteocles and Lycurgus to the ephebes. As witnesses to their famous oath, the ephebes invoked, in addition to a series of gods, 'boundaries of the homeland, corn, barley, vines, olive-trees, fig-trees'. They are thus brought into close association with other products of that native soil by which they too were reared, of which they too are seen as products. Two propositions would now be widely accepted about the controversial history of the ephebate: a form of the institution already existed in the first half of the fourth century (and doubtless much earlier too); but it was extensively reformed by the 'law of Epicrates' in the early Lycurgan period. The first point is proved by Aeschines' reference to his own service as an ephebe in the 380s or 370s, and by various pre-Lycurgan traces of the 'ephebic oath', most notably an explicit citation of it under that name by Demosthenes in 343; the second is made highly probable—although all we strictly know about Epicrates' law is that it was mentioned by Lycurgus in a speech—by, in particular, the sudden outburst in the late 330s of honorary decrees in favour of the ephebes and their various supervisors.[123] Both points are confirmed by a passage in Xenophon's *Poroi*, which already in 355 seems to show young men training and racing and doing guard duty and patrolling the borders, as did the later ephebes, but without yet receiving a state maintenance-allowance for doing so. A form of training that had been (perhaps) intermittent, unpaid, and for that reason doubtless voluntary, was now given

---

[122] 1, 15, 25.

[123] Aeschin. 1.49, 2.167; Dem. 19.303 (cf. P. Siewert, *JHS* 97, 1977, 102–11); Reinmuth, *Ephebic Inscriptions, passim* (but his dating of his no. 1 to 361/0 is generally rejected: cf. Rhodes, *Commentary Ath. Pol.*, 494, n. 35). Epicrates: Lycurgus V.3 Conomis (= Harp. s.v. *Epikrates*). The oath is accessible as Tod, *GHI* II.204.

public support, and became—at least for those of hoplite status and above—a compulsory two years of full-term service.[124] No source brings Lycurgus himself into an association of any kind with the institution; but the concern to train up the young shoots of the land as 'shield-bearing inhabitants, reliable in (any) hour of need' seems quintessentially Lycurgan.

By the late second century, no festival, so to speak, was complete without the participation of the ephebes, as we learn all too fully from the honorary decrees.[125] To what extent did they owe their ceremonial role to the law of Epicrates? The Lycurgan 'new model ephebes' were certainly involved from the start in at least one form of festival activity: for two dedications survive which commemorate victories won in torch-races by two different teams of ephebes in 333/2, one probably at one of the festivals of the city, the other at the *Nemesia* at Rhamnus.[126] But the important passage of Xenophon already mentioned shows that the 'proto-ephebes' too spent their time, under the charge of gymnasiarchs, in training for just such torch-races. Whatever other rites they may have performed (one striking suggestion is that they provided the tragic choruses), it looks as if the torch-race, that display of speed and dexterity and teamwork, was the quintessential ephebic form.[127] Here then the law of

---

[124] See P. Gauthier, *Un commentaire historique des Poroi de Xénophon* (Geneva 1976), 190–95, on *Poroi* 4.51–52; for good summaries of the debate see e.g. Rhodes, *Commentary Ath. Pol.*, 494–95 [+]; J. J. Winkler in id. and F. I. Zeitlin eds., *Nothing to Do with Dionysus?* (Princeton 1990), 25–33. Details of the 'proto-ephebate' have largely to be guessed, but N. V. Sekunda points out, *ZPE* 83 (1990), 152, that the division between 'gymnasium' and 'countryside' service (of each of which the post-Epicratean ephebes did a year) is already present in Xen. *Poroi* 4.51–52.

[125] See Pélékidis, *Éphébie*, 211–56 (add now two important texts from the late third cent., *SEG* XXVI 98; XXIX 116).

[126] C. Habicht, *AM* 76 (1961), 143, no. 2 (= *SEG* XXI 680; Reinmuth, *Ephebic Inscriptions*, no. 6) (from the Ceramicus); *IG* II².3105 + *SEG* XXXI 162 (from Rhamnus), on which see O. Palagia and D. M. Lewis, *BSA* 84 (1989), 333–44 (who discuss further comparable victory reliefs dedicated at Rhamnus: their caution about the games concerned, 344, seems unnecessary now that a *gymnikos agon* at 'the greater *Nemesia*' is attested, *Prakt* 1989 [1992], 31, no. 15.9). Note too Reinmuth, *Ephebic Inscriptions*, no. 15, which seems to show the ephebes *en masse* attending an early set of Amphiaraic games: cf. D. M. Lewis, *CR* NS 23 (1973), 255.

[127] Xen. *Poroi* 4.52 confirms the explicit statement of Σ Patm. on Dem. 57.43 (*BCH* 1, 1877, 11) that the various torch-races were performed by 'those about to marry' or 'ephebes': cf. Sekunda, *ZPE* 83 (1990), 149–58, who stresses the interest in this context of the mockery of the unfit torch-runner in Ar. *Ran.* 1089 ff. (but his inference that not all torch-races were relays is unconvincing). For torch-racing as characteristic of the young of a social élite see too Ar. *Vesp.* 1203–1204. 'Bull-lifting', by contrast, later characteristic of ephebes, is assigned simply to '200 Athenians' in *IG* I³.82.30. Other rites: see e.g. Palagia, *BSA* 84 (1989), 338, n. 17, on the Parthenon frieze. Tragic chorus: J. J. Winkler, 'The Ephebes' Song', in id. and Zeitlin eds., *Nothing to Do with Dionysus?* 20–62; this brilliantly presented hypothesis is, however, finally unconvincing; for, if tragic choral dancing were as intimately related to ephebic training as Winkler argues, the tragic festival would almost necessarily have been

Epicrates brought no change, except perhaps a new enthusiasm; and it may be that ceremonial tasks such as escorting the ancient image of Athena to the sea were only added to the ephebic programme after the fourth century (for the institution retained the form given to it by the law of Epicrates for only a short period, soon changing from a military training for most, if not all, young citizens into a kind of finishing-school for a social élite[128]). But one detail shows with a model clarity how, already in the fourth century, the patriotism of the ephebes was to be grounded upon piety to the city's gods: before entering their first year of service, they were taken upon a tour of the shrines of the city.[129] If that practice was an innovation of the Lycurgan period, it well expresses its spirit; if it is older, we see again one of the traditions from which Lycurgus' piety derived.

organized as a competition between tribes; and Winkler needs to explain why the link between ephebes and tragedy has disappeared by the time, during the lifetime of classical tragedy, when our evidence for the ephebate becomes abundant. (For other criticisms see P. Vidal-Naquet, *PCPS* NS 32, 1986, 137, esp. D. Lewis's suggestion, 144, n. 105, that the Pronomos vase, Winkler's key text, in fact represents dithyramb.)

[128] On the date of the second reform see P. Gauthier, *Chiron* 15 (1985), 151–61, esp. the conspectus of views in 161, n. 46; cf. C. Habicht, *ZPE* 93 (1992), 47–49: a change to a single year of service at the ephebe's own expense probably already occurred in 307.

[129] Arist. *Ath. Pol.* 42.3.

Beyond the Death of Alexander

When should a history of Athenian religion come to an end? One date that is obviously inappropriate is 323. Could one seriously contemplate trying to give a feel of fourth-century religion without reference to Menander and the *Characters* of Theophrastus?[1] Radical political change doubtless affects almost every area of life in the long term, but it does not overturn long-established social forms overnight.[2] Even politically, the division at 323 is in some ways too sharp (though one must certainly allow that the forced restriction of citizen rights for much of the period between 322 and 307 was a drastic change, with, we must assume, great though unobservable consequences for the religious life of the dispossessed). If it is objected that Menander's prosperous and unpolitical men and women are, surely, a world away spiritually from the fellow citizens of Pericles, one may answer that the audience of Demosthenes, according to the orator, resembled them all too much. Εὐετηρία 'prosperity', a Hellenistic ideal already honoured by a statue at Athens in 299/8, perhaps first appears in a denunciation by Demosthenes of the false values of his contemporaries.[3] The conventional division disguises the sense in which the Hellenistic world was born before Alexander was. One advantage of studying the religious practices of a single city is precisely that the continuities are much more obvious than if the eye flits from novelty to novelty up and down the Greek world.

One religious phenomenon, however, of the last years of the century may appear revolutionary indeed: we must consider this apparent counter-case at once. Before 323, little if any cult had been paid

---

[1] Cf. Millett, *Lending and Borrowing*, 20. [2] Cf. Gauthier, *Bienfaiteurs*, 5.
[3] Dem. 8.67, 10.49 f.; cf. Demochares *FGrH* 75 F 4 (on Demetrius of Phaleron). Statue: A. E. Raubitschek, *Hesperia* 35 (1966), 242, no. 2; cf. *IG* XI.2. 105 1–2 (Delos, 284 BC), *SEG* XXX 1121.10 (Entella, early third cent.), and, for the goddess *Eueteria*, *Bull. Ép.* 1966, no. 137 (with citation of Wilhelm). For the ideal of an '*agora* full of *agatha*' see already Ar. *Pax* 999. For earlier senses of the word εὐετηρία (agricultural abundance; physical good condition) cf. LSJ. A trireme already bore the name in 373, *IG* II².1607 B 6.

to living men at Athens. Clement records that the Athenians voted to 'prostrate themselves before [προσκυνεῖν] Philip at Kynosarges'. What underlies this may be no more (and might be less) than a decision to set up a statue of the king in the famous precinct at Kynosarges of Heracles, Philip's supposed ancestor.[4] In 324, a proposal to worship Alexander was certainly debated, because we know from contemporary sources that Demosthenes first 'forbade the recognition of any except the traditional gods' but subsequently said 'the people should not dispute Alexander's right to honours in heaven'; he 'allowed Alexander to be the son of Zeus and of Poseidon, if he wanted'. The proposal was inspired by a belief that Alexander desired such honours ('if he wants'), even if not necessarily by an actual request from the king. Demosthenes' change of mind (which the jibe about 'son of Poseidon' proves not to have been a change of heart) was due, many moderns suppose, to prudential considerations, those summed up in an epigram attributed to Demades: 'take care lest by guarding heaven you lose the earth': Alexander's goodwill could not be put in jeopardy at a time when the fate of Athens' cleruchy on Samos hung on his decision, and by a thread. Doubtless the same hard argument swayed the assembly (though no trustworthy source actually states that the decree was passed).[5] It was through 'compulsion' again, according to Hyperides, that heroic honours were granted to Alexander's 'servant', the dead Hephaistion.[6] There was in fact no tradition at Athens of treating

[4] Clem. Al. *Protr.* 4.54.5; for different views see e.g. Nilsson, *Geschichte*, II.142; H. S. Versnel, *Mnemosyne*, 4th ser., 26 (1973), 273–79; J. N. Bremmer, ibid. 30 (1977), 369–74; E. A. Fredricksmeyer, *TAPA* 109 (1979), 39–61; Badian, 'Deification', 67–71 (whom I follow); M.-F. Billot in M.-O. Goulet-Cazé and R. Goulet eds., *Le cynisme ancien* (Paris 1993), 73, n. 8 [+]. Versnel and Bremmer argue that the supposed honour played on the negative connotations of Kynosarges (ἐς Κυνόσαργες for instance meant roughly 'go to blazes'). But were actual decrees passed in such a tone? Evidence for worship of Philip elsewhere is also controversial: see Fredricksmeyer, *TAPA* 109 (1979), 39–61, and Badian, 'Deification', 38–41, and add *SEG* XXXVIII 658.

[5] On all this see Badian. 'Deification', 54–55 [+], and now G. L. Cawkwell, 'The Deification of Alexander the Great: A Note', in I. Worthington ed., *Ventures into Greek History* (Oxford 1994), 293–306. Contemporary sources: Din. 1.94; Hyperides, *Contra Dem.* fr. 7 col. xxxi (cf. xxxii), which gives the date. Cawkwell argues that the latter two apophthegms of Demosthenes quoted in the text derive from a different context, a debate about the heroization of Hephaestion (enjoined by the oracle of Ammon). But this would not have been the most natural occasion on which to ἀμφισβητεῖν τῶν ἐν οὐρανῷ τιμῶν Ἀλεξάνδρῳ. Later sources of uncertain reliability (written out in A. D. Nock, *JHS* 48, 1928, 21–22), add that the proposal was to make Alexander a thirteenth god and that the proposer was Demades, who was subsequently fined; they also quote sarcasms of Lycurgus (in fact now dead) and Pytheas about the proposed 'god'.

[6] *Epitaphios* col. viii.21; cf. E. J. Bickerman, *Athenaeum* 41 (1963), 70–85 = id., *Religion and Politics in the Hellenistic and Roman Periods* (Como 1985), 473–88; Habicht, *Gottmenschentum*, 29, 249 f.; Cawkwell, 'Deification of Alexander', 300. Since Hyperides here says that the Athenians were forced to see sacrifices performed to mortals (i.e. Alexander) and

historical mortals even as heroes, if we except the two tyrannicides and the war-dead on the one hand, and on the other the poet Sophocles, host of a god.

(Alexander's treasurer Harpalus built a cenotaph of famous magnificence for his mistress Pythionike at Athens, as well as a tomb at Babylon. One of these constructions he treated, according to malicious contemporaries, as a 'temple' with an altar dedicated to 'Aphrodite Pythionike'—the 'famous temple of the whore' as it is called in a fragment of one Python's satyr play *Agen*. We cannot be sure that Pythionike became Aphrodite at Athens (and not just at Babylon, or in the mouths of Harpalus' enemies). But the Athenians could anyway scarcely prevent Alexander's powerful friend from spending his money, and addressing his dead lover, as he pleased.[7])

Demetrius of Phaleron, regent of Athens from 318 to 307 and a native Athenian, received no divine cult, although a personality cult of novel type is certainly indicated by the 300 statues with which he was honoured. (The smelting of them after his death, all but one, became a theme for sententious reflection.[8]) The liberation of Athens by Demetrius Poliorcetes in 307, however, brought a transformation.[9] Poliorcetes and his father, Antigonus Monophthalmus, became the patrons of two newly created tribes, Demetrias and Antigonis; and unlike the heroic eponyms of the two Clisthenic tribes the two newcomers were gods—the two Saviours (*Soteres*), honoured as such henceforth with priest and altar and procession and sacrifice. Their images intruded on two sacred places: beside the statues of Harmodius and Aristogeiton in the *agora*, and on the very robe presented to Athena at the *Panathenaea*.[10] When Demetrius returned in 304 to rescue the city from siege by Cassander, he was granted new honours: the right to reside in the Parthenon; and an altar (probably) of 'Demetrius Descendent' at the spot where he first

to honour their servants (Hephaestion) as heroes, it is sometimes concluded that cult of Alexander, in contrast to that of Hephaestion, occurred only outside Athens. But 'we have been forced to see' stresses powerlessness, not necessarily lack of direct involvement.

[7] Theopompus *FGrH* 115 F 253; Python *TrGF* 91 F 1 (a setting at Babylon is perhaps suggested by line 5, but I do not see that lines 11–13 in themselves exclude Attica). For the cenotaph see Plut. *Phoc.* 22.1–2; Paus. 1.37.5; Dicaearchus in Athen. 594e-595a; A. Scholl, *JdI* 109 (1994), 254–68 [+]. Charges of this kind had, interestingly, become common currency in political abuse: Demosthenes 'erected a shrine' to the assassin of Philip, according to Aeschin. 3.160.

[8] See F. Wehrli ed., *Demetrios von Phaleron* (Basle 1949), frs. 21–24, 54–55: the survivor is *IG* II².2971 = *SIG*³ 319 = fr. 20 Wehrli.

[9] Main sources: Plut. *Dem.* 10–13, 23.4–5, 24.9–10, 26, 46.2; Diod. 20.46.2. For further details and the chronology see the admirable discussion of Habicht, *Gottmenschentum*, 44–55.

[10] Plut. *Dem.* 10, 46.2; Diod. 20.46.2: for epigraphic references to the joint cult see Habicht, *Gottmenschentum*, 45, n. 12. Plutarch's claim that Athenian years in this period were dated by reference to the priest of the Saviours has, however, been shown by inscriptions to be wrong.

alighted. (The doubt concerns not the fact but the date.) His subsequent victories in the Peloponnese evoked, as an inscription has recently shown, a further annual commemorative sacrifice 'to the *Soteres*'. A decree passed by the 'Athenian volunteers' who served in, most probably, these campaigns apparently calls on other Greek states too to accord Demetrius similar honours, and insists that 'those responsible for the sacrifices performed *on behalf of* King Demetrius should also sacrifice *to* Demetrius the Saviour' in the most magnificent way.[11] A little later, he asked and was permitted to pass through all the grades of Eleusinian initiation at a single ceremony (only the daduch Pythodorus daring to speak in opposition). It was probably in this period that the assembly decreed, on Stratocles' proposal, that messengers approaching him from the city were to be styled 'sacred ambassadors' and that 'any instruction of King Demetrius should be pious in respect of the gods and lawful towards men'.[12]

A last set of honours probably dates from the final period of his control of Athens, beginning in 294. His comings to the city were to be celebrated like those of Demeter and Dionysus; the *Dionysia* were restyled *Dionysia and Demetrieia*, and a month and a day were named for him too; and it was apparently in 292 or 291 that, on Dromokleides' motion, a sacred embassy was sent to seek an 'oracle' from the 'saviour god' on a religious issue (Delphi itself being inaccessible). In or near 291 again he was greeted with a famous hymn, in ithyphallic metre, that contained the lines 'the other gods are far distant, or lack ears, or don't exist, or pay no heed to us: but you we see present here, not in wood or stone but in reality'.[13] The same ithyphallic hymn speaks of his 'friends' as 'stars around the sun': three of these 'friends' (figures in fact of some importance from other Greek states) were also honoured with 'hero-shrines and altars' in Athens. One of the three friends in turn founded a temple of Phila Aphrodite (in honour of Demetrius' wife, Phila) at Thriai, west of Athens.[14]

---

[11] Plut. *Dem.* 23.3–5, 10.4–5 (cf. Habicht, *Gottmenschentum*, 49); *SEG* XXX 69 (cf. *Hesperia* 59, 1990, 463–66); Moretti 7. The small bronze coin-type which shows Demetrius wearing the Corinthian helmet also characteristic of Athena (E. T. Newell, *The Coinages of Demetrius Poliorketes*, Oxford 1927, 25, 40–41) derives from Cyprus and should not be linked closely with events in Athens.

[12] Plut. *Dem.* 26; 11.1; 24.9–10.

[13] Plut. *Dem.* 12.2 (but Plutarch's claim that the *Dionysia* were simply renamed *Demetrieia* is apparently disproved by an inscription, Habicht, *Gottmenschentum*, 52, n. 38); ibid. 13 (cf. Habicht, *Untersuchungen*, 34–44); Demochares *FGrH* 75 F 2 and Douris *FGrH* 76 F 13, whence Powell, *Coll. Alex.* 173–74 (cf. Habicht, *Untersuchungen*, 35, n. 5).

[14] Demochares *FGrH* 75 F 1 (cf. Habicht, *Gottmenschentum*, 55–58); Athen. 255c (cf. Alexis fr. 116 K/A). The identification of this shrine with the one still visible at Daphni is

The Athenians were not the only Greeks to make successors of Alexander heirs too to his divine honours, nor even the first.[15] But theirs is a uniquely well-documented case—which is why it has seemed right to repeat the many details that are, so uncommonly, recorded. In some respects it can count as a model example. 'Ruler-cult' (an expression open to contestation—but something is needed) is a product of the confrontation between city-states and immensely powerful individuals outside them on whom they are in various ways dependent for their very survival.[16] In this respect the relation is exactly analogous to that between a city and its traditional gods. Athens' dealings with Demetrius illustrate in the most dramatic way these close encounters between city and external power. In 307 and 304 he gained the city by force of arms, in 294 he brought it back to allegiance through a horrific siege, and he was at times actually resident in the city in all his power and splendour. Typical again is the way in which ruler-cult is represented as being not, in fact, a mere response to power but an expression of 'honour' and 'gratitude' in response to the immense benefits conferred on the city by the king.[17] (The possibility thus arises of seeing the cults as expressions of a spontaneous upsurge of feeling; but this kind of expression of gratitude, like any other, might or might not be sincerely felt.[18]) In 307 and 304 Antigonus and Demetrius 'liberated' Athens from other masters; in 294 Demetrius treated the rebellious city with a gentleness quite unexpected after a hard siege. Even the recently discovered decree that records the Athenians' decision later in the century to 'honour with godlike honours' Antigonus (Gonatas), victor over the city in the Chremonidean war, explains that this 'saviour of the people' 'continues doing good to the Athenian people'.[19] These two factors together surely explain why the Athenians were so much

unfounded: see L. Robert, *Hellenica* 2 (1946), 30, n. 3. Demochares speaks also of 'shrines of Leaina and Lamia Aphrodite' (these being two courtesans): where? According to Polemon fr. 15 Preller *ap.* Ath. 253b it was the Thebans who founded a shrine of Aphrodite Lamia.

[15] See *OGIS* 6, from Scepsis, of 311.

[16] See Price's admirable study, *Rituals and Power*.

[17] See Habicht, *Gottmenschentum*, 165–71, 230–36; Gauthier, *Bienfaiteurs*, 46–49. For such 'enthusiasm' at Athens see (in addition to the literary texts relating to Demetrius) Moretti 7; Polyb. 16.25–26 (arrival of Attalus I); and *e contrario* the remarkable account of the cursing of Philip V and the whole Macedonian dynasty in Livy 31.44.2–45.2 (Habicht, *Studien*, 142–50). On the 'benefits' later conferred by Ptolemy III and Attalus I see Habicht, *Studien*, 105–12. The Athenian cleruchs on Lemnos founded temples of Seleucus and his son Antiochus in gratitude for liberation from Lysimachus: Phylarchus *FGrH* 81 F 29.

[18] Cf. F. W. Walbank, *Chiron* 17 (1987), 381.

[19] See B. C. Petrakos, *Prakt* 1989 [1992], 31, no. 15: a decision of the Rhamnusians, on the motion of Elpinikos Mnesippou Rhamnousios, proposer of Moretti 25 of 236/5, to 'sacrifice to Antigonus and wear crowns' at the athletic competition of the *Great Nemesia*, in consequence of the Athenians' decision summarized in the text.

readier to honour Demetrius than Alexander (whom none the less they had honoured, very probably). Alexander was in Asia, Demetrius at or within the gates: the crucial difference did not lie in the theological sphere.

What, by contrast, is rare (though not necessarily untypical) is that Demetrius' godhead demonstrably did not go uncontested. Athens remained a city of deep political divisions. In 307 Demetrius may have been greeted as liberator with almost universal enthusiasm, but by 303 there was bitter opposition, in the name of 'democracy', to Athens' dependence on the fiat of the absent king. One symptom is a famous attack on Demetrius' chief Athenian supporter, Stratocles, by the comic poet and diplomatist Philippides:[20]

> he who compressed the year to a single month,
> [*a reference to the decree authorizing Demetrius' irregular initiation*]
> who treated the acropolis as a tavern
> and introduced the call-girls to the Maiden,
> because of whom the frost scorched the vines,
> because of whose impiety the *peplos* split in the middle,
> he who made the honours of the gods mortal:
> this is what subverts the democracy, not comedy.

The language of the attack is religious (the ancient conception of impiety causing ill weather is even deployed), the motivation, as the last line shows, political also.[21] Indeed it is ultimately to polemic from such quarters that we owe Plutarch's long and indignant account of the servile 'flattery' practised by Demetrius' supporters. His second period of rule (from 294) was later described as a time of 'oligarchy', and ended in revolt;[22] adulation of the charismatic leader was at its height, as in the ithyphallic hymn, at a time when his dominance was in fact by many most bitterly resented. A certain excess attached to some of the honours accorded to Demetrius, even in the judgement of a posterity well used to the phenomenon of ruler cult. In part no doubt this excess was due to uncertainty in handling an idiom that was still relatively new. But Demetrius' supporters were also driven to extremes by the pressures of political struggle.[23]

---

[20] Philippides fr. 25 K/A: cf. Shear, *Kallias*, 47–51.

[21] Cf. Habicht, *Gottmenschentum*, 213–21. Habicht argues that there was no opposition at this date to the principle of granting divine honours to men; only strong disagreement, on political grounds, whether a particular individual merited them. But even if we disallow the possibility that Callisthenes' famous protest in Arrian, *Anab.* 4.11 reflects contemporary feeling (P. A. Brunt, Loeb Arrian I.540; Badian, 'Deification', 28–32), the language of Philippides here and of Hyperides (*Epitaphios*, col. viii.21) and of the accusers of Aristotle (n. 87) is religious, whatever their motives.

[22] Shear, *Kallias*, 52–55; Habicht, *Untersuchungen*, 22–33, 43–44.

[23] Cf. Plut. *Dem.* 24.6–12. On this excess see Price, *Rituals and Power*, 223–24 (on sacrifices made 'to' not 'for' Monophthalmos and Demetrius: on this distinction cf. n. 33).

A notorious instance of such excess is the claim of the ithyphallic hymn that the 'other gods', dead or ineffective or indifferent, have been supplanted by Demetrius. To moderns the idea that god-kings and traditional gods were rivals has an intuitive appeal, and the hymn is constantly cited, almost *de rigueur*, as an emblem of the changed religious attitude of early Hellenism. But even if one looks at the matter in these terms, the antithesis is obviously too extreme. The gods who *ex hypothesi* had failed the Greeks were the city-protecting gods.[24] To Demeter, for instance, Demetrius was no rival; the ithyphallic hymn itself, inconsistently, speaks of her daughter with respect, and piety as well as impiety is displayed even by the king's irregular initiation at Eleusis.

The exaltation of the mortal god at the expense of the Olympians in the *ithyphallos* is anyway—and this is the crucial point—quite untypical.[25] Perhaps it should be seen in a context of festival excess,[26] like the outrages piously inflicted on the Olympians in old comedy. We should remember anyway that temporary disillusionment with a god or gods is a well-attested feature of popular polytheism.[27] But much more typical of the normal relation between monarch and gods is the kind of non-competitive association found, for instance, in the renaming of the *Dionysia* as *Dionysia and Demetrieia*; or in the decision of the Athenians in 304 to sacrifice, 'for the safety of those on campaign', to Athena Nike, Agathe Tyche, and the Saviours; or in the description of the honours later conferred on Antigonus Gonatas as '*equal* to those of the gods'.[28] Even Demetrius' intrusions upon the Parthenon and Athena's sacred robe perhaps tend in the same direction, though much more crudely. And, where no kings are present, there city-holding gods are still credited with saving miracles, just as before.[29] There can be no better corrective to the *ithyphallos* than the dossier of texts and inscriptions that relate to the defeat of the Gallic invasion of Greece in the early 270s: just as in 480–479, the gods intervened repeatedly to save the Hellenes from the barbarian

[24] So Habicht, *Gottmenschentum*, 230–36.

[25] Cf. Price, *Rituals and Power*, 38; F. W. Walbank in *CAH*³ VII.1 (1984), 94.

[26] Cf. Ferguson, *Hellenistic Athens*, 143; *aliter* Dodds, *Greeks and the Irrational*, 242, and 258, n. 32.

[27] See Versnel in id., *Faith, Hope and Worship* (Leiden 1981), 37–42; and for Athens, Thuc. 2.47.4.

[28] Above, n. 13; *SEG* XXX 69 (cf. n. 11); above n. 19 (on ἰσόθεοι τιμαί, an expression now first attested at Athens in connection with ruler-cult—though for other contexts see Ch. 8, n. 55—see Habicht, *Gottmenschentum*, 196, n. 23).

[29] Cf. the several instances in Habicht, *Gottmenschentum*, 231–32 (who draws a different conclusion).

horde.[30] Saviour kings could be assimilated to saviour gods precisely because saviour gods still had power.[31]

In Athens itself, the *Panathenaea* remained the great symbol of national identity and focus of patriotic feeling. Foreign kings paid graceful tribute to Athena's city by donating the most valued products of their own land for use at the great festival: Lysimachus in 298 sent Macedonian timber for the mast of the Panathenaic boat, Ptolemy in 282 or 278 gave Egyptian linen-cord for its rigging. When King Pyrrhus entered the city in 286, his first act was, of course, to climb the acropolis and make sacrifice to Athena.[32] After Athens' defeat in the Chremonidean war, forms of ruler-cult (suspended doubtless in the period of independence from 287–262) re-emerged: the cult of 'the Soteres' revived, Antigonus Gonatas, as we have recently learnt, received 'honours equal to the gods' (hitherto no more had been attested than public prayers 'on behalf of' him and his family and later of his son Demetrius), and in the 220s, after the break from Macedon, games were named for Ptolemy III, who also became eponym of a tribe.[33] As far as we can tell, these rites and games took their place in the festival cycle peacefully and without controversy.

The events of 307 to 287, therefore, are not quite the watershed that they may appear. After a period of some confusion, traditional cults and cults of god-kings settled into a mode of co-existence. And it was, in all seeming, through external circumstance, not a development or decline in belief, that the efflorescence of ruler-cult at Athens occurred at just the time that it did. That argument, of course, merely pushes the critical period earlier, if one believes that the very possibility of ruler-cult could not have emerged without a crisis in traditional belief. As is well known, the first harbinger of what was to come was the rechristening of the *Heraia* on Samos as *Lysandreia*, probably at the end of the fifth century, not long after

---

[30] See e.g. *SIG*[3] 398, Paus. 10.19.5–10.23, Diod. 22.9; and in enormous detail G. Nachtergael, *Les Galates en Grèce et les Sôtéria de Delphes* (Brussels 1977). More generally see M. Rostovtzeff, *A Social and Economic History of the Hellenistic World*[2] (Oxford 1953), 1122–23.

[31] Contrast Dodds, *Greeks and the Irrational*, 242 'when the old gods withdraw, the empty thrones call out for a successor'.

[32] Lysimachus and Ptolemy: see Robert's brilliant comments, *REG* 94 (1981), 397 f., on *IG* II[2].657.13–15, and *SEG* XXVIII 60.67–70 (on the chronology of the latter see C. Habicht, *ClAnt* 11, 1992, 70, n. 10). Pyrrhus: Plut. *Pyrrh.* 12.6–7, cf. Shear, *Kallias*, 75.

[33] See Habicht, *Gottmenschentum*, 45, n. 12 and 192; id., *Untersuchungen*, 72, n. 19 and *IG* II[2].1299.10–11 (*SIG*[3] 485) (add now *SEG* XXXIII 115.23–24); p. 274–5 below. Antigonus: n. 19 above—a surprise; since it has often been noted that in general the honours accorded to Antigonus Gonatas (no friend of Greek liberty) are extremely modest.

the proclamation of a proto-euhemerism by Prodicus of Keos.[34] Fortunately this problem of origins[35] can be evaded here, by appeal to subsequent history. The crisis, if crisis there was, was of the type from which the patient emerges changed, perhaps, but still capable of long life.

We revert to the original problem. Where should a line be drawn? Framed so generally the question is unanswerable. Only in respect of particular enquiries into particular aspects of religious life can an answer be attempted.[36] The major festivals persisted late into the Roman period: the heortologist will need to follow them thither. For the intellectual historian, the break had already occurred, with the emergence of the first philosophical schools. This book must seek a conclusion by looking at the changes and continuities that affect its own particular subjects.

First, social forms. As units of political organization, demes and tribes survived right until the later Roman empire, phratries at least until the mid-second century BC.[37] But as centres of collective life they had all lost most of their importance by the end of the third century BC—if we assume, as we should, that any thriving social body at this date would pass decrees and record them on stone. The demes in general vanish from the record around the middle of the third century (though one or two individual demes are still active in the second).[38] The rites and shrines and myths of the Attic countryside do not disappear altogether, of course; what is lost is the individual demesman's automatic association, through the publicly financed sacrificial calendar of the deme, with a local mini-pantheon of gods and heroes. And the cults of the countryside did in fact in the long term suffer seriously, to judge from the bodily transportation of several of the finest extra-Athenian classical temples to the *agora* in the Augustan period. Recent archaeological studies suggest that Attica

[34] Douris *FGrH* 76 F 71 and 26; *AA* 1965, 440; Habicht, *Gottmenschentum*, 3–6, 243–44. The reservations of Badian, 'Deification', 33–38, seem to undervalue the importance of the renaming. Prodicus: see A. Henrichs, *HSCP* 79 (1975), 115–23, on *P. Herc.* 1428 cols. ii–iii. But note that Prodicus' deified benefactors are culture heroes, not (like Euhemerus') kings.

[35] For an excellent introduction see F. W. Walbank, *CAH*³ VII.1 (1984), 84–98 (*Chiron* 17, 1987, 365–82 is a related German version); cf. M. Flower, *CQ* NS 38 (1988), 123–34.

[36] Cf. Veyne, *Writing History*, ch. 3.

[37] Demes and tribes: see Traill, *Political Organization, passim.* Phratries are still mentioned in the latest citizenship decrees, of about 150 (e.g. Osborne, *Naturalization*, D 112, 113). The new procedure adopted thenceforth (cf. Osborne, III/IV.184–85) leaves us uninformed about the formalities of registration.

[38] Whitehead, *Demes*, p. xxvii. Both texts he cites concern religion; one is from Eleusis, which was the least likely of all demes to lose its identity (*IG* II².949), one from the city deme Melite (*Hesperia* 11, 1942, 265, no. 51).

outside Athens already suffered large-scale depopulation in the third century, that time of war and poverty.[39] Around 300, and perhaps a little later, a clutch of texts still attest phratries busy with feasting and their own problems of organization and finance,[40] but there is no clear trace of them after that. (One may suspect, however, that a festival as popular as the *Apatouria* would not vanish quickly.) As for the tribes, their religious organization had been shaken up by the creation of Antigonis and Demetrias in 307 (and further upsets were to follow).[41] The members of the demes that were transferred to the new tribes had in principle to forgo their association with an eponymous Attic hero, in favour of a Macedonian king. Such changes could, however, be weathered, as the history of the new Clisthenic creations shows. The representatives of the tribe on the council maintained a cult of 'the eponymous hero', and many competitions, a focus of enthusiasm, were still tribally organized in the second century; but tribal decrees become rare after about 250, and one may wonder whether sacrifices that brought together all the members to feast in honour of the eponymous hero still occurred.[42]

As demes and phratries and tribes vanish as active entities from the epigraphic record, so other bodies rise into prominence. Most conspicuous are the various Attic garrisons—above all, those of the forts of Rhamnus and Sunium. The composition of these garrisons varies—ephebes, mercenaries, Macedonians, citizens all appear, in various permutations—as does their function: sometimes they guard Attica, sometimes they are a guard set over it by the kings of Macedon; but beneath these changes the fort or 'fortified small town' has a continuing life of its own, stronger than that of the contemporary demes.[43] As a counter case, an instance of the continuing vitality of local groupings, one might cite the surprising information

---

[39] Transportation: see T. L. Shear Jr., *Hesperia* 50 (1981), 361–63; W. B. Dinsmoor, *Hesperia* 51 (1982), 410–52; J. M. Camp, *The Athenian Agora* (London 1986), 184–87. Depopulation: Lauter, *Landesgemeinden*, 129, 142; Lohmann, 'Country Life', 30, 38. For the survival of some deme rites see Paus. 1.31–39.3; and note e.g. H. Lauter, 'Ein ländliches Heiligtum hellenistischer Zeit in Trapuria (Attika)', *AA* 1980, 242–55.

[40] Theophr. *Char.* 30.16; *IG* II².1241; *SEG* XXXII 150.

[41] See W. K. Pritchett, *The Five Attic Tribes after Kleisthenes* (Baltimore 1943), 13, n. 1; Traill, *Political Organization*, 26–31. *Hesperia* 32 (1963), 14–15, no. 13 (*c*.200) is remarkable: a decree honouring a member of the tribe Ptolemais is to be posted in the Eurysakeion, tribal headquarters of Aiantis, to which his deme had belonged before the creation of Ptolemais.

[42] Eponymous hero: *Agora* XV, *passim*. Competitions: see e.g. *IG* II².956–65; Pickard-Cambridge, *Dramatic Festivals*², 74. Decrees: Jones, *Public Organization*, 66–67 (for an exception see n. 41). Tribal feasts did, however, survive the abolition of the liturgies by Demetrius of Phaleron: see *IG* II².1165.

[43] See Pouilloux, *Rhamnonte*, 79–92; R. Osborne in Murray/Price, *The Greek City*, 277–85; and on the role of generals in local religious life, Ch. 11, n. 108 above. 'Fortified small town': so Lohmann, 'Country Life', 39.

(which we owe to Delphic inscriptions) that the Marathonian
Tetrapolis late in the third century continued, or more probably
revived, its ancient custom of dispatching a sacred embassy or
Pythais to Apollo.[44] But such interstate religious diplomacy is rich
men's work, and it is just as plausible to see the limited reflorescence
of the Tetrapolis as a complement to the decline of the demes.
Similarly, in the second half of the second century, several of the
surviving *gene* were to enter on an Indian summer which continued
in some cases deep into the imperial period.[45]

What of private associations?[46] Do elective religious clubs take up
the slack left by the loosening of traditional civic ties? Non-citizen
associations, commonly worshipping 'foreign' gods, certainly
underwent a boom in the period from about 305 to 250. Such groups
had existed before, but many more now appear and pass decrees—
which reproduce the typical forms of the host culture, the protocols
of the democracy, with a startling fidelity.[47] Greek metics, non-
Greeks, and slaves or ex-slaves all find a place, though perhaps not
often a shared place, in these societies. Citizen associations too are
not rare, but in the majority of cases remain of a traditional type.
Groups of '*orgeones* of Asclepius' are first attested in this century, as
are 'Asclepiasts' and 'Amphieraists'. But the society of *orgeones* of a
healing-hero was a long-established form in Attica. Groups named
from gods, entry to which was commonly by choice and payment
rather than by birth, already existed in the fourth century (the
Panistai of Menander's *Dyscolus* being the clearest example). But in
the third century, when a vast expansion might have been predicted,
no single instance is recorded (except the Asclepiasts and
Amphieraists just mentioned, who are of special type). The only real
novelty to mention is the foundation of a society of citizen *orgeones*
of the Great Mother in the Piraeus, and perhaps another such in the
city. Of course it is particularly credible in this area that we may be
misled by forced dependence on a single category of evidence. The
best that can be said is that the inscriptions certainly do not indicate
a revolution.

What is much more striking is, surely, the fact that it remains
broadly possible to sort the clubs into 'citizen' and 'non-citizen'.
Socially and intellectually, one might infer from Book 1 of the
Republic, rich Athenians and rich metics had much more in common

[44] See App. 3 below.
[45] See introd. to App. 2 below, and J. K. Davies, *CR* NS 23 (1973), 229.
[46] For details see App. 4 below.
[47] Cf. R. Osborne, in Murray/Price, *The Greek City*, 275–76. Such external conformity
need not of course entail internal acceptance (as feminist critics have stressed in other contexts).

than either group had with the citizen poor. And it is clear from New Comedy that travel outside Attica had become commonplace for the propertied classes. Yet with one exception (of 269/8 or the following year)[48] it is not until early in the second century that we find the distinctions of civic status certainly put aside, even in a private religious club. And even after the appearance of the first mixed association, many remained exclusive.

What of the largest of all worshipping groups, the citizen-body itself? In the classical period, in theory and to a large extent in practice, the right to 'eat sausages at the *Apatouria*'[49] and enjoy the other religious perquisites of citizenship was acquired by birth alone. The rare manufactured Athenians were foreign benefactors granted a title of honour which they were usually unlikely to make practical use of. From about 229, it has been argued, persons who might exploit their citizenship in ways useful to the city (businessmen and traders) become more prominent in the honours lists.[50] But it was only after 166 (an epochal date in the life of the city, when *rapprochement* with Rome made Athens rich again) that the old principles were formally relaxed, and in practice even then only in favour of the prosperous. In the 150s and 140s, metics appear among the *hieropoioi* for the *Athenaea*, *Romaea*, and *Ptolemaea*—festivals, no doubt, of designedly international appeal. And while 'made' Athenians had originally been excluded from political and religious office, one Telesias of Troezen, who was granted citizenship in 140/39, went on to serve as a priest, an overseer of Zeus Soter and an organizer of the Dionysiac procession. From about that date, decrees granting citizenship vanish altogether, and the right became available to the prosperous, it is generally supposed, on request.[51]

A continuity which has never been doubted is that Hellenistic Athens remained a city of festivals. The third-century traveller Heraclides, in his encomium of the city, speaks (in the choppy prose of the school of Hegesias) of 'festivals of every kind . . . many ways to spend the time, continual spectacles'. Late in the century, in the

---

[48] See p. 340 below. The continuing outsider status of non-citizens even when rich is a sub-theme of Millett's admirable *Lending and Borrowing* (though his concern is of course the fourth cent.). The picture of group formation in Hellenistic Rhamnus drawn by Robin Osborne in Murray/Price, *The Greek City*, 284 'all lines of distinction were bent and even obliterated' does not seem generalizable to Attica as a whole.

[49] Ar. *Ach*. 146.

[50] Osborne, *Naturalization*, III/IV.144–45 (for the traditional criteria see 147–50); but cf. P. Gauthier, *REG* 99 (1986), 131–33.

[51] Metic *hieropoioi*: *IG* II².1937–38. Telesias: *IG* II².971 (Osborne, *Naturalization*, D 102). The original exclusion: [*Dem*.] 59.92; Osborne, *Naturalization*, III/IV.173–76. Citizenship on request: ibid. 144–45.

honorary decree for distinguished Euryclides of Cephisia, special mention was made of his care for such 'spectacles'. Even Demetrius of Phaleron had organized a spectacular Dionysiac procession, led by a mechanical snail.[52] (By contrast, we do not know how public were the *Aphrodisia* held at Athens by another future philosopher-king, Antigonus Gonatas, at some time before 287; they were certainly luxurious. And Demetrius Poliorcetes' decision in 290 to hold the Pythian games in the city, since the Aetolians debarred him from Delphi, is obviously a special case, a characteristic instance of that king's lawless piety.[53])

The organization of the festivals, however, had been reformed in a way which affected the relation of the rich to the cults of the city very considerably. Demetrius of Phaleron, it seems, abolished the wasteful liturgies: expenses henceforth were to be met from public funds, while administrative responsibility was to fall on a single elective magistrate, the *agonothetes*. In the inscription which first attests the change, we read that 'the *demos* was *choregos*' for the *Lenaea* of 307/6. But the ideal expressed in that phrase was little more than pseudo-populist rhetoric. In practice, public funds almost never sufficed, and the city became dependent on men of wealth and civic ambition who would 'submit to' being elected agonothete and subsidize the festivals by 'spending not a little from their own resources'. The agonothete in 307/6 was the great benefactor Xenokles of Sphettos, and late in the third century Euryclides spent no less than 7 talents in the office.[54] We cannot begin to assess the full practical consequences of these changes, the number of minor rites, for instance, that may have been discontinued. Doubtless the scale of the transformation can be exaggerated: many cults must still have had their traditional revenues from rented land and levies; and if major festivals were not seldom postponed, that was because of the wars and political crises of this terrible century rather than a simple lack of funds.[55] But we constantly now hear of sacrifices performed

---

[52] F. Pfister, *Die Reisebilder des Herakleides* (Vienna 1951), § 1; *IG* II².834.23 (*SIG*³ 497); Demetrius frs. 34 and 132 Wehrli (and cf. fr. 30).

[53] Athen. 101e–f, 128b (Habicht, *Untersuchungen*, 73); Plut. *Dem.* 40.7–8 (where note both Plutarch's disapproval, and Demetrius' appeal to the Athenians' traditional association with Apollo πατρῷος).

[54] See *IG* II².3073 (*SIG*³ 1089; Pickard-Cambridge, *Dramatic Festivals*², 120) for Xenokles (on whom see Ch. 11, n. 105 above): for his successors *IG* II².657.39–50 (*SIG*³ 374); 798.18–19 (= *SEG* XXXIX 125); 834.4–7 = *SIG*³ 497 (Euryclides); cf. 968.42–47, and in general Pickard-Cambridge, *Dramatic Festivals*², 91–93; Veyne, *Pain et cirque*, 275; Shear, *Kallias*, 39, 84. G. Steinhauer argues that the abolition of the *choregia* is already implied by the new decree of 315/4 of the deme Acharnae that he publishes: *ArchEph* 131 (1992), 179–93. On ὑπομένω cf. L. Robert, *Le sanctuaire de Sinuri* (Paris 1945), 33.

[55] See Shear, *Kallias*, 11, n. 11, and 37–38, and *SIG*³ 485.31–32 (*IG* II².1299), with Dittenberger's n. 7.

or shrines restored through the generosity of individuals: agono-thetes, of course, but also taxiarchs, a Macedonian garrison-commander, generals, a trierarch, an unnamed deme-patriot.[56] Unforced munificence was, of course, not unknown in the classical period, on the part, for instance, of liturgists (trierachs among them) who showed themselves magnificent beyond what the law required. But the very way in which payments 'from one's own resources' have now become a normal subject of commendation in honorary decrees indicates a practical erosion of the ideal of publicly financed (*demoteles*) cults.

Priesthoods were affected in similar ways. Explicit changes are, it is true, not attested until the early imperial period, when we find the priesthood of Asclepius, which had rotated annually between the tribes in a model instance of democratized religion, transformed into a post tenable for life.[57] But already in the third century a conspicu-ous number of the holders of that priesthood (the only one that can be observed in any detail) are persons of some wealth and promi-nence; and in the second, individuals are sometimes said to have 'submitted' to holding the post or 'liturgy'.[58] In the 230s an annual priest of Artemis Kalliste is praised for dedicating a stone altar 'from his own resources'; priests recruited from *gene* too might need to show similar generosity, as too might 'supervisors of the Mysteries'.[59] Most striking is the case of the cult of 'Demos and the Graces', founded in the 220s or 210s, on the initiative, doubtless, of the brothers Euryclides and Micion, the dominant political figures of the day. Euryclides, who is praised for spending money on sacred buildings, very probably met the costs of construction, and may have been first priest; however that may be, in 194 or thereabouts his son held the priesthood, and silver coins issued by his great-grandson as mint-master in 122/1 bear the Graces as their device.[60]

---

[56] *Hesperia* 2 (1933), 156, no. 5; Moretti 18.12, 25.7–8; *IG* II².1299.13 (*SIG*³ 485); *Prakt* 1990 [1993], 21, no. 1.11, 13; Moretti 29.13; *IG* II².1215.13.

[57] Aleshire, *Asklepieion*, 85; and on the similar case of Artemis Kalliste, Ch. 8, n. 28.

[58] Third cent.: see e.g. the entries for 260/59 to 247/6 in Aleshire, *Asklepieion*, 372, with the relevant entries in the prosopographic register in Aleshire, *Asklepios*. In the fourth cent. prominent priests are less common. Second cent.: R. O. Hubbe, *Hesperia* 28 (1959), 182–83, on *SEG* XVIII 21, 27, 29 (on the verb cf. n. 54 above). *IG* II².1046 (*SIG*³ 756) of 52/1 records an instance of voluntary euergetism by the priest.

[59] *IG* II².788.13. *Gene*: *IG* II².776.19–20; *SEG* XXIX 135. Supervisors of Mysteries: above, Ch. 11, n. 109; cf. *Hesperia* 11 (1942), 265, no. 51.6 for the generosity of a 'priestess of the Thesmophoroi' (city, or deme?) *c*.180. Posidippus fr. 28. 21 K/A assumes that the wives of 'conspicuous' men (ἐπιφανής) may be priestesses; see too Ch. 11, n. 109 on Diodorus fr. 2.23–30 K/A.

[60] *IG* II².834.25–26 (*SIG*³ 497.25–26), 4676 and 2798 (and for the brothers' interest 844.36–42). The coins: C. Habicht, *Chiron* 21 (1991), 8: and see Habicht, *Studien*, 85–93. Note, however, that the device was not invariably present on coins issued by members of the family (Habicht, *Chiron*, 21, 1991, 8).

Apparently the family had a special relationship of some kind[61] with this pre-eminently public cult. In the fifth century, surely, a lasting place in the ceremonial life of the city was not to be acquired, whether by wealth or merit.

After about 300, large numbers of familiar Attic festivals are never mentioned by name except in antiquarian contexts. A very provisional list of disappearing festivals might include *Kronia*, *Synoikia*, all the *Herakleia*, *Genesia*, *Apatouria*, *Oschophoria*, *Hieros Gamos*, *Diasia*, *Dipolieia*, and *Brauronia*.[62] (Several of these do indeed appear in the calendar frieze, of late Hellenistic date, now built into the church of Haghios Eleutherios; but we cannot assume that it reflects contemporary practice.) Of course, festivals are only likely to be mentioned in inscriptions if they involve the official participation of representatives of the people; and on this basis it was only to be expected that most of the festivals in that list would slip out of view. Only in regard to *Synoikia* and *Dipolieia* does the argument from silence have much weight. On the other hand, Plutarch claims in the *Life of Theseus* that various quite minor rites commemorating events in the hero's career are performed 'even now': a procession of maidens to the Delphinion, the *Oschophoria*, the *Metoikia* (i.e. *Synoikia*), the *Boedromia*, and a sacrifice to Theseus' *paidagogos* on the day before the *Theseia* themselves.[63] Possibly he is using a variant of the 'ethnographic present', whereby in academic discussion the Nuer still 'do' what they did when visited by Evans-Pritchard fifty years ago; but the case would be rather extreme, as Plutarch had himself studied in the city of his Nuer and could scarcely have imagined them still frozen in the customs of his hypothetical Evans-Pritchard, a Hellenistic antiquarian source.[64] Until the matter has been

---

[61] For permanent priesthood assigned to benefactors of a cult see *Bull. Ép.* 1955, no. 163 (Istros, third cent. BC), 1963, no. 169 (Istros, second cent.); *LSCG* 61 (Gytheum, first cent.); and *SIG*³ 898. For comparable archaic cases see Hdt. 3.142.4 and 7.153.2.

[62] But evidence for some of these may well have escaped me. The *Thesmophoria* are attested by implication by a decree of Melite of *c.*180 (n. 59); the *Anthesteria* by Philodemus *De Pietate* 550–59, 808–10 Obbink (Epicurus fr. 169 Usener) (a ref. I owe to Jan Bremmer) and still by *IG* II².1368.130, 13139; the *Thargelia* by *LSS* 14; the *Pyanopsia* or a memory of them are implied by *LSCG* 52.9. Otherwise decrees in honour of the ephebes are the main source (Ch. 11, n. 125). The *Brauronia* almost certainly did cease, the sanctuary having become unusable through flooding in the third cent.

[63] 18.1; 22.4; 24.4; 27.3; 4. Note too 17.7 (*Kybernesia*) and 21.2 (Delian dance; there are also many καὶ νῦν's applied to toponyms and suchlike). But note the past tense used of the *Hekalesia* in 14.2; also the inscriptional confirmation of a similar claim in *De Malign. Hdt.* 862a about a procession to Agrae (Deubner, *Attische Feste*, 209), and the highly circumstantial ἔτι νῦν of *Phoc.* 22.2.

[64] A point stressed to me by Christopher Pelling in kind response to an enquiry. On Plutarch's use of his sources (much less mechanical than used to be supposed), see Pelling's remarks in *JHS* 99 (1979), 74–96.

thought about systematically, as has never been done, there is no way of knowing the actual fate of most of the disappearing rites; very probably there would not be, even then.

Another striking instance of vanishing evidence may be mentioned here. Private sculpted dedications on the acropolis, so abundant in the sixth and fifth centuries and still not rare in the fourth, vanish completely in the third century (if we accept the datings given in the corpus of inscriptions).[65] Even after allowance has been made for the notorious unreliability of dating based on letter-forms alone, a steep decline in quantity would doubtless have to be recognized. Yet, as we have seen, Athena and the *Panathenaea* continued to symbolize Athenian identity in the third century as much as they had ever done; and another festival of the goddess, the *Athenaea/ Chalkeia*, was in fact to acquire new prominence in the second century. And on the acropolis itself a new form of monument became popular: the statue set up by proud parents in commemoration of the service of a daughter as *arrephoros* of the goddess.[66] At first sight, therefore, we are faced with a division of a quite new type—but of a type often considered typical of the Hellenistic age—between religion's civic forms and the private beliefs and emotions of the worshippers. The very abruptness of the supposed change, however, should surely give us pause. Are other explanations possible? The disappearance of elaborate grave-monuments in Attica was, we know, a consequence of legal restrictions introduced by Demetrius of Phaleron.[67] Is the disappearance of sculpted dedications from the acropolis at about the same time a related phenomenon? But in the Asclepieum they persist, even if they change in character (marble votive reliefs largely disappearing[68]). Is it possible that Demetrius, or another, specifically forbade the dedication of marble monuments on the acropolis other than statues of *arrephoroi* and the like? That hardly seems in keeping with Greek ideas of piety. Or did the pillaging of temple treasures by Demetrius Poliorcetes and Lachares[69] dim the lustre of the sacred place for a while? (But why then the *arrephoroi*?) The problem remains tantalizingly irresolvable.

[65] *IG* II².4318 ff.

[66] *Athenaea/Chalkeia*: see C. Habicht, *AM* 97 (1982), 171–84. *Arrephoroi* (in fact *errephoroi* in the early instances): e.g. *IG* II².3461, 3466, 3471.

[67] Cic. *Leg.* 2.66, Demetrius fr. 135 Wehrli (the only source: Demetrius' abolition of the choregic system is not directly attested at all); on fourth-cent. monumental graves see Scholl, *JdI* 109 (1994), 239–71. Another reform of (probably) Demetrius was the institution of γυναικονόμοι who, in association with the Areopagites, in principle supervised 'meetings in private houses at weddings and other sacrifices' (Philoch. *FGrH* 328 F 65: cf. Jacoby ad loc.; Ferguson, *Hellenistic Athens*, 45; E. Bayer, *Demetrios Phalereus der Athener*, Berlin 1942, 51 ff.). Unlike the restriction on funerary architecture, this reform was soon swept away.

[68] So A. Koerte, *AM* 18 (1893), 244–45.   [69] See Ch. 11, n. 95.

Some new cults arose, of course, as others declined, in the third century as in any other. Ruler-cult aside, the visible innovations are in fact not very numerous. Most of the new gods who appear (Sarapis, for instance) are confined to societies of non-Greek worshippers.[70] Such is the position of Sarapis when he first appears in a decree of 'Sarapiasts' of 215/4, though in this case we also hear a little later of a public cult (in some sense no doubt a product of the city's warm relations with the Ptolemies).[71] The great festivals of Delian Apollo and Amphiaraus of Oropus now lay outside Athenian control; this may be why shrines of Amphiaraus are now attested in Attica itself. The pair Zeus Soter and Athena Soteira continues to grow in popularity; and a new cult (as it seems) of 'Aphrodite Leader (of the People)' is attested late in the century both in the city (linked with '*Demos* and the Graces') and in Rhamnus.[72] We have already met the cult of 'Demos and the Graces [*Charites*]', first mentioned in the archonship of Archelaus (? 212/1) but perhaps founded shortly after the liberation of Athens from Macedonian rule in 229. On one level this new cult is a transparent translation into religious language of the political ideals of the day. The Athenian people, innumerable honorary decrees over the previous hundred years had declared,[73] knows how to pay back favours (*charites*) to its benefactors, by granting them privileges and honours. This is then a cult of

[70] See App. 4 below.

[71] Sarapiasts: p. 340 below. Public cult: *IG* II².4692 (*c.*200 Dow; 'unassignable', Tracy): cf. Paus. 1.18.4, Σαράπιδος ἱερὸν, ὃν Ἀθηναῖοι παρὰ Πτολεμαίου θεὸν εἰσηγήσαντο. See S. Dow's fundamental study, 'The Egyptian Cults in Athens', *HThR* 30 (1937), 184–232, the results of which in essence still stand (cf. F. Dunand, *Le culte d'Isis dans le bassin oriental de la Méditerranée*, II, Leiden 1973, 4–10; add now *SEG* XL 199, from Rhamnus). Slight signs of Athenian interest in Egyptian gods other than Ammon are found in Ophelion fr. 6 K/A (perjury by Isis), Theophilus fr. 8.6 K/A (an oath by Apollo, Horus and Sabazius), Menander fr. 139 Koerte (praise of Sarapis); Timocles fr. 1 and Anaxandrides fr. 40 K/A mock animal worship. It is tempting to associate the establishment of an official cult with the enthusiasm for the Ptolemies of the period beginning in 229 (see C. Habicht, *ClAnt* 11, 1992, 68–90, at 76; and for the 'desire of independent communities to show friendship to the Ptolemies by adopting the Alexandrian deity', P. M. Fraser, *OpAth* 3, 1960, 29, 49), but we have only a *terminus ante quem* for the foundation, and Egypt had been important to the Athenians throughout the third cent. (so Habicht, *ClAnt* 11, 1992, 68–90; Dow notes a citizen Sarapion born *c.*250 in *IG* II².820, though a down-dating by some twenty years would now be defensible [Tracy, 134]). As with Bendis (cf. Ch. 8 above), one question is whether the introduction of a cult should be given a quite precise niche in diplomatic history or seen in the context of broader interaction between two nations.

[72] See Ch. 8, n. 105 (Amphiaraus) and Ch. 11, n. 81 (Zeus Soter). For Aphrodite Hegemone see *IG* II².2798 (Travlos, *Pictorial Dictionary*, 79–81); *Prakt* 1990 [1993], 21, no. 1.12, 33, cf. *Ergon* 1992 [1993], 3. The goddess must have borrowed associations from the Attic Grace called Hegemone, Tod *GHI* II.204.19, cf. Habicht, *Studien*, 89 n. 59; note too Athena Archegetis (Ch. 7, n. 67), Heracles Hegemon (Xen. *Anab.* 6.2.15 and often), Hermes Hegemonios (Ch. 11, n. 72); also *IG* II².1242.9 (Lambert, *Phratries*, 294).

[73] See already *IG* II².223.13–14 (of 343/2).

'the people and favours repaid' or 'the people and gratitude', and honorary decrees for benefactors are duly displayed in the grateful people's shrine. At Claros too the precinct of the Charites was used for the same purpose; and in Teos in 204 or 203 a sacrifice to the goddesses was explicitly associated with the repayment of favours to King Antiochus III and his queen. An early beneficiary of the people's new way of expressing gratitude may have been King Ptolemy III, whose aid was so essential towards the preservation of Athenian autonomy in the mid 220s. In the reserved seats in the theatre of Dionysus, the priest of Demos and the Graces sat with the priest of Democracy on his left and the priest of Ptolemy III and Berenice on his right, very probably on a bench donated by the first priest of the new cult himself.[74] But the Graces had been goddesses long before they became embodiments of the principle of political gratitude or obligation; and it is surely plausible that the new cult exploited these older associations, and indeed could not have come into existence without them.[75]

Did festivals change in character? Did they become, in a still-greater measure than before, events at which citizens were mere spectators? This is the century in which the professional 'artists of Dionysus' are first attested, and in which citizen dithyrambic choruses perhaps disappeared from the *Thargelia*. But drama had always tended towards professionalism, since the choruses and actors were not tribally recruited; there continued to be citizen dithyrambic choruses at the *Dionysia*; and at athletic festivals there were still good numbers of competitions open to Athenians alone, particularly the young.[76] Above all, the ever-increasing involvement of the ephebes with the festivals shows how clearly they remained occasions of civic display.

A characteristic development in the third century throughout Greece is the foundation of festivals that are explicitly described as a commemoration, ὑπόμνημα, of recent great events. The Delphic

[74] Display: see Wycherley, *Testimonia*, 59–60 (first in *IG* II².844.39–41 [*SIG*³ 535–37], the strict *terminus ante quem* for the cult's foundation: Habicht, *Studien*, 93). Claros and Teos: *SEG* XXXIX 1243 col. v. 45; P. Herrmann, *Anadolu* 9 (1965), 38.31–42: cf. L. and J. Robert, *Bull. Ép.* 1969, nos. 495 and 496, and eid., *Claros*, I (Paris 1989), 60; Gauthier, *Bienfaiteurs*, 66, n. 217; also Habicht, *Studien*, 91–93, who stresses the association of cultic Graces with gratitude already found in Arist. *EN* 1133ª2. Theatre: see Maass, *Prohedrie*, on *IG* II².4676 and 5029a (note that there were three seats and so three distinct priests).*

[75] So L. and J. Robert, as cited in the previous note. Specific proof in Athens is lacking, unfortunately: on the traditional cult of the Graces there see Habicht, *Studien*, 85–90. For their association with Athena (Nike?) see *LIMC* s.v. *Charites*, nos. 11–13; L. Beschi, *ASAtene* NS 29–30 (1967–8), 531–36.

[76] On drama and dithyramb see Pickard-Cambridge, *Dramatic Festivals*², 74, 90 n. 6, 279; id., *Dithyramb*, 76. Athletics: third-cent. evidence is hard to find, but for the revived *Theseia* of the second cent. see *IG* II².956–65. Ephebes: above, Ch. 11, n. 125.

Soteria, 'commemoration' of the repulse of the Gauls, is the model instance.[77] At Athens, the poet Philippides as agonothete in 284/3 established an 'additional competition' for Demeter and Kore as a *hypomnema* of 'the liberation of the people' (an all but certain supplement) from Demetrius Poliorcetes. (The liberation occurred by stages, and Demeter and Kore were probably chosen as honorands because Eleusis had only just been recovered.) At some time after 229, Euryclides 'introduced a competition' which was doubtless again a commemoration of the liberation of that year. And already in 304/3 the Athenians had voted that the *prytaneis* of Akamantis should henceforth sacrifice in Elaphebolion each year as a *hypomnema* of the 'good news' (of Demetrius' victories in the Peloponnese) reported during their prytany.[78] But the novelty here is simply the explicitness with which the festival's commemorative function is recognized. As we have repeatedly seen, much the commonest motive for the introduction or extension of a cult in the fifth or fourth century was as a kind of war-memorial.

It is here perhaps that the festival *Diogeneia* should be classified. Diogenes was the commander of the Macedonian garrison who in 229 'sold' Piraeus and Mounichia and Salamis and Sunium to the Athenians for 150 talents, thus leaving Attica entirely free of foreign troops for the first time for almost seventy years. 'Diogenes the benefactor', as he was named on a seat of honour in the theatre, was remembered, in the words of a verse inscription, as the man 'through whose deeds our native land saw again its ancient freedom'.[79] The festival named after him, often mentioned in the late second century, is surely likely to have been founded soon after the great event.[80] Though formally an expression of gratitude to a benefactor (to whom sacrifice was made), the *Diogeneia* was probably in practice a festival of liberation.

The most elaborate and long-enduring festival introduced in the third century was the *Ptolemaea*, created at some date before King

[77] For others see Habicht, *Gottmenschentum*, 231–32.

[78] *IG* II².657.43–45 (*SIG*³ 374): cf. Shear, *Kallias*, 84–85; *IG* II².834.24 (*SIG*³ 497); *SEG* XXX 69, with the corrections of C. Habicht, *Hesperia* 59 (1990), 465.

[79] Plut. *Arat.* 34.4–6; Paus. 2.8.6; *IG* II².5080 (theatre seat), 3474 (verse inscription: ? about 125). Cf. Osborne, *Naturalization*, III.91–93; Habicht, *Studien*, 79–84; Gauthier, *Bienfaiteurs*, 63–65 (who records the view of L. Robert that Diogenes was a native Athenian). The old view that the theatre seat (for 'Diogenes the benefactor', not priest or descendants of the same) was intended for his use while still alive appears to have recovered epigraphic credibility: see Tracy, 5, 22 (against Maass, *Prohedrie*, 54, n. 100, 139 f.)

[80] First in a victory-dedication of 117/6 (*Ergon* 1991 [1992], 5, cf. 6), thereafter in numerous ephebic decrees (*IG* II².1011.14 etc.). The building named after him is first mentioned in 106/5, when it needed repairs (*IG* II².1011.41, cf. Pélékidis, *Éphébie*, 265). Conceivably the *Diogeneia* was the *agon* founded by Euryclides (Ferguson, *Hellenistic Athens*, 295, n. 3).

Ptolemy III's death in 221. It joined the *Panathenaea*, the *Dionysia*, and the *Eleusinia* (this last a new promotion to this level) as one of the four showcase festivals, at which public honours were proclaimed; participation was solicited from states throughout the Greek world that wished to display their goodwill or loyalty to the king.[81] Such a festival named for a king is, of course, unparalleled in earlier centuries: in 421/0, for instance, it had been Hephaestus who had been honoured by a series of new competitions. But, its name aside, the *Ptolemaea* was a festival of popular traditional type, and slipped easily into the familiar succession of 'spectacles'. And it too, because it commemorated the aid given by Ptolemy in the struggle against Macedonian domination in the 220s, was another celebration of the city's own liberty.

Nothing is more characteristic of classical Attic religion than its abundance of hero-cults. What becomes of them? In the vast majority of cases, they disappear permanently from view in the third century, with the disappearance of the deme calendars. The cults did not necessarily vanish along with the calendars that recorded them; but they doubtless suffered from the decline of the demes themselves as organizers of religious life. Documents issued by groups of *orgeones* of heroes (never admittedly very numerous) in effect cease early in the third century. On the other hand, healing-heroes, and not just the almost-gods Asclepius and Amphiaraus, continued to flourish; the *Epitaphia*, the *Theseia* and the Salaminian *Aianteia* remained major festivals in the second century BC (or were elevated to that level at that date);[82] and dedications are still made 'to the hero' (who is usually anonymous).[83] Some of these last may in fact have been addressed to healers; but it is probably in this period that,

---

[81] See Moretti 30.11, 31.10, 33.49; *SEG* XXVIII 75.17; for its later fortunes, Habicht, *ClAnt* 11 (1992), 83–85 (and now *Ergon* 1991 [1992], 5–6). Solicited: see L. Robert, *Études épigraphiques et philologiques* (Paris 1938), 62–69. Aid: cf. n. 71. On the *Eleusinia* in the third cent. see M. Thompson, *Hesperia* 11 (1942), 213–29.

[82] See Pélékidis, *Éphébie*, 229–39, 247–49; and on the *Theseia* (which he argues to be in effect a new festival) G. R. Bugh, *ZPE* 83 (1990), 20–37. Note too the offerings to the dead of Marathon, *IG* II².1006.26–27, 69–70. Contrast G. V. Lalonde's archaeological case for the neglect of minor hero shrines in the *agora*, *Agora* XIX, p. 9. Attica provided no evidence for S. E. Alcock's study of 'Tomb Cult and the Post-Classical Polis', *AJA* 95 (1991), 447–67, at 451.

[83] See *SEG* XXI 754, statue of a son dedicated 'to the hero' by his mother ('s. III a': associated with the 'doctor hero' in *SEG*, on grounds not stated); ibid. 794, a dedication 'to heroes' (*c*.100); *SEG* XXI 633, *eranistai* 'to the hero' (? early second cent.); *Hesperia* 15 (1946), 221, no. 48, a general to the hero-general, with the probably similar dedication *SEG* XXI 792 (respectively undatable and early second cent., Tracy); *MdI* 85 (1990), 105–107, no. 9 = *SEG* XXXVII 143, a dedication to an ἐπήκοος ἥρως made by Simylos on behalf of Lacrates (*c*.280 according to the editor: but is ἐπήκοος paralleled so early?).*

for instance, the 'hero-general' first announces himself. And though the characteristic form of hero-relief disappears from Attica at about the same time (it lives on elsewhere), this change too appears too sudden to be explained by a change in belief; we should remember that the sculpture market had probably been disrupted by the sumptuary reforms of Demetrius of Phaleron.[84]

In Attica, unlike many regions of the Greek world, the practice of saluting large numbers of the recently dead as 'heroes' never became established.[85] Apart from 'Diogenes the benefactor' and the briefly heroized companions of Demetrius Poliorcetes, only two sets of new heroes were, to our knowledge, created in the Hellenistic period: wealthy Dionysius of Marathon and his father, heroized early in the second century by the society of Dionysiasts that they had perhaps founded; and three members of another powerful Marathonian family, honoured in the first century by a specially established college of *Heroistai*.[86] No doubt there were several other instances, but these two suggest that unusually rich and powerful figures succeeded in reserving the honour for themselves. The special status of the hero was not, therefore, weakened by dilution.

Late in the fourth century, hostilities between the Athenian people and the philosophers had been renewed. According to his ancient biographers, Aristotle was indicted on a charge of 'impiety', and withdrew to Chalcis 'lest the Athenian people sin a second time against philosophy'. The same charge was brought against Theophrastus in 319/8, but the prosecutor Hagnonides scarcely got a fifth of the votes. And in 307 Sophocles of Sunium briefly secured the passage of a law (rejected, however, as illegal the following year) whereby 'no philosopher (in one version: 'no sophist') might conduct a school without permission of the assembly and people'.[87] The real point at issue, it is all but universally agreed,[88] was the philoso-

---

[84] Cf. Dentzer, *Banquet couché*, 361–62. For the decline of a particular form of dedication (the marble votive relief) an explanation of this type appears possible (cf. n. 68). The effect might be oblique, the reform leading to a change in taste and fashion.

[85] See R. Lattimore, *Themes in Greek and Latin Epitaphs* (Urbana, Ill. 1942), 99; and cf. *SEG* XXVIII 234. But see now the qualifications of C. Sourvinou-Inwood, *'Reading' Greek Death* (Oxford 1995) 206, n. 389.

[86] See App. 4 below. That 'hero' need not have been a mere courtesy title in such cases is shown in a very important discussion by Graf, *Nordionische Kulte*, 127–35.

[87] Aristotle: e.g. Hermippus *ap*. Athen. 696a–f, fr. 48 in F. Wehrli's edn. (*Hermippos der Kallimacheer*, Basle 1974), D.L. 5.5; cf. Clinton, *Sacred Officials*, 21 [+]. Theophrastus: D.L. 5.37; Aelian, *VH* 8.12 (which sets the trial before the Areopagus). Sophocles: Pollux 9.42; D.L. 5.38; Athen. 610e–f, with citation of Alexis fr. 99 K/A [+]; cf. C. Habicht, *Hellenistic Athens and her Philosophers* (David Magie Lecture 1988, Princeton), repr. in his *Athen in hellenistischer Zeit* (Munich 1994), 236–37.

[88] O. Gigon, *Vita Aristotelis Marciana* (Berlin 1962), 75, is a rare agnostic.

phers' sympathy with undemocratic regimes, that of Macedonia above all. In each case the move against philosophers was made at a moment when the Macedonian yoke had temporarily been lifted; the prosecutors of Aristotle and Theophrastus were Demophilus and Hagnonides, prosecutors also of the pro-Macedonian Phokion; and Demosthenes' nephew the ardent democrat Demochares spoke unsuccessfully in defence of Sophocles' repressive law.[89] There is little reason to suppose that, political though the motives of the prosecutors may have been, the anxieties which they sought to exploit in the jurors were of a different character: jurors too doubtless had strong views about the political disposition of the philosophical schools.

Whether any religious feeling was also in play is hard to tell. According to Hermippus, an early (third-century) though not a reliable source,[90] the politician Demophilus was put up to accuse Aristotle by the hierophant Eurymedon (who later often appears as the actual accuser); but according to the same source (and many subsequently) the philosopher's supposed offence lay in the composition of a paean, a literary form proper only to the gods, in honour of a mortal, the tyrant Hermias of Atarneus. Even his formal 'impiety', therefore, lay neither in his theological beliefs nor in his attitude to the Eleusinian cult but in a particular expression of his infamous love of tyrants. Some suppose that the whole story of an indictment is an invention, Aristotle having in fact spontaneously withdrawn from Athens after Alexander's death, fearing the worst.[91] Nothing is recorded of the particular form of Theophrastus' supposed impiety. And the main thrust of Demochares' robust defence of Sophocles' law seems simply to have been that, whether one considers politics, warfare, or morality, philosophers are equally worthless.[92]

Diogenes Laertius tells of difficulties encountered by two foreign philosophers at Athens at about this time. Stilpon the Megarian was summoned before the Areopagus for denying, on quibbling grounds, that Phidias' Athena was a god; the Areopagites, unimpressed by his defence that she was not a god but a goddess, ran him

[89] Plut. *Phoc.* 38.1; for extracts of Demochares' speech see Athen. 215c, 508f–509; Euseb. *Praep. Evang.* 15.2.6, p. 347 Mras.

[90] See n. 87 above. Theological offences only appear much later in the tradition: I. Düring, *Aristotle in the Ancient Biographical Tradition* (Göteborg 1957), 344; A. H. Chroust, *Historia* 15 (1966), 186–87. It is not in this context that the charge (Lycon in Euseb. *Praep. Evang.* 15.2. 8, p. 347 Mras) that Aristotle sacrificed to his dead wife 'as the Athenians do to Demeter' is mentioned (cf. D. W. Wormell, *YCS* 5, 1935, 87).

[91] So apparently Wehrli on Hermippus fr. 48; Chroust, *Historia* 15 (1966), 191–92. But the role of Demophilus sounds authentic.

[92] See n. 89 above.

out of town. Theodorus 'the atheist' playfully accused the hierophant of 'revealing the Mysteries', and would have been summoned
before the same body but for the intervention of Demetrius of
Phaleron; according to one Amphicrates, however, he was in fact
condemned and executed, while Diogenes himself in the next chapter speaks of him as having been expelled by the Athenians.[93]
Should we infer that judgement in cases of impiety had been transferred to the Areopagus in the late fourth century? Or had that body
always had authority to railroad undesirable foreigners out of town
untried? Or is the Areopagus, here as elsewhere, being credited with
quite fictional powers?[94] There are other traces of increased activity
by the Areopagus in this period, and it is quite conceivable that the
oligarchic reformers of the late fourth century had spurred on the
ancient council to exercise its traditional function of supervising the
city's religion more vigorously. From such anecdotes, however—
illustrations, above all, of the philosophers' irreverent wit—there is
no precise history to be extracted.

No later philosopher was, to our knowledge, prosecuted or harried for his religious views. Some shifting of the boundaries of what
was publicly acceptable seems gradually to have occurred. Already
during the fourth century the adjective δεισιδαίμων had changed
from praising a man as 'god-fearing' to censuring him as 'superstitious'. A word therefore existed, for the first time, to stigmatize some
supposedly religious practices—certain forms of healing, of
purification and of divination above all—as foolish and even impious.[95] Philosophic polemic may have had some influence on this
recoining: Diogenes the Cynic was supposedly a scourge of just such
practices,[96] and it is in Theophrastus' *Characters* that the
Superstitious Man first steps before us. Truly sacred things, such as
initiation at Eleusis, sometimes, it is said, felt the lash of Diogenes'
tongue.[97] In the main, however, this was a critique that traditional
religion could assimilate very comfortably. The chief victims—

[93] D.L. 2.116, 2.101–102 (= Demetrius of Phaleron fr. 43 Wehrli): expulsion of
Theodorus, in unstated circumstances, also in Philo, *Quod Omnis Probus Liber Sit*, 127–30.
M. Winiarczyk, *Philologus* 125 (1981), 66–69, partially harmonizes the tradition by suggesting
that Theodorus was persuaded by Demetrius of Phaleron to pre-empt investigation by leaving Athens; Wehrli too takes Demetrius' involvement to be historical.

[94] On all this see Wallace, *Areopagos Council*, 107–108, 204–205. The association of the
Areopagus with the *gynaikonomoi* in an oligarchic law (see n. 67) gives some support to the
view that its powers were actually extended.

[95] See Nilsson, *Geschichte*, 796 [+].

[96] See e.g. D.L. 6.24, 37, 42–43, 48, 61; Clem. Al. *Strom.* 7.4.25.1: for more Cynic material see J. F. Kindstrand, *Bion of Borysthenes* (Uppsala 1976), frs. 25–33, with the commentary.

[97] D.L. 6.39 (cf. Kindstrand, *Bion*, 229). It is not clear whether Diogenes' contempt for
seers would have led to contempt for Delphic prophecy (as expressed much later by
Oenomaus, commonly accounted a Cynic).

wandering purifiers and seers—were, precisely, not part of the formal structure of civic religion. And it is clear from New Comedy
that jokes at their expense, very much in the spirit of Diogenes and
Theophrastus, became perfectly acceptable.[98]

Epicurus, one might have thought, was a different matter.
Posidonius and other ancient critics held that it was 'for fear of
falling foul of the Athenians' that Epicurus, a closet atheist, insisted
so vehemently that the gods exist. As it happens, that long-
discredited view has recently been revived, in much subtler form, on
philosophical grounds.[99] Yet the proposition that the gods care
nothing for human affairs was scarcely less subversive than outright
atheism; and this, of course, Epicurus boldly proclaimed, declaring,
by the reformer's characteristic strategy, that he was conducting this
reversal of traditional piety in true piety's name.[100] Did the
Athenians not know, or not care? The only knowledge of Epicurus
that the poets of New Comedy reveal concerns, perhaps predictably,
his doctrine that pleasure is the goal.[101]

The continuance of traditional cult Epicurus, of course, supported, as did all the philosophical schools, except possibly the
Cynic.[102] Yet no philosopher understood the gods who lay behind
the cult traditionally. This metaphorical interpretation of established cult must in course of time have had wide influence in Attic
society, as ever more young men of the propertied classes passed
through the philosophical schools. Philosophy even became
respectable, as long, at least, as it sided with virtue against pleasure.
Zeno the Stoic, if a decree preserved in Diogenes Laertius is genuine, was awarded a gold crown and a public funeral, Chrysippus
was granted citizenship and, again, state burial, and it became a
common practice to send philosophers on diplomatic missions. In
the 140s we find a cluster of Stoics, Panaetius of Rhodes among
them, serving as *hieropoioi* for a public festival (the *Ptolemaea*), and

---

[98] See Parker, *Miasma*, 207, and 224, n. 90.

[99] Posidonius fr. 22 Kidd, cf. Cic. *ND* 1.85 with A. S. Pease's note. For philosophers
unwilling to expound their theological views 'in the street' or 'before a crowd' see D.L. 2.117,
with Kindstrand, *Bion*, 225. Revived: see A. A. Long and D. N. Sedley, *The Hellenistic
Philosophers* (Cambridge 1987), I.147–48.

[100] *Epistle* III (Menoeceus), 123–24.

[101] Baton fr. 5, Damoxenus fr. 2.62 (the whole fr. parodies Epicurean language),
Hegesippus fr. 2 K/A: cf. A. Weiher, *Philosophen und Philosophenspott in der attischen Komödie*
(Diss. Munich 1913), 74–78.

[102] See e.g. Epicurus frs. 12, 13, 169, 387 Usener. On the Cynics see M.-O. Goulet-Cazé,
'Les premiers cyniques et la religion', in ead. and R. Goulet eds., *Le cynisme ancien* (1993),
117–58: she concludes that Diogenes' views about the gods are unknowable (he may have been
agnostic) but that he certainly regarded gods as irrelevant to the good life ('insignifiance des
dieux', 150) and made 'absolutely no concessions' to traditional religion.

by the last quarter of the second century it was even expected that the ephebes should attend lectures at the Lyceum and the Academy.[103] This acceptance of the philosophers implied an acceptance, or at least a toleration, of their metaphorical interpretation of the traditional forms of anthropomorphic cult. This is not to say that the metaphorical interpretation became, as it were, official; but it evidently took its place among the group of wholly acceptable possibilities. The expansion of that group is, no doubt, one of the most fundamental changes that took place in the Hellenistic period.

We have rejected the conventional division at 323 and have been scanning the third century in search of an alternative—without success, it seems. Numerous changes appear, but no clear line of fracture. One may wonder, indeed, whether the problem is not when classical religion gives way to Hellenistic but whether it does: whether, that is, the convention of dividing histories of Greek religion into two chronological sections rather than three or four or ten has any substantive justification.

Life being finite, however, some divisions have to be made. And, in terms not of substantive history but of evidence, an overwhelming case can be made for drawing a line somewhere between 300 and 250 BC. The great attraction of studying the religion of classical Athens is not so much that it is either Athenian or classical as that it can indeed be studied, in some detail. By contrast, we noted earlier that nothing at all is known of the history of a good number of important festivals in the third century and beyond. An incomplete sketch of a panorama of the religious practices of the classical period can be drawn; for the Hellenistic period, no more can be attempted than isolated views. And the loss is not only, or even centrally, one of factual information about the conduct of this or that rite. The charm of our vastly diverse sources for classical religious attitudes is that enquiry is not pinned down to this level. The multiple perspectives opened by literary and artistic and historical and documentary sources are very largely reduced, in the Hellenistic period, to that provided by inscriptions alone. Actual experience, however, will doubtless not have been simplified to the same degree.

As it happens, the period in question saw the death, in old age, of the last and greatest representative of a literary genre of especial relevance to this study. Throughout the fourth century, Atthidography

---

[103] D.L. 7.10–12 (cf. A. Erskine, *The Hellenistic Stoa*, London 1990, 83); Osborne, *Naturalization*, III/IV.90, 201; Erskine, *Hellenistic Stoa*, 88; *IG* II².1938 (cf. T. Dorandi, *ZPE* 79, 1989, 87–92); *IG* II².1006.19–20 etc., with Pélékidis, *Éphébie*, 266–67. On all this see now Habicht, *Hellenistic Athens and her Philosophers*.

had been a means for Athens to look at itself, by way of a historical narrative. Accounts of myth and cult always had an honoured place in these histories, proof of the Athenians' sense of their importance for what the city was and meant. And the *Atthides* provide, or would have provided, precious instances of 'native exegesis' of rituals by members of the governing class. Philochorus, the last known Atthidographer, was a trained seer, who believed that Nicias' disastrous mistake in Sicily was due not to heeding an omen but to misinterpreting it. An instance of his own activity is preserved in his own words:

At the beginning of the next year, an omen occurred on the acropolis. A dog entered the temple of Athena Polias and, going into the Pandroseion, climbed on to the altar of Zeus Herkeios under the olive-tree and lay down. It is a tradition among the Athenians that dogs should not go up to the acropolis. At about the same time, a star was visible in the sky for a period of time during the day, though the sun was shining and the weather was fine. I was asked about the meaning of the omen and the apparition and said that both portended a return of exiles, not as a consequence of revolution but under the existing constitution. And this interpretation turned out to be fulfilled.

(The exiles in question are the partisans of Demetrius of Phaleron; the date of their return is probably 292/1.[104]) In addition to the *Atthis*, Philochorus wrote monographs on a wide range of religious topics: *On Divination, On Sacrifices, On Festivals, On Days, On Competitions at Athens, On Mysteries at Athens, On Purifications, On Dreams*.[105] No more for Philochorus than for Lycurgus, evidently, was the Olympian religion played out. (That he rationalizes details of myths is by no means a counter-indication; an educated believer would not do otherwise, at this date.) He died in the 260s, at Antigonus Gonatas' instigation, suspected of sympathy for King Ptolemy. The same decade saw the deaths of Alexis and Philemon, two of the last great representatives of New Comedy (as well as of Epicurus and Zeno, who concern us less).[106] The execution of Philochorus shows that he was a figure of some weight, even in the eyes of the world. Our history can take the death of this pious citizen as its conclusion.

---

[104] Philochorus *FGrH* 328 F 135, 67; cf. Shear, *Kallias*, 54–55.

[105] See Jacoby's list in *FGrH* IIIb suppl. (text), 242. For Jacoby's assessment of his religious attitudes see ibid. 225–27.

[106] See H. Heinen, *Untersuchungen zur hellenistischen Geschichte* (Wiesbaden 1972), 204–205.

APPENDIX 1

Rattle-Shakers

About a dozen Late Geometric Attic vases, almost exclusively pitchers, show a ritual which has been associated with heroic cult. Details vary, but the fundamental element is a seated figure (usually male), who holds in each hand and apparently brandishes a spindle-shaped object, probably a rattle. In most cases two such rattle-shakers face each other over a centrepiece. This is most commonly (4×) a square or rectangular chequered object, over which a pair of 'Dipylon' shields may be shown, but the centrepiece can also be (1× each) a cauldron, a vessel, a vessel on a small table, and a pair of Dipylon shields, and in one example it is missing. Occasionally the rattles are replaced by a lute, and a bird or pair of birds may perch on the centrepiece (perhaps merely to fill space).[1]

Even apart from the problem of the 'rattles', these scenes are very puzzling. The central chequered object has not been conclusively identified,[2] and thus the principle by which other items can substitute for it inevitably remains unclear. That a ritual is depicted seems certain; that the ritual is in a broad sense funerary, with the shield symbolizing the dead man, is very

---

[1] See J. M. Cook, *BCH* 70 (1946), 97–101; W. Hahland, *Festschrift für Friedrich Zucker* (Berlin 1954), 177–94; J. Boardman, *JHS* 86 (1966), 4–5; G. Ahlberg, *OpAth* 7 (1967), 177–86 (with full illustrations; on the North Syrian reliefs that she plausibly adduces as an iconographic influence cf. Dentzer, *Banquet couché*, 34–46); Coldstream, *Geometric Pottery*, 71–72; S. McNally, *AJA* 73 (1969), 459–64 (a new type, permitting the association of two further vases). Rattles: see J. E. Harrison, *Themis: A Study of the Social Origins of Greek Religion* (Cambridge 1912), 77 f., Cook, *BCH* 70 (1946) ('instruments of rattle or clash'; Boardman prefers cymbals). The common bottle-shaped (?) 'rattles' (see Kurtz/Boardman, *Greek Burial Customs*, 76–77 with 352) may be related. Hahland argued for 'vases of pomegranate form' (of a known type) used for sprinkling, but could only offer a far-fetched explanation of why one was held in each hand (by several officiants).

[2] For Cook and Ahlberg, it is a table (used for a funerary or commemorative meal) with a cloth hanging down over its sides. But (the history of table-cloths aside!), even if the frame or border round three sides of the check pattern can, when present, be interpreted as a table, it is absent in two representations out of four. (Conversely, the presence of this border seems to rule out a carpet.) Boardman suggests the tomb; but square or rectangular tomb-monuments are not attested at this date (for their emergence in the seventh cent., see Kurtz/Boardman, *Greek Burial Customs*, 79–84), and the seats imply an indoor scene. Hahland, *Festschrift für Friedrich Zucker*, 184, thinks of low rectangular structures used as tables in *heroa*; these structures are hypothetical, and they leave the check pattern unexplained. In representational scenes in Attic Geometric, check pattern is most commonly (perhaps exclusively) used to represent fabric, the bier-cloth at the *prothesis* (see G. Ahlberg, *Prothesis and Ekphora in Greek Geometric Art*, Göteborg 1971, 60).

plausible;[3] that it honours not a single newly dead individual but a group of ancestors or a hero can be no more than an attractive suggestion, until we have identified the chequered object more securely. The warrior-shields would well suit ancestors or heroes; but the chairs (sometimes accompanied by footstools) perhaps suggest a domestic setting (and so mourning for the recently dead) rather than a *heroon* or a ritual area in a graveyard.[4]

[3] So Cook, *BCH* 70 (1946), 99 (why two shields, however?). His main argument, that the pitcher is an intrinsically funerary form, is hard to accept; note, however, that one pitcher stylistically related to the rattle group bears a *prothesis* (Coldstream, *Geometric Pottery*, 72, no. 10).

[4] Ancestors: Hägg, *Greek Renaissance*, 193, in a discussion of circular ritual areas in graveyards. Hero: so Hahland, *Festschrift für Friedrich Zucker*, rightly stressing, 193, n. 23, the symbolic role of shields in hero-cults. The 'Dipylon' form of the shield is not decisive: see A. M. Snodgrass, *AM* 95 (1980), 51–58 [+]; J. Boardman in W. G. Moon ed., *Ancient Greek Art and Iconography* (Madison 1983), 27–33; Snodgrass, *An Archaeology*, 151–53.

APPENDIX 2

The Gene*: A Checklist*

As a collection of material, the learned book of J. Töpffer, *Attische Genealogie* (Berlin 1889), has not been supplanted. But the elaborate speculation in which it abounds makes it a difficult work to use; and a substantial amount of new evidence has accrued. F. Bourriot's *Recherches sur la nature du génos* (Lille 1976) contains valuable discussions of many *gene*[1] but not a systematic presentation. A summary of the main facts (in large measure a mere précis of Töpffer) may be found useful. All the groups that Töpffer or others since him have identified as *gene* are (it is hoped) included; but where the identification is wrong or uncertain the group is relegated to a second list, B, of 'Uncertain and Spurious *Gene*'. Inevitably, the division between lists A and B is not clear-cut. Of the forty-seven *gene* accepted in A, some doubt attaches to the *Mesogeioi, Pamphidai, Philaidai*, and *Phreorychoi*, and (for the classical period) the *Bakchiadai, Gephyraioi, Erysichthonidai*, and *Pyrrhakidai*. And it is certainly possible that one or two of the groups known only from a single lexicographical reference were in fact *oikoi*.[2] The thirty-three names listed under B are very mixed in character. Some (such as *Ionidai*) are nothing but scholarly figments; more are the names of human groups that certainly existed, but the character of which is uncertain. Doubtless some of these were in fact Attic *gene*; but which, we cannot know.

A large number of *gene* are known exclusively from entries in lexicographers, Hesychius above all. These entries must derive in part from Attic orators or the lexica to them (so e.g. that for *Brytidai*), much more extensively from the various writers περὶ γενῶν (see *FGrH* 344–45, with Jacoby), of whom Drakon (no. 344) will probably be the earliest, if, as is likely, he is the same as the Δράκων Βατῆθεν known from several inscriptions and datable 'c. 175–111' (*LGPN* II, *Drakon* [5]). The production of such genealogical literature coincides with a revival of the *gene*, or some among them, in the late Hellenistic and Roman periods (see, for instance, the entries for the *Gephyraioi, Erysichthonidai, Eumolpidai, Kerykes, Pyrrhakidai* below; and Ch. 12, n. 45 above). Particularly characteristic of Hesychius is the description of a group as γένος ἰθαγενῶν (which occurs seventeen times); Hesychius' systematic deployment of the concept is (to judge from the *Thesaurus Linguae Graecae* data base) unparalleled, though the use of ἰθαγενής in the sense αὐτόχθων, γνήσιος (Hesychius' own gloss,

---

[1] As does now Humphreys, 'Genos' (cf. Ch. 5, n. 1).

[2] For a certain case of an *oikos* to which a group-name of patronymic form was applied see Dem. 43.19, 79 on the *Bouselidai*.

ι 380) goes back at least to the fifth century (see LSJ). In five cases the specification 'at Athens' is added; in five further cases the group in question can be shown on other grounds to be certainly or all but certainly Athenian (*Kerykes, Kephisieis, Koneidai, Lykomidai, Charidai*), and never is a demonstrably non-Athenian group so described. It is therefore commonly and reasonably assumed that the γένη ἰθαγενῶν can all be counted among the Attic *gene*,[3] the expression deriving perhaps from the περὶ γενῶν literature. Whether all the recognized γένη counted as being ἰθαγενῶν by these criteria can only be guessed; Hesychius' usage looks haphazard.

Some *gene* are absent from Hesychius but appear in other lexicographical sources (*Theoinidai, Koironidai, Krokonidai, Philleidai*); and the information that he gives is demonstrably incomplete (see Ch. 5, n. 11). The following *gene* appear to escape the lexicographical net entirely: *Bakchiadai, Gephyraioi, Erysichthonidai, Mesogeioi* (whatever they were), *Philaidai, Pyrrhakidai, Salaminioi*. Nothing can be made of individual omissions; but it is odd that no less than four of the limited number of *gene* that demonstrably shared in the late Hellenistic revival (*Bakchiadai, Gephyraioi, Erysichthonidai, Pyrrhakidai*) should be absent, if this was the period when the περὶ γενῶν literature began to be produced. Or was some 'invention of tradition' taking place by which Hesychius' source remained somehow unaffected?

A: Certain and Probable *Gene*

Αἰγειροτόμοι. ἰθαγενεῖς τινες Ἀθήνησιν (Hesych. α1699).

Ἀμυνανδρίδαι. γένος ἐξ οὗ ἱερεῖς Ἀθήνησιν (Hesych. α 3849). Amynandros is a credible but unattested heroic name (Kearns, *Heroes of Attica*, 66, n. 11); it is also borne by historical Athenians.[4] The *genos* (so described) supplied the priest of Cecrops, according to a catalogue of the Augustan period which is also interesting in showing how widely the *gennetai* were distributed among the demes (*IG* II².2338.8; the fragmentary contemporary decree *BCH* 51, 1927, 246 adds nothing).

This Amynandrid priest of Cecrops almost certainly served as the 'priest of the eponymous' hero of the tribe Cecropis, as R. Schlaifer demonstrated in a brilliant study (*HSCP* 51, 1940, 251–57) the conclusions of which are strongly supported by more recent discoveries (see *Agora* XV, 12–14, where, however, Schlaifer is overlooked). He pointed out that whereas certain tribes consistently chose the eponymous priest from within the tribe, others were served by an outsider (again, as we can now add, consistently): in the latter case, he suggested, a *genos* that had furnished a priest for the hero before Clisthenes created the tribes simply retained its privilege. The case of the *Amynandidrai* and Cecropis fits the theory perfectly: a cult of

[3] The omission by Töpffer, unaided by the database of the *Thesaurus Linguae Graecae*, of *Selladai* (and *Kallais*) was probably inadvertent.

[4] For the evidence supporting all such claims in this App. see *LGPN* II.

Cecrops controlled by a *genos* is attested, while the eponymous priest of Cecropis was an outsider late in the third century and again, very probably, early in the first (see Meritt/Traill, *Agora* XV, 12–14). For a parallel instance unknown to Schlaifer see below s.v. *Eteoboutadai, ad fin.*

Ἀνδροκλεῖδαι. γένος Ἀθήνησιν (Hesych. α 4750). At Athens no more is attested; the name Androcles is common. At Ephesus, Androclus, son of the Athenian King Codrus, was honoured as founder, and his descendants enjoyed special honours (see especially Pherecydes *FGrH* 3 F 155 and its context in Strabo 14.1.3–4 [632–33][5]).

Ἀνταγορίδας.[6] γένος Ἀθήνησιν (Hesych. α 5302). The name Antagoras is common in the Aegean islands (for a mythological instance see Plut. *Qu. Gr.* 58, 304d); three Athenian Antagoroi are known, the first in *IG* II².1544.8 (332/1).

Βακχιάδαι. Known only from *IG* II².2949, an altar bearing Dionysiac motifs and found in the precinct of Dionysus Eleuthereus, inscribed Πιστοκράτης καὶ Ἀπολλόδωρος Σατύρου Αὐρίδαι πομποστολήσαντες καὶ ἄρχοντες γενόμενοι τοῦ γενοὺς τῶν Βακχιαδῶν. These two brothers had been Πυθαϊσταὶ παῖδες (proof also of considerable social standing) in 128/7 and 138/7 respectively (see J. v. Freeden, *ZPE* 61, 1985, 215–18, who sets our dedication in the period 123/2–121/0). Von Freeden argues that the dedication commemorates two distinctions of the brothers, separate though close in time, and both associated with Dionysus: their role in organizing, as ephebes, the great procession at the *City Dionysia*; and their appointment as annual *archontes* of a *genos* whose allegiance to the god is revealed in its very name. (It would follow that they became *archontes* shortly after leaving the ephebate.) On this view we know nothing at all of the actual activities of the *genos*, since even the 'procession' of the inscription is taken away from them.

There were also Bacchiads in Miletus (Hesych. s.v. Βακχιάδαι) as well as the well-known family in Corinth (cf. *RE* s.v. *Bakchiadai*); neither group seems relevant to ours.

Βουζύγαι [MSS Βουζυγία]. γένος τι Ἀθήνησιν ἱερωσύνην ἔχον. Βουζύγης γάρ τις τῶν ἡρώων, πρῶτος βοῦς ζεύξας τὴν γῆν ἤροσεν καὶ εἰς γεωργίαν ἐπιτήδειον ἐποίησεν. ἀφ' οὗ γένος καλεῖται Βουζύγαι (*Anecd. Bekk.* I.221.8, etc. The new Photius, β 226, and Σ Aeschin. 2.78 apparently confuse the Bouzygai with the Eteoboutads). On the hero Bouzyges see Kearns, *Heroes of Attica*, 152 [+]. A member of the *genos* continued to perform a 'sacred ploughing' each year below the acropolis (on which the hero's plough was dedicated, Σ Aeschin. 2.78): Plut. *Praecepta coniugalia* 42 (144a) Ἀθηναῖοι τρεῖς ἀρότους ἱεροὺς ἄγουσι· πρῶτον ἐπὶ Σκίρῳ, τοῦ

---

[5] Cf. Prinz, *Gründungsmythen*, 195–96, 320 ff.; Smarczyk, *Religionspolitik*, 352, ns. 54, 55.
[6] The similar accusative in Hesychius' lemma Βρυτίδας comes from [Dem.] 59.59.

παλαιοτάτου τῶν σπόρων ὑπόμνημα, δεύτερον ἐν τῇ ʿΡαρία, τρίτον ὑπὸ πόλιν τὸν καλούμενον Βουζύγιον (cf. Ael. Arist. 37.16, p. 308 Keil, Βουζύγης τῶν ἐκ τῆς ἀκροπόλεως). While ploughing, he uttered the proverbial (as they became) βουζύγειοι ἀραί (*Paroem. Graec.* I.388, no. 61): ὁ γὰρ βουζύγης Ἀθήνησιν ὁ τὸν ἱερὸν ἄροτον ἐπιτελῶν ἄλλα τε πολλὰ ἀρᾶται καὶ τοῖς μὴ κοινωνοῦσι κατὰ τὸν βίον ὕδατος ἢ πυρὸς ἢ μὴ ὑποφαίνουσιν ὁδὸν πλανωμένοις (cf. Eupolis fr. 113 K/A, Diphilus fr. 62 K/A with note). Σ Ael. Arist. III, p. 473.25–27 Dindorf also associates the *genos* with the sacred ploughing at Eleusis: Βουζύγαι καλοῦνται οἱ τὰς ἱερὰς βοῦς τὰς ἐν Ἐλευσῖνι ἀροτριώσας τρέφοντες . . . τὸ δὲ γένος τοῦτο ἦν ἱερόν.

Around 37 BC the *genos* of *Gephyraioi* consulted Delphi on behalf of a 'Bouzyges and Priest of Zeus at the Palladion' (*SEG* XXX 85.10–11, 18–19); the same combination of titles also appears in *IG* II².3177 (perhaps a related text) and 5055, and *IG* II².5075 offers a 'Priest of Zeus Teleios, Bouzyges'. The intervention of the *Gephyraioi* suggests a blurring of the lines between *gene* characteristic of the period,[7] but it is likely that the priesthoods of Zeus at the Palladion and Zeus Teleios belonged originally to the *Bouzygai*: an 'Athenian called Bouzyges' helped Demophon to bring the Palladion to Athens in one account (Polyaenus 1.5, and see Burkert, *Zeitschr. f. Religions- und Geistesgeschichte* 22, 1970, 356–68).[8] For the possibility that members of the *genos* escorted the Palladion annually to the sea see below s.v. *Praxiergidai*. In a text of the second century AD, '*Bouzyges*' appears in a list of Eleusinian priesthoods and offices (*IG* II².1092 B 32).

In that last text, the *Bouzyges* is apparently a functionary rather than a member of a *genos*. And the other references to *Bouzygai* in the texts of the Roman period just cited can readily be taken in the same way: a '*Bouzyges* and priest of Zeus at the Palladion', for instance, would be the holder of two sacred offices. Bourriot, *Génos*, 1281–91, has accordingly questioned whether there ever was a true *genos* of *Bouzygai* (as the lexicographers, alone, declare) rather than an office of *Bouzyges*. Some doubt is, certainly, justified. But a *genos* could bear a functional rather than a patronymic name (cf. *Kerykes*); the circumstances of the Roman period cannot necessarily be retrojected; and one would in fact expect such a function to be vested in a *genos*.

Two prominent politicians of the late fifth and early fourth century were *Bouzygai* (the only two known before the Roman period):[9] Demostratos who spoke in favour of the Sicilian expedition (Ar. *Lys.* 397; cf. Eupolis, *Demes* frs. 103, 113 K/A); and Demainetos, general in the Corinthian war (Aeschin. 2.78: cf. Davies, *Propertied Families*, 104–105). It is clear from these passages, even the abusive ones, that 'Bouzyges' was a title of distinction.

---

[7] See Ferguson, 'Salaminioi', 51–52; B. D. Meritt, *Hesperia* 9 (1940), 93–95; Bourriot, *Génos*, 1286–90; and s.v. *Eteoboutadai* below.

[8] For doubts about the antiquity of this tradition see Humphreys, 'Genos'.

[9] Pericles was not one: see Bourriot, *Génos*, 1270–75.

Βρυτίδαι. Attested as a γένος in [Dem.] 59.59–61 (whence derive several notices in lexicographers); seven γεννῆται from six different demes are named, of whom one was demonstrably rich (Davies, *Propertied Families*, 408).

Γεφυραῖοι. Herodotus' little digression (5.57–61)[10] on the origin of Harmodius and Aristogeiton, who were γένος τὰ ἀνέκαθεν Γεφυραῖοι, is much the most important source. By general consent the Gephyraeans were an immigrant group, though their original home was (and is) controversial.[11] In Herodotus' view they were expelled from Tanagra on the arrival of the Boeotians, an event dated by Thucydides sixty years after the Trojan war (1.12.3). They came to Athens, and were granted citizenship 'on fixed terms' by the Athenians, who excluded them from 'numerous but insignificant' privileges. καί σφι ἱρὰ ἐστι ἐν Ἀθήνῃσι ἱδρυμένα, τῶν οὐδὲν μέτα τοῖσι λοιποῖσι Ἀθηναίοισι, ἄλλα τε κεχωρισμένα τῶν ἄλλων ἱρῶν καὶ δὴ καὶ Ἀχαιίης Δήμητρος ἱρόν τε καὶ ὄργια (5.61).

Herodotus insists that the Gephyraeans had shrines and rites confined to themselves. They are, therefore, something of an embarrassment for the modern theory which denies that the cults controlled by a *genos* were in origin its private *sacra*. One possible response is to press the text of Herodotus: he does not describe the *Gephyraioi* as a *genos* (cf. Bourriot, *Génos*, 343–44), but sees them rather as something exceptional, an immigrant group whose strangely isolated religious practices invite particular comment. It should, however, be noted that these immigrants had already been settled in Attica for well over half a millennium on Herodotus'

---

[10] Derived from Hecataeus according e.g. to Jacoby on *FGrH* 1 F 118.

[11] Cf. Davies, *Propertied Families*, 472–73. According to Herodotus, the Gephyraeans themselves claimed to derive from Eretria; but in his own view they were Phoenicians who had come to Boeotia with Cadmus and settled at Tanagra. Herodotus' theory about their immediate origin seems to have been accepted in later antiquity: it finds some support in the tradition that Tanagra had once been called Gephyra (Steph. Byz. s.v. Γέφυρα· πόλις Βοιωτίας. τινὲς δὲ τοὺς αὐτοὺς εἶναι καὶ Ταναγραίους φασίν, ὡς Στράβων [9.2.10 (404)] καὶ Ἑκαταῖος [*FGrH* 1 F 118]. ἀφ' οὗ καὶ Γεφυραία ἡ Δηώ; *Etym. Magn.* 228.58 s.v. Γέφυρα, which derives the name from bridges across the Asopos), and in the evidence (but only of the Roman period) for worship in Boeotia of the Gephyraeans' goddess Demeter Achaia (see Schachter, *Cults*, I.163, 170–71), who is so far unattested elsewhere in Greece outside Attica. Legend surrounded this mysterious and glamorous people: on their migration from Tanagra, Demeter herself indicated where in Attica they should build their city and her shrine (*Etym. Magn.* 180.34 s.v. Ἀχαιά); they had once (Pausanias Atticista δ 23 Erbse: a new testimonium in the new Photius δ 723) been 'tithed to Delphi by the Athenians', where they were told to follow a herd of cattle and settle where they first reclined, in Tanagra as it turned out—a puzzling story, possibly designed to give the group an ultimate origin in Athens. *Etym. Magn.* 229.5–7 s.v. Γεφυρεῖς is also problematic: δῆμος Ἀττικός· ὅθεν καὶ Γεφυραία Δημήτηρ. εἴρηται ἀπὸ τοῦ ἔχειν γέφυραν, δι' ἧς ἐπὶ Ἐλευσῖνα κάτεισιν οἱ μύσται. There was in fact no deme Γεφυρεῖς, though there could have been such a village (Traill, *Political Organization*, 86, 115). If Demeter/Deo *Gephyraia* (cf. Steph. Byz. cited above) had any association with the Gephyraeans, the epithet was presumably a (perhaps quite recent) alternative to *Achaia*, and had nothing to do with the well-known (see e.g. *RE* s.v. *Gephyrismoi*) Eleusinian bridge; but if it derived from the bridge, 'Demeter as honoured at the bridge during the great procession', it had nothing to do with the *genos*.

chronology, and included men such as Harmodius and Aristogeiton of the highest social distinction. In these terms no small number of noble Attic families would turn out to be composed of immigrants.

If by contrast the Gephyraeans were indeed a *genos* in the technical sense in Herodotus' day, three interpretations are possible: (1) the modern theory is wrong; (2) Herodotus is wrong when he insists on the exclusivity of the Gephyraeans' cults; (3) even if some of their cults were exclusive, they also controlled other, public cults (and it was this which made them a *genos*). In support of (2), it can be noted that early in the fourth century the deme of Marathon (not far from Aphidna, Harmodius and Aristogeiton's deme) was sacrificing to Achaia (*IG* II².1358 = *LSCG* 20 B 27).[12] Is it possible that Herodotus has mistaken the special relation that existed between a *genos* and certain cults for an exclusive one?

'The Gephyraeans' appear as creditors on a mortgage stone of the fourth century.[13] This confirms the existence of an identifiable association of *Gephyraioi*, but tells us nothing of its character. By the Roman period they were certainly a flourishing *genos*. For their letter to Delphi from the time of Augustus, which seems to indicate an association with the *Bouzygai*, see above s.v. *Βουζύγαι*. Later still we find a ἱερεὺς διὰ βίου Ἀπόλλωνος Πατρῴου Γεφυραίων καὶ Δαφνηφόρου (*IG* II².3629–30, cf. *Bull. Ép.* 1972, no. 133), and a dedication Ἀπόλλωνι Γεφυραίῳ (*IG* II².4813). The priestesses of Demeter Achaia and Demeter Kourotrophos Achaia, known from theatre-seats (*IG* II².5117, 5153), were presumably members of the *genos*. Uncertain conjectures in a corrupt fragment of Antiochus/Pherecydes (*FGrH* 333 F 4) would associate them with a Palladion.

Διογενίδαι· γένος Ἀθήνησι ἰθαγενῶν (Hesych. δ 1863). Diogenes is, of course, a common post-heroic name.

Ἐρυσιχθονίδαι. Erysichthon was a son of Cecrops who was mythologically particularly closely associated with Delos: see Phanodemus *FGrH* 325 F 2, with Jacoby's commentary; Kearns, *Heroes of Attica*, 162. The *genos* first appears among those that sent representatives to the *Pythais* of 97/6 (*SIG*³ 728 D¹). In 91/0 they listed those of their young men who had acted as ἀμφιθαλεῖς (*IG* II².4991: carved on the reverse, it has been noted, of a document relating to Delos). Delian inscriptions of the Augustan period show us a father and son who served successively as ἱερεὺς τοῦ Ἀπόλλωνος διὰ βίου ἐκ τοῦ γένους τῶν Ἐρυσιχθονιδῶν (*Inscr. Dél.* 1624 bis; 2515–18; the identification was made by P. Roussel, *BCH* 53, 1929, 179–84). From 166 until (at least) about 100 the priesthood (the most important in the island) had been annual. Perhaps it was formally assigned to the *genos*, in an antiquarian spirit, at the same time as life-tenure was introduced. If so, the arrangement probably broke down, since subsequent life-priests of Apollo

[12] But the apparent allusion in Ar. *Ach.* 709 is probably corrupt: see E. K. Borthwick's discussion and brilliant conjecture (cf. Hdt. 7.117) αὐτὸν Ἀρταχαίην, BICS 17 (1970), 107–10.

[13] G. R. Davidson, *Hesperia* Suppl. 7 (1943), 1, no. 1 = M. I. Finley, *Studies in Land and Credit in Ancient Athens* (New Brunswick 1952), 160, no. 147.

do not advertise themselves as Erysichthonids and were probably not members of the *genos* (see Bruneau, *Recherches*, 64; Roussel, *BCH* 53, 1929, 184, on Tiberius Claudius Theogenes).

At the *Pyanopsia* and other rites of Apollo, the *eiresione* was carried by an *amphithales*, who is likely to have been the one recruited from the Erysichthonids (see N. Robertson, *AJP* 105, 1984, 385 ff.); and given the association of the *genos* with Apollo one can guess that it may have filled one of the god's several priesthoods.

'Ετεοβουτάδαι. This *genos* claimed a much closer association than did almost any other with the central figures of the great mythological period in which Athens' identity was shaped. Erechtheus and Boutes were sons of King Pandion I and Zeuxippe; on his death they divided the inheritance, Erechtheus receiving the kingship, Boutes the priesthood of Athena and of Poseidon Erichthonius (Apollod. 3.14.8–15.1; but for other genealogies see Kearns, *Heroes of Attica*, 153). In another source we hear of a *pinax* dedicated in the Erechtheum by a member of the *genos* in which its descent was traced ἀπὸ Βούτου [τούτων MSS] καὶ Ἐρεχθέως τοῦ Γῆς καὶ Ἡφαίστου ([Plut.] *X Orat.* 843e). The 'hero Boutes' had an altar in the Erechtheum (Paus. 1.26.5), and *IG* II².5166 (fourth cent. according to *IG*), a seat found in that region and inscribed Ἱερέως Βούτου, attests even a priest (presumably an Eteoboutad)—unless indeed Hesych. β 990 βούτης· . . . καὶ ὁ τοῖς Διπολίοις τὰ βουφόνια δρῶν is based not on mere confusion with βουτύπος but on an actual use of βούτης to designate a sacral officiant (Kearns, *Heroes of Attica*, 69, n. 23, thinks of the priest of Poseidon Erechtheus). By the Roman period the noble birth of the Eteoboutads was proverbial (Töpffer, *Attische Genealogie*, 117 f.), and their prestige can already be detected in the fourth century: Aeschines mentions that his own phratry 'shares altars with the Eteoboutads, who provide the Priestess of Athena Polias' (2.147), and Demosthenes points out that one Pyrrhos was executed, Eteoboutad though he was (21.182).

This special nobility of birth is of course associated with the extraordinary religious privilege that the *genos* enjoyed: it filled the priesthoods both of the city's guardian goddess, Athena Polias, and also of the god who disputed with her for primacy in Attica, Poseidon Erechtheus—he too, despite his defeat, honourably lodged on the acropolis (Apollod. 3.15.1; [Plut.] *X Orat.* 843; etc.). In addition to their separate functions, the priestess of Athena and the priest of Poseidon Erechtheus were jointly involved (with the priest of Helios) at one festival, the *Skira*, and on this occasion further members of the *genos* apparently participated: we are told that 'the Eteoboutads' carried the parasol under which the three priests walked out to Skiron (Lysimachides *FGrH* 366 F 3 *ap.* Harp. s.v. Σκίρον). It is not known whether the assistants of the priestess of Athena, the Κοσμώ and Τραπεζώ (Harpoc. s.v. Τραπεζοφόρος; Hesych. s.v. Τραπεζώ), were also Eteoboutads.

About the early history of this privileged *genos* regrettably little is known. (Thus attempts to account for its special eminence are wholly speculative.[14]) Some connection evidently existed between the *genos* and the Clisthenic deme Boutadai, in which its most prominent family was registered. (But since other Eteoboutad families were registered elsewhere, the *genos* must already have been dispersed in 508.) To judge from the well over twenty Clisthenic demes that bore names of patronymic form, it was common for place-names to derive ultimately from prominent local families; but a name could cling to a place long after the family that gave it was extinct, and this is one of the very few cases (Philaidai is another, Semachidai perhaps a third) where a deme-name can be associated with an attested *genos*. The locality was doubtless known as Boutadai before Clisthenes; in consequence of the reform, an ordinary inhabitant became not merely '*x* of Boutadai' but '*x* the Boutad', and this change may have spurred the *genos* to rechristen itself 'true Boutads'; but we need scarcely infer an intent on the part of Clisthenes to dilute the prestige of the old aristocracy.[15]

The most famous Eteoboutad was the orator Lycurgus, of the deme Boutadai; of his forebears, nothing certain is known except that two of them, Lycomedes and Lycurgus, distinguished themselves enough to receive public burial (Ps. Plut. 843e), this earlier Lycurgus doubtless being the politician often mentioned in Old Comedy who was executed by the thirty tyrants (Ps. Plut. 841a–b, cf. Davies, *Propertied Families*, 350). (The family burial-plot has recently been discovered:[16] interestingly these blue-blooded men—who bore a fine array of wolfish names—are identified by deme and not by *genos* even on their gravestones.) This family seems to have possessed moderate wealth, but not more, and not even that can be said of the other group of Eteoboutads known from the classical period, the relations of Lysimache the priestess of Athena (Davies, *Propertied Families*, 348, 169);[17] the comedian Alexis does, however, introduce a parasite who preys on 'Demeas son of Laches, Eteoboutad' (fr. 205 K/A). No source says that the Lycurgus who headed the faction of *Pedieis* in the sixth century was an ancestor of the orator (cf. Bourriot, *Génos*, 1308–10); but he comes from the right part of Attica, and the name is rare enough in other families to give the connection some plausibility.

No relationship can be traced between the priest of Poseidon and the priestess of Athena Polias until the late second century, when the two posts were filled by a brother and sister, Medeios and Philippe (Ps. Plut. 843b). It is commonly supposed that the priesthoods traditionally belonged to two distinct branches of the *genos* (so e.g. Davies, *Propertied Families*, 348–49);

---

[14] The common theory that makes them descendants of the Athenian royal line is criticized by Bourriot, *Génos*, 1327–44, who points out that Athenian tradition knows nothing of a royal family of *Boutadai*. But Bourriot's own suggestion (based on the deme-name) that they were a pre-Clisthenic local group of the city itself scarcely explains why they alone acquired such eminence.

[15] Cf. Roussel, *Tribu et cité*, 71, 275.

[16] See A. P. Matthaiou, *Horos* 5 (1987), 31–44 (*SEG* XXXVII 160–12).

[17] The offence of Pyrrhos, an Eteoboutad who was executed, was to have served as a juror, illicitly, while in debt to the state; he needed the money, Demosthenes explains (21.182).

but our knowledge of the succession of priests and priestesses, unusually full though it is, is none the less too fragmentary for the case to be certain.[18]

The transmission of the priesthoods is remarkable in two further ways. The siblings who filled both posts in the late second century were children of a Eumolpid exegete (Ps. Plut. 843b), who must himself have been a Eumolpid, not an Eteoboutad. At this date, therefore, entitlement to an Eteoboutad priesthood seems to have been transmissible in the female line;[19] a similar relaxation of the patrilineal principle can be seen in other *gene* in the same period.[20] The second point derives from [Plut.] *X Orat.* 843e–f: κατῆγον τὸ γένος . . . τὰ ἐγγυτάτω ἀπὸ Λυκομήδους καὶ Λυκούργου . . . καὶ ἔστιν αὕτη ἡ καταγωγὴ τοῦ γένους τῶν ἱερασαμένων τοῦ Ποσειδῶνος ἐν πίνακι τελείῳ, ὃς ἀνάκειται ἐν Ἐρεχθείῳ. τὸν δὲ πίνακα ἀνέθηκεν Ἄβρων ὁ παῖς αὐτοῦ [Λυκούργου] λαχὼν ἐκ τοῦ γένους τὴν ἱερωσύνην καὶ παραχωρήσας τῷ ἀδελφῷ Λυκόφρονι. καὶ διὰ τοῦτο πεποίηται ὁ Ἄβρων προσδιδοὺς αὐτῷ τὴν τρίαιναν. It seems to be implied that Lycomedes and the two Lycurgi had all held the priesthood of Poseidon; and this certainly passed successively to two of the orator's sons. Similarly, most of the known priestesses of Athena Polias (also Eteoboutads) belong to a single family. Such hereditary transmission is obviously incompatible with true sortition from the *genos* as a whole. And yet use of the lot appears to be attested both by λαχών in Pseudo-Plutarch (which is admittedly not decisive in itself: see Töpffer, *Attische Genealogie*, 126) and by a reference in a fragmentary fourth-century decree of Erechtheis to [τὸν ἱερέα τὸν ἀεὶ] λαχόντα (*IG* II².1146.4), who ought from the context to be the priest of Poseidon Erechtheus. (It used to be common to associate this text with a postulated tribal priest of Erechtheus distinct from the Eteoboutad. But we now know—see below—that no such distinct priest existed.) These data can be reconciled on the hypothesis that the mode of selection was in fact κλήρωσις ἐκ προκρίτων, allotment from a pre-selected group. This method (attested for deme priesthoods) may have been the norm among all the *gene*:[21] in the rare explicit references, no prin-

---

[18] The succession: Ps. Plut. 843; D. M. Lewis, *BSA* 50 (1955), 7–12; Davies, *Propertied Families*, 169–73, 348–53; and on the priestesses see now S. Aleshire, 'The Demos and the Priests: The Selection of Sacred Officials at Athens from Kleisthenes to Augustus', in *Ritual, Finance, Politics*, 325–37. Uncertain: cf. Bourriot, *Génos*, 1337–44; Aleshire, 'The Demos and the Priests', promises a study in which she will associate the priestess of *IG* II².3461.6 with the family of Lycurgus.

[19] For further cases, later in date, see Töpffer, *Attische Genealogie*, 125–27. In the case of Medeios and Philippe, it is unclear how far back the male Eteoboutad blood lies. Lewis, *BSA* 50 (1955), 5, argues that Penteteris, a priestess of Athena of the first half of the (?) second cent. BC, was qualified by descent in the female line from the fifth-cent. priestess Lysimache; but the association is not mandatory.

[20] Cf. n. 7 above; and on the chronology of the development, Ferguson, 'Salaminioi', 51–52 —but note the qualification s.v. *Mesogeioi* below, *ad fin.*

[21] So Aleshire, 'The Demos and the Priests'. Demes: Dem. 57.46–48, 62 (our only evidence on deme practice). Sortition is attested for the *Salaminioi* (*LSS* 19 12–13), and in the prehistoric state was normal, according to Aristotle, *Ath. Pol.* fr. 3 Kenyon (one source for this fragment, *Lex. Patm.* 152 s.v. γεννῆται, includes a specific reference to Eumolpids and Kerykes and Eteoboutads, which may, however, be an interpolation). For restricted

ciple of selection other than the lot is ever mentioned, but the phenomenon of quasi-hereditary transmission of certain priesthoods at certain periods is observable in two, and perhaps three, other cases. The process whereby the short list of names to go forward to the lot was arrived at may have varied, between *gene* and within *gene* at different periods: in extreme cases, the list perhaps contained but a single name (cf. Bourriot, *Génos*, 1342, n. 593).

One 'priest of the eponymous' hero of the tribe Erechtheis is now attested by name, and turns out not to be a member of the tribe: Ἀριστώνυμος Ἀριστωνύμου Πιθεύς (*Agora* XV, nos. 98–99: 'c. 250', according to *Agora* XV; but '215–205' in Tracy, 67). According to Schlaifer's brilliant theory (see above under *Amynandidrai*) he ought therefore to be a member of a *genos*, in this case the Eteoboutads; and given the tendency of names to run in families it is suggestive that another Aristonymus appears among the third-century descendants of Lycurgus ([Plut.] *X Orat.* 843b, Ἀριστώνυμος Συμμάχου, J. Kirchner, *Prosopographia Attica* (2 vols., Berlin 1901–3), no. 2189, cf. the stemma ad no. 9232; Davies, *Propertied Families*, 353, with table iv). He could conceivably be the father of our man, though Pseudo-Plutarch mentions only one son (Charmides).

A 'field of Athena Polias' which is said to 'belong' to the *genos* (an odd joint-ownership) appears to be attested in the second century AD (*Agora* XIX H23–24, apparently copied from fifth-cent. texts).

Εὐδάνεμοι/Εὐδάνεμοι. Known as a *genos* only from the pseudo-Dinarchan διαδικασία Εὐδανέμων πρὸς Κήρυκας ὑπὲρ τοῦ κανῶς (Dion. Hal. *Din.* 11, p. 315.1 Usener/Radermacher). Their association with Eleusis is confirmed by a puzzling passage of Arrian, which appears to attest an altar belonging to the *genos* in the Ceramicus at Athens, and another dedicated to their patronal hero 'on the plain' at Eleusis: ἐν Κεραμεικῷ . . . οὐ μακρὰν τῶν Εὐδανέμων τοῦ βωμοῦ. ὅστις δὲ μεμύηται ταῖν θεαῖν ἐν Ἐλευσῖνι, οἶδε τὸν Εὐδανέμου βωμὸν ἐπὶ τοῦ δαπέδου ὄντα (*Anab.* 3.16.8; cf. Wachsmuth in *RE* s.v. *Eudanemoi*). Proclus (*In Ti.* 65 f., 1.213.23–24 Diehl) refers to αἱ τῶν Εὐδανέμων εὐχαὶ παρὰ Ἀθηναίοις addressed to the gods responsible for winds. The only other reference is the obscure notice Hesych. ε 6744: Εὐδάνεμος· ἄγγελος [MSS: ἰθαγενεῖς Latte] παρὰ Ἀθηναίοις. In favour of interpreting the name (to be aspirated therefore at the start) as 'sleep wind' Töpffer compares Hesych. α 4879: Ἀνεμοκοῖται· οἱ ἀνέμους κοιμίζοντες· γένος δὲ τοιοῦτόν φασιν ὑπάρχειν ἐν Κορίνθῳ.

Εὐμολπίδαι. On Eumolpus see Kearns, *Heroes of Attica*, 163. From the middle (*IG* I³.6 C), perhaps the beginning (*IG* I³.231.22), of the fifth century there are numerous references in decrees to 'the Eumolpids'. The fees

transmission of the posts of daduch and (?) hierophant see ns. 25 and 49; similarly, the priest-hood of Hippothoon, almost certainly vested in an unknown *genos* (cf. s.v. *Amynandridai* above), became *de facto* hereditary in the second cent. BC (B. D. Meritt, *Hesperia* 21, 1952, 363).

that they and the *Kerykes* may charge for initiating (μυεῖν) candidates for the Mysteries are regulated (*IG* I³.6 C 20–31 = *LSS* 3 C); they perform sacrifice to Eleusinian heroes, on the occasion perhaps of the *Eleusinia*, in a fragment of Nicomachus' revised sacrificial code (*LSS* 10 A 60–74); they 'expound' (ἐξηγοῦνται) sacred matters (see below); along with the *basileus*, hierophant, daduch, and *Kerykes* they supervise the delimitation of the sacred *orgas* (*IG* II².204. 14 = *LSCG* 32); they probably record the names of initiates (*IG* I³.386.161–62); with the *Kerykes*, they are said by Isocrates (*Paneg.* 157) to make the famous proclamation debarring killers and barbarians from the sacred rites.[22] In most cases we may suppose that the work was not done by the Eumolpids *en masse*;[23] but for the state what mattered was the delegation of responsibility to the *genos*, which might then delegate further among its own members.

The role of τὰ γένη τὰ περὶ τὼ θεώ (*IG* II².2944.10–11, third cent.) is stated in very general terms in a provision of the political settlement of 403: ἐπιμελεῖσθαι δὲ [τοῦ ἱεροῦ] Κήρυκας καὶ Εὐμολπίδας κατὰ τὰ πάτρια (Arist. *Ath. Pol.* 39.2). Because of their concern for the cult, they passed decrees in honour of its (and their) benefactors (*IG* II².1231, for an outsider; on honours for hierophants, see below). The impeachment brought against Alcibiades supposedly accused him of parodying the Mysteries παρὰ τὰ νόμιμα καὶ τὰ καθεστηκότα ὑπό τ᾽ Εὐμολπιδῶν καὶ Κηρύκων καὶ τῶν ἱερέων τῶν ἐξ Ἐλευσῖνος (Plut. *Alc.* 22.4). Thus the two families[24] were seen in a sense as not merely executors but also sources of legitimate religious tradition. The special role of the two *gene* was still recognized in the fourth-century decree which established the board of ἐπιμεληταὶ τῶν μυστηριῶν: they were to be four in all, two chosen from 'all the Athenians', and one each from the two families (*Hesperia* 49, 1980, 258 ff. = *SEG* XXX 61 A fr. a+b 29–37; cf. Arist. *Ath. Pol.* 57.1) They also of course enjoyed perquisites: each Eumolpid received a μέρις from the sacrifices at the Greater and Lesser Mysteries (*IG* II².1231).*

The Hierophant of the Mysteries was selected from the Eumolpids, by a method unfortunately unknown.[25] He often worked in concert with the

[22] But cf. n. 29 below.

[23] *IG* I³.6 C 30–31 specified which members of the two *gene* had the right μυεῖν; but the specification has to be supplied (h[οἱ ἂν hεβ]ῶσι *IG* I³, *alii alia*). The new decree *Hesperia* 49 (1980), 258–88 = *SEG* XXX 61, if correctly supplemented in A 27, shows that all members had this right; one might, however, rather expect a continuation of the topic of the preceding lines. If Andocides' claim, in *Myst.* 132, to have initiated (μυέω) strangers means, as it should in context (cf. MacDowell ad loc.), that he performed the act in person (rather than merely paying the fee), then we have confirmation both that Andocides was a *Keryx* and that all *Kerykes* (and so all Eumolpids) were empowered μυεῖν. For this view see W. Dittenberger, *Hermes* 20 (1885), 31–32, with Töpffer 83, n. 3; for the other, Davies, *Propertied Families*, 27 [+].

[24] On the co-operation of two societies in one cult see the work of N. Forsberg, *Une forme élémentaire d'organisation cérémoniale* (Uppsala 1943).

[25] See Clinton, *Sacred Officials*, 45. Apparent instances of 'hereditary' succession occur, but only very spasmodically.

genos[26] and in a sense represented it, as the daduch represented the *Kerykes* (though the two *gene* often combined in honouring a satisfactory hierophant[27]). Like an ordinary Eumolpid, he was involved in 'caring for the shrine' as well as in ritual duties; but even when acting as a kind of administrator[28] he was still above all a ceremonial figure, the embodiment of sacred tradition. The hierophant and the daduch jointly represented the shrine before the world: they 'proclaimed' the forthcoming celebration of the Mysteries in the Stoa Poikile,[29] invited participating states to send a tithe of first-fruits to Eleusis (*IG* I[3].78 [= *LSCG* 5] 24 ff.), and in 350/49, after a war with Megara over violation of the sacred *orgas*, were chosen, by agreement with the Megarians, to mark out its limits anew (Philochorus *FGrH* 328 F 155).[30]

The hierophant was, of course, the central officiant at the Greater (and Lesser?) Mysteries, where he 'revealed the sacred things'. He is also attested as 'announcing', at Athens, the Eleusinian festival of *Proerosia* (*LSCG* 7 A 4–7: late fourth cent.); participating, apparently, in the Athenian festival of *Pyanopsia*, along with the 'priestesses from Eleusis' (ibid., A 14–19); organizing a *lectisternium* for Plouton (of course an Eleusinian god) in Athens (*IG* II[2].1933–34, both late fourth cent.; ibid. 1935, 2464, Roman period[31]); conducting the 'sacrifice and procession of the *Kalamaia*' at Eleusis in company with 'the priestesses' and the demarch of Eleusis (*IG* II[2].949.10, 164/3 BC); and attending the *Thargelia* at Athens along with the daduch and οἱ μετὰ τούτων ἥκοντες (*LSS* 14.36, 129/8 BC). It is likely that the hierophant had not been involved in all these rites in, say, the fifth century, but was subsequently invited to participate because of the great prestige of his office and of the cult he served.

The Eumolpids also provided the ἐξηγηταὶ ἐξ Εὐμολπιδῶν. There are several references to exegesis by 'the Eumolpids' in the fifth century (*IG* I[3].78 [= *LSCG* 5] 36–37; Andoc. *Myst.* 115–16 [by implication]; [Lys.] 6.10); but the specific post of Eumolpid exegete is first attested in the fourth century (in *Hesperia* 49, 1980, 258 ff. = *SEG* XXX 61 A 38–40), and was perhaps first created at the end of the fifth.[32] (Whether the earlier exegesis would have been performed by the *genos* as a whole or by prestigious individuals within it, or even in certain circumstances by any individual Eumolpid, we can only guess. In so far as 'exegesis' merely involved explaining Eleusinian traditions to outsiders,[33] any Eumolpid could

---

[26] Note *SEG* XXII 124 (re-edited by Clinton, *Sacred Officials*, 24), where line 14 stresses the participation of the *genos* in one of his activities, and line 11 appears to refer to συγγραφαί of the *genos* defining certain of his duties. Cf. the fragment *IG* II[2].1044.

[27] *IG* II[2].1235, 2944; *IG* II[2].1236 is a joint decree in honour of a benefactor of the cult.

[28] See e.g. *IG* II[2].1013.48–49, and previous note.

[29] So Σ Ar. *Ran.* 369. But Isoc. *Paneg.* 157 ascribes the proclamation to the 'Eumolpids' and 'Kerykes'; Dittenberger suggested, *Hermes* 20 (1885), 14, n. 2, that they may have uttered an ἐπίφθεγμα (cf. Lucian, *Alex.* 38).

[30] Cf. Clinton, *Sacred Officials*, 18.

[31] Clinton, ibid. 20, n. 65, also mentions *Hesperia* 11 (1942), 75, no. 38.

[32] See Clinton, *Sacred Officials*, 89–92 [+].

[33] Cf. *SEG* XXX 61 A fr. a+b 38–40.

doubtless perform it; but the creative development of traditions, the creation of Eumolpid 'case-law', must have been more regulated.) A late formulation probably gives the content of such exegesis correctly as τὰ ἱερὰ
καὶ πάτρια (*IG* II².3490): not sacred law in general, but the traditions of the
Eleusinian cult. Only two specific applications of such exegesis are known:
one concerns the form of a new sacrifice (*IG* I³.78 [= *LSCG* 5] 36–37), the
other the penalty for an offence against the rules of the sanctuary (Andoc.
Myst. 115–16). This second case is complicated, because the self-appointed
exegete was not in fact a Eumolpid, and the 'ancestral law' which he
claimed to expound was perhaps a fabrication; it was certainly no longer
valid, having, as Andocides shows, been supplanted by a written law. The
punishment supposedly prescribed by the ancestral law was 'death without
trial'. If this 'law' either was a genuine tradition or resembled one, the
Eumolpids may once in effect have claimed the right to have Athenian citizens executed on request for certain offences against the cult.[34] However
that may be, penal exegesis would have been restricted in scope by the
growth of written laws of the state; we certainly do not hear of any instance
in which the 'unwritten laws, according to which the Eumolpids
expound'[35] which Pericles had supposedly urged courts to use against
offenders ([Lys.] 6.10) were in fact penally applied.

Demosthenes 22.27 lists procedures available in cases of impiety as
ἀπάγειν, γράφεσθαι, δικάζεσθαι πρὸς Εὐμολπίδας, φαίνειν πρὸς τόν
βασιλέα. Of a Eumolpid court empowered to hear all cases of impiety we
would surely hear more: this tribunal doubtless adjudicated on offences
against the Mysteries alone, and could perhaps only impose such penalties
as exclusion from the shrine (cf. J. H. Lipsius, *Das attische Recht und
Rechtsverfahren*, I, Leipzig 1905, 62, n. 34; 143, n. 31).

It is plausible on general grounds—but no more—that the hierophant's
female equivalent, the *hierophantis*,[36] was a Eumolpid.

Although it was eminently respectable to be a Eumolpid ([Dem.]
59.116), we know of only one member of the *genos* who was perhaps rich
enough to perform a liturgy,[37] and of none who was politically influential.
The interventions of Eumolpids in public life all concern religion, and usually the Eleusinian cult itself; in this respect, however, their role is notable.
It is true that it was by instruction of the state that the 'priests and priestesses' of Eleusis cursed the profaners of their Mysteries in 415 (and were

---

[34] Note, however, the possibility (which Jacoby, *Atthis*, 245, appears to favour) that the
'ancestral law', if genuine, was simply a now-outdated law of the state. But in that case, why
was 'exegesis' required?

[35] On this phrase see M. Ostwald in E. N. Lee, A. P. D. Mourelatos, and R. M. Rorty eds.,
Exegesis and Argument: Studies in Greek Philosophy Presented to Gregory Vlastos (*Phronesis*
Suppl. 1, 1973), 89–91.

[36] See Clinton, *Sacred Officials*, 86–89.

[37] Archias ([Dem.] 59.117); but the liturgies ascribed to him and his ancestors are left very
vague, and Davies, *Propertied Families*, does not include him. For his untimely political intervention see Ch. 10, n. 12. It has also been noted that one of Pericles' accusers, according to
Heraclides Ponticus (Plut. *Per.* 35.5), bears the same name as a fourth-cent. hierophant: see
LGPN II, s.v. *Lakrateides*, (2) and (4).

forced to uncurse Alcibiades in 411);[38] but it was of their own volition that the Eumolpids and *Kerykes* stood forth to oppose the recall of Alcibiades (Thuc. 8.53.2), to support therefore the claims of religion against a particular view of what was advantageous for the state, in a way virtually without parallel in Greek religious history. Certainly, we should not imagine the two families as a kind of priestly community—so far as we can judge, very few members of either even lived at Eleusis; but the unique sanctity and prestige of the cult that they served sucked them in, and gave them a unique sense of corporate devotion to the interests of the two awesome goddesses.[39] The unknown speaker of [Lysias] 6 was the great-grandson of a hierophant (54), and thus, unless the connection was maternal, a Eumolpid himself: the speech attacks Andocides, another profaner of the Mysteries, with fierce and narrow piety. We learn incidentally from the speech that the speaker's grandfather, certainly a Eumolpid, had once given advice to a court on how to proceed against 'a Megarian who had committed impiety' (54). (Was this a further instance of 'Eumolpid exegesis'?). It was even claimed that in the fourth century the hierophant Eurymedon played a part in the move to prosecute Aristotle for impiety (see Ch. 12, n. 90). This is why the Athenians so scrupulously consulted the Eumolpids or the hierophant on so many issues concerning the shrine. They were tradition and orthodoxy embodied.

Εὐνεῖδαι. Λυσίας ἐν τῷ κατὰ Τελαμῶνος, εἰ γνήσιος· γένος ἐστι παρ' Ἀθηναίοις οὕτως ὀνομαζόμενον. ἦσαν δὲ κιθαρῳδοὶ πρὸς τὰς ἱερουργίας παρέχοντες τὴν χρείαν (Harp. s.v. Εὐνεῖδαι). Later lexicographers (e.g. Hesych. ε 7007) add that the *genos* was named from Euneos son of Jason. Pollux 8. 103 in a list of four types of herald includes οἱ δὲ περὶ τὰς πομπὰς ἐκ τοῦ Εὐνειδῶν γένους. It was one of the *gene* that provided Pythaists for the *Pythaides* of 106/5 and 97/6 (*SIG*³ 711 D 1 37–40, 728 D 1). By the Roman period there were two priests of Dionysos Melpomenos, one ἐξ Εὐνειδῶν, one ἐκ τεχνειτῶν (*IG* II².5056, 5060). Since the *Euneidai* are thus associated with Dionysus, and could also according to Pollux act as heralds, Töpffer, 184, argues that the 'sacred herald' of [Dem.] 59.78, who administers an oath in connection with the sacred marriage of Dionysus, ought to be a Euneid (but Humphreys, 'Genos', thinks rather of one of the Eleusinian *Kerykes*).

Was a Euneid summoned whenever music was required at a public festival? It is more plausible that the lexicographers are over-general, and that the *genos* only participated at specified rites (possibly only those of Dionysos Melpomenos).

Their ancestor the Lemnian King Euneos, son of Jason and Hypsipyle,

---

[38] Plut. *Alc.* 22.5, 33.3; [Lys.] 6.51: the first and last of these passages speak of 'priests and priestesses', the second of Eumolpids (so too Nepos, *Alcibiades*, 6.5).

[39] Cf. Foucart, *Mystères d'Éleusis*, 224 f., with the qualifications of Clinton, *Sacred Officials*, 114 f. On residence see Clinton, *Sacred Officials*, 8: only one attested priest or priestess bears an Eleusinian demotic (about the ordinary members of the *gene* we have no evidence).

is already mentioned in Hom. *Il.* 7.468. He was a descendant, through his mother, of Dionysus, and according to Euripides in *Hypsipyle* (a play in which he is a character) was taught music by Orpheus (fr. 64 col. ii 98–101, p. 48 Bond). Dionysus appeared in the *exodos* of that play, and may have instructed Euneus to go to Athens to practise his musical art (Euripides, *Hypsipyle*, ed. G. W. Bond, Oxford 1963, 20). Cratinus wrote a *Euneidai*, but a fragment that has been thought to describe the *genos*, τέκτονες εὐπαλάμων ὕμνων (fr. 70 K/A), is ascribed to a different play of Cratinus, *Eumenides*, by the source which quotes it.[40]

Ζευξαντίδαι. γένος ἰθαγενῶν παρὰ Ἀθηναίοις (Hesych. ζ 126). An Athenian *genos* ending in -ντίδαι appears to have sent representatives to the *Pythais* of 106/5 (G. Daux, *Delphes au iiᵉ et au Iᵉʳ siècle*, Paris 1936, 551–54, correcting *SIG*³ 711 E): Ζευξαντίδαι and perhaps Ἀφειδαντίδαι (q.v., in sect. B) are the attested possibilities. Zeuxas is not found either as a mythological or historical Attic name.

Ἡσυχίδαι. γένος ἰθαγενῶν παρὰ Ἀθηναίοις (Hesych. η 921). The main source is Polemon *ap. Σ* Soph. *OC* 489, where the silence, ἡσυχία, that characterizes the rites of the Eumenides/Semnai is discussed and is said to be the reason why the Ἡσυχίδαι, ὃ δὴ γένος ἐστὶ περὶ τὰς σεμνὰς θεάς, lead the procession in honour of these goddesses. We are told that they make a preliminary sacrifice of a ram to Hesychos before the main sacrifice to the Semnai; we then, after a lacuna, hear of a 'shrine' (of Hesychos?) 'beside the Kyloneion [?] outside the nine gates', of a 'priestess' (?), and through a quotation of Callimachus fr. 681 Pfeiffer of a college of female Ἡσυχίδες who make wineless cake-offerings to the goddesses.

The obvious interpretation, that 'Hesychos' is a projection from the silence characteristic of the rite, has been challenged; it is none the less very likely to be correct (cf. Friedlaender in *RE* s.v. *Hesychos*).

This procession (of date unknown) to the shrine of the Semnai was apparently one of the most splendid of the year. *Hieropoioi* of high status were also recruited from outside the *genos* to serve the Semnai, probably on this occasion;[41] Philo insists that only free men and women of irreproachable life took part in the procession, and that the sacrificial cakes were prepared (presumably a later touch) by the most reputable (δοκιμώτατοι) among the ephebes (*Quod Omnis Probus Liber Sit*, 140; Deubner, *Attische Feste*, 214, n. 8). The participation of the ephebes is now confirmed by inscriptions of the late third (*SEG* XXVI 98.9) and second centuries

---

[40] The ascription is accepted by K/A, who vindicate the existence of this play against earlier doubts.

[41] Dem. 21.115, Dinarchus VIII fr. 2 Conomis *ap. Etym. Magn.* s.v. ἱεροποιοί, Photius s.v. ἱεροποιοί. Their number apparently varied (Wallace, *Areopagos Council*, 109, suggests that it increased in the Lycurgan period): Demosthenes speaks of three, Dinarchus of ten, Photius says they were τὸν ἀριθμὸν ἀόριστοι. The selection was made by the Areopagus because of its proximity to the shrine, according to *Σ* Dem. 21.115; the two known to us (from the sources just cited) were none other than Demosthenes and Lycurgus.

(*Hesperia* 15, 1946, 199, no. 40.16–17; 24, 1955, 228, line 26). It seems, therefore, unlikely that Polemon meant to say (cf. sect. B s.v. *Eupatridai*) that 'Eupatrids' were excluded from the festival as a whole, though they may well have been from some part of it. The great procession is doubtless evoked at the end of Aeschylus' *Eumenides*, though Aeschylus deliberately stresses the participation of the whole people and so neglects the specific role of the *genos*.

Θαυλωνίδαι. γένος ἰθαγενῶν Ἀθήνησιν (Hesych. θ 139). Cf. Hesych. β 998 s.v. βουτύπον· πυθμήν† Ἀθήνησι ἐκαλεῖτο, ἐκ τοῦ Θαυλωνιδῶν γένους καθιστάμενος.[42] There is an obvious connection with one version of the aetiological legend for the ritual of *Bouphonia* performed at the *Dipolieia*, according to which the original blow was struck by one Thaulon (first in Androtion *FGrH* 324 F 16). Problematic though the division of functions at the *Bouphonia* is (see sect. B s.v. Δαιτροί), there is no reason to doubt the existence of an autonomous *genos* of *Thaulonidai* who supplied this, the most important of all *boutupoi*. The post is probably distinct from that of Priest of Zeus Polieus, though the late evidence that we have is scarcely conclusive (contrast Töpffer, *Attische Genealogie*, 158, and Deubner, *Attische Feste*, 161 f.[+]; also Scherling in *RE* s.v. *Thaulon*).

Θεοινίδαι. Photius s.v. Θεοίνια· ἱερὸν Διονύσου· ἀφ' οὗ καὶ γένος. The existence of this *genos* had been doubted until they were securely identified by S. C. Humphreys in a decree from Athens, perhaps of the second century BC, praising a ἱέρεια τῆς νύμφης (probably—but cf. Kearns, *Heroes of Attica*, 67, n. 15[43]—the Νύμφη whose shrine has been uncovered on the south slope of the acropolis: Travlos, *Pictorial Dictionary*, 361–64): see *AJA* 100 (1979), 213–15. New light therefore falls on Harp. s.v. Θεοίνια· Λυκοῦργος ἐν τῇ διαδικασίᾳ Κροκωνιδῶν πρὸς Κοιρωνίδας· τὰ κατὰ δήμους Διονύσια Θεοίνια ἐλέγετο, ἐν οἷς οἱ γεννῆται ἐπέθυον· τὸν γὰρ Διόνυσον Θεοῖνον ἔλεγον . . . (On the little-known festival of *Theoinia*, wrongly identified by Harpocration with the *Rural Dionysia*, see Deubner, *Attische Feste*, 148.) It had hitherto been debated whether the γεννῆται were the members of all the *gene*, or the *Krokonidai* and *Koironidai* (see Bourriot, *Génos*, 1071–74); it now becomes natural to identify them as *Theoinidai*. Kearns, however (*Heroes of Attica*, 67, n. 15), cites Dionysius Scymnaeus, *TrGF* 208 F 1, μὰ τὰς Θεοίνου καὶ Κορωνίδας κόρας, in support of the association between *Theoinia* and the *Koironidai* (who, she speculatively suggests, in fact called themselves *Koronidai*, to stress the link with the Koronides Korai).[44] The γέραραι of [Dem.] 59.73, who prepare

---

[42] On the textual problem, which does not in fact affect the central connection between βουτύπος and Θαυλωνίδαι, see Deubner, *Attische Feste*, 161.

[43] And Humphreys, 'Genos', notes that on archaeological evidence the shrine may have been obsolete by the date of the decree.

[44] Note too her tentative suggestion that 'Theoinidai was a new name assumed by the Koironidai after the fracas of the *diadikasia*, in order to make their cultic affiliations and claims

the wife of the *basileus* for her marriage with Dionysus, ought also to be *Theoinidai* (Humphreys, 'Genos'), since they swear that they will 'celebrate the *Theoinia* according to tradition'.

Κεντριάδαι. Cf. sect. B s.v. *Δαιτροί*. Of the three '*gene*' named by Porphyry, the *Kentriadai* are the group most likely to have been a true *genos* (cf. Deubner, *Attische Feste*, 170). Though a specialized function in the ritual of the *Dipolieia* can possibly be detected in their name, the connection can only be indirect; for they are not simply 'prickers, spurrers' (as a cult functionary would be called), but 'descendants of Spurrer'. And they are independently described as 'a family of heralds' and 'among those concerned with the Mysteries/mysteries'.[45] Töpffer combined these last two notices to identify them as a subgroup of the 'Heralds concerned with the Mysteries', i.e. the *Kerykes*. But as it happens an inscription explicitly refers to the activity of heralds at the *Dipolieia*;[46] and a lexicographer could almost certainly have applied the term 'mysteries' to that festival (see Töpffer, 153). 'Heralds' could surely have performed the role of 'driving the cattle round the altar' that Porphyry ascribes to the *Kentriadai*. Probably, therefore, we should recognize in the *Kentriadai* a second *genos*, along with the *Thaulonidai*, entrusted with ritual duties at the great ancient festival.

Κεφαλίδαι. γένος Ἀθήνησιν (Hesych. κ 2396). They possibly had some association with the sanctuary of Apollo at Daphni, which had supposedly been founded by the descendants of Cephalus in the tenth generation (Paus. 1.37.6–7); Cephalus himself received cult at Thorikos (Kearns, *Heroes of Attica*, 70, 177). For the possibility that Cephalus' associations with western Greece and Odysseus (Aristotle fr. 504 Rose; Hellanicus *FGrH* 323a F 24) reflect a tradition of the *genos* see Humphreys, 'Genos'.

Κήρυκες. The *Kerykes* appear far earlier than any other *genos*, in a remarkable fragment attributed to Solon's *kurbeis*: ἐν δὲ τοῖς κύρβεσι τοῖς περὶ τῶν Δηλιαστῶν οὕτως γέγραπται· καὶ τὼ κήρυκε ἐκ τοῦ γένους τῶν Κηρύκων τοῦ τῆς μυστηριώτιδος· τούτους δὲ παρασιτεῖν ἐν τῷ Δηλίῳ ἐνιαυτόν (Athen. 234e–f = Solon fr. 88 Ruschenbusch). The *Kerykes* already therefore formed part of the personnel of Athenian public religion in the 590s (if the law is indeed Solonian); and they had a role in the cult of Apollo Delios as well as that of Demeter. The obscure last words of the phrase τοῦ γένους τῶν Κηρύκων τοῦ τῆς μυστηριώτιδος raise the further possibility that the lawgiver associated the name of the *genos* with a particular function, that of proclaiming the 'mystic truce' (σπονδή being idiomat-

---

still clearer'. Humphreys, 'Genos', similarly suggests that *Krokonidai* and *Koironidai* may have merged in the third cent. to form the *Theoinidai*.

[45] πατριὰ κηρύκων (Photius s.v. *Κεντριάδαι*); τῶν περὶ τὰ μυστήρια (Hesych. κ 2230). For πατριά = family in Phot. cf. (with Burkert, *Homo Necans*, 139, n. 17) id. s.v. Εὐμολπίδαι· πατριὰ Ἀθήνησιν.

[46] *IG* I³.241.17: cf. n. 91.

ically omitted after ἡ μυστηριῶτις;[47] the normal expression, however, was the plural, αἱ μυστηριώτιδες σπονδαί. A Δαιδôχος appears among the companions of Theseus on the François vase (A. Minto, *Il vaso François*, Florence 1960, 173).

But if the *Kerykes* were originally 'heralds of the sacred truce', they subsequently acquired new privileges and ceased to be closely associated with their eponymous function. (The later *spondophoroi*, a little-known body, were apparently recruited from both the great Eleusinian *gene*, not the *Kerykes* alone.[48]) In the classical period, they constantly acted in conjunction with the Eumolpids, as did the daduch (chosen from their number) with the Eumolpid hierophant. As a result, most of the relevant evidence has already been cited in the discussion of the Eumolpids. Items specific to the *Kerykes* are few (and fuller evidence might well provide Eumolpid parallels even for these few). A sacred law from the early fifth century possibly regulates their perquisites at Greater and Lesser Mysteries and at the *Stenia* (*LSS* 1 A; but note the much more cautious text of *IG* I³.231). They had an οἶκος at Eleusis (*IG* II².1672.24–25). They passed, of course, honorary decrees of their own (*IG* II².1230, *SEG* XIX 119). In the Roman period they flourished exceedingly (see e.g. W. Dittenberger, *Hermes* 20, 1885, 35–40; D. J. Geagan, *ZPE* 33, 1979, 93–115).

The daduch was selected from the *Kerykes*, by a process (not known in detail) that allowed particular families to dominate the office at particular periods.[49] Of his ritual duties other than those associated with the Mysteries themselves, the most remarkable was to urge the faithful to 'summon the god' at a festival of Dionysus, the *Lenaea*.[50] We also hear that the daduch used the 'fleece of Zeus' in certain purifications (perhaps associated with the Mysteries), and that in the second century he attended the *Thargelia* in Athens with the hierophant (Suda s.v. Διὸς κώδιον, cf. Parker, *Miasma*, 284–85; *LSS* 14.36).

The 'Herald of the Initiates' and the 'Altar-priest' were also *Kerykes*; and by the Roman period the *genos* was also filling a spectacular series of lesser posts, some associated with the cult at Eleusis and some (such as 'Herald of Pythian Apollo') independent. By the late second century BC they were also furnishing Pythaists.[51] How much ancient tradition there is

[47] Cf. C. A. Lobeck, *Aglaophamus* (Regimontii Prussorum, 1829), 213, note n.

[48] *IG* II².1236.14 (second cent.): τοῖς γένε]σιν ἐξ ὧν οἱ σπονδοφόροι ἐκπέμπονται (apparently the Eumolpids and *Kerykes*); a hierophant's services to the *spondophoroi* are also praised in *IG* II².1235 (third cent.), a joint decree of the two *gene*. It is of course possible that a Eumolpid had always accompanied the *Kerykes*, as a symbol of the sacred promise.

[49] See Clinton, *Sacred Officials*, 67 (cf. W. Geominy, 'Eleusinische Priester', H.-U. Cain, H. Gabelmann, and D. Salzmann eds., *Festschrift für Nikolaus Himmelmann*, Mainz 1989, 253–64, at 257–59); cf. Ferguson, 'Salaminioi', 52–53; Bourriot, *Génos*, 1342, n. 593; and s.v. *Eteoboutadai* above, n. 21.

[50] Σ Ar. *Ran.* 479; for the role of the *Epimeletai* of the Mysteries at the *Lenaea* see Arist. *Ath. Pol.* 57.1 and Pickard-Cambridge, *Dramatic Festivals*², 27.

[51] The key text for all these lesser priesthoods is the decree of 20/19 BC honouring the daduch Themistocles, most recently ed. by Clinton, *Sacred Officials*, 50–52; they are discussed by P. Roussel in *Mélanges Bidez* (Brussels 1934), 822–37. Pythaists: *SIG*³ 711 D¹ 32; 728 D¹; 773.7. Herald of Pythian Apollo: first attested as a post of the *genos* in *Delph* 3(2) 110.

in all this is uncertain; but as we saw they are found active outside Eleusis, dining in the temple of Apollo Delios, in the first allusion to them, in Solon.

In contrast to the Eumolpids, the *Kerykes* numbered among them one family of outstanding wealth and power. Revealingly, at least two members of it were accordingly chosen as daduch: Kallias 'Lakkoploutos', 'richest of all Athenians', general, ambassador; and his grandson of the same name, general, ambassador, playboy, and patron of the most advanced thinkers of his day.[52] This luxurious friend of Protagoras and Socrates is a striking figure to find holding high Eleusinian office; and though he was involved in the prosecution of the impious Andocides, religious outrage scarcely seems to have been his motive (Andoc. *Myst.* 117–23). (On the possibility that Andocides was himself a *Keryx* see n. 23 above.) But Xenophon shows him duly deploying Eleusinian themes when sent in his old age as ambassador to Sparta (*Hell.* 6.3.3–6). A less unusual representative of orthodox piety perhaps was the later daduch Pythodorus, who stood out courageously if vainly against the proposal to allow Demetrius Poliorcetes to pass through all three stages of initiation in a single day (Plut. *Dem.* 26.3).

Κηφισιεῖς. γένος ἰθαγενῶν (Hesych. κ 2580).

Κοιρωνίδαι. Cf. s.v. Κροκωνίδαι.

Κολλίδαι. γένος ἰθαγενῶν (Hesych. κ 3338). Wilamowitz wondered whether they might be associated with the deme Kollytos (*Kleine Schriften*, V, pt. 1 (Berlin 1937), 291 n. 1); he also (*Aristoteles und Athen*, Berlin 1893, II.183–84) tentatively identified Κολλυτίδες Ἀρχενείδες in *IG* I³.779 (early fifth cent.) as a *gennete*, rather than the bearer of a demotic of primitive quasi-patronymic form (cf. Whitehead, *Demes*, 74, n. 63). Neither suggestion is compelling.

Κονεῖδαι (Töpffer: MSS Κονείδη). γένος ἰθαγενῶν (Hesych. κ 3504). Κονείδης or Κοννίδας was the παιδαγωγός of Theseus, and received the offering of a ram on the day before the *Theseia* (Plut. *Thes.* 4, cf. Hesych. κ 3505 s.v. Κονείδης; Kearns, *Heroes of Attica*, 120, 178).

Κροκωνίδαι and Κοιρωνίδαι. Anecd. Bekk. I.273.7 ff. s.v. Κοιρωνίδαι· γένος Ἀθήνησιν, ἀπὸ Κοίρωνος, ὃς ἦν ἀδελφὸς Κρόκωνος. καὶ Κροκωνίδαι γένος ἱερὸν Ἀθήνησιν. ἀμφότεροι δὲ ἦσαν παῖδες Τριπτολέμου. Most of our knowledge of these *gene* is owed to the chance that they engaged in a famous law-suit in the fourth century: Harp. s.v. Κοιρωνίδαι· ἔστι Λυκούργῳ λόγος οὕτως ἐπιγραφόμενος "Κροκωνιδῶν διαδικασία πρὸς Κοιρωνίδας", ὃν ἔνιοι Φιλίνου νομίζουσιν. ἔστι δὲ γένος οἱ Κοιρωνίδαι, περὶ ὧν Ἴστρος ἐν τῇ Συναγωγῇ τῆς Ἀτθίδος [*FGrH* 334 F 15] φησίν· ὠνομασμένον δ' ἂν

59.6 (= *SIG*³ 773: early Augustan), but the post already existed in the earlier *Pythaides* and probably already belonged to the *genos*.

[52] For details see Davies, *Propertied Families*, 254 ff.; Clinton, *Sacred Officials*, 47–50.

εἴη ἀπὸ Κοίρωνος, ὃν νόθον ἀδελφὸν εἶναί φασι τοῦ Κρόκωνος, παρ' ὃ καὶ ἐντιμοτέρους εἶναι τοὺς Κροκωνίδας τῶν Κοιρωνιδῶν. ὁ δὲ τὸν λόγον γεγραφώς, ὅστις πότ' ἐστιν, τρισὶν ὀνόμασί φησιν αὐτοὺς προσηγορεῦσθαι· καὶ γὰρ Κοιρωνίδας καὶ Φιλιεῖς καὶ Περιθοίδας. A speech of the same title attributed to Dinarchus was perhaps delivered on the other side.[53] Very probably Lycurgus' speech bore the alternative title περὶ τῆς ἱερωσύνης, which will indicate the point at issue (see Lycurgus VII. 1a and 1b Conomis, with the editor's references). A wide range of religious occasions and offices were mentioned in the two speeches (the festivals *Procharisteria* and *Theoinia*; the *genos Kunnidai*; the post of οἰνόπτης; the hierophant), but we do not know their relevance to the dispute between the two *gene*. Of the two alternative names that the *genos* supposedly bore (it is not clear whether a tendentious orator or a confused lexicographer is the source) Peirithoidai was in fact a deme; Töpffer suggests that Philieis may have been a phratry.

A report about the hero found in Paus. 1.38.1–2 is very likely to derive ultimately from speeches associated with the court-case, since we happen to know that Lycurgus mentioned the same deme Skambonidai (Harp. s.v. Σκαμβωνίδαι) to which Pausanias also refers: καὶ διαβᾶσι τοὺς Ῥειτοὺς [on the way from Athens to Eleusis] πρῶτος ᾤκει Κρόκων, ἔνθα καὶ νῦν ἔτι βασίλεια καλεῖται Κρόκωνος. τοῦτον Ἀθηναῖοι τὸν Κρόκωνα Κελεοῦ θυγατρὶ συνοικῆσαι Σαισάρᾳ λέγουσι. λέγουσι δὲ οὐ πάντες, ἀλλ' ὅσοι τοῦ δήμου τοῦ Σκαμβωνιδῶν εἰσιν. ἐγὼ δὲ Κρόκωνος μὲν ἀνευρεῖν τάφον οὐχ οἷός τε ἐγενόμην . . . This report raises genealogical difficulties (since according to the standard tradition Saisara would be Krokon's aunt), one way of resolving which is to suppose that it asssumes a Krokon who is not a son of Triptolemus (cf. Jacoby on Istrus *FGrH* 334 F 15, n. 2). On that view we can reconstruct claim and counter-claim of the two *gene* (so Kearns, *Heroes of Attica*, 67[54]): the *Krokonidai* declare the archegete of the *Koironidai* illegitimate, and perhaps question whether the *genos* is anyway correctly so named (Harp., cited above); the *Koironidai* declare Krokon's association with the cult to be by marriage only. See further s.v. *Theoinidai*.

Anecd. Bekk. 1.273.25–27 (and Photius) have the entry: κροκοῦν· οἱ μύσται κρόκῃ καταδοῦνται τὴν δεξιὰν χεῖρα καὶ τὸν ἀριστερὸν πόδα, καὶ τοῦτο λέγεται κροκοῦν (Phot. adds οἱ δὲ, ὅτι ἐνίοτε κρόκῳ καθαίρονται). Töpffer's suggestion is very attractive (though no ancient source makes the connection) that it was from this ritual activity, performed by his descendants, that Krokon derived his name.

[53] Blass's objection, *Die Attische Beredsamkeit* III, pt. 2² (Leipzig 1898), 299 f., that in that event the title should have been Κοιρωνιδῶν διαδικασία κτλ. is scarcely compelling. The *testimonia* (not present in Conomis' edn. of Dinarchus, no. XXa, p. 106) are Harp. s.v. ἐξούλης and ἱεροφάντης. From the latter we learn that the hierophant was mentioned; but this is not ground enough to identify the speech with the διαδικασία τῆς ἱερείας τῆς Δήμητρος (a Philleid) πρὸς τὸν ἱεροφάντην (a Eumolpid) = no. XXXV Conomis.

[54] But I am less certain than she is that the tradition recorded in Pausanias is 'designed to demote Krokon'.

In a fourth-century decree, the *genos* praises the members of a commission that it had appointed to build a shrine of Hestia (*IG* II².1229). Possibly some connection existed between the *genos'* cult of Hestia and the role of the hearth in broader Eleusinian cult and myth (cf. Richardson, *Hymn to Demeter*, 233); but Töpffer's suggestion that the παῖς ἀφ᾽ ἑστίας of the Eleusinian cult was a Krokonid is wrong, as several inscriptions show beyond question (see Clinton, *Sacred Officials*, 113).

Κυννίδαι. γένος Ἀθήνησιν, ἐξ οὗ ὁ ἱερεὺς τοῦ Κυννείου Ἀπόλλωνος (Hesych. κ 4592, cf. Harp. s.v. Κυνίδαι = Lycurgus VII.4 Conomis, Suda κ 2707 Κυννίδαι); cf. *Anecd. Bekk.* I.274.16 (= *Etym. Magn.* 545.51–52) Κυννίδαι· γένος ἱερὸν Ἀθήνησιν, ἀπὸ Κύννου ἢ Κυννίδου ἥρωος. Cf. Suda κ 2706 (= Phot. s.v. Κύνειος): Κυννήειος· Ἀπόλλων Ἀθήνησιν οὕτως λεγόμενος, ὃν ἱδρύσατο Κύννις (Κύνης Phot.), Ἀπόλλωνος καὶ Παρνηθίας νύμφης, ὡς Σωκράτης ἔν ιβ'· θεμένης τῆς Λητοῦς τὰ βρέφη ὑπὸ κυνῶν ἁρπασθῆναι. τοῦ κνυζηθμοῦ γὰρ αἰσθομένους κύνας καὶ ποιμένας ἀνασῶσαι τῇ μητρί. ὀνομασθῆναι οὖν ἐν Ὑμηττῷ ἀπὸ τῶν κυνῶν. Κράτης ἐν τῷ περὶ τῶν Ἀθήνησι θυσιῶν οὕτω γράφει· τὸ δὲ Κυνήειόν ἐστιν Ἀπόλλωνος Κυνηείου, τὸ ἐκ τοῦ θυννείου γινόμενον. τοῦτο δέ ἐστι τὸ θυννεῖον ἀλήσιον (Ἀλῆσι Photius). καὶ γίνεται πρόσοδος μεγάλη. ταύτην ἡ πόλις εἰς θυσίαν καταχωρίζει τῷ Ἀπόλλωνι τῷ Κυννείῳ Ἀλῆσι, οὗ Δημήτριος ὁ βασιλεύς (text as printed in Adler's Suda; for the authors cited see Tresp, *Kultschriftsteller*, 63, 212).

This very corrupt entry obviously combines two quite distinct explanations of the epithet. The localization of the cult on Hymettus implied by the first (unless indeed the phrase is corrupt) can perhaps be reconciled with the second, as Töpffer suggests,[55] if we take Halai as Halai Aixonides, a coastal deme close to the southernmost outcrop of the mountain; a legend about Leto and the birth of Apollo also attached to nearby Cape Zoster. But Crates' derivation of Κύννειος from θυννεῖον is of course fantastic, and it would surely be a strange coincidence if the fact that supposedly underlies it, the financing of a sacrifice to Apollo Kunneios from tunny-revenue, were authentic.

There is no more Attic evidence about the *genos* or the god. But the cult of Apollo Kunneios is attested in Corinth (*IG* IV.363) and at Temnos in Asia Minor (Poly. 32.15.12; L. Robert, *Études anatoliennes*, Paris 1937, 90–91).

Κωλιεῖς. γένος ἰθαγενῶν, ὅπερ ἦν ἐκ Κωλιάδος (Hesych. κ 4817). A fourth-century [hορ]ός [χ]ωρίο [Κ]ωλιέων (provenance unknown) has been found (A. E. Raubitschek, *Phoros Meritt*, New York 1974, 137–38), and they appear in a fragmentary context in a sales-tax record in connection with property at Phaleron (?: *IG* II².1598.23–24). They may have supplied the priestess (*IG* II².5119) in the famous cult of Aphrodite Kolias (Ar. *Nub.*

---

[55] But his attempt to refer the tunny-sacrifice (to Poseidon) mentioned by Antigonos of Karystos *ap.* Athen. 297 to Halai is misguided, as 88a shows.

52, *Lys.* 2 with *Σ*; Paus. 1.1.5; etc.) at Cape Kolias. *Κωλιάς* had also been a naukrary (Phot. s.v. *Κωλιάς*; *Anecd. Bekk.* 1.275.21). (There were also *Κολιάδαι* or *Κωλιάδαι* on Aegina, *IG* IV.6 = *Schwyzer* 112, who has the correct interpretation.)

Λυκομίδαι. γένος ἰθαγενῶν (Hesych. *λ* 1391). They controlled the Mystery-Cult at Phlya. Our most important information about them comes, unfortunately, from late sources. Plutarch records that *ὅτι μέντοι τοῦ Λυκομιδῶν γένους μετεῖχε [ὁ Θεμιστοκλῆς] δῆλόν ἐστι· τὸ γὰρ Φλυῆσι τελεστήριον, ὅπερ ἦν Λυκομιδῶν κοινόν, ἐμπρησθὲν ὑπὸ τῶν βαρβαρῶν αὐτὸς ἐπεσκεύασε καὶ γραφαῖς ἐκόσμησεν, ὡς Σιμωνίδης ἱστόρηκεν* (Plut. *Them.* 1.4). Pausanias adds that they sung 'the hymns of Orpheus' and, it seems, Pampho in accompaniment to their rites, and that the only genuine work of Musaeus was that to Demeter written for them (9.27.2, 30.12; 1.22.7, cf. 4.1.5, where we learn that Musaeus' *Hymn* described Phlyos as an autochthon).[56] There was also a shrine at Phlya of Apollo Daphnephoros, at which the trierarch Lycomedes son of Aischraios, doubtless to judge from his name a member of the *genos*, made a famous dedication of spoils from Salamis (Plut. *Them.* 15.3); but it does not certainly follow that the *Lycomidai* controlled that too. Members of this Lycomedes' family remained prominent in public life down to the end of the fifth century (Davies, *Propertied Families*, 346–47).

The only testimonium from the classical period is the mortgage stone *IG* II².2670, which merely confirms that the group existed and had associations with Phlya. The *genos* flourished under the Roman empire (see *IG* II².3559, a joint honorary dedication of Lycomids and Eumolpids), and it is very likely that the Mystery-cult and its mythology were extensively reshaped in the Hellenistic or Roman period. The ensemble that Pausanias records at Phlya of ten altars, in two temples, dedicated to gods bearing recherché epithets sounds post-classical,[57] and the presence in the shrine of an image, bearing a tendentious inscription, of the mysterious founder and reformer of mysteries Methapos[58] (perhaps supposed to be a figure of the mythological period—but the inscription certainly postdates 370 and is probably much more recent) is a further reason for suspicion (Paus. 4.1.5–9). There is little hope, therefore, of penetrating back to the Mysteries in their early shape (and one may even feel some suspicion about the supposed association of the glamorous Themistocles with the *genos*[59]).

---

[56] On the cult see too Hippol. *Haer.* 5.20.4 (= Orph. fr. 243 Kern), with M. J. Edwards, *ZPE* 88 (1991), 30–33.

[57] 1.31.4, cf. Nilsson, *Geschichte*, 669. This complex was doubtless the centre of the Mystery-cult, though Pausanias does not say so explicitly.

[58] See e.g. Kern in *RE* s.v. *Methapos*.

[59] This is not, however, to endorse the attempt of Bourriot, *Génos*, 1260–63, to deny that for Plutarch (*Them.* 1.4) Themistocles was a member of the *genos*. A less pessimistic view about the possibility of reconstructing the cult has been taken by I. Loukas in several writings, most recently 'Meaning and Place of the Cult Scene on the Ferrara Krater T 128', in R. Hägg ed., *The Iconography of Greek Cult in the Archaic and Classical Periods* (Athens 1992), 73–83.

Μεσόγειοι. The *Mesogeioi* are a cult association known from three decrees of the late fourth (?) and third centuries (*IG* II².1244–45, 1247). Their centre was a Herakleion, not further identified in their certain documents; a further decree which has been associated with them mentions the 'Herakleion in the *kyklos* at Cholargi' (*IG* II².1248), but as there is no independent ground for ascribing this text to them it is a *petitio principii* to identify the two Herakleia. Their main festival was a ἑορτή of Heracles which comprised a sacrifice (for which 'ox-purchase' had been necessary), a procession, 'distribution of meat', ἐπικόσμησις τραπέζης, and some use of wine. A priest of Heracles and a priest of Diomos who are praised by the Mesogeians for their role in the festival are likely to have been members of the association; and we also hear in the same context of *mnemones*, a *purphoros*, a *koragogos* and an 'ancestral herald'. The most important official, however, was the annual 'archon of the *Mesogeioi*', who was chiefly responsible for organizing the festival and also performed further 'traditional' sacrifices (unspecified both as to content and occasion) to 'gods and heroes'. The association also had a *tamias*, who doubtless administered the 'revenue from the god's property' (*IG* II².1247. 30); this property perhaps included an *agora* (1245.8).

R. Schlaifer pointed out that the *Mesogeioi* have no point of contact with the Mesogeia apart from their name (*CP* 39, 1944, 22–27; cf. S. Dow and D. H. Gill, *AJA* 69, 1965, 103–14). He suggested, therefore, that they were not, as had been thought, a local association, but a *genos*: the attested members are of high social standing, the officials find parallels in other *gene*, and, above all, the only restoration that respects the στοιχηδόν in *IG* II².1244.7—unless we postulate the rare exception of an iota not allowed its own space—is γένει (or the implausible οἴκωι), not κοινῶι. We can add the point that the Mesogeians' festival of Heracles sounds quite elaborate enough to be a minor public rite; honours were even proclaimed at the festival (*IG* II².1247.13), surely not merely to the assembled Mesogeians. Perhaps they administered the attested festival *Herakleia at Diomeia* (Ar. *Ran.* 651), as the role at their rite of the 'priest of Diomos' might suggest. (On Diomos see Kearns, *Heroes of Attica*, 156.) Diomeia is an unlocated city-deme (if we reject the, as it seems, unfounded identification of its Herakleion with that at Kynosarges[60]), and could well have encompassed the region a little west of the modern National Archaeological Museum (see *AJA* 65, 1965, 110) where two of the Mesogeians' decrees were found.

It is, however, a not negligible difficulty that the daughter of Polyeuktos, archon of the Mesogeians in 275/4, was a priestess of Athena Polias (see Davies, *Propertied Families*, 171 f.); thus he himself according to traditional rules was an Eteoboutad. Perhaps, Schlaifer suggests, those irregularities in the transmission of priesthoods and/or membership of *gene* certainly observable in the late second century had already begun in the

---

[60] See my note in H. D. Jocelyn ed., *Tria Lustra* (Liverpool 1993), 25–27. The earliest decree (*IG* II².1244) of the *Mesogeioi*, however, was found at Kamatero, i.e. towards Acharnae, and Humphreys, 'Genos', wonders whether the group (which she regards as of recent origin) moved thence to the city in the third cent.

third (cf. s.v. *Eteoboutadai* above); or perhaps the *Mesogeioi* were a branch of the Eteoboutads. The question must remain open.

Παμφίδαι. Inferred from Hesych. π 287 s.v. Παμφίδες· γυναῖκες Ἀθήνησιν ἀπὸ Πάμφου τὸ γένος ἔχουσαι. Cf. the Ἡσυχίδες recruited from the *genos* Ἡσυχίδαι (above).

Πάροικοι. γένος τι Ἀθήνησιν (Hesych. π 935, between παρικτόν and παριλλαίνουσα).

Ποιμενίδαι. γένος ἐξ οὗ ὁ τῆς Δήμητρος ἱερεύς (Hesych. π 2725). The cult of Demeter here mentioned is quite unidentifiable. No relevant mythological Poimen is known.

Πραξιεργίδαι. οἱ τὸ ἕδος τὸ ἀρχαῖον τῆς Ἀθηνᾶς ἀμφιεννύντες (Hesych. π 3205). No hero Praxiergos is known, but the name was borne by the *archon* of 471/0. Hesychius refers to the festivals of *Plynteria* and *Kallynteria*, as we see, for instance, from Plut. *Alc.* 34.1: δρῶσι δὲ τὰ ὄργια [the *Plynteria*] Πραξιεργίδαι . . . ἀπόρρητα τόν τε κόσμον καθελόντες καὶ τὸ ἕδος κατακαλύψαντες. In the fifth century, the Praxiergids sought and obtained permission from the people to inscribe an oracle concerning them, and their *patria*, on a *stele* on the acropolis (*IG* I³.7, *LSCG* 15). The oracle refers both to their (presumably) traditional task of 'putting on the *peplos*' and also to certain sacrifices; if the approach to Delphi was recent and provided the occasion for the *genos*' request to the people, the enquiry presumably concerned the sacrifices. The fragments of the *patria* relate to ritual perquisites and duties. The *genos* reappears epigraphically, not very revealingly, in the third century BC and again in the second/third century AD (*IG* II².776.18–20; 3678); the earlier text mentions a θυσία πάτριος (doubtless at the *Plynteria*), and both show the *genos* in close association with the priestess of Athena Polias.

The Praxiergids surely provided the Λουτρίδες· δύο κόραι περὶ τὸ ἕδος τῆς Ἀθηνᾶς· ἐκαλοῦντο δὲ καὶ πλυντρίδες· οὕτως Ἀριστοφάνης (Hesych., Phot. s.v. Λουτρίδες), who were obviously active at the *Plynteria*, and perhaps too the Κατανίπτης· ἱερωσύνη Ἀθήνησιν· ὁ τὰ κάτω τοῦ πέπλου τῆς Ἀθηνᾶς ῥυπαινόμενα ἀποπλύνων (*Etym. Magn.* 494.25, cf. *Anecd. Bekk.* I.269.29).[61] There was a procession at the festival, which is probably to be identified with that at which ephebes 'escorted Pallas to the sea and back' μετὰ τῶν γεννητῶν (sc. the Praxiergids).[62] A case has, however, been made for associating this 'Pallas' not with the image of Athena Polias but with the Palladion, which was supposedly washed in the sea by King Demophon before being finally established in its shrine;[63] in that event, the γεννῆται in

---

[61] But if this was a permanent post, as Ziehen suggests (*RE* s.v. *Plynteria*, 1062), rather than a function associated with the *Plynteria*, there is less reason to connect it with the *genos*.

[62] *IG* II².1011.11; for further allusions cf. Pélékidis, *Éphébie*, 251.

[63] By W. Burkert, *Zeitschr. f. Religions- und Geistesgeschichte* 22 (1970), 356–68 (accepted in Parker, *Miasma*, 27 and P. Brulé, *La fille d'Athènes*, Paris 1987, 105–106). Burkert

question would be *Bouzygai* (q.v.). The procession was organized, at least in the early Hellenistic period, by the Νομοφύλακες (Philochorus *FGrH* 328 F 64b),[64] a board of magistrates who had nothing to do with either *genos*.

The *Plynteria* are associated aetiologically with Aglauros daughter of Cecrops (Hesych. s.v. Πλυντήρια; *Anecd. Bekk.* I.270.3–5), and one might therefore expect the *genos* to supply Aglauros' priestess; but see s.v. *Salaminioi* for the possibility that she was in fact a Salaminian (q.v.).

A number of Praxiergids (from three different demes) appear in an obscure context in a dedication to Heracles by Τιμόθεος Τεισίου of the mid-fourth century (*Hesperia* 7, 1938, 92, no. 12: cf. *LGPN* II, *Teisias* [19]), if [τῶν Πρα]ξιεργιδῶν is correctly read on a very worn stone.

Πυρρακίδαι. They are first known from two small circular religious monuments, with entrances, found on Delos; one is inscribed Τριτοπάτωρ Πυρρακιδῶν Αἰγιλιῶν (presumably 'of Aigilia', an Attic deme), the other Νύμφαι Πυρρακιδῶν (*Inscr. Dél.* 66–67). P. Roussel dates both monuments to *c.*400 (*BCH* 53, 1929, 167–79: not in fact a time of Attic control of the island). Without further evidence we might assume the *Pyrrhakidai* to be native Delians (particularly as they still had property on the island in the second century BC, *Inscr. Dél.* 1416 B 1 57). But they reappear in the late second century BC, amid known Attic *gene* (*Kerykes*, *Euneidai*, and interestingly *Erysichthonidai*), sending Pythaists to Delphi (*SIG*³ 696 A, 697 B, 711 D¹ 30, 728 C). Humphrey, 'Genos', wonders whether they moved to Athens only in the second century BC (Αἰγιλιῶν being therefore a late addition to their early monument). The hero is known only from Hesych. s.v. Πύρρακος· ἥρως κατ' Ἐρυσίχθονα γεγονώς, where it is interesting to find him associated with the eponym of another *genos* that had strong Delian connections. For a full discussion see Bourriot, *Génos*, 1161–71.

Σαλαμίνιοι. The *Salaminioi* are the Attic *genos* of whose affairs we know most, by a large margin; and yet they nowhere appear in the literary record. Our information comes from three inscriptions: an honorary decree perhaps of the late fourth century (*IG* II².1232: cf. *Hesperia* 7, 1938, 62), and

attempted to show, from chronology and nomenclature, that the rite attended by the ephebes was demonstrably not the *Plynteria*. But the negative argument fails, as B. Nagy, *Historia* 40 (1991), 288–306 and M. Christopoulos, *Kernos* 5 (1992), 36–38, have shown; and the case for a procession associated with the Palladion rests merely on the story that the image was washed by Demophon (Σ Patm. Dem. 23.71, cited by Burkert, *Zeitschr. f. Religions- und Geistesgeschichte* 22 (1970), 364, n. 31). The similarities between the disputed rite and the *Plynteria* are so great—both involved a procession, manipulation of an image of Athena, and an active role for *gennetai*—that it seems easiest to identify the two. (For a third, but topographically implausible, suggestion see Nagy, *Historia* 40, 1991; his argument that the ephebes could not have been involved in a gloomy, secret rite such as the *Plynteria* underestimates the extent to which mixture of mood often characterizes Greek ritual.)

[64] Most moderns date the institution of this board (against the ancient evidence, which speaks of Ephialtes) to the last quarter of the fourth cent.: see e.g. Rhodes, *Commentary Ath. Pol.*, 315.

the record of two arbitrations between the two branches into which, as it appears, the *genos* was divided, the 'Salaminians ἀπὸ (τῶν) ἑπτὰ φυλῶν' and 'the Salaminians from Sunium'. The report of the first arbitration (*Hesperia* 7, 1938, 3–5, no. 1: = *LSS* 19 [+], *SEG* XXI 527, *Agora* XIX L4*a*), which occurred in 363/2 BC, covers ninety-eight lines and is our major source (it is cited in what follows by line-number alone); the second, from the year of the archon Phanomachos (? 265/4), is a briefer text concerned with the division of property at or near Sunium, and is chiefly of interest in showing a development in terminology—the arbitrators refer to the two branches as two distinct *gene*, and both are frequently identified not just as Σαλαμίνιοι but as Ἀρχαιοσαλαμίνιοι (*Hesperia* 7, 1938, 9–10, no. 2 = *Agora* XIX L4*b*; for the reading Ἀρχαιοσαλαμίνιοι see G. Daux, *REG* 34, 1941, 220–22).

From the honorary decree we learn that the Salaminians displayed decrees in the temple of Athena Skiras and in the 'Eurysakeion'; that they had *hieromnemones*; and that they were rich enough to award a gold crown worth 1,000 drachmas. The great arbitration (for a full translation of which see Ferguson, 'Salaminioi', 5–8) covers the following topics:

1. (8–16) *Priesthoods.* Four priesthoods, those of Athena Skiras, Heracles at Porthmos, Eurysakes, and probably one joint priesthood of Aglauros, Pandrosos, and Kourotrophos[65] are to be common to the two groups for ever; a new priest or priestess is to be appointed by lot from the two groups when an incumbent dies.

2. (16–19) *Property.* The shared property (land at the Herakleion at Porthmos [cf. 93], a salt-flat, an *agora* 'at Koile') is to be divided between the two branches.

3. (19–27) *Financing and division of sacrifices.* The meat of sacrifices paid for by the state or 'received by the Salaminians from the *oschophoroi* and *deiphnophoroi*' is to be equally shared between the two branches; the cost of sacrifices paid for by the Salaminians from rent (of the property in 2) is to be divided equally.

4. (27–41) *Priestly dues.* The perquisites and fees due to the priests of Heracles and Eurysakes (which are specified) are to be paid equally by the two branches.

5. (41–52) *Arrangements concerning the cult of Athena Skiras and the festival of* Oschophoria. After removal of the traditional number, the 'loaves in the shrine of Skiras' are to be distributed among the priests, priestesses, other officiants, and the two sections of the *genos*; and an *archon*, who will in turn appoint the *oschophoroi* and *deipnophoroi*, is to be chosen by lot alternately from the two halves.[66]

6. (52–65) *Miscellaneous provisions.* The priest of Eurysakes is also to serve 'the hero at the salt-flat'. Joint rights and duties of the two groups in

---

[65] 11–12 implies a single priestess serving all three figures; in 45–46 Kourotrophos is separated from the other two, but what appears on the stone is bizarre Greek and odd sense, and has probably been misinscribed.

[66] Jacoby's suggestion that ἄρχοντα in 47 is subject rather than object of the verb (n. 2 to comm. on Philochorus *FGrH* 328 F 14–16) founders *inter alia* on the absence of the article.

relation to repairs, records, the leased land, and 'the preparatory sacrifice for the competition' are confirmed. Thrasykles is to continue as sacred herald.

7. (80–95) *Sacrificial Calendar*. On the proposal of Archeleos, the sacrificial calendar of the *genos* and the priestly dues are recorded, so that the sums to be expended for sacrifices from the rent of the leased land shall be clearly known.

We learn incidentally that the *Salaminioi* had two annually appointed *archontes*, one drawn from each branch (69–70, 74, ? 82; as we have seen, they also seem to have appointed a separate *archon* to organize the *Oschophoria*, 47–57).

The second arbitration regulates the rights of the two *gene*, as they are now described, to the *temenos* of Heracles at Porthmos near Sunium and its surroundings: we hear of a threshing-floor (to be duplicated), gardens, a well, fields (presumably the substantial area mentioned as leased out in the earlier arbitration), and a ἱερὰ ἄρουρα; and also of the salt-flat and *agora* known from the earlier text.[67]

From these documents, the Salaminians emerge as, above all, a religious association, concerned with priesthoods and cults. Though they own a substantial property at Sunium, no use for the revenue from it is mentioned except to meet the expenses of the cult, about 530 drachmas a year.[68] The only immediate secular advantages that Salaminians gain from membership of their *genos* are, perhaps, the right to use such amenities as the salt-flat and the threshing-floor and the *agora*.[69] Their religious calendar, by contrast, is unexpectedly ample. Twenty-three sacrifices financed from Salaminian funds are listed, probably occurring on eight separate days during the year and at at least four different sites, at a total cost of 530½ drachmas. These self-financed festivities must primarily have concerned the Salaminians themselves (even if some of them occurred on the occasion of public rites).

It is, however, equally clear that the Salaminians were involved in various ways with the cults of the city. Most obviously, they administered the public festival of *Oschophoria*, celebrated at one of their own centres, the temple of Athena Skiras at Phaleron; and given that the male *oschophoroi* and female *deipnophoroi* who had a role of honour at the festival were appointed by a Salaminian (47–50), it is very probable that these and other officiants (the 'basket-bearer' and the [?] millers, 46) were drawn from the

---

[67] For proposed identifications of the Herakleion, the salt-flat, and now the *agora* in the Boundazeza and Limani Pasa regions up the coast a few miles north of cape Sunium, see J. H. Young, *Hesperia* 10 (1941), 163–91; E. Ch. Kakavoyiannis, *ArchDelt* 32, 1977 [1982]/*Mel.*, 206–207; on the newly discovered *agora*, about 80×60 m. in size, see M. Salliora-Oikonomakou, *ArchDelt* 34, 1979 [1986]/*Mel.* 161–73; Travlos, *Bildlexikon*, 406, 426–29.

[68] Cf. Ferguson, 'Salaminioi', 35. We know that they also spent money on repairing shrines, inscribing decrees and (*IG* II².1232) honouring their members.

[69] The questions of what these utilities were used for or were worth, and of what kind of group would have owned them, have never been discussed. The newly discovered *agora* (see n. 67 above) which has been tentatively identified with the Salaminians' is unexpectedly grandiose.

genos itself.[70] At their otherwise unknown festival, the *Herakleia* at
Porthmos, animals were contributed both by the *genos* and by the city (87);
doubtless, therefore, non-Salaminians also attended.

Their priests and priestesses too all served cults that were in some sense
public. The shrine of Eurysakes at Melite (the *genos'* second centre) was
also the place of display for decrees of the tribe of Eurysakes' father Ajax
(*Hesperia* 7, 1938, 94–95 no. 15).[71] We have just seen that the city contributed victims to the festival of Heracles at Porthmos. Athena Skiras was,
of course, through the *Oschophoria* a public goddess. The case of the
'priestess of Aglauros and Pandrosos and Kourotrophos' is more complicated. In our other evidence the post of public priestess of Aglauros is distinct from that of priestess of Pandrosos (and, except in the late *IG*
II².5152, the cult of Kourotrophos is separate again); and it is hard to see
why these goddesses should have been served on the acropolis by women of
the *Salaminioi* rather than, say, of the *Praxiergidai*. And yet the
Salaminians' priestess did not minister to the Salaminians themselves, who
made no sacrifices to either Pandrosos or Aglauros (and only a modest
πρόθυμα to Kourotrophos), and allowed her no priestly dues from their
own funds. Perhaps the joint priesthood of Aglauros and Pandrosos, here
attested in the fourth century, had been divided by the third century when
our other evidence for the public cult begins. It is perhaps a faint pointer to
an original association between the two posts that one of the two known
priestesses of Aglauros comes from the same deme as the one known priestess of Pandrosos.[72] Or perhaps the Salaminian priestess served in a different but still public cult, that of a deme, for instance.[73]

The priestesses, in contrast to the priests, receive no dues from the *genos*.
It has been very plausibly inferred that they received them from the city
instead (Ferguson, 'Salaminioi', 57). The priests are, as it were, employees
of the *genos*, the priestesses of the city. But as we have seen there was a public aspect even to the cults served by the priests; and they may in fact have
received further dues from the city.

Among the *Salaminioi* attested in the inscription, several are known from
other evidence and must have been comfortably circumstanced; and we can
very tentatively identify a patron of Pindar, Timodemus, as a member of
the *genos*.[74] But we know no Salaminians of real consequence, unless the

[70] So Ferguson, 'Salaminioi', 34. Whether the city contributed any victims at the
Oschophoria is uncertain. The *genos* did not, formally at least; the only source specified is 'from
the *oschophoroi* and *deipnophoroi*', 20–22, and where they got the victims from is not said (private contribution by individual Salaminians, according to Ferguson, 34, n. 3; perhaps they
provided them themselves).

[71] Ajax appears with Melite on the name vase of the Codrus painter (*ARV²* 1268, 1): see
e.g. U. Kron in M. Schmidt ed., *Kanon: Festschrift Ernst Berger* (*AntK-BH* 15, 1988), 298.

[72] *IG* II².3459 (Aglauros); *SEG* XXXIX 218 (Pandrosos); for the other priestess of
Aglauros cf. *SEG* XXXIII 115, with D. M. Lewis, *ZPE* 52 (1983), 48.

[73] So Kearns, *Heroes of Attica*, 139, and similarly S. C. Humphreys, *ZPE* 83 (1990), 246,
n. 5.

[74] See Ferguson, 'Salaminioi', 14; Davies, *Propertied Families*, 167 f., 209 f., 568. They
should not be taken as a representative sample: the *genos* would naturally choose its most gen-
teel members to swear the oath. Timodemus: cf. sect. B below, s.v. *Timodemidai*.

conjecture that Alcibiades belonged to the *genos* (sect. B below, s.v. *Eupatridai*, n. 94) is correct. The origins of the *genos* remain wholly mysterious. The central puzzle is that, on the one hand, several of their gods and heroes (Eurysakes, Athena Skiras and Skiros, Teucer) appear to be authentically Salaminian, while on the other they provide priests for ancient public festivals of Attica and even perhaps of the acropolis. An explanation is commonly sought in Athens' long and ultimately successful struggle with Megara in the seventh and sixth centuries for possession of Salamis: the strategically important island had to be ideologically incorporated, whether the mechanism was that an Athenian association adopted Salaminian cults and a kind of Salaminian disguise (Ferguson, 'Salaminioi', 43–47),[75] or that actual Salaminian immigrants were admitted to Attica on conditions of high privilege (M. P. Nilsson, *AJP* 59, 1938, 385–93 = id., *Op. Sel.* II.731–41; Jacoby, n. 2 [p. 193] to comm. on Philochorus *FGrH* 328 F 14–16: cf. in general Bourriot, *Génos*, 574–94). In the same spirit, Salaminian Ajax was to be made an Athenian tribal hero as late as 508/7 (Hdt. 5.66.2); he was indeed sometimes given an Athenian father, Aktaios, or even Theseus.[76] Ajax's sons Eurysakes and Philaios had themselves supposedly emigrated and handed over their island to the Athenians in gratitude for their reception in Attica (Paus. 1.35.2, Plut. *Sol.* 10.3, etc.: cf. Ferguson, 'Salaminioi', 16). That myth certainly provides a charter for the Athenians' claim to Salamis, perhaps too for the presence of the *Salaminioi* in Attica. But it is not impossible that the *genos* were true immigrants from a much earlier period.[77]*

The division of the *genos* into two groups is a further unsolved problem. Those 'from Sunium' (70–73) were all registered in that deme, near the property and shrine of the *genos*; those from '(the) seven tribes' (73–79) were more dispersed, and do not seem to have been based either around the sanctuary of Eurysakes at Melite or of Athena Skiras at Phaleron. The phratry to which members of the *genos* belonged seems to have had its centre at Alopeke, just south of Athens (see below). Ferguson took the 'seven tribes' as those of Clisthenes (13: 'what else can they be?'); but seven is a significant number, and it seems more likely that the 'seven tribes' is an archaic organization (perhaps of Salamis itself) otherwise unknown than that a group of Salaminians should have wished to rename itself in this way on being dispersed among the Clisthenic tribes (Jacoby, n. 2 [p. 193] to comm. on Philochorus *FGrH* 328 F 14–16).[78]

We may conclude by listing the sacrifices financed by the *Salaminioi*

---

[75] Cf. the incorporation of Aeacus into Athenian cult during the conflict with Aigina, Hdt. 5.89.

[76] Cf. Kron, *Kanon*, 298.

[77] Cf. C. Sourvinou-Inwood in R. A. Crossland and A. Birchall, eds., *Bronze Age Migrations in the Aegean* (London 1973), 217 f.; S. C. Humphreys, *ZPE* 83 (1990) 247; R. Osborne in *Placing the Gods*, 154–59; and for the general possibility of such immigration Manville, *Citizenship*, 135–44.

[78] The Clisthenic interpretation is doubted also by A. Andrewes, *JHS* 81 (1961), 9, n. 31, and Robertson, *Festivals and Legends*, 124, n. 16.

from their own funds, with a brief commentary. If we accept Ferguson's convincing articulation of the text (22), they met on eight separate occasions. All details listed here appear in the inscription (80–93) except those in square brackets. The three columns list recipient, victim, and cost in drachmas; the stone itself lists further small sums for wood.

1. MOUNICHION [before the 18th] at Porthmos

Kourotrophos	Goat	10
Ioleos	Sheep, burnt	15
Alkmene	Sheep	12
Maia/Nurse	Sheep	12
Heracles	Ox	70
Hero at the Salt-Flat	Sheep	15
Hero at Antisara	Piglet	3½
Hero Epipyrgidios	Piglet	3½
(Alternate years Ion	Sheep)	

2. 18th MOUNICHION [at Melite]

Eurysakes	Pig	40

3. HEKATOMBAION, at the *Panathenaea* [at Athens]

Athena	Pig	40

4. 7th METAGEITNION [at ?]

Apollo Patroos	Pig	40
Leto	Piglet	3½
Artemis	Piglet	3½
Athena Agelaa	Piglet	3½

5. [8th?] BOEDROMION [at Phaleron]

Poseidon Hippodromios	Pig	40
Hero Phaiax	Piglet	3½
Hero Teucer	Piglet	3½
Hero Nauseiros	Piglet	3½

6. 6th PYANOPSION [at ?]

Theseus	Pig	40

7. At the *Apatouria* [at Alopeke?]

Zeus Phratrios	Pig	40

8. MAIMAKTERION [at Phaleron]

Athena Skiras	Pregnant sheep	12
Skiros	Sheep	15

1. This, the only Suniac festival, is also shown by the scale of the offerings to have been the greatest of the year. It was the main occasion when the *genos* transacted its business, to judge from the dating of the second arbitration 'at the *Herakleia*' (*Agora* XIX L4*b*2). Sacrifices are made to Kourotrophos (the familiar preliminary), to Heracles in company with his

mother Alcmene, his charioteer Ioleos, and, it seems,[79] his nurse ($\mu a i a$), and to three heroes of the locality. Why Ion is also honoured in alternate years is unclear. Other sacrifices, not listed, were made at public expense (87), which is perhaps a hint that non-Salaminians also attended the festival. One might very tentatively wonder whether it comprised games, as did the *Herakleia* at Marathon; a victory dedication showing deeds of Heracles has been found in the vicinity.[80]

2. On the association of the *genos* with the Eurysakeion at Melite see above. The cult of Eurysakes, a Salaminian abroad *par excellence*, was doubtless a main focus for the *genos'* sense of ex-patriate identity—if that indeed is what they were. About the specific circumstances of this sacrifice nothing can be said.

3. It was as members of demes, not of phratries or *gene*, that individuals were entitled to a share of the public sacrifices at the *Panathenaea*; but we learn from this passage that other groups could meet for private festivities on the margin of the public.

4. At a sacrifice that primarily honours Apollo, the other two members of the Delian *famiglia sacra* characteristically receive subsidiary offerings. No specific reason, by contrast, can be given for the presence of Athena. Her title $A\gamma\epsilon\lambda\acute{a}a$ is otherwise unattested, as is, in cult, her common Homeric epithet $\dot{a}\gamma\epsilon\lambda\epsilon\acute{\iota}\eta$, to which $\dot{a}\gamma\epsilon\lambda\acute{a}a$ is perhaps related. The 'meaning', i.e. presumed etymological origin, of both has been much discussed (cf. G. S. Kirk's note on Hom. *Il.* 4.128). Neither perhaps signified anything very clearly to hearers or worshippers, in which case what they 'meant' was primarily tradition. (Is there a pun in the offering of a $\beta o \hat{v} s$ $\dot{a}\gamma\epsilon\lambda a\acute{\iota}\eta$ to Athena in *Il.* 11.729?)

Shrines of Apollo Patroos belonging to specific *gene*, to specific phratries, and to the state are all attested (cf. sect. B below s.v. *Elasidai* and e.g. Paus. 1.3.4). Ferguson argued that the Salaminians, lacking a priest of Apollo Patroos of their own, must have used the public shrine in the *agora*. But a special priest was surely not needed, and either the *genos* or its associated phratry (see 7 below) is very likely to have had its own altar somewhere.

The seventh of each month was sacred to Apollo, and it is very plausible (so Mikalson, *Calendar*, 36) that the day of our sacrifice was also that of the *Metageitnia*, a minor festival in honour of Apollo Metageitnios held on an unspecified day in this month. One can see an attraction for the immigrant Salaminians in assembling during a festival in the name of which ancients heard the idea of 'change of neighbourhood';[81] but the uncertainties are too many for it to be worth speculating further.

5. Poseidon Hippodromios, the main honorand, probably takes his name from the hippodrome at Echelidai in the Phaleron region. It is widely

---

[79] See M. P. Nilsson, *AJP* 59 (1938), 392; Kearns, *Heroes of Attica*, 35, suggests that the whole festival is 'kourotrophic'.

[80] See Young, *Hesperia* 10 (1941), 169–71; but the 'competition' of the first arbitration (61) is presumably that of the *Oschophoria*.

[81] Plut. *De Exil.* 6, 601b–c, with an aetiological story of a move from Melite to, probably, Diomeia; cf. L. Radermacher, *SBWien* 187 (1918), 1–17; id., *Glotta* 25 (1936), 198–200.

agreed[82] that these sacrifices are in some way related to the tradition, and ritual practices, recorded by Philochorus (*FGrH* 328 F 111) *ap*. Plut. *Thes.* 17.6. According to Philochorus, Theseus built hero-shrines at Phaleron, near the shrine of Skiros of Salamis, for a pilot Nausithoos and look-out Phaiax whom Skiros had given him; and in their honour a festival *Kybernesia* was celebrated. Philochorus' account is a model instance of the reinterpretation of an older tradition, for which skill at seafaring was associated above all with the Phaeacians, in terms of the newer source of ritual meaning, the legend of Theseus. More specifically, it shows with almost unique clarity the influence of a particular group in shaping tradition: for the appropriation of Nausithoos and Phaiax as Salaminians can scarcely have any other origin than our *genos*.[83] Are the sacrifices of our inscription to be identified therefore with the festival *Kybernesia* mentioned (but not dated) by Philochorus? That question needs to be broken down into three: (1) Are the gods and heroes of the inscription substantially those honoured at the *Kybernesia*? (2) Was the *Kybernesia* organized by the *Salaminioi*? (3) If not, did the two celebrations occur at the same time? In answer to (1), the only difficulty is the offering to Teucer, a Salaminian hero but not a patron of navigation. Nauseiros and Nausithoos can scarcely be dissociated, and it is more than likely that the *Kybernesia*, a named festival, in fact had the god Poseidon rather than the two heroes as primary honorand.[84] In answer to (2), probably not; the Salaminians have priesthoods of none of the gods or heroes concerned, and do not on this occasion receive victims provided by the state. If the *Kybernesia* was indeed a festival of Poseidon, the *Phoinikes* (see below) who held a priesthood of the god at Phaleron may well have organized it (so Ferguson, 'Salaminioi', 27, followed e.g. by Kearns, *Heroes of Attica*, 39). In answer to (3), if the gods whom the Salaminians honour are essentially those of the *Kybernesia*, with the addition perhaps of Teucer, it is very likely that the occasion was the same too: a meeting of the *genos* on the margins of a public rite, therefore, like those at the *Panathenaea* and *Apatouria*. But if the answer to (1) is no, then there is little reason to say yes to (3). The more we dissociate the Salaminians from the *Kybernesia*, however, the less easy it becomes to understand their influence on its aetiological legend.

6. The *Oschophoria* in Plutarch's account (*Thes.* 22.2–4) commemorates an event that immediately preceded Theseus' return from Phaleron to the city, which Plutarch dates to 7th Pyanopsion. The festival has in consequence regularly been dated to 7th Pyanopsion or thereabouts, and Ferguson argues (28) that it fell on the same day as our sacrifice, with which it ought therefore to have some connection. But the whole argument for locating the *Oschophoria* surely underestimates the freedom with which

---

[82] See now Kearns, *Heroes of Attica*, 38–40, who discusses Jacoby's scepticism, and topographic problems, in 38, n. 137.

[83] Ibid. 39.

[84] *Aliter* Jacoby, ns. 1 and 9 to the commentary on Philochorus *FGrH* 328 F 111; Robertson, *Festivals and Legends*, 122, n. 7.

aetiology could manipulate heortological facts.[85] All that can be said about the Salaminian sacrifice, at an unknown site, is that it falls in a time of year rich in Thesean associations, two days before what Plutarch calls (*Thes.* 36.4) 'the greatest sacrifice to Theseus', i.e. probably the *Theseia* (Mikalson, *Calendar*, 70).

7. This entry raises the issue of the relation between *genos* and phratry. The *Apatouria* was celebrated by the phratries at their separate centres throughout Attica (Ch. 7, n. 10 above). It seems to follow that, if the Salaminians could eat together at the festival, they must have belonged to a single phratry (so Andrewes, *JHS* 81, 1961, 9–10). This conclusion squares neatly with the other evidence for close association between *gene* and phratries (p. 64 above). Two of the Salaminians known from our document almost certainly appear in an incomplete list of members of a phratry that very probably had its base at Alopeke.[86] Our sacrifice therefore doubtless took place at Alopeke. It provides a second certain instance (cf. 3 above, and for possible cases 4 and 5 too) of a meeting of the *genos* during the course of a festival primarily celebrated by a different body.

8. These two cults, though located at Phaleron (Philochorus *FGrH* 328 F 111; Paus. 1.1.4), had the strongest possible associations with Salamis: Skiros was a primeval king of the island (see Kearns, *Heroes of Attica*, 198), Athena Skiras perhaps its leading goddess (Hdt. 8.94.2; see further Ferguson, 'Salaminioi', 18–20). The goddess' shrine at Phaleron was the second place of display for the decrees of the *genos* (*IG* II².1232) and site of the most important rites of the *Oschophoria*. It is not inconceivable that our sacrifices should have coincided with the *Oschophoria*, once the festival has been unpinned from its traditional date in Pyanopsion (see above). More probably this is a private meeting of the *genos*.

Σελλάδαι. γένος ἰθαγενῶν (Hesych. σ 389).

Σπευσανδρίδαι· γένος ἰθαγενῶν (Hesych. σ 1488). Speusandros is attested as a historical, not a mythological name.

Φιλαίδαι. The 'Philaids', presumed to be a *genos*, often appear in modern accounts of Athenian history. But the matter is complicated. A powerful οἰκίη (Herodotus' word) of the sixth and fifth centuries, that of Miltiades, traced its ancestry to Philaios son of Ajax (Hdt. 6.35.1; Pherecydes *FGrH* 3 F 2: on them see Davies, *Propertied Families*, 294–312, and on their genealogy Thomas, *Oral Tradition*, 161–72). In D.L. 10.1 we read that the philosopher Epicurus was γένους τοῦ τῶν Φιλαϊδῶν, ὥς φησι Μητρόδωρος

---

[85] Cf. Calame, *Thésée*, 149; doubts also in Mikalson, *Calendar*, 68–69 and Robertson, *Festivals and Legends*, 123, n. 8.

[86] *IG* II².2345: cf. S. C. Humphreys, *ZPE* 83 (1990), 243–48. Admittedly the Alopeke hypothesis starts from an identification of homonymous father–son pairs of the type criticized in Ch. 7. n. 11 (in relation to this very text), but the name Ktesikleides is rare enough to lend the identification some plausibility. Lambert, *Phratries*, 82–84 questions the consensus that a phratry list is what *IG* II².2345 is.

[third cent. BC] ἐν τῷ περὶ εὐγενείας. The use of γένος there might in principle be non-technical (cf. sect. B s.v. *Alkmaionidai*), but there is no reason to think it so, since it is not to 'the Philaids', a term he does not use, but to a smaller unit, the family of Miltiades, that Herodotus applies the term οἰκίη (cf. M. W. Dickie, *Phoenix* 33, 1979, 195–96). Conversely, there is no justification in saying that 'the Philaids' exercised political power; all we can say is that one *oikos* which we may presume to have belonged to the Philaids did so. We know of no priesthood associated with the *genos*, but when our knowledge of the *genos* itself is based on a single reference, that is scarcely surprising. There was also a deme *Philaidai*.

Φιλλεῖδαι. γένος ἐστιν Ἀθήνησιν· ἐκ δὲ τούτων ἡ ἱέρεια τῆς Δήμητρος καὶ Κόρης, ἡ μυοῦσα τοὺς μύστας ἐν Ἐλευσῖνι (Suda φ 319, etc.). On the duties of this extremely important Eleusinian priestess see Clinton, *Sacred Officials*, 76. A fragmentary inscription of the Roman period which contains the only other reference to the Philleids has been supposed to indicate that other *gene* too might supply the priestess; but too much of the inscription is lost for this interpretation to be at all certain.[87]

Φοίνικες. γένος τι Ἀθήνησιν (Hesych. φ 692); cf. the Dinarchan speech Διαδικασία Φαληρέων πρὸς Φοίνικας ὑπὲρ τῆς ἱερωσύνης τοῦ Ποσειδῶνος (Dion. Hal. *Din.* 10, p. 312.4–5 Usener/Radermacher). M.-F. Baslez ('Cultes et dévotions des Phéniciens en Grèce', in C. Bonnet, E. Lipiński, and P. Marchetti eds., *Studia Phoenicia*, IV: *Religio Phoenicia*, Namur 1986, 291) intriguingly suggests that these *Phoinikes* are in fact a society of ethnic Phoenician worshippers of Poseidon, settled at Phaleron. But it is not easy to imagine circumstances in which such a society and a deme could have come into conflict over title to a priesthood. The received view that they are a *genos* is probably therefore correct. On the possibility, suggested by the sacrificial calendar of the *Salaminioi*, that the *Phoinikes* administered the festival *Kybernesia* see p. 315 above; if so, their priesthood was of Poseidon Hippodromios. Töpffer notes the curious coincidence that in Ialysus on Rhodes too a priesthood of Poseidon was hereditary in a *genos* of Φοίνικες who had supposedly been left behind by the founder of the cult, Cadmus, to serve it (Diod. 5.58.2).

Φρασίδαι [eds.: φράσις δέ MSS] γένος Ἀθήνησι (Hesych. φ 841).

Φρεωρύχοι. γένος Ἀθήνησιν ἢ οἱ τὰ φρέατα ὀρύσσοντες (Hesych. φ 876). The comedian Philyllios wrote a Φρεωρύχος; one may wonder whether the supposed *genos* may not be a product of misunderstanding.

---

[87] *IG* II².2954, as interpreted by Clinton, *Sacred Officials*, 74. But even if the restoration in line 3, whereby 'the priestesses' are chosen from more than one *genos*, is correct, the lost beginning may have mentioned further priestesses: we need not suppose that a single priesthood was attached to more than one *genos*.

Φυλλίδαι. γένος ἰθαγενῶν (Hesych. φ 995). Cf. *Anecd. Bekk.* 1.314.7–8: Φυλλίδαι τί ἐστιν; γένος ἱερὸν ἀπὸ Φυλλίδος ἢ Φυλλέως. The answer looks like guesswork, as Töpffer observes (309); but as the Thracian princess Phyllis, who was loved and left by a son of Theseus, can scarcely have given her name to an Attic *genos*, we can do no better.

Φυταλίδαι. γένος παρὰ Ἀθηναίοις (Hesych. φ 1063). A little west of Athens towards Eleusis, Phytalos entertained Demeter in his house and was given a fig-plant in return. An epigram on his tomb recorded the encounter, concluding:

ἐξ οὗ δὴ τιμὰς Φυτάλου γένος ἔσχεν ἀγήρως (Paus. 1.37.2).

The line appears to confirm the existence of a historical *genos*. We also hear of mythical Phytalids, who entertained and purified Theseus at the altar of Zeus Meilichios near the Cephisus on his return from killing Sinis (Paus. 1.37.4, Plut. *Thes.* 12), and who as a reward were entrusted with the charge of a sacrifice to him which was to be financed by contributions ἀπὸ τῶν παρασχόντων τὸν δασμὸν [to Minos] οἴκων (Plut. *Thes.* 23.5; see on this passage K. Ziegler in *RE* s.v. *Phytalos*). According to an elegant suggestion of Nock (*ap.* R. Schlaifer, *HSCP* 51, 1940, 236–38) we have here the *aition* for an attested tax to finance a sacrifice, τὸ τέλος τῆς πεντεδραχμίας τῆς τῷ Θησεῖ (*Agora* XIX P26.479). The *oikoi* unfortunately cannot be identified, and nothing more is known about the role of the *Phytalidai*. For the possibility that the *genos* first acquired this function in connection with the bringing home of Theseus' bones in the 470s see p. 169.

Χαρίδαι. γένος ἐξ οὗ ὁ ἱερεὺς τοῦ Κραναοῦ (Hesych. χ 82). The obscure King Kranaos supposedly died in Lamptrae, where Pausanias saw his μνῆμα (1.31.3; see further Kearns, *Heroes of Attica*, 179). Charias is a common Attic name.

Χιμαρίδαι. γένος τι Ἀθήνησιν (Hesych. χ 475). For Chimaros as a (non-Athenian) proper name of the historical period see *LGPN* I.

B: Uncertain and Spurious *Gene*

Ἀλκμαιωνίδαι. γένος ἐστὶν ἐπιφανὲς Ἀθήνησιν ἀπο Ἀλκμᾶνος, *Anecd. Bekk.* I.378.11; ⟨Ἀλκμαιωνίδαι· γένος Ἀ⟩θήνησιν, ἀπὸ Ἀλκμαίωνος τοῦ κατὰ Θησέα Hesych. α 3097 (cf. Harp.). For the controversy on the status of the Alcmeonids see M. W. Dickie, *Phoenix* 33 (1979), 193–209 [+]. The arguments for seeing them as an *oikos* are (1) that they are so described by Pind. *Pyth.* 7.5/6 Snell/Maehler, Hdt. 6.125.5; (2) association with them was possible through the mother (Pericles, Alcibiades); (3) their original eponym seems (*pace* the lexicographers) to have been the historical Alcmeon, from whom all known Alcmeonids are in fact descended (cf. Thomas, *Oral Tradition*, 146); (4) they are associated with no known priesthoods (indecisive). The chief counter-argument is that they are described as a *genos* by various sources, beginning with Arist. *Ath. Pol.* 20.1, 28.2. Bourriot, *Génos*, 553–69 suggests that from the mid-fourth century a process of 'gentification' of *oikoi* took place (cf. Dem. 43.19, 79, on the *Bouselidai*, of whom, however, the term *genos* is not used). But an *oikos* could not have become a *genos* through a mere linguistic shift at a date when *gene* still had a defined legal status. Given the strong grounds for seeing the Alcmeonids as an *oikos*, we must suppose, with Dickie, *Phoenix* 33 (1979), 203 f., that the use of *genos* in *Ath. Pol.* is non-technical.

Since a member of the family, Megacles I, was *archon* in the pre-Solonian period (Thuc. 1.126.8–12; cf. Hdt. 5.70–71), he and his descendants were perhaps (see p. 63) *gennetai*, of (we must conclude) an unknown *genos*.

Ἀφειδαντίδαι. Known only from *IG* II².1597.19 (fourth cent.), the sale of a piece of land at Kothokidai (a deme probably located north of Eleusis) by Λεόντιος Καλλιάδου ᾿Επικηφίσιος, the Ἀφειδαντιδῶν ἐπιμελητής. Apheidas was an Attic king slain by his illegitimate brother Thymoites, who in turn surrendered the throne to Melanthus, father of the last King Codrus (Demon, *FGrH* 327 F 1, with Jacoby). The *Apheidantidai* could just as well be a phratry as a *genos* (though note sect. A s.v. *Zeuxantidai*), as were the groups named from figures comparably placed in Attic mythology, the *Medontidai* and *Thymaitadai* (cf. Lambert, *Phratries*, 363).

Βαρθει. γένος ἰθαγενῶν (Hesych. β 230). Taken, unconvincingly, by Töpffer, 308, n. 1, as a corrupt doublet of the entry β 1272 s.v. Βρυτίνας = Βρυτίδας. H. Diels, *Hermes* 26 (1891), 247, n. 1, tentatively suggested a corruption from the postulated Βαρίδαι (q.v.).

Βαρίδαι. Tentatively identified by H. Diels, *Hermes* 26 (1891), 247, n. 1, from an aetiological legend of the cult of Artemis Mounichia, according to which one Βάρος ἢ ῎Εμβαρος agreed to sacrifice his daughter to Artemis to stay a plague ἐπὶ τῷ τὴν ἱερωσύνην τὸ γένος αὐτοῦ διὰ βίου ἔχειν; he then cunningly offered a disguised goat in her stead (Pausanias Atticista fr. 35 Erbse, and derivative sources printed e.g. in A. Brelich, *Paides e Parthenoi*, Rome 1969, 248–49).[88] We have no independent evidence about the priesthood. The difficulty is that the legend contains a double aetiology, both for certain practices of the cult and also for the proverb ῎Εμβαρος εἶ, 'you're a shrewd fellow'; and the relation between these two explanations is not clear. Was Embaros originally associated with the cult, or was a distinct proverb only subsequently attached to it? Only in the first case, probably,[89] can we believe in a *genos* of *Baridai* (or rather, perhaps, *Embaridai*). In favour of this view, the question has been put: 'Why on earth would anyone seeking to explain the proverb "You are . . . an Embaros", with all the

---

[88] Recent discussions of the myth (Brulé, *La fille d'Athènes*, 182–86; K. Dowden, *Death and the Maiden*, London 1989, 20–24) have not considered the priesthood.

[89] Unless we suppose that the connection arose through a chance resemblance of names between e.g. *Baridai* and Embaros.

world to choose from, have turned to the priesthood of Artemis Mounichia
and foisted upon them a fictitious ancestor?' (W. Sale, *RhMus* 118, 1975,
276). It can perhaps be countered that the element of supposed deception
in the ritual itself, the sacrifice of a goat in lieu of a girl, was itself sufficient
to draw in the cunning Embaros aetiologically. The reservation of the
priesthood to his descendants would then be a further (fictitious) manifes-
tation of his shrewdness. The question must be left open.

Βρύθακες [Βρυτακίδαι Meineke]· ἢ χιτῶνες βομβύκινοι ἢ γένος ἰθαγενῶν
(Hesych. β 1234). Rejected rather peremptorily by Töpffer, 308, n. 1, as a
confusion with the Βρυτίδαι.

Γλαυκίδαι. This group and the *Epikleidai* appear on a mortgage stone of
unknown provenance (*IG* II².2723) as two of five sets of lenders, the others
being an individual and two groups of *phrateres*. They might be either *gene*
or phratries. Lambert, *Phratries*, 78–79, 197–98, neatly suggests that, on
the hypothesis that both were *gene* attached to one phratry (cf. Ch. 5, n. 30),
the loan can be seen as one in which five subgroups within a single phratry
combine to aid a fellow-member, according to a familiar pattern of mutual
aid within a group. One might even take them for *oikoi*, since Glaukos and
Epikles were common historical names, and reach the same conclusion;[90]
but there are no obvious parallels for such collective financial activity by an
oikos.

Δαιτροί. According to Porph. *Abst.* 2.30, three *gene* (his word) performed
the ritual of *Bouphonia* at the *Dipolieia*: the *Kentriadai* (cf. κεντεῖν, goad),
who drove the ox round the altar; the *Boutupoi*, who slew it; the *Daitroi*,
who prepared the ensuing feast (δαίς). Töpffer, however, denied that
Daitroi, *Kentriadai*, and *Boutupoi* were the names of true *gene*: they were
rather cultic titles indicating functions which members of differently
named *gene* might on occasion assume. There is strong independent evidence that the *boutupos* was a functionary recruited from the *genos* of
Thaulonidai (q.v., sect. A). *Daitros* too, 'banquet man', is a functional
name, and though *gene* could bear such names (witness the *Kerykes*, or
Theoinidai) the parallel case of the *Boutupoi* gives grounds for doubt.
Töpffer argued, on insufficient grounds, that the *Daitroi* (and also the
Kentriadai) were drawn from the Eleusinian *Kerykes*.[91] They could in fact,

[90] A mysterious Glaukos does, however, receive an offering in *IG* I³.255.14 (cf. Kearns,
Heroes of Attica, 153); he is more likely to be relevant than the mythological Attic Glaukos
adduced by A. v. Premerstein, *AM* 35 (1910), 107 from *Etym. Magn.* s.v. Γλαυκώπιον, probably a late invention designed to explain Γλαυκώπιον as a name for the acropolis. And it seems
more natural to link the *Epikleidai* with the common name than with Hesych. ε 4858:
Ἐπικλείδια· ἑορτὴ Δήμητρος Ἀθήνησι.

[91] Several items (some discovered after Töpffer wrote) have been cited to show that the
Kerykes were associated with the *Dipolieia*. (1) On the *Kentriadai*, see sect. A above. (2) Athen.
660 a–b states ὅτι δὲ σεμνὸν ἦν ἡ μαγειρικὴ μαθεῖν ἔστιν ἐκ τῶν Ἀθήνησι κηρύκων· οἵδε γὰρ
μαγείρων καὶ βουτύπων ἐπεῖχον τάξιν, ὥς φησιν Κλείδημος ἐν Πρωτογονίας πρώτῳ (which
follows, *FGrH* 323 F 5). Töpffer read Κηρύκων, and inferred that members of the *genos* were

if not a *genos* themselves, have come from any other (perhaps unrecorded) *genos*. For the possibility that a society of *Dipoliastai* attested in the late fourth century is to be associated with these *gene* see App. 4 below.

Δεκελειεῖς. A *genos* of this name was briefly (contrast *Rh. Mus.* 45, 1890, 384, n. 1) postulated by Töpffer, *Attische Genealogie*, 289–91. But the literary texts (Hdt. 9.73, Lys. 23.2–3) which have been held to distinguish a group of 'Deceleans' from the demesmen do no such thing (see Hedrick, *Demotionidai*, 45–47: *aliter* still Lambert, *Phratries*, 112–16), and whatever the controversial Δεκελειῶν οἶκος of *IG* II².1237.42 may have been (cf. s.v. *Demotionidai*) there is no strong reason to see it as a *genos*.

Δημοκλεῖδαι. This group is known only from the fifth-century boundary-stone of their shrine of Artemis Orthosia (*IG* I³.1083: found north-east of Hymettus at Κατζουλιέρτης). The goddess' main function was probably to set children straight on their feet, but that is a good which *genos* and phratry could have desired alike.

Δημοτιωνίδαι. This group is known only from *IG* II².1237, three decrees concerned with preventing and correcting the admission of unentitled persons to a particular phratry. The first decree (of 396/5) prescribes that a scrutiny of the membership-list 'in accord with the law of the *Demotionidai*' should continue. Any individual whom 'the *phrateres*' vote out may appeal 'to the *Demotionidai*' (who also keep the authoritative membership-list). In such a case, the 'house of the Deceleans' will choose five representatives to put the case against the candidates; if the appeal fails, the appellant will be subject to a large fine (1,000 drachmas) to be exacted by 'the priest of the house of the Deceleans'. Several functions are also assigned to an unspecified priest who, being regularly associated with the phratriarch, is likely to be the priest of the phratry. Two conclusions (most influentially drawn by H. T. Wade-Gery, *CQ* 25, 1931, 129–43 = id., *Essays in Greek History*, Oxford 1958, 116–34: cf. A. Andrewes, *JHS* 81, 1961, 3–5) lie close to hand: (1) 'the *phrateres*' and 'the *Demotionidai*' are distinct, since the latter judge an appeal against a decision of the former; (2) the name of the phratry concerned is 'the house of the Deceleans', since any appeal

the *Daitroi* (= *mageiroi*, cooks) and *Boutupoi* (but this is certainly not true, as Töpffer elsewhere acknowledges) of the *Bouphonia*. The continuation of the fr., however, where Clidemus does not appear to have a particular *genos* or rite in mind, seems to prove that Jacoby was right to read κηρύκων. And to speak of the *Kerykes*, Athenaeus (who lacked the benefit of capitals) would almost certainly have introduced the term *genos* (cf. e.g. Theodorus' work περὶ Κηρύκων γένους, and other works of similar title listed by Töpffer, 1, n. 1) (3) The calendar fr. *IG* I³.241.17 (*LSCG* 17 A *b* 8) records a payment κέρυχσιν ℎοὶ Διπολιείοις . . . . Here too, if *Kerykes* were meant (as is often supposed), one would expect the term *genos* to be used. (4) A fr. which seems to belong to the *boustrophedon* calendar which apparently stood in the City Eleusinion refers to a (?) [βου]τύπος and, two lines later, to Zeus Polieus or his festival (*IG* I³.232.24–27 = *LSS* 2 A *c* 10–13). The firmest of these items is (4), and even this proves at most that some connection existed between the Eleusinian cult and the *Dipolieia*, not that the *Daitroi* were *Kerykes*.

against the decision of 'the *phrateres*' is to be contested by the house and since it seems economical to identify the document's two priests, the presumed phratry priest and the 'priest of the house of the Deceleans'. If conclusion (1), which most concerns us, is accepted, the *Demotionidai* can scarcely be anything other than a *genos*. It can only be escaped by supposing either (*a*) that appeal was indeed made back to the phratry against the phratry's original decision or (*b*) that 'the *phrateres*' who make the original decision are to be understood as 'the relevant subdivision of the *phrateres*', not the whole body. Neither alternative to (1) is easy; but one cannot interpret with much confidence a perhaps loosely drafted decree that was issued in an abnormal situation (the aftermath of the Peloponnesian war, in an area of Attica that had been occupied by Sparta) and presupposes much knowledge of particular circumstances hidden from us. If the *Demotionidai* are in fact a *genos*, it seems to be by its own choice that the phratry submits to this external jurisdiction (the decree begins 'the *phrateres* decided').

The decrees have recently been re-edited from the stone, with full commentary and bibliography, by Hedrick, *Demotionidai*. Hedrick supports alternative (*a*) to conclusion (1), and suggests that 'the house of the Deceleans' is in fact the deme Decelea (demes, however, had a plurality of priests, not one alone). Lambert, *Phratries*, ch. 3, argues for alternative (*b*): the document is issued by 'the house of the Deceleans', a semi-autonomous subgroup of the phratry of *Demotionidai*; 'the *phratores*' in the early lines are therefore 'those *phratores* [who belong to the house of the Deceleans]'.

Εἰκαδεῖς. See p. 337.

Ἐλασίδαι. This group possessed a *temenos* of Apollo Patroos, known from a fourth-century inscription found at Cephisia (*IG* II².2602). An anonymous phratry is known from an inscription first recorded in a collector's garden also in Cephisia (*IG* II².1240); but it is not sure that the latter stone was in fact found there (see Hedrick, 'Phratry Shrines', 244), and even if it were, the identification of the two groups would only be a possibility. As both phratries (*IG* II².4973) and *gene* (Dem. 57.67, *LSS* 19.88, *IG* II².3629–30) honoured Apollo Patroos, the status of the *Elasidai* is indeterminable (cf. Bourriot, *Génos*, 1066–67). Two obscure Trojan Elasoi (Hom. *Il.* 16.696; Paus. 10.26.4; Töpffer, *RhM* 45, 1890, 383–84) are scarcely likely to have anything to do with them.

Ἐμβαρίδαι. Cf. Βαρίδαι.

Ἐπικλείδαι. See under Γλαυκίδαι.

Ἐτιονίδαι. Known only from *IG* I³.1016 [+], a dedication by ὁ θίασος [Ἐ]τιονιδῶν, perhaps made to Heracles and probably deriving from the Herakleion near Phaleron. *Thiasoi* are unparalleled in *gene*; they are known as subdivisions of phratries, but not in association with a patronymic group-name. The *Etionidai* may well have been a '*thiasos* of Heracles' (cf. App. 4 below, ns. 3–4, and Lambert, *Phratries*, 88–89).

Εὐεργίδαι. This group[92] is known from the early fourth-century *horos* of their precinct of the Tritopatreis: ὅρος ἱερὸ Τριτοπατρέων Εὐεργιδῶν (*Agora* XIX H20). We know another group, the *Zakyadai*, from a very similar text (*IG* II².2615, provenance unknown). It is tempting to interpret both as *gene* by analogy with the *Pyrrakidai* (q.v.), a *genos* that certainly had a cult of Tritopator. But there is no obvious reason why phratries should not have honoured their Tritopatores, as even demes were to do (*LSCG* 18 D 43–44; 20 B 32, 53: cf. Bourriot, *Génos*, 1171–72; Lambert, *Phratries*, 369).

Εὐπατρίδαι. From a historiographic tradition that begins for us with Arist. *Ath. Pol.* (13.2), the *Eupatridai* are known as the aristocratic caste that supposedly monopolized power and office until the reforms of Solon. The adjective εὐπατρίδης appears quite commonly in poetry, particularly in Euripides, in the sense of 'well-born'. It has, however, often been thought that alongside the caste (or a memory of it), there existed a distinct *genos* of Eupatrids. But none of the texts adduced is decisive. The Χαιρίον Ἀθεναῖος Εὐπατριδόν known from his sixth-century gravestone in Eretria (*IG* I³.1516) could evidently have belonged either to caste or to *genos*. Isocrates appears at first sight to attest a *genos* when he says that Alcibiades πρὸς μὲν ἀνδρῶν ἦν Εὐπατριδῶν, ὧν τὴν εὐγένειαν ἐξ αὐτῆς τῆς ἐπωνυμίας ῥάδιον γνῶναι, πρὸς γυναικῶν δ' Ἀλκμεωνιδῶν (16.25). But Isocrates was not obliged to choose exactly parallel forms of expression in the two limbs of his sentence, if he thought that the generalized grandeur of Eupatrid origin shed more lustre on Alcibiades than the name of a particular *genos*.[93] (The argument sometimes offered, however, that Alcibiades cannot have belonged to a *genos* of Eupatrids because he was demonstrably a member of another, the *Salaminioi*, is inconclusive.[94]) The word is certainly applied to a contemporary, without indicating that he belonged to a specific *genos*, in Xen. *Symp.* 8.40, where Callias of the *genos* of *Kerykes* is described as εὐπατρίδης . . . τῶν ἀπ' Ἐρεχθέως, ἱερεὺς θεῶν οἳ καὶ ἐπὶ τὸν βάρβαρον σὺν Ἰάκχῳ ἐστράτευσαν (so O. J. Todd in the Loeb: εὐπατρίδης, ἱερεὺς θεῶν τῶν ἀπ' Ἐρεχθέως MSS). In Xen. *Oec.* 1.17 it has the vague sense 'well-born' familiar from poetry.

In the late second century BC, a *genos* of Eupatrids again appears to be attested by a Delphic text in which 'Pythaists from the Eupatrids' head a

[92] But Humphreys, 'Genos', suggests that *Euergidai* here is just an adjective qualifying *Tritopatreis*.

[93] So H. T. Wade-Gery, *CQ* 25 (1931), 82–85 = id., *Essays in Greek History* (Oxford 1958), 108 ff., followed by Davies, *Propertied Families*, 11, and Bourriot, *Génos*, 407–22; contrast Jacoby, *Atthis*, 263, n. 156.

[94] We hear from other sources that Alcibiades traced his descent from Eurysakes or Ajax (Pl. *Alc.* 1.121a, Plut. *Alc.* 1.1, Didymus *ap.* Σ Pind. *Nem.* 2.19), and this, it is argued, proves that he was a member of the *genos* that was closely associated with Eurysakes, the *Salaminioi*. But the ancestry that an individual family might choose to claim could include links in the female line and thus be quite distinct from that of the *genos* to which it belonged (Dittenberger, *Hermes* 20, 1885, 6). We can at least conclude that in all probability Alcibiades was a γεννήτης.

list which continues with Pythaists from three known *gene*, the Pyrrhacids, *Kerykes*, and Euneids (*SIG*³ 711 D¹: other allusions in Delphic texts are less clear). But the four groups need not be equivalent: general representatives of the aristocracy, in first position, are followed by members of *gene* that had particular sacral duties or particular associations with Apollo. And if the Delphic Eupatrids are not a *genos*, we need not postulate that two of them who are elsewhere attested as members respectively of the *Bouzygai* and (very probably) the *Kerykes* belonged to more than one *genos*⁹⁵ (see A. Wilhelm, *AnzWien* 1924, 124–26; G. Daux, *Delphes au iiᵉ et au Iᵉʳ siècle*, Paris 1936, 551–54). On the ἐξηγηταὶ ἐξ εὐπατριδῶν, not attested before the early Roman period, see Jacoby, *Atthis*, 27 f.

One important text remains. Σ Soph. *OC* 489 reports τοῦτο ἀπὸ τῆς δρωμένης θυσίας ταῖς Εὐμενίσι φησί. μετὰ γὰρ ἡσυχίας τὰ ἱερὰ δρῶσι καὶ διὰ τοῦτο οἱ ἀπὸ Ἡσύχου θύουσιν αὐταῖς, καθάπερ Πολέμων [fr. 49 Preller] ἐν τοῖς πρὸς Ἐρατοσθένην φησὶν οὕτω· τὸ τῶν Εὐπατριδῶν γένος οὐ μετέχει τῆς θυσίας ταύτης. εἶτα ἑξῆς· τῆς δὲ πομπῆς ταύτης Ἡσυχίδαι, ὃ δὴ γένος ἐστὶ περὶ τὰς Σεμνὰς θεάς, τὴν ἡγεμονίαν ἔχουσι. If the argument thus far is sound, *genos* is here probably being used, as it easily might be (cf. [Plut.] *X Orat.* 834b),⁹⁶ in a non-technical sense to describe the caste. (The immediate recurrence of the word in a technical sense in reference to the *Hesychidai* is certainly uncomfortable; but the closeness of the juxtaposition is probably due to abbreviation.) May we draw the important conclusion that there existed at least one non-Eupatrid priestly *genos*, since the *Hesychidai* officiated at a rite from which the Eupatrids *en masse* were excluded? That would not be safe, when the text is so abbreviated: τῆς θυσίας ταύτης may have been, in context, only a small part of the rite, and there is independent evidence that the Eupatrid Lycurgus participated in a festival of the Semnai very probably to be identified with this one (cf. s.v. Ἡσυχίδαι).

Εὐφρονίδαι. The early fifth-century herm *IG* I³.1007 = *CEG* 307 declares that it was made by Kallias Εὐφρονίδεσι. That word has been taken either as an epic dative plural (with -εσι for -εσσι) from feminine Εὐφρονίδες, an otherwise unattested group of nymph or Eumenides-like figures (so e.g. Hansen), or as an old Attic dative plural (i.e. -ησι) from Εὐφρονίδαι (so e.g. Hiller). The second interpretation is clearly preferable (see K. Mickey, *Studies in the Greek Dialects and the Language of Greek Verse Inscriptions*, Diss. Oxford 1981, II, ch. 2, 24, n. 62): an -εσσι dative is only once found in epigraphic verse before 400, at a date well after our inscription, in a piece that is indisputably verse, and in a word, Χαρίτεσσιν, that is very familiar in that form from Homer (*CEG* 428, Cos, late fifth cent.), while the dative of the group for whom the monument is made has a parallel in

---

⁹⁵ But the phenomenon of dual membership is too well attested (see n. 7) for this objection to be decisive in itself.

⁹⁶ But contrast C. A. Hignett, *A History of the Athenian Constitution* (Oxford 1952), 316.

Schwyzer 112 (Aegina, fifth cent.), Κολιάδαις. But we are still left uncertain about the character of these *Euphronidai*. Euphron is a common Attic name.

Ζακυάδαι. See under *Euergidai*.

Θυργωνίδαι. οἱ δὲ Τιτακίδαι καὶ Θυργωνίδαι φρατρίαι τινὲς καὶ γένη ἄδοξα. εἰς γὰρ εὐτέλειαν ἐκωμῳδοῦντο· οὐχὶ δὲ δῆμοι, ὥς τινες οἴονται (*Etym. Magn.* 760.33–35 s.v. Τιτακίδαι). But since both names were in fact (cf. Traill, *Political Organization*, 88, 122) those of post-classical demes (which had doubtless existed earlier as villages, and could thus have been butts of comedy), we should probably reject *Etym. Magn.*'s claim rather than attempt the speculative compromise that they were both demes and phratries or *gene*.

Ἰκαριεῖς. The existence of a group of Ἰκαριεῖς (whether *genos* or phratry or *oikos*) distinct from the deme has regularly been inferred (see e.g. Töpffer, *RhM* 45, 1890, 384; D. M. Lewis, *Historia* 12, 1963, 32, n. 93) from the form of expression in *IG* II².1178: ἐψηφίσθαι Ἰκαριεῦσιν ἐπαινέσαι Νίκωνα τὸν δήμαρχον . . . καὶ ἀνειπεῖν τὸν κήρυκα ὅτι στεφανοῦσιν Ἰκαριεῖς Νίκωνα καὶ ὁ δῆμος ὁ Ἰκαριέων τὸν δήμαρχον . . . But Ἰκαριεῖς can scarcely change from the name of the demesmen in the first line to something different within the same sentence; we seem rather to be dealing with an artificial form of expression in which the Ἰκαριεῖς are no more distinct from the δῆμος Ἰκαριέων than is Nikon from the δήμαρχος. 'The καί should not mislead; the Ἰκαριεῖς honour him (1) as an individual (2) as δήμαρχος; and for this it is more appropriate for them to appear as ὁ δῆμος' (Professor D. A. Russell, who kindly considered the problem at my request; so too now Lambert, *Phratries*, 367).

Ἰωνίδαι. Unjustifiably identified (cf. Bourriot, *Génos*, 572, n. 327) as a *genos* by Töpffer on the sole basis of a conjecture by Meier in Σ Areth. Plat. *Apol.* 23e (p. 422 Greene): Λύκων μέντοι πατὴρ ἦν Αὐτολύκου, Ἰωνίδης [MS Ἰων] γένος, δήμων Θορίκιος. But in other expressions of the form '*x* as to genos' in these scholia (an unlikely place indeed to find *genos* used in the specialized Attic sense), *x* is an ethnic (cf. the Σ on 18b); and we learn later in the same scholion that Lykon was attacked in comedy as a ξένος.

Καλλαῖς. γένος ἰθαγενῶν (Hesych. κ 460). '? Κωλιεῖς', Latte.

Κωδειῆς. γένος ἰθαγενῶν Ἀθήνησιν (Hesych. κ 4782). Rejected by Latte as a doublet of κ 4817 Κωλιεῖς (q.v., sect. A).

Κωμάδαι. This group is known only from a fifth-century inscription found at Tatoi (below Decelea): hορός τὸν Κομαδὸν ἱερόν (*IG* I³.1086 bis: punctuation is uncertain).

Λαξάδαι . . . Ἀθήνησι (Hesych. λ 280). According to Latte, a corrupt doublet of λ 196 Λακιάδαι (the deme).

Μεδοντίδαι. According to legend, the *Medontidai* (Hesych. μ 518, οἱ ἀπὸ Μέδοντος Ἀθήνησι; Vell. Paterc. 1.2; Paus. 4.5.10, 4.13.7) were the dynasty who ruled Athens after the death of the last King Codrus, holding the archonship first for life and later for periods of ten years; they took their name from Codrus' son Medon. Inscriptions show that a group Μεδοντίδαι still existed in the historical period (*IG* I³.1062, 1383; *IG* II².1233), and this was, not surprisingly, long identified as a *genos* claiming royal descent. A more recently published document, however, has brought a surprising but unambiguous reference to a κοινὸν φρατέρων Μεδοντιδῶν (*Agora* XIX P5.17). Perhaps there was also a *genos*, it has been suggested (Jacoby on Hellanicus *FGrH* 323a F 23, n. 70); but no source in fact claims that the dynasty of *Medontidai*, which is mentioned only in relation to the prehistoric period, survived as a *genos* into classical times.

Μητιονίδαι. A mythological family who drove King Pandion I into exile (e.g. Apollod. 3.15.5). No trace of them survives in the historical period.

Οἰκάται. An Οἰκατῶν ἐπιμελητής appears in the same document as the Ἀφειδαντιδῶν ἐπιμελητής (see above).

Παιονίδαι. According to Pausanias, Paion and Alcmeon were among the Neleids who fled to Athens when expelled from Pylos by the Heraclidae, καὶ τὸ Παιονιδῶν γένος καὶ Ἀλκμεωνιδῶν ἀπὸ τούτων ὠνομάσθησαν (2.18.9). The Alcmeonids certainly existed, though their status as a *genos* is controversial; but the name Παιονίδαι is otherwise only attested as that of a deme.

Πυρρητιάδαι. Tentatively inferred by Töpffer from the archaic dedication *IG* I³.665 Λεόβιος ἐποίεσεν Πυρετιάδες. But, other difficulties aside, the artist is quite likely not even to be an Athenian.

Σημαχίδαι. δῆμος Ἀττικῆς, ἀπὸ Σημάχου, ᾧ καὶ ταῖς θυγατράσιν ἐπεξενώθη Διόνυσος, ἀφ' ὧν αἱ ἱέρειαι αὐτοῦ (Steph. Byz.; on Dionysus' reception by Semachus see too Eusebius as quoted by Jacoby on *FGrH* 328 F 206). This is a puzzling notice. Stephanus seems to imply the existence of a *genos* in which the priesthood of Dionysus was vested. But his explicit statement that Semachidai was a deme is correct (cf. Traill, *Political Organization*, 112). Possibly we should acknowledge here a further rare case of homonymy between deme and *genos* (cf. sect. A s.v. *Eteoboutadai*). A Σημαχεῖον is attested (shrine or mine?) in south-east Attica (*IG* II².1582.54, cf. R. J. Hopper, *BSA* 56, 1961, 218 f.); its relation to the deme, of controversial location, is uncertain.

Τιμοδημίδαι. A group mentioned in Pind. *Nem.* 2 (line 18), an ode in honour of Timodemus of Acharnae. They are in all appearance an *oikos* descended from an identifiable historical Timodemus, not a *genos* (see Roussel, *Tribu et cité*, 56). Indeed, since praise of Salamis is unexpectedly introduced in *Nemean* 2, and at least two *Salaminioi* were settled at Acharnae, it is plausible that Timodemus the Timodemid was a *Salaminios*.

Τιτακίδαι. Cf. s.v. *Θυργωνίδαι*.

Χαλκίδαι. *γένος* (Hesych.). As Hesych. mentions some non-Attic *gene* (e.g. α 1401, 2017, 4879), Töpffer's assumption that the *Chalkidai* are Attic (he adduces the Athenian Metion's son Chalkon, *Σ* b Hom. *Il.* 2.536) is no more than probable. Other *gene* of no fixed abode in Hesychius are the *Krontidai, Nyktidai,* and †*Πορθομιν*.

APPENDIX 3

Local Religious Associations

The known local associations, other than demes, are:

THE TETRAKOMIA OF THE PHALERON REGION. 'Tetrakomoi'
is commonly supplied as the missing twelfth 'city of Cecrops' in
Philochorus *FGrH* 328 F 94 (see Jacoby ad loc.). This was an organization
of four demes based on a shrine of Heracles, at which (doubtless) they competed annually in a distinctive dance, the τετράκωμος ὄρχησις. The competition was taken seriously enough for victory dedications to be made in
the fourth century. No other rites of the association are known.

The main literary source is Pollux 4.105: ὁ δὲ τετράκωμος, τὸ τῆς
ὀρχήσεως εἶδος, οὐκ οἶδα εἴ τι προσῆκον ἦν τοῖς Ἀθήνησι τετρακώμοις, οἳ
ἦσαν Πειραιεῖς, Φαληρεῖς, Ξυπεταίονες, Θυμοιτάδαι. Steph. Byz. s.v.
Ἐχελίδαι mentions the τετράκωμον Ἡράκλειον near the Piraeus, and we
learn further that the τετράκωμος ὄρχησις was a blend of music (μέλος) and
dance, sacred to Heracles, associated with war or victory, and accompanied
by the flute (Poll. 4.99, Hesych. s.v. Τετράκωμος, Tryphon *ap*. Ath. 618c);
interestingly, it was also known as τέσσαρες κῶμοι (Hesych.)

It is natural to refer the name Tetrakomoi to the inhabitants of the four
'demes', that had perhaps before Clisthenes been κῶμαι, named by
Pollux.[1] (The formation of the compound adjective follows the regular
τιμή/ἄτιμος principle; the association itself should be called τετρακωμία,
cf. Strabo 9.2.14 (405), though the word is unattested in this context.) But
the position is complicated by inscriptions found at a site north-east of the
Piraeus which has been convincingly identified, from their contents, as the
site of the τετράκωμον Ἡράκλειον.[2] The most important (*IG* II².3103)
begins Ξυπεταίονες ἐνίκων, gives an Athenian archon date (Aristophon,
330/29), lists—with patronymics but not demotics—four κώμαρχοι,
including Φίλτων Αἰσχύτου and Πάμφιλος Αἰσχύτου, and on the reverse
five κωμασταί, again including the two sons of Aischytos. Another (*IG*
II².3102), a marble base for a tripod, records Φ]αληρεῖς ἐνί[κων and goes

---

[1] Note, however, that on Lewis's view (n. 5 below) the *komai qua* members of the
Tetrakomoi had different membership-lists from the homonymous Clisthenic demes, so that
e.g. a man of the 'deme' Phaleron could be 'komarch' of the *kome* Thymaitadai.

[2] See A. A. Papagiannopoulos-Palaios, *Polemon* 1 (1929), 44–52, 107–109, 232–37, who
publishes *IG* II².2830, 3102, 3103, and *IG* I³.1016; on the find-spot, identical in each case
(*pace IG* II²), see ibid. 234 and cf. G. R. Stanton, *Chiron* 14 (1984), 37; a relief fr. showing
Heracles' club and lion-skin was later seen nearby (see *Polemon* 3, 1947/8, 17–21, where some
very fragmentary further inscriptions are also published, including *IG* I³.242 of '490–480').

on to list names without demotics; another similar base (*IG* II².2830) names one ἐπιμελητής each from Thymaitadai and Piraeus, and perhaps honoured representatives of the other two demes in missing parts.

That these are monuments of victories in a competition between the four demes seems beyond doubt: all four are attested. But the κωμασταί of *IG* II².3103 introduce complications, as they cannot be dissociated from a κῶμος. How are we to explain these allusions to both κωμαί and κῶμοι in the documents of the Tetrakomia? A neat explanation would be that the four demes/*komai* were each represented in the competition by a troupe known (through a popular etymological assimilation) as a *komos*. What becomes of the 'komarchs' on this view? Other evidence suggests that they should be 'village-chiefs', persons with practical as well as ritual responsibilities; for a κωμάρχος from near Aphidna is attested in the administrative context of a sales record, and these same records (the *rationes centesimarum*) present three κώμης ἄρχοντες from unnamed κῶμαι in the Tetrakomia region whom it is natural to identify in function with that κώμαρχος and our κώμαρχοι.[3] But it is perhaps not inconceivable that the village-chiefs also became '*komos*-leaders' on the ritual occasion.

A difficulty arises, however: it seems impossible to distribute the four *komarchoi* of *IG* II².3103 between the four demes. As they are listed without demotics, and include what look like a pair of brothers, they must surely all be members of one deme, victorious Xypetaion.[4] Thus we must unwillingly conclude either that a single *komos/kome* could have four *komarchoi* or that one at least of the four demes of the Tetrakomoi was itself subdivided into *komoi* or *komai*. One elaborate suggestion is that the division occurred, for festival purposes only, by a kind of symbolic duplication: each quarter of the whole was itself divided into four parts, *komoi*, so that the whole Tetrakomic competition was fought out between four sets of τέσσαρες κῶμοι (so Papagiannopoulos-Palaios, *Polemon* 1, 1929, 44–52). But the *rationes centesimarum* again appear to show that even outside the ritual context one *kome* could have more than one *komarch*.[5]

On any view, it seems almost certain that the presence of κῶμοι (implied by κωμασταί) in a competition between κῶμαι must be due to assimilation rather than mere coincidence; that perhaps is the reason why here, uniquely, κῶμοι are found associated with a god other than Dionysus.[6]

---

[3] *IG* II².1594.44, 1598.8–22; cf. P. Roussel, *RA*, 6th ser., 18 (1941), 226–31.

[4] In saying, *RA*, 6th ser., 18 (1941), 227, that there is 'nulle impossibilité' in brothers belonging to different demes, Roussel is presumably postulating a father who changes deme by adoption: possible, but far-fetched.

[5] *IG* II².1598.8–22 (on readings see D. M. Lewis in M. I. Finley ed., *Problèmes de la terre en Grèce ancienne*, Paris 1973, 192, n. 3). Roussel, *RA*, 6th ser., 18 (1941), argues that the *komai* of this passage are subdivisions of Phaleron (itself of course a *kome* within the Tetrakomia), D. M. Lewis, *Historia* 12 (1963), 33, n. 104, and in Finley ed., *Problèmes de la terre*, that they are some of the four deme/*komai* of the main τετρακωμία (cf. n. 1); but even Lewis's view leaves one *kome* with two *archontes*.

[6] Cf. Pickard-Cambridge, *Dramatic Festivals²*, 44 f.

THE TRIKOMIA OF THE EUPYRIDAI. This association is known only from Steph. Byz. s.v. Εὐπυρίδαι· τρικώμους δὲ τούτους ἐκάλουν, Εὐπυρίδας Κρωπίδας Πήληκας. The three demes named by Stephanus lay west of Acharnae. See too the next entry.

A TRIKOMIA IN THE ERCHIA REGION (?). *IG* II².1213, a fragmentary decree found at Spata, attests τρίκωμοι and a τρικώμαρχος. A second τρικωμία, otherwise unattested, has therefore been postulated in the region (by P. Bicknell, *REG* 89, 1976, 599–606). But *IG* II².1213 is physically so small that it is very likely to have strayed from the territory of the preceding group (so R. Schlaifer, *HSCP* 54, 1943, 45, n. 39; Lauter, *Landgemeinden*, 137).

THE EPAKREIS (?). The deme Plotheia made contributions to a religious association of Ἐπακρεῖς (*IG* I³.258.30), which was the name of a Clisthenic *trittys* (*IG* II².2490: not now in *IG* I³.1128). But it is not clear that the *trittyes* had religious functions (Ch. 7, n. 4 above), and an alternative explanation is available in this case. Philochorus lists Ἐπακρία as one of the twelve cities of Cecrops, after the Marathonian Tetrapolis (Philochorus *FGrH* 328 F 94); lexicographers (e.g. Suda ε 1936) appear to treat the Ἐπακτρία χώρα as a tripolis or tetrapolis (admittedly in muddled contexts), and the deme Semachidai is named as belonging to 'the Epakria' (Philochorus fr. 206). Thus it has long and plausibly been supposed that the Clisthenic *trittys*-name Ἐπακρεῖς was borrowed (as was the *trittys*-name 'Tetrapolites') from a pre-existent religious association, and that it was to this that the Plotheians contributed (Wilamowitz, *Aristoteles und Athen*, Berlin 1893, II.154; cf. R. J. Hopper, *BSA* 56, 1961, 217–19; W. E. Thompson, *Mnemosyne*, 4th ser., 22, 1969, 150–52). From a new honorary inscription (*SEG* XXXII 144, fourth cent., from Mygdaleza nr. Stamata: οἱ δημόται. Ἐπακρέες. [ ] εἰς Ἀπολλώνια ἄρξαντα—which constituent deme is referred to is unknown) we now know that the Epakrians appointed an *archon* to organize specific festivals, an apparently archaic practice also found in the local league of Athena Pallenis (q.v.). We do not know whether the Epakrians had any further communal rites other than these *Apollonia*,[7] nor who the members of the association were, other than Plotheia and, probably, Semachidai. The *Apollonia* were funded by contributions from the participating demes and were possibly trieteric (*IG* I³.258.25–31: cf. *Gifts to the Gods*, 140, n. 32); no more is known of them.

THE LEAGUE OF ATHENA PALLENIS. The cult of Athena Pallenis at Pallene is ancient and celebrated. The associated league is known from extracts, quoted in Athenaeus, of the 'king's laws' that regulated its festival, and from a mid-fourth-century inscription in which its functionaries

---

[7] The Plotheians in the inscription cited list a series of festivals, including the *Apollonia*, for which they set aside funds. But there is no knowing whether any of these other than the *Apollonia* were Epakrian rites.

(probably of a particular year) are listed. The surviving 'king's laws' (laws of the *archon basileus*) appear to be fifth-century reworkings of earlier originals.[8]

We know much more of the organization of the festival than of its content. The *basileus* 'saw to the appointment of *archontes*' for the festival (king's laws), presumably each year. According to the most likely interpretation of the inscription, one *archon* was recruited from each of the demes Gargettus, Acharnae, Pallene, and Paeania. These *archontes* in turn recruited 'parasites' 'from the demes' (king's laws). 'From the demes' in context doubtless meant 'from the restricted number of demes traditionally involved', and in other parts of the laws a group of parasites from Acharnae is assumed to exist; yet the twenty-eight parasites of the inscription come from a wide range of demes, and share no obvious common feature except surprisingly high social status.[9] Conceivably the festival had been opened out between the date of the king's laws and of the inscription. Two further groups (we do not know how recruited), 'old men' and 'women married to first husbands', joined the *basileus*, the *archontes*, and the parasites in 'supervising' an unrecorded activity.

The activities of the parasites are veiled in textual uncertainty. 'From their own part' (the meaning is obscure) 'they levied a *hekteus* of barley each'; they also, of course, banqueted, possibly on an ox selected from a sacred herd; the parasites from Acharnae sacrificed to (unexpectedly) Apollo, and also rendered him their *hekteus* from the barley-levy, 'for *thargelia* [cakes]' according to a bold emendation of a corrupt phrase. These scraps of information merely tantalize.

THE DEMES AROUND HEKALE. See Ch. 7, n. 34 above.

THE MARATHONIAN TETRAPOLIS.[10] The Tetrapolis, one of the supposed 'twelve cities of Cecrops', was honoured with a monograph by Philochorus (*FGrH* 328 F 73–77). It was supposedly founded by Xouthos the father of Ion (Strabo 8.7.1 [383]). The one surviving decree of the association, of the early second century BC, was to be displayed both on the acropolis and in the Dionysion at Marathon (*IG* II².1243), which we can therefore presume to have been its cultic centre; the one surviving dedication, by the 'Tetrapoleans to Dionysus', was found near Marathon and must derive from this shrine (*IG* II².2933 = *SIG*³ 930). An annual *archon*

---

[8] For details see R. Schlaifer, 'The Cult of Athena Pallenis', *HSCP* 54 (1943), 35–67—an admirable study of Athen. 6.234d–235d; and G. R. Stanton, *BSA* 79 (1984), 292–98, who re-edits the inscription (unknown to Schlaifer) *AM* 67, 1942 (1951), 24–29, no. 26. On cult 'parasites' see Schmitt Pantel, *Cité au banquet*, 100–104.

[9] Twelve demotics can be restored with near certainty, and many more surely appeared; Stanton, *BSA* 79 (1984), 296, considers the possibility that representation was tribal. Social status: of the six certainly identifiable parasites, five appear in Davies, *Propertied Families*.

[10] Cf. W. Wrede in *RE* s.v. *Tetrapolis* [+]; Jacoby on Philochorus *FGrH* 328 F 73–75.

was appointed (and apparently, by the second century, more than one), and four *hieropoioi*, one from each of the constituent demes.[11]

It is uncertain whether the association had once organized all the religious activities that took place within its territory. No explicit connection is ever made, for instance, between the Tetrapolis as an organization and the important Marathonian *Herakleia*. And in the post-Clisthenic period the constituent demes, headed by their demarchs, celebrated their own rites, sanctioned but not apparently shared by the Tetrapolis as a whole (see p. 111). Probably the individual '*poleis*' had always had their own festivals, with Tetrapolitan ceremonies functioning, as it were, as local *Panathenaea*.

The most remarkable feature of the Tetrapolis' activities is that it sent independent θεωρίαι to Delphi and to Delos, after observation of omens 'in the Python at Oinoe' and 'in the Delion at Marathon' respectively. These sacred ambassadors were perhaps drawn from specified *gene* (Philochorus *FGrH* 328 F 75). At the end of the third century Delphi honoured the Tetrapolitans for their traditional 'friendship to the god and the city' (*SIG*³ 541: cf. Ch. 12, n. 44), and the association was still represented in the sacred embassies again sent by Athens, after a long interval, from the end of the second century BC (*SIG*³ 541, n. 1; perhaps the independent θεωρία of the Tetrapolis had by now lapsed[12]).

It is an unresolved puzzle that the association's sacred calendar (*IG* II².1358 = *LSCG* 20) was found at Kukunari, well outside Tetrapolitan territory.[13]

KYDANTIDAI AND IONIDAI. A joint decree of these two smallish demes has recently been published (A. P. Matthaiou, *Horos* 7, 1989, 7–16 = *SEG* XXXIX 148), in which they resolve to honour the two κωλοκράται of 331/0 BC and the priest of Heracles, all members of Kydantidai, who καλῶς καὶ φιλοτίμως ἐπεμελήθησαν τῶν Ἡρακλέων τῶν τε σπονδ⟨ε⟩ίων καὶ τῶν θερινῶν. The decree is to be posted in the Herakleion.

Joint deme-decrees, local κωλακρέται (and the spelling), and the festivals of Heracles here named are all novelties. Nothing else seems to be known of the religious life of either deme. As to their relation, various possibilities can be envisaged,[14] but the easiest seems to be not a general *communio sacrorum* but participation by the men of Ionidai in a pair of rites celebrated at a Herakleion of the Kydantidai.

---

[11] Archon: *IG* II².1358 B 39–40 (*LSCG* 20); *IG* II².2933; contrast *IG* II².1243 (of *c*.190, Tracy). *Hieropoioi*: *IG* II².2933. For the identity of the 'four *poleis*' see e.g. Strabo 8.7.1 (383), Steph. Byz. s.v. Τετραπόλις. On the 'Dionysion' cf. Ch. 6, n. 29.

[12] So L. Ziehen, *RE* s.v. *Theoria*, 2230.

[13] It does not help to identify Kukunari with Hekale (see the notes to *IG* II² ad loc.), given that the association of 'demes around Hekale' (above) is otherwise treated as quite distinct (as it certainly is geographically) from the Tetrapolis.

[14] Matthaiou, *Horos* 7 (1989), 9, suggests that the two demes controlled the shrine in alternate years.

APPENDIX 4

Private Religious Associations

Attica is full of private religious associations that bear a confusing variety
of names: there are groups of *orgeones*, of *thiasotai*, of *eranistai*, of '*theastai*'
(an invented name for groups named from a god such as Asklepiastai) and
so on. The names matter little. *Eranistai*, for instance, are simply members
of a group that is financed by contributions from the members; but societies
of *thiasotai* and *theastai* often depended upon such *eranoi*, and in their
decrees it is common to find their members referred to as *eranistai* or their
leader described as *archeranistes*.[1] The title *orgeones* is a partial exception,
since groups of *orgeones* may once have enjoyed special privileges in relation to phratries, and a certain social cachet probably continued to attach to
the name; but already at the end of the fourth century we find a decree of
orgeones which speaks of the association as a *thiasos*.[2] There is also, as we
shall see, an early attested group of non-citizen *orgeones*, though a special
explanation is available in that case. Conversely, the same name (*thiasos*,
eranos) may cover a diversity of actual forms. The questions that need to be
asked about any society are 'Who belongs to it, and by what right?', 'How
durable is it?', 'What type of god does it honour?', 'What non-religious
functions does it perform?', 'What does it own (in particular, does it own its
own shrine), and how is it funded?'. The following brief survey of the possibilities will be very broadly chronological. This arrangement may serve as
an antidote to the view that the private association is a distinctively
Hellenistic phenomenon, a symptom of the collapse of the city as organizing centre of religious life.

We will start with the forms of association attested in the fifth and fourth
centuries. Groups of *orgeones* of the type that seems to have been traditional
were discussed in Chapter 7. They were apparently hereditary groups of
citizens devoted to the cult of a hero, whose shrine they owned. We also
hear of '*thiasoi* of Heracles', to one of which (in the one case where principles of admission are attested) a step-son was introduced by his step-
father.[3] These were doubtless often hereditary or (step-sons being
admissible) quasi-hereditary, though they perhaps need not have been so
exclusively. Aristophanes' first play, *Banqueters* (Δαιταλῆς), was named
from a group who 'dined in a shrine of Heracles and then got up and
became the chorus'. They were perhaps members of such a *thiasos*;

---

[1] See e.g. *IG* II².1297.10, 1335.5; *SEG* XXXII 149: refs. to *archeranistai* are very numerous.

[2] *AJA* 69 (1965), 104.

[3] Isae. 9.30: cf. Ferguson, 'Attic Orgeones', 70, n. 12, and A. Andrewes, *JHS* 81 (1961), 11.

certainly it is likely that the main cult-activity of the *thiasoi* was dining in honour of the great diner Heracles. A fine cult-table survives, from about 400, which declares that it belongs to 'Simon of Kydathenai, priest of Heracles, and the society [*koinon*] of *thiasotai*', who are then listed to the number of fifteen. The *'thiasos* of Etionidai' which made an offering in a shrine of Heracles in the Phaleron region in the mid-fifth century is doubtless another such group. If so, we can perhaps tentatively infer that the *thiasoi* met and dined in public Herakleia, not in shrines of their own.[4]

From these hereditary or semi-hereditary groups we turn to others that are elective (though family traditions doubtless often played a part too). Informal *thiasoi* brought together for particular rites were discussed in Chapter 9.[5] The accounts that we have of them are hostile, and the organizer of such a *thiasos* was in some danger of prosecution. One criticism that was made was that men and women participated together; and the barrier between citizen and metic might surely also have been broken. Whether any such *thiasoi* outlived the particular rite for which they were assembled is not demonstrable; it is certainly credible that some did.

Doubtless *theastai* should also be included, even though we know little about the two earliest attested instances. First come the *Dipoliastai*, whose *epimeletai*, both citizens, appear as vendors in a sales record of *c*.330;[6] the society was perhaps based at Phlya, home deme of one of the *epimeletai* and site of the plot of land that they sold. They evidently (witness the sales record) owned property, but are surely unlikely to have had a private shrine of Zeus of the City. Possibly they had sacral functions in connection with a public shrine of the god or at his festival, the *Dipolieia*.[7] In that event they would be comparable to the Pythaists or Hebdomaists or Deliasts associated with Apollo. (Indeed it has been suggested that the society of *Dipoliastai* simply brought together the various individual *gene* that were involved in the great festival.[8]) But would such a group own property? Perhaps they met to sacrifice (in a public precinct?) during the *Dipolieia* (and possibly on other occasions too). Are they then no more than a diningclub? We must come back to the problem of the relation between diningclub and religious association. In principle, at least, the common fund of the Dipoliasts probably existed to finance sacrifices to Zeus Polieus.

The other early *theastai* are the *Paianistai*, or much more probably *Panistai*, who are shown approaching a public cave of Pan in Menander's

---

[4] *Banqueters*: see testimonia iii to Ar. *Daitaleis* in K/A's edn. (cf. *IG* II².1267, a fragmentary decree of δαιταλεῖς or Δαιταλεῖς) . Table: *IG* II².2343; for prosopographical speculations about the members see S. Dow, *AJA* 73 (1969), 234–35; H. Lind, *MH* 42 (1985), 249–61 (with a photo). Etionidai: *IG* I³.1016; cf. App. 2 B above. A. D. Nock seems to underestimate the extent to which private associations made use of public shrines (*HThR* 29, 1936, 72–77 = his *Essays on Religion and the Ancient World*, Oxford 1972, I. 430–34).

[5] See pp. 161–3. Men and women: p. 162 above, and cf. perhaps the *thiasos* of Aeschines' mother (Ch. 9, n. 25 above, with H. Wankel, *ZPE* 34, 1979, 80).

[6] *Hesperia* 9 (1940), 331, no. 38.5.

[7] For theast names formed from a festival see Poland, *Vereinswesen*, 62.

[8] So Humphreys, 'Genos'. Pythaists: see E. Voutiras, *AJA* 86 (1982), 229–33. Deliasts: p. 88 n. 84 above. Note too the hypothetical Βορεασταί, Ch. 9, n. 14.

Dyskolos (230). No more can be said of them than that, unfortunately. But Dipoliasts and Panists together appear to show that there were citizen clubs honouring Greek gods in the late fourth century.

Possibly there also existed *Sabaziastai* in 342/1. At the same site as a decree of an association of *Sabaziastai* of 102/1 was found a dedication 'Dedicated by the *hieropoioi* in the archonship of Sosigenes [342/1]: Nikon, Eutychides, Demokles, Mantitheos'.[9] Prima facie this society too should be of Sabaziasts. Citizens or aliens? No other alien society has left any trace of its existence so early (though some must indeed have existed); on the other hand, the absence of demotics suggests—but fails to prove—that the *hieropoioi* were non-citizens. An exclusively non-Athenian society could not have owned a shrine at this date without the express permission of the assembly,[10] which there is no sign that the Sabaziasts had received; but the argument for identifying this group as Sabaziasts depends precisely on the premiss that a shrine existed, the same in 342 as in 102. None of the questions raised by this text can be answered.

We should also note the possibility that there were citizen *orgeones* of Bendis alongside the Thracian group which will be mentioned below.[11]

What of dining- and drinking-clubs? Were they in any sense religious associations of the type we are considering? We know the names of several such, of the late fifth and early fourth centuries: *Noumeniastai*, *Tetradistai*, *Dekadistai* (all named from the day of the month on which they met) and probably *Agathodaimonistai* (from the Agathos Daimon to whom third libations were poured).[12] They could apparently acquire a more formal structure: we have the beginning of a decree of banqueters or Banqueters (Δαιταλεῖς) and a fragment relating to a dining-club of citizens in the Piraeus, and the *Dekadistai* were property owners.[13] The hell-fire clubs of *Autolekythoi* and *Ithyphalloi* and *Triballoi* are inversions of the type, as is observed in a fragment of Lysias in connection with the *Kakodaimonistai*: they met and dined on days of ill omen, and 'called themselves *Kakodaimonistai* instead of *Noumeniastai*'.[14] Such groups obviously will have made libations and perhaps sacrifices (though they probably did not own shrines), and may have claimed the patronage of a particular god. The

[9] *IG* II².2932 (tentatively accepted by E. V. Lane, *Corpus Cultis Iovis Sabazii*, II, Leiden 1985, 26, no. 52). They are registered as citizens in *LGPN* II.

[10] See below, on *IG* II².337 (the formulation of which gives the argument from silence some force).

[11] See Ch. 9, n. 65 above.

[12] Lysias fr. 53 Thalheim, V Gernet/Bizos; Alexis fr. 260 K/A; Menander *Kolax* fr. 1 Sandbach; *IG* II².2701.8, Wilhelm's palmary conjecture in Theophr. *Char.* 27.11. *Agathodaimonistai* are implied by Lysias fr. 53 (so G. M. Calhoun, *Athenian Clubs in Politics and Litigation*, Austin, Tx. 1913, 32). Νεομηνιασταί are already now attested, unexpectedly, by graffiti in sixth-/fifth-cent. Olbia: E. I. Levi *et al.*, *Ol'viya. Temenos i Agora* (Moscow 1964), 140, and 142, fig. 9.

[13] *IG* II².1267 (but this may relate to a *thiasos* of Hercules, n. 3 above); *IG* II².2350 (cf. L. Robert, *EphArch* 1969, 7–14 = Robert, *OMS* VII.713–20); 2701.8.

[14] Dem. 54.14, 39; Lysias fr. 53: on their world see O. Murray in id. ed., *Sympotica* (Oxford 1990), 149–61.

Ithyphalloi, says Demosthenes with an obscene pun, 'initiated each other to Ithyphallos' (or 'with an *ithyphallos*'), and the name-day chosen by clubs of *Tetradistai* type seems always to have been sacred. The fourth of the month, for instance, was dedicated to Aphrodite and Hermes, and a fragment of Menander duly presents *Tetradistai* feasting together during the festival of Aphrodite Pandemos.[15] The bad boys had a taste for sacrilege which might represent an inversion of religious practices found in more orthodox societies: the *Triballoi* ate polluted relics,[16] and it was in such milieux that the parody of the Mysteries took place.

Hebdomaistai were mentioned earlier. They are known from a fourth-century relief of Apollo dedicated in, perhaps, the Pythion at Marathon by 'the *Hebdomaistai* in the year of . . .'.[17] Initially, they sound like something quite different, not a spontaneously created dining-society but a college, recruited annually or periodically, attached to a shrine (like the 'parasites' of certain cults, perhaps). Yet there may after all be some analogy between *Hebdomaistai*, feasting no doubt at Apollo's festival, and *Tetradistai* feasting at Aphrodite's.

Still, none of this is enough to show that any one of the *hetaireiai* was a religious association in the sense that its formal purpose was to honour a god or hero. The gap between the two forms is possibly bridged by a society known as the *Eikadeis*; even if it is not, this group demands our attention as an unquestionable religious association of a type quite different from those seen so far. They are known from a decree, of 324/3, found near Hymettus; two *horoi* of their 'common property' from the same region; and the roughly contemporary record of the sale of a plot of land on Salamis by ἐκ Σαλαμῖνος Εἰκαδέων βούλ[αρχος], one Olympiodorus son of Eumelus.[18] (Does this last text imply a separate Salaminian branch?) The decree contains a denunciation of certain members of the group who, contrary to their oath and 'the curse which Eikadeus swore', have borne witness in court 'to the detriment of the common property of the *Eikadeis*, from which they sacrifice to the gods'. The *archontes* of the group for that year are to display the decree in the shrine (otherwise unknown) of Apollo Parnessios. Obviously the name of the *Eikadeis*, 'twentiethers', derives ultimately from the twentieth of the month, one of Apollo's sacred days. At first sight, then, they belong in a series with the *Tetradistai* and the rest, and we have the proof that such a group could indeed be a true religious association with common property to support a cult. There is a complication, however. In the case of the *Eikadeis* an intermediary intrudes between the day and the group, in the form of (we must assume) the founder-hero Eikadeus,[19] whose curse the members fear. So we cannot simply assume that whatever

[15] Dem. 54.17; Menander, *Kolax*, fr. 1 Sandbach. Not much can be done with the information that the members of the club evoked in Lys. 8 engaged (5) in a συνθεωρεῖν to Eleusis.
[16] Dem. 54.39.   [17] See Voutiras, *AJA* 86 (1982), 229–33.
[18] *IG* II².1258, 2631–32 (this is probably the property mentioned in the sales record *Agora* XIX P26.384, 395: cf. B. D. Meritt, *Hesperia* 5, 1936, 409); 1596.12.
[19] He is attested only here; but see *RE* s.v. *Eikadios* for another hero closely associated with Apollo.

is true of the *Tetradistai* is likely also to be true of the *Eikadeis* (whose history may be much more complicated), and vice versa. Possibly they were in fact a hereditary group of *genos* type.[20] (*Archontes* are also found in *gene*.)

However that may be, the text suggests one further intriguing possibility. The particular court-case at issue in the decree concerned, it is true, the society's own property, and this is all that members were sworn, under threat of the curse of Eikadeus, to defend. But one may wonder whether there was not strong pressure on them to aid each other in legal affairs of other kinds too. In that case, religious society would merge with the kind of sworn society for mutual aid in court cases (and elections) that is notorious from Thucydides.[21]

We must now set a class of document aside. Several instances of collective dedications by a group of *eranistai* are known. One that falls in our period is a stele bearing a relief of Zeus and inscribed '*Eranistai* dedicated to Zeus Philios in the archonship of Hegesias [324/3]' (*IG* II².2935). *Eranistai* could, it is true, constitute a lasting religious society with officers and regular sacrifices and so on. But it is not certain that such a society exists whenever *eranistai* appear, even if the context is religious.[22] The *eranistai* who made the dedication to Zeus Philios may have been primarily united by any one of the many, mostly secular, forms of co-operation that could be described as an *eranos*; sometimes, perhaps, the *eranos* was formed precisely in order to finance an offering. The same doubt applies to collective dedications made by *eranistai* who were mining-slaves at Laurion.[23]

The associations considered so far have been of citizens (though non-citizens may have participated in some informal *thiasoi*). But there were also groups of foreigners honouring foreign gods. In 333/2 the merchants of Kition sought and obtained the permission of the assembly to buy land on which to found a shrine of their Aphrodite, 'as the Egyptians have founded a shrine of Isis'.[24] Both groups must have constituted a *koinon* or *thiasos* of some kind. There are also the *orgeones* of Bendis, *orgeones* these of a quite untraditional type. They worship a goddess, not a hero; they, or a group of them, are non-citizens; and they resolve to solicit applications for membership 'so that there may be as many *orgeones* of the shrine as possible'.[25] Clearly the old rule that anyone admitted to a group of *orgeones* must also

---

[20] So Lambert, *Phratries*, 365: 'a geminated *genos* with some members on Salamis, others elsewhere'.

[21] 8.54.4.

[22] So rightly Poland, *Vereinswesen*, 28 f. On secular *eranoi* cf. Millett, *Lending and Borrowing*, 153–59.

[23] *IG* II².2937–40: see S. Lauffer, *Die Bergwerkssklaven von Laureion*² (Wiesbaden 1979), 177–92 (who makes a good case for the group having a more than momentary existence). Cf. 2354 ('fin. s. IIa', Tracy), a dedication to an unnamed recipient by a '*koinon* of *eranistai*' consisting of thirteen women and ten men without demotics, one of them named Syros; and *SEG* XXI 633 (early second cent. BC) 'The *eranistai* to the hero', followed by a complete list of ten male names without demotics; also *IG* II².2934, a collective dedication to the Nymphs by οἱ πλυνῆς.

[24] *IG* II².337; cf. Ch. 10, n. 69 and Ch. 11, n. 92 above.

[25] *IG* II².1361, late fourth cent. Cf. Ch. 9, n. 63 above.

be automatically admitted to an associated phratry did not apply in this case. On the other hand, like traditional *orgeones*, those of Bendis own and administer a shrine. In this they are also like the merchants of Kition and other foreign groups. They are allowed the probably more honourable title of *orgeones*, it has been argued, because, uniquely, they have a role in an Athenian public cult.[26]

The most obvious development in the third century is a dramatic expansion of non-citizen groups. The first surviving decree issued by such a group dates from 302/1, and it has been suggested that they first acquired formal rights of association in 306, as a by-product of the failure of Sophocles of Sunium's attempt to muzzle the philosophical schools.[27] But that right had by implication already been acknowledged in the case of the Egyptians and Kitians and Thracians by the 330s, as we have seen. Surely the movement attested by those cases was merely gathering speed. *Thiasos* is the typical third-century term for such a society. Sometimes they are exactly of the type just discussed, societies of foreigners gathered round a native god. Aphrodite and Adonis are honoured, it seems, by Phoenicians, the only named worshipper of Zeus Labraundios of Caria is a Carian, and two of the three known *thiasotai* of the Phrygian hero Tynaros bear foreign-sounding names.[28] But we also now find non-citizen Greeks, and eventually slaves, figuring in such associations. The two named members of a *thiasos* of the Mother of the Gods in the Piraeus, for instance, are a Troezenian and a Heracleot, while in another (deity unknown) we find a Salaminian and an Olynthian.[29] Several *thiasoi* seem to be composed in large part of slaves.[30] In fact no member of a group described as a *thiasos* is demonstrably a citizen in any of the quite numerous third-century inscriptions that speak of the institution. (One citizen *thiasotes* appears, however, in a text of 194/3, apparently the last where a word of the root *thiaso-* is found.[31]) It is doubtless because the members of such associations often lacked kin close to hand that they were sometimes bound to attend, or help to finance, each other's funerals.[32]

[26] Cf. pp. 170–1 above; and on 'non-traditional' *orgeones*, Ferguson, 'Attic Orgeones', 95–121. There may, however, have been another group of non-citizen *orgeones*, those who honour a Μαρωνίτης in *IG* II².2947 (*c*.200).

[27] IG II².1261; Ferguson, 'Attic Orgeones', 67. On Sophocles' measure see Alexis fr. 99 with K/A [+].

[28] *IG* II².1261 (302/1) (cf. Ch. 9, n. 29), 1271 (third cent.), 1262 (301).

[29] *IG* II².1273 (cf. Ch. 9, n. 145), 1263 (301/0).

[30] See *SEG* XXIV 223; Ch. 9, n. 66 above (the *thiasos* from Salamis); n. 33 below. For other non-citizen *thiasotai*, see *IG* II².2943.7–8, (?) 2352.

[31] *IG* II².1323. The readings in *Hesperia* 16 (1947) 63, no. 1 and *SEG* XXI 533 are doubtless wrong. For further *thiasos* inscriptions (not yielding names of deities) see *IG* II².1263 (301/0), 1275, 1277 (? 278/7), (?) 1278, 1318, 2347 ('post med. s. iv a'), (?) 2348–49, (?) 2351–52, 2936 ('fin s. iv a'), (?) 2943; *Hesperia* 15 (1946), 214, no. 43, *SEG* XXI 532 (227/6).

[32] See *IG* II².1275, 1277.15, 1323.10: cf. M. N. Tod, *BSA* 13 (1906–7), 336, and on *IG* II².1327.10 ff. Ferguson, 'Attic Orgeones', 115. *IG* II².1275 requires the members, vaguely, to protect one another from wrongdoing.

Such non-citizen *thiasoi* typically honour 'foreign' gods. At the centre of their communal life there is normally a shrine which they own—necessarily, since there was no temple of Zeus of Labraunda, for instance, at Athens until the *thiasotai* provided one (a very presentable one, with a portico, in this case). But Greek gods are found too, and it may be that in these cases the society met in a public precinct. (Slave *thiasoi* evidently did not control private shrines.) A group of *eranistai*, whose only named member is an *isoteles*, sacrifice to 'Zeus Saviour and Heracles and the Saviours'; there are 'Artemisiasts' whose only named member is a Cyrenaean; and a *thiasos* at Eleusis consisting predominantly, it seems, of slaves sacrificed to '[ ] and Zeus Soter and Hygieia'.[33] This last group, in the hard days of the Demetrian war (238/7 or thereabouts), met, monthly, in the private house of their treasurer, who had apparently 'received the sacred objects' for the purpose. Was this normal, or would they have assembled in public precincts in better times?

One Piraeus society honours some of its members for their work on extending the temple of Ammon, and decrees that these honours should be proclaimed 'at the sacrifice of Amphiaraus'. Neither of the two named members is given a demotic, though one has a patronymic, and they are likely to be non-citizens.[34] Was the 'sacrifice of Amphiaraus' one performed by the society itself? In that event, this is the only instance where one such group is involved with two unrelated gods. Possibly the private society was exploiting the opportunity to make a proclamation at a public rite (cf. Aeschin. 3.41).

Citizen groups also increase somewhat. *Orgeones* of Asclepius (most of them interrelated) appear at Prospalta, and Asclepiasts at the city Asclepieum;[35] whether there is a functional difference, the *orgeones* administering a local shrine, the Asclepiasts merely using a public one, can only be guessed. *Amphieraistai* are recruited to repair the shrine, and revive the cult, of Amphiaraus in the fortress at Rhamnus.[36] These were not surprising developments, given the place that *orgeones* had long had in the cult of healing-heroes. It is more interesting that a shrine of Magna Mater in the Piraeus is now under the control of a group of citizen *orgeones*, and flourished under this management for centuries.[37] (We have already noted the possibility that there may have been citizen *orgeones* of Bendis in the fourth century.) A further group of *orgeones* (of unknown status) of an unnamed goddess is attested around the middle of the century. And at the end of it,

---

[33] *IG* II².1291 ('med. saec. III': 'the Saviours' are probably the Dioscuri, cf. *IG* XII.3 Suppl. 1333; Moretti, II.126); *IG* II².2942 ('s. III'); *SEG* XXIV 156, with L. Robert, *ArchEph* 1969, 14–23 (*SEG* XXXII 149: Robert *OMS* VII.720–29). For *thiasoi* and Greek gods cf. *IG* II².2939/4339 ('s. iv'), a dedication to Athena Organe by one Bacchios when 'crowned by his *thiasotai*'.

[34] *IG* II².1282 (263/2 or 262/1). But *LGPN* II, allows them citizen status.

[35] *IG* II².2355 ('s. III a.?'), 1293 (*SEG* XVIII 33: 'med. s. III'), cf. 2353.

[36] *IG* II².1322 (Ch. 9, n. 83 above).   [37] See Ch. 9, n. 146 above.

a citizen priestess appears to be ministering to a group of *orgeones* (of Magna Mater again?) in Athens itself.[38]

In none of these groups did citizen demonstrably mix with non-citizen. If there were citizen *orgeones* of Bendis, they formed a distinct group from the Thracians. In the second century, by contrast, mixed associations became commonplace. And there is in fact one clear instance of mixing in the third, a dedication to Artemis made in the year of Philip (269/8 or thereabouts) by four *hieropoioi* of an unknown (but doubtless private) worshipping-group in the Piraeus: two are citizens, one an *isoteles*, one a man of Soli.[39] One must also allow that in most of the third-century groups too few persons of identifiable status are attested for it to be certain that members were exclusively of one class. Special uncertainties arise when members of a society are listed without Attic demotics but bear non-servile Greek names. The comfortable doctrine does, indeed, exist that at this date a person without demotic is a person without citizenship; and in respect of honorary decrees or other contexts where an individual is on prominent display it has perhaps some force. That criterion would establish that the officials of the *Sarapiastai*, who lack demotics even when honoured, are not citizens.[40] But when applied to membership-lists (paid for by the letter) it may be less trustworthy. In the list of members of a mixed society of *c.*150–130, for instance, demotics are added to distinguish homonyms, not to mark status: those who lack them do so not necessarily because they lack citizenship, but because no other member of the group happens to share their name.[41] Thus there must be some doubt about the status of the *thiasotai/eranistai* (male and female) who met, almost certainly, in the public shrine of Artemis Kalliste in the 240s and 230s.[42] Their decrees name an *archeranistes* and the proposer of a decree, both without demotics. These two then are probably non-citizens, by the criterion accepted earlier. But it is not quite certain that this conclusion can be extended to the full list of fifty-eight members. This is particularly unfortunate when they are such a good example of a *thiasos* based upon a public shrine.

Late-attested need not be late-created, and traditions have a certain shaping force: it may be prudent to end by looking briefly at the associations of the second and first centuries. *Thiasos* as a designation disappears; *eranistai* by contrast (who are often also *theastai*) proliferate, and terms such as σύνοδος become more frequent. Mixed societies, as we have noted, are

---

[38] *IG* II².1289, with Ferguson, 'Attic Orgeones', 84–86; *SEG* XVII 36, of 212/1 or *c.*200 (Tracy, 253).*

[39] *IG* II².2859.*   [40] So S. Dow, *HThR* 30 (1937), 197, on *IG* II².1292 (215/4).

[41] *IG* II².2358, cf. Poland, *Vereinswesen*, 304 (a point uncharacteristically overlooked by Dow, *HThR* 30, 1937).

[42] *IG* II².1297–98 (? 237/6 and 244/3): cf. Poland, *Vereinswesen*, 308–309. These two texts seem certainly to derive from two similar *thiasoi* attached to the shrine of Artemis Kalliste, even if not from the same *thiasos* (A. Wilhelm, *ArchEph* 1905, 201). The contrast with the demotic-bearing priest in 1297 is not decisive: he is not a member, and cf. anyway *IG* II².2343. 2347 (unnamed god) and 1265 (*eranistai*) raise the same problem.

henceforth commonplace.[43] Some groups exclusive to citizens are still created, and citizens still predominate in many mixed societies. Non-citizen associations, of the type hitherto known as *thiasoi*, now bear different names, and become perhaps rather less common. About the activities and organization of several of the attested groups nothing is known (important though their documents may be prosopographically).[44] We will look only at those that are more revealing.

The Dionysiasts or *orgeones* of Dionysus are first attested in 185/4 by a decree honouring their life-priest and great benefactor, Dionysius of Marathon.[45] They are a select band of rich citizens, equipped by courtesy of Dionysius with a luxurious shrine in the Piraeus at which they met monthly. The shrine was in the courtyard, it seems, of Dionysius' own house; before its construction, meetings may have happened in the house itself. Membership is fixed apparently at fifteen, with son in principle succeeding father (an unexpected reappearance of the hereditary principle). A second decree follows Dionysius' death: the life-priesthood is to pass to his son, and the *orgeones* are to consider how he himself may be 'heroized', and his image set in the shrine 'beside the god, where his father is'. (This image of Dionysus beside which heroized mortals were set had been 'added' by Dionysius 'in accordance with the oracle of the god'.) This society, so dominated by one great family, is likely to have been founded by them not long in the past.

Much humbler apparently is a *sunodos* of Heracles, which admitted as new members in 159/8 five citizens, two Antiochenes, and seven or eight persons of unspecified origin (some probably slaves). From a few years later comes a membership-list, containing over ninety names of both sexes, of an unknown society. The *archeranistes* and his son the priest are both Antiochenes, but citizens of high status also belong (as also does a 'Daos').[46] Two documents of 112/1 reveal groups of seafarers: a 'society of shipowners and traders who pay the contribution to Zeus Xenios', and a 'house' (*oikos*), whose members are also called οἱ κατακλειμένοι, 'banqueters', which honours those protectors of sailors the Great Gods (and a deity beginning with A). Both are fundamentally non-citizen groups (though the former has a citizen treasurer).[47]*

In 102/1, the Sabaziasts of the Piraeus resolved to place a list of *eranistai* 'in the shrine' (the one they owned, or habitually used?). The list survives

---

[43] See *IG* II².1323 = *SIG*³ 1103 (194/3); *SEG* XXXVI 228 (a σύνοδος of Heracles, 159/8); *IG* II².2358 ('c. 150'), 1335 (102/1). *IG* II².1327.33 (? 178/7) attests a foreign *epimeletes* in the citizen society of *orgeones* of Magna Mater.

[44] e.g. *AJA* 64 (1960), 269 (59/8); *SEG* XXXVII 103 (52/1).

[45] *IG* II².1325–26 (*SIG*³ 1100–1101, *LSCG* 49), cf. 2948: cf. Ferguson, 'Attic Orgeones', 115–19, and on the shrine, Garland, *Piraeus*, 146.

[46] *SEG* XXXVI 228 (οἰκογενής in line 8 may be a description, not a name); *IG* II².2358 (n. 41 above).

[47] *IG* II².1012 (*SIG*³ 706); *Hesperia* 30 (1961), 229–30, nos. 28–29 = *SEG* XXI 535–36 (cf. J. Velissaropoulos, *Les nauclères grecs*, Paris 1980, 104–106 and esp. Robert, *EphArch* 1969, 7–14 = Robert *OMS* VII.713–20). The named members of the *oikos* are foreign; the worshippers of Zeus Xenios (NB) have a citizen *proxenos*.

complete, and shows that the society, exclusively male, consisted of thirty-six citizens (some ex-ephebes, that is to say fairly prosperous), thirteen non-citizens, one 'public slave', and three persons of unspecified origin. A Phoenician/Greek bilingual text of 96 BC from the Piraeus set up by the '*koinon* of the Sidonians' honours one Diopeithes/Shama'abaal for erecting a portico to the (unnamed) god's temple. In 95/4, in the Piraeus again, we meet *orgeones* of 'Syrian Aphrodite' (doubtless a fairly recent introduction). All that emerges is that the goddess had a Corinthian priestess, honours for whom were proposed by a male citizen. '*Heroistai* of Diotimus and . . . and Pammenes', three dead members of an extremely prominent Marathonian family, are attested in 57/6. The *archeranistes* is a son of one of the heroes, but the group, in some financial difficulties it seems (or is it meanness of the rich?), resolves to recruit new Heroists on payment of a fee. We end with a society of sixty Soteriasts, founded in 42 or thereabouts by a citizen who remained its leading figure and patron for the next five years. The five named members are citizens; like the earlier *thiasos* of Artemis Kalliste, it was based at what appears to have been an existing *temenos*, of Artemis Soteira.[48]

[48] Sabaziasts: *IG* II².1335. Sidonians: *IG* II².2946; J. C. L. Gibson, *Textbook of Syrian Semitic Inscriptions*, III (Oxford 1982), no. 41; for the date, Tracy, 247. 'Syrian Aphrodite': *IG* II².1337, cf. Ferguson, 'Attic Orgeones', 119–21. Heroists: *IG* II².1339—on the family cf. *LGPN* II, s.v. *Zenon* (*Marathon*) and *Pammenes* (*Marathon*). Soteriasts: *IG* II².1343 (*SIG*³ 1104), cf. 4695.

Addenda

An asterisk at the end of a paragraph or note in the main work refers the reader to an addendum here.

5 n. 16 On the problem of definition see now S.B. Aleshire, 'Towards a definition of "State Cult" for Ancient Athens', in R. Hägg ed., *Ancient Greek Cult Practice from the Epigraphical Evidence* (Stockholm 1994), 9–16.

9 n. 30 The location for the 'ancient agora' implied by Apollodorus (*FGrH* 244 F 13) is, in all seeming, incompatible with that which has come into favour since Dontas's discovery in 1982 of the 'true Aglaurion' (see e.g. C. Schnurr, *ZPE* 105 (1995), 131–38); but the only testimony to the existence of an ancient agora is precisely that of Apollodorus. So, *pace* the statements on p. 8 and elsewhere, recent developments have if anything strengthened the probability that Apollodorus was speculating to explain a cult-title of Aphrodite, not exploiting authentic knowledge of archaic Athens.

9 n. 31 T. L. Shear, ''Ἰσονόμους τ' Ἀθήνας ἐποιησάτην': The Agora and the Democracy', in W. D. E. Coulson *et al.* eds., *The Archaeology of Athens and Attica under the Democracy* (Oxford 1994), 225–48, at 226, draws an opposite conclusion to Morris's: this must have been the home of the living.

34 n. 21 C. M. Antonaccio, *An Archaeology of Ancestors* (Lanham, Md. 1995), has now appeared; for Attic material see especially pp. 102–26, 166–68 (Phrontis), 186–97 ('sacred houses'). She denies that the eighth-century enclosure wall at Eleusis (p. 35 above) is a mark of reverence, given that five of the tombs within had recently been looted.

50 n. 30 The 'totalitarian' vision of the *polis* endorsed here (and e.g. on p. 215) is disputed by M. H. Hansen, *The Athenian Democracy in the Age of Demosthenes* (Oxford 1991), 61–64, 79–81. But he allows that religion is a partial exception to his conception of the citizen's unrestrained 'personal or private freedom'.

71 n. 13 For a post-Pisistratean date for the temple of Athena see too now W. P. E. Childs in Coulson ed., *Archaeology of Athens*, 1–6.

72 n. 19. T. Hayashi, *Bedeutung und Wandel des Triptolemosbildes vom 6.–4. Jh. v. Chr.* (Würzburg 1992), 20–22 and K. Clinton, 'The Eleusinian Mysteries and Panhellenism in Democratic Athens', in W. Coulson ed., *Archaeology of Athens*, 161–72, at 162, now argue for a down-dating of the *telesterion* to the late Pisistratid or early democratic period.

73 n. 22 Shear, 'Agora and Democracy', now argues that the *agora* first acquired important political buildings (*bouleuterion, stoa basileios*) under the young democracy.

73 n. 24 Hayashi, *Triptolemosbild*, 19–20, argues that the city Eleusinion may pre-date Pisistratus.

97 n. 126 Cf. Hayashi, *Triptolemosbild*, 15–29, who ascribes all developments in the cult to the Pisistratids or the young democracy rather than to Pisistratus.

109 n. 28 Cf. the addendum to p. 192 n. 145.

124 n. 13 H. Beister, 'Neue Aspekte zur Beurteilung der Kalliasdekrete (*IG* I³ 52)', in *ΠΡΑΚΤΙΚΑ ΤΟΥ Η' ΔΙΕΘΝΟΥΣ ΣΥΝΕΔΡΙΟΥ ΕΛΛΗΝΙΚΗΣ ΚΑΙ ΛΑΤΙΝΙΚΗΣ 'ΕΠΙΓΡΑΦΙΚΗΣ*, II (Athens 1987), 51–56, tries to set the institution of a central board of 'Treasurers of the Other Gods' into a similar context of 'die Einschränkung oder gar Verdrängung begrenzter lokaler bzw. gentiler Institutionen durch solche der politischen Gesamtgemeinde'. But he underestimates the importance of T. Linders' argument (*The Treasurers of the Other Gods in Athens and their Function*, Meisenheim 1975, 12–16) that the cults concerned had perhaps all already been publicly administered; and he has to explain the evidence she deploys for the continuing existence of local administration, in parallel with that of the central board, as a sign that the aims of the Callias decrees were only partially fulfilled. I hope to make good my neglect of these questions of cult administration elsewhere.

126 n. 20 Use of the lot in the choice of priests is treated by Plato (*Leg.* 759b) as a form of divine selection. On that view there would be no need to see it as derivative from democratic practice. But see the sceptical remarks of Hansen (*Athenian Democracy*, 49–52), about this understanding of the lot (whether for choosing priests or magistrates).

127 n. 21 The priesthood of Artemis Agrotera too was probably annual in the 2nd cent. BC (*Hesperia* 6, 1937, 457–58 no. 7. 12), and W. S. Ferguson speculatively suggested, from a juxtaposition of *IG* II². 1297 and 788, that the priesthood of Kalliste rotated tribally (*Klio* 7, 1907, 213–14). Note too that the system of tribal rotation was applied to numerous cults on Delos when the Athenians reacquired control of the island in the 2nd cent. BC (Aleshire, *Asklepieion*, 76). Another cult for which dating by priestess is common is that of Eileithyia (*IG* II².4682, etc.).

131 n. 33 See too now R. Stupperich, 'The Iconography of Athenian State Burial in the Classical Period', in Coulson ed., *Archaeology of Athens*, 93–103.

140 n. 73 Cf. now M. H. Jameson, 'Theoxenia', in Hägg ed., *Cult Practice*, 35–57, at 51–53 [+].

143 n. 85 *IG* I³.391 records very small returns ἀπὸ τὸ σίτο τῆς ἀπαρχῆς for the years 422/1–419/8: on the problem see most recently K. Clinton, 'The

Epidauria and the arrival of Asclepius in Athens', in Hägg ed., *Cult Practice*, 17–34, at 32.

160 n. 29 V. Pirenne-Delforge, *L'Aphrodite grecque* (Athens 1994), 351–52, 363–66, stresses that a cult of Adonis (so named) in Cyprus is attested only in literary texts of the Roman period (Paus. 9.41.2; Steph. Byz. s.v. Ἀμαθοῦς). So even when practised by foreigners the 'foreign' cult may have been affected by Greek myth, which regularly associated Adonis with Cyprus via Aphrodite.

174 n. 76 Cf. now Z. H. Archibald, 'Thracians and Scythians', in *CAH*² VI (1994), 444–75.

177 n. 85 Clinton, 'Epidauria', discusses the arrival of Asclepius in detail. He points out, with regard to the role of Sophocles, that *IG* II².3195 (late 1st cent. AD) attests a commemorative ritual of ὑποδοχή and μύησις of Asclepius. He opposes the correction δ⟨ρ⟩άκ[οντα] in *IG* II².4960.13. Above all he adduces six lines from an unpublished sacred law, probably a fragment of Nicomachus' first codification of 410–404. As restored it records substantial payments made Ἐπιδα[υρίοις] to Δέμε[τρος ἱερείαι] ἱιερ[ομνέμοσι], ἀκο[λούθοις], and φρ[οροῖς]. Clinton identifies the ἱιερομνέμονες and φροροί with Epidaurian officials attested e.g. in *IG* IV² 40–41, and infers that the Athenian *Epidauria* were so named because of the actual (and, if he is right, very unusual) participation of functionaries of the Epidaurian cult.

179 n. 94 See the addendum to 177 n. 85.

185 n. 116 Beschi's identification of Sophocles/Dexion on the Telemachus monument is endorsed by F. van Straten, *Hierá Kalá* (Leiden 1995), 70–71.

188 n. 127 The cult of Ἀφροδίτος and Ερμαφροδίτος known in Athens in the 5th and 4th cents. (Phot. α 3404, citing Ar. fr. 325 and Pherecrates fr. 184 K/A; Theophr. *Char.* 16.10; *AM* 62, 1937, 7 no. 5) derived, if we believe Philochorus (*FGrH* 328 F 184) and later commentators, from Cypriot cults, which certainly existed, of bisexual deities: see Pirenne-Delforge, *L' Aphrodite grecque*, 67–70. It should doubtless have been mentioned as another 'foreign' cult. E. Vikelas's important monograph *Die Weihreliefs aus dem Athener Pankrates-Heiligtum am Ilissos* (*AM-BH* 16, Berlin 1994) has now been published. The case for a significant foreign element in the cult does not seem to me to have been made out.

192 n. 143 For another probable cult place of Mother in Athens itself see *SEG* XLI 121.

192 n. 144 The grave monument (Piraeus Museum 3627, ex Athens NM 1030) which bears *CEG* 566 shows the deceased woman holding a temple key, approached by a girl who holds out a large round tympanum to her (C. W. *Clairmont, Classical Attic Tombstones*, 6 vols., Kilchberg 1993, no.

1.934). Three other Attic funerary monuments show a dead woman holding, as it seems, a tympanum: Piraeus Museum 217 (*IG* II².12292; Clairmont, *Tombstones*, 2.362); Athens Nat. Mus. 3287 (from the Dipylon region: Clairmont no. 13); Ashmolean Museum Oxford 1959.203 (Clairmont no. 14). The last of these also shows a lion seated beneath the dead woman's chair. If all these women were, like the first, priestesses of Cybele, the number associated with the single cult surprises, only about ten or eleven priestesses in all by Clairmont's count being identifiable on tombstones (*Tombstones*, VI.147–48). If some were only devotees, we have important evidence that this was indeed (cf. 198 n. 166) a special devotion. (I owe knowledge of these monuments to J. B. Connelly's monograph [in preparation] on priestesses, and am most grateful to the author for discussion.)

192 n. 145 A preliminary report on the inscriptions from the shrine of (Herakles) Pankrates has revealed a society of citizen *orgeones* based there. But a κοινὸν τῶν θιασωτῶν and an organized group of ἐρανισταί also appear. The officers of the latter in 300/299 were Mys, Apollodorus of Miletus, Eunostos of Thebes, Demophilus of Heraclea, Dionysius, Konon of Heraclea (*SEG* XLI 171); two ἰσοτελεῖς are mentioned in other texts from the shrine. See A. G. Kalogeropoulou in *ΠΡΑΚΤΙΚΑ ΤΟΥ Η' ΔΙΕΘΝΟΥΣ ΣΥΝΕΔΡΙΟΥ* II, 298–304 (with full summary in *SEG* XLI 247).

196 n. 157 The nickname 'Ammon' borne by Hipponikos I (Heraclides Ponticus fr. 58 Wehrli ap. Ath. 536f–537c) may indicate that Ammon was already consulted in aristocratic circles *c*.500 BC (so Davies, *Propertied Families*, 256–58, and M. Zorat, 'Atene e il santuario di Ammone', in L. Braccesi ed., *Hesperia*, I, Rome 1990, 89–123); but A. B. Bosworth, in I. Worthington ed., *Ventures into Greek History* (Oxford 1994), 22, thinks that a guest-friendship between Hipponikos and a Cyrenaean would suffice to explain the name.

196 n. 159 The identification of the altar is disputed by M. Osanna, 'Il problema topografico del santuario di Afrodite Urania ad Atene', *ASAtene* NS 48–49 (1988–89), 73–95 (where the character of the goddess' cult is also discussed).

198 n. 166 See the addendum to 192 n. 144.

222 n. 16 On the panhellenic standing of the Mysteries in this period see Clinton, 'Mysteries and Panhellenism'.

228 n. 40 Olga Palagia, 'No Demokratia', in Coulson ed., *Archaeology of Athens*, 113–22, now associates the giant torso with Agathe Tyche.

240 n. 81 'Soteles the Athenian' and his troops made dedications to Zeus Soter, Poseidon and Artemis Soteira (Soteles alone made another to Poseidon Asphaleios) at Failaka in the Gulf of Kuwait late in the 3rd cent. (?): see *Failaka. Fouilles Françaises 1986–1988* (Lyon 1990), 193–95.

246 n. 101 'Coins for the *Eleusinia*': these coins have been updated to 'the second quarter of the fourth century' and associated with the the Mysteries rather than the *Eleusinia* by J. H. Kroll, *AJA* 96 (1992), 355–56; cf. Clinton, 'Mysteries and Panhellenism', 169.

273 n. 74 'Die mit dem Demos verbundenen Chariten sind . . . als der personificirte Begriff der Dankbarkeit zu fassen (Arist. Eth. Nicom. V,8)': W. Vischer, 'Die Entdeckungen im Theater des Dionysos zu Athen', in id., *Kleine Schriften*, II (Leipzig 1878), 363 (from *Neues schweizerisches Museum* 1863, III). The Teos decree is now available as *SEG* XLI 1003 C/D 29–44.

275 n. 83 An inventory of *c*.325 from the agora is tentatively associated with the hero general by D. M. Lewis, *ZPE* 36 (1979), 131–34.

294 A collective payment 'to the Eumolpids' appears in the Eleusinian accounts *IG* I³.386.12.

312 Was the deme of Sunium a favoured home for νεοπολῖται? See Anaxandrides fr. 4.4. K/A (on mutability) πολλοὶ δὲ νῦν μέν εἰσιν οὐκ ἐλεύθεροι,/εἰς αὔριον δὲ Σουνιεῖς, and Hdt. 6.90 on the settlement of pro-Athenian Aeginetans at Sunium early in the 5th cent.

340 n. 38 Note too the addendum to 192 n.145.

340 n. 39 Possibly the ἐρανισταί of Pankrates were a mixed group; but it is far from certain that the Mys and Dionysios of *SEG* XLI 171 (see addendum to 192 n. 145) were citizens.

341 I overlooked *AM* 66 (1941), 228 no. 4 (cf. Ferguson, 'Orgeonika', 163), a decree (found in Athens) issued in 138/7 by *orgeones* of Aphrodite. The only named member, the ἐπιμελητής , is from Heraclea; he is said to have made sacrifice 'on behalf of the Athenian people' as well as on behalf of the society of *orgeones*.

Select Index of Sources and Monuments

A. LITERARY TEXTS

Note too the entries under individual authors in the subject index.

B. INSCRIPTIONS

Subject Index

Greek words are positioned alphabetically as if transliterated into English. Please look for Greek names beginning with kappa under both C and K.

abstractions, personified, cult of 228–37
Academy region:
    altar of Eros 74
    PG and G cults in 18, 33
Acharnae, Mycenaean remains 11
    and league of Athena Pallenis 331
    see also Menidi
Achniadai (phratry) 106
acropolis:
    buildings of 19, 40, 69–71
    dedications on 18, 40, 71 n. 17, 271
    Mycenaean 11
    (?)residence of Pisistratus 72 n. 18, 84
administrators, religious 78, 127, 244–5
    see also *Dionysia*; Mysteries; Zeus Soter
Adonia 160 n. 29, 162 n. 33, 194, 197–8
Adonis 160, 194
    Phoenician cult of 160 n. 29, 338
Adrasteia 172, 195, 197
Aeacus 157
Aegeis 119
Aegeus (tribal eponym) 118
Aegina:
    Athenian wars with 157
    horoi from 144
    social groups in 63 n. 26
Aeschines:
    on Amphipolis 225–6
    mother of 159
Aeschylus, *Oreithuia* 157
Agathe Theos 231 n. 49
Agathe Tyche 231–2, 243, 244
Agathodaimonistai 335
Agathos Daimon 231, 232 n. 52
Agdistis/Angdistis 198 n. 163
agermoi, see collections
Aglauros:
    and *Plynteria* 308
    state priestess of 311
Aglauros, Pandrosos, and Kourotrophos,
    Salaminian priestess of 309, 311
agonothetes 268
agora, Athenian:
    first use of 68
    hero shrines on site of 34–5

panathenaic route through 91
    in sixth century 73
    see also Apollo Patroos; Zeus, in agora
agora, old 8–9, 22 n. 46
agora, of *Salaminioi* 310
Agoracritus 188, 191
Agrae, Mysteries at 97, 188, 194
agriculture, originates in Athens 99
Aianteia 153, 187, 275
Aiantis:
    sacrifice by 103
    tribal sanctuary of 119
Aidos 232, 235
Aigeirotomoi (genos) 285
Ajax (tribal eponym) 118, 312
    at battle of Salamis 153
    see also *Aianteia*; Aiantis
Akamantis:
    sacrifice by prytaneis of 103, 274
    tribal sanctuary of 119
Akamas 226
    as tribal eponym 118
Akeso 182
ἅλαδε μύσται 238
Alcibiades, ancestry of 312, 323
Alexander, divine honours for 257
Aliki 33 n. 18
Alkmaionidai:
    genos or *oikos*? 61–2, 318–19
    and Delphi 127
    and Theseus? 85 n. 73
Alkmene, sacrifice to 313
Alopeke, phratry of 316
'Altar-priest' (at Eleusis) 301
Amazons 138
Ammon 195–6, 339
Amphiaraea 149, 247, 250
Amphiaraus:
    at Athens (priest) 148 n. 105, 272
    at Oropus 25, 146–9, 244, 247, 250
    at Rhamnus 176
    sacrifice in Piraeus 339
    at Thebes 147
Amphiareum at Oropus, hero reliefs from
    183 n. 109

BLOOD ON THE CURB

A

Mystery

JOSEPH T. SHAW

cover by Stockton Mulford

BLACK MASK

2020

Table of Contents

Blood on the Curb

1

LUIGI BUSANO SET the glass on the table beside him, brushed his right forefinger across his mustaches, and leaned back in his chair with a comfortable sigh. He was a short, deep-chested man with stout limbs. His round face, the jowls full and the chin cleft, seemed made for smiles.

The room was low-ceiled, stuffed with furniture. The sills were high and the windows themselves were each cut into a dozen small panes. But there was a carpet on the floor; the sofa and one of the chairs were upholstered in horsehair; a canary sang in a cage, and on the ledges were potted geraniums. Busano's glance was possessively content as it swept these evidences of moderate comfort and returned to the elder of his two guests.

"Ah—that was good, Dominick, no?"

The elder Cardani nodded soberly. "We do not drink such fine wine often."

Busano threw back his head and burst into laughter, "But this is an occasion."

"A birthday? You should have told us."

"No, no, no. You call upon me—and Paul, over there; and he has brought his violin. In a little while he will play, and I shall sing; eh, Paolo?"

"You are always happy, Luigi," Dominick Cardani said.

"Me—I am very content. Eight, no, ten—Giovanna was one year over there—ten years ago I leave much trouble behind me. I find no trouble here. I have Maria, Vanna, Tulio, and now my *bambino.* I make myself a good business. Not a great deal, but enough for us all. Why should I not laugh and sing?"

His rounded mouth left the question for a moment in the air.

"And you, Dominick," he went blithely on, "you make good clothes; you do well in your business; you have a nice family—*corpo di bacco* you are not ill-natured, yet you do not smile, even when you take wine such as this. Ha, ha! Sober; always you are sober. Like Paolo over there."

Busano shrugged, glanced with a quick frown at the empty bottle, then turned his head to call over his shoulder: "Maria! *Uno momento, angela mia!*"

In half a minute, while Busano remained expectantly poised in the same position, the door opened. A woman, young although in full maturity, appeared and paused on the threshold. Thick black brows frowned a little over large black eyes. Her cheeks were ruddy. As a girl she might have had some claim to beauty, but now stoutness robbed her of much of its semblance. Busano pressed fingertips to his lips, opened them to waft her a kiss.

"Is the *bambino* awake, my love?"

His wife nodded to Dominick Cardani and the dark-haired, quiet youth seated a little aside from the two men.

"He is in the shop with me," she said shortly.

"Tulio and Vanna?"

"Tulio will have supper with his small friend. Vanna is not back since school, and already she is a little late. Is that what you want of me?"

"But one more little thing, my angel. Another bottle just like this. It is not often that Dominick and Paolo come to visit me. And we will have music."

Maria frowned again, not prettily.

"You will drive all the people away with your singing, Luigi," she scolded. "Already they say that you laugh and sing all the time and get fat and do not so much work as I."

Busano roared with laughter, pressing his hands to his sides. "I grow stout, maybe; because I am in good spirits and do not worry and mope." He wiped tears from his eyes; then pushed up his mustaches. "But my singing—bah! They are jealous. They know I should be in grand opera. And they will crowd around when Paul plays and I sing. You will see. But the bottle, my little pet. I always do better when people around me are happy—and I would have Dominick smile."

"Such nonsense!" came gruffly with the closing of the door.

"Ah, she is one fine woman," Luigi said heartily. Then he held a finger close to lips and nose and spoke in lowered tone. "She is very funny, my Maria. To hear her talk one might think she is cross, a scold. But it is not so. It is her way, and she will have her little joke with Luigi who works very hard, I tell you. Only I much prefer to laugh than to cry, and the silly people do not understand. Me—I do not like those fellows to paint the devil on the wall—even my Maria." This last was a whisper, with a glance at the closed door.

"Is she then worried?" Dominick Cardani asked quickly.

"Pouf! Such silly talk!" Busano shrugged his heavy shoulders, and his mood became merry again. "Ah, Paolo; shouldn't you take out the violin and make it in tune?"

The dark-haired youth, who had been listening attentively without contributing a word to the conversation, looked up.

"I think it is already in tune, Mr. Busano," he said in a pleasant tone. "I will try it when you are ready."

"Benito Pianelli," Dominick Cardani said, "tells Paul there is much good cause to worry. He thinks the situation is growing worse. He believes the New York police would do something if they could but are helpless."

Busano waggled a forefinger reprovingly. "Paolo, Paolo, if you listen much to Benito Pianelli you will be a fighting man and not a great musician. This Pianelli. I will not say that he is not a good man; he has always been loyal to his friends. He is getting a little gray now. When he was younger, they say, he was very good with the stiletto. What does he teach you, Paolo?"

Young Cardani was listening with a curiously thoughtful expression behind bright eyes. He was a little slow in replying, glancing once at his father.

"He teaches me many things, Mr. Busano," he said finally. "Some things of the hand; some of the mind."

"Ha!" Busano exploded. "So he would take you from me, this Pianelli—I who have set my heart that yours should be a career of which we of our race could be proud, a career that has been denied me although I have the talent. But what does he teach you, lad? Perhaps it has done no harm, for, see, you still keep up with your violin. Tell us."

"Mr. Pianelli says," Paul began very slowly, as if careful that his repetition should be exact, "that we owe a great debt to this country to which we have come. He says that our people are mostly kindly and gentle, honest, good and peace-loving, but that unfortunately there are some evil ones among us who, in the eyes of the people here, are giving their reputation to our whole race. He believes that we ought to do something about it."

"Bravo! Bravo!" Busano applauded heartily, clapping his

thick hands. "A very, very fine sentiment, Dominick. And some day we must think about it. But, Paolo, that is not all he has taught you. A little of the stiletto, no?"

"Oh, yes," Paul answered more confidently. "He has shown me many tricks. Particularly he has shown me what an unarmed man can do when he does not have to think of his weapon, and I am not afraid of a man armed with knife or pistol if I can get close enough to him. If I am armed with either, I can kill. Mr. Pianelli has been very kind to me."

"Brrr!" Busano shivered. "*Sangue diavolo!* In another moment you will have me, Luigi Busano, as sober as you two. Ah!" with obvious relief as the door opened and Maria appeared, bearing the coveted bottle and as well a frown of distinct disapproval.

He took the dust-covered bottle gently and set about opening it with great care.

"There is the business," Maria reminded him, "and I had a customer to wait upon. There will be more now, and somebody must see to them." She turned toward the door.

"But another little moment, my angel," Busano implored her. "Call Margherita; have her care for the shop. You bring in another glass and the *bambino*. He loves so to hear me sing and to be tossed on my foot. But hurry, Maria *mia*. And is Vanna come?"

"No, she is not yet back. Well, I suppose to have peace I must come." She closed the door more softly than before. Busano glanced slyly at Dominick Cardani.

Almost lovingly he poured a little of the wine into his glass, filled Cardani's and then his own. He glanced toward Paul, but the youth said, "No, thank you," and Busano sat holding the bottle until the door was again opened and Maria came in, glass in one hand, a black-eyed, chubby baby clasped to her ample bosom.

Busano filled her glass, set the bottle on the table, raised his glass to both, and drank slowly, smacking his lips he placed the glass at one side. Then he reached forth both arms and took the baby from his wife, coddling it closely to his big chest, rocking forward and back and cooing to it with chuckles of delight. Maria took a chair on the further side of the table and watched them dully.

"So, Paolo," Busano called merrily, closing one eye against a probing finger, "we are ready."

Young Cardani stepped across the room and commenced to unfasten the plain case. He was a strongly built lad in his early twenties, of medium height, with square, solid shoulders. His hands were large, the fingers blunt, but as he took up bow and violin and began to thumb the strings, his touch was light and sure.

"Again, Paolo," Busano called. "That E string; a very, very little flat, no?"

Paul bent his ear closer, nodded without looking up, and adjusted the peg a hair. He ran his thumb across the strings, one after the other, then glanced at Busano who nodded beamingly.

"My ear," he said, "is very particular."

Paul hunched the instrument beneath his chin and swiftly ran a double octave. The black-eyed baby ceased tugging at Busano's flowing mustache and turned around in wonderment. Then, with his chubby hand still holding its vantage grip, he commenced to jump up and down, crowing delightedly.

With some difficulty and with tears in his eyes, Luigi finally disengaged the little fingers and, placing the baby on his knee, with greater safety to himself, proceeded to smooth his hair. Maria Busano laughed unexpectedly, a full-throated sound.

"Ah," Busano said, "it is good for us all to be so merry."

During this, Paul remained waiting, bowing with lightest touch, his dark eyes dreamily on the Busanos but his thoughts evidently on the tones he produced, for his expression was far-away and made no response to their actions.

Busano had crossed one stout leg over the other knee and now balanced the baby on his swinging foot. Clasping both tiny hands in one of his own, he maintained the baby's balance and attention while he drank again.

"And now, Paolo," he cried, "we are ready. But of course my favorite—*Funiculà*. Give me, if you please, the first tone.... A-a-a-h.... *Bene!* It wasn't necessary, but the *bambino* expects it. We are ready, *bambino mio?* So, Paolo...."

Young Cardani struck the opening chords and swung into the sweeping melody. Busano caught up the song, and Maria took fire and hummed the words with passable spirit, even if her throaty contralto was not altogether in tune.

> *Stasera, Nina mia, sono montato....*
> *Te lo dirò?*
> *Colà, dove dispetti un cor ingrato*
> *Più far non può...*
> *Colà, cocente è il foco, ma se fuggi,*
> *Ti lascia star,*
> *E non ti corre appresso è non ti struggi*
> *A riguardar.*
> *Lesti! Via, montiam su là!*
> *Funiculì—funiculà.*

On the last note Busano raised triumphantly to the higher octave, at the same time giving his foot a flip so that the baby was propelled through the air to land on Busano's broad chest.

The muffled sound of hand applause and *"Bravo! Bravissimo!"* came from somewhere beyond the closed door.

"You hear, Maria *mia?*" Busano cried delightedly. "It is as I promised you. They listen and applaud. We shall do it again."

The sounds from without ceased suddenly. Then came a knock on the door. It was not opened, but a voice called:

"Signore Busano; you will come, please, and quickly."

"Peste!" Busano growled. "It is that Margherita. It will be that someone wants that I should bake a cake, and the stupid one cannot take the order. Maria, be so kind, I beg of you. We must have our song again, eh, *bambino?* But of course. Now, Paolo...."

Maria's swarthy face shed its placid smiles and assumed once more what seemed to be the frown of trade and occupation; yet she closed the door gently as she went out.

Young Cardani had glanced up quickly at the note of vague excitement in Margherita's voice, which appeared to have escaped Busano. He looked slowly around at his father, then at Busano who was smiling broadly and again balancing the chubby baby on his foot. Paul nodded, as his eyes met Luigi's, and struck up the refrain in which Busano's tenor joined lustily.

> *Lesti! Lesti! via, montiam su là,*
> *Funiculì, funiculà, funiculì, funiculà-à....*

A woman's scream pierced the note, rose above it in crescendo, knifed it to an abrupt silence, leaving Busano with open mouth and arms suspended and widespread.

A dull, heavy thump, in the room beyond, fell upon the silence, accompanied by another sharp cry, shorter and in different voice.

"Jesus Maria!" Busano gasped.

He looked moderately alarmed for a moment, then smiled, a little uncertainly.

"I think perhaps it is a mouse," he said. "She is very afraid of the mouse."

Dominick Cardani rose quickly from his chair. Paul at once lowered bow and violin, stepped directly to the stand where he had left the case. He carefully placed bow and instrument in it, fastened it, and looked around.

It was apparent that Luigi Busano had caught alarm from the decisive attitude of the two Cardanis, for he now came slowly to his feet, staring doubtfully at the door. He started toward it, but he seemed mentally handicapped by the baby in his arms, as if aware that it was something he should not take with him to the room beyond, yet uncertain about going without it.

Dominick Cardani took the child from him, and Busano darted through, leaving the door open behind him. The Cardanis heard his choked exclamation of dismay, but they did not hurry to follow. Dominick looked about, discovered a crib behind a screen, and deposited the baby in it, soberly waggling a finger at its surprised wailing. Then he went to the door, and Paul, who had waited silently, accompanied him.

On the threshold they paused.

Busano was on his knees bending over Maria, who lay flat on her back beside a table. Her head was turned to one side, and her eyes were closed. Obviously she had fainted. Busano stroked her hair back from her forehead, patting her cheeks and babbling in a voice of much concern.

"Maria *mia,* my little one. What happened you, my pet? Wake up. Wake up. It is Luigi, your Luigi who calls. What frightened you, *preziosa mia?* Nothing shall harm you now that Luigi is here."

As this exhortation appeared of little avail, with sweat streaming down his round cheeks he set to chafing her hands, rubbing her arms, yet never ceasing his worried endearments.

A little at one side stood the servant, Margherita, her tall, thin form bent, sobbing into her handkerchief. What could be seen of her face was a mask of terror. Busano seemed unconscious of her presence, for he did not question her.

Young Cardani's keen eyes observed the girl's stricken attitude, and he suddenly frowned. His glance returned to the woman and lit upon a torn wrapper or envelope that lay beside her. His eyes raised higher, to the table surface.

Close to the edge, as if dragged thus far and then abandoned, was a sheet of paper recently twice folded but now opened, disclosing on it three small objects of such grisly aspect that the lad drew in his breath sharply and the color fled from his cheeks.

An instant he was shaken; then his eyes blazed, his mouth drew into a straight, grim line. Raising his hand, he gripped his father's arm hard. Dominick Cardani twisted his head quickly, then turned to look in the direction Paul was silently pointing. He looked, and started violently.

"*Santa Madre di Dio!*" he muttered.

The sound of the exclamation, although low, pierced Busano's bewilderment. He turned his head slowly toward them, a half smile on his face as if in acknowledgment of their sympathy. He saw, however, that their glances were beyond and not on him. Puzzled, he raised himself a little and looked where they were staring.

Suddenly he screamed.

Still on his knees, he scrambled past his wife's senseless form to the table. His two hands were raised, then came down as fists, heavily, on the table. He beat his forehead on the edge, again and yet again, while his big arms cradled protectingly, but did not quite touch, the three frail little fingers with their bloodied ends.

2

THE CARDANIS STEPPED resolutely forward. Dominick drew a handkerchief from his pocket and reaching inside Busano's arms, gathered the pitiful relics, rolled the handkerchief around them and laid them at one side.

Pressing close to his father's shoulder, Paul peered keenly down at the paper which Dominick was spreading flat upon the table. Paul fought against the impulse to shudder at the smear of fresh blood, that partially obscured the writing, and even bent closer over it, studying its condition of coagulation to determine the time factor thereby suggested.

Paul then stooped, picked up the wrapper, and examined it. The outside bore simply the name of Luigi Busano and was without postage or other positive indication of its carriage, as he had expected. On the inside were faint stains of the same reddish-brown color.

He glanced at his father, saw that his lips were moving as he slowly deciphered the message, and turning stepped to the weeping maid and grasped her firmly by the arm. She raised miserable eyes to him. She was still holding the handkerchief to her mouth, vainly attempting to stifle the hysterical sobbing she could not control. He shook her a little.

"Tell me," he said in low tone. "Who brought this?"

"I—I do not know, young Signore," Margherita whimpered. "There were several who came to buy. When they left and all were gone, I looked on the counter and it was there."

"Who were the customers?"

"I—I do not remember."

"Men or women?"

"I think—oh, Signore, I can't think."

"Try to remember," Paul said, and turned back to the table.

With his head bowed to the edge, Busano was babbling incoherently, shaking with broken sobs. Paul's father pushed the paper toward him, and, with a little difficulty, he read the crude scrawl:

> "Each time we have asked, you have laughed. We warned you twice and still you laughed. This is the third time and if you find it a joke you can laugh again. But if you do not have $1000 ready to be given us we will send you more jokes like this and you will never see your daughter alive. We are watching you and will know at once what you decide. A doctor's care is needed. It is you who are delaying it."

Dominick Cardani's thick forefinger pointed to the only form of signature, a roughly drawn hand in black ink. He looked at his son. Paul nodded. Dominick stepped past him and laid his hand firmly on Busano's shoulder, gripping hard. Without raising his head, Busano tried to shake off the clasp.

"Dio misericordioso!" he moaned.

With head bent as if watching Busano, Paul raised his eyes so that he could glance through the large window in the room, by which one could see the entrance and an end of the shop.

A crowd of curious ones were jammed in the outer doorway, craning to see what they could make of the tableau with its aspect of tragedy. None had so far ventured inside the shop. Mostly they were women, with several men behind, whom

Paul could not see so clearly. Giving no indication that he was aware of this silent audience, Paul let his glance fall on Busano's still, bent form.

Dominick had pulled the suffering man back a little from the table so that his arms, without its support, drooped at his sides; his head hung slack on his chest. Cardani shook him vigorously, and Busano partially lifted his head, glancing up sidewise, with dull eyes and loose mouth.

"Come, come, Luigi," Cardani said firmly. "Take hold of yourself. Vanna has been hurt, it is true; but now you must get her back, and quickly."

This brought Busano slowly to his feet.

"What do you mean?" he demanded hoarsely.

Cardani pointed to the table.

"Have you not read what is there written?"

Busano glanced hesitantly in the direction indicated, to look quickly away. He compelled his eyes to wander further, saw the rolled-up handkerchief, then glanced back at the paper. He seized it in both hands and pressed the stained sheet to his lips.

"Blood of my Vanna," he groaned. *"Povera Vanna mia!"*

Cardani gripped his arm in his powerful clasp.

"Read it, man. Read it."

Busano held the paper before him in both shaking hands, then turned streaming eyes to his friend.

"I cannot," he whispered. "Tell me, I beg of you—"

Cardani read the message to him.

Busano turned swiftly upon him. Anger had dried his eyes.

"Blood of the devil!" he cried. "What is this they ask! They take my little girl, my poor little girl. They cut off her fingers and send them to me. And now they tell me I must give them money, my savings from my hard work, that I may have her back!"

He clenched his hands into fists and beat them savagely against his chest, so that the blows resounded hollowly.

"What has she done that she should be so hurt?" he screamed. "And what have I done, I, Luigi Busano, to be so treated? I, who have harmed no one, who am good and kind to my neighbors? It is because I sing and laugh to make people happy, they do this to me! It says so there. Happy! I, who thought I was happy—"

Paul glanced again through the window. The women were commencing to slink away, with glances askance. Some crossed themselves as they hurried on. Paul looked back into the room.

"Luigi Busano," Dominick said sternly, "there is no time for that now. Get control of yourself. Do you realize that you must act at once if Giovanna is to come back at all?"

A low moan from the floor drew his attention to Maria. He turned to the quaking if now silent maid.

"Margherita," he said swiftly. "Take her to the next room, get her to lie down, and keep her quiet."

Together they helped her to the cheerful room they had so recently quit, where Cardani left her to the care of the maid.

Busano was now leaning back against the table, huge arms folded, head sunk on his chest. His eyes watched Cardani's approach with an up-from-under look.

"Come," Cardani said briskly. "This message says you must have one thousand dollars in readiness to deliver if you wish to see Giovanna alive. Are you prepared to do that, Luigi? Can you get the money at once?"

Busano heaved a deep sigh that caused his head to bob oddly with the movement of his chest.

"It will ruin me," he gasped hoarsely. "It is all I have saved."

Cardani turned to the table, reaching for the paper.

"It said here," he muttered, as if to himself, "something about you being watched—"

Paul touched his father's arm, and when he had Dominick's eye, nodded toward the big window. Cardani followed the glance.

As if left by the receding crowd of curious women, a man was standing in the open outer doorway. He was tall and rather thin, with sharp features in profile. He leaned against the jamb, with one heel also pressed against it, which cocked his knee before him. A derby was pushed back on his head. Between his thin lips was a long cheroot which he rolled slowly back and forth. In their full view, with his head bent and eyes fixed apparently on his cocked knee, the man's whole expression and attitude suggested faintly amused indifference.

"*Si bene!*" Cardani breathed.

Paul was staring hard at the stranger with eyes of black agate. Unconsciously his fists were clenched at his sides.

As if finally aware of the steady scrutiny, the tall man leisurely took the cheroot from his mouth, flicked the ash, and turned his head. As he met the glances of the two Cardanis, his lips twisted in what was less a smile than a mocking sneer. Paul took a step forward. His father restrained him. The man let his foot fall and pushed himself erect. He entered the shop and approached the inner door.

"Luigi," Cardani said, in low tone, "go now for the money. I think the messenger is here. Do not, however, come in until I call you."

Busano walked heavily from the room as the stranger came

to the door and carelessly pushed it open. Neither of the Cardanis spoke.

"Seems like you are having some trouble here," the man said lightly.

"I guess you know what it is all right," Paul told him.

The man darted an angry, evil glance at the lad. He met only a stony stare. He shrugged bony shoulders and turned to the older man.

"Just goin' by," he said, "when I saw a crowd here and heard that fat man yellin'—"

"I wonder," Paul said, "if you will yell when your fingers are being cut off."

"Be quiet, Paul," his father admonished. "This is not our affair."

"Yeah," the man snarled, "but that fresh kid will damned soon find it is his affair if he don't watch his mug. I come in to see if I could help, but I'll walk right on again if that brat opens his yap again. I don't have to take it."

"You can help," Cardani told him steadily, "if you will carry the message that the money will be paid for the safe and immediate return of the girl."

The tall man shrugged and attempted a sly grin of innocence.

"Don't know what you're talkin' about, brother," he said, "but it just happens I might guess. Fact is I was in a poolroom, never mind where, and I heard some words dropped that might tie in with this. I guess I could find the same fellers again, but I'm damned sure I won't if there's any followin' or spyin' on me. I want it understood I ain't mixed in this at all. Get me?"

It was Cardani's turn to shrug. "All right," he said. "Suppose you go back to your friends and tell them that I will meet them any place they say and give them the money when they give me the girl—safe."

"If you got the money," the man suggested, "you might save time, if that means anything to you, by giving it to me now."

"The girl—safe, or no money," Cardani told him sternly. "No one will follow you. We will wait here."

"Huh—I'm only tryin' to do somebody a favor," the man said in a tone he attempted to make sound aggrieved. He knocked ashes on the clean floor and leered at Cardani.

"I think," Dominick said softly, "that you had better go now and go quickly."

The man shrugged, moved a little toward the door, then paused.

"All right. If I see the same fellers may be you'll hear from them. You'll meet 'em with the money, is that it?"

"Yes," Paul told him. "With the money for the girl—safe."

Paul watched the man as he left the shop with a leisurely step of careless indifference. As he disappeared Cardani turned to his son.

"Perhaps we have done wrong," he said worriedly. "The little girl will need quick attention. It might have been better if I had taken the money and gone with him."

"They're only a short distance away," Paul said quietly, and when his father looked at him in amazement, he pointed out: "That letter came by messenger—possibly this same man. The blood was still wet. See; it is now dried. We will have the answer in fifteen or twenty minutes."

"Then—" Cardani began, but was interrupted by the sudden opening of the door from the living room.

Maria, wild-eyed and disheveled, staggered in.

"Vanna—Vanna!" she screamed hoarsely. She stared insanely around the room. "Why—is she not here? You told me, you promised me she would be back! Oh, what have they done to her, my poor, innocent little baby? Have they—have they—"—her voice sank to a gasping whisper—"killed her?"

"Have patience, Maria," Cardani said calmly. "In just a little while."

A door at the end of the room opened. Luigi Busano came softly in. His round face was very sober; his eyes troubled.

Maria ran to him, shrieking. Clutching fingers reached out but did not quite touch his face.

"Oh, you miserable one!" she screamed. "It is your fault, all your fault, that this trouble has come to us, that our little Vanna is being murdered. When the notes came to us you laughed. You scolded me when I worried, I, who love our babies and slave for them—you who think only of how to laugh and how to sing. Oh—oh—merciful Mother of God!"

Busano, miserable and perplexed, gave way before her reaching hands. Cardani caught her wrist.

"Listen to me, Maria," he said a little sharply. "In this fashion, you do not help. Go and lie down in the room a little while longer."

She clung to his arm with her head bent to it, weeping. Her faltering steps followed his as he led her to the door. "You are kind, Signore Cardani," she babbled.

Dominick closed the door gently behind her.

"You have the money, Luigi?" he asked briskly.

"It is here," Busano answered dully. "One thousand dollars. There is only a little left now. I shall take it to the bank tomorrow."

"Give it to me," Dominick said, and Busano handed him a packet of old bills, mostly of very small denomination.

"You understand," Cardani said, "that I will go with the messenger and will pay it only if Vanna is given to me—safe. Now," he added more quickly, "it is best that he should not see you or talk with you. He might demand more when he sees that you have this. From me he cannot get it. Go into the room with Maria. See to her; keep her quiet. I will do what I can."

Busano did not move to obey. Slowly he took from his pocket a knife, unclasped it, and placed one hand on the long, gleaming blade. His usually mild eyes were a little wild. Saliva flecked his lips.

"I swear," he began, "on this blade and the blood of—"

Paul sprang swiftly to him and caught his arm.

"No, no, Mr. Busano," he said quickly. "Don't take the oath of vendetta. This is America. There are other ways. Here—let me have it."

Young Cardani's strong fingers disengaged his grasp, took the knife, closed the blade and put it unnoticed in his own pocket.

"Go quickly now, Luigi," Cardani said from near the window. "I think he is coming. When we have left, it would be well to send someone to bring Tulio."

3

THE LIVING ROOM door closed behind Luigi as the tall stranger appeared in the shop entrance. He glanced once sharply into the room and, apparently satisfied, turned into the shop. A fresh cheroot was between his thin lips, and as he opened the door and entered he let smoke drift from mouth and nostrils. He looked at the Cardanis in turn, with a hard glitter in his sharp eyes.

"In the first place," he said harshly, "if you try to tie me in with this thing it will be just too bad."

Cardani shook his head. "We heard your story. That is all we know."

The tall man took the cheroot from his mouth and spat on the Busanos' freshly scrubbed floor. He tried to appear cold and calm, but his eyes darted from object to object; the motions of his hands were quick and nervous.

"All right then, and it better be so," he said gruffly. "Well, I found the feller and he said he knew where a girl was being held. He talked to someone and told me I was to bring the money and the girl would be turned loose."

Cardani shook his head.

"I go with you and take the girl or there isn't any money."

The tall man laughed. "How do I know you have any money?"

Cardani drew the packet from his pocket and riffled the edges of the bills, then returned it. The man's eyes glittered.

"Well," he said, "I guess you fellers are sensible. Come on; I'll see if I can find him again.... But wait a minute." He turned, scowling. "What's that boy going to do while we are gone? It don't mean anything to me; at the same time I don't want to do any explaining to some copper."

"No," Paul said quietly before his father could speak. "I'm going with you."

"Huh? Well that'll be just fine."

Dominick started to demur, but Paul argued that he would be needed if Giovanna should not be able to walk.

The tall stranger, with long strides, led them up the street to the first alley, into which they turned. At the other end they emerged on a back street. Crossing that, they traversed another alley to a still more deserted street where dwellings gave way to stores and lofts that were already closed for the night. Dusk had fallen. Widely separated gas lights gave pools of flickering illumination on the cobbled ways, but the alleys were dark and littered.

For perhaps ten minutes they followed this latter street which, in a long arc, curved inward with respect to the point of their departure. Making show of studying the buildings, their guide finally paused before a small and apparently disused warehouse. Glancing up, Paul saw faint light behind a grimy, cobwebbed window. The street was very quiet. When their footsteps ceased, they heard no other sound.

The tall man said, "You wait here till I see if it's the right place."

He disappeared behind the door, and they heard his groping steps ascending. Under the meagre light of a distant lamp, Paul began to scrutinize the face of the building and its neighbors to right and left and across the cobbled street, as if he would fix the place securely in his memory. With scarcely a pause, however, descending steps grew louder. The door creaked open, and the tall man rasped at them, "Come on up. I guess they're here."

Without hesitation, Dominick and Paul pushed forward, but the man, turning, checked them in the doorway.

"There's just one thing first, brother," he said, leaning beyond them and glancing up and down the street. "I don't know these fellers any more than you. Like I said, I heard a man talkin' and took your message on a chance. You keep it that way, and I won't tell 'em anything about you. You won't see 'em, but if you act funny and don't come through quick, they'll come pilin' out on you, and I can't help that."

"I believe we understand each other," Cardani said, a little impatiently.

"All right; come on…. Close that door behind you, kid, and don't slam it."

Within, there was a stale, musty smell of straw or hay that had lain long undisturbed. Indirect light from above showed faintly the top of a fairly broad stairway. What lay immediately before them was a well of blackness. It might have been a hallway with doors or an open storeroom. What the darkness might hide, they could only conjecture; they could not see.

Their feet, groping for the first steps, found treads that were narrow and worn; but once fairly started, they went up quickly.

The stair ended on a landing. Straight ahead was a closed door. At the left an open door provided the light by which they had ascended. They followed their long-legged guide through this into a room bare of everything except an upended box on which stood an ordinary stable lantern.

The grimy window which Paul had noted from below was

at one end of this room; at the other was a partially opened door with other light behind it that showed only rough floor boards. From apparently close beyond it, however, came a low, half-muffled, whimpering cry and the indistinguishable growling of a man's coarse voice.

"All right," the tall man said testily, "shell out."

"The girl," Cardani said tersely and glanced toward the door.

The tall man shrugged, stepped across, and pushed the door wider. With one hand on the jamb, he thrust head and one shoulder out of sight. Words passed, which the Cardanis could not catch. The man reached inside, turned and faced the room, and the little Busano girl was now beside him.

She was erect only through the support of the hand that gripped her arm hard. Her legs were bent limply; her chin was on her chest. Her eyes were closed in a chalk-white face. Her pale lips were parted, whence came incessant whimpering complaint. Her unsupported arm hung straight, its hand cloth bound. The cloth was mostly soggy crimson.

Paul drew in his breath sharply. His father gave no sign.

"Satisfied?" the man said sharply, and started to turn back.

"Wait!" Cardani called.

He stepped swiftly to the doorway, careful to stand at one side of it with a shoulder to the opening. He drew the packet of money from his pocket, held it in view.

"Give the girl to Paul," he said. "I will pay you here."

The man twisted his head to look into the further room and evidently received an affirmative signal, for he dragged the girl across the floor. Paul took her into his arms. He made no move to leave the room.

The tall man stepped hurriedly back to Cardani. The money

was passed. Dominick waited imperturbably while the man thrust it, bill by bill, through the doorway to someone unseen. When the last had disappeared, a deep voice growled, "Check," and the door was closed.

Cardani strode swiftly toward his son, ignoring the tall man who leaned against the frame and watched with a triumphant leer. Drawing a handkerchief from his pocket, Dominick twisted it, then bound it tightly around the girl's wounded arm. Little Vanna's complaint had stopped. Her head swung loosely as Cardani took the slight form from Paul's arms and started toward the door.

Paul followed slowly until his father commenced the descent. Then he turned around and came back into the room. In the lantern's pale light, his eyes were inscrutable black pools. His head was bent a little, as if listening. Beyond the closed door, the sounds of footsteps grew fainter as they receded toward the rear. Paul advanced a slow step.

Snapping his back against the door frame, the tall man pushed himself erect and came forward to meet Paul. His sallow face was suddenly flushed; his shifting eyes a little puzzled.

"Want to talk more with me, do you, son?" he asked, mockingly. "Well, now, that's fine."

He came on, and without breaking or hastening his stride, launched a sudden kick at the lad's groin.

As the blow started, Paul's stocky body half turned, slid sidewise, and he struck savagely with his right fist.

Under the impetus of the swinging leg, that met only space, and the sudden blow on the mouth, the man's body spun as if on an axis. He thumped heavily to the floor, causing the lantern to jump and its flame to flicker dangerously.

The tall man scrambled to his feet, with blood trickling from his mouth corners. His face was a writhing mask of fury. Surprise and rage clogged his foul words with incoherence.

His hand thrust into a pocket, whipped out with a clasp knife. He snapped the blade open and darted forward.

Paul gave a slight backward movement, as if about to turn and run for it. Then he sprang under the upraised arm, caught the wrist with his right hand and helped its descent. His left arm twisted under and around the tall man's forearm, with that hand clamping on to the bony wrist. His hands twisted suddenly, then his right hand plucked the knife from the loosened finger muscles.

Paul's movements were so swift and sure, his grip so perfectly applied, that the man had no time for independent action. He cried sharply once with pain, and instinctive reflex caused him to strain against the grip. But immediately Paul's binding arm slipped out of its hold; his fingers caught the ends of the man's long fingers before he could snatch that hand away, and Paul drew the keen blade hard across them, close to the knuckles, the sharp steel cutting into the bone.

The tall man screamed. He jerked the hand away, stumbling backward. He caught his right wrist with the other hand, holding it out before him, staring wildly at the dangling fingers with their four streaming wounds.

"I knew you would yell when you got it," Paul said calmly. His eyes were very bright. "You didn't fool us," he added. "You're as much of the gang as those other rats who kept out of sight. Only you've got a mark now, and a whole lot of people are going to know what it means."

He raised the knife menacingly and the tall man scrambled

backward, turned and rushed for the second door. He bumped into it and went plunging into the darkness beyond.

Paul listened briefly, heard the man's stumbling steps and no indication of his companions' return. Closing the knife blade, still holding it in his hand, he went hurriedly down the stairs; and so rapid had been the action that he overtook his father a few paces from the door. Over his shoulder, Dominick gave his son a quick, searching scrutiny, but said nothing.

Between intervals of silence, sounds hammered at them out of the night. From the distant Bowery came once the roar of an elevated train, diminishing shortly to a faint, long-drawn-out rumble. The quiet of an alley engulfed them, broken only by the swift patter of their footfalls. As they emerged on another thoroughfare, a street car clanged past an intersection, with the metallic thud of wheels, the clack—clack of steel-shod hooves trotting on the cobbles, the tinkling of the horses' bells.

4

WHEN THEY CAME, there was no light in the bakeshop, and the shade in the big window was closely drawn. Busano was waiting in the darkened doorway. His outstretched arms reached to take Giovanna, but Dominick anticipated him.

"She has only fainted I think," he said. "You should get a doctor at once."

"He is here now—with Maria," Luigi said in subdued tone. "Dr. Luciano. I went for him."

"Get him," Cardani said sharply, stepping into the lighted room and still holding the motionless child. "And keep Maria away until he has seen her."

Busano bustled to the door of the adjoining room, opened it, and beckoned. Immediately Dr. Luciano came out. He was a portly man of middle age, with kindly, smiling face.

"Place her here," he said with professional briskness, stooping to open his bag. He indicated the table which still held the nucleus of dining accessories, oil and vinegar cruets, a sugar bowl, salt and pepper, and Dominick Cardani's handkerchief with its grisly burden.

Dr. Luciano set his opened bag on the table, close beside the girl's insensible form. He gestured to the maid, and as she cleared away the table things, he took from his bag stethoscope, instruments, bandages, and bottles of odd sizes.

The doctor's glance swept the little girl's face keenly.

"Luigi," he directed, "get me some hot water as soon as possible; and a clean basin and bowl. And you, young man," to the boy Tulio who had crept close and was kneeling with hands grasping the table edge, his round black eyes fixed on his sister's face, "go to your mother while she makes the bed ready."

While he talked, Dr. Luciano's hands were not idle. Now he divested himself of his coat and waistcoat and rolled up the sleeves of his white shirt, disclosing thick wrists and muscular, hairy forearms. With the room finally cleared of most of its occupants, he let his glance rest keenly on Dominick Cardani. "I should like you to help me," he said.

Dominick nodded and came forward to stand by the table.

Paul found a chair and seated himself unobtrusively a little at one side. He watched closely while the doctor cut away the crude tourniquet and the semblance of a cloth bandage, exposing the still bleeding finger stumps. Paul shifted his glance to Luciano's face, noting the quick frown, narrowed eyes, and compressed lips as the portly doctor examined these mute evidences of wanton outrage.

Busano came in with bowl and basin and a pot of steaming water. He approached and stood by the table with averted eyes until Cardani relieved him of the articles. Luigi then came over to draw a chair close beside Paul, sitting with elbows on knees and face sunk in his cupped hands.

At Luciano's gesture, Dominick held Giovanna's wrist suspended while the doctor turned some of the water into the bowl and poured into it dark liquid from a bottle. Taking the wrist, he submerged the mutilated hand, moving it gently around and around.

Under the strong antiseptic, pain revived the girl's senses. She began to moan at first, then her cry became a scream of agony.

Dr. Luciano relinquished the wrist to the silent Cardani.

With one hand he gently stroked Giovanna's forehead, talking steadily, soothingly to her the while; with the other he delved into his black bag, producing a rather large bottle of white opaqueness, and a rolled-up towel. He paused to glance over at Busano, who now was sitting bolt upright with straight, tensed arms and clenched hands. His head was raised high; tears welled between his closed lids.

"Luigi," Dr. Luciano said quietly, "I wish you would go in and tell Mrs. Busano that we are getting on nicely. I wouldn't want her to interrupt us just now. Stay with her. I will call you if anything is needed."

Paul watched Busano stumble from the room, and was then aware that the doctor's glance was on him.

"Young man," Luciano said, "see if you can find me a paper— any kind. And bring it here, please."

Paul stood up with alacrity. His quick eyes lit upon a news- paper and he stepped to it. At the doctor's nod, he brought it to the table. Dr. Luciano again gestured, and Paul relieved him, stroking Giovanna's head. Her screams had now sunk to a sobbing, whimpering cry.

Paul watched the doctor skilfully shape the paper into a cone and wrap the folded towel about it. He held it aside while he felt of the little girl's pulse; then un-stoppering the large bottle, he sprinkled some of its contents inside the cone which he held for a few moments over Giovanna's mouth. Paul took a backward step away from the potent ether, but he did not avert his eyes.

"What is your name, young man?" Luciano asked him in a low tone.

"Paul Cardani."

The portly doctor nodded and smiled, with a glance at the elder man.

"I knew the last name," he said. "You're as alike as two peas. Now, Paul, do you think you can stand this?"

"Yes, sir."

Giovanna was quiet now. Her head was turned to one side. Her eyes were closed and she was breathing regularly. Luciano placed the cone aside.

"When I tell you," he said to Paul, "sprinkle more of the ether inside, and hold it as I did."

He turned quickly to his work, and Paul marveled at the swift deftness of those thick fingers.

A new tourniquet was applied on the thin forearm. Then the loose tissue of the first finger was cut away, little splinters of bone removed. The delicate work of tying the severed arteries followed, and finally a flap of skin was drawn over the stump and sewn.

With one finger carefully bound with gauze, Dr. Luciano again tested the pulse. Then he nodded to Paul who prepared the cone and held it until Luciano said, "Enough."

Dr. Luciano looked with kindly eyes at Paul.

"You do not seem to mind this, my boy. That is unusual for your age, and I do not believe you are hardhearted."

The air in the room was close and filled with the mingled odors of olive oil cooking and of freshly baked bread, the cloying scent of ether and the smell of the antiseptic.

Paul smiled. "I do not see how it is possible that you can do what you have done."

Luciano sighed. "This poor little thing," he said softly. "I could wish for greater skill."

In due time the second and third fingers were finished and the three bandaged together. The doctor's main work for the moment was completed.

He smiled at his two assistants. "Without you two," he said, "I could hardly have done the work here." He looked down at the motionless little form. "I should have taken her to the hospital, but Maria would have gone wild. It is the best that I could do. I think it will be all right.... Last week I had a case exactly like this; and constantly stab wounds, hurts from bombs and fire." He shook his head.

Luigi came in with soft tread. Maria was at his shoulder, her whole soul in her round dark eyes. Luciano met them with a warm smile.

"We are all ready for bed now," he said in a cheerful voice.

"Yes, Dr. Luciano." Her eyes were on Giovanna. She approached the table slowly.

"Oh, Doctor," she gasped. "Why is she so still and—"

He laughed with great good-humor, reassuringly. "It is the ether; it has not yet worn off. Perhaps she will be a little ill from it. That does not matter. Take her now, Maria.... So. You won't hurt her. Don't worry. I'll be in after a little while. Luigi, help her."

Dr. Luciano closed the door upon Maria and turned back to the Cardanis who were standing silent and incurious.

"Paul," he said briskly, "pour the water over my hands, will you?"

By the time he had washed and dried his hands, resumed waistcoat and coat and was gathering up his instruments, Busano returned.

"We will go now," Dominick said. "Get your violin, Paul."

Paul brought his hat and violin case, stepped to the second door, and beckoned. The maid followed them through the shop and bolted the door after they had gone out.

The two walked a block in silence. Then Paul stopped and turned to his father.

"Will you please take this home for me?" he asked. "I am going to talk with Mr. Pianelli."

Without a word, Dominick took the instrument case. They separated.

5

IT WAS QUITE dark when Paul Cardani turned off Mulberry into a cross street that threaded further into the Italian quarter.

He walked at a steady pace, neither hurried nor loitering. He appeared thoughtful and a little absent-minded; yet no face that passed escaped his notice. From time to time passersby looked closely at him, but Paul did not appear to notice them at all.

Once when two furtive-eyed men brushed close by, quickening their steps as they almost touched him, he thrust his right hand into his coat pocket, paused and swung sidewise, ostensibly facing a shop window. Slowly his head turned as his eyes followed the retreating figures, and it was not until they had passed the block and continued on that he resumed his way.

After a few minutes he turned into a quieter street where the buildings were smaller. Part way down the block, he stopped abruptly at a door that was close beside the still illuminated window of a wine and cheese shop.

He stood motionless in the partial shadow for a full minute while his eyes searched the way he had come. Then turning the knob, he stepped quickly into a small hallway lighted by a single gas-jet on the first landing above. He closed the door softly, mounted the stairway with swift, easy step, and knocked on the one door there. It was opened shortly by a gray-haired, slightly bent woman. She peered intently with shortsighted eyes at Cardani's stalwart figure motionless in the flickering light.

"Is Signore Pianelli at leisure, Carlotta?" he asked gently.

Instantly a beaming smile stirred a thousand wrinkles in her withered face. "But of course, Signore, to you. Come." She closed the door, then pattered along before him. "He is smoking over his coffee. His supper was late tonight."

She led the way from the short hallway across an anteroom with a linoleum-covered floor and opened a door at one side.

"It is the Signore Paul," she announced, certainty of his welcome apparent in her quavering tone.

Paul turned to pat her shoulder, then strode in.

Benito Pianelli was seated at a table which bore white linen, silver, and cut glass. It was lighted by four candles in silver sconces. As he turned toward his visitor he presented a striking appearance. Piercing black eyes of peculiar intensity vitalized an intelligent face with high forehead that was crowned by snow-white hair brushed straight back. His nose was aquiline, with delicate nostrils. His thin-lipped mouth was partially shadowed by Victor Emmanuel mustaches as white as his hair. He looked both a soldier and a student.

Paul stepped up to him, and they shook hands with a quick, firm grip. Pianelli did not rise; neither did his lips change expression. But his eyes were bright as he looked up keenly into Paul's serious face.

"Ah, my young sergeant of police," he said in gentle tone, "I have been wondering when you would find time to come again."

"I should have come sooner and often," Paul said, "had it been a matter of my own wish."

The older man filled Paul's liqueur glass, saw that the cheroot he held was out, and dropped it into a tray.

"You have news for me tonight, Paul," he said quietly. "Anyone less familiar with you than I would not guess it. But I observe that you have an air of repressed excitement which is very rare with your temperament. Once only before have I detected it. That was the night you came to me direct from the Busanos'. Ten years ago, was it not? Poor little Vanna. She was married only last month."

"Twelve."

"Twelve years ago, then. We talked half the night, discussing what could be done with the situation. That night you came with your decision made—to abandon your desire of becoming a musician in order, as you then said, to follow Luciano's footsteps in the service of our poor people here. You became a policeman, a patrolman, later a detective."

Pianelli pushed his coffee cup aside and sipped his Benedictine. Paul was silent, his eyes brooding.

"A courageous fellow, Luciano," Benito Pianelli resumed. "A man of intelligence and education and of very sympathetic heart. He deserved a better end."

"Only last week," Cardani said softly, "I sent his killer to be executed." He drew a long, deep breath. Then he shifted his position a little and took a meagre sip of the smooth old liqueur. "It was a baffling case for a while," he said. "My suspicions and information pointed to a certain man, but following the advice you gave me when I first started, Signore, I was not prepared to arrest him and take him into court until I had unbreakable evidence to convict.

"With the exception of one point I had everything; motive, opportunity, his presence at the time of the murder, witnesses except to the actual deed. The one obstacle was that the fatal blow was struck with the left hand. There could be no doubt of that—and the man was right-handed. Then I discovered that while using the right hand ordinarily, he lacked the strength in the fingers of that hand to grip the knife and deliver such a blow. It was Vittorio Ferrara."

"Ah!" Pianelli exclaimed. "I recall. He was the one who held the little Busano girl." His eyes sparkled. "It was the first occasion you had to put to the test the little trick I showed you. Ha! And you cut more cunningly than you knew. The scum! The good doctor once pulled him through a sickness, and his only pay—the knife.... I am glad to hear of it."

Pianelli stood up, disclosing a slender figure of slightly more than Paul Cardani's height. With unexpectedly lithe step he moved to the sideboard, opened a narrow box, and took from it a thin cigar.

"You still do not smoke, Paul?" he asked.

"No, thanks."

"You had much help from Luciano?" Pianelli asked quizzically.

Paul glanced up quickly, then nodded. "A great deal; and I am still making use of it." He sighed unconsciously. "I think I brought it on him.... During the past few years, when they gave me more and more cases in this section, I saw him on every possible occasion. He obtained much information from people where I was unable to get it myself. I was not always in uniform, but they knew me and became suspicious—and he paid the penalty for it. I went to see him too often."

He broke off; sighed unconsciously.

"People thought he was a physician only," he went on, when Pianelli did not speak, "a doctor with a smile and sympathy for everyone. And he was respected and loved. Few imagined he was ever serious except when his work demanded it. Probably it will never be known what a man he really was, what he sacrificed—at the end even his life—to stop the attacks upon those who were too ignorant, too helpless to defend themselves.

"Even I, at Ferrara's trial, could not dispute the motive of robbery and show the real reason that lay behind his assassination. If I had, the people would have idolized him, but the other criminals would have been warned. I am not finished with them."

"Pouf! Luciano was a soldier. What he did was not for glory. It would have been stupid if you had done otherwise. The work he started is only fairly begun, and you have only touched the fringes of it."

Pianelli turned to flick the ash from his cigar, then swung upon Cardani aggressively and vitally alert.

"It was Luciano's constant fear," he said, "that these loose bands would organize. We estimated that there were five thousand members of the Mafia and Camorra in this city, with probably six times that number throughout America. The societies are not kept up here as abroad, but all these men are familiar with organization and its advantages."

Pianelli had come to his feet now and was pacing the room, lost in frowning thought. Cardani with secret enjoyment watched the play of strong emotion on the older man's face; the fierce bristling of the white mustaches as the thin lips worked beneath them; the blazing penetration of the black eyes; the alert poise and quick step; the firm set of the chin. Here was a man unafraid.

Presently the fiery old gentleman stopped beside the table,

rapped once, smartly, with his knuckles on the cloth, and reseated himself.

"There are," he said, "two, possibly three, reasons why, for the past twelve years or so they have operated in small bands independent of each other. The first is jealousy; between themselves, competing for the same object, and of the large portion of the spoils which a man at the head of an organized group would take for himself. The second is the lack of a man powerful enough, and evil enough, to forge and control single leadership. And the third possible reason is that, up to recent times, they have not felt the need of an organized force to combat the law. The authorities are efficient, but they do not understand our language, our people. They have considered us all alike. Thus the criminals have been practically immune from suspicion and arrest.

"Mark you, Paul," he added with slow emphasis, "I placed all this in the past. Conditions are changing. They grow bolder, come more into the open. Some of these bands have been drawn together, have melded into larger groups. From that it is only a step to an agreement between gangs—association, organization."

Cardani nodded, soberly. "I was about to say as much."

"Very well," Pianelli said briskly. "Assuming it is so, before we go further into that, let us examine our opposition. The really dangerous men opposed to you are numbered in the scores. The rest are rabble, *canaglia*. They are slinking, cowardly rats. They slash with that harmless-appearing but abominable invention—a pencil sharpener, with its short blade. They do not use the knife or the pistol. They rob at night or in isolated places; they use every form of trickery to steal money. They add to the general terror, but they are petty criminals who can easily be stamped out when your police understand matters better.

"The others are different," he continued. "Those are the killers. They do not deal in petty hold-ups; they go for bigger game, greater loot. They mutilate and murder to intimidate so as to extort money easier and in larger sums. They also kill suspected informers; they kill for vengeance, and if threatened.

"Those are the men who form your real enemy. They are the men who have headed the most ruthless bands; they are the ones who will lead organized groups when Luciano's great fear becomes reality. Whether you have evidence or not, such men should be known by you and watched."

Cardani smiled slightly. "I know," he said. "Let me tell you what I am doing. Regularly Italian papers come to me and I keep them filed. When I read that a notorious criminal has escaped the police over there, I expect him sooner or later here. I gather all possible information about him; his appearance—a picture if available; the types of crimes he has committed there, for then I will know what to expect of him here.

"Each man," he explained, "has a favorite criminal weapon—the bomb, the knife, the pistol, or the torch. The crimes that occur by these different weapons are usually distinct. In a bombing or fire there is rarely a murder by the knife or shooting. In a kidnaping, the knife is used, to mutilate or murder. It is the typical weapon of the kidnaper. It is silent and does not draw attention to the location.

"You once said to me, Signore, 'By their weapon you shall know them.' I am proving the truth of this. You taught me to trace a knife to its source, the fragment of a bomb to its maker, a pistol to its purchaser; and with these leads it is not difficult in time to track down the actual criminal.

"For some time now there have been very few major crimes in the quarter that could not be set down to gang operation; and I'll tell you why I believe they are organized. Formerly an interval of weeks might occur between bombings, or two might take place the same day. Within the past six weeks there have been six, scattered over the quarter, and no two in the same twenty-four hours. It is the same system with fires, with extortion, blackmail, and kidnaping.

"If I can capture any men at the scene of a crime, I do not bring them at once to trial even if I am certain of their conviction. I hold them for evidence against their leaders, to discover through them, if possible, the identity of those leaders. It is the only way the gangs can be broken. From my lists of criminals who have fled the Italian police during the past several years, I have already the names of several who might head the gangs operating with a known weapon. Five criminal activities, five gangs, five leaders. If I could get something more than this mere suspicion, I would know how to seek evidence that would prove which are the men I want." He passed a hand across his damp forehead. "Coremo, Tasso," he repeated slowly, "Biretti, Spiro, and Vira are the men I most suspect. If they are the real leaders, if I can prove it, I will smash the gangs."

"One against five," Pianelli said brittlely. "And each of the five with anywhere from a dozen to forty men." He slapped his hand, hard, on the table. "It would seem," he said, "that they have proceeded more rapidly and further with organization than I had supposed. I fear they may crush you, Paul; for such a force, united, is many times more difficult to combat than twice the number separated." He dismissed the sombre thought with a smile and a quick gesture of snapping fingers.

"You can make sure of association when you observe that the different gangs do not trespass on each other's territory or type of victims. Whether they are also acting under single leadership is more difficult to discover, and the organization then would be more difficult to disrupt—impossible until you get that one man himself."

Under his bushy white brows, Pianelli's eyes were intensely bright.

"Such a man," he went on, "would work under cover. He would be more dangerous, craftier, more subtle, worse than any and all of his followers. He would be a man they would fear, a man who would kill at the slightest insubordination, for in that way alone could he himself be safe. Therefore a man who has already killed, a master criminal; probably one who has been high in Neapolitan or Sicilian circles of crime. He should not be difficult to identify."

Cardani shook his head. "There has been no man come to this country in recent years worse or more forceful than Spiro, Tasso, or Coremo; and none of these is powerful enough to hold the others. No; I don't think there is any single leader yet."

Pianelli shrugged.

"I should not want to be too confident of that, Paul," he said softly. "And if he is not already here, I should watch for his coming."

Cardani nodded soberly; then smiled. "I must go now."

"Ah, but the news," Pianelli reminded him.

"Oh, yes. I had forgotten." He paused to look steadily at his friend, while a smile appeared and grew on his strong features.

"At last they have given me all I could ask. I am permanently in plain-clothes, with advanced rank. A lieutenant. All Italian cases are to be referred to me to handle as I see fit. I report only to my highest superiors, the inspector and the commissioner himself."

"My warmest congratulations," Pianelli said dryly.

Cardani's smile broadened.

"Wait. I am to organize and head a secret squad of Italians, for my work solely. I am to choose these men myself and am allowed six to start with."

Pianelli, who had been lounging, came to his feet. His eyes were points of flame.

"Now," he said, a little hoarsely, a rare betrayal of emotion, "your chances to live and make headway are, I think, somewhat better than the one to a thousand odds I had considered them."

6

CARDANI WAS GIVEN his own office, on Lafayette Street right around the corner from Police Headquarters at 300 Mulberry. With his new activities to be secret, as far as possible, his official quarters could be neither obvious nor pretentious. They were not.

An old, long unused, three-storied warehouse was taken over. Cardani moved into the top floor. Although in a different section, its approach reminded him strongly of that other disused storehouse where with his father, Dominick Cardani, he had rescued the mutilated Giovanna, little daughter of the singing baker.

On the ground floor, rubbish was cleared away; as well as any old boxes or barrels behind which an enemy or spy might lurk. Otherwise it was left alone, with its large single room in the back and its office and narrow hallway from which stairs led to the second story, also a deserted space, and on to the third.

There a large front room was partitioned off for Cardani's own use, a smaller one for his two first assistants, and a third for the general purposes of the rest of his men, including sleeping quarters.

To these new-old quarters Paul brought his whole accumulation of criminal records, a rather amazing collection gathered through many years. There were examples of hand-writing of all manner of criminals and of men merely on his suspected list: letters written abroad; unsigned notes and messages of threat and extortion; communications of a business nature with signatures that might prove important; missives apparently without significance yet of possible use.

Then there were specimens of every known weapon employed by the Blackhanders in their nefarious operations: knives of all makes, pistols, bombs. His ten years of devoted study had made Paul an expert in each.

On one wall was a map of Italy; in his files, papers published currently in that country, exhaustive notes and records, photographs and descriptions; on his shelves, such works on criminology as he had been able to acquire.

Here were no sheets of music, no operas, no violin. These were all in his modest and not distant living quarters which saw him little enough in his waking hours.

The establishment of his force and equipment in these "secret" quarters took a long time for its final accomplishment. It proceeded mostly at night. His days were taken on cases, in court, in the pursuit of wanted criminals, or, when not more actively engaged, in ceaseless roaming through Mulberry Bend, Five Points, and its environs, the whole quarter where crime was rampant throughout the twenty-four hours.

During this period, in his spare time Cardani proceeded with the instruction of the six men he had chosen from long acquaintance. These selections, in each instance passed upon and approved by Benito Pianelli, were made for intelligence, trustworthiness, physical ability; and for the reputation of the men among the people whom Paul had set himself to protect.

It was a monumental work of preparation, never to be fully achieved; for each day brought its new complications, its different problems and equations. The reign of terror was approaching its peak....

SHADOW SLANTED AT an acute angle from the eaves of the old warehouse, falling athwart the upper half of the third-story windows, leaving the lower portion shot with hot light. Beneath the raised sashes, warm air, heavy with moisture, sifted into the room behind, bearing the multifarious odors of the neighborhood.

Paul Cardani, in neat white shirt and black tie, was leaning back in an ordinary hard-bottomed chair. His keen eyes were watching Dick Ocelli and Peter Largio, his two first assistants, to whom he had been explaining his plans.

Ocelli straightened. He was a clean-limbed, lithe fellow in his late twenties, with smooth olive skin, black wavy hair, and dark eyes that were unusually bright and intelligent appearing.

"I guess I see what you're after, Lieutenant," he said, in deceptively soft tone.

"The point now," Cardani said, "is this: working alone I have had to follow every case as it came up, without any particular system. With you two and the other men finally having some idea what it is all about, I am ready to take these gangs, one after the other. We won't neglect anything that comes under our feet, but right now we are concentrating on the knife men, because we have more on them at the moment.

"In the lockup over on Mulberry, we have at least half a dozen caught in knife attacks. I have enough to convict and send up every one of them, but I'm delaying their trials, holding their punishment before them, in hopes of a squeal. They haven't told us much yet, but as soon as we land one from the top, we can start the whole bunch spilling and tie the big ones up. And that killing over on Leonard last night is our chance."

"What was that, Chief?" Largio asked. "I just got back from that macaroni fire in Harlem, you know."

"Francesco Carmello and his brothers," Cardani explained, "had a wineshop on Leonard near Baxter. Frank lived in a back room behind the shop; the others upstairs. They've made payments on threats before. This time they refused a large demand. Last evening, around closing time at nine, there were half a dozen strangers who had drifted in a couple at a time. A woman customer left. Then one of the strangers closed the door and stood by it. The rest grabbed Frank, rushed him into the back room, cut his throat, and beat it.

"I spent the morning there," Paul resumed, "but that's all I've got on it so far. If the killer had left his knife, I could get him, but he didn't. We haven't located the woman customer yet.

"One of the brothers says he was upstairs. The other told me he was opening a case in the basement, and when he heard Frank yell he came up only in time to see the men going out. That is what they say. My guess is they could give us at least descriptions but are too scared to talk. A patrolman on the beat came in while I was there, and that didn't help matters."

Paul thumped a heavy hand on the table.

"Six men wouldn't go on a premeditated killing like that without some leader. Each one of those six knows the others and knows which one was the murderer. We've got to land one of them. We've got to get more information, and I'm very sure the Carmellos could give it to us."

"I know Tito Carmello," Ocelli said quietly.

"Does he know you're in police work?" Cardani snapped.

"Not the least idea. We play pool sometimes, and once went to a dance together."

"Drop all other work. You know what to do; you know how I would go after it. If you can, bring Tito over here, so I can get at him."

"If I could do it the way you do," Ocelli murmured, "I'd already be the chief at Headquarters."

"Never mind that," Paul said sharply. "Get after it and do your work. Excuses won't go if you don't come back with something."

He stood up, a powerful figure packing a hundred and ninety pounds of hardened muscle that didn't show. He stepped across the office to a peg where he had hung coat and vest. The coat sagged badly from a weight in the right-hand pocket. He took both down and drew a silver watch from a vest pocket.

"Almost twelve," he announced, frowning. "I go to Benito Pianelli. For lunch. I haven't made an engagement like it for years, but he has never yet asked me to come without reason.

"You know where it is," he added, setting his hat on the table and brushing his hair with his hands before the single small mirror. "Over on Norfolk near Seward Park. Send me word if you get anything and if I'm delayed."

He buttoned his vest and smoothed down the coat; then, apparently after giving the matter thought, removed a revolver from the right pocket and thrust it into a hip pocket of his trousers, not without a little, unconscious shake of the head.

He strode toward the door, a substantial man of neat appearance. Before he opened it, however, he thrust his right hand into the side coat pocket. Ocelli, as if watching for this gesture, nodded at Largio and grinned.

Paul hurried down Lafayette and turned east on Houston, with the intention of taking the Bowery line down. Near Mott, a big brewery truck was drawn up at the curb, and almost mechanically he stopped to look at the pair of splendid dappled grays.

The driver was just easing a heavy keg from the flaring truck side. He was young, husky, with reddish hair and laughing, reckless eye. Cardani watched the keg come down and thump solidly on the cushion set to break its fall, but with less rapidity in its descent than would have been the case had it not been for a stalwart back and a pair of muscular arms.

The driver half straightened, winked at Cardani, and began to roll the keg across the sidewalk to the saloon. Cardani glanced back at the horses, saw that both heads were stretched expectantly toward him, and remembered a barrel of apples outside a fruit shop next to the saloon.

As he turned, his quick eye caught a hurrying figure just disappearing around the corner into Mott. Before he could even speculate what if anything this might mean, in his line of vision two doors ahead, the whole front of a low building suddenly flew out over the sidewalk.

Accompanying this startling phenomenon, the blast of a stunning explosion seemed to strike him with physical force, slapping him in the face and chest, rocking him back on his heels.

Cardani's recovery was instantaneous, automatic. His response was action. He had a sidelong glimpse of the big horses rearing upward, their pawing forelegs feathered from fetlock to huge hoof. He heard an angry oath in rich brogue, the slap of running brogans, even the thump-thump of the abandoned keg as it started rolling toward the curb. But Paul was already running. It seemed to him that he was running when the first bits of shattered glass struck brick and cobblestone with a sharp, penetrating tinkle.

As he advanced he saw a man beyond the broken store front hastening toward him, and instantly recalled the figure hurriedly rounding the corner before the blast. He saw at once, however, that this man was taller. Others, men and women, were pouring excitedly from near-by doorways. Across the street a restaurant began to disgorge its early noonday patrons; and all were converging on the damaged shop.

Cardani was the first to arrive. As he came up, a man was staggering through the yawning opening that now lacked frame of window or door, or even wall boards. Cardani hurried to meet him on the broken threshold, seeing no other human form beyond him, only a meaningless jumble of smashed fruits and bottles, splintered glass, boards, and sticks, a welter of plaster from which a white dust filled the air.

The shopkeeper's face was slightly blackened and streaming blood, yet he seemed unaware of any hurt. His one evident desire was to get away from there as speedily as possible. Paul checked him with a restraining hand against his chest. The round, staring eyes appeared not to see him at all. The man pawed at Cardani frantically, uttering curiously choked, inarticulate sounds.

"Steady!" Cardani said sharply, pushing the man a little back. "The damage is all done now. What led up to this?"

Paul was aware that many others were crowding close in behind him with a murmur of excited voices. He gave them no heed. He wanted to catch this man off guard on the rebound, surprise information from him that would be difficult to get in a more sober moment.

"Why—why," the shopkeeper stuttered. "I don't just seem to know. It came too sudden. I was just turning—"

"I mean before this happened. You've been getting threats, haven't you? You have made some payments?"

"Yes, yes. I paid them twice. Only this time they asked twice as much. They—"

"Did anyone come to see you?" Cardani interrupted. "Or did they just send notes?"

"Notes—yes, that was it. I got a note yesterday sayin' if I didn't pay by last night, this would happen. And now—"

"Have you kept any of those messages?"

Cardani's broad shoulders filled the space at the top of the steps that had been the shop's entrance. None tried to get past, yet he could feel them jostling close, chattering excitedly. He was trying desperately, by his own rapid questions, to hold the shopman's attention while he had it.

"Not the first ones," the shopkeeper answered mechanically. "I think I still got this last one, wondering what I could do, because I didn't have the money."

"Just before the explosion, a man came into your shop?"

"Yeh. Sure. I'd forgotten him. Was noon, an' no one else here. He wanted somethin' that was in the back of the shop. I got it and was just turnin' round when it let go. Come to think of it, I don't remember seein' him afterwards. S'pose he got blowed up?"

"No; I saw him running away. What did you think he looked like?"

"Well, lemme see." In apparent effort to remember, the shop-keeper's glance wandered beyond Cardani. Watching closely, Paul saw him suddenly stiffen, his face, where not covered with blood and soot, grow white, saw horror and fright come into his eyes. "I—I can't seem—to think," he faltered.

Cardani whirled around, suspecting instantly what had happened. The tall man, whom he had earlier seen hastening toward the explosion, was just turning away into the crowd that jammed the sidewalk from wall to curb.

Cardani's right hand shot out, clamped on the man's shoulder, and threw him face around. The same hand drew back and struck hard, the heel smashing against mouth and nose.

The man staggered a little, then snapped erect, snarling with rage. He was inches taller than Cardani, of fairly heavy build, and well dressed. His long face with its lantern jaw was dark, swarthy, and slightly pockmarked.

"What d'you think you're doing, copper?" he demanded belligerently. "Don't fool yourself that you can get away with it."

"I know what I'm doing," Cardani told him, pressing a little closer. "You put the sign on that man, scared him so he wouldn't talk. What have you got in this?"

"That's right," a voice cried from the edge of the crowd. "I saw him. The Sicilian death sign."

The tall man, scowling fiercely, started to turn in that direction. Cardani again pulled him around and slapped him hard on the mouth. He made a move toward a pocket, and Cardani dropped his hands.

"Go ahead, reach for it," he taunted, crowding nearer. "Come on; come on. You're a brave man. You only make a little sign, and a man is afraid to talk. Why don't you show us what you will do? See—my hands are at my side. What've you got? A knife? A pistol? Come on; do something, you rat, or you'll never be able to frighten anyone again."

He swung his open hand again, with a resounding slap; a greater humiliation than a blow. Then he clamped a viselike grip on the stranger's arm above the elbow and swung him around until they were close, face to face.

"You called me copper," he said, in a tone that carried to the crowd, "and you probably know that I never pull a man unless I have enough on him to send him to the chair or to jail. I know you're in on this deal. I haven't enough on you now, but I'm on your trail from this moment. Get wise and beat it away from here, back where you came from. Stick around and I'll land you."

He turned the man to face the crowd.

"Look at this thing, men," he called. "Look at him carefully, all of you. He is the kind that slinks around at night and sticks a knife in your back. Remember his face. You don't have to be afraid of him or his signs. Just face him, and he will run."

Cardani shook the man violently, and the crowd yelled their delight. Here was something new, unheard of. One of the dreaded Blackhanders, for as such they recognized him, publicly shaken and cuffed like a truant schoolboy.

Still holding him, Cardani led the pockmarked man through the crowd to the curb, cuffed him once more, and shoved him hard into the street. The man stumbled and jostled against the young Irish truck driver who, with his team evidently under control, had just come up. The swing of a heavy brogan helped the tall man on his way. He half paused and scowled back. The husky lad stepped toward him.

"G'wan now, ye dhirty dago," he growled. "Ye make me ashamed of me Eyetalian grandmither. Or stand up an' take it."

The tall stranger slunk hastily off without another backward glance, found a convenient alley, and disappeared. Cardani watched his going with frowning, thoughtful eyes.

"Do you know who that fellow was?" he asked.

"They call him the Wolf," the truck driver answered readily enough, "and he's supposed to be bad. That's his reputation anyway, but I don't know anything he's done."

Lupo! That was the alias that had been hammering at the back of his mind. He had remembered the features from a picture in his files. A name he had found to attach to the perpetrator of old crimes overseas and on his suspected list here, but without any recent information. Lupo!

Cardani sought the shopkeeper and was told that the man had gone. Someone said he had left to see a doctor.

A patrolman came up to disperse the crowd, and Paul went further into the shop. From the effects, he suspected the character of explosive used and after diligent search discovered a twisted and broken bit of iron pipe. Satisfied, he stepped over the débris to the sidewalk.

The patrolman recognized him, saluted, and asked for orders.

"Routine," Cardani told him and turned away.

Absent-mindedly he was actually retracing his steps toward his own office when abruptly he recalled his delayed luncheon engagement. With a muttered exclamation, he swung about and fairly ran to the Bowery.

A few minutes later he was knocking at the familiar door on the first landing.

Carlotta promptly opened to him. "Oh, Signore," she cried, in very obvious relief. "We feared that something bad had happened to you."

She conducted him toward a room in front. Cardani still

carried in his hand the fragment of iron pipe, which he had been examining on the way down. Reminded of it when he took off his hat, he transferred it to a pocket. Carlotta opened a door and announced him.

After the brilliant noonday street glare, the room which he faced was a little dark to his eyes. He stood for a moment on the threshold, very erect, very stern in the abstraction that still held him.

Benito Pianelli, always cool and smart in appearance, came with outstretched hand to greet him.

"You are a little late, my young friend," he chided affectionately.

"I'm sorry," Cardani said bluntly. "I started soon enough but ran into—an interruption."

Pianelli turned a little aside, bowed with his inimitable courtesy.

"Permit me," he said. "Signora Alfredo, may I present my esteemed young friend, Lieutenant Cardani?"

Cardani bowed over the frail white hand that was extended to him, smiled at the bright-faced, gray-haired little lady.

"And," Pianelli murmured, "Signorina Ravino."

Surprised, Cardani turned and looked into the warm eyes of the most gloriously beautiful girl, he instantly told himself, it had ever been his fortune, or regret, to meet.

7

"MY BROTHER WAS disappointed, Lieutenant," Signora Alfredo said. "He was coming to meet you. Only at the last moment, when we called for him, a business matter came up and he could not leave."

"He asked us to give you his respects and apology," Signorina Ravino added. She turned her head a little to look up at him; her eyes smiled into his.

"I too regret having to miss him," Cardani said somewhat blankly.

They were at table now; the two ladies at Cardani's left and right, Pianelli opposite. Cardani's mind was altogether in a whirl of conflicting thoughts. He had come entirely absorbed in the many problems of the crowded morning, every one of which demanded his attention and study. Ocelli's visit to the kin of the murdered Carmello held possibility of the first important "break," which Cardani had long awaited. There was the bomb to be traced; the shopkeeper rounded up. And most important of all was this new figure, the Wolf, who had stalked so confidently on to the stage of this most recent crime.

Actually he had crossed the threshold with the name of Lupo on his lips, expecting to dispose of a hurried luncheon, discuss meanwhile all these matters with his friend and confidant, Pianelli, then rush back to his office.

Abruptly his thoughts and speculations were arrested and without his volition shunted into other channels. Unprepared and without warning, he was brought face to face with this charming girl, whose presence was as unexpected and refreshing as a breeze in midsummer. It was outside Cardani's experience; yet, caught thus off guard, his response was spontaneous, as automatic as his reflexes in action. The girl was rarely beautiful without doubt. She was also of a class that had been quite outside his sphere. And yet she was treating him with unreserved friendliness, made possible of course only by the impeccable medium of their acquaintance, the aristocratic Signore Pianelli.

Hot Calabrian blood flowed in Paul Cardani's veins. It had boiled in combat and in peril, congealed in dread for the pitiful fate of others, and had never hitherto been warmed by an emotion more tender.

Now the mind of the serious lieutenant was a bit chaotic. His own eyes were on fire as they met the girl's friendly glances. Yet behind their gleam was a peculiar, sombre sadness, possibly reflecting a sense of the sorrow that might be his if he lost himself completely. Although he did not know it, the girl caught something of this, which she found vastly more intriguing than the mere ardent glances of a new admirer.

"He is Giulia's father," Signora Alfredo was explaining. "Damiano Ravino, the banker, you know."

"Of course," Cardani said, a little mechanically as he responded to the warmth of that name—Giulia. Then a tardy thought pulled him abruptly alert.

"I should very much like to know him," he said, after that momentary pause. "As a matter of fact, I have been planning for some time to talk with a few of the bankers in this quarter, if I could meet them on a confidential basis. They could give me valuable information."

"How so?" Pianelli asked.

"The sudden withdrawals of amounts, particularly from long savings, that are not for business purposes."

"You mean," Pianelli said dryly, "payments for extortion, ransom, and blackmail."

Cardani nodded, and instantly regretted that he had introduced the suggestion when he saw Giulia's smile fade. "We need not speak of that now," he said.

She looked at him with a new light in her expressive eyes. "I wish you would. Before you came, Mr. Pianelli was telling us—so many interesting things."

"Indeed, yes," Signora Alfredo contributed. "He says that you are devoting your whole life to fighting this terror which is dominating the poor people here. We think it is magnificent, a noble sacrifice."

Benito Pianelli coughed behind his hand. "I am very certain," he said in his dry tone, "that I didn't intend setting up Paul as a hero. You flatter him, Signora."

Giulia said nothing, but her eyes were telling what her red lips neglected to express.

"I have never thought of it in that way," Cardani said, instantly sober. "It is just my work, like that of a doctor, or a banker," he added with a laugh.

"You will meet Damiano," the Signora cried. "And I am sure he will help in any way he can. He is much upset over these continued outrages, and he knows well what you have been doing, Lieutenant, as do all of us."

"It will not be information a banker can readily give," Pianelli said. "I can understand its value to you, Paul, especially if the payments could be traced, and perhaps, discreetly, some of our banker friends might be persuaded to co-operate. It's an idea to think about. Of course you, better than anyone else, understand its danger."

"Thoroughly. And for that reason I have delayed seeking it. But let's not speak of it now." He turned to Giulia. "Are you fond of music, signorina?"

"Indeed I am," she responded quickly. "And Mr. Pianelli says that you play the violin exceptionally well."

He laughed, glad of the lighter turn to the conversation. "In my younger days, Luigi Busano, a neighborhood baker with a really remarkable tenor, tried hard to make a musician of me. To be candid, my own inclinations were, and always will be, I suppose, in that direction. My good friend here, however, favored a more useful work."

Giulia was looking at him with that provocative, sidewise, upward tilt of her pretty head. "But you still keep up your violin, do you not, Lieutenant? Oh, you must."

Cardini's dark eyes grew dreamy. "Yes, I still play, a little," he said. "Whenever I can, whenever I feel that I might be discouraged, when the world seems all wrong." He shrugged broad shoulders, as if in quick apology for his mood. "Then everything gets bright again."

"Poor Luigi," Pianelli said in his brittle tone, which told nothing whatsoever of what he might feel. "I doubt if he has once sung since that night of Giovanna's mishap those many years ago."

"What was that?" Giulia asked Paul.

He frowned a little, then smiled into her eager eyes. "It is a story that doesn't belong in such a pleasant time. Tell me; do you go to the opera?"

"Surely," she said vivaciously. "When Aunt or Father or my brother Vincent can be persuaded to take me.

"I wish sometime we might go together," Paul said wistfully.

Giulia smiled, blushed, then glanced at her aunt.

However, before the Signora could frame any polite evasion, Carlotta, whose biscuit Tortoni and delicious coffee had already been consumed, entered, paused a pace from the table, and looked expectantly at her master. Pianelli nodded.

"It is for Signore Cardani," she said, and gave Paul a sealed envelope.

With a blunt, "Excuse me," Cardani hastily tore it open, withdrew the half sheet it contained, and read to himself:

"Tito is here. He saw Tasso.

Ocelli."

Absent-mindedly Paul rose to his feet. His dark eyes glowed strangely. His mouth was suddenly grim and hard. Abruptly he became aware that the three were looking at him curiously. He quickly resumed his seat.

"An urgent call?" Pianelli thoughtfully inquired.

"A break!" Cardani said, in low tone but with almost explosive intensity. A brief silence followed.

Benito Pianelli bowed to the two ladies, pushed back his chair, and rose.

"I fear," he said, "that we must excuse the lieutenant to his duty."

Cardani bowed low over Signora Alfredo's hand as she expressed her pleasure at meeting him. Then the Signora stepped a little aside with her host while Paul turned to Giulia.

She extended her hand, and Cardani thrilled at the slight response to his strong grip. Her eyes, which had been laughing so merrily, were strangely sober as she steadily met his look.

For a brief moment while he was silent, she was not quite certain what she wanted to say. Then impulse decided the matter. "You are going into danger," she said simply. "I know it. Please be careful."

The light in his dark eyes was unrestrained. "At least," he said very quietly, "I shall not be afraid now."

The door closed gently behind him, and he descended the stairs swiftly.

Before he reached and opened the outer door, his right hand was thrust into his coat pocket and rested on the butt of the revolver which he had transferred thence. He was alert once more, his whole mind intent on the grim business before him.

8

A FORTUNATE CIRCUMSTANCE had given Cardani two new leads; the fragment of bomb, which he still carried, and the new figure in the vicious circle— Lupo. In spite of his haste to get to his office, Paul knew that it was imperative to attempt to get further information on his way thither.

As Cardani came up, a patrolman was standing before the blown-out front of the ill-fated shop, twirling his stick on its thong and looking blankly at the disordered interior. Paul glanced beyond him. The stout figure of the shopkeeper, with bandaged head and face lugubrious where it showed at all, was poking among the débris. Two boys were making creditable effort to help. Paul touched the policeman on the arm.

"Stick around," he said in low tone.

The officer interrupted his twirling to salute, then resumed it with scarcely the loss of a measure. Cardani went inside.

The shopkeeper twisted his head quickly at sound of the step, recognized his earlier inquisitor, and hastily turned the other way. Cardani stepped close.

"I want to talk with you."

The shopkeeper glanced toward the street, then turned partly to Cardani, without facing him. His expression was both worried and sullen.

"This ain't your trouble, Mister. I can't tell you anything."

"I'm making it my trouble," Cardani told him, a little sternly. "You don't want this to happen again, do you?"

"That's just it. I don't. That feller saw me talking to you and put the sign on me. I ain't going to get caught at it again. So, *ex*-cuse me." He started to turn away.

"You're not afraid of Lupo, are you? Didn't you see him slink away like a gutter rat?"

The shopkeeper whirled all the way around. He was visibly shaken.

"Is that who it was? I didn't— Oh, God save me! Please, Mister, haven't I—"

"What do you know of Lupo?"

"Nothing! Nothing!" Desperation made him angry. "Ain't I had trouble enough? Why the hell don't you leave me alone!"

Cardani studied him for a moment."What are you planning to do?" he asked in quieter tone.

"Can't you see? My boys and I are tryin' to clean up." He glanced at Cardani, saw nothing but a calm, unruffled expression. "I guess you mean all right, but it ain't safe to be seen talkin' with a copper—not around here."

"Are you going on with your business, when you get the place cleaned up?"

The shopkeeper sighed heavily. "I dunno. I dunno what to do. I'd sell it, if I had any other place to go. But I'm fixed here, and if I get goin' again they'll come back an' hit me for more money." His face, between the strips of bandage was a picture of despair.

"Haven't you anyone to help you?"

"Sure. My brother, who lives with me, is comin' any minute."

"How'd you like to go away for a few days, while he's putting it in shape again, and let this scare blow over?"

"What'd I go on, an' where?" He waved a hand comprehensively. "This'll cost every cent I got. Don't make fun o' me, Mister."

Cardani turned away. "All right," he said. "I'll see you again. What is your name?"

"Stefano Bellini. But don't make it too soon."

Outside, Cardani signed to the patrolman to follow him out of sight of the shop. "Bellini's brother will be along in a few minutes," he said. "When he comes, take Bellini to Headquarters. Tell him the law requires him to make out a report. Tell Inspector Sherwin to take care of him for me and to hold him for questioning."

The patrolman saluted, and Cardani hastened toward his office, chafing over the time lost, even if it was not wasted.

He found Ocelli and Largio seated beside the table in Cardani's own office with Tito Carmello between them. He was a man of about twenty-eight, of slender build and intelligent face. Tragedy showed in the dark eyes he raised to Cardani; that and a trace of fear as well. The lieutenant shook hands with him soberly.

"I'm glad you came, Carmello," he said simply, and turned to his desk where he busied himself for a few minutes, making notes on the shopkeeper Bellini and on Lupo, but in reality to allow Carmello to become used to his presence.

After a while he pushed the papers aside and took his chair over to the three young men. Their low-voiced conversation ceased at his approach. He seated himself with a show of leisurely assurance.

"On my way over this noon," he said, addressing no one of the three in particular, "I ran right on to a bombing. I have a piece of the bomb which I can trace; I have the victim comfortably quartered where he can safely give me the information I need, and I have turned up a new man. Altogether it was a break."

He turned more directly to Carmello and smiled confidently. "And you are providing me with another."

Tito Carmello made a deprecatory gesture. "Dick has been talking to me," he said, in a very low tone. "I didn't want to hold out on you this morning, Lieutenant—but—you know how it is."

"I know how it is."

"Dick has shown me another side," Carmello went on. "I don't believe there is any chance for me after this, but I don't much care. They will get me sooner or later; but they got Frank, and I want them to pay for it. I wanted to do it my own way. Dick talked me out of that. He told me he had brought his own trouble to you, and, well, he persuaded me to come and talk with you."

"Ocelli is right," Cardani said. "This is America. I am an officer of the law here. At the same time I am of your race, Carmello, brought up as you were, with exactly the same ideas and the same prejudices. All that is different here."

He broke off to turn to Ocelli. "How did you come in?" he asked.

"Back way, from Crosby."

"That is fine. Now, Carmello, they are not going to be able to reach you for a few days, and in that time with your help I'll put them where they can never touch you."

Carmello looked his doubt.

"In this way," Cardani said briskly. "When you tell me a few things I need to know, I want you to go back to your home. Largio will go with you, and another of my men will follow you. Tell your brother to pass the word that you are going out of town for a few days to arrange to have Frank's body taken away. Tell him it is necessary that he should attend to all other arrangements. Then come back with Largio. He will take you to Mulberry Street where you will have comfortable quarters and be safe while we round up this gang."

For the first time, Carmello's eyes brightened a little.

"If it will get the man who killed Frank," he said bitterly, "I will do anything you say, Lieutenant."

"It will do just that," Cardani promised him. "Now tell me your story. It's getting late and I have a lot to do. Besides I want you under cover as soon as possible."

"I was down in the basement, as I told you. I heard the scuffling of feet going toward the back, and came to the stairs. Then I heard Frank yell, once. I came up to the top and looked out. I saw a man I knew was Michele Tasso run out from the back room. He had a knife in his hand and"—he faltered a little—"it was dripping blood. He wiped it as he went along and put it in his pocket before he reached the door.

"There was another man standing there. He opened the door, and he and Tasso, followed by three or four other men, ran out, and the last man closed the door. I came into the shop, and then Guido came downstairs. We—found Frank."

"Did you recognize any of the other men?"

"I—I don't think so. I knew something awful had happened when I saw the knife, and nothing seemed very clear to me after that. But I had seen Tasso first. I can swear he was the man. And the man at the door. I would know his face if I saw him again, but I don't know who he was."

"Wait a moment," Cardani said, and moved his chair back to the desk. He wrote hurriedly and in a few moments brought over to the table the statement as Carmello had given it to him. Carmello read it.

"What is that for?"

"That is so, in case something should happen to me, they will still get Michele Tasso. Sign it, Carmello, and you two fellows witness it."

Without further hesitation, Carmello affixed his signature and, the paper properly witnessed, Cardani locked it in a drawer. His stern features showed not the slightest sign of his elation.

"Pete," he said to Largio, "I want you to understand this and make no mistake about it. I don't have to tell you Tito Carmello's importance to us, do I?"

"No, Chief. I got it."

"He has to go back to his home to get that story started so Tasso's crowd won't get suspicious and hide out. If it wasn't for that, I'd put him under cover now. Until he is turned over to the inspector's care, I'm putting his safety in your hands. I'll send one man to cover you. Dick, call Ceruti."

Ocelli stepped to the door opening into the squad room and came back with a short, thick-set man in his twenties. Ceruti had coal-black eyes, a broad, low forehead, and a square jaw. He looked like a prizefighter or a wrestler.

Cardani explained what he wanted briefly. "Ceruti, I want you to tail Carmello and Largio until they get back to Headquarters. Keep about ten paces behind them." He turned to Largio. "Pete, don't let Carmello out of your sight for an instant. Keep your eyes open for any sort of attack and your pistol handy. We can't take chances now. If you get to Headquarters before I do, explain matters to Inspector Sherwin personally. That's all boys."

Ocelli opened the door to the stairway, and Cardani called to him.

"Hustle down, Dick, and see these fellows out the back way. Look out yourself first."

After the men had gone, Cardani stood in the same position, his eyes fixed sombrely on the closed door, seeming not to see it but to be looking far beyond its barrier. He drew in a long, deep breath, let it escape slowly from his lips. Then he turned to his desk, lighted the gas lamp, and got busy with his files.

By the time he had got out and brought to the desk photographs, descriptions, and all information he had on "Mike the Knife" Tasso and Lupo, Ocelli returned.

"They got away all right, Lieutenant," Ocelli said in a matter-of-fact tone, although his eyes were keen and bright with excitement.

Cardani nodded. "There's the file on Tasso. Let the rest of the squad see it. Then send them out in different sections to try to locate him. Tell them to work carefully so as not to alarm him. You can do that later. Now I want to tell you something else."

He then told him every detail of the bombing, particularly the part played by the mysterious Lupo, and the disposition he had made of the unhappy shopkeeper.

"Lupo," Ocelli repeated. "First time I've heard that name."

Cardani pointed to his desk. "Get what you can out of that file. It's old stuff. I think he's new here or been keeping under cover. When you're out, see if you can get some line on him. Now take that Tasso file and study it. I want to look up Lupo further."

It was getting late in the evening, but neither man spoke of hunger. After a time there were steps on the landing outside and Largio came in with Ceruti. Cardani shot a keen glance at their faces, then unconsciously drew a deep breath of relief.

"All locked up for the night, Chief," Largio said lightly.

Cardani nodded. "Had your supper?"

Ceruti said, "Had mine early. If you don't need me I'll go back in the squad room and turn in bimeby."

Largio said, "No; and neither have you."

"Take the evening off if you want to," Cardani told Largio. "Before you go, I want both of you to take a look at these two." He indicated the files. "Tasso is wanted for first degree. I want him located. Make your inquiries carefully, but keep your eyes and ears open."

In a few minutes the men left; Ceruti to go to the general room and to bed, for at least one man was in the loft throughout the twenty-four hours, and Largio down the stairs.

9

CARDANI STOOD UP.

"I'll run over to Headquarters. Want to get Tasso's warrant started. If Inspector Sherwin is in I may be a few minutes longer. Get your men started; then wait here, Dick, and we'll go out for a bite."

Ocelli nodded, watched Cardani put on his hat, and smiled when the lieutenant thrust his right hand into his coat pocket before opening the door.

Cardani made the gesture unconsciously. It was a habit that a score of attempts on his life had fixed on him. He closed the door and started down the stairs, his mind immersed in a whirl of plans and speculation. He trod lightly, for his weight, yet his footsteps echoed dully in the stairwell and the empty rooms of the warehouse, accentuating the silence that followed the noisy day's departure.

But Cardani was insensible to this impression. His thoughts were on the opportunities which the last few hours had brought him; the chance so soon for the secret squad to justify its existence.

He came down the second flight, turned on the landing. Absorbed as he was, habit raised his eyes to glance ahead.

His keen look caught the slightest flicker of shadow. In the same instant he sank to one knee. As he ducked he saw a prolonged streak of light start from the stairhead and leap toward him. He heard the breath of the passing blade; its dull thud into the wall behind. Then the crashing report of a pistol shot smothered the sound.

On his knee, Cardani fired twice through his pocket, saw the flame of the answering shot. A form pitched forward from the stairtop to the landing. He heard the smack of descending steps.

Peering between the rough banisters he had a quick, clear view of the fleeing man. With the speed of a camera he caught the shape of the hat, the short, thick figure with its slouching shoulders. Cardani could have shot him in that moment. Instead, he groaned loudly and let his body thump noisily to the floor.

Instantly, silently, he was on his feet, racing catlike up the way he had come. He met Ocelli midway of the second flight.

"Get man on first landing," he whispered, and sped on.

Ceruti, half dressed, threw open the squad room door at the top. Cardani pushed past him, ran to the rear of the loft. Darkness was behind him as he thrust his head out the window and looked below.

Dimly he saw a figure pass along a narrow alley that flanked the warehouse. It disappeared past the wall of the building fronting Crosby Street.

Cardani pushed through the window to the fire escape, went down it swiftly with a balanced weight that made no sound. As he gained the alley, the narrow oblong of light at the street end was unobstructed by human form.

He ran lightly to the end, peered cautiously around to his left. He had guessed right. That squat figure, topped by the shapeless soft hat, had turned downtown.

Cardani glanced quickly around. Several loiterers were in sight, but they seemed indifferently intent upon their own affairs. Evidently the alarm given by those crashing reports a minute earlier was confined to the other block. He looked in the other direction. His quarry was walking steadily onward. His pace was neither hurried nor slow. Cardani started to follow.

It was soon apparent to him that the man ahead either felt certain of no pursuit or feared to arouse suspicion by acting otherwise than as a casual pedestrian. They traversed several blocks, and not once did he look behind. Then Cardani lengthened his stride and began to cut down the distance that separated them.

From his years of experience Paul Cardani was an expert trailer. Not one of the many who passed him could possibly have suspected that he was as ruthless in his pursuit as the would-be killer in his recent attempt at assassination. His right hand was still in his pocket, gathering the cloth in a fold to hide the telltale powder-burned hole. It also grasped the revolver butt. Cardani was ready to shoot on the instant should his quarry turn, discover him and show fight, or seem about to escape.

But Paul did not want to kill. He had made that decision in a split second on the stairway. On the point of shooting, it had flashed across his reason that this man was not acting on his own initiative. He had been sent, and he would return to report. It followed that he would lead to the men who had ordered the killing.

Remembering the thrown knife, Cardani first suspected that the pursuit might lead even to Michele Tasso, now wanted for murder. But a circumstance bothered him. A pistol man and a knife man had made the attack together. A single man might be armed with both, but never in Cardani's experience had he hitherto known members of the two distinct gangs to act in unison.

His mind flashed back to the noonday hour, to that mysterious figure that had come so unexpectedly, so confidently on the scene. Lupo. Lupo, so far unplaced, could be acting now between the gangs—an adjutant for the higher power.

Lupo, or "Mike the Knife." This pursuit might lead to either. Which one Cardani did not much care. But he was suddenly more eager than ever to penetrate the hideout to which the man ahead was unknowingly taking him. To whomsoever the killer would report, that man Cardani could arrest for conspiracy to murder. Then he would have a further link in the chain.

He was only half a block behind his man now.

They had crossed Spring and Broome, were approaching Grand. Cardani had to make a quick decision. Before entering the actual rendezvous, the killer would make sure that he wasn't followed. Trailing behind him, Cardani could not escape that scrutiny. To gain his purpose, he must allow the killer to go in without suspicion. It was the only way by which he could surprise him with his chief and implicate the other man.

Cardani knew the quarter like a book. There were hideouts, basement saloons where no honest man dare enter, on Leonard near the intersection of the street they were now on. If the killer were seeking one of these, after crossing Grand he would go straight ahead. Should he turn east—there was a notorious crook meeting place on Mulberry, just below Hester. There were several others, of lesser repute if no less evil purpose, in the same section on lower Mulberry.

The man crossed Grand and turned left.

Cardani, with his head twisted slightly in the other direction, went straight on. Once beyond the corner, he quickened his stride. He turned east on Howard, crossed Lafayette to Hester, hastened past Baxter, and turning right on Mulberry found a dark recessed doorway. He had cast the die and waited now with stolid patience.

There was no flood of lights here. The staggered gas lamps, with their protected mantels, were widely separated by interval spaces of dim illumination.

Cardani knew that if he had guessed wrong, a few moments only would prove his mistake. Men approached and passed from either direction. Then on the opposite sidewalk appeared the squat figure with its slouching shoulders and shapeless felt.

The man passed a few doors, then turned abruptly and went down two steps toward a basement entrance. There he stopped. For a long moment, he scanned his back trail, looked all about him while Cardani hid his left hand and bent his head so that the white blur of his face should not show.

When he looked up the man had gone. Faintly to his ears came the sound of a closing door.

Cardani waited half a minute, then crossed over. He walked swiftly to the place where his quarry had disappeared, saw the steps leading down to the basement entrance. To the left of the door were two unlighted windows. Above them a sign read "Wood, Coal, Ice." At the right was the sheer stone flank of steps going up to a squalid tenement. Cardani went down.

His left hand grasped the knob, turned it, eased the door open without noise. He stepped in and closed it softly behind him. He paused to accustom his eyes to the blank darkness. Then, at some paces ahead, he made out a faint glimmer of light. His left hand swept to one side and touched the panels of a door. That would be the entrance to the business blind. Stepping softly he crept slowly ahead.

He came to the source of the dim illumination and saw that it came through the cracked panel of a door in the wall at his right. From beyond it came an indistinct murmur of voices. He stood motionless, listening, scarcely breathing. He heard the clink of glass and bottle, but no footstep. The passage reeked with the odors of stale beer and liquor.

He saw, by the crack, that the wood of the door was not thick. The light touch of his left-hand fingers found an ordinary knob. He did not turn it. He thought the chances were that it would be locked.

As yet unsuspected, he could go back the way he had come, get to the nearest drug store, and in a very few minutes have a raiding squad from Headquarters. He did not even think of it.

Instead he grasped the knob again, leaned back the full length of his arm. His fingers twisted at the instant his powerful shoulder hit the door. He crashed it open and went in with it.

His feet struck thick sawdust, spread a little, and set firmly. His right hand lifted the pocket of his coat where it held, poised. His eyes flashed around.

He was in a low-ceilinged room of rectangular shape.

Ten or a dozen men sat in small groups at bare, rough tables under two hooded kerosene lamps slung from the ceiling. There was a bracket lamp close by the door; another at the end of a crude bar of unfinished planking where a sour-faced man stood. Every eye was on the intruder. For some seconds, it was a silent, frozen tableau.

Cardani was the first to break it.

The pistol held in his pocket, while plainly evident, showed that he had not come with the intent to kill. He had counted on that. He did not want to drive some fear-maddened rat into sudden action, exploding the whole works beyond his control. Now, after those first few seconds, he dominated the situation.

Big, powerful, cool eyes unafraid, he held every man motionless.

Cardani's first swift glance had picked out the man he sought; at the furthest table to his right. Without obvious intention, his eyes on everyone, he commenced to move along the wall in that direction.

"You," he said, and his left hand pointed, "come out from behind that bar. Stand in front of it and keep your hands still."

He waited, tense, poised, until the sour-faced man complied. Then he continued his sidewise movement.

"I am not here to hurt anyone," he said. "Keep quiet and you won't get hurt. Start anything and I'll shoot the first man that makes a move out of turn."

He reached his objective, slipped behind the table. From where he now stood he had all the men more closely bunched before him. And he was careful that no one should cover another. Not a man of them had spoken. No one had moved; except that all eyes followed him as if the men were automatons under a single control.

He stepped close to the man who had led him here. Stooping a little, his eyes watchful on the room, his left hand sought and found the pistol in the man's pocket. He transferred it to his own and stood erect, motionless for a long moment.

Instantly he was conscious of a general relaxation, which was what he sought. He had tried to make it appear that this was a pinch; that one man only was wanted, the rest to be let alone unless they interfered. Searching their faces, Cardani found no indication of such intention—as yet.

He stepped back a pace, to keep his own gaze more level, then let his glance fall to the killer's sole table companion. His eyes widened; then grew narrow and hard.

This was not the expected Lupo or "Mike the Knife" Tasso. But with his abnormally keen memory, Cardani recognized him instantly. It was Francesco Vira, high up on Cardani's list of the pistol gang.

Cardani raised his eyes quickly, hoping that Vira had failed to note his recognition. He was not yet quite ready for his desperate act.

These men before him, no longer scowling belligerently, seemed disposed to let him take the gunman on the pinch. But without doubt they were Vira's men. To take Vira as well might be an entirely different matter. But that was Cardani's intention nevertheless.

With the same cool authority, he drew the revolver from his pocket and cocked it. He stepped close behind Vira's chair and indicated the gunman.

"Stand up," he ordered, "and turn your back to me."

The man, white-faced, shaking a little, stood up and turned.

Cardani's cold gaze swept the room. Still there was no change that he could see in the men's attitude of sullen acquiescence. He raised the pistol to waist level. It was close by Vira's ear, but Vira made no motion. His head was bent. He seemed undesirous of attracting Cardani's special attention.

"You, there," Cardani called sharply to the man furthest from him, "go over to that back wall. Face it. Put your hands against it, above your head. And keep in mind I can hit a fly from here…. All right, you, next."

One by one they filed over until even the sour-faced barman was lined against the wall, backs to the room; all except Francesco Vira and his gunman.

With the last man in position, Cardani's left hand went downward, thrust inside Vira's collar, the knuckles hard against Vira's spine. With little seeming effort, Cardani raised him straight out of his chair, set him on his feet. At the same moment, he pressed the cold round muzzle of his revolver against Vira's neck.

"March!" he said.

The gunman, taking it for his command, started off. Cardani shoved Vira close behind.

"Clasp your hands up before you," he whispered harshly in Vira's ear. "One bad move and you'll get it."

He watched the silent line against the wall as they approached the door. When close to it, he spoke to the squat man in the lead.

"Take that lamp out of the bracket. All right. Now stand back to the door and let me out first. You men," he called, "keep your heads inside. I'll shoot the first one that sticks out."

Cardani pushed Vira into the passage, ordered the gunman to back through and close the door. Once this was done, he rushed them both for the exit and got them to the sidewalk with the least possible delay. There he told the gunman to throw the lamp away; then hustled both men up the street.

10

THE MORNING BROUGHT no definite news of Tasso. One lead, however, held possible promise. Late in the evening Ceruti had come across a friend who, in the course of conversation, complained of a group of men living near him. Returning to his home one midnight this man saw some members of the group hold up a man. They all flashed knives, robbed their victim, then inflicted a severe knife wound in his arm. Evidently they were the terror of the neighborhood; no one molested them; no one ventured too great curiosity concerning themselves or the house which they occupied.

Ceruti's friend worked during the day. Ceruti had arranged to meet him in the evening, go with him to his home, and look things over. The other squadmen had even less to offer. Paul sent them out again and went around the corner to Headquarters.

Commissioner Redfield was a big man with barrel chest, square head, and heavy jowls. His manner was brusque, hurried, and energetic. He spoke explosively, as if he was continually angry or petulant. He took his work very seriously.

Inspector Sherwin was a grizzled veteran who had earned an undying reputation in his captain's rank when Broadway's mid-section was the Tenderloin. He had also helped Paul Cardani qualify for his first uniform. Both men held him in highest esteem and were responsible for the broad scope of his present duties.

For their benefit Paul outlined the status of his various

current activities, particularly his run-in with Lupo and the attack upon himself that followed so quickly, in which members of two separate gangs participated.

He turned to Sherwin.

"Inspector, can you put Vira away where a habeas corpus can't reach him for a while?"

"What do you want that for, Lieutenant?" Commissioner Redfield demanded.

"I look upon the evidence I could get in time from Vira as even more important than Vira's conviction. I can convict him, but I can't break him if his lawyers get to him."

"All right, Sherwin. Attend to it."

"I have talked with the shopkeeper, Bellini," Cardani said. "He feels safe under your wing, Commissioner, and has opened up. This man Lupo has twice tried to sell him protection. Lupo also made a slip. He saw how easily Bellini was scared. He threatened him with two names. Listen. One was Coremo, the bomber; the other, who I suspect leads the kidnapers—and Bellini has children—was Rafaelle Spiro. I'm afraid, Commissioner, that Bellini should be your guest until we round up at least this man Lupo. If we let him go we will lose a valuable witness."

"Damn it, man, you want the city to run a boarding-house. All right. That's the sort of boarders we want."

The Commissioner jerked his big body to more upright position, glared at Cardani through his rimless glasses.

"Now you listen to me, Lieutenant. You are trying to cover a hell of a lot of territory. Right now you are rounding up the man Tasso for murder of Carmello's brother. You have taken Vira, with his gunman, and you'll want to compile the case against them. You have new evidence against the bombers and want to push that while it's hot. You have turned up a new man—what the devil's his name—Lupo. He's selling protection, and you suspect he's the go-between man for the mythical head of this whole slimy mess."

"I see what you mean, Commissioner. I should take one at a time and finish it. Meanwhile the rest would get away from me. They're all hot, right now."

"I agree with that. It's the only way you can smash the whole works. Now; you have the co-operation of Inspector Sherwin and myself. You can call on a platoon of the Headquarters force any time you need them. I wish you would make use of them. You can call on the reserves at any precinct in an emergency. The point is—can you use any more men in your own squad? Could you get them without loss of time?"

Paul looked up, surprised. "I can use two more very well. I know where to put my hands on them."

"All right. Go get them."

"Thanks, Commissioner. I can't ask anything more." Paul stood up.

"I'm not finished, Lieutenant."

Paul resumed his seat.

"You have taken on yourself enough to occupy a dozen men, but here's something more. We've just been discussing it. For some time past there has been a flood of bad money throughout the East. This you have known. What you don't know is that Federal men have arrested passers simultaneously in three Jersey cities and Philadelphia. They have advised me confidentially this morning that their information points to the source not only in New York but also somewhere right in this quarter. The chief is coming over in two or three days. Perhaps we may learn something to help him meanwhile. That is all, Lieutenant. Luck to you."

Inspector Sherwin accompanied Cardani to the outer door. "Narrow escape you had last night, Paul."

Cardani shrugged. "Eternal vigilance—"

"—is the price of life," Sherwin finished dryly. "Ocelli tells me that the knife struck exactly at the height of your chest, with a bullet hole on either side of it. You got off lucky. You killed the knife man and took the other." He shook his head. "You could have had a platoon last night. Don't forget that again."

"There wasn't time."

Sherwin laid a hand on Paul's powerful shoulder. "Take care of yourself, boy," he said gruffly. "We need you."

Paul turned to face him. "I have a work to do," he said simply. "I think I'm going to finish it."

FROM HEADQUARTERS CARDANI walked downtown to Hester. He carried with him the pipe fragment which he had picked up in the bombed fruitshop.

Like every successful detective he knew the value of sources of information. Years earlier, even before he was assigned to the quarter, he had cultivated such sources all over the section. For the most part he relied upon the honest people, the potential or actual victims of the outrages; yet some of his most vital information came from quite a different sort.

Thus, he knew the advisability of leaving undisturbed a known meeting place of the worst types, of permitting a petty crook to remain at large. The justification for this was obvious.

Experience had proved over and again that if these avenues were all closed, he could not penetrate far into the underworld of serious crime.

Cardani had fairly certain knowledge where many of the bombs were made. He had not raided these places. Others, unknown to him, would immediately spring up. He had methods of reaching them, however, and the information that came to him indirectly had helped toward numerous arrests.

On Hester Street he stepped into a small machine-shop. A slender, wiry man, with wispy mustache and stringy hair, the shop's only occupant, turned from his lathe, recognized his visitor, and switched off the power. Without explanation, Paul handed over his bomb fragment. The man carried it to the better light of a window. He studied it for a few moments, smelled of it, then came back with a shake of his head.

"I don't place it. I don't believe it came regular."

"Can you check it?"

"Sure. I can ask."

"What do you make of it?"

The machinist smelled of it again, turned up one end which showed faint trace of a broken thread.

"Soup; and I'm bettin' they used a firecracker fuse. Not much of a job."

He glanced at the lieutenant briefly, then averted his eyes. "I'll tell you something. They ain't been puttin' out so much lately; not for the last three, four months."

Cardani frowned. "There have been more bombings in the last three months than there were in the six previous to that."

"That's what I'm gettin' at."

"You mean the users themselves are now making them?" He

studied the other for a long moment. "You wouldn't have any line on these home makers?" he asked very softly.

The machinist's face grew hard. "Not a chance in the world, Mister. If I knew I'd forget so damned quick I couldn't remember. But I don't."

"You have three places to check. Can you do that?"

"Sure. That won't do me no harm."

"I'll get around after noon," Cardani told him, and left.

In place of returning directly to his own offices, he went north and east, crossing the Bowery. He was after his two new recruits.

He had two young men in mind. One was Tulio Busano, son of Paul's old friend the singing baker, who was now a sturdy lad of twenty.

With the persistence of his race, Tulio had never forgotten or forgiven the injury done his sister. This resentment, gathering strength with more mature understanding, was not abrogated even by Ferrara's punishment, the man who had inflicted it. Tulio wanted revenge, and Cardani feared that he would be quite apt to seek it on Ferrara's like. Paul believed that he could turn this deep-grounded feeling to better purpose.

Moreover the lad was ideally situated for Paul's present need. His father, Luigi, had long since abandoned a bakery for consumers' trade. He had cut off all personal contacts. He was now a baker for restaurants and shops. Tulio was one of his salesmen. His calls on the trade now would excite no suspicion; and it was among these small merchants that the bombers' activities were especially directed.

Paul's business at the Busanos' was concluded in short order. Their trust in him was complete. With his father's sanction,

Tulio promised to report at the Lafayette Street offices under cover of darkness that evening.

Cardani's second quest was completed with scarcely greater difficulty but with more time consumed in explanation. Here he sought a similar entry to the majority victims of the arson gang—small shop and factory operators. The man he wanted had been employed by a wholesale supply house but was now idle. A few years older than Tulio Busano, as even a distant relative of Benito Pianelli his trustworthiness was amply vouched for. This youth, John Orlando, also agreed to be on hand that evening.

Finding himself in the neighborhood of Seward Park, with the noon hour well advanced, Paul dropped in on Pianelli for a chat and lunch. Only twenty-four hours earlier Paul had left here with entirely new and strange emotions. Memory pressed hard upon him—of dark eyes, a wealth of rich brown hair, smiling lips.... Wherever he looked about the familiar place he seemed to see Giulia's face; but he spoke of their yesterday's guests not at all, and Pianelli tactfully avoided their mention.

Paul left and hurried back to Hester Street.

He found the machinist returned to his lathe. His report to Paul was brief and to the point.

"What I thought," he said, and handed back the pipe fragment.

"Not regular, then?"

"Home-made."

Something in the man's manner gave Paul the idea that he had more on his mind and was in doubt whether or not to tell it. Following his hunch, Paul talked on, making no move to leave. The lathe man answered absent-mindedly; then abruptly turned away. He went over to a tap that emptied into an iron sink beside the shop's rear window. Stooping, he drank from the pipe. Paul could see him, with his head sidewise, at the same time looking through the window.

Closing the tap, the machinist walked past the door and with seeming carelessness pushed it to. He then came back to where Paul had remained standing by the lathe. He leaned one grimy hand on the machine and in place of looking at the lieutenant faced the window.

" 'S funny," he said, in noticeably lower tone, "but I got me a job while I was out. Feller wants me to go to Buffalo to install some machinery."

Cardani made no comment.

"Leavin' tonight. May be gone a month. May be gone a year." He hesitated again, then shifted his weight to lean a little closer to Paul. "One o' those guys I saw is goin' outta th' business. He's sore 'bout something. I don't know what o' course, an' I ain't guessin'. But anyway he thinks you been pretty white to him. Never bothered him, he says."

He paused again; then blurted out in a whispered breath, "He says if you want a big maker you can look for him 'tween Cherry and Water, Rutgers an' Jefferson."

He swung away abruptly, reached overhead, and pushed a stick. The lathe spun into purring revolutions.

Paul's eye lit on a six-inch length of brass pipe on a near-by bench. He walked over and picked it up. It looked like a piece of waste. He took it, at the same time drawing a five-dollar bill from his pocket, which he rolled. Passing the machinist, he gave him the bill and without a word left the shop.

For a block he carried the brass pipe end ostentatiously in sight, then tossed it into a refuse can.

11

OCELLI AND LARGIO, Cardani's two first assistants, were waiting for him when he climbed the stairs to the third-story office. Paul took the bomb fragment from his pocket, dropped it on the table between the two men. He pointed to the broken piece of metal.

"I've had this checked. As I thought, it was homemade. I'm told the gang are making their own bombs, in quantity, in one place. That adds up that they would have to have some unsuspicious means of bringing the material and explosive in and of taking the finished bombs away. It wouldn't be by hand. It would be by wagon or truck, probably also employed in some other, harmless business."

He paused; then abruptly shifted the subject.

"The commissioner has allowed me two new men. They will report after dark tonight. One, Tulio Busano, will work on the bombings. His father is a wholesale baker, and he calls regularly on the trade in this whole quarter. Ocelli, you get out your records on places bombed the last few weeks. Leave out Bellini's. Tell Busano where to go and what you want. Tell him particularly to bring in any written threats he can get his hands on.

"The other man goes to you, Largio. He is John Orlando. Have him work the same way on the fires. Both of you listen: I want of course any men who can be caught with the goods. But even more than that I want evidence that will build up cases against the gang leaders. Threat letters signed or not. I believe Coremo heads the bombers. I think Tony Biretti leads the torch crowd. In my files are letters written and signed by both those men. Get the idea now?"

"Sure we do, Chief," Largio said. Ocelli nodded.

Cardani consulted his watch. "Ocelli, get these two names to the commissioner before he leaves; Busano and Orlando. Get their papers and badges. Better go now. Hurry back. I'm sending Largio out on something. You may have to follow it up. Here."

Paul scribbled the two names with their respective addresses, and Ocelli left.

Paul stood, gazing absent-mindedly at the floor. Largio watched him a few moments, then broke into his thoughts.

"Want I should go out with this new guy tomorrow, Chief, and show him the ropes?"

Paul raised his glance slowly; shook his head. "He already knows enough about it to go alone. Tell him what I just told you. Tomorrow you're a huckster."

"A—? Wow!" burst from the irrepressible Largio. "What 'm I going to sell? Here y'are, people. Come arunning. Seven for a nickel—dozen for a dime."

"Do you know where you can borrow a pushcart for the day?"

Largio thought for a brief moment. "Sure," he said with a wide grin. "I got an uncle in the business."

"Fix it up tonight so you can start early. Get yourself right for the part. Where you are going it will be as much as your life is worth if you don't look and act the real thing, and you can't tell who might spot you. Besides you would ruin my plans."

"What's the gag, Chief?"

"You are going to work just one block from daylight until

after dark; all four sides of it. I want you to spot every cart, wagon, or truck that comes to that block or goes away from it during the day. Especially watch for any drivers that go into buildings. Note the places where they call or leave. If you can, find out whether or not the calls are entirely legitimate. If you can't finish it in one day, Ocelli will take up where you leave off. In that case you will have to make a complete record for him. Get it?"

"I get that, Chief; but—"

"You have forgotten. I'm told that bombs are being made in that block by Coremo's gang. In this way we can probably spot the exact place."

"Then call the army, huh?"

"I'll take care of that end. You find it."

"Where is it, Chief?"

Paul repeated the boundaries given him by the machinist.

"Whew!" Largio whistled. "That's over toward Corlears. One sweet spot."

"Want Ocelli to take the first turn?"

"Not a chance. He'd give it away. His family don't know the trade. Me—I used to push the cart around for the old gent when I was a kid. Once I run away with it and was just divvying up with the boys when he caught me. He whaled hell outta me. I'll do the trick, Chief."

A step sounded on the landing outside. Ocelli came in. He laid two long folded papers on Cardani's desk, fished a couple of badges from a pocket, and placed them beside the papers. Then he handed an envelope to the lieutenant.

"Inspector got this himself just as I was leaving," Ocelli explained. "Said everything he had was in there, and if you couldn't spare the time, to let him know and he would send someone else."

Paul nodded, slit the envelope with a blunt forefinger, and took out the single sheet. As he read the message, in spite of his usual control, his expression changed markedly. His ordinarily sombre features relaxed into more cheerful lines. Then a puzzled look crept into his eyes. With the sheet held absently, he started to pace the floor, head bent in speculation. Once he stopped; reread the message carefully; then resumed his pacing.

Largio stood up. "Well, Chief, I better be getting along to look over my stock—'less you want me for something else."

Paul glanced up quickly under frowning brows. He thrust the letter into his pocket and came over. "Just a moment."

He explained Largio's morrow's mission to Ocelli. "If," he said to the latter, "Largio doesn't turn up anything the first day, you or one of the other men will have to take it on. It will be less apt to arouse suspicion. Don't make any mistake about it. In a thing as important as this they are sure to have watchers out."

"Aw, give me a chance, Chief," Largio pleaded. "You don't need anyone else on this."

Paul turned on him a little grimly. "Ocelli pulled a good one when he brought in an iron-clad first degree on Tasso. You have just as big a chance on this; and you can spoil everything if you bungle it. Just don't muff it."

"It's in the bag, Chief," Largio said with a slight swagger.

Paul looked at him, and his glance softened. "Be careful, boy," he said, unconsciously repeating Inspector Sherwin's own admonition to himself. "Don't push your luck too far. You could get in bad trouble over there. All I want is information; but I want that right."

"Be seeing you, Chief." Largio saluted with a flourish and left.

With the closing of the door, Paul resumed his puzzled reflection.

Ocelli watched him for a while, then commenced to move papers and files around on the table, putting things in order. The sounds finally caught Paul's attention, awoke him from his abstraction. He drew the letter from his pocket and proceeded to give a transcript of its contents.

"The banker, Damiano Ravino, wants me to call at his home as early as possible this evening."

"Humph. Is that all? Thought it might be a murder."

"Yes."

"Want me to go? You have those two new fellows coming in tonight, you know."

"No-o." Paul tried to put no particular inflection in his refusal. "He's pretty important, I believe. Besides I've been wanting to get in touch with some of the bankers in the quarter. I'll explain it to you some other time."

He put his desk in order, closed it, and got his hat. He smoothed down his coat carefully, feeling the bulge of the revolver, noting the wrinkles its weight had formed. He looked at his watch.

"I'll have to run along. Wish you would stick here, Dick. Have one of the men bring you in some supper. If I am delayed, talk with the boys along the lines I spoke of. Have 'em report first thing in the morning."

Paul hastened along Lafayette toward the house where he had his modest living quarters. He liked the old street with its casual trees taking space from the brick sidewalks. Each had its brick-ringed circle of bare earth; its trunk wire guarded. Somehow Lafayette seemed a little aloof; not, however, in the sense of a suburban village. In a moment one could slip from it into the arterial rush that was Broadway.

And that particularly appealed to Paul Cardani. He wanted always to be near the greatest activity, yet able to step aside from it at will. He thought what very little meaning in fact his dwelling held for him. He decided that something must be wrong if one's home did not seem important. Actually, he reasoned, a man should have a place apart from the busy affairs of the day, where he could enjoy music and books and meditation.

Care and attention should be given such a home. It should not be merely a place where one slept. Even if a man were alone, it should be a proper environment for a family. He grew a little wistful with the thought.

In his rooms, he threw off suit and shirt, washed face and hands in cold water that he turned from a pitcher into the bowl. Walking about, he put on a clean white shirt, found a tie that was almost new. Half dressed, his eye fell on a sheet of music he had recently bought but had so far lacked opportunity to try.

Led on by this, he looked around for his violin case and frowned at the light coating of dust it had gathered. He stole a glance at his watch, hesitated; then took out the instrument, tuned it deftly, and softly played an old air that was familiar to him—a deep-toned melody that seemed to be particularly in keeping with dark eyes and dark hair....

Replacing the violin, he took down a neatly pressed suit and hurriedly completed his dressing. He transferred money, papers, revolver, and keys from the discarded clothes, which he set aside for pressing. He caught up his hat and was about to leave when again his roving glance fell on the new music sheet. He debated whether he should take it with him; then decided it wouldn't do to have it observed that he had assumed he would see Giulia.

12

THE ADDRESS WAS a little south and west of Tompkins Square. Paul found the number on a two-and-a-half-storied brick building of peculiarly fresh and neat appearance.

Shades, half drawn, disclosed lace curtains. Against the subdued light within, the panes looked clean and spotless. A trim railing, painted black, led up the few steps. The double outer doors were opened. The vestibule was paved with freshly scrubbed marble blocks, and behind the single glass of the grilled inner doors a lace curtain was drawn tight.

Paul touched the button at one side.

A maid, in cap, apron, and black dress, admitted him. He asked to be announced to Mr. Ravino. Evidently his call was expected. He was ushered immediately into a cozy living room at one side of the carpeted hallway. As the maid withdrew, Paul remained standing.

With no delay at all, he heard light steps approaching. Giulia entered. Paul stepped forward eagerly to meet her, his eyes telling him that his memory had scarcely done justice to her.

Giulia smiled a little, took his hand in a warm, brief clasp. She said, "I'm so glad you came. I was afraid they might have to send someone else. I do not know the police at all."

He looked with much concern into her dark eyes, keenly noted their worried expression.

"I hope there is no trouble."

"I hope not. Father will tell you. He will be here in a moment. Was it only yesterday that we were so jolly at Mr. Pianelli's?

He is such a dear; and he feels so terribly responsible for you. Please—shall we sit down?"

Paul followed her and took a chair near the divan on which she seated herself. He was disturbed. He recognized, beneath her light words and friendly manner, a restraint that told of anxiety. What it might be he couldn't conjecture, and he did not want to ask her. He felt a little ill at ease.

"Perhaps I came too early. It is hardly seven."

"It was good of you to come so soon." Giulia tried to smile; then her lip trembled, and she caught it between her white teeth. "Ah, here comes father now."

She sprang to her feet, and Paul stood up.

Damiano Ravino came swiftly into the room. He was a rather small man, very carefully dressed in a dark suit. He had gray hair, a trimmed grayish mustache, and dark eyes behind rimless glasses.

Without waiting for Giulia's introduction, he came directly to Cardani and extended his hand.

"It was good of you to come, Lieutenant," he said, in quick, precise manner. "I've heard a great deal of your work, and it's all good. My sister and Giulia have both told me of meeting you at Pianelli's yesterday. I was sorry I could not be there. It was impossible. Let us sit down. I do not wish to take more of your time than necessary."

"My time is quite at your disposal," Paul murmured.

Ravino drew up a chair facing him. "I sincerely hope this will prove of no importance. In which case, Lieutenant, I will present you with my thanks and apologies. However, we are all considerably disturbed, and with the troublous times there seemed nothing else to be done."

He paused. Cardani made no comment. With a side-wise glance he observed Giulia take a handkerchief from her dress and press it to her lips.

"It concerns my son Vincent," Ravino resumed. "He did not return to his home last night. He has not been at the bank all today. We have not had the least word from him or from anyone else regarding him. He rarely is absent from home, and never before, not one single time, has he stayed away without first advising us. Then too there is his absence from his duties at the bank."

"I suppose you have inquired of his friends?" Paul asked quietly.

"He has no friends with whom he would pass the night and whole day. He has no habits that would cause him to neglect either his home or his business. He is very fond of his home and extremely interested in his work."

"Could any business of the bank have caused him to see an out-of-town client, which perhaps did not give him opportunity to notify you of his intention?"

"No, I am sure it was not that. He is now a teller. His work is entirely in the bank."

"How old is he?"

"Four years older than Giulia; twenty-three."

Paul was aware of Giulia's increasing perturbation. It seemed to him that as her father now presented the matter it was assuming a much greater seriousness than she had suspected. He tried to get her mind off that phase by the manner of his questions.

"Is he in love?" he asked bluntly.

"Never!" Ravino denied emphatically.

"Father—" Giulia said hesitantly.

"What is it, child?"

"I think I ought to tell something that Vince told me once, in confidence."

"Tell it by all means, if it is of importance."

"Vince told me, a few weeks ago, that he liked a certain girl very much. He said that he didn't love her; that he didn't want to let himself fall in love with her, because he could never ask her to marry him. She was not at all of his class. He said she understood that too; that they were merely friends. He said he would stop seeing her soon; it would be better for both."

"I can't see anything of importance in that, Giulia. Just a boy and girl friendship."

"It might do to look into it, however," Paul suggested.

"I do not see why. My boy is of the highest character."

"It was from that point of view that I made the suggestion. There might be an act of chivalry involved."

"I do not see it. However, let us leave it for the moment. I have made all possible inquiries. I dislike to admit it, but I can only decide that Vincent has not absented himself willingly; that he has been forcibly taken. It is for that reason, Lieutenant, that I asked the inspector if possible to have you assigned to the case. I have been told that you know more about these affairs than any other man on the force. And naturally I should expect to reward you personally if successful."

Paul's face flushed under his perennial tan.

"That isn't necessary, Father," Giulia said quickly.

"I am only too glad to be called into it," Paul said, more to Giulia than to her father.

"Well," Ravino said impatiently, "can you come to any other conclusion than the one I mentioned?"

"Although we shall act at once on that assumption," Paul said a little stiffly, "that is the last thing we will want to admit. So far I haven't any facts on which to base any conclusion, except the fact of your son's unexplained absence, which I sincerely hope will prove of no importance at all. For example, you have received no demands of any kind for his safe return, have you?"

"None at all. We have received no word. Does that signify anything?"

Paul managed a smile. "It would be the usual thing if he had been kidnaped. You see, we have no facts yet."

He stood up, and the two rose with him.

"What will you do?" Ravino asked. "Will you begin work on it tomorrow?"

"We will begin work on it as soon as I return to my office."

"Wait a moment, Lieutenant," Ravino said abruptly. "My sister insisted on saying a word to you. I will call her."

He left the room with his quick, nervous step.

Giulia turned to him, stepped close, and laid a hand on his arm. Her dark, troubled eyes searched his.

"You are much worried, aren't you? For us, of course. You think that—that because they haven't sent any demand, it might mean—something—terrible?"

Paul placed his big hand over hers.

"Please don't worry," he said very earnestly. "And believe me when I say that this concerns me as closely as it possibly could. We have no facts yet. Therefore there is no cause to worry now."

She withdrew her hand, slowly. "You are very good. Just your being here, taking a part in it, has already made me feel better."

"I have some new music," he said, to change the subject. "I

wanted to bring it to you; but I wasn't sure I'd be lucky enough to see you."

"Some other time, I'd be awfully glad to see it. You will bring it, won't you? When—oh, when everything is calm again."

"Have you a picture of your brother I could see?"

She turned and took a small photograph from the mantel. "You may keep this until you come back again."

"And will you give me the name and address of that girl of whom you spoke?"

"DePasso; Maria dePasso, I think. I don't know just where she lives. Not far from the bank, Vince once said. She works in the bank and may live in one of those houses on Rivington. I believe Vince could have loved her—only he knew father would never consent to it. He is very proud."

Paul looked deep into Giulia's eyes, but their expression was both impersonal and inscrutable.

Signora Alfredo came in with her brother, pressed Cardani's hand warmly with both her own. She was a little tearful and managed only a few words expressing her thanks to the lieutenant for coming to them in their trouble and her devotion to her boy, Vincent.

13

THE TWO NEW men, Busano and Orlando, were with Ocelli. Paul told all three of the missing young banker and gave each definite and immediate work to do.

He was starting on a cold trail, now more than twenty-four hours old. The logical place to begin was at the bank and at an hour when young Ravino's associates and neighborhood acquaintances were around. This would have to be deferred till morning. The chances of cutting the trail now were practically hopeless; yet Paul's concern was such that he would not wait.

In his own mind he shared the fears of Giulia and her father that something serious had befallen the young man. That seemed the only logical explanation for his absence. The characters of the father and sister, the description of the boy both had given him, precluded a score of other reasons. No, Paul told himself, if Vincent Ravino was soon to return, he must be found.

He did not believe that Vincent could have been waylaid if he had started directly from the bank, long before dusk, to go home. From this he reasoned that young Ravino's first steps were taken either willingly or through the persuasion of some person in whom he had confidence. If an attack had occurred it must have taken place later in the evening or at night. What had transpired meanwhile was what Paul now sought to discover.

He further reasoned that if Vincent had followed any purpose except a purely personal one, he would without doubt have advised his father. Giulia had supplied the personal reason. Paul shrewdly guessed that the young man had arranged a last meeting with the girl. Under the circumstances Vincent would keep this to himself. It would also seem to him sufficient justification for his absence for a few hours.

If the dePasso girl could be found, she could confirm or disprove this conjecture immediately. If correct, she could tell where and at what time Ravino took his leave of her, from which point they could seek to trace his further movements.

Explaining this fully to his men, Paul sent Ocelli to search for Maria dePasso. He despatched the two other men to visit the restaurants in the vicinity of the bank, of a type young Ravino would patronize. For himself Paul sought out and interviewed the patrolmen on their beats in a wide radius from Rivington and Second Avenue, and even talked with two in the vicinity of young Ravino's home. He learned nothing.

Around midnight he returned to his office. All three men had preceded him and were waiting. They reported the same lack of success. Ocelli had made a house-to-house canvass for several blocks on Rivington and found no trace of the girl. Tulio and Orlando found the better restaurants closed. Those they visited knew nothing of the young banker. There seemed nothing more to be done that night.

Paul was back in his office at six in the morning.

No one was there. Largio, he knew, would be out with his pushcart, trying to locate the dangerous bomb gang. Ocelli should be in shortly. The squad kept early and late hours. Paul stepped into the sleeping quarters and found Ceruti in one of the cots. At his shake, Ceruti sat up, rubbing his eyes. He followed him into the private office. He had interesting news.

Ceruti, the evening previous, had called at the home of his friend who had complained of the gang of thugs living close by.

"They got a whole house by themselves," Ceruti said. "Six or may be a dozen of 'em. There's a road or something running between two streets, with a kind of circle midway. Their house is on this circle and has an exit to an alley behind it. I got a hunch they could also go out on the roof to the houses each side, as they're all about the same level. If they had watchers you couldn't get near 'em front or back without being spotted. And it would take a coupla platoons to cover all the holes out."

"Did you see them, get any idea what any of them are like?"

Ceruti was getting more awake now, and in the same ratio his enthusiasm grew.

"Sure. This fellow told me a lot too. He lives directly opposite. That's what he was kicking about. He don't feel safe, especially after that stick-up he saw 'em pull. Just after we got there— we were watching from his dark room—about six of 'em came out, and in an hour they went back in again. A little later, three more came out. I saw 'em when they were in a light, and I'm telling you, Chief, one of 'em was this guy Tasso. I saw his face good and I'll swear it."

"Did your friend see any of the men in the stick-up enter that house afterward?"

"Sure. It was dark and rainy. He was just getting home. He saw a bunch brace this feller, and he sneaked behind one of the stoops. Afterwards they went right into the house."

"You think you recognized Tasso?"

"I know it. Tall, thin guy with a big nose and long chin. Little black, beady eyes. Scar at one corner of his mouth. He came across the street. There was a light in the window next door, and he took a quick look in. That's when I spotted him. That's his description, isn't it?"

Paul nodded. He had come to the office thus early, seething with the mystery of Giulia's missing brother. It was a brooding worry which the fruitless search of the night before had not lightened. He was eager to take up the daylight trail; but this was something that could not be ignored.

Tasso was wanted for first-degree murder. His capture would mean the first big blow at the knife gang.

"Have you any idea," he asked, "what hour would find most of them in?"

"Tasso and his two men came back in a little while. We waited till long about two, but we didn't see anyone else come out or go in. Looks to me as if they were all sticking pretty close, and my guess is that the whole bunch would be in before seven or after nine."

"We'll take them tonight. I will arrange with Headquarters for all the men we need. Can you get in your friend's house in daylight without being seen, in a back way?"

"Sure. That's the way we went in and I came out last night."

"Take one of the other men with you and get in there around noon. Count the men coming out and going in. Probably just after dark will be the time to strike. If you are pretty certain that most of them are in at that time, send your man to meet us."

"There's a drug store right around the corner. My friend says they're all right. You could be there."

"All right. Give me the address. Also give me the exact location and address of the house. Make a plan of the whole place before you leave. I'll be at the drug store, but I'll have the men ready to strike from both sides. You've done good work, Ceruti. I only hope you are right about Tasso."

"I'm sure of it. I'd know that guy anywhere."

"Well, make that plan as clear as you can. I'm going to Headquarters now."

As he turned toward the door, there was a knock on the panel. Paul opened and a patrolman in uniform appeared. He saluted.

"Thought I'd find you in, Lieutenant. Call just come in to Headquarters. Man on Spring Street beat, west, rung in he's found a murder case. Sergeant's gone over, and they sent me for you. Sergeant said they wouldn't touch nothing till you got there."

"Just where is it?"

"Close to Sullivan. On the street. You'll see 'em there."

Paul swung around. "Take charge here, Ceruti, until I get back. When Ocelli shows up, send him right over. You heard the place."

Paul started down the stairs with the patrolman.

"You going over?" he asked.

"Gotta get back. Me—I don't mind shootin' a guy when I have to, but I don't like pawin' him over after."

As they reached the foot, Ocelli was just coming in the entrance. Paul told him to come along. On the way over he told him of Ceruti's discovery and the plans for that evening. He said, however, that the most important part of the day's work was to push the search for the young banker.

Notwithstanding the early hour, a little crowd was gathered on the Spring Street sidewalk, advertising their destination. As they approached, Cardani saw a uniformed policeman facing an alley entrance. The men crowded behind him were craning their necks to see. Coming up at their backs, Cardani spoke sharply to the officer.

"Healey, get this crowd away. Send them to their business. They haven't anything to do with this—or have they?"

The men had swung about at his voice, with an air of belligerence. At his last words, they commenced to move away. He looked at every man's face closely until the place was cleared, then stepped to the alley mouth.

A few paces in from the sidewalk, a Headquarters sergeant was bending over what appeared to be an ordinary flour barrel. He glanced over it to Cardani and Ocelli.

"Got a funny one here, Lieutenant," he said sourly.

The two secret squad men went close. As they rounded the end of the barrel furthest from the entrance, they saw that a man's body had been wedged into the unheaded container. With considerable difficulty the three men finally extricated it. As they turned it face up, Cardani started back with a fierce exclamation; a display of emotion that none of his associates had ever seen him make before.

"Recognize him, Lieutenant?" the sergeant asked.

Ocelli was silently looking his concern.

Cardani nodded. He turned to Ocelli. "It's Vincent Ravino," he said.

"My God!" Ocelli echoed. "How is that possible?"

The sergeant straightened up. "Case you were workin', Lieutenant?"

Cardani passed his hand, hard, over his working features, then became at once stern and composed.

"I'll take full charge of this, Sergeant," he said. "Phone to the morgue and tell the coroner to make a quick examination, then have the body taken to the boy's home. I'll give you the address when I'm ready. I'll want you to have a wagon take this barrel to my office. Meanwhile, have the patrolman keep everyone away. That's all, Sergeant."

Cardani, with Ocelli's help, proceeded to the examination. Turning the body slightly, he saw what he had earlier glimpsed. The knife was still in the wound, near the back on the left side, below the ribs. A terrific blow had been struck, as a portion of the handle had entered with the blade, which was easily possible with the weapon common to the knife men.

Cardani, the detective now, uttered a low exclamation of satisfaction. He glanced at the hilt keenly.

"We'll have to leave that for the coroner," he told Ocelli. "Get it back to me as soon as possible. We can't make any mistake about it. We must know that this is the murder weapon. Get it yourself from the coroner."

"Yes, Lieutenant," Ocelli murmured.

"This is a break," Cardani breathed. "More than I could have expected. He can't escape me now."

He paused a moment in sudden thought. Then repeated, as if to himself, "He can't escape me now."

He began to take things from the murdered man's pockets; change, a fair amount of money, keys, a small wallet with cards, and a few letters. Cardani left the latter for more leisurely examination. He reached then into an inside pocket, and a puzzled frown grew on his forehead. He glanced sidewise at Ocelli who caught the expression and bent closer. Cardani withdrew his hand with a thick sheaf of new banknotes, a surprising amount.

Curiously, frowning more deeply, he riffled the edges, noting the face amounts, roughly guessing the total. He turned them face up and bent over them, studying the topmost intently. After a time he stood up, sighed unconsciously. He had given the other pocket things to Ocelli to carry. He put the sheaf of bills into his own pocket.

"Now," he said curtly, "let's have a look at the barrel."

It was standing on end, open end uppermost.

Cardani peered inside and observed a thick brownish stain a little way down, with a trail of it to the bottom. He pressed a finger against it, at side and bottom, to note its stage of coagulation. He said nothing as he grasped the edge of the barrel, turned it slowly around, and examined the whole interior carefully. He then gave his attention to the outside, going over it inch by inch. He set it on end and stood erect.

"Note these points carefully, Ocelli," he said. "I want you to trace it. A flour barrel that is brand new and has never been used. There is no sign of flour inside and"—he pointed a hand toward the body without looking that way—"there is no flour, not even dirt on the clothing. There is a little dust on the front of the coat and trousers, but not from this barrel."

He leaned forward and indicated with a finger. "There is a small stencil. I should say offhand it is the cooperage mark. Remember it so you can identify it on others, or make a copy to be sure. It might be a separate cooperage or a shop attached to a flour mill. Look for a stock of new barrels either with ends temporarily in or out altogether. If you find some with ends, look for an extra set that might come from this one."

Ocelli looked around, not for the purpose of seeing anything in particular, but as if to help him in his thought.

"There is a flour mill, I think, over nearer the Hudson and in this section west of Broadway. Should I go there first?"

"You won't go there at all," Cardani said shortly. "You have overlooked the fact that this is the north side of the street. There is no possibility that they would have carried that burden across the street. They came from the other direction. I should say well east of Broadway and little, if any, north of the Spring Street line. Come."

Cardani left the alley, stepped across the sidewalk to the curb. He bent over and looked closely at the rough surface of the street close in to the curb. In a moment, he knelt down, and Ocelli squatted beside him. Cardani pointed.

In black dirt that lay between the cobbles and in places overlapped them was the plain mark of a narrow, flat tire. Cardani stood up and followed it a short way in both directions. He came back to Ocelli.

"It curves in to the sidewalk there"—he pointed—"and curves away there. It was a light, rather high wagon, I think, drawn by a single horse. There are no hoof marks near the tire, which there would be if it had been a pair."

He turned abruptly and, bent over, walked slowly across the sidewalk and into the alley as far as the barrel. He took up the barrel and examined its lower edge carefully. Then he came back to Ocelli, who had not moved.

"It was carried in, I think," Cardani said. "I can be sure when I get a microscope on the barrel. Make sure that nothing touches the side of it when it is taken in."

He paused and sent a swift glance about him.

The patrolman on the beat had been reïnforced by a man from Headquarters. The two stood at a little distance from the alley entrance, forcing the few passers-by to detour into the street. Cardani turned back to Ocelli.

"That is a job," he said, and there was weariness in his tone, "for you, Largio, or one of the others. But you get this now. First we have to find where this barrel came from. Then we can guess pretty close what streets they took coming here.

"A light, high wagon, with a single horse, with two men, or one very strong man, came over that route some time after midnight. Somewhere along the way some men must have seen it.

"We've got to find those men. While you are waiting here for the Medical Examiner, try to get a clear tire track that will show some nail mark or irregularity. As soon as you get the barrel and knife to my office, go after the first thing—where that barrel came from. Better look from Second to the East River, and between Hester and Division and East Houston. My hunch is that as soon as we find that girl's address, it will be pretty close to the line from there to Tompkins Square."

Cardani stopped speaking and stood gazing blankly into the street.

After a little while Ocelli asked, "Where can I find you later on, Lieutenant?"

Cardani turned his head slowly.

"I am going now," he said, "to see Ravino—at his bank." His shoulder muscles stiffened; then quickly he relaxed and spoke more easily, although his tone was cold.

"I'll get the girl's address and stop at Headquarters on my way back. You can get me there or at the office. When you get to the office, send Busano, the new man, out on those restaurants again. Ceruti hasn't anything to do until noon. Tell him the whole story. I want him to work around the Ravino bank and try to pick up young Ravino's trail when he left the bank at closing time."

He paused, thought for a moment, then went on:

"Ceruti says he has spotted Tasso, located his hideout. We'll raid that this evening. If Largio gets anything today on the Coremo gang, we'll take that, perhaps, tomorrow night. But what we are on now is more important than either."

Cardani slapped his coat where the sheaf of new bills lay in an inside pocket, turned and walked resolutely away, shoulders squared, head erect.

14

CARDANI WAS ADMITTED without delay into the office of the president. Still neat in appearance, Ravino nevertheless looked worn and gray, palpable evidence of a sleepless night of worry. The eyes he raised at Cardani's approach were haggard, stricken with anxious foreboding, and Cardani, seeing, felt that his news was anticipated.

He told his story at once, omitting details.

Ravino, as Cardani had earlier observed, was a man of unusually strong character, yet the shock to him was great.

As soon as possible Cardani started to take his leave, but before going requested that he be allowed to call upon the banker that evening.

"It is distinctly out of place, Lieutenant," Ravino answered, in stifled tone. "I am not interested in revenge, or in further helping the law that has failed me in my greatest need. There is nothing that can be done now.

"I would not ask it," Cardani said, "if it was not important to you."

"I do not understand. I cannot talk with you now. All right; come if you must."

Cardani stopped briefly in the outer office, learned the address of Maria dePasso, and was advised that she had not been in for two days and was no longer employed there.

As he was leaving he observed that the news was already out. Preparations were being made to close the bank to business at once.

From the bank, Cardani went directly to Headquarters and was immediately closeted with Commissioner Redfield and Inspector Sherwin.

He reported the fruitless search of the preceding night and its tragic end in the early morning. Both listeners were very serious.

The commissioner slammed his fist on to the desk top, with a force that made the objects on it hop.

"This is going too far," he rapped angrily. "When they feel so safe that they reach out and coolly murder men of that standing, it is time for something drastic to be done. It is time they were blasted."

He jerked erect, paced the floor for a few turns, stopped, with knuckles rapping the desk as he spoke.

"It isn't that I'm not satisfied with you, Lieutenant. I am. You have more murder convictions to your credit than any five men on the force. Your arrests and convictions the past year for lesser crimes run into the hundreds. But still this goes on and grows worse."

He stopped for a deep breath that puffed out his cheeks before he exhaled it. "When the inspector," he went on, "was in the Tenderloin he looked on the nightstick as the greatest dissuader to crime. I haven't heard that he has since changed his opinion, and if he has not, I am in agreement with him.

"Here at Headquarters, as well as at the precincts, we have a bunch of Irish lads and Swedes to whom a stick or a club is a weapon as natural as their fists. Just show them a lot they can work on, Lieutenant. That is all I ask of you. If they crack a few innocent heads, all right. It will be justified when we throw the fear of God and the law into these throat-slitting hoodlums."

"It happens," Cardani said quietly, "that I have a raid planned tonight. One of my men is sure he has spotted Tasso, the murderer. He is holed up with half a dozen or a dozen of his men."

"Now, damn it, that is something!"

The inspector, in his turn, came to his feet. "Give me the details, Lieutenant," he said, "and I'll handle it in person. And I'm only hoping one of 'em will start shooting or throwing a chiv around. And if they don't—well, imagination sometimes goes a long way. What's the dope, Lieutenant?"

Between them they completed the arrangements in a very few minutes. Two platoons would be sent as quietly as possible to a selected rendezvous, while the inspector with half a dozen plain-clothesmen would meet Cardani at a place they agreed upon. Their moves from that point would be left to circumstance.

"Now about this young banker," Sherwin said, when details of the Tasso raid were settled. "How do you place it, just another extortion case?"

"Not at all. I think this is the vital clue we have been hoping for."

"What is that?" Redfield demanded. For the past few minutes he had been listening absent-mindedly.

"I believe," Cardani said slowly, "that when we solve the murder of Vincent Ravino we will reach the top!"

"You think you can solve it?"

"I am sure of it."

"Why?"

"The murderer left the knife."

The commissioner gave a short laugh. "I can't follow that,"

he said, "but I've known of you working that miracle before, so we'll accept it. On what do you base the other assumption?"

"The murder was committed with a weapon and in a manner common to Mafia and Camorra. That links it to the Black Hand here. Now there are certain activities practiced only by the highest in authority in those organizations abroad, and naturally it would be the same here. One is protection. Another is counterfeiting and the passing of bad money."

"Counterfeiting!" the commissioner exploded. "D'you mean to say you've got a lead on that?"

Cardani drew the sheaf of new notes from his pocket, placed it before the two men. "What do you make of them?" he asked.

Each took a bill, examined it critically. After a moment they looked at each other and nodded.

"That," the commissioner said to Cardani, "is the bad ten we were warned of by Washington. What about it?"

"I took them myself from the body of Vincent Ravino. Before that, his body was bent double in the barrel. I think," he added softly, "that is the second mistake the murderer made."

"Could it be possible," Redfield asked, somewhat hesitantly, "that the murderer didn't know they were there? Was there any other money on him?"

"Answering your first question, Commissioner," Cardani said coldly, "in my own mind I am sure they were placed there after Ravino was killed. For the sake of the courts, I will make certain this evening."

"But we are raiding this evening," Inspector Sherwin blurted out.

"That won't take long," Cardani said coolly. "As to the second question, there was about a hundred dollars in bills and some change. Nothing seemed to have been taken from him."

"I believe he is right," the inspector said. "I can't see this thing as clearly as the lieutenant, but it looks pretty important to me."

Cardani laid his clenched fist on the desk softly. "I'll stake my life," he said, "that when we put our hands on the killer of Vincent Ravino we will have the leader of this whole organization. And at last I am convinced that there is such a leader."

The commissioner looked at Cardani with narrowed eyes; then he turned to Inspector Sherwin.

"Important enough," he said, "to notify Washington at once." He reached for the telephone.

"Just a moment," Cardani said quickly. "I am very certain that I can handle this best myself."

"I think so, too. But this is something that concerns the Government, and they must be notified. I will do all in my power, Lieutenant," he added, "to see that you direct this case and its investigation. But, by God, you're going to have help." He paused, with his hand on the instrument.

"You took in one killer last night, a leader of a gang. You have rounded up another and expect to get him tonight. You have told me that your men are trying to locate the secret place of a third. And now you not only have a fresh murder case on your hands, but are hitting at the very head of this criminal organization responsible for hundreds of murders, for the greatest wave of terror this city has ever known."

He took up the receiver. "Get me," he bawled in a tone that must have carried a goodly distance toward the goal of the prospective conversation, "Washington; the Department of Justice. And snap it up."

He looked at Cardani and grinned amiably. "You needn't wait, Lieutenant. I'll see that you are advised. I expect you have a busy day ahead of you."

"I guess," the inspector drawled, "if he tried to tell us about it, it would take the rest of the morning."

Cardani stood up. He took half a dozen of the spurious bills and put them in his pocket. "I'll need these later," he said, and left.

Back at his office, Cardani found that Ocelli had come and gone on the quest assigned him and had despatched Ceruti on his errand of inquiry near the bank. One of the older squad men was in charge. He nodded toward a corner where the barrel had been set in a safe place by itself; then he showed Cardani the drawer in his own desk in which Ocelli had deposited the murderer's weapon.

Cardani took out the knife and spent an hour over it, using a microscope, referring to his notes, finally comparing it with the numerous similar weapons he had gathered. Before he laid it carefully aside, he knew not only its manufacturer but could also make a shrewd guess as to what retail house had handled it and the approximate year of its purchase. He made notes of his findings with the purpose of checking them later.

He then turned his attention to the flour barrel and submitted it to the same minute examination. The microscopic study provided more negative than positive evidence, seeming to confirm all that he had told Ocelli.

Neither the side nor the edge of the closed end gave any indication that the barrel had been rolled with its burden, establishing that it must have been carried into the alley. Furthermore, there was no lint on the outside of the staves, which there would have been if a single man had borne it.

From time to time messengers came to the office bringing reports that often required immediate answer. Some called on Cardani with every attempt at secrecy, bringing a word of threat received, or the message itself, or bits of important information he had sought to obtain and entrusted to others to get for him.

He handled all these matters with surprising celerity and without serious interruption to the progress of his study.

After the barrel was put aside he turned to his files, particularly the old Italian papers. Since his first discovery of the counterfeit notes, one thought had been hammering at the back of his mind. With the sight of that sheaf of fresh bills, and his quick realization that they were not genuine, the conviction had flashed upon him that there *must* be a definite head to the great criminal organization. Since that moment he had racked his mind to conjecture who that head might be.

Now he commenced to go through the papers, beginning a year earlier and going backward as to time. Pianelli, in describing potentially such a man, had said that in all probability he would have been high in criminal circles abroad before fleeing hither to start his evil work anew. Cardani had kept this in mind.

As he read account after account, he checked each possible name either with his memory or with notes readily at hand. He had exhausted much of his material and had not found a single person of proportions fitting the part and at the same time available for its purposes. For the moment he was baffled; but he had the clue which in itself, if properly followed, should lead eventually to the man's identity.

15

TOWARD NOON CERUTI returned.

The lieutenant glanced up, then his eyes narrowed keenly. Beneath Ceruti's slight swagger there was an air of restrained excitement; in his eyes a gleam of triumph. Cardani waited.

"My luck still seems to be holding, Chief," Ceruti announced lightly.

"How's that?"

The squad man swung up a chair, placed it beside his superior, took his time seating himself. "Well, I think I got this case all cracked and sewed up."

Cardani looked his interest but said nothing. Ceruti went on.

"Ocelli gave me the dope, told me what you wanted. I shoulda been on this last night, but I was chasin' Tasso. Well, this young Ravino left the bank at regular closin' time, crossed over and stood on the sidewalk in front of a restaurant. Bimeby a girl from the bank come along and joined him, and they went into the restaurant. They'd eaten there together before, and the waiters knew 'em both.

"Maria dePasso's the girl's name. They fooled around a lot, talkin' low till it got time to eat, then had supper. Here's what's important, Chief; the way they acted to each other. The young feller seemed to be makin' a lot of apologies, and the girl didn't look none too happy. She cried a little. She didn't break right out bawlin', but the waiter saw her wipin' her eyes plenty."

Ceruti eased himself forward slightly. "That's what gave me the right dope, Chief. They went off to a theatre somewhere, but there didn't seem any good findin' that. Feller at the restaurant told me of an Avenue drug store where he'd seen her tradin', and I got her address there. Over on Stanton, near Clinton."

"Did you see her and talk with her?"

"No. I didn't think you'd want me to go as far as that, Chief." Cardani nodded.

Ceruti hitched well-creased trousers over his knees. "But I went to the house where she lives with her mother," he said. "And I got acquainted with an oldish lady there. She gave me the dirt. Seems this young Ravino got the girl in trouble and don't want to marry her. His father's rich and proud, and his sister's a high-stepper in society. That marriage wouldn't go. Vincent's been tryin' to buy her off, and the girl won't take money."

Ceruti leaned back for a better view of the lieutenant and to enjoy his triumph. When Cardani still made no comment, Ceruti leaned forward again. "There's the whole dope, Chief; motive, everything. This here vendetta idea is still pretty strong with most of the people in the quarter. You know yourself how they hate to ask help of anyone outside the family. The man who done this trick for Vincent, you'll find, is one of the girl's relatives.

"Soon's I cracked it," he continued, "I stopped right there. I know you don't care for the credit, Chief, but you like to handle 'em when they get hot. It oughtn't to be much trouble locatin' the right guy, and you'd have your own ideas of the angle to go at it."

Cardani sat silently for long moments. The strong fingers of his right hand played idly with one of the numerous clasp-knives he had brought to the desk to compare with the murderer's weapon and not yet put away. His dark eyes were brooding, but to the man watching him closely they gave no indication of his thoughts. Finally he dropped the knife and turned more directly to his young assistant.

"In any case of this sort," he said, slowly and carefully, "where you have certain apparent facts not contradicted by others, they point to an obvious conclusion, and there is a great temptation to make a hasty decision. Remember this, Ceruti. You have done well, and I believe you will go far in this work."

Ceruti started to interrupt. Cardani held up his hand. "Acting on the evidence given you, your steps were logical and your reasoning sound. The first step now is to prove or disprove the truth of these statements. I will see the dePasso girl as soon as possible."

"I was goin' to say," Ceruti broke in, "that while I didn't go any further there, the old lady sent me to a feller in a store on the corner, and he gave me the same story. I think he was her son, or nephew or something."

Ceruti stood up. He looked a little chagrined. "I guess you don't like my story, Chief."

Cardani shook his head. "It may prove very important. If it turns out to be untrue, it will be just as helpful. It happens that I have clues in this case pointing in another direction. I, too, was tempted to a hasty conclusion. Now we'll have to consider both. Get your lunch, Ceruti. Take that other new man, Orlando, with you for messages and get up to your post."

He explained where and when he could be reached, what was necessary for Ceruti to know of the plans agreed upon between himself and the inspector, then dismissed him.

Alone, Cardani yielded momentarily to the sombre thoughts pressing upon him. His sympathy for Giulia Ravino was most acute, proving, if proof were needed, the extent of his feelings for that dark-eyed girl. He could readily picture her anguish at the murder of her brother. If to that anguish was to be added the disgrace of scandal, her misery would be crushing. And Cardani now knew that scandal threatened from two distinct and totally different causes.

While the attitude of the elder Ravino toward him had not particularly appealed to Cardani, still his belief in Giulia and her family inspired him with utter faith in the murdered Vincent. He did not fear the truth in either matter. He was aware, however, that suspicion and rumor unchecked swiftly develop into scandal that survives in part even after its denial.

Cardani was essentially a man of action. He shook off the momentary mental depression with a shrug of his powerful shoulders. He was going to devote the evening to finding out what he could of the counterfeit money. Now he reached for his hat, intent on immediately settling the question of the story Ceruti had turned up. He set out for the address the squad man had given him.

Maria dePasso was a pretty girl of transparent character and naïve intelligence. At his first keen look at her, Cardani was convinced that the ugly rumor was utterly without foundation. However, he was not content to leave the matter to his own convictions.

The girl herself opened the door to his knock at the second-floor apartment. Her manner was simple and composed, although she showed evidences of grief. He introduced himself, explained that he had called to make certain inquiries. She led him into a small, neat living room. A grayish-haired woman was sewing in one corner. Maria introduced her mother and asked the lieutenant to be seated.

Cardani had anticipated speaking with the girl alone. Having seen her, he was glad for the presence of the older woman.

"We are investigating last night's unfortunate murder," he began, without other preliminary. "You can speak frankly with me, Miss dePasso. I have no idea of involving you in any way in the matter. I am simply after facts. I understand that you dined with Vincent last evening and later attended a theatre with him. Please tell me about it."

She seemed not the least surprised at his knowledge.

"Yes," she said. "I had a date to meet Mr. Ravino after the bank closed. He said he wanted to talk with me. I met him in front of the restaurant; we had an early dinner and went to the theatre afterwards. He brought me home. We walked all the way down, and I think it was about half-past eleven when I got in."

She glanced at her mother, who nodded and said, "Just half-past."

"If it was not too personal, would you mind telling me something of your talk?"

"I'd rather not," the girl said quickly.

"He probably has a reason for asking," her mother interjected.

"I know you were friendly," Cardani said. "Were you and Vincent engaged?"

"No. We didn't even think of it," the girl said impulsively, and added, "I suppose it won't make any difference now. Mr. Vincent has always been very good to me. He was the most perfect gentleman I've ever known. I don't know why he was so kind to me. He said he liked me, and he told me that—that he had better not see me any more as he was afraid he might come to like me too well. That was what he wanted to tell me.

"Perhaps he thought that I expected he would ask me to marry him, but of course I knew better than that. I just enjoyed our friendship and never thought of anything beyond that."

"Did you notice whether he seemed to have something on his mind that worried him?"

"Only what I have told you. I am sure there was nothing else."

"Of course your mother understood the situation; but what did your other relatives think about it? You have a brother, possibly, or some cousins?"

"No. My mother and grandmother are my only relatives."

"You are better-looking than most girls. Didn't you know any man who would have liked to be your suitor, and who would have resented Vincent Ravino's treatment of you?"

"Why, he never did the slightest thing that anyone could possibly resent. We were never alone; that is, away from other people, and he always acted like the gentleman he was. Besides, I don't know any other men well."

From the corner of his eye, Cardani observed that Maria's mother had stopped her sewing and was regarding him closely.

"Just what did you mean by that, Lieutenant?" she asked.

"In cases as serious as this, we have to run down all sorts of clues and rumors."

"And is there any rumor about Maria?"

Cardani turned to face her more squarely. "A person said that Mr. Ravino might have been the victim of vendetta. I am personally in charge of this case, and I am satisfied that it is not so."

Maria was slow of comprehension; her mother was quick. "Maria can swear on the Holy Madonna there is no truth in it," she said, "and I know it."

Cardani bent his head a little, then turned to Maria. "You say he left you at eleven-thirty. Do you know where he was going then?"

"Home, of course. That is, I think so. We walked down, as I told you. He wanted to walk some more, but he said it was too late for me."

"Did you see anyone on the street when you came in, anyone you would remember?"

"I think we passed some people, but I am not sure. There are always people on the street in the evening. I don't remember anyone in particular."

Cardani stood up. "I am very much obliged to both of you," he said.

"I have a neighbor," Maria's mother said, "who has always been unfriendly toward me and jealous of anything Maria or I might have. She would be one to say such a thing, and now," she added a little bitterly, "I suppose she will be happy that Maria has lost her position at the bank."

"I think," Cardani said, "it may be possible to do something about that."

He shook hands with both and left.

As he reached the ground floor a sharp-faced, gray-haired woman opened wide the door she had been holding ajar. She put fingers to her lips and jerked her head over her shoulder. He stepped into a small hallway but did not close the door.

"I saw you goin' up stairs," she said in a low tone, "and I thought I just better stop you an' tell you the truth 'bout it, 'cause I know what you went up for."

"Madam," he said, "I am Lieutenant Cardani of the police force. This morning you told one of my men a vicious lie. More than that you sent him to one of your relatives to get the same story. If there is any more of it, I will have you both brought into court."

He closed the door on a much frightened woman.

When he reached his office later in the afternoon, Ocelli had not returned. He busied himself with routine matters until dusk commenced to gather, when a message came in from Ceruti.

"Tasso hasn't come out," it said. "I think the whole bunch is in."

Cardani relayed the message to the inspector at Headquarters, with the added note that he would leave in ten minutes for the appointed rendezvous.

The acknowledgment was promptly received. Cardani continued his work until the time had expired, then called a man in from the squad room and put him in charge, with instructions to have Ocelli and Largio wait for his return.

His preparations for the expected raid were simple. He looked to his revolver, saw that it worked properly and that five of its chambers were loaded, returned it to the right-hand pocket of his suit coat, and put some loose cartridges in the left-hand pocket.

16

CARDANI WAITED IN a drug store not far from one end of the short street with its circle of houses midway of the block. Ceruti had drawn a plan of the location for him. The suspected hideout was exactly in the center of one side of the circle. The house where Ceruti was watching was directly opposite it.

He was consulting the plan when the inspector, accompanied by half a dozen plain-clothesmen, joined him. They gathered around.

"Are your platoons posted, Inspector?" Cardani asked.

"I personally saw them in position. They are split into halves. The ends of the alley and the ends of the street are all covered. At the signal they will converge simultaneously on front and rear and enter the house."

"I think we will have to do it on time. A signal might allow some to escape."

"How do you want to work it?"

"First, I want four of these men on the roofs. Two will enter houses at each end of the street and work toward the center. We will give them ten minutes to get into their positions. Then three minutes after I leave here, the platoons should start to move. Call it exactly thirteen minutes from the moment these four men start. Can you get word to the platoons, Inspector?"

"Certainly. But what do you propose to do?"

"I am going directly to the house."

"That's too damned dangerous."

"I don't think so. I speak the language, and you don't. I'll ask questions, try to engage somebody in conversation, with the door open. The men will be right behind me, and we can rush it."

"Thought this was my raid," Sherwin grumbled. "All right. Have it your way."

He detailed the four men who were to cover the roof, told the remaining two to check their watches and get word to the split platoons.

"Get going," he growled. "And tell 'em if they gotta shoot, to be damned sure what they're hitting. I don't care how they use their sticks as long as they use them."

Ten minutes later Cardani replaced his watch in his pocket and started out. He turned into the short street and saw that it was only dimly lighted. He kept to the side on which the suspected house stood. He walked without haste, one hand in his pocket, to all appearance a casual pedestrian.

As he reached the edge of the circle he glanced to the opposite side, at the window where Ceruti should be watching. It was in darkness. A loosely flapping curtain showed faintly behind the partly opened window.

He looked toward the end of the short street. Not a man of the platoon could be seen. He had passed men, huddled close in the shadows, on his way in. Hardly a minute of the three had elapsed.

The house he sought had a short stoop. As he turned toward it he observed that no lights showed in any of the front windows. The door was a flimsy affair of painted boards, evidently covering a more substantial structure.

Cardani ascended the few steps, found a bell-pull at one side, and drew it out. There was no response that he could hear.

He waited a moment, then rapped solidly on the wood with his left-hand knuckles. He waited another short interval, tried the outer door, found it unhasped, and pulled it open. A solid door showed behind. He pounded on that. The sound echoed in the quiet street.

His ears, keenly alert, heard footsteps approaching the door. He thought, too, that there was some sound in the room at the right, one of whose windows, at a slant, faced him.

A rough voice behind the closed panels rasped, "Whatda you want? Ain't nobody lives here 'cept me."

"If you are the caretaker," Cardani shouted, purposefully, "I got to leave a paper with you. From the gas company."

"Don't burn no gas."

"Have to leave it just the same. Take it and let me get away."

There was a short hesitation, during which Cardani caught the movement of a dim shape in the window close beside him. Then there was the sound of the bolt being shot. The door opened enough for a grimy hand to stick through. The same voice growled, "Gimme it an' get th' hell outta here."

Cardani shoved a foot into the opening. At the same time his left hand clamped on to the man's wrist, and he jerked powerfully. The man's arm came through, and Cardani twisted it to one side, holding it so that the man could not get back to close the door.

The window close beside him at his right splintered. Sidewise he caught the gleam of metal on knife or pistol. Simultaneously a round hole appeared in the unbroken portion of the pane, and a pistol shot crashed from across the street behind him. It was quite evident that Ceruti had been watching.

Cardani shot once through his pocket at the window, then

gave his attention to the man whose arm he was gripping. The fellow was twisting and writhing, and soon Cardani was aware that he was being helped in his endeavor to escape, from behind.

He heard voices now in the house, excited yelling. He heard also running steps in the street behind him. Abruptly he straightened the arm from where it was bent around the frame, lunged with all his weight against the door, and went in with it.

The space before him was in total darkness, yet he knew by sounds that men were there. Still keeping that hold on the wrist that was trying vainly to tear loose, he drew his right hand from his pocket, gauged the distance by the arm, and struck heavily with the revolver.

He felt the blow land solidly, felt the man slumping down. Twisting powerfully with his hold on the wrist, he threw the falling man past him to crash limply on the threshold and block the closing of the door. With the same movement he flung himself to one knee just as a pistol flashed almost in his face.

There was a sharp curse behind him, the tramp of feet on the steps, the sudden yelling of many voices.

Cardani, crouched, fired once, aiming low. The flash showed him the dim forms of men crowded into the hallway, the approximate position of those nearest him. In the darkness that succeeded, he sprang forward. His outstretched left hand touched an arm, gripped. He swung his clubbed pistol again.

Something struck hard between his left arm and body, with the sensation of a knife slitting the cloth. It was a vicious blow, aimed at bowels or heart; the thrust of an expert knife man, made from below with an upward swing. Paul clamped his arm to his side with all his strength, imprisoning momentarily his unseen assailant's hand with its deadly weapon.

Slipping the revolver into his pocket, he gripped both hands on forearm and wrist in the hold Pianelli had once taught him. He twisted. The knife came from the cramped fingers and fell to the floor. The action was a matter of seconds.

In the darkness the man's left fist crashed into Paul's face. He caught the arm with his right hand, twisted the man's left arm behind his back, tripped him, and threw him heavily to the floor just as the rush from the doorway swept over and past him.

The place was in uproar. Men shouted and yelled; a milling crowd stormed in the narrow hallway. Glass and wood splintered. Then feet stamped on the stairs in a mad rush upward. Added to the bedlam there was the sound of heavy blows on wood in the back of the house.

"Make a light!" That was Inspector Sherwin's stentorian voice. "Look out for Cardani! Quick there. Rush 'em, men!"

A match flame flared near the open doorway. An instant later a hissing gasjet gave greater illumination. Immediately a great yell went up from the invaders. Nightsticks swung and struck as the rush of the fighting policemen carried the battle toward the rear of the hall.

The inspector near the doorway took command.

"Into that room at your right!" he shouted. "That's enough. Up the stairs there, Murphy, Riordan, Svenson! Two more of you. Make a light as you go. Get every one of 'em and bring 'em down.... Get back there!" he yelled over his shoulder. "Outside. Watch the windows. A couple get down to the basement door and stay there till we come through."

Cardani, kneeling on his captive, with his left hand still clamping an arm, saw that the rush had passed him. Then men from the alley platoon came bursting into the back hallway, driving two of the thugs before them. Caught between the two forces, they were quickly subdued. Inspector Sherwin pushed swiftly past, rallying the men into some sort of control for a systematic search of the whole place. The battle on the ground floor was over, but up above, noise of the mad pursuit still went on, with yells and shouted orders, a great stamping of feet. Above these sounds came suddenly the reports of two pistol shots on the roof.

A hand fell on Cardani's shoulder. He turned his head quickly.

"You all right, Chief?" Ceruti asked anxiously. And when Cardani nodded silently, "Who you got there?"

"I am going to look now."

He got to his feet, raising the man with him. Ceruti was the first to see his face.

"Wow!" he yelled. "Take a look, Chief."

The man, now upright, was taller than the lieutenant although of slighter build. Cardani twisted him about. He saw a long face with small, black eyes, prominent nose, and lantern chin. There was an old scar long healed at one corner of the mouth.

"Ah, Tasso," Cardani said quietly. "We are very glad to see you."

"Mike the Knife" Tasso twisted vainly in Cardani's powerful grasp.

"Let go of me, damn you," he snarled. "You'll pay for this, copper. What th' hell do you mean breaking into a private house and beating up these innocent men?"

"Ceruti," Cardani said, "take the cuffs off my belt and slip 'em on."

Tasso threw himself violently around, and when he could not free his arms tried to butt Cardani's face with his head.

Cardani brought the man's wrists together; there was a metallic click, another.

"You can't do this to me," Tasso yelled, beside himself with fury. "You can't hold me. I'll be out in a day, and perhaps you think I'll forget this, you damned yellow-hearted copper."

Ceruti slapped his face hard.

"I think, Tasso," Cardani told him, "that first-degree murder will hold you—until they want to get rid of you for good and all."

"First degree nothing," Tasso jeered. "You been hittin' the pipe."

"Ceruti," Cardani said, "look out for that man."

He nodded toward the door where the man he had first knocked down was sitting up, rubbing his head dazedly. Ceruti caught hold of him, lifted him to unstable feet, and brought him over beside the lieutenant and his important prisoner.

A light had been made in the front room across the hallway. Sherwin was just coming down the stairs. There were still one or two prostrate forms on the floor. Other men, with bleeding heads and faces, were held by the patrolmen.

"Inspector," Cardani called. "Let's get them all in that front room. I'd like to check them before they go in."

In a few minutes a full dozen sorry-looking captives were lined up against the wall. Of them all, only the leader, Tasso, had escaped a beating. Two had to be held up; a third had a bullet wound in the shoulder.

"Are you sure this is all?"

"That's all. We've covered every inch of the place from basement to roof, every room, every closet, and we saw to it they couldn't double back on us."

Cardani passed slowly along the line of cowed, beaten men, studying each one carefully, calling on his truly remarkable memory for any familiar features. If he recognized any, his inscrutable eyes gave no sign. He came back to the inspector and drew him a little aside.

"We have Tasso," he said. "He's the tall one this end of the line. I'll go in with him personally. I'd like to put him in solitary for a day or two, and I don't want any lawyer getting to him. Can you fix it on the arraignment, say for forty-eight hours at least?"

"Lieutenant," Sherwin said, "you can have any damned thing you want. This is the biggest haul we've yet made. I only hope we can make something stick on all of 'em. If we can't, at least they've had a damned good lesson in crime."

"I wish you would have them booked apart from each other. Then they may not get the idea to lie about their names. I know some of them and have charges on them. When I get all the names I'll know more about them. And I'll have plenty of witnesses to look them over. You have been a great help to me, Inspector."

"Help, hell! You left me in the rear ranks. But I didn't stay there long. I sneaked after you. That was a damned-fool thing you did, Paul, but I guess we'd have had trouble if you hadn't got that door open. When you rushed it, I was right behind you—just in time to see that pistol go off."

Cardani turned on him quickly. "I heard somebody swear. Did that bullet get you?"

"Only a nick in the shoulder," the grizzled inspector said lightly. "Nothing at all."

He moved over and glanced out the window. "Wagons are here," he announced. "All right, boys. Get going."

Two men to a prisoner, the jubilant officers led their captives forth. The street outside was crowded from curb to curb, from one end to the other. Under the inspector's direction, the building was locked rear and front, the patrol wagons dispatched, and the return march to Headquarters started.

Tasso was taken to Headquarters between Cardani and Ceruti. Cardani saw his prisoner safely put away and then joined his squad man. They walked together to the corner, where Cardani stopped.

His eyes were very warm as he looked at his young assistant. "You've done fine work," he said. "I'll see that it is in the report. I want you to go back to the office and wait for me. Have Largio and Ocelli also wait if they come in. I have an errand. I won't be long."

Ceruti started to speak, but the lieutenant had already turned away.

17

PAUL WAS SHOWN into the living room by the maid. The room itself was dimly lit, and the whole place was somberly quiet. He remained standing. Through the day and the exciting events of the early evening, he had succeeded to some extent in keeping his thoughts from dwelling on Giulia and the effect upon her of this terrible tragedy.

Even in his ordinary life Cardani was neither pitiless nor without sympathy. In crises of heart-rending suffering, to all outward appearance he was cold, unsympathetic. This was his manner. Inherently, he had the delicate emotional balance of the musician. He had recognized this and sternly trained himself against it. It had become automatic with him, a part of his developed character, to preserve his cool judgment under all circumstances, and he accomplished this through the concentration of his thoughts strictly upon his duty.

Now, in Giulia's home he was finding the repression of his natural feelings a most difficult matter. He did not want to face her. He hoped that he would not have to look on her grief-stricken face. He had done everything in his power, the night before, to find her brother, to avert the tragedy he half suspected. That effort did not weigh with him now. He had a sense of failure in the first task she had entrusted to him.

He had not wanted to come here at this time. Only the knowledge that he might be of help to her had brought him. He had seen this the moment the spurious notes were in his hands. He knew that if he did not act quickly, some other official of the force or a Secret Service operative would come in his stead and press the questions that must be asked with real if unconscious brutality.

To Cardani, in his perplexity, the minutes of waiting dragged interminably. After what seemed to him a very long while, he heard quick footsteps approaching, and Damiano Ravino entered the room. His sorrow seemed not to have softened but to have hardened the banker, at least in his attitude toward an outsider, as Paul knew he must be considered.

Ravino spoke without greeting. His voice was pitched low, but its tone was harsh, impatient.

"I do not understand why you should come at this time. When you insisted this morning, I was too shocked to refuse you. If I had thought of it again up to this moment, I should have asked the inspector to prevent it. Please make this intrusion as brief as possible."

"If I had not come," Cardani said quietly, "some other officer, a stranger to you, would have been obliged to."

"That would make no difference to me. Suppose you explain why you invade this home of sorrow and be gone.

Cardani withheld his reply momentarily. His quick ear had caught a lighter step. He waited, while the banker watched him with obvious irritation.

"Father," Giulia's low-toned, choked voice called, "are you in there?"

"I am busy, my dear," Ravino answered. "Lieutenant Cardani of the police has insisted on coming here, on a matter of business."

"Oh!" she said from the threshold. "He has come here— tonight!" She came into the room.

Cardani tried not to look at her directly, but his eyes seemed drawn to her by a power greater than his own. He bowed deeply, silently.

"Oh!" she choked, coming nearer him. "How could you come to us now! How could you ever come to us again. You, with your great reputation of helping others, who were going to do so much for us." Her breast rose and fell as her emotion mounted. "I had such faith in you. It was only last night—last night! You told us not to worry; that everything would be all right, that you would go out at once and—and find him. Why did I ever believe you! Last night I did not worry. Then— then—this morning— How can you be so cruel as to let me see you!"

"We searched more than half the night," Cardani said miserably.

"But you found nothing—you accomplished nothing. And with all this—I have to bear, I, who leaned upon you, have lost faith in you. And now you come, when it is terrible even to think of you, to think what you might have done."

With great effort she checked her tears, found some measure of control. She spoke to him again, but her voice was low, infinitely tragic.

"But what can you do now? What is there that can be done— when it is too late?"

"Yes," Ravino said with some asperity. "There is nothing that can be done now. Have the kindness to leave us."

"There is still something that can be done," Cardani said steadily.

"For—Vincent? Oh, no, no, no. Don't be so heartless. Don't you know that people can suffer?"

"Let us have an end of this," Ravino said shortly. "You are a policeman. Everything—tragedy, suffering—is all one with you in your exaggerated estimation of your duty. Can't you understand, sir, that we want nothing of it? Come. I will show you out myself."

Cardani did not move. "Signorina," he said, and some unsuspected quality in his tone held them both, "I hoped that you would not let me see you tonight. I did not want to look on you in your suffering. I did not want to annoy you with the sight of me. I had to come, for your sake, for your father's sake; for there is yet something that can be done for—your brother."

Giulia, speechless, looked at him with wide, tear-filled eyes.

"Explain yourself, sir," Ravino snapped.

Cardani turned slowly toward him. "If the signorina will permit, I should prefer to speak to you alone, Mr. Ravino."

"No, no!" Giulia gasped. "If it concerns—Vincent, I want—I must hear it."

"Come, come," Ravino snapped. "I cannot endure this longer. Speak up, man. What more can you do for my son?"

Cardani looked once at Giulia, then turned to the banker. "We can save his honor," he said simply.

Giulia, horror-stricken, reached out blindly for a chair, found it, and sank into it, her eyes fastened upon him.

Ravino came a step nearer the lieutenant. "What do you mean?" he demanded hoarsely. "My son is above reproach." He seemed about to break into more violent speech. Cardani checked him.

"I believe that with all my heart," he said. He thrust a hand into his pocket, held it there momentarily. "But some explanation must be made at once, to satisfy the Government authorities, before any story starts that would hurt that reputation. You can give me the answer that will satisfy them. I did not want to go to any one else, to let anyone else even know about it."

He drew out the counterfeit bills, offered them to the banker. Giulia looked on wonderingly, one hand pressed to her lips. Ravino took them, mechanically listed them through for the amount. He glanced up at Cardani.

"Well, what does this mean?" he asked. "Where did they come from?"

"I, myself, took them from your son's pocket."

"But what of it? There is here a hundred dollars. It isn't surprising that he should have that money with him."

"That is only a part of a thousand dollars that was in the sheaf."

"But—are you suggesting that he had taken money that did not belong to him—even a thousand dollars?"

"Look at them more carefully, please," Cardani said.

Ravino glanced at him quickly, then stepped close to the shaded light. He took off the topmost bill, turned it over, scrutinizing front and back. Suddenly he frowned. Where the light struck his cheek it showed gray. He came back to the lieutenant.

"It is—counterfeit?" he asked between tight lips.

Cardani heard Giulia gasp. He did not look at her.

"Yes."

"What—what do you think?" the banker asked, badly shaken. "Did you—did you—" He was struggling for control, but he looked very old and gray and worn.

"I do not for one moment," Cardani said gently, "entertain

the idea that he was doing anything with them. I do not believe that he ever knew they were in his possession. But the authorities will want more than my belief. You can help, sir, in this way. Can you tell me if these, or any similar bills, have appeared at your bank? Would you be in a position to know absolutely if they had not?"

The banker drew a long, deep breath. For the first time he looked at Cardani with an absence of antipathy.

"I thank you, Lieutenant," he said in a steady voice. "I see exactly what you mean. I understand, too, why you felt it necessary to—call upon me at once. I am in a position to know, and I can assure you, without question of doubt, that no such bills have yet been taken in or offered to the bank."

"I was sure of it," Cardani said softly. "Now I am in position to confirm it. Thank you, sir."

He took back the bills, which he returned to his pocket. He was about to take his leave when he found Giulia standing beside him.

"Won't you please tell me what this all means?" she asked.

"It means," her father said, "that the lieutenant found these counterfeit notes on—Vincent. The authorities had to be notified at once. He knew that an investigation would be begun, and that an ugly rumor might be started if he could not squelch it in time. Therefore he came to me."

Giulia caught her breath with a little gasp. "I— But—"

"Please," Cardani said a little huskily. "I can't express myself very well. I can't say how I feel for you both."

"But you have shown it," Ravino said. "I am very much in your debt, Lieutenant."

Unconsciously Giulia had placed her hand on Paul's arm.

"Why," she gasped, "your coat has been cut—and there is a hole burnt in your pocket! You have been—"

"I'm sorry," Paul muttered. "I forgot. We took in a mur—that is, we captured some gangmen this evening."

She held out her hand to him. "Good night, Lieutenant."

18

PAUL STOPPED ON the upper landing, just outside the door to his private office. The door, he noted absently, was not closed firmly; it stood a mere crack ajar. Voices sounded behind it. For the moment he gave them no heed.

He was still under the spell of the thoughts which had accompanied him, step by step, back from Giulia Ravino's stricken home. Heretofore he had conquered such feeling, made it subservient to the iron purpose of his duty. This had struck through his control. He was bitter, resentful. For the first time that he could remember he felt that his efforts were futile, unavailing. He had sought to protect many. In reasonable measure he had been successful. But in this one great crisis, where the victims should reasonably have been aloof from harm, he had failed; he had been too late.

He knew that the mood was wrong, knew that his work still lay ahead of him. He was aware that he had merely paused momentarily, to step aside and allow human sympathy to have its way with him. He could not replace, but he could try to make amends.

He brushed his calloused palm hard across his sweaty forehead. He marshaled his wayward thoughts, separated them. He made himself listen. That was Largio's voice inside. He recognized it now. Largio, he forced himself to remember, had been sent to push a cart through the four short streets of a single block, to find a certain hideout, the secret place where a gang was working, making bombs; Coremo's gang. He had been anxiously awaiting Largio's report. Strange that he had forgotten it even for a minute. He leaned closer to the open crack.

Largio was saying: "Yes, sir, Bob. I'm a merchant, I am. Listen. I sold me twelve suspenders, a package of safety-pins, a toothbrush— Gee, that was a hard one. I don't believe the old geezer himself coulda done that. A baby's—"

Paul pushed open the door.

Ceruti and Ocelli were seated in chairs leaning back against the table. Between them a man slouched in a chair faced the opposite way, feet on the table— But could that be Largio?

A too large, soft black hat, gray at the edges, came down well over the ears, showing fringes of long, unkempt hair beneath. A face dark, smirched with grime and dirt; filthy collar with flamboyant red tie; a patched coat too large, too long in the sleeves; ill-fitting, baggy trousers, patched and darned, with the cuffs several times rolled. Runover shoes, holes in soles and uppers, rested on the table edge. The man cocked his head around.

Feet and chair legs came to the floor with a bang. Largio stood up, saluted, and grinned.

"Any luck, Largio?" Paul asked quickly. Somehow, in these first words spoken, his voice sounded strange to himself.

"These fellers," Largio said, "have been trying to get it outta me. It's a long story, Chief, and I wanted to wait for you, so's I'd tell it only once. I been tellin' them how I made a dollar and forty-nine cents."

Cardani looked keenly at Largio, saw the smile in his tired eyes, and nodded.

"Sit down," he said briskly, "and let me have it."

"If you don't mind, Chief." Largio grimaced. "These ain't my regular shoes, and my feet got blistered on them damn hot cobbles." He reclaimed his chair.

Cardani stood beside him, leaning against the table.

"I was out at daylight," Largio said. "But you don't want that. Well, I checked everything on wheels that went outta that block or came to it." His tone grew more serious. His thick brows drew together.

"Every time a truck or a cart drew up, I nosed in to see what was doing. If one of them went away from a place, I went as far as I thought I ought to find what they had taken away. One I thought was foolin' me. It took away stuff from a vegetable and fruit store, a big place. I had an idea there might be a place in the back. I went in there and looked around. There wasn't.

"I tell you, Chief, I covered everything that touched that block from daylight till after dark, and I'll take my oath that every damn one of 'em was on legitimate business—except one that mightn't 'a' been."

Largio hitched himself up in his chair and swore as a bare spot of his foot touched a knot in the rough floor. Cardani watched him without comment. Ocelli and Ceruti were following every word.

"I'll tell you about this one, Chief," Largio continued. "There's an old building, kinder like a warehouse, on Cherry near Jefferson. It's two stories and long. I got a look at it from the other side later on. The front is sorter square; then from one side the long part of it runs back. There ain't many windows in the back part, and some of 'em are broken. But I saw a couple next to each other that were all whole an' painted black inside.

"What led me to it was this. When I first got there, on the street I mean, I saw a ragpicker drive his wagon outta the front end. He had one horse and the regular cart. He stopped outside and went back and locked the double doors with a key. Then he went off.

"I pushed my cart past him. That wagon wasn't just empty, as I thought it shoulda been. There was some kinder junk in the bottom an' some old coats over it. I dunno why, but that made me suspicious, and I kept an eye on the place when I could. Long about nine, a coupla men and a woman came to it, opened the doors, and left them open. I pushed past 'em and saw they were sorting rags inside.

"Bimeby I came back, stopped there, and tried to sell 'em something. I couldn't, but I got a look at the place; that is, this front end. There was a stall for the horse, some hay, room for the wagon, and a place where the rags were set in two piles. There was a door that was shut at the right as I looked in. These people didn't seem to like me hangin' around, least I may've imagined it, and I went on.

"Just about dark, long after the place was locked up, this ragpicker came back. He had a full load and it looked legit, dirt and all. He unlocked the door, drove in, fooled around a minute or two, prob'bly feeding the horse, came out, locked up, and went off."

Largio shrugged elaborately.

"I dunno. As far's I could see it looked like regular business. But, Chief, that's the only wagon, truck, go-cart, or baby carriage that was in that block today that I didn't see exactly what they were carrying. I'll go back tomorrow, if you say so; but I gotta get me different kind of shoes."

Cardani was thoughtfully silent for a long minute. "I don't think it will be necessary," he finally said. "That lead looks pretty good to me, and after that wholesale take-in this evening, we'll have to work fast. We'll try it out."

He glanced at Ocelli; then at Ceruti. "Ceruti, you'll have to handle this. Pick a man from the squad to work with you. In the morning, Largio, take them to a place where they can't be seen but can see this ragpicker come out. Once you have spotted him for them, leave them and come back to the office.

"Ceruti, you keep on the ragpicker all day. When he gets his load, and you think he is starting back, arrest him and bring him in. Tell him it is on account of his license. Don't pick a place too close to his shop; as far away as possible, if his load is big enough. Have your man stay by the wagon until we relieve him. But don't let him get on to either of you all day until you pinch him. That's all, boys. Ocelli, wait a minute. I may have to run over to Headquarters."

Largio, yawning heavily, went out with Ceruti.

Cardani turned to Ocelli and nodded.

"I found something," Ocelli said, "but they were telling me you grabbed Tasso and about a dozen of his crowd. I missed that."

"What you were on was more important. Let's hear it."

Ocelli sighed wearily, then hitched himself more upright in his chair.

"I started from Hester, and worked north and east. Long in the afternoon, in fact close to dark, I found a cooperage place. It was 'bout the fourth one I'd looked over. The others were all working and didn't have this mark. This one seemed to be shut down. It's over on Stanton, near where there's talk they're going to make a park.

"There was a high slat fence in front of a yard. I came near going right past it; then I saw some barrels piled under an open shed. At the other end of the yard is a small brick office and a cooperage shop in between. The office windows looked dirty. Anyway there was no one around, not even a watchman."

Cardani said nothing; his eyes were very bright.

"I finally found I could slip the latch on the gate," Ocelli went on. "It was pretty dark under the shed, but I lit some matches and looked the barrels over. They had the same stencil. They were new and never had anything inside of them. All I looked at had the ends loose fastened, and I found an extra set on the ground."

"Did you bring them in?"

"They're on the table there, in the newspaper."

Ocelli reached for them, but Cardani was before him. Throwing off the wrapping, he tried them on the murder barrel. They fitted exactly. Cardani drew a long breath. He glanced at his watch, and shrugged. Ocelli got somewhat slowly to his feet. Cardani swept him with a keen glance.

"Tired?"

Ocelli grinned. "I guess I can make it if you can." He pointed to the lieutenant's rent coat. "And I didn't collect anything like those, either. Somebody try a knife on you?"

Cardani made a wry grimace. "That's the second time my attention has been called to it." He ignored the question. "We'll need matches and candles, won't we?"

"Yes; or a lantern would be better. I'll get one from the squad room."

19

ON THE WALK across town, it occurred to Cardani that he had so far been without dinner, and he could not recall whether or not he had missed his lunch as well. The matter was remedied with little loss of time, and the two were plodding on again.

"According to the examiner," Cardani said once, "the trail from the time of the murder is forty-eight hours old. The transportation of the body brings it twenty-four hours nearer and gives us another lead. The barrel was not in the Spring Street alley prior to last night. We are getting closer."

A few minutes later Ocelli said, "That's the place we're coming to now."

Midway of the block, on the south side of the street, they were approaching a high fence of separated upright strips. Ocelli led the way to a gate, reached an arm inside, and after a little manipulation raised the latch and swung it open. Cardani followed him into a yard with the buildings which his first assistant had described. Ocelli pointed to one end.

"There're the barrels over there."

Cardani nodded and glanced toward the opposite end. "Did you look into that building?"

"No. I looked at the office windows from the street but couldn't see inside."

Cardani started toward the low brick structure. Only faint illumination from the nearest street lamp reached them here, and when they came within twenty feet of the building they were in complete shadow.

"Wait here a moment," Cardani said. Turning, he stepped to the fence, walked beside that, and approached the door close by the wall. He could see the dim blur of a broad stone step. He sank to one knee, struck a match, and bent close. After a brief moment he blew out the flame and, still kneeling, called softly to Ocelli, "Come the way I did," and when Ocelli was beside him, "We have come to the right place."

He struck another match and pointed to a round, brownish stain on the stone. Raising the cupped flame he indicated another similar spot on the second step and blew out the light.

"The murder was committed here—inside."

"How d'you happen to come here, first thing?"

"They had to have some place to talk. If the killing was done on the premises at all, it had to be here."

Paul came slowly to his feet, mounted the two steps, and put his hand on the doorknob. It turned under his touch, and he pushed the door inward. He took one step inside, struck a third light, and carried it low to the floor.

"Come inside and close the door," he said to Ocelli, and moved only to give him room. "Now light the lantern and stay just where you are."

When Ocelli had complied they saw that they were in a low-ceilinged square room, of the approximate size of the building itself, holding mute but irrefutable evidence of tragedy. A not large oblong table stood in the center, with one end toward them. At the ends of the table and a little to the right of it, two upright chairs had been pushed back. Between these two chairs, a third was overturned on the floor and was not far from the wall on that side. Between this latter chair and the table there was a very large brown stain.

Cardani saw this much without moving. He sent a quick glance around, noted that the shades of the office's three windows were closely drawn, and turned to Ocelli.

"Pull down that curtain on the door behind you. They have left this evidence for forty-eight hours. Not much chance of their coming back now, but I can't take that chance. The whole story is here. Go outside, stand in the shadow. If anyone comes into the yard, don't let him get away from you. I'll call you."

The instant the door was softly closed, Paul set to work. Half an hour later when he called Ocelli in, his eyes were bright with an expression of triumph which he made no effort to conceal.

"Not a single person been by either way," Ocelli said. "Found something, Lieutenant?"

Cardani nodded. "It was probably the same the night of the murder. Now listen carefully. Tomorrow come here, bring a photographer. Make a plan and have pictures taken of the points I show you.

"Now; young Ravino sat there in the middle, between two men. His back was to the telephone you see on that shelf on the wall. That big stain shows where he fell and lay until they carried him out. Those smaller stains leading to the door were the blood dripping from his coat. They placed his body for a moment on the step outside. We'll find further marks, at least of the barrel end, in daylight.

"A left-handed man, smoking a cigar, sat at Ravino's left. He was, I believe, the actual murderer. I'll come to that later. At Ravino's right sat a man smoking cigarettes. I judge that all three came here together and stayed about fifteen minutes, or a little less, before the murder was committed. During that time they may have argued and discussed, but there was no violence even threatened. The attack, as sudden as it was brutal, was completely unsuspected by the victim."

"Whew-w!" Ocelli gasped. "How'd you get all that, Lieutenant?"

"I believe I can tell what was talked about as well as the motive for the sudden killing. First, however, as to the time and the men. You see, at the right of where Ravino sat, a quantity of cigarette ash, the short butt of one, and still another where the cigarette lay and burned itself out. At the right of the chair, to Ravino's right, is about the same amount of cigarette ash. There is also a short butt which a man's foot has pressed. At this end of the table, at the left of the chair here, is a lot of cigar ash but no butt. All three smoked approximately the same length of time."

Cardani drew a long breath. Ocelli was watching him with wide, amazed eyes.

"Here is what I think happened," Cardani went on. "Recall young Ravino's state of mind. He was half in love with Maria dePasso; he was a man of high principle and fine character. He had just made it plain to her that they would have to break off their friendship; that no good could come to her from it. He felt that his action, while right, was in a way brutal, and this disturbed him deeply.

"He left her, careless of himself, indifferent. He was accosted by these two men, who had been following him, waiting for just this chance. They told him something about the girl and himself, sufficient, whatever it was, to persuade him to go even to this out-of-the-way spot to discuss it further. There is no other conceivable reason why he should have come here willingly, as he did.

"Today Ceruti ran on to a vile rumor of their relations. It was untrue, but I believe these two men thought it was true, and that through it they could persuade Ravino to their purposes; that is, to pass some of their counterfeit money through his father's bank. They got him here and sat down to broach their proposition.

"Now as to their positions, and why I believe the left-handed cigar smoker did the killing. A right-handed man will frequently hold his pipe in his left-hand fingers, but a cigarette or cigar smoker flicks the ashes off with his superior hand, an unconscious habit formed from the time he first begins to smoke.

"I'll finish quickly now. The wound was in Ravino's back, nearer the left side. The blow was struck so viciously that a portion of the haft entered the wound. If he had feared the attack, he would have backed to the wall, and the wound would have been in front. No; he spurned their proposition, sprang to his feet, kicking over his chair, and turned to reach the telephone. I have reason to believe," Cardani added, in a curiously hard tone, "he wanted to call me.

"On that instant, the cigar smoker signed to his confederate to let him have his knife. Behind Ravino's back, with lightning quickness the knife was passed and the blow struck."

"Just a moment," Ocelli interrupted. "You're too fast for me. How do you know that?"

"The man originally at Ravino's right could not have given that particular blow, with such violence, with either hand without getting into a position where Ravino would have seen him. The cigar smoker could not have delivered it if he had been right-handed. And the actual murderer would not have left his own weapon in the wound later to betray him.

"When we find the owner of that knife we will have the accomplice. To save his own life he should lead us to the real killer. And when we have him we will have the leader of this whole rotten organization. He is the cleverest killer I have ever trailed.

"In that fraction of time he was right enough to get the other man's knife. He probably pretended panic in order to rush his companion away so that he would forget that his knife was left behind. Yet while doing so he was shrewd enough to plant that bunch of counterfeit notes, to take advantage of that opportunity to put the Federal agents off his trail, knowing of the arrests they have recently been making.

"I tell you, Ocelli, that such a man is a master criminal, a master mind, the very highest in authority. At last," he added savagely, "we are on the trail of a man big enough, vicious enough, to be the leader who I knew must exist.

"He is here, in this country, in this city. We must get him."

He stopped abruptly. Light leaped in his black eyes. "Listen, Ocelli. Benito Pianelli and I talked over this very matter, the kind of a man who could organize and lead this enormous gang here. I went back in my memory; I searched all my files. I studied information on every big criminal who had come here in recent years. Ocelli—I did not go back far enough.

"That man who sat in the chair there, smoking his expensive cigar, leading young Ravino on until he himself had gone too far, then like a flash murdering him—that man, Ocelli, has been in this country for years. During all this time, slowly, craftily, he has laid his plans. Never once, before, has he done one careless act that would disclose his identity. I am sure of that. In five years there has not been one murder of an important person in this quarter that I have not solved. And now he is big enough, sure enough of his power and position, to do the striking himself. God! if I could only get a glimmer of who he is!"

He broke off. Taking some old envelopes from his pocket, he carefully collected into each the separate cigarette ashes and butts, identifying them respectively. He did the same with the cigar ashes, took one more keen look about the place, and turned to the door. With a hand on the knob he paused.

"I'll want both you and Largio on this," he said. "You begin here; I'll start Largio on the back trail from where the barrel was left. Last night, some time after midnight and before daylight, the wagon I described to you left this yard and went over to that alley on Spring near Sullivan. There were, I believe, two men on the job. Somewhere along the route someone saw them. I want that wagon found, its driver brought in."

20

IN THE AFTERNOON following his investigation at the cooperage plant, Paul was summoned to the commissioner's office at Headquarters. There, besides Commissioner Redfield, he found Inspector Sherwin and a stranger. Cardani was at once introduced to Chief Thomas of the Federal Secret Service.

"Lieutenant," the commissioner began, "Chief Thomas has come over to take personal charge of tracing this counterfeit money to its source. I have promised him all possible co-operation. If you have obtained any additional information since I talked with you yesterday, I wish you would give it to him."

Cardani did not reply at once. His eyes were lowered to the desk in deep thought. The others watched him silently; the chief of the Secret Service with shrewd, speculative look. Finally the lieutenant raised his eyes to his superior, glanced at the other two.

"I have," he said, "additional information. In my opinion it is the most important that has yet come into my hands."

He turned to the Secret Service man. "I don't want to obstruct your work, Mr. Thomas. In fact, I believe we should work together as closely as possible. I only fear that a premature movement might disrupt my own plans, which are rapidly coming to a crisis."

"Explain yourself, Lieutenant."

Cardani outlined, for the benefit of the man from Washington as well as of his two superiors, his conception of the whole criminal organization and stated his belief that he was now definitely on the trail of its head. He then explained in all its details the murder of young Ravino and told of his discoveries of the previous evening.

"I believe," he said, "this proves that Mr. Thomas and his men are very close on the trail of the counterfeiters. Placing those bills on the murdered man was a desperate and reckless move. It shows they are feeling the pressure. The trail is hot.

"At the same time the whole circumstance proves to me that in one chair sat the very head of this Black Hand outfit; in the other his chief assistant and probably the man who would have the plates."

"How is that, Lieutenant?" Chief Thomas asked.

"The murder was not premeditated as a murder. The attempt was first to persuade or force young Ravino to pass the notes off through his bank. That would not have been entrusted to a subordinate. When they saw they had failed, they killed. Then they planted the bills on his body, had it transported to another section. No subordinate would have dared to do that. No one but the head himself would have thought in that instant of the chance to put you off his trail in that manner.

"How about the assistant having the plates? That is what interests me primarily."

"The head of this outfit would be too shrewd to keep the plates anywhere near himself. After all, that is only one of his many activities. On the other hand, he would have taken with him on such a job, where murder might have to be done in their own protection, no one but the man closest to him. Such an associate would logically have custody of the plates."

Under half-shut lids, the eyes of Chief Thomas were very bright. "Got any idea who these two men might be?"

"Who the leader is, I haven't the least suspicion. As to the other man, I can only guess."

"Well, I kinder think I'd like to string along on your guess, Lieutenant. Shoot."

Cardani told of his first meeting with the man called Lupo, of the bombing of the fruitshop, and of the attack on him by members of two distinct gangs that followed so immediately.

"In addition to this," he added, "Lupo is the only criminal I know, of his apparent importance, that I cannot place in some activity or another."

"What's he look like?" Thomas demanded curtly.

Cardani gave a very careful description of which Chief Thomas made notes.

"What you are afraid of," he said shrewdly, "is that if we come busting in after this plate crowd, it might flush your big bird before you have a gun on him or even know what he looks like when he comes out of cover."

Cardani nodded silently.

The chief of the Secret Service cracked fist into palm. "You've got the thing twisted around, Commissioner. My department will give Lieutenant Cardani every assistance of which it is capable. Now, Lieutenant, how do you want to go about this? What do you want me to do?"

"I think that your men who are making these outside arrests of the shovers of the queer should keep up their work and perhaps increase it; also that they should continue their drive toward the headquarters of the gang without coming in too far—yet. At the same time, as an entirely separate thing, I'd be glad of any help you could give me to locate this Lupo. But I don't think the men who are on the bill passers should do this job, too."

Chief Thomas nodded. "How about arrests of passers in the city—too close, Lieutenant?"

"All the better; if they don't go too far into the East Side."

"What makes you say that?"

"Ravino was murdered on Stanton, east of Second Avenue. His body, with the bills, was taken over into that other section, on Spring near Sullivan."

"We have a hunch," Chief Thomas said slowly, "that the headquarters is east of Third Avenue and south of East Houston. All right; I'll have a dozen men come over from Washington right away. If the commissioner can spare me a little office, I'd rather locate here than in the Federal Building. Want to talk it over further this evening, Lieutenant?"

Cardani told of his plans for the evening. "After that, I'd be glad to."

"Just a detail, huh?"

"Yeah," Inspector Sherwin said dryly. "I went on one of the Lieutenant's little details last night, and was damn' fool enough to follow him into a hideout with a dozen men behind the door and nearly got my head blown off."

"What are they using mostly?" Thomas asked.

"In rare cases some nitro. Generally it's dynamite sticks melted down—soup; or just plain blasting powder with a fire-cracker fuse. The home-made kind, that we're going after, are usually sawed-off pipe lengths sealed. Last week we found a Chianti bottle filled to the neck with blasting. The fuse went out an inch short."

"So you're going to bust into a joint with nitro, dynamite, and blasting powder lying around. How long shall I wait for you, Lieutenant?"

"I don't think I'll be very late," he said.

He nodded to the commissioner, stood up to take his leave, turned again to the chief of Secret Service.

"I hope you don't think I'm butting into your territory."

Chief Thomas shook hands with a hard grip. "I wish I had all six of you over in Washington, Lieutenant."

"Not while I'm Commissioner of Police in New York," Redfield declared.

Cardani left the office, went along the corridor, and climbed stairs to a room that had been assigned to Tito Carmello. He stopped only for a short chat; then paid a similarly brief visit to the shopkeeper whose place had recently been bombed. These were two important witnesses; one against Tasso, who was already in custody; the other against the mysterious figure called Lupo, whom Paul hoped soon to have behind bars. From there he returned to his own offices.

Toward dusk Ocelli and Largio returned. Starting from opposite ends they had worked toward a common center, met, and come in together. Neither had anything definite to tell, although both had leads which might be followed to possible advantage.

Ocelli had learned of four young men, with one of whom he thought he had slight acquaintance, who had crossed town late on the night in question, coming from a ship at her pier on the North river. Whether they had walked east on Spring Street, whether they had seen anything of importance to the detectives, were matters to be determined. Ocelli had encountered difficulty in finding the one of the quartette whose name was familiar to him. He had deferred the matter temporarily to report.

Largio's most promising quest, after hours of haphazard inquiry, had been in a few saloons and cafés along the route with the idea of discovering late patrons. He wanted to pursue the search further at an hour corresponding with the approximate time the wagon had passed on its fateful journey.

Paul had barely finished his instructions for carrying on the work when Ceruti came in escorting a medium-sized, very dirty, and apparently much frightened man. Long hair straggled over a grimy forehead and dirt-stained neck. Baggy, ill-fitting coat and trousers, tattered and disreputable, composed his chief attire, ending in old, worn shoes. In his blackened hands he twisted a battered black felt. He glanced with blinking eyes from his captor to the lieutenant, before whom Ceruti brought him.

Paul, looking at him keenly, thought he detected an animal-like craftiness in the man's shifting eyes. He turned to his assistant.

"What've you got here?"

"This feller's supposed to be a ragpicker. I don't know how I happened to notice him, but I thought he was acting kind of suspicious. He stopped at a place over yonder—it wasn't a tenement or a house at all. After a while he brought out something and stuffed it in under his pile of rags. It didn't look like rags or bottles or anything like that. I followed him then and finally decided I'd better bring him in."

Cardani nodded soberly. "Who do you work for?" he demanded abruptly.

"Nobody, meester," the man whined ingratiatingly. "I my own boss."

"Where do you keep your horse and wagon?"

"On Hester Street, near Sec'nd Avenue."

"Live there?"

"N—yes, meester."

"Let's see your license."

Warned by the man's slight start, Cardani flashed a glance at Largio, who was standing a little behind Ceruti, the latter having pushed forward with his prisoner. The man reached his right hand into a pocket, withdrew it, thrust it into another. His fingers groped around, then suddenly flashed out with an open clasp-knife. With surprising agility, he whirled around toward the door.

Largio, however, was prepared. His right hand clamped on the man's wrist, bent the arm backward, twisting it. The knife clattered to the floor. Ceruti grasped the other arm, and they held him writhing and snarling.

"All right," Cardani snapped. "Take him into the detention room, strip off those rags, wash his face, give him a set of overalls, and run him over to the lockup. Charge, assault with a deadly weapon. Ocelli, you and Largio attend to this, but send two of the men from the squad room over with him. I want you in here as soon as you fix him up."

As soon as the door closed upon the three, Paul glanced at Ceruti. His expression was one of keen, alert satisfaction. Ceruti began his story without further invitation.

"We got the wagon over near Second. I wasn't fooling, Lieutenant. You oughta look into it. I'll gamble there's dynamite in that package he stuck under the rags. Want to go now?"

"Is young Busano in the squad room? Step in and see. Bring him in, and get the clothes, shoes, and hat they take off that ragpicker."

Wonderingly, Ceruti stepped briskly out to return in a

few minutes with Busano and the clothes, which he carried gingerly with the tips of his fingers and dumped in the first convenient place. Young Busano looked inquiringly at the lieutenant. Paul waited until Ocelli and Largio returned, then nodded toward the young man.

"Nearest the size and build we have, isn't he?"

Largio was the first to understand. "Same height, I'd say. Might pass for the build, but my gawd, what a difference! But say, Chief, when we washed that guy's face he looked like a different man."

"I thought so," Cardani said dryly. He turned to Busano. "Tulio, I have a dirty job for you, but it won't be any worse than mine. Want it?"

"You bet I do," the young man said quietly.

"You can drive a horse?"

"Sure. I handled one of the delivery wagons at the bakery when I was fourteen."

Cardani glanced at Ocelli and Largio, nodded toward the bundle of clothing. "Make him look as much like that ragpicker as you can. Don't waste any time."

"Gee, boy," Largio murmured as he caught up the clothes, "you're going to itch."

Paul turned at once to his own preparations. From a lower drawer of his desk he brought forth a pair of overalls, a loose coat of the same material, and a steamfitter's cap. He donned these over his regular clothes and saw to it that the loose fit did not hamper his movements. He drew his revolver, made sure that its mechanism was working smoothly, and that it was loaded to the empty chamber on which the double-action hammer rested. He added a blackjack from the drawer, which he put in a trousers-pocket, and transferred a police whistle from his own coat to the one that was now outside.

He reached for the telephone that was connected with Headquarters. When he hung up, Ceruti, who had been watching every movement closely, could no longer hold in.

"Mind telling me what you plan, Lieutenant?"

Cardani shrugged. "Tulio is going to drive me into that shop. I can't tell what will happen after that."

"But, my God, Lieutenant, you are not going into that bunch of bomb-makers alone? You'll get blown to hell in a hack."

"Best way to go about it. We can't just raid them. Too much danger of something going wrong."

Ocelli and Largio came in with a creditable-looking ragpicker between them. Largio was laughing; young Busano was making evident effort to resist scratching.

"Listen carefully, now," Paul said, a little sharply. "We are all going over where Ceruti left the outfit. I'll want to look it over, so we'll start from there. There are two platoons waiting at Headquarters. Ocelli, you will lead one; you, Largio, the other. When Tulio and I start, you two come back to Headquarters. Keep your two groups separate, with a guide in between. You don't have to hurry. I think the timing will be about right. Ocelli, your men will cover the front of the building. When you see Tulio lock up and come out, wait five minutes, then send your guide back to bring up the men. Spread them out well. Don't let a man get away whatever happens. Largio, you do the same in the rear. You'll have to use your own judgment in placing your men. You know the layout there. Understand?"

"Yes, sir. But—"

"All right. Let's go."

21

THEY FOUND CERUTI'S helper waiting in a poorly lighted side street, idly parrying the pert questions of a group of gutter urchins. A rather decrepit-appearing horse was munching the sparse grass at the curb; behind him the ragpicker's wagon was full. A few pennies sent the children scurrying around the block.

Ocelli stepped at once to the back of the wagon and, with head averted, fumbled among the close-packed rags. He drew out a stiff paper-wrapped parcel about two feet long. He set this gingerly on the soft dirt of the sidewalk, and Lieutenant Cardani unfastened the string that bound it. Beneath the paper was a burlap bag, and when this was unwound six or eight sticks of dynamite were disclosed.

"Thought so," Ocelli muttered.

"Did you spot the place where he got it?"

"Sure thing; but I didn't pinch him until he was well out of sight of it."

The lieutenant commenced to rewrap the parcel in the same manner in which it had been found.

"Tomorrow," he said, "see Inspector Sherwin. Lead half a dozen men over there and bring in everyone in the place."

"Right. Want me to take this back to Headquarters when I go in—or to our offices?" He picked up the package of dynamite.

"Put it back in the wagon, after I get in." Paul turned to the other men who were watching silently and in some little awe.

"Largio, tell Tulio Busano here just where he is to go. Describe that building to him so he won't have to hesitate and look around. Tell him exactly what he is to do inside, where to leave the wagon, where to put the horse."

Largio hesitated a moment, then faced Cardani. His rounded face was very serious. "Lieutenant, I know that place inside and out like a book. You don't know it at all. Let me do the riding in, and I can open the way for the rest of you. Besides, if Busano makes a break I can set it right."

"Thanks, Largio," Cardani said dryly. "This is my end of it. You fellows do your parts exactly as I have told you, and we'll have a chance to pull it off. We have lost time enough. Give the dope to Busano and, Tulio, make all the motions and noise of locking the door, in case there is a watcher there, but leave it unbolted."

While Largio passed on the information in careful detail, Cardani, with the help of Ocelli, concealed himself entirely beneath the pile of filthy rags. He lay close to the bottom, his head near the back. He drew his revolver, held it in his right hand before his face. His left hand held a handkerchief loosely over eyes, nose, and mouth. Ready, he instructed Ocelli to place the parcel of dynamite beside him, taking care that it would not shift to the side and that there were plenty of rags beneath it.

"Get going," Cardani's muffled voice came to them, and the wagon commenced its jolting journey.

Grim thoughts accompanied Paul Cardani on that seemingly endless trip. If he could forget for a minute that package of deadly explosive, the swaying of the frail cart would bring it against his side in forceful reminder. That, however, bothered him not at all. He knew there was practically no chance of mishap because of it en route; the danger lay in what might happen from it at the journey's end. Of course he could have sent it to Headquarters; but he had brought it along for very definite reasons.

For one thing, it would complete the chain of evidence in case the bomb-makers should lack other explosive in their secret factory for the moment. Paul also had an idea that it might be useful as bait to lead him to the inner sanctum of the mob.

Slow minutes filed past, to the faint click of the horse's hoofs, the creaking, jerking rattle of the old contraption on wheels. Tulio Busano was driving at a walk, carefully. He did not know what made dynamite go off, and he had no wish at the moment to discover.

Beneath the rags, Cardani was finding breathing difficult, since he found it desirable to press his handkerchief close to mouth and nostrils to filter the dust and keep out a measure of the nauseous odors. The layout of the section by streets was as clear in his mind as if he were studying a map before him. He beguiled the tedious progress by noting the turns, to right and left, reckoning distances between, naming the streets in his mind as one followed the other.

After a time he commenced to anticipate the end and found himself not many seconds in advance. Abruptly the rickety old vehicle came to a stop with a jolt that caused its burden to slide forward a little. The wagon heaved as young Busano stepped down. A moment's pause, while Cardani visualized the young man fumbling at the lock, then it moved forward up a slight incline, came to a level, and stopped again. Once more it moved, this time backward. It turned for a very short distance, and then it stopped.

Paul had kept track of its ingress, its turning, and backing. From Largio's description, he knew just where were rag pile, stall, and, most important, that door at the right of the entrance leading to the rear of the adjoining building.

Carefully he swept the rags away from his face, inched closer to the back until his head and his right hand that held the revolver were free. He turned both in the direction where that door should be, and waited.

The only light came from the dim illumination of the street through the open doors. It was faint at this point, which was some distance from the nearest lamp. Cardani did not try to distinguish objects; that was of no importance now. He could hear Tulio fumbling at the harness of the horse, loosening the breeching, unfastening the traces. He wondered if the young fellow's fingers were trembling, for he seemed inordinately slow.

However, while noting Busano's progress, Paul was listening for other sounds, above all the first faint, jarring tread of distant footsteps approaching the other side of the door, which, according to Largio's observation, should now be closed. He did not hear them—at once.

The horse, finally, was unharnessed; whether led by Tulio or from its own instinct, it started for its stall. The heavy steps sounded hollowly on the worn floor. Under cover of the noise, Cardani freed himself entirely of his foul covering, eased himself silently over the back to the floor. His keen eyes pierced the dusk, located the door exactly where his memory had placed it.

Tulio was at the big doors now; he had closed one half and was swinging the other, when Paul's alert ears picked up the sound that he had been expecting and hoping would come, but not too soon. Steps were coming along some passage beyond the partition. He wanted to call to Tulio to hurry, to get away and escape discovery that would not only defeat Cardani's plans but might readily cost both their lives.

Through hearing alone, he timed young Busano's leisurely closing of the door and the approach of those footsteps, while he himself spun into action. As he had climbed from the wagon he had observed that it was backed close against a considerable pile of rags, apparently awaiting the sorters. He slid soundlessly behind this pile, crouching low, feeling around to make certain that his footing would be clear.

The outer door banged; there was the rattle of the key in the lock, a sliding rasp as it was withdrawn. And almost at the same instant the door from the passage came open; the place was flooded with light. By comparison with the previous darkness, the sudden illumination seemed brilliant, and Paul crouched lower still, letting his breath make no sound.

He could not see beyond his rag-pile, but he heard the steps come inside, the door close quietly. Shadows danced grotesquely as the light advanced.

"You wantta see that guy?" a voice rasped hoarsely.

"Naw. I'm damned glad he's gone."

"Wonder what made him so late. The boss was gettin' nervous."

"Dunno. He left fast enough anyway. Look where the damned fool dropped the harness."

"T'hell with that. Let's get the stuff an' get back."

"Say, why d'they want this extra? We got 'nough back there to blow hell outta anything."

"Guess the boss wants to send a special present to that fox, Cardani. D'you hear what happened last night? One o' the boys was just tellin' me—when the boss weren't 'round."

"Yeah. They took Mike the Knife and some of his boys. Looks like an inside tip-off to me. I know who wants his place."

"All right. Let's quit the gabbin' an' shag this stuff inside. If he's brought it, the dirty louse. I don't like something 'bout that guy. I'll bet he gets us into trouble some day. His eyes're too damned shifty."

"Hell with him. You hold th' light, an' I'll get it out."

Inch by inch, Cardani got the blackjack from his pocket into his left hand. He knew now what he would try to do. He shifted as the men approached the wagon end and squeezed between it and the impenetrable if frail barrier that hid the lieutenant's tense form.

The horse was munching steadily, with an occasional stamp of a foot. That and the men's thick breathing were the only sounds. Cardani had to act quickly now if at all.

Softly, noiselessly, careful not to disturb the rag pile, he skirted it around to his left, crept closer.

"This looks kinder damned funny," one of the men muttered. "He ain't packed it like usual. Hold that steady, damn it, will you?" There was a grunt as the man reached further in. "Yeah. Here it is."

Cardani was almost at their backs now, his approach as soundless, as unsuspected, as that of a jungle cat. One man, at his right, was standing upright. He held the lantern. The other was twisted sidewise with one arm thrust far in. His head was turned to the side. Cardani could see one eye. He saw the eye suddenly widen, grow startled. He leaped the last few feet, struck once, a second time, accurately, a light flick of his left wrist, heavily with his revolver-weighted right.

The bows thudded dully. There was no other sound. One man lay over the wagon tail; the other slumped softly to the rag pile. Paul whirled, caught the falling lantern as it slipped from inert fingers, righted it, and set it at one side where he had light for the work in hand.

Both men were unconscious. Cardani found strong strips of cloth from the rag pile, twisted them, bound the hands and legs of the two men. Groping in their pockets he found handkerchiefs, fashioned them into gags, secured them firmly in place. He worked swiftly, silently, without waste motion. When he was finished, he rolled them apart from each other, covered all but their heads with rags. He was ready now for the next step.

Drawing the dynamite package from its place of concealment, he stripped off the outer paper wrapping, which he rewound around rags and a stick he picked up. It made about the same bulk. He shoved this under his left arm, caught up the lantern with his left hand. His right held his revolver, no longer concealed in his pocket.

He moved over to the side door, opened it, stepped through. A short passage confronted him. He followed it to a turn to his right. Half a dozen steps led downward. He descended to a landing with a turn to his left and the same length of stairway leading upward to a door.

He went up, pushed the door open, and stepped into a passage of considerable length. Turning sidewise, he got the lantern behind him and looked along the passage. At a little distance from him, there was faint illumination that came from one side.

Cardani walked straight onward, shuffling his steps a little, trying to imitate the coming of more than one man.

He came to the source of illumination, saw that it came from cracks in a weathered door. With a single deft movement, he stripped the lantern of its chimney until its flame was bare.

Setting the hot glass on the floor at his feet, he turned the doorknob, pushed the door wide, and stepped inside.

At his first glance, it seemed to him that fully a score of men were gathered in the long room in which he found himself, busy with various occupations. The light was plentiful but carefully guarded. His one swift look over all picked out a lathe, a rack of pipes, a long shelf with shorter pipe lengths, bottles, a litter he lacked leisure to identify.

Not one man glanced up at the moment of his entry. A second later a tall man at one end twisted his head slowly, then screamed in alarm. Heads shot up; men came to their feet, then froze in strained attitude.

Cardani's pistol muzzle swept back and forth, covering man after man. His eyes were everywhere, but not for an instant did he pause. He eased the package under his left arm to the floor. He lowered the open flame close beside it, set his foot against the lantern.

"I'm here to shoot," he yelled. "Hands 'way up—everyone!"

The menacing revolver, at steady arm's length, swept down the line, back and forth, paused momentarily where there was the slightest hesitation. All hands were aloft, but Cardani read desperation in the eyes glaring at him in bitter hatred, as well as fear.

"Stand as you are!" he told them. "Try anything, any one of you, and I'll shoot to kill. You know what I have at my feet. A touch of my foot, and fire takes it. That nitro on the shelf over there. I can't miss it."

He waited a tense moment, studying the effect of his threats. He didn't like what he saw. One or two of the men were close to hysteria; a third, a low-browed swarthy man, looked as if he were weighing a desperate chance. Paul lacked opportunity more than to glance at individuals, his swift look making what it could of their attitudes, their expressions. But he knew that the leader, that Coremo himself, was over at his right, cold, calm, although his eyes blazed, watching, waiting.

Cardani drew the whistle from his pocket, blew three swift blasts. He dropped it from his lips, tensed forward, the revolver cocked.

Men swayed at the sound. Some glanced swiftly toward Coremo. One commenced to blubber. The swarthy man partly lowered his hands, began to turn slowly to one side. His eyes were on Cardani, reckless, desperate. A little removed from him, on the shelflike counter, was a smallish bottle containing a white, oily liquid. If he could reach it, hurl it when Cardani's attention was momentarily diverted—

Paul seemed to read his thoughts. He let his eyes flicker at the man. There was a shadow of movement over to his right, near where Coremo was standing, a swaying of hands in the air, the slow shifting of a body. Cardani sent a swift glance that way but caught the start of the swarthy man's quick motion even as his eyes began to leave him.

There was a crash of splintering glass just behind the man. Half of the window burst inward. A heavy pistol swept downward in a half arc, cracked on the man's outstretched wrist, then steadied on his heart. Largio's head came through the opening. His eyes were black, shot with dancing light.

"Steady there, you!" he called to the man who had yelled once with pain, then faltered backward. "Your number's up. All right, Chief. I got 'em covered from this end. Watch it! Your *right!*" he shouted suddenly.

The warning came an instant after Cardani had caught the swift movement. A man who had been swaying slowly to right and to left, suddenly ducked, slid behind Coremo, and came partly upright with a pistol in his hand.

Past Coremo, the lieutenant saw the man's arm and shoulder. He shot instantly, the report making thunderous sound in the narrow space. The man screamed, staggered more into view, one hand clutching his shoulder, with blood already showing between his fingers. The thud of the pistol on the floor came like a faint echo to the report.

Cardani stepped away from the light powder smoke, a little nearer Coremo. There were sounds, now, of yells and shouts from back and front, the pounding of feet in the passage outside, hammering blows on a door at the far end of the room. Cardani turned more squarely to face Coremo. The leader's face was pale. Fear was commencing to creep into his eyes, drenching the blazing hatred.

The passage door burst inward. Ocelli first, then men of the platoon came piling through. A panel of the stouter rear door was splintered. A hand came through, pushed the bolt, and a rush of uniformed figures, nightsticks drawn, followed its opening.

Under cover of Cardani's revolver, Coremo was searched, knife and pistol taken from him; then his right wrist was handcuffed to the left wrist of a big, red-haired sergeant. One after another Coremo's men were manacled and led into the stable, where the first two men whom Cardani had encountered were beginning to recover consciousness. The march to Headquarters started.

Cardani and his two first assistants waited. They were still looking over the deadly paraphernalia when a man from the newly formed Bomb Squad arrived to take over.

22

CARDANI HAD DEVELOPED a third-degree method of his own. It did not include physical violence, although its threat might be invoked. In principle it was purely mental. It was designed to utilize the mind of the prisoner to wreak his own havoc, working upon his reason as well as his fear.

It consisted in placing clearly before the man a picture of his own inescapable plight, proving to him beyond peradventure of doubt that conviction stared him in the face, and then showing him the measure of punishment called for by his crimes. This was not done all at once or solely by word of mouth. It was gauged shrewdly to the character of the man in question, the strength of his mental resistance. He began first with Tasso, against whom a writ for first-degree murder was being prepared.

Tasso was incarcerated where no lawyer, sent by associates now at large, could reach him. So far as they had knowledge he might already have been executed or shot, so completely had he disappeared. Lawyers, familiar antagonists of Cardani in the courts, searched frantically for him, as they were likewise doing for Vira and Coremo. The precinct records yielded nothing. Tasso had been booked and was being held under a different name.

His cell was alone, away from other prisoners. Its corridor was dark, its silence broken only at regular intervals three times a day when a jail attendant, dumb to all questions, brought him meagre food. He was left thus for forty-eight hours.

From his records, Cardani prepared the progress of his planned visitations. He had scores of witnesses to outrages in which Tasso was either a participant, or where known associates of the leader had been apprehended. He had two or three witnesses of extortion demands made by Tasso himself, when violence had followed shortly.

Cardani selected the witnesses for his present purpose carefully and drilled them in what they were to say. At the end of the forty-eight hours he was ready.

At fifteen-minute intervals, one group followed the other, each with its separate story, recalling to the prisoner the pitiful incidents of his gory trade, crying aloud now for the justice that would no longer be denied them.

The last of the parade came and departed. Half an hour passed. Then Cardani came with Tito Carmello. This witness, who would send the murderer to the chair, had needed no coaching. Through the undisturbed days of his waiting his feeling had crystallized into a single purpose that was not vengeance but the desire for just punishment.

Carmello used no invective as he faced his brother's killer. And he was without fear. Calmly, almost stoically he recited the details of the crime, describing Tasso fleeing with the bloody knife, his gesture, his expression as he left the victim who had done him no wrong.

When they turned silently away, Tasso was in tears, broken. He sensed their going and rushed to the bars, pleading frantically with Cardani to come back. Only the dull sound of their retreating steps answered him.

At daybreak Cardani returned and entered his cell. Tasso was haggard, his eyes shifting wildly from object to object. Utterly shaken, he appealed to Cardani to aid him, to limit the charge to his lesser crimes.

Cardani disregarded his pleading. As if he had not heard, he went on to tell his conception of the whole vicious organization in a way that convinced his hearer that he spoke from complete knowledge. He repeated the words he had overheard spoken by members of Coremo's gang when he lay concealed behind the rag pile; that Tasso's capture was due to an inside tip from a man who coveted Tasso's place. Then deftly Cardani sought for names.

Tasso told him many, unknowingly supplying links that had long been missing from the lieutenant's chain of information. Despite his despair and his apparent willingness to placate his captor by any means, he would not or could not divulge the identity of the mysterious leader. And for the time being Cardani had to be content.

Almost concurrently he applied the same method to the two other imprisoned leaders, Vira and Coremo. From the former he obtained information comparable to that given by Tasso. With Coremo he had better fortune. Confronted by victim after victim, maimed and crippled by the terrible weapon with which he had wrung blood money from so many, caught inextricably in the web of evidence which under Cardani's skilful direction was woven around him, the bomb-maker finally broke completely.

The information dropped from Coremo's trembling lips not only pieced out his whole gang's organization, hideouts, and places of operation, but also definitely identified the man Lupo as the adjutant of highest authority, the man who brought orders from the head, stipulated lawyers for defense of their men, collected a percentage of their takings for the supreme leader.

Who this leader might be, the whining Coremo asserted over and over again that he did not know. He took oath on whatever he yet considered sacred that he had not the slightest suspicion of the man's personal identity. Whether Cardani believed him or not, he at least recognized that he could get no further at the moment.

Fatigued as he was by the days of ceaseless mental effort he had given to wrest these confessions, he nevertheless lost no time in hastening to his own quarters to pick up again the clue threads surrounding the Ravino murder.

Ocelli and Largio were playing seven-up. They put away the cards when they heard his step.

"All right, boys," Cardani greeted them. "Let's have it."

Largio gestured to his companion.

"I found the fellow I was looking for yesterday," Ocelli began. "He and his three friends were returning from the docks late. He remembers seeing a wagon with one horse, two men on the driver's seat, on Spring the other side of Broadway. He didn't notice, or couldn't remember, more than that, except that it was going west.

"One of his friends works in the Bronx, the other two in Jersey. He is getting their addresses for me, and I'm to see him this evening. I'll keep after it."

Cardani nodded. "And you, Largio?"

"That's about all I got too, Chief. I've talked with maybe fifty men who were out that late along the route. Two remember seeing the wagon; one on Rivington east of Third; the other between Elizabeth and Mott. They don't remember any sign.

One thinks he would know it again and one of the men on it, but the description he tried to give me would fit a dozen. I got their names and addresses, and they will come when I want 'em."

"That means," Cardani said, "we'll have to find it by some other means, then call them for identification. All right. Ocelli, you follow your end of it. If you can get any better description, I'll give you a couple of men. If you find someone to tell you the color of the horse, it will be easier. We must find that wagon and one of those two men.

"Largio, you know where Maria dePasso lives. Work between her home and that cooperage. I want someone who saw Ravino and the two men who met him. Maria says that people were on the street when she came home. Talk with her. She may be able to help. Some person who was in that section between the time Ravino left the girl and half a hour or an hour later must have seen three men together. Get that person. Stay with it. What we want is a description of those three men or any one of them. Got it?"

"I got it, Chief." Largio stood up. "Be seeing you."

He went out.

Ocelli had the rest of the day until evening before taking up again the work to which he was especially assigned. Cardani took from his desk the murder weapon that had ended the life of young Vincent Ravino. He handed it, carefully wrapped, to his first assistant. He then gave him brief notes, signed by himself, to three addresses.

"These men," he explained, "will tell you for me what they know. Don't tell them what that knife means. Get any information positive or negative. Either way it will check what I already suspect. Leave your report if I am not here."

For the next hour he busied himself bringing up to date the records of the torch gang's very active operations. Until the last few days Largio had been assigned especially to this field. Working closely with the lieutenant, between them they had actually anticipated the setting of fires in one or two instances and had arrested a number of men in the act.

Like many of his other prisoners, these men were booked and held pending the accumulation of other evidence. Their conviction would have been a simple matter. Cardani wished to use them to involve the larger gang. With the additional information now before him, he decided that he was about ready to confront these prisoners, force further facts from them, and lay plans for the capture of the arson mob.

With this work finished, the lieutenant turned again to his earliest files of Italian newspapers. He might be engaged on a thousand different occupations, but incessantly, in the back of his mind, one query obtruded—who could be the mysterious head of the appalling organization of crime?

Paper after paper he examined and returned to his files. Every report of a prominent criminal who had escaped justice abroad, or whose activities there had suddenly ceased, he studied with minute care. He looked at pictures, photographs, and sketches, weighing the power in evil of the types shown, constructing a mental estimate of individuals, comparing one with another.

23

FAR FROM SATISFIED, he was still in the midst of this work when a call came that a prisoner was asking urgently for Lieutenant Cardani. Although he was engaged upon a most important task, Paul set it aside without a moment's hesitation. He had a sudden hunch; and he always played his hunches.

He never knew whence would come vital information; his experience had taught him that it could emanate from most unexpected sources. Often he had befriended men under arrest awaiting trial, such as the one now calling for him, who, gaining confidence in his fair dealing and wishing to help themselves, had given him material assistance.

In a few minutes he presented himself at the precinct house on Clinton Street between Delancey and Broome. Sergeant Cassidy at the desk greeted him warmly. He led the way to the cell tier.

"Dunno what's the matter with this guy, Lieutenant. He's in a hell of a stew, ever since his old woman come in to see him. And a funny thing; he made a big secret of it. He didn't want any o' the other lads we got in here to know he wanted you. Well, here he is. Go inside if you wanta. Rattle the door when you want out."

The sergeant unlocked the cell door and locked it again after Cardani had entered.

The lieutenant found himself facing a short, thickset man with broad, low forehead, flat nose, and square chin. His black eyes were very bright, worried, and a little wild in their look.

With his memory for faces and details, Cardani recalled the circumstances of the man's arrest a week or two earlier.

The prisoner eagerly caught Cardani's arm, urged him as far from the door as the space would allow.

"Listen, Lieutenant," he began in a low, husky voice. "Th' boys tell me you're a square shooter. You're out to get us, an' that's all right; but they tell me you know how to keep your tongue behind your teeth an' don't go back on your word."

"What's your name?"

"Toni Zapretti. They got me on a hold-up with a knife, and maybe I'll get a stretch. That's all right. But will you keep a thing to yourself?"

"I can, if it's the right thing to do. What's on your mind?"

"Lissen. There's some fellers I been playin' with you ain't got on to yet. Don't ask me 'bout them. Won't do any good. But this's what they done to me. They know I been jugged, an' they're 'fraid I'll shoot my mouth. They've taken my little girl. Carlotta's only eight, an' all I got. They sent word to me by my old woman if I spill they'll give her the works."

He paused, glanced apprehensively toward the cell door, then turned more toward the wall.

"They oughta know me better, but that's what they done. And I know those fellers. If somebody tells 'em I been lippin', an' somebody don't like me damn sure will, they'll slit her throat like that."

He snapped his fingers.

"If they get any kinder idea I sent for you, they'll do it, too. You gotta work fast. I want you to get her. Take her to her mother, an' they'll beat it to Jersey. I don't care what they do to me, an' if I go up they can't reach me for awhile. So what the hell. I want my little girl outta there."

"All right. Tell me about it."

Zapretti leaned closer, lowered his voice to a hoarse whisper. "I'm tellin' you something now, Lieutenant, but I gotta do it. There ain't nobody else to help me. They got two places; one where they take kids when they wanta hold 'em a while or get rid of 'em. It's over by the river." His voice sank to a faint, barely audible breath as he gave the address and described the place.

"You gotta get inside 'fore they know it if you do any good, an' you gotta go alone, or they'll spot you comin' an' get suspicious. When they brought me in here they took my stuff away from me. There was two keys. You want the short one. There's always two fellers there, 'cept round meal times one goes out for food. You get there at six."

Cardani regarded the man soberly. Here was a chance that he had long awaited. Zapretti by his own admission was of the kidnap gang which so far had proved peculiarly elusive. Cardani, it is true, had made numerous rescues, had effected a number of arrests, but he had not made serious inroads on the gang itself.

With the information he now possessed he could strike a telling blow. By playing on the man's agony, he could probably wring more from him. He chose to play it another way.

"All right. What's your wife's address where I can take the child if I get her?"

Zapretti told him.

Without another word Paul turned and rattled the door. Sergeant Cassidy, who must have been waiting not far away, promptly let him out. In the office Paul asked for Zapretti's effects. Among them he found the two keys described. He took the shorter one, returning the rest to the police officer, who was watching him curiously.

"Couldn't tell a guy what's up, could you?"

"I'm playing a hunch. You'll know about it if anything comes through. And, Sergeant, there were some more men brought in about the time Zapretti was taken. Can you shut off their visitors for a few days?"

"Can and will, Lieutenant. Glad of an excuse. Say, if you need any o' the boys where you're goin', gimme a ring."

"I might at that, Sergeant. Thanks. 'Bye."

Cardani glanced at the clock, saw that he could get to his destination by walking, with a little time to spare, and set out. He found the neighborhood readily enough. The address he sought was one door from the corner down a short side street that gave no sign of tenement occupancy. The corner, with windows on both streets, was taken by a tobacconist's, which seemed the only retail shop in the immediate vicinity.

Cardani walked past, on the opposite side, not hurrying particularly, but with the air of passing through to a definite destination. He turned his head neither to right nor left, but his keen eyes missed little. The tobacconist's, he decided, was a lookout station. It could be manned at all hours of the twenty-four since there appeared to be living quarters on the second floor of the mean, two-storied wooden building. Along the street were a couple of small machine-shops, one or two loft buildings apparently for dead storage, and several nondescript structures whose former use was problematical as they now seemed abandoned.

He crossed over at the end of the block and turned the corner. Ahead of him the way ran the length of two building lots to the East River. He went as far as the alley running back of the building he had come to visit, saw that it was merely a dark passage between walls. Save for a few footprints in the dirt, it gave no sign of frequent use. He had seen no person since first entering the street. Altogether the whole immediate section seemed deserted.

He came back to the corner. Having observed a partially open door to a disused building, he stepped directly to this place of concealment. The space inside was utterly dark, but after listening a moment he gave it no further thought. He found a weathered crack in the door, saw that it gave him a view along the face of the buildings and set himself to wait.

He consulted his watch, found that it was close to six. In a very few minutes a man came out of the building next to the tobacco shop, sent one swift glance down the block, turned, and disappeared around the corner at a leisurely pace.

Cardani waited thirty seconds only, then walked swiftly forward, keeping as close as possible to the wall line. The key was ready in his left hand; his right was sunk in his pocket. As he came near he flattened himself to the wall and extended his left hand to the lock. The door was flush, and he had no difficulty in reaching it.

He worked the key softly, felt the catch slip, and with his right hand turned the knob. The door opened noiselessly, as if the hinges were oiled. Getting his right hand back to his pistol butt, he pushed the door wider, slipped inside. He closed it without sound and relocked it from within, returning the key to his pocket.

He found himself in a sort of crude vestibule with its inner door ajar. He moved to this, paused listening, and was instantly aware of a voice somewhere beyond. The words were indistinguishable, but the talking continued. He tried the door gently, found that it also gave no sound, and pushed it slowly open.

Before him was a square room that seemed once to have held merchandise. At one side an unrailed set of stairs led upward. Beyond the stairway, toward the rear of the building, light showed an inch-wide streak at a door edge. From beyond the door came the sound of the voice, a low, snarling, guttural rumbling.

Cardani kept close to the wall, where the chances of a board creaking were less, and crept carefully forward. As he advanced, words of the talker became clearer to him. Apparently it was a one-sided conversation. There were no questions asked; no answer, in words, made.

"Stop yer bawlin', you dirty little brat. Won't do you no good, an' it makes me sick. See this knife, don't ye? Keep it up, an' I'll slit that throat o' yourn from ear to ear. Aw right, if you wanta cry I'll get the knife ready, good an' sharp."

There was the sound of metal rasping on metal, a little, half-smothered shriek, the slap of a blow.

"You're goin' to get it anyway, fer a lesson to yer gut-spillin' father. Jest wait till it gets dark, an' the water is black an' cold. But when yer goes inta it yer won't know nothin' 'bout it, with yer throat wide open an' th' blood drippin'—"

Cardani had reached the crack of the door. He could see a little of the room beyond. A child huddled miserably against the wall, face hidden by trembling hands, through whose fingers tears were steadily falling. A big man stood close before her, his back partially to the lieutenant. He was bent above the child, gloating. One hairy hand held a knife, but the child, with her eyes covered, could not see it.

The man began to talk again, to taunt his helpless victim, driving her terror to the point of hysteria. Under cover of the sound and with the advantage of the big man's preoccupation, Cardani eased the revolver from his pocket, got it flat in his hand, put his left hand on the door edge. He pushed it wide, sprang the two paces that separated them. He struck heavily as the man started to turn.

That one savage blow was enough. Senseless, the man began to slump. Cardani caught him, eased him to the floor. The little girl tore her hands from her face, shrank backward with stricken eyes. Her mouth opened to scream her fright. Paul spoke quickly.

"All right now, Carlotta. Don't scream. We're going home. I came to get you. He can't hurt you now."

The child ran to him, grasped his arm in hands that trembled violently, pressed close against him.

"That's the girl," he said quietly. "But now we must hurry."

He cast swiftly about him, saw some strands of rope beneath a rough table. A heavy weight at one end gave sinister suggestion. He caught up the knife from the floor where it had fallen, cut the rope free, bound the man's arms and legs. Finding a handkerchief, he stuffed it into the man's mouth, secured it in place with a cloth. He was little worried whether or not the child's captor might suffocate.

He crossed the room to the rear door, saw that it was heavily bolted inside. It was the work of a moment to get it unlocked and open. The lamp-light showed a couple of steps leading to the dirt of the alley.

"Now, Carlotta," he said, "we're going home this back way. We'll have to be very quiet, for that other man may come back. But you keep close to me and don't be afraid. Step out the door. Wait there for me."

The child obeyed instantly. Paul got his bearings, blew out the light. In spite of the man's bulk Paul raised him easily to his powerful shoulder. He eased through the doorway, pulled the door closed behind him. The child, still terribly frightened, started to whimper her protest that the bad man should be brought along. Cardani soothed her with a word, and she caught his free hand.

Seemingly unhampered by his burden, he hastened out of the alley, turned to the waterfront, and hurried along it for several blocks. There he set his still unconscious prisoner to the ground. He drew his own handkerchief from his pocket and bound it over the man's eyes, forming at the same time a bandage of a sort for the cut scalp. Taking his whistle from his pocket, he blew it shrilly.

In a few moments, up the street a little way, a patrolman appeared, caught sight of Cardani's waving arm, and broke into a run. He came up blustering, billy in hand.

"What the hell you got here, cully?" he began.

Cardani cut him short. "Lieutenant Cardani of Headquarters. What is your precinct?"

"Thoirteenth, sor," with a salute.

"Ring the wagon. Get this prisoner to Sergeant Cassidy. Tell him I sent him in and will see him about the booking. Tell him I said to give the man no information whatever, and that the charge is serious."

"Yis, sor. Shall I lave him here while I get the wagon?"

"Where's your call box?"

"Nixt corner."

Cardani stooped, swung the man up again, and started off.

"Aw, let me have him, sor."

"Run along and get your call in. I'm in a hurry."

Finally relieved of his prisoner, Cardani led the little girl over to the Avenue, where in a few minutes he was lucky enough to find a closed carriage, apparently returning from a call. He gave the driver the address of Zapretti's wife.

Before the tenement, the lieutenant remained in the carriage, preventing the curious from catching even a glance of the little girl. He sent the driver up to get the woman, with word to bring her bag. She was down in a moment. Her eyes were stricken, staring straight before her a little blankly. She seemed numbed with fright and worry.

Cardani cautioned her sharply to silence until they could get away from the crowd which the strange sight of the vehicle had quickly gathered. Once around the corner, however, she took the child in her arms, rocking back and forth as she smothered it against her ample bosom.

At the lieutenant's direction, they went directly to the precinct house. Accompanied by Sergeant Cassidy, he led the child and her mother before Zapretti's cell. He left the three together a moment while he explained matters to the sergeant, directed that the new prisoner be kept apart, and asked that a man be detailed to see Mrs. Zapretti safely to the ferry.

As he turned to leave, Zapretti signaled to him. Cardani stepped close. Zapretti thrust a big, hairy hand through the bars, gripped the lieutenant's hard.

"Come see me," he whispered hoarsely, "before I go up. You're white."

24

EVERY DETECTIVE OF experience knows that the breaks form a most important part of the solution of a big criminal case. They count upon them in their work, and the more clever they are, the more alert they hold themselves to catch the significance of facts or evidence that may turn up unexpectedly before them.

Cardani was not satisfied to leave his discovery of the mysterious personage he was seeking entirely to a break, but for the moment at least he had to be content. Meanwhile he decided to push his plans to round up the last two formidable leaders—Biretti of the arson gang, Spiro of the kidnapers. And Lupo. All of the older squad men were quietly seeking information about Lupo. The Federal Secret Service men, directed by Chief Thomas himself, were concentrating on that search.

All the wheels of his complex machinery of crime-fighting were turning; not one was idle. Not even those of silence and aloofness that were working relentlessly upon the spirits and minds of his formidable captives, Vira, Tasso, and Coremo.

Cardani consulted his watch. It was still early. He had a moment's respite. He might even take the evening off without detriment to his work. He turned to his desk, picked up a letter which he had momentarily laid aside.

It was a note from Giulia Ravino, thanking him for the flowers he had sent, suggesting that he call if he should find the leisure, bringing his violin and the music of which he had spoken. They were very quiet and lonely, she said. They were not going out at all. His call would not be an intrusion. And she owed him amends for her hasty words. The invitation was confirmed in a brief postscript by Giulia's aunt, the Signora Alfredo.

Subtly Cardani's expression changed as he reread the missive, but not to a look of happiness. He could not visualize happiness in the outcome. To him Giulia Ravino appeared as unattainable as she was utterly desirable. He recognized poignantly their difference in class and position, culture and breeding. With his rude upbringing, he was keenly sensible of his lack of polish. He did not pause to reason that polish is primarily a veneer, ultimately a veneer unless substantiated by stolid substance beneath.

Paul Cardani thought straightforwardly. He was fully aware that the whole emotional side of his nature was given irrevocably to Giulia Ravino. It would be the one love of his life. But, he told himself relentlessly, even if by some miracle it should be reciprocated, it would be unfulfilled. He could not, would not, subject one whom he treasured so deeply to the dangerous vicissitudes of his own existence, pledged as it was to the accomplishment of one purpose.

To him, to be in the presence of Giulia Ravino was like listening to a glorious symphony with a theme of melancholy that left him unsatisfied and distraught, with his whole soul yearning for something he could not define, let alone hope to attain. Yet, regardless of its effect, he knew that he would seek it over and over again.

After a little while, Ocelli came in. Cardani went over his reports carefully, sifting the helpful from the negligible, advancing materially his search for the source of the weapon.

Ocelli had done his work well. With the information he had brought, Cardani could confidently show the weapon for identification to Coremo, the admitted associate of the suspected owner, Lupo. But that would be deferred a little. He wanted time to work more havoc on Coremo's resistance for this important step.

After Ocelli had gone, the lieutenant left the office in charge of one of the men from the squad, called punctiliously at Headquarters, where he confirmed the fact that nothing of importance claimed his early attention, and went on to his own rooms.

It was yet early in the evening when he presented himself at the brick house off Tompkins Square, a stalwart figure in neatly pressed blue. His freshly shaved face had lost its look of fatigue and worry. He looked alert, competent, and dependable.

The white-capped maid showed him at once into the living room, where Giulia, her father, and the Signora Alfredo rose to extend their quiet greetings. Giulia's rich coloring was slightly paled. To Paul Cardani she appeared gloriously beautiful, her dark eyes a little haunted, pleading.

He laid his violin case aside, came back, and took the chair indicated. Damiano Ravino at once launched into a subject which Paul had earlier broached to Giulia.

"I have been talking to some of my banking associates, Lieutenant. They are keenly aware of the present situation. The continued depredations are causing serious interruptions and losses in various businesses in the locality, which are being felt by the banks. Insurance is high and difficult to obtain. Destruction of property calls for withdrawals of capital for rebuilding.

"The two or three men with whom I have so far spoken

know the splendid work that you are doing. They are agreed that in common interest you should be given every possible support to bring this crime wave speedily to an end. If they can be assured that attention will not be called to them, they will give you such information as seems to them proper. For myself, you can call upon me freely for whatever you desire. I shall leave to your own discretion to safeguard what is now left of my small family."

Cardani nodded soberly. Damiano Ravino had changed. He seemed to have aged by ten years. His manner was still alert but carried the air of prolonged weariness. There was not a vestige of the somewhat provocative intolerance which had marked the lieutenant's first impression of him.

"I can give that assurance," he said. "As a matter of fact such information as they might give me would only be suggestive and could do no harm if not repeated, which of course would not be done."

"I will then write letters to them for you. These men are friends, business acquaintances of long standing. In addition there are several private bankers with whom I am less acquainted, although my name should get you entrée to them. I refer particularly to Walter Brindisi, the Rossi brothers, and Sebastiano Gambroni. The last, Gambroni, I know scarcely at all. He is a comparative newcomer among us. Within the past two years he bought the private banking business which he now manages. I am told that he is quite wealthy, and therefore he probably controls some important accounts. I will speak with these men if you think it advisable."

"I think you have done enough, Mr. Ravino. I advise strongly against speaking to anyone beyond a close personal friend in whom you have confidence. We are beginning to get closer to the higher circles already. With the great amount of money involved, we cannot tell what lines even in the banking field they may cross."

Ravino regarded him soberly. Paul was aware that Giulia was watching them both, listening apathetically. Beyond the first greeting she had spoken no word. He wished that he might talk with her. He wondered what he should say.

"We have read something of your recent doings in the papers," Ravino said. "It would seem to have been enough to break any ordinary organization, but the crimes have not ceased. You walk in constant danger," he added.

Cardani smiled, shook his head. He noted that Giulia closed her eyes for a long moment.

"No, although it might be so if I were unprepared. As it is, it is just like any ordinary business. You get so you don't think about it." From the corner of his eye he saw that Giulia was looking at him again. "I can't estimate the time, but I think the end is almost in sight."

"Ah!" Ravino stood up. At the door he turned around. "I wish you would have some music." He looked at Giulia. "It won't do my little girl any good to go on like this. Cheer her up, Lieutenant, and I will be obliged to you. I will write the letters now."

Giulia watched his going. Then she glanced up at Cardani and smiled a little, her eyes sparkling with moisture. "Will you play something—anything?"

Signora Alfredo caught herself in the midst of a sigh. "Yes, please do, Lieutenant," she said, with an attempt at brightness.

He got up, crossed the room, and took the instrument from its case. He tested the strings, turned to them, and smiled.

"Now, don't expect too much. I was my one and only pupil."
He struck a few chords lightly. "Here's one—I believe I haven't
played it since I was a kid. It was a favorite of my old friend
Luigi Busano."

Without further hesitation he launched into a merry air
from *Rigoletto*, "La Donna e Mobile." He played it softly
but with boisterous tempo, giving everything he could to its
cheery swing. At the end they were both smiling, which was
the reward he sought.

"But that was excellent," Signora Alfredo declared.

She stepped to the piano, hunted through sheets of music
until she found what she wanted, then seated herself on the
bench. "Will you let me try one with you, Lieutenant?"

He came and looked over her shoulder. "*Ciribiribin*. Hm.
Well, I'll try."

She gave him the key notes, and he retuned the violin. They
played the piece through once, then a second time, and Giulia
clapped her hands.

Her aunt swung around on the bench, looked up at Paul. "I
think we did that very well." She got up. "Now, Giulia."

The girl came to her feet, walked slowly to the bench which
her aunt had relinquished, and seated herself. Her slender,
well-formed fingers wandered gently over the keys without
striking them. She glanced up at him.

"What shall it be?" he asked, trying hard to keep from his
voice what he knew must be in his eyes as he looked down at
her.

A little color came into her cheeks. Her long dark lashes hid
her eyes as her glance returned to the key-board. "Didn't you
bring something—the one you spoke of?"

He laid the violin on the piano, crossed to the case, and came back with a music sheet. "It's by Eduardo Di Capua. *O Sole Mio.*"

"Oh, I'd love that."

He placed it on the rack, picked up the violin. "It has the piano and violin arrangement. I haven't tried it yet."

Her fingers touched lightly the first and last chords. "I think we can do it." She smiled up at him. "If not the first time, later anyway."

They played it slowly at first. Gaining confidence, they swept through it a second time with more expression, each seeking the other's time and emphasis. As they finished, Signora Alfredo was standing a little at one side, with averted glance.

"I will ask Maria to fetch us some tea and cake," she said very quietly and left the room.

Paul placed his violin and bow on the piano. As he turned about, Giulia was standing, close beside him. Their eyes met and held, telling, asking, pleading.

Scarcely aware of the impulse, of the first motion, Giulia was suddenly in his arms, her lips pressed to his. Then her head was on his breast. She was sobbing, trembling, clinging close.

His strong arms held her steadily. His lips swept her hair, pressed her forehead.

"Giulia!" he whispered huskily. "Oh, my love, my love. I tried so hard not to let you know. I'm not worthy of this."

Her moist eyes came up to meet his; her head was bent back a little. Her hands slipped up to his shoulders.

"Paul," she said. "It was this from the first day. And now I need you so. I'm frightened and lonely. I need your strength and courage. I wouldn't want to live without you."

"It was so with me—from the first moment I saw you. I felt it was utterly hopeless. Your position, and mine. Your refinement and the coarseness of my life and work. The dangers I love you too much to let you share. To see you again and again, I knew would be only torture. My strength? I couldn't resist it. To have you for my wife—ah, that was beyond my wildest dream, my dearest hope. I'm not worthy of you, Giulia."

"Hush!" Her finger pressed his lips. "Paul, I know you. These terrible times have made me see clearly, far beyond mere appearances, in everything. You are the finest man I've ever known, have ever hoped to know. I shall be proud of you—if you want me."

He pressed her to him gently, kissed her lips and forehead almost reverently, led her to a chair and stood beside her.

"I want you," he said very quietly, "more than anything else life could possibly hold for me. I feel that I am utterly selfish in asking. I have no more judgment. Happiness has swept that away from me. I shall talk with your father—let him decide."

She caught his wrist, pressed his hand to her warm cheek. "Not now, Paul. Not tonight. Wait a little while. I do not want now to think of questions, of decisions. And I have already decided. It shall be nothing else, no matter what happens—if you still want me. Now I want to think only of this happiness. It helps me. It gives me strength only to think of you—that you love me. You do?"

"Oh, my love, my love," he whispered.

"What, no more music?" Signora Alfredo spoke from the doorway. She came in slowly.

"Only its discussion, Auntie dear." Giulia's tone was light; her eyes very bright. She did not, however, glance toward her aunt. Cardani stepped away a pace, waited until the signora had seated herself.

"Maria had everything almost ready. It's such a relief to find a maid who anticipates," Signora Alfredo chattered cheerfully on. "But we must repeat this evening, Lieutenant, whenever you can find the time to spare. Damiano is really anxious that Giulia should take up the opera again. The season is on, but I haven't been able to persuade her."

"I wish you would let me take you both to a performance."

"That would be delightful, Lieutenant. Don't you think so, Giulia?"

"Yes. Whenever—he has the time."

"May I send word the first evening I am free? I shouldn't want to make an engagement and then break it."

"That is the only way we should want you to do it," Giulia said. "And whatever evening it is you will find us ready."

The maid came in, set a light table with a white cloth before them. When she returned with a large silver tray with tea things, Damiano Ravino joined them. He gave to Paul the several letters he had written.

Later, through the hours of the night when Paul did not seek to sleep, he thought he could recall every slightest incident of that most eventful evening of his life. But whether he drank tea or water, ate cake or *ravioli,* he had not the least idea.

25

HAVING PRIMED HIS forces for action all along the line, it was perhaps not surprising that, moving simultaneously, events broke fast. Yet Cardani himself was hardly prepared for the deluge of activity that suddenly swept down upon him.

Messages, reports, a train of informers and witnesses stormed the third-floor offices on Lafayette, testing the stocky lieutenant's executive ability to the utmost. Each individual matter demanded his personal knowledge and attention; he could ill afford, in what he hoped was the final push, to neglect one.

Early in the morning, Ocelli brought in the four young men who had passed the wagon transporting Vincent Ravino's body from the cooperage shop to the Spring Street alley. Amalgamating the impressions of the four, a fairly definite description was obtained of the single horse and wagon and even of the general appearance of the two men on the driver's seat.

On top of this, a saloon-keeper, interviewed by Largio and to whom Cardani was favorably known, brought in a patron who independently confirmed the description already given and added the important detail of a certain marking on the side of the wagon seat.

That was enough. Instructing the witnesses to be ready for a call to identify, Cardani assigned two of the squad men to Ocelli for a swift search through the quarter for the murder vehicle and its drivers. He even arranged for secret incarceration of the wanted men, or suspects, in view of their importance in the chain of evidence he was implacably welding about the yet unknown murderer of Giulia's brother.

Ocelli and his men left. Ceruti and young Tulio Busano came in, bringing with them a man of substantial appearance.

A destructive fire, of indubitably incendiary origin, had occurred the previous evening. Ceruti, happening to be in the office when the report was received, had followed it up automatically. The man he had brought in was the owner of the burned factory, who gave to the lieutenant a written message of threat he had received several days earlier and ignored.

Cardani compared it with specimens in his files. Expert in chirography, he checked it at once with the handwriting of the gang leader himself, Biretti. Satisfied that the comparison would stand in court, he made plans for Biretti's capture that evening.

The general locality of Biretti's hideout, within the space of several buildings, was already known to the squad. Cardani believed that, following the spectacular fire, the leader and his closest men would lay low for a day or more, keeping in their quarters. It was the opportunity he sought.

Ceruti, who had scouted the knife men so effectively, was assigned the task of finding the exact hideout and of discovering if possible the presence of its occupants. He was told to report his progress without delay. Meanwhile, the lieutenant would arrange with Headquarters to hold a platoon in readiness for this service.

Young Busano had also brought in threat letters which he had picked up in his previous day's rounds. One Cardani added to the Biretti file; the two others he could not readily identify and laid aside temporarily. But he had immediate work for Busano of another nature.

There was the kidnapers' hideout for children to be scouted. Paul wanted very much to learn of the effect produced by the mysterious abduction of Zapretti's child and her brutal captor, of the afternoon previous. While he had purposely delayed this investigation, it was important to him to know whether or not the gang had taken alarm and abandoned the place altogether.

Tulio was instructed to roughen his appearance to that of a laborer. From his father's establishment he could procure a horse and wagon of nondescript appearance. He was to take a load of old iron pipes and unload them in one of the unused store-houses close to the building in question. He was to arrive before twelve, work lazily, if necessary eat his lunch on the job, at any rate remain through and beyond the noon hour. His orders were to note, without arousing suspicion, every detail possible of any person leaving or entering the place.

And all this while messages flowed in from Headquarters and precincts in the section; a hold-up here, a stabbing there, a night burglary, a daylight shop robbery, face slashing, a batch of immigrants tricked by the time-worn bandanna shift. Routine which kept the lieutenant's spare men scurrying, but which he handled in his stride.

With barely a pause for a hasty snatch of lunch he yet found time for a quick visit to his rooms. Here he selected the most treasured volume from his choice if small store, a book well thumbed from careful reading, therefore infinitely more personal than a fresh copy. Thence to a florist; and the two packages soon found their way to the brick house off Tompkins Square.

Men of his small command marveled at his unflagging energy from early morning through the day, used as they were to his iron resistance to fatigue. From his unsmiling, almost sombre features, his cold, dispassionate handling of affairs, they could not guess that beneath it all his heart was singing, that he was looking upon his work with new zeal, with renewed confidence in the value of its purpose, and with impatience for its early completion.

In late afternoon, Largio came in with the insouciant air which Paul had come to associate with some work well done. Hard on his arrival the phone rang. Paul interrupted Largio's leisurely beginning to answer.

It was Ceruti calling from a drug store. He not only had discovered Biretti's hang-out, but as well had found a friend in the neighborhood. A clerk in a local shop had provided him with the information he most desired; knowledge that a number of men were in the hideout. His friend, Ceruti said, had also described several of the men, one of whom Ceruti was certain matched the picture he had seen in the office files of Biretti. In addition he had sketched a rough plan of the building they occupied, with its front and rear exits.

Cardani asked Ceruti the address of the drug store, told him to wait there, then to return when relieved by Largio. He hung up.

Largio apparently had forgotten his urge for a theatrical beginning, for he launched directly into the meat of his report. "Well, Chief, I think I got something for you. I'll skip now telling you how I came to it, 'cept I found the feller's girl first. Anyway I got a guy who saw three men together the night of the murder.

"He was saying good night to his girl in one of those convenient double doorways. There was a gas lamp at the foot of the steps. This—did I tell you?—was only 'bout a block from the cooperage place and a little while before midnight.

"Anyway he had the outer door a little open, 'count of the girl's folks being out and expected any minute. When he heard steps on the sidewalk, he took a peek. Three men were coming along, close to the light, and he saw them well.

"Listen." Largio hitched himself more upright from his slouching position in the chair. "The one in the middle answers to young Ravino. I didn't tell him any names and didn't ask any when he said they were all strangers to him. The feller on the outside, he said, was pretty big, with a long jaw and a dark face which looked as though he'd had chicken-pox or may be smallpox, at that."

"Lupo!" Cardani breathed.

"Uh-huh. That's what I thought. And now get this. The feller on the inside was a kinder dapper guy with a quick step and dressed as though he had plenty. Little over medium height, plump, well-fed build, rather roundish face; and the guy told me this—says he thinks he saw a thin, straight, white scar from the corner of his left eye down on his cheek. Anyway, he was sure his hair showed gray at the side under his bowler.

"If the feller I talked with," Largio drawled, well aware of the effect his words were producing, "hadn't been kinder nervous who was coming he wouldn'ta taken such a good look. And I say a nervous guy like that has his use after all."

Paul's look was faraway. His mind was racing over the many pictures he had examined countless times, searching for even faintest resemblance. Muscles were bunched at his jaw angles; his mouth was a straight hard line. Presently he shook his head. His eyes returned to Largio. And Largio sobered and averted his own glance from their piercing intensity, which seemed not to see him but to bore through and beyond him.

Paul stood up. With a rare display of feeling, his right hand rested on Largio's shoulder, closed in a grip that made Largio wince in spite of himself.

"Nice work, Pete. That's our first sight of the big chief; and it fits. He would be like that. Deceptive. Will the man you found appear if wanted for identification?"

"He'll tell you anything you want, Chief; but he'd rather not face anyone."

"Well, we'll see. Now I'll shoot you out to relieve Ceruti." He gave the address. "Send him right in. We'll start the raid as soon as I get his report. Before you go off tonight I'll want you to write the full description the man gave you, with his name and address. Perhaps in writing it you can recall some detail you forgot to mention. You've done a great day's work. I'm proud of it. Now hurry out there."

"Thanks, Chief. Be seeing you."

Cardani closed his desk and hurried over to Headquarters. First arranging that a platoon should be assembled and held in readiness for the forthcoming raid, he next sought Chief Thomas of the Secret Service, whom he found on the point of leaving the office assigned to him.

Inspector Sherwin, learning that the lieutenant was at Headquarters, came in and joined them. "What's this shenanagin you got on for tonight, Lieutenant?" he asked.

Cardani explained, then told him of the fire the evening previous and his belief, now confirmed, that the gang would hole up for a short while, affording an opportunity to catch many of them together. That, he said, was the reason why he

wanted to push the raid at once, without waiting even for darkness to mask their approach.

"Well, now," Chief Thomas said, "if you're at all right about
that other feller, Lupo, maybe that's what he's doing too. We're
getting pretty close to his hole, but we haven't found anyone
who's seen the cuss lately."

"That's what I have come to see you about. We have."

"You have what?" Sherwin demanded.

"Found someone who described him as a man walking with
young Ravino shortly before the murder."

"Judas Priest! That's a break."

"How close are you to him, Chief?"

"One of three houses on one street, or may be one of two
on the street that backs it. We haven't been pressing too close.
You didn't want us to."

"I think," Cardani said slowly, "that we'd better take him
now; say in a couple or three days. Will that give you time to
get his exact location?"

"I can get it any time we want to push it. You aren't afraid of
scaring your big man off, huh?"

"Lupo's become too important to lose. Can you spare some
good plain-clothesmen for the chief, Inspector?"

"Anything he wants, except the City Hall, and may be I
could get him a slice of that. What's on your mind, Lieutenant?
Perhaps he doesn't want any help."

"I can't afford to lose Lupo at this stage. At the same time I'd
like to give him a couple of days more to see if he might lead us
somewhere, especially at night, late, when I'd want him tailed.
Meanwhile, I'd like to have the stations covered, the ferries and
the docks where there 're boats sailing."

"That's all taken care of," Chief Thomas said, "ever since I got my men in. If you want this guy tailed, I could use a couple of good pick-up men, so my men won't be spotted." He shook his head a little doubtfully.

"Today," he went on, "we took in a couple of passers in Jersey and another in Philly. That means the stuff is still going out, or they're working off what they had. Either. I've gone about as far as I ought to, Cardani. My job is to get those plates. I've been playing it on your hunch this guy's got a boss. If we pinch him and miss the plates, we don't know where to look unless you know the boss. If I wait much longer I'm going to hear from Washington. I'm telling you, I'll be damned glad when you say to put the squeeze on this guy."

"If I don't find anything in forty-eight hours," Cardani said steadily, "we'll take him."

"Huh!" Sherwin exploded. "Got something up your sleeve, you old fox?"

"N-o. It's just that things are breaking fast. I had three turns of luck today. I believe we have the arson gang leader cornered; we have men who spotted that wagon, and this about Lupo. We're closing in and are bound to get the big break soon. I'd like to wait for that; but it wouldn't be fair to the chief here. Besides I can't lose Lupo now."

"Oh, hell," Thomas said. "Day or two more wouldn't matter. That feller can't get away from me now. It's only I'm damned curious to see what he's got in his hole."

The grizzled inspector was watching Cardani shrewdly. "All right, keep it in your muzzle," he growled. "Go ahead now and have your party. Want me along with you?"

Cardani smiled. "No, thanks, Inspector. You take too many chances."

Sherwin gave him a jab in the ribs, and swore. "And that," he said, "hurt my wrist more than it did you. Man, you're iron."

"That," Cardani said lightly, "is because I don't eat too much and don't sit in a chair all day."

"By God! I believe you've got something up both sleeves. I haven't seen you grin like that in months. And just going out to raid those hooligans, too. I know damned well something's come over you."

"Lieutenant," Chief Thomas said softly, "remember, if you stop a bullet or get a chiv in the ribs this evening, my party comes off tonight, so help me."

"Forty-eight hours, Chief." Cardani stood up. "Inspector, would you mind ordering that platoon right over to my building? I've been waiting for my man to come in. He should be there now. Good night, gentlemen. Pleasant dreams."

"Pleasant hell," Inspector Sherwin growled after him. "I've a damned good mind to order you to stay here and let the platoon do the job. Only they'd probably muff it, and you'd get sore at me. Careful, boy."

26

THE ARSON GANG hideout, as Ceruti described it, was a somewhat narrow house of three stories, flanked by an alley. A tobacco shop occupied all of the front except the space required for the house entrance. The shop had doors on both the street and alley, and from it, according to Ceruti's informant, there was probably an entrance to the house itself.

Often, the man told Ceruti, his curiosity had been aroused by seeing more men come out of the shop than he had observed entering it. There had been no trouble with the occupants of the house, he said, but the place did not have a savory reputation. It was shunned, and, under the wave of terror, men would have nothing to say about it.

In the rear of the house was the usual back yard with a shed for storing wood. Behind that, a second alley ran between the rows of buildings, at right angles to the street-to-street passage.

Cardani assigned Ceruti to the sergeant leading half the platoon, with instructions to move up on the rear and cover that end and both alleys. The lieutenant himself led the other half directly to the drug store, where Largio was waiting. This, fortunately for their purpose, stood on a street corner, with an entrance concealed from the three-storied house and with a window from which Largio had been watching the doors of house and tobacco shop. He reported that no person had come from the house itself, and no more from the shop than had entered it.

Cardani's orders to the platoonmen were to wait until they

had seen him and Largio enter the tobacconist's. Then to proceed directly to the house door, ring for admittance, and if not answered break their way in. Accompanied by Largio, he set out at once.

Crossing the street, they walked leisurely toward their goal. As they reached the alley, Cardani glanced down it and saw the other half of his small force approaching from the further street. The timing was right. The afternoon had advanced toward evening. No lights were yet on, but the interior of the tobacco shop was in dusk. As they entered, a man, the only occupant at the moment, stood behind a showcase and counter on the side next the house wall. When they were inside, the platoonmen would begin their approach. The two detectives had to work fast.

Largio stepped directly to the counter, rapped a coin on the glass case. "Gimme a pack of Sweet Caps," he demanded. When the shopkeeper made no immediate move to comply, Largio glanced up at him.

The man was watching Cardani, who was making a swift survey of the place. Largio saw suspicion in the close-set, black eyes and rapped again sharply.

"Hey! Sweet Caps, I said. Come awake, will you?"

"I heard you," the shopman said without looking at him. "Say, what do you want, feller?"

Cardani jerked his head sidewise to indicate Largio and stepped forward toward the house wall, where, near the rear corner, a dark cloth hung from the low ceiling to the floor.

"Say, you," the man repeated sharply to Cardani. "That anything to you?"

Paying no heed to the excited, angry voice, the lieutenant

reached out his hand and swept the cloth aside. Behind it was disclosed a door set flush with the wall but still discernible.

Largio saw the shopkeeper's quick movement as he bent forward and stretched a hand beneath the counter, saw his arm tense as he pressed something upward. Largio leaned over, grasped the wiry wrist, and drew it back. He was not quick enough. The alarm had been given.

Cardani glancing over, caught the situation immediately. "Take him, Pete," he snapped, and turned his attention to the door, which seemed to have neither knob nor latch.

Largio yanked the man over the counter, whipped bracelets from his own belt, and, seeing an upright pipe in one corner, dragged the man to it and cuffed his arms around it.

Cardani, baffled for the moment, turned around. "We're officers," he said sharply. "How does this door open?"

"Officers be damned," the man snarled. "You'll get yours in a minute."

Largio slapped him hard on the mouth. "Think so? Take a look out that window."

He pointed across the street where eight stalwart figures were moving purposefully along. Largio made his hand a fist, pushed it against the shopkeeper's nose, twisted it hard.

"Better be good, feller, while you got the chance. Speak your piece and speak it damn quick. How do you get in that door?"

The man's face had paled perceptibly. He turned his head, glanced wildly over his shoulder.

"Piece o' metal back o' the showcase," he whispered. "Stick it in the slot an' lift up."

Low as were the words, Cardani's keen ears caught them. He sprang to the counter, found the metal strip. Back at the door, he saw the narrow slot which he had missed before. Thrusting in the metal, he felt it engage a latch, but before lifting it, he drew his revolver from his pocket. By that time Largio was beside him.

"Better wait a second, Chief," he said in a low tone. "The cops are just crossing over. They'll be at the door in a minute."

Cardani had no intention of waiting. He stooped low. "Keep back to one side, Pete," he said swiftly, pressed the metal, and pushed against the door.

It swung readily inward against a well of pitch blackness that was instantly split by a sharp flash from somewhere a little above him, with the startling crash of a pistol shot.

Cardani scrambled through, with Largio close behind him, slamming the door as he got out of its way.

Paul fired once in the direction of the flash just as a second shot burst from that higher level. Largio reached out his left hand, located the lieutenant's shoulder, then his own pistol crashed three times in quick succession. The sound of a sharp cry and steps running upward mingled with the echoing reports. An instant later there came a heavy pounding at their left and a hoarse demand to open up.

"Let 'em in, Pete," Cardani ordered, moving forward. "The stairs must be there. Cover the door we came through. Don't let anyone get away."

"Better look out, Chief. They can shoot down from that stair-head and can see you when—"

He stopped talking. From higher in the building and toward the rear a sudden fusillade interrupted him. From the rapid reports it seemed as if three or four pistols were in action.

Faintly, in an interval of comparative silence, yells sounded in the back yard; then the crash of an answering volley.

"Judas Priest!" burst from Largio. "The sons of guns were ready for us. Will you hear that now!"

Cardani was no longer beside him. He had groped his way in the darkness until he located the stairs, then turned back to the door which was directly opposite their foot. Slipping the bolt, he threw off the chain that guarded it. He twisted sidewise, sent two quick shots in the direction where he guessed the stairhead was, and threw the door wide open.

"Come on, men!" he yelled. "Largio, watch that side door!" Then he sprang for the stairs he could now see and started running upward. A rush of feet and shouting men stormed after him.

He reached the top without meeting opposition. There he paused for a moment, peering along the faint corridor. A couple of closed doors were at one side. He turned, stretched out his open left hand, restrained the men pushing upward to join him.

The firing in the building had ceased. Occasional shots were still coming from the back yard, followed by the crash and tinkle of breaking glass. From somewhere above there was the dull sound of movement.

"Below there," the lieutenant called. "Two of you men go back down. One outside to watch the basement exit."

He turned toward the rear of the house, came to a window with closely drawn shade. He allowed that to run up and, standing at one side, raised the sash, waved a hand, then peered out.

Below, some of the platoonmen had taken shelter behind the small shed; others were peering around the walls of the closest buildings, pistols ready, alert. Cardani thrust his head out.

"Come on!" he shouted. "Break in that rear door. Two of you wait outside. The rest come up. Clean out everything as you come!"

Turning back, he stepped along the corridor, signed to his men to silence. The sound of movement from above had ceased. For the moment there was intense quiet.

"If there is any more shooting," he yelled, "we'll kill every man in the place."

No answer came from above. Below there was a sudden splintering crash as some heavy object struck the rear door; another, then the sound of heavy footfalls tramping into the house.

One of the men lit a gasjet in the corridor. Cardani flung the nearer door open. With revolver ready, he stepped boldly in. Two men were standing beside a window, one holding a bleeding arm. He walked to them, felt them over roughly. No weapon was on them or in sight. He herded them out, where the patrolmen handcuffed them together.

Paul entered the second room, found it empty. As he came out, the burly sergeant who had mounted the rear stairs, pushed through the men and joined him.

"We're cleanin' out the rooms downstairs an' the basement, Lieutenant, like you told us. Where's the rest of 'em?"

Paul pointed upward with his revolver barrel; where the stairway led to the third floor. Without a word, he started up at a run. He heard a growling curse, the sound of steps following, but he went onward without a backward glance.

At the top was another corridor, blank, running away into greater darkness. Cardani made out a gas-jet, turned the cock, and lighted it. The flame showed a door right at hand. He flung it open, saw the first of a group of men crowding close together, their faces dark, sullen. No weapons were in sight; their hands were at their sides. They stood silent, motionless, watching him, their eyes blinking a little in the light.

Paul's revolver was out of sight, although his hand grasped it in his pocket. He did not know until later, when he chanced to glance around, that the big sergeant stood close to his shoulder, his heavy service pistol raised and ready.

"Make a light in there," he ordered sharply.

After a short delay, a man further back in the crowd scratched a match, a jet hissed and flared. Paul stepped boldly in. A dozen or fifteen men faced him, still in that motionless, sullen pose. He glanced at them sharply. They could be waiting for a quick, simultaneous break, a sudden blasting of their pistols, a rush for freedom. Watching them keenly, he stepped a little to one side, grasped the first, and pushed him roughly toward the door.

"All right, Sergeant," he called over his shoulder. "Take them and pass 'em down."

"Hey, men," the sergeant bellowed. "Get the cuffs on 'em, get 'em down, and hold 'em."

Cardani sent the second and the third man stumbling toward the door, where the burly sergeant, pistol still in hand, propelled them further. Then the group began to shift, to dissolve, and move of its own volition to the exit. This abrupt surrender with no word spoken, without resistance, all acting as one, bothered the lieutenant. He had not before experienced anything quite like it. Usually, in raids of this sort, especially after the gun battle that was put on, one man, small groups would fight it out to the last, cursing, threatening, complaining.

Suddenly he caught the idea. They were acting under orders.

Someone with an authority they recognized had told them to quit and go in peaceably, no doubt promising sufficient defense in court; had advised them to dispose of their weapons, for although both Paul and the sergeant slapped each man as he passed, there was not a concealed pistol or knife in the lot. Whether that was true or not, Paul told himself, they would find out later. At the moment a more important matter concerned him.

He had looked swiftly over the crowd, he had scanned more closely each face as it went by him. Biretti, the leader, the man he wanted more than all the rest, was missing. He was not one of the two first taken downstairs. He had not been in the crowd here; not since the lieutenant had come into the room.

He grasped the last man as he was about to pass through; caught his shoulders and swung him violently around. His hands gripped hard, biting into muscle. He bent his face close.

"Where is Biretti? Where did he go?"

The man squirmed and twisted, wincing under the pressure. "He ain't here. I haven't seen him."

Paul rocked his head with a sharp slap. "You lie. I know he was here. Where has he gone?"

"I tell you I ain't seen him. He hasn't been here at all. Beat hell outta me, an' I'll tell you the same thing. He ain't here."

Cardani's hard look bored into the shifting eyes. Suddenly he flung the man from him through the doorway.

"Hold him for me, Sergeant. If we don't find Biretti, I'll get it out of him. He's lying, and I know it."

"What's the matter, Chief?" This was Largio who had worked his way up past the push on the narrow stairs.

"Did you see Biretti down below there?"

"No; and I've seen everyone they've pulled out of closets and the wood-bin. Didn't you find him here?"

Paul turned away. The suspicion that the wily leader had outwitted him, had managed somehow in the general fracas to make his escape, angered him beyond measure. But the hot rage that sent blood to his face did not blunt his judgment, his keen manhunter's sense of the way of fugitives.

That he had been here, Paul was morally certain. With every nook and corner curried, it was just as obvious he was here no longer. Therefore he had gone out. But how, with all possible exits covered? All except—

Paul ranged that highest floor. He looked through the two other rooms toward the front of the building; sleeping quarters with frowsy, unkempt cots. Back in the room where they had made the big take, he opened the door of a closet in the rear wall. Garments were hanging there. He swept them from their hooks.

Light did not enter here in sufficient strength, and he lit a match. By its flickering light he examined the back wall, saw a small round hole in a narrow board into which he might thrust a finger. There was no knob, no latch, but a portion of that back wall seemed to him to have the markings of a crude door.

His match went out as Largio squeezed in behind him.

"Close the door, Pete," he said in low tone, and took his revolver from his pocket as the light from outside was cut off. "Get a match ready to strike. Ready?"

"All set, Chief."

Paul had marked the spot; now he set his shoulder against the place, shoved hard. The door gave easily without hinges, fell inward with a great clatter. Paul, with his own effort and the little resistance of the door, stumbled to his knees. His free hand came down hard on the rough edge of a joist. He held himself there, raised his pistol.

"Match, Pete!"

Largio reached his hand through the opening he sensed was there, scratched the match, held it high, cupping it with his hand to keep the light off the lieutenant.

Before Cardani was a ten-foot stretch of unfinished attic ending in a blank wall. His glance swept swiftly around. It was bare of any obstruction, empty of the man he sought.

"Hold it, Pete. Get another going. I've got it. Quick!"

With the light Pete Largio provided, Paul stepped on a single board that gave a catwalk across the narrow beams toward the rear of the building. A few feet along this, he stopped and peered upward.

He was directly under a trap, and he saw instantly that the hasps that had fastened it were now hanging loose. He gave a low exclamation of satisfaction. Largio pressed close beside him, also peering up. The house, as Paul had earlier observed without giving it particular thought, had a mansard roof with a level top. Whether it gave access to an adjoining roof was a matter to be determined without delay, for without doubt someone had recently passed out this way.

"Must've been a ladder here," Paul whispered, "and they pulled it up. Get a couple chairs, Pete. One, if it's all you find in that first room. Hurry," he added, unnecessarily as Largio was already at the opening.

"Hey, Lieutenant! Where the hell are you?" a voice bellowed from the room just beyond.

Largio reappeared, pushing a chair before him.

"Tell the sergeant to come here, Pete; and not to make too much noise."

Paul lighted matches while Largio came into the attic, followed by the big sergeant, who was grumbling to himself.

"What the hell you got here?" he growled as he crept up beside them.

Paul pointed upward, took Largio's chair and set it, shakily at best, directly beneath the trap. "You fellows hold it. Get your shoulders together so I can step on 'em."

He held a match while he stepped a little gingerly on the chair. When he tried to straighten, he found that his shoulders could reach the trap and that his arms had a good purchase against it. He shifted his pistol to his breast pocket, with the butt sticking handily out. Both men were braced, bent over, gripping the seat and back of the chair. Paul saw just where the big sergeant's shoulder was, the step he must take to reach it, and blew out his match.

Placing the palms of both hands against the flat under surface of the trap, he pushed upward, hard. The trap did not give at all, but the chair wobbled crazily. One of the sergeant's big feet slipped off the narrow joist edge, went down through lathing and plaster until he himself brought up astride it, in the midst of unrepeatable blasphemy.

Cardani came down, caught himself catlike, and was partly supported by Largio. He lighted another match, while the sergeant extricated his foot with some difficulty and the aid of more profanity.

Largio grinned at the red-faced, discomfited policeman.

"It's all right," Paul murmured. "Someone's sitting on that trap. Which means he can't get off the roof. We've got him.

Pete, bring over that door. Should've used it before." He stepped a little to one side to give Largio room.

"Got him, hell!" the sergeant growled. "Well, I'll get him off his perch anyway."

Before they saw his intention, he had whipped out his service revolver and fired straight up at the trap. The report in the narrow space was deafening. As it died down they heard footsteps shuffling hastily along the room above their heads.

"I moved him all right, by God," the sergeant crowed. "Now let's get him."

With the chair now more securely in place, Cardani mounted once more. This time, against his pressure the trap gave readily. He eased it up a little. Instantly there came the crash of a pistol shot. Splinters stung Paul's face.

Supporting it with his left hand, Paul drew his own revolver. Through the crack he held open, he made out a chimney against the early evening light. It seemed to him the shot had come from that direction, that he could see an uneven shape at one edge. Aiming at the bricks, lest his bullet go beyond, he fired a single shot. The uneven shape disappeared.

"Stand up here, Pete," he ordered, and when Largio was beside him. "Cover that chimney while I go up. Sergeant, get my right foot on your shoulder."

"You're crazy as a loon," came from below him, but he felt his foot lifted, placed on a meaty shoulder.

Paul went through and stood on the roof. Pistol ready, he started to circle toward the chimney on the narrow roof top. An instant later Largio was beside him.

"We'll take him from both sides," Largio said, and moved

over. "You hold him here, Chief, and I'll get behind him." His tone was loud enough to carry.

Paul caught him, held him back.

"Come on, Biretti," he called. "Throw your pistol and step out. We've got you."

There was a moment's hesitation.

"You'll shoot me anyway."

"Throw out your pistol and we won't shoot. Wait another minute and we will come, shooting."

A heavy object clattered on to the slates. A figure showed at one side of the chimney. Paul stepped straight to the man, grasped his arm, while Largio slipped around the chimney behind him.

"Scratch a match here, Pete," Paul told him.

In the flare he peered closely at his prisoner's face.

"All right, Biretti. March!"

The big sergeant received him below the trap, slipping on handcuffs without delay.

Biretti, the fourth gang leader, was taken.

27

PRESSURE WAS BEING brought by the District Attorney's office with regard to the many prisoners being held, even though the matter had the sanction of Headquarters.

The District Attorney himself was in entire sympathy with the plan Paul was working out to smash the whole organization, and made inquiries only when it was advisable. But after all, he pointed out, there were recognized methods of law and procedure that must be observed. Therefore formal charges must be made and the prisoners brought before a jury for indictment.

Paul had no fear of losing the indictments. His cases against each were too well grounded. Nevertheless he was now obliged to complete them in presentable form for the court. And while he had every assistance Headquarters and the legal department could afford, the work demanded his constant personal attention. He alone was conversant with all the facts and the manner in which the charges could be made lawyer-proof.

Day and night he gave to it with unremitting fervor, in a fever of anxiety to make an end of it and get on with his other work. None knew better than he that a criminal organization of this type could be a mushroom growth so long as its fungus roots were undisturbed.

Given time, new leaders, just as evil, just as powerful, would be enlisted from the original source. The ranks could be even more easily recruited. Under the direction of that still unknown chief in command, a new and perhaps more menacing organization would be speedily built on the structure of the old and launch its operations. Small wonder that Paul Cardani fretted, drove himself and his assistants relentlessly. Simultaneously he endeavored to carry on the outside work, drawing the net closer and closer, leaving no loopholes unguarded.

Ocelli and his men brought in the two drivers of the murder cart. They were put away against the time when Paul hoped to have his all-important prisoners. Young Busano came In with his report on the kidnaper's juvenile hideout. He had seen two men emerge. One answered closely to the description of the suspected leader, Spiro; the other, to that of the companion of the man whom Cardani had so forcibly abducted.

Paul had plans to close in on the place, set a trap, and capture what he could. For the moment he was too occupied to put them into execution.

He set Largio and Ocelli, when he could possibly spare them, to roam the quarter in a wild hunt for the mysterious chief of whose rather vague description they were now possessed.

And with it all, he yet found time to send messages to Giulia, small presents of not too obvious significance, and to gladden his heart with her notes when a late hour of the night finally found him in his rooms, alone.

On the second day following Biretti's capture, Chief Thomas sent him word that the man Lupo was definitely located, was holed up without question of doubt. That evening Paul went with the Secret Service men and several of his operatives.

The work of preparation had been so efficiently done, the ground so effectively covered, that the capture was a simple matter and not in the least spectacular. Lupo at heart was a coward. Even when cornered, as Paul had earlier shown, he would not fight.

When Cardani and Thomas gained access to the house, burst through the door of his room with drawn revolvers, Lupo raised his hands and submitted to the manacles with only vocal remonstrance. But the Secret Service men made their haul. The plates and a large amount of spurious currency were uncovered after a short search. Lupo himself was spirited away to the secret cell which earlier had held Tasso.

And there Paul left him, temporarily, to be worked upon by his own method of third degree, whose first steps were silence and solitude. He was elated, for now the end was almost, almost within his grasp. Yet he preferred not to confront Lupo, to wring from him the confessions and admissions he knew he could obtain, until he had at least the name of that one man above them all.

Back again at his desk, after a few days more of the same hectic concentration, his cases were complete and dispatched to the District Attorney's office. The decks were once more cleared for him of their drudging routine.

That afternoon, his first free moment, he called at the house off Tompkins Square. And he found that Giulia's love for him was anything but a figment of dreams. Both were now of the same mind. Paul at once set out for the banker's offices on Second Avenue.

Damiano Ravino had indeed greatly changed. Above his pride, his ambition, he wanted happiness for the child that now remained to him. Also, alert to the possibilities of the matter, he had taken counsel with Paul's lifelong staunch friend, Benito Pianelli.

So, within a very few minutes after Paul was admitted to the private office and had presented his case, he came out, radiant, scarcely crediting his fortune. Giulia alone was nominated the arbiter, and in Giulia's decision Paul had ample confidence.

He hastened back to her with his news. They agreed upon a short betrothal, an early marriage. They also arranged to go that evening to the Metropolitan.

It was a gala performance. For perhaps the first time since boyhood Paul gave himself entirely to full enjoyment. His mind, his whole soul was filled with the rhapsody of the music and Giulia's nearness. He had thought of no other thing on earth or in heaven. For once, the sombre downtown days, even his own set purpose, were forgotten.

Finally the music ended. The rhapsody continued. Unhurried, arm in arm, they allowed the gay throng to bear them slowly to the exit doors, to the foyer. Abruptly he felt the arm pressed close in his stiffen in quick tension. Surprised, he glanced sidewise at Giulia's face. Her color, rich all evening, had paled slightly; her long lashes were lowered over downcast eyes. He felt her arm tremble. Instantly he sought the cause. He glanced in the direction she had been facing the moment before.

A man in full evening dress, with opera cloak thrown open, was lounging against the rail before the closed ticket office. His dark eyes fixed on Giulia were brilliant with admiration; their look almost predatory.

Paul saw all this in a flash; yet continued to look. He was partly shielded by some person who stood between, although the stranger's gaze was for Giulia alone. Paul saw a well-rounded figure of a little more than medium height, a smoothly shaven face with full cheeks; hair gray at the temples beneath the opera hat; a thin, white scar line from eye corner straight down the cheek.

A sudden sensation chilled Paul's blood; then set his pulses madly pounding. A spring, impelled by vision of that face, released a shutter; memory instantly brought him recognition.

He did not recall a description that had recently been given him. Memory went far beyond that, back to the days of his childhood. Seconds only passed; merely the space of time while figures shifted and intervened. Yet in that meagre period, an old drama was re-enacted before his mind's eye.

He saw a thinner face, a leaner form. He was in the fields and meadows of Calabria.

A neighbor's child had been taken by a Mafia band. The neighbor, with Paul's own father, had gone to a lonely spot to pay the ransom and receive the child. Paul, hardly more than a child, unsuspected, had followed.

Concealed behind a bush, he had watched the men meet. This man before him now was that leader, hard, forceful, a cruel sneer on his face, the scar a livid welt. Paul saw the money paid, the band, laughing, walk away. He saw his father stoop and pick a limp form from the ground. Paul saw the dangling arm, blood streaming from the mutilated hand, the kidnapers' callous method of intimidation. Sickened he shrank back. Then rage possessed his childish heart.

The band was just disappearing over a low hill. Paul set out in pursuit, without purpose or aim. He felt that he must follow them, to witness, perhaps, the inevitable punishment he knew must overtake them. Screened from discovery he saw them pause on the edge of the not distant monastery grounds. One of the men took a sack from his shoulder, shook out a monk's black cassock, which the young leader donned. The rest of the band disappeared in the wood.

With cowl over his head, his crossed hands fumbling the string of beads, the scarred leader set out slowly toward the monastery wall. Curiosity now getting the better of him, Paul followed. It was near the noon hour. Most of the monks were still in the fields. The place seemed deserted as Paul crept to the massive doorway, peered cautiously in, saw the pseudo holy man walking slowly away from him down a long dim corridor.

From the further end a man and woman, in civilian dress, were approaching. Why they should have come, how admitted, perplexed Paul, but he had little time to ponder this. As the three met, the man and woman paused, asked some question. The false monk's reply was as quick as it was unexpected.

His left hand, thrust into the bosom of his cassock, whipped out with the gleam of steel. Swiftly it rose and fell, struck into the heart of the unsuspecting victim. The woman screamed, a sound that haunted Paul's dreams for many a night. She turned, ran desperately down the corridor, her cries ringing frightfully. The murderer sprang after her. Once, twice, his hand rose and fell. She stumbled, lay prone, motionless.

Paul saw no more. Blindly he rushed into the bright sunshine, back the way he had come. The whole scene in all its details, the murderer's face were stamped on his childish mind in indelible memory. A man now, he recalled them instantly as he looked upon the same features still wreathed in their predatory expression as the man's glance rested upon Paul's lovely companion.

The throng shifted. Figures came between. Himself unobserved, Paul led Giulia to the sidewalk, presently found a carriage and helped her in. He gave the address in a voice that trembled slightly. He was exultant, triumphant. Here was the man who could be, must be, the secret leader of the great criminal organization.

Paul's careful search of all available records had eliminated all others. He had not come upon this man's record. This, the murderer of a rival leader in the formidable Mafia, and his wife, as Paul had later learned, must be the man. Suddenly he recalled the description given by Largio's witness of one of the two men who had accompanied young Ravino, Giulia's brother, on his last walk. It checked. That old scar, just as Paul had seen it in his childhood, would now be the thin, white line which the face still carried. Only such a man could have planned the organization, directed its operations and effected such frightful outrages.

At last the unknown leader was a mystery no longer. Paul had seen him, face to face. He did not for an instant doubt or question his conviction. He was certain of it. Now he had only to identify him.

Giulia laid a soft hand on his arm. "You are quiet, dear. Did anything disturb you?"

"That man who stood before the ticket window as we came out, who looked at you so closely—have you ever seen him before?"

"Oh, my dear, don't let that trouble you. I was so ashamed at the way he looked at me. I've seen him once with father. Father knows him slightly, I believe. He is Gambroni, Sebastiano Gambroni, the wealthy private banker. I'm sure I never want to see him again."

28

PAUL CALLED REDFIELD at his home and found that the commissioner himself had just returned from the opera. Paul told him the matter was most urgent, that he must talk with him at once. The commissioner invited him to come out.

Before starting, Paul's phone call awakened Inspector Sherwin, drew him growling from bed. Paul interrupted his grumbling, told of his immediate appointment, and asked Sherwin to join him at the commissioner's house.

When the three were seated in the library, Paul told them of his discovery, of his certainty that now he knew his man.

"But, my God, Lieutenant," Commissioner Redfield exploded. "You must be mistaken. Here is a man of position, reputed to be wealthy, rich enough at least not to dabble in crime. It would be fantastic, the height of absurdity, to accuse such a man of murder, of heading these Black Hand affairs. We would be the laughing-stock of the whole city, to say nothing of suits for damages. Man, you're crazy!"

"Commissioner," Paul said very slowly, "that is the man. I swear it. I know it. Who knows how he made his money, how he is making it now? I'll take my most sacred oath that Sebastiano Gambroni is the man we want.

"His description fits exactly with the description of a man seen with Lupo and young Ravino the night of the murder, within a short time of it, and in that same vicinity. I hadn't told you this. I wanted more to put with it. I have it now.

"Here's another thing; something that had escaped my mind.

This Gambroni answers the description of the man who was rumored to be connected with that affair of the Mafia and Black Hand in New Orleans, when Chief Hennessy was murdered and eleven of his killers were strung up by the citizens after the jury was intimidated and had acquitted them. This man escaped then; nothing was heard of him afterwards. But that would explain where he has been since he fled Italy for the killing of Cuoculo and his wife.

"That is the man, Commissioner. I'll stake my reputation, my life on it. I know it."

"If you're so sure of it," grumbled Sherwin, repressing a yawn, "why the hell didn't you pinch the ———— and let us all go to sleep?"

"We can't to it that way," Paul replied promptly. "We haven't enough on him yet to hold a minute in court."

Frowning, Commissioner Redfield made an impatient gesture. "What is it you want us to do, Lieutenant?"

"Put the best plain-clothesmen you've got on him, day and night. Not one of our squad; not one of his countrymen. Men that won't make a slip, who can tell us every step he takes; who comes to see him, at his home or office. Where he goes and whom he sees, particularly late at night."

"Well, I don't see that any harm can come from that. And I don't believe any good will, either. I can't agree with you, Lieutenant. Everyone must make a first mistake. I think this is yours."

Paul smiled. "If you will do that, I won't ask any more; except to see every report that comes in. I will do my own work in another way."

"And can we go back to bed now?" Sherwin grumbled.

Paul clipped him on the shoulder. "You're not so sleepy as you want to appear, Inspector. I believe you agree with me."

"You've never gone wrong on a man yet, boy, as long as I've known you, and I've known you quite a few years. I'll put the tails on this guy if he's the biggest banker in town, if the commissioner gives the word."

Redfield looked at both from under frowning brows. "If you should happen to be right—" he muttered, half to himself. Then aloud: "You've got to be right. What's more, you've got to consult me before you take any definite steps, no matter what your men report. All right, Inspector. Take what men you need. If your reports continue to be negative, call 'em off before we get into trouble. Good night."

Inspector Sherwin rode part way downtown with Cardani, who continued to the cross street leading to his own offices. Ocelli was in Paul's own office, chair cocked against the wall, feet propped on the table, reading a work on criminal cases. He said that Largio had come in late and was now sleeping on one of the back cots. Paul aroused him and brought him in.

With doors closed, speaking in low tones Paul recited the events and his discovery of the evening, including the assistance the commissioner had promised.

"If he's that guy," Largio said, "he'll be too foxy, Chief. They won't get a thing on him."

"I think so myself, with one possible exception. Lupo is out of the way. Gambroni may seek another contact man. On the other hand, he'll know about Lupo's arrest and the finding of the plates and bad money. He'll probably do nothing for a few days but cover up his tracks. He'll play to the limit the other side of his double rôle. And if he does that, it will tell us something.

"What I want to tell you boys is this: lay off looking for the man Pete's witness saw. I've found him. The biggest break we've yet had. We'll concentrate now on building the murder case against him."

"But what you got there, Chief?" Largio objected. "Nothing but a theory and a half-baked guy's word that he saw a man like that near the crime. Ain't enough."

Paul smiled. "We won't try it that way. The case we will build up will be against Lupo, for first-degree murder; the killing of Vincent Ravino. Ocelli has got the two men who drove the murder wagon. Gambroni never ordered them to do that. Lupo. We have the knife. My theory and every other circumstance suggest that the knife was not Gambroni's, but Lupo's. Do you begin to get it now?"

Largio smote the table with hard knuckles. "By damn, I get it. We'll convict Lupo and let Lupo—"

"Exactly."

"So what, Lieutenant?" Ocelli asked. His eyes were very bright.

"We'll let the commissioner's men trail Gambroni for a week or so. By that time I'll know about all there is to know on the knife. We'll put those two wagon men over the hurdles and find out just what they will spill. We have enough on them to make them come through. We have the plates found with Lupo and the bad money which we can match with the notes found on young Ravino. I want you, Pete, to get friendly with your man. He probably remembers Lupo better than Gambroni. Show him Lupo's picture. Get him ready to swear to it. Meanwhile, we will let Lupo stew.

"He is where no one can find him. No communication will

reach him; not one word will be exchanged with him until we are ready. Lupo at heart is yellow. I think he will be ready for us when we come, with what we will have to show him."

"Say, Chief," Largio asked with quizzical air, "don't you ever sleep?"

A rare smile swept over Paul's sombre features. "Plenty. But not so much when the trail is as hot as it is now. But that's no reason why you shouldn't, and we'll make an early start in the morning, and every morning until Sebastiano Gambroni is put where he can do no more mischief."

EVERY SKILL THAT Paul could command was set to close the net of unbreakable evidence around Lupo. He worked his men as he did himself, indefatigably. He planned the case he was to present to the prisoner as if Lupo were the suspect, the real criminal; yet every step taken he knew was bringing him closer to his final goal, the annihilation of the master mind of evil, Gambroni.

And every day he had evidence of the frantic search being made for Lupo. He let the rumor creep out that Lupo had been spirited away by Federal men who wanted him on the counterfeit charge. Chief Thomas sent Paul word from Washington of the inquiries his men had received, through prisoners, stool pigeons, even lawyers. Notwithstanding that, precinct men and Headquarters itself reported similar interest in the whereabouts of the man who had acted between the gangs and their supreme head. Paul heard and smiled grimly. If he had ever questioned its wisdom before, Paul knew now that his course with Lupo was the best. It was the one link to Gambroni. Gambroni feared it.

The inquiries could not be traced, not beyond a certain point. In each instance, some reason was given. But Paul did not care. He was satisfied that he knew their source; and the very fact of their existence proved to him that his theory was correct; that the chief and not the lieutenant was the real killer. He was closing in on Gambroni.

And each day he visited Giulia; sometimes for dinner or for lunch. Signora Alfredo was very pleased; Benito Pianelli, for once, enthusiastic. The day was set. The wedding would be as quiet as possible. But some of the family's relatives and closest friends would come. Also Commissioner Redfield and Inspector Sherwin insisted on being present. Pianelli, of course; the Busanos; and all of the squad who could be spared from duty.

It dawned at last. After the ceremony the party drove to the house off Tompkins Square for the wedding breakfast. What with Pianelli's reminiscing, the many little side conversations that developed in the family group, the many toasts, time fled rapidly. Dusk was falling when the bride and groom set out. As the carriage swung down Lafayette and drew up before their door, the street lights were just coming on.

Finally they were alone in the apartment. Within a few minutes there was a knock at the door, and Paul hastened to answer it.

The young shopkeeper from downstairs handed him an envelope with the word that a man in civilian clothes had just left it, saying that he could not wait for an answer as he was carrying a similar message to one of the other men. Paul thanked him, closed the door, and tore open the envelope with sudden misgivings.

"What is it?" Giulia called from a doorway beyond.

Paul was frowning. "It's from Ocelli. He says that an urgent matter has just developed with one of the prisoners we are holding and asks if I could come to the office for a few minutes and tell him what to do."

He turned, walked slowly to a set of drawers, and mechanically took his revolver from the topmost, dropping it into his pocket. Giulia was watching him with eyes that were a little startled in spite of her effort to be at ease.

"Must you go now?"

"I have ordered a telephone. They are slow in their installations. It will be in, they promised, next week. If I had it now I could attend to this without going out. There is none downstairs. The nearest is in the drug store a couple of blocks away. I suppose I can get there and back as quickly as I could phone. I won't be long."

He kissed her, caught up his hat, and hurried down the stairs.

He had gone two blocks, turned the second corner, when he heard running footsteps behind him. The street was a little dim. He waited until the steps were close upon him, then swung about quickly, his right hand in his pocket. He told himself that he had half expected something like this.

But it was no enemy that came rushing up to him. It was the shopkeeper's son, bareheaded, his eyes wild in a white face.

"Quick, Signore," he panted. "They have taken—taken the young Signora."

Paul grasped his shoulders. "Speak fast!"

"You were but just out of sight. A fight broke out up the street. I was watching it. Then I realized that an automobile was at the door. I went to look. Three men were just putting the Signora inside. Her head fell back; she seemed to have fainted."

Paul took two steps back up the street, stopped suddenly, swung around.

"Had they started off before you left to get me?"

"Yes, yes. They went away at once. But they were not out of sight when I—"

"Which way did they go?"

"Toward Broadway."

Paul tore the message from his pocket, thrust it into the lad's hand.

"Run to my office. You know where it is. On the third floor. Give this to anyone there. Tell them your story. Tell them to get to Headquarters and put out the alarm to all the stations. Tell them what the car was like. Do you understand?"

"Yes, yes."

"Run!"

Paul turned in the other direction, east, hurrying at his utmost speed along Spring, toward Delancey.

29

IT SEEMED TO Giulia that Paul must hardly have left the building when the sounds of some street altercation caught her attention. She stepped to a side window to look out. She could see some men scuffling, others quickly gathering. A light knock at the door swung her around.

As she crossed the floor, she wondered if Paul had returned to reassure her over the disturbance. She slipped the catch and opened the door.

The sight of three strange men startled her to silence. Before she could move, could catch her breath to scream her terror, they were upon her. One grasped her throat roughly, clapping a coarse hand over her mouth. Another held her shoulders. A cloth was thrust to her nostrils, closing over them. It was wet, with a sickish sweet smell. The grip on her throat relaxed. After two or three spasmodic breaths she lost consciousness.

She awakened to the rush of wind and jolting motion. The sound of flapping curtains was in her ears. She tried to move and found she could not. Her arms were bound. A hatted head was a little distance before her, another faced in the direction she looked. She saw the sheen of a windshield, the glaring path of headlights down which she was speeding, the flashing passage of objects within her narrow range of vision.

A scream rose in her throat, was throttled in her mouth. She could breathe only through her nostrils without difficulty. Some cloth or rag was stuffed into her mouth, bound in place by something tight around her neck.

At intervals light flashed through the windows of the side curtains. She sensed a presence at either side and turned her head to the right. A man taller than she was pressed close to her, his hand gripping her arm. She caught a glimpse of a hawklike nose, a thin-lipped mouth that was curled in a sneer, a flash of black eyes that seemed to gloat over her. She looked straight ahead.

The machine was not traveling fast. There was other traffic; a street car passed, several trucks, carriages, an occasional automobile. She guessed they were on Broadway; she could not tell just where. A right-hand turn was taken; then one to the left. There were no car tracks here. The traffic was lighter.

Giulia saw they were approaching a park, iron-railed. She had merely a glimpse of it when a rough hand was clapped over her eyes.

"Not that it will do you a damn bit of good," a voice said hoarsely in her ear. "But just in case."

Giulia did not recoil. She could move only a little, and she thought it was useless. She felt the swing of the car as it turned sharply right, left, left, right; then the hand was removed.

"Some dame, eh, Spiro?" That was the man at her left. She hadn't seen him yet. "And a bride, too. Wot d'you think o' that!"

"Tie your mouth," the man at her right growled. "Wait till we get her there."

"Ain't I waitin'! Oh, boy!" He continued to chuckle until the man he had called Spiro snapped, "Shut your mouth an' watch your side. We could get in a jam yet. Can't you get a little more outta her, Toni?"

"Doin' all I dare now," the driver let drift over his shoulder. "Don't want to get pinched fer speedin', do you? You kin see we're up to near twenty-eight."

"Aw right. An' if you see a cop, slow down; but don't stop for nothing."

Giulia scarcely heard. Her heart choked her with its terror. That name—Spiro. She had heard Paul mention it, when he was telling her father and Pianelli of the captures they had made, the one gang leader still at large. The most heartless and cruel of them all. The most wanton in his outrages. Terror gripped her again, stark fear that chilled her blood, bathed her whole body in cold perspiration, choked her breathing.

They would kill her of course. As they had killed Vincent. But—what else? They couldn't be taking her for ransom; or why should they have waited until her wedding day? Paul was not rich. It was her father who had money. And they must fear Paul. That was it. They were striking at Paul, through the only weak link in his strong armor.

A hand brushed her hair. She had no hat. A cloth was whipped around her head, covering her eyes, bound tightly. The sudden touch aroused her when the world was beginning to toss black before her swimming senses. Her pulse quickened again. She tried to think, to conjecture where they were, where they were going.

Blindfolded, she set her mind to follow their course; anything to keep it from her terror, to rescue her senses from unconsciousness.

She seemed to recall that the car had turned once, to the right, when she had felt herself fainting. That was the only turn for a long while that she could remember. Now it was turning again, and once more to the right. She reasoned then that after a considerable ride uptown, they had swung to the east and were now paralleling their earlier course downtown. Back to the quarter. Of course. It was logical.

Soon she became aware that the car was slowing. Abruptly it swung to one side and stopped.

"All right, Toni?"

"Aw right, boss. Your side. Street ahead looks clear. Can't see behind well. Better be quick."

Giulia heard the curtains at her right being ripped from their button fastenings. Hands grasped her, lifted her from the seat, moved her a short distance, and then placed her upright on another seat. She heard the quickening of the motor. It seemed to be drawing away. A door was shut. A voice called, and the vehicle started onward to the sound of horses' hoofs.

She had been transferred from automobile to carriage. That would be a hard trail to follow; impossible, in time.

This was to be the last part of the ride. Giulia knew that. When they should stop again, it would be for the last time. They would be at their planned destination. Sitting rigidly upright, muscles tense, she tried to steel herself for that moment.

They seemed now to be taking a slowly winding course to the left. That would mean a curving street. No word was spoken within the carriage. No one had spoken since the shift. There were no outside sounds from the street; nothing but the slow beat of the horses' hoofs, the impatient clucking of the driver, the creak of harness and carriage springs, the noise of the wheels on cobbles.

She found herself listening for other sounds; evidence of another vehicle, other human beings. She heard nothing. A hand gripped each of her arms, never relaxing, never removed. A turn was made to the right. The man Spiro swayed closer against her shoulder. The horses walked on. Then, suddenly, the carriage stopped. They had arrived.

The carriage swayed as a man stepped down from the box. She heard his footsteps at one side; the faint click of a lock.

The carriage door at one side was opened. The hand that was Spiro's lifted her partly erect, drew her toward that side. She was helped out. Again the hands were about her arms, guiding her steps. She walked without resistance, thinking to keep from them any idea of her desperate intent. She was led up several steps, forward into air that was damp and moldy, heavy with staleness. They paused. There was the sound of the door closed, of the scratching of a match.

The cloth was taken from her eyes, and she blinked in the faint, uncertain light. She did not glance at her captors but saw a wall that had once been plastered but was now streaked and gray, with open patches showing the laths beneath. A little to her right was the beginning of worn stairs, leading upward.

Giulia waited, hoping that now they would also unbind her arms, at least remove the terrible gag that was commencing to make her choke. She would plead with them. No, that would be useless. She would offer them money, any sum, that would set her free, unharmed. But that—

Her thoughts were interrupted. A hand pushed her roughly forward, toward the stairs.

"Up you go, my lady. Right to your boodaw." The man laughed raucously. This was not Spiro. It was the man at her left; the subordinate.

Her feet touched the first tread. She started slowly upward, impelled by Spiro's grasp of her arms, pushed roughly from behind when she appeared to falter. Another match, behind her, was lighted. That was the third man, the one who had ridden with the driver, who unlocked the door. She remembered now that she had heard the carriage driving off even before she had entered the foul old building.

They reached the landing, went along the passage, and started up another flight. The match went out. Spiro cursed in the momentary darkness until another was lighted.

"You fellers coulda brought candles," he growled.

"Don't worry, Boss," the man close behind her chuckled. "We'll have all the light we'll need in 'bout a minute."

The third man laughed noisily.

"Shut up," Spiro told them. "Wait till we get behind the door. Might be somebody come along."

"Not a chance."

"Well, shut up now, an' don't forget I'm boss."

"Aw, but you ain't goin' to be mean. Remember, we gotta make this guy Cardani good an' sore, so he'll lissen to reason."

"Damn you, Jake; shut up! Cut that noise till we get inside. Then I'll talk to you."

"Oh, aw right, as long as you ain't mad."

Giulia's whole body weakened suddenly. If it had not been for the arm that dragged her upward irresistibly, she would have fallen.

They reached the third landing, paused, turned to the left. A heavy oaken door, incongruous in this place, faced her.

Spiro fumbled with a key. The flickering match light faded, was extinguished. Spiro swore in a low, growling, savage tone.

"Aw, don't be nervous, Boss," the second man told him, as he struck another.

The key was fitted, the lock clicked. As the door was opened, the little flame was again extinguished.

Spiro drew her roughly into the darkness.

"Come in, you fellers," Spiro called. "Shut that door. I'll get the light goin' myself. You damn bunglers would knock the jet down."

From behind her, there came the sound of a match struck on a rough wall. Light sprang up quickly, with a sharp, hissing noise.

"Damn this gas! Fulla air."

Giulia flashed a glance over her shoulder. Spiro had his hand to the petcock; his two companions were watching him. She looked resolutely in the other direction.

She saw a long, rather narrow room. There was a rug on the floor, a table, several chairs, a couch. She looked further, toward the end of the room. She started slightly.

There, deep in the far corner, it seemed to her that a shape had suddenly gained substance. Her eyes widened. Truly a man stood there. Motionless. Not clearly seen. This must be the head, the chief of them all, waiting until they brought her to him. Waiting—

Her heart leaped suddenly, choking her. There was something vaguely—Giulia's senses were reeling. Everything was getting black—

A sharp exclamation sounded from behind her. Giulia felt herself falling.

"Damn you!" Spiro shrieked. "You devil, Cardani!"

Flame spurted before Giulia's closing eyes. There was a thunderous crash. Another from close behind her. The thud of something falling heavily on the floor. Twice more, in quick succession, flame streaked from that far corner. All other sound was drowned in the two reports. As the echoes died, there was agonized cursing behind her; another heavy fall.

But Paul's arms were about her, lifting her, setting her on her feet. He placed her on a chair, swung away from her to step toward the three men.

Spiro was dead. Paul had shot that once to kill; twice more to wound. Jake and his companion were moaning. One grasped a wounded shoulder. Blood ran between his fingers. The third man was lying on the floor. Both hands were clasped to his thigh. Paul searched them, took knives from both. He picked from the floor the pistols which they had drawn too late, caught up Spiro's fallen weapon, and came back to Giulia.

Gently, deftly, he removed the gag and the rope which had cut and numbed her arms. He chafed her wrists, talked to her quietly, smiling down at her.

Paul bound and gagged the two wounded men and led Giulia out, extinguishing the light and locking the door behind them. Once outside, they hurried along the deserted street. Paul's pistol was reloaded in the emptied chambers; his hand was on the butt in his side pocket. But Giulia walked bravely now. Paul was here, beside her.

After a while they found a carriage. Paul scrutinized the driver closely, then gave the Lafayette Street address.

When Giulia asked Paul for an explanation, he told her the story of the repentant kidnaper, Zapretti, of the rescue of his child, and of the two keys to the secret hideouts.

30

PAUL AND OCELLI stood in the dark, silent corridor. At one end, that from which they had come, a single light burned dimly. It cast their shadows before them, on the hard, flagged stone floor, past the door to the cell where Lupo was.

For nearly ten days Lupo had been left to the meagre consolation of his own dark thoughts. Men had come to him at intervals; jailers with food and water. He had spoken to them, cursed them, cried out to them; but none had answered a single word.

Paul signaled over his shoulder. An attendant came and put on a light before Lupo's cell, illuminating the interior. He went away. Still Paul waited until he heard movement in the cell, saw Lupo's hands at the bars. Then he and Ocelli walked slowly forward until they confronted the prisoner.

Lupo's face was drawn and haggard; his eyes feverish. His hands trembled in their clasp of the bars. He recognized Lieutenant Cardani. His face twisted; then blazed in sudden anger.

"You can't do this to me," he croaked. "If I got twenty years comin' to me, take me out of here. Let me start 'em. I ain't done nothing callin' for solitary. You're afraid to let me see my lawyers. They'll break you for this."

"Get over there on your cot, Lupo," Paul said quietly, "and sit down."

Lupo glared; then turned and did as he was bid.

Paul took keys from his pocket, unlocked the cell door. He and Ocelli stepped in, closed it behind them with their prisoner.

Ocelli stood back, leaning against the wall with folded arms. His smoldering eyes were fixed steadily on Lupo.

Paul stepped to the cot and seated himself beside the prisoner. For a long while there was silence in the cell. Lupo himself finally broke it.

"Well, copper," he snarled, "if you're goin' to preach to me, go ahead. If you think I'm goin' to spill anything, you're crazy. I ain't got nothing to tell. I don't know anything. And if you stay here a week, I still ain't got anything."

After another long interval, while Lupo averted his eyes from Ocelli's unshifting look, Paul asked quietly:

"What do you think is going to happen to you, Lupo?"

"Happen to me? Why, hell; I got caught with those plates, didn't I? They weren't mine. I didn't have anything to do with them. I was visitin' a friend that night when you busted in. Maybe I can prove the truth of that in court, when I see my lawyers. If you got me framed, and I can't, I suppose I'll be soaked a twenty stretch."

"Oh, no. You're wrong, Lupo. You won't get any twenty years. You won't get any term. From here you will go to the courtroom. From there you will go to the chair. It won't take long, Lupo."

"The chair!" Lupo gasped. He laughed, a weird sound in that place. He looked at Paul, saw his stern, sombre features, the implacable expression in his eyes. "You got me framed!" he screamed suddenly. "It ain't true. You gotta let me see my lawyers. I ain't done nothing, and I can prove it!"

Paul turned his head slowly toward Ocelli, nodded slightly. Ocelli stepped to the cell door and whistled once, not loudly.

"Stand up, Lupo," Paul said suddenly.

Lupo came to his feet, astonished, trembling in spite of himself. Paul caught his arm, led him close to the cell door.

Presently there were footsteps in the corridor, approaching. Largio came along. There was a young man with him. They stopped before Lupo, looking at him closely.

"That's the man," the young fellow said snappily. "I'm sure of that nose and chin, that pocked face. That's the man I saw late at night, over on Stanton, walking with young Vincent Ravino and another man a short time before Ravino was murdered in that cooperage office. I'm ready to swear that's the man."

Paul led Lupo back to the cot, forced him to sit. Lupo's face had gone white. He was babbling.

"That ain't true. I don't know what he was talking about. I was never over there, where he said. I never saw this other fellow—what'd he say his name was? The word of one feller like that don't mean anything."

"No?"

Paul nodded again to Ocelli. Again Ocelli signaled, and Paul once more led Lupo to the bars.

This time Largio came with two rough-looking men, of the lowest class. They too looked long and searchingly at Lupo.

"'At's de guy," one finally muttered. "Damn him! He got us in dis trouble. He come to us, hired us to take a barrel from de place where dey make barrels out on Stanton. He wanted us to dump it up on de docks on West Street. Paid us ten dollars apiece for de job."

"Yeh," broke in the other man. "We didn't know wot was in de barrel, Mister. Bimeby, crossin' Broadway—it was late at night, see?—four young guys come along an' looked at us kinder suspicious. I said to Rocco, here, we'd better see wot the hell we're carryin'. We went along a piece an' took a look. My gawd, Mister, when we see wot we had, we dumped it pretty damn quick. An' dat's de guy got us to do it. I'll go to court an' swear it."

"An' so'll I," chimed in his companion. "I know dat guy. I'd never miss him. Dey calls him Lupo. An' I want to see a loop round his lousy neck."

Back on the cot again, Lupo was sobbing protestations of his innocence. Paul allowed him to babble on. There was the whole night before them; another night if necessary.

When Lupo had exhausted his pleas and invective and had reached some measure of quiet, Paul took a sheaf of banknotes from his pocket. "Did you ever see these before, Lupo?"

"Course I never did. What's that now you're trying to put on me?"

"No? They are counterfeit. Their numbers run in sequence with the counterfeit bills Chief Thomas of the Federal Secret Service and I found in your possession. These notes that I have here were stuffed by you into young Vincent Ravino's pocket after you had killed him. They were found in his pocket by me when his murdered body was taken from the barrel, into which you had forced it."

Lupo, as Paul Cardani had first seen, was a coward. When he commenced to realize the unbreakable case being built up against him, for first-degree murder, one bit of evidence after another forging the inescapable chain, his shrieks and moans, his frenzied agony might have been pitiful if it had not been at the same time revolting and nauseating.

Paul sat motionless, silent, through the tirade. Ocelli never moved from his position against the wall. Whenever Lupo glanced that way, Ocelli's sober gaze was on him, like just vengeance waiting.

The minutes passed, crept into hours, while Lupo alternately stormed his protestations of innocence and wept at the undeserved fate that was being thrust upon him. After a time he sprang to his feet, began a restless pacing of the narrow confines of his cell.

Neither Paul nor Ocelli left his place. Only their eyes followed him, accusing, sure. Whenever Lupo turned he met the look of one or the other. He threw himself finally on to the cot again, sat bowed over, face in hands, fingers thrust into his hair.

Another long period passed. Lupo stirred, raised his head, glanced at the silent man beside him. Paul turned slowly toward him. In place of the counterfeit notes, his hand now held a clasp-knife, its long blade stained a rusty brown. Lupo took one look at it; then started back, with indrawn breath. He strove desperately to control himself.

"Recognize it, Lupo?"

"No, no, no! I never saw it before. Why should I?"

"That," Cardani said, "is the knife you plunged into Vincent Ravino's back when he turned to reach the telephone. That is the knife that I found in his back when his body was taken from the barrel."

"No, no! It isn't true! It's not my knife. I never saw it before."

"Strange. It's strange that you should deny it, Lupo, when Coremo and Tasso and Vira all have identified it as your own knife, recognizing it by its peculiar handle and the mark you put on it, having even seen it in your possession within a short time. They have all made depositions to that effect and signed them. Strange that you can't remember when you bought it from John Costa, on Elizabeth Street.

"That is your knife, Lupo; and with it you killed Vincent Ravino in cold blood. Listen, Lupo. I will tell you just how it happened."

Carefully, watching the prisoner's face for any indications of error, Paul reconstructed his theory of the manner in which the murder had been committed. He commenced at the beginning, telling the purpose, to force the counterfeit on the young banker, which ultimately resulted in his murder. He recited how they had lain in wait for the young man, how they were seen leading him to his doom.

Then he described the little office, placed each of the three men in their respective positions; told what they smoked; even related the false rumor against Ravino, through which they had hoped to gain their ends.

He came to the climax. He related how Ravino had spurned their offer, denied the calumny against the girl he had befriended; how he had leaped from his chair, swung to the telephone, when, Lupo, drawing the knife, had struck the fatal blow.

And all through the recital, Lupo listened, not once interrupting or denying. Watching him covertly, Paul saw the effect that was being wrought upon him, saw that he was rapidly approaching a hysteria of abject terror.

And at the close, Lupo blurted out, "My God, Cardani; you were there!"

Instantly overcome by realization of this confession, Lupo broke into a wild torrent of raving words.

Paul waited, and when it ceased, said, "No, Lupo. I was not there. Another man was."

Lupo glanced at him, with a peculiar gleam in his harried eyes.

All through his story, Paul had told of the third man without mentioning him significantly. He had given meagre descriptions of this third man, as if he were not of great importance. Now he leaned closer to the prisoner.

"Sebastiano Gambroni," he whispered, "was there, Lupo."

After that, Paul fell silent. He sat immoble, sombre, waiting.

For countless minutes, Lupo's haunted eyes quested every corner, every wall and stone of his bleak cell. Time and again his wildly roving glance returned to this implacable man who, to his tortured mind, represented fate.

It was well toward morning when the break came. Lupo, in complete despair, tossed his arms before him, slumped to a slouching figure.

"Gambroni," he whispered, through parched lips, "took the knife from me. He did it."

After that, the end was easy.

An Interview with Joseph T. Shaw

Editor of Black Mask magazine—by Ed Bodin

THIS AFTERNOON WE have an enjoyable assignment. We are going to call upon one of the cleverest, friendliest and most popular editors in the all-fiction field— not only an editor and a gentleman, but an editor with a keen sense of humor—namely Joseph T. Shaw of *Black Mask* magazine, whose new book, *Danger Ahead,* released a few days ago has already found a fine reception.

We give the taxi-cab driver more than the usual tip as he fights his way through the tangled traffic of upper Fifth Avenue and shoots into Madison Avenue near 57th Street. We enter the Ley Building at 578 Madison, and an express elevator brings us quickly to the 11th floor.

The beautiful blonde receptionist of *Black Mask* and associated magazines, soon gets Mr. Shaw on the inter-office phone and nods her head as she says: "Mr. Shaw will see you at once— go right in."

As usual, the editor of *Black Mask* is up to his neck in manuscripts as he sits at his huge desk beside the wall where at least a hundred covers of *Black Mask* are trained and hanging in neat arrangement. They give off an atmosphere of virility and action.

Up comes Mr. Shaw's hand for a real handshake. No matter what he is ever doing, whether reading, dictating or talking to the President of the Writers' Union—he's never too busy to greet a guest with that uprising palm that bespeaks friendship and welcome. His grey-streaked hair and mustache add dignity to his middle-age appearance as he invites us to be seated.

"Mr. Shaw," we begin—"the readers of *Author & Composer* have come for a short visit this afternoon for a personal chat and message to carry back home."

"Fine," he smiles. "I always knew that real people like *Black Mask*—that's why we intend to keep the reputation it has gained as the leading magazine in its field."

We answer quickly. "You don't have to tell us—we know that *Black Mask's* fiction whether it is an adventure, western or detective story, finds its place in homes from the White House to the mechanic's cottage."

Mr. Shaw interrupts at this point. "Yes," he says—"I've always wondered what a composite picture of the *Black Mask* readers would look like."

"A typical red-blooded virile American—fit he-man comrade for the many animated women who also enjoy the thrill of *Black Mask* fiction."

But we soon get to the point of the visit and we put the first query: "What chance has the unknown writer to click with *Black Mask?*"

"Best in the world," replies the editor, "if he carries the *Black Mask* standard of craftsmanship as well as the story. You see— *Black Mask* demands fine workmanship. The names in the author list of our magazine, are found in the *Saturday Evening Post, Collier's, Liberty* and the best magazines in the country; but names don't mean much unless the story is there too. That's why leading writers consider it a distinction to be on *Black Mask's* contents page."

Then Mr. Shaw makes this vital point: "Remember—when I read a story by a new author, I don't read it from the standpoint of that one story. I read it also as an example of that writer's workmanship. He might not click with that story—but if he writes *Black Mask* quality, he will know about it—for I am always looking for the fellow with the flair."

When asked to mention names of his writers he most preferred, Mr. Shaw replied quickly: "This wouldn't be fair to the many *Black Mask* writers—for one never knows when one of the authors who write *Black Mask* quality, will step ahead with a story that is exceptional. All my writers are fiction masksmen—that's why so many writers who get their first breaks in *Black Mask,* soon appear in the *Post* and others, along with their *Black Mask* appearances."

We interrupt at this point and ask: "The best way, therefore, to know *Black Mask,* is to read a copy?"

"Not exactly—but rather study the technique of the *Black Mask* writers—not one issue, but a dozen—and suddenly you will feel that fiction punch that tells why their stories were purchased. You'll find that expert swing and delivery in every story in *Black Mask.* Until you can sense it and duplicate it—you are not quite ready to click."

"Now as to the best lengths to try," we ask. "We presume the short would stand a better chance?"

"Yes, *Black Mask* doesn't like novelettes over 15,000 words—and, of course, seldom does the new fellow hit the bull's-eye with that length. His best bet would be the 6,000-word story, or a little less."

THUS IT IS plain why *Black Mask* magazine holds such a high reputation in the all-fiction field. The editor is not just a purchasing agent of virile, adventure, western, detective or border stories that are usually found in such magazines—but a Judge of the Supreme Court of two-fisted fiction who knows quality as well as story substance and considers them with the eyes of his readers. As a popular author himself he has both the author's and the editor's vision.

So don't send ordinary material to Joseph T. Shaw. While he wants to be friendly and helpful—his judgment cannot be fooled by inferior quality of workmanship or weak stories. When shooting at *Black Mask,* you are shooting at as fine a market as there is in the magazine field—and Mr. Shaw intends to maintain that reputation for *Black Mask.* Don't overburden him, or impose upon his good nature. He will meet you more than halfway—but you've got to show him that you have the flair.

Made in the USA
Monee, IL
18 October 2020